"IF I HAVE GOT TO GO AND FIGHT, I AM WILLING."

"IF I HAVE GOT TO GO AND FIGHT, I AM WILLING."

A Union Regiment
Forged in the Petersburg Campaign

The 179th New York Volunteer Infantry
1864-1865

EDWIN P. RUTAN, II

RTD Publications LLC
Park City, Utah

Copyright

Published by RTD Publications, LLC
Park City, UT 84098

Maps prepared by Brian A. Dawe
Design by Michelle Rayner, cosmicdesignllc.com
Typeface: Garamond

First Print Edition December 2015
ISBN 978-0-9862722-2-6

Electronic Book Edition March 2015
ISBN 978-0-9862722-0-2

INTRODUCTION TO THE PRINT EDITION

If I Have Got to Go and Fight, I Am Willing was conceived of as an electronic book in order to present more effectively maps and other visual materials related to the experience of the men of the 179th New York Volunteers. The e-book has thirty high resolution, enlargeable maps, most of which are in color, and more than one hundred eighty high resolution photos and other illustrations, some of which are in color. In order to produce the print edition at a reasonable cost and to include only those visual images which can be reproduced in print with high quality, all of the maps and over one hundred of the visual images from the e-book have been omitted from the print edition.

However, readers of the print edition will have free access on our website (www.179thnyvolunteers.org) to all of the omitted maps and images. Each map or image that has been omitted from the print edition is identified at its place in the text by brackets with the caption of the omitted item. If interested, the reader can use the caption to quickly access the map or image in the "Gallery" tab on the website.

Thus, we have reversed the publication process. Civil War books typically are published initially in print format and then offered as e-books without adding the visual enhancements that the electronic medium offers. By starting *If I Have Got to Go and Fight, I Am Willing* as an e-book, we have provided high resolution maps and images in numbers and with a richness unrivaled by the typical Civil War book. Our website enables the reader of the print edition to access those maps and images with a level of quality not available in print.

The reader may discuss *If I have Got to Go and Fight, I Am Willing* and other Civil War subjects with Ed Rutan and Brian Dawe and other readers on our blog – 179thnyvolunteers.blogspot.com.

To ...

... James C. Rutan, my great-great-grandfather; Edwin Ellsworth Rutan,
my great-grandfather; Edwin P. Rutan, my grandfather; and Peter Grant Rutan,
my father; – citizen-soldiers who served our country in four wars.

... Christopher Grant Rutan, my son, a "citizen-volunteer" who served our country
in the Peace Corps.

... Amelia Breese Rutan, my great-great grandmother, who also served in the Civil War
as she stood and waited.

... Helen Hall Rutan, my mother, a member of America's Greatest Generation,
who served our country during World War II by working in a factory.

"Well if I have got to go and fight I am willing to go."
--Abner Roberts, an eighteen-year-old farmer from Howard

"The explosion was the most grand and awful scene I ever witnessed."
--Newton Spencer, a newspaperman from Penn Yan, on the Battle of the Crater

"[I]f you cood just see the wounded that is here coming every our it would scare you.
... I must confess it a grate deal wors than I did think it cood be."
--Daniel B. Lee, a thirty-year-old farmer from West Almond

"I have the Inflamatory Rheumatism and Remittent fever.
My right foot & hand was swelled up like cushions, the Doctor lanced them
and there run a half pint of blood and matter from them."
--John Cook, an eighteen-year-old farmer from Newfield

"[It] is raining yet, and the prospect is fair that it will rain --forever."
--Lt. John Andrews, a twenty-two-year-old recent college graduate from Reading

"It was no Play Spell to do it, rather those Gray Coats fought like tigers."
--William Tuck, a twenty-one-year-old farmer, on the final assault at Petersburg

"It is all right. Tell them I died fighting for the old flag."
--Lt. Col. Franklin Doty, reputed last words after being mortally wounded on April 2, 1865

TABLE OF CONTENTS

ILLUSTRATIONS & MAPS

Detailed publication information is provided in "Illustrations & Maps" page 460 et seq.

PREFACE

The 179th New York Volunteer Infantry was raised in the spring and late summer of 1864. The 179th's service in the field began with the Army of the Potomac's change of front from Cold Harbor to Petersburg in June 1864 and ended with the surrender of the Army of Northern Virginia in April 1865. The 179th New York fought in six battles during the Petersburg campaign, including the Battle of the Crater.

I became interested in the 179th New York Volunteers because my great-great-grandfather, James C. Rutan, served in Company A. As I began my research, I realized that I wanted a much broader understanding of the experience of the men as soldiers than regimental histories of famous units typically provide. A regiment with a well-earned reputation for bravery in one or two days of battle solidified by canonization over the past one hundred fifty years was not necessarily the best candidate for the objective examination of the soldiers' broader experience that I planned to undertake. The 179th New York Volunteers – which has previously been the subject of just a bare bones pamphlet published in 1900[1] – provided a fertile field for that broader approach because no reputation preceded it.

The first regimental histories were written even before the Civil War was over as the terms of enlistment of the soldiers who joined the army in 1861 expired. Veterans wrote book length histories of many regiments between the end of the war and the early 1900s, but relatively few qualify as serious historical studies.[2]

Regimental histories written during the last fifty years are generally more objective, but tend to focus on the battles with little attention to the social, cultural and political dimensions, which were also important parts of the soldiers' complete experience. Even the best regimental histories, such as Warren Wilkinson's *Mother, May You Never See the Sights I Have Seen* (the Fifty-Seventh Massachusetts Veteran Volunteers); Richard Moe's *The Last Full Measure* (the First Minnesota Volunteers); and Richard F. Miller's *Harvard's Civil War* (the Twentieth Massachusetts Volunteers), which do take a broad sweep, still give relatively little attention to support from the home front, medical care, the role of the soldiers' religious faith, the importance of the soldiers' vote in the 1864 election, and the post-war pension system. Some military subjects, such as desertion and prisoners of war, also received limited treatment.[3]

Works such as Drew Gilpin Faust's *This Republic of Suffering: Death and the American Civil War*, Steven E. Woodworth's *While God Is Marching On: The Religious World of Civil War Soldiers*, and Eric T. Dean, Jr.'s *Shook Over Hell: Post-Traumatic Stress, Vietnam and the Civil War* examined in depth aspects of the Civil War soldier's experience which have received only passing attention in the past.[4] This project includes these and other subjects traditionally under-emphasized in regimental histories in order to provide a more complete history of the experience of the soldiers in the 179th New York Volunteers.

My research also uncovered new voices to relate their Civil War experiences. The soldiers of the 179th New York Volunteers left behind a fair amount of first hand material that has been untapped. None of the soldiers of the 179th made it into Bell Wiley's *The Life of Billy Yank*, for example.[5] Not only has there been no previous serious history of the 179th New York, but in all the books about the Civil War battles and campaigns that I have read, I recall only one quoting a soldier from the 179th – and only a five word phrase without attribution at that.[6]

The most vigorous of these untapped voices was Newton B. Spencer, a newspaperman before the war. Spencer reminded the Union army's top brass that they were commanding citizen-soldiers and thinking-bayonets.[7] He wrote a scathing critique for his hometown newspaper, the *Penn Yan Democrat*, of the performance of the Army of the Potomac's commanders at the Battle of the Crater. The pseudonymous "Ord." (probably Nathaniel P. T. Finch) also mixed pointed criticism of the military hierarchy with his reports for local newspapers on the more mundane aspects of the 179th's experience.

As a college student when the war broke out, John Andrews agonized over whether he should enlist to save the Union. He finally joined the 179th as a second lieutenant in the fall of 1864. The extensive factual detail and mature reflections in his "War Journal" and correspondence, along with his college diary, could justify a book by themselves.[8] I have relied heavily on his thoughts.

Diaries and letters written by less educated soldiers in the 179th are no less insightful. The simple statement in William Lamont's letter to his parents that "he could enjoy a letter from home every day" speaks for generations of soldiers serving far from home. The terse diary entry by William Larzelere that "our regt was mostly destroyed" and the letter home from Daniel B. Lee that "all of the regiment is cut to pieces" tell it all for what happened to the 179th New York Volunteers on June 17, 1864.

This history of the 179th New York Volunteers also provides a more robust visual presentation than regimental histories typically do. Drawings by the "special artists" for newspapers such as *Harper's Weekly*, contemporary photographs, and maps supplement the verbal descriptions provided by the soldiers. I decided to publish *If I Have Got to Go and Fight, I Am Willing* as an electronic book in order to provide many more maps, photos and illustrations than the economics of print publishing typically permit.

There is one sense in which the 179th New York Volunteers may have a reputation which precedes it. The 179th New York was a so-called "high-number" regiment, i.e. a regiment recruited in the latter part of the war when the draft was in place and high bounties were paid for volunteering. As Bruce Catton noted in *A Stillness at Appomattox*, "[t]he old-timers in the Army of the Potomac disliked conscripts and utterly despised high-bounty men." and "these 'high-number' regiments were never accounted the equals of the ones with lower numbers, which had enlisted in 1861 or 1862."[9]

The disdain that veterans who enlisted in 1861 and 1862 held for the soldiers of the high number regiments continued to be held by some veterans after the war ended. The Union Veterans' Union, a less prominent organization than the Grand Army of the Republic, initially limited its membership to veterans who had seen combat and who had enlisted prior to July 1, 1863 "before high bounties were offered."[10] In an 1884 Memorial Day address delivered in Canandaigua, New York, an area where some of the soldiers of the 179th had come from (and some of whom may have been in the audience), the speaker distinguished between those soldiers who volunteered early in the war and those who came later, referring to the former as "noble men – patriotic men, unselfish men – breasting the storm of bullets, with higher motives than the bounty ... impelling them."[11]

Some historians have also taken a less than complimentary view of the high-bounty men. Ella Lonn referred to them as mercenaries, a term many Americans associate with the Hessians fighting for the British during the Revolution.[12] In one of the most widely read books on the Civil War, James McPherson wrote that: "Relatively few of the bounty men or substitutes actually became cannon fodder, however, for many deserted before they ever got into action and others allowed themselves to be captured at the first contact with the enemy."[13]

Catton did note that several of the high-number regiments "made excellent records." He specifically noted that the Army of the Potomac's Ninth Corps, in which the 179th served, refilled its ranks with these high-bounty soldiers and "does not seem to have lost its old fighting quality with the transfusion." He stated that "[i]t would undoubtedly be a strong overstatement to say that all of the men brought in by the draft and bounty were useless," but still ended with the conclusion that "[y]et if there is exaggeration in the complaints there is not very much exaggeration." [14]

The 179th New York Volunteers certainly was not a famous unit like the Iron Brigade or the 20th Maine. [15] However, the 179th New York Volunteers were no mere rear echelon or garrison soldiers. The 179th lost heavily during the Petersburg campaign. In its first battle at Petersburg, the 179th suffered approximately forty percent casualties among those engaged. The 179th suffered another twenty percent casualties in the Battle of the Crater and fifteen percent in the final assault at Petersburg on April 2, 1865. [16] This book demonstrates that the 179th New York was a "high number" regiment that fought.

The main purpose of this book, however, is not to glorify – or even justify – the men of the 179th. As Margaret Humphreys recently wrote, "The war, for those who fought it, was less about heroism and more about the daily grind of disease, hunger, death, and disability." [17] In the end, my main purpose is that the reader understand more deeply and more broadly the reality of the soldiers' experience and respect what they endured.

"IF I HAVE GOT TO GO AND FIGHT, I AM WILLING."

———◆———

Volunteer Enlistment Form (Stephen Compton)

CHAPTER ONE

Civil War Draft, Bounties and Citizen-Soldiers

The tradition of the citizen-soldier in the United States goes all the way back to the minutemen at the Battles of Lexington and Concord in the American Revolution. As Gary Gallagher explained in a recent book about the Union side of the Civil War, "Americans cherished few things so much as the idea that their national history, unlike those of all the European powers, rested on the republican virtue of citizens willing to sacrifice in times of military crisis." [1] In the memory of Americans living today, that "willingness to sacrifice" reached its zenith during World War II and its nadir during the Vietnam War. [2] In the post-Vietnam era, the United States now pursues its military needs with a professional army, as evidenced by the wars in Iraq and Afghanistan. But the Civil War was fought by the citizen-soldier and the "thinking-bayonet". [3]

In his memoirs, General Ulysses S. Grant remarked on the difference between the American and the European soldier:

> The armies of Europe are machines: the men are brave and the officers capable; but the majority of the soldiers in most of the nations of Europe are taken from a class of people who are not very intelligent and who have very little interest in the contest in which they are called to take part. Our armies were composed of men who were able to read, men who knew what they were fighting for, and could not be induced to serve as soldiers, except in an emergency when the safety of the nation was involved, and so necessarily

must have been more than equal to men who fought merely because they
were brave and because they were thoroughly drilled and inured to hardships. [4]

When the Civil War began in 1861, the federal government was hardly prepared for war.
Moreover, the Union's capital was located within a border state with definite leanings toward
the Confederacy (Maryland) and across the river from a state that had seceded (Virginia). The
regular army of the United States had only sixteen thousand soldiers spread mainly across frontier
outposts west of the Mississippi. In addition, nearly one-third of the regular army officers resigned
to serve the Confederacy. [5] As a result, President Lincoln necessarily had to rely on the states
remaining in the Union to provide an army to defend Washington and defeat the Confederacy.
Lincoln called for seventy-five thousand soldiers on April 15, 1861 to serve for three months
to "suppress the rebellion." [6] The states responded with more than ninety thousand men, but
within a month the President called for another five hundred thousand soldiers. Calls for
troops in the hundreds of thousands would come again and again until the end of the war. [7]

The wave of patriotic fervor after the attack on Fort Sumter stimulated sufficient enlistments
to meet the calls for troops at the beginning of the war. The newly raised state units typically carried
the designation "volunteers," as in the 23rd Regiment of Infantry, New York State Volunteers
(popularly known as the Southern Tier Rifles). However, as the war continued past its anticipated
short duration and with the shocking number of casualties in battles such as Antietam and
Fredericksburg in the latter part of 1862 (12,000 Union soldiers killed or wounded in each battle),
it became clear that volunteer enlistments would no longer suffice. As James McPherson observed:
"The men likely to enlist for patriotic reasons or adventure or peer-group pressure were already in the
army" and "[w]ar weariness and the grim realities of army life discouraged further volunteering." [8]

The Confederacy adopted the policy of forced conscription in 1862 and the Union
followed a year later, in March 1863. [9] The U. S. Congress had in effect authorized a draft in
1862 as a back-up to a call for three hundred thousand state militiamen, but the call had been
met and a draft became unnecessary. [10] Under the 1863 Enrollment Act all males between the
ages of twenty and forty-five were subject to the draft unless they "were mentally or physically
impaired, the only son of a widow, the son of infirm parents, or a widower with dependent
children." [11] The Act was administered by assigning quotas to districts basically following
existing congressional districts. Males were enrolled on lists and divided into two classes – Class
One included men between the ages of twenty and thirty-five and unmarried men between
thirty-five and forty-five, while Class Two included everyone else subject to the draft. [12]

The draft posed an awkward challenge to the theory of American democracy. Citizen-soldiers
were supposed to come forward and volunteer in response to calls for troops, not wait to be
conscripted. For a community that could not fill its quota with volunteers, a draft was a mark of
shame because it demonstrated the community's lack of patriotism. Newspapers in the upstate
New York communities where the 179th New York was raised trumpeted the need to avoid a draft.
When a new regiment was authorized in 1862 with the backup draft to the militia call in effect, the
Havana Journal exhorted: "RALLY! MEN, RALLY! And save Schuyler County and the 27th Senate
District from the disgrace of a draft. You can do it; up and at it!" [13] Following the February 1864
call for five hundred thousand men, *The Hornellsville Tribune* challenged its readers:

> Shall the town of Hornellsville, or any other town in the 3d Assembly District,
> be disgraced by another draft? ... Shall it be said that, while a large portion of
> this State has filled its quota by volunteering, the conscript officer's services
> were required to make the 3d Assembly District do its duty? Men of Steuben,

arouse. [14]

The *Watkins Express* spoke of the need to:

> avoid an odious and humiliating conscription. ... The volunteers *can be obtained if the proper effort is made by all.* It is no time to remain inactive and trust to fortune or circumstances. Each citizen has a duty to perform to the community in helping in every way possible to promote enlistments. (emphasis in original) [15]

The *Dunkirk Journal* called for "immediate and active exertions" to avoid enforcement of the draft. [16] After the July 1864 call, the *Ontario County Times* expressed the hope that "no effort will be spared to obtain the required number of men in time to avert the draft" and added the exhortation "Fill up the ranks, boys." [17] A month later, the *Times* reported that the efforts were going well and concluded that "Old Ontario may therefore be safely counted out of the draft." Even the *Penn Yan Democrat*, representing the 'War Democrat' wing of the party, proclaimed that: "'A long pull, a strong pull and a pull by all together,' will save Yates County from the conscription and give the thinned ranks of the army 280 more men." [18]

The violence of the New York draft riots in July 1863 is well-known. However, there is no indication of violence in opposition to the draft in the areas of New York State where the 179th was recruited, although the draft certainly was not popular.

Communities brought strong social pressure to bear on potential volunteers. D. B. Tuthill, a supervisor for the town of Jerusalem in Yates County, wrote the following address which was published in the *Yates County Chronicle*:

> Young Men of Jerusalem: Your country is in peril. Black-hearted traitors threaten her very life. Her gallant armies need to be reinforced. ... Shall [our quota] be filled, as it hitherto has been, by noble-hearted volunteers; or shall the Government be compelled to resort to a compulsory draft? Hitherto the patriotisam of Jerusalem has voluntarily responded to all calls of our country. Shall the present one be an exception? I trust not...
>
> Will you not now step forward and enroll your name among the worthies now in the service of your country? Shall it be said of you, that when the very liberties of our country – nay, those of all mankind, are at stake, you ignobly refused to give a helping hand until you were compelled by the strong arm of Government. Is that a spirit worthy of your Revolutionary Grand-sires? Would you prove worthy descendants of such an illustrious ancestry or fit associates of your gallant brothers now in the field, periling their lives in defense of our country? Shall it be said of you that in the grandest national struggle the world ever saw, destined to fill the grandest page of history, that living, as you did, in those times, your selfishness was so mean, your patriotism so little, and your cowardice so great, that you took no part in the grand struggle, but suffered all the honor to be achieved by those whose names will forever shine on the page of their country's history, while yours will descend forever to the grave of oblivion? [19]

War Meetings were held locally "for the purpose of agitating the question of enrollment and encouraging volunteers to come forward and enlist." Shortly after the February 1864 call, the town of Italy in Yates County held a war meeting that generated fourteen new recruits– "enough to nearly or quite fill up the quota of the town." The *Yates County Chronicle* reported: "Well done, Italy." [20]

Soon to be Lieutenant John Andrews attended a war meeting in North Hector (Schuyler County) while he was recruiting for the 179th New York.

> The war meeting was a good one, the ladies aiding largely by their presence. The hall in which the meeting was held was not large but it was densely packed. An old gray-haired Judge addressed the meeting in a very long, dry, but intensely loyal speech wearying the patience of even those most anxious to enlist. Being called upon I followed with a few remarks, mostly with reference to my business. We then went to work filling out enlistment papers and when we finished, which was at nearly twelve o'clock we found that seventeen had enlisted. Along towards the last some extra inducements were offered to the 'next one.' Mr. Adams gave two or three five dollar 'greenbacks' and when they were urging the seventeenth one he threw down a fifty dollar one (the last he had) and persuaded the man. [21]

The federal, state, and local governments recognized that they could not rely on moral suasion alone. They resorted to the historical practice of paying volunteers a bounty to enlist. Payment of a bounty was justified because citizen-soldiers needed the means to provide for their family while they were away from home serving their country. [22] The federal, state, county and ultimately even town governments each provided a separate component of the total bounty.

The bounties were aggressively promoted. A large ad in the February 26, 1864 *Penn Yan Democrat* for the 179th New York Volunteers touted the "Large Bounty" of $677. [23]

For unskilled laborers, this was an extremely large sum of money. In 1860, a farm laborer in Elmira was paid between $12 and $16 per month. By 1865, shortages of civilian labor had nearly doubled farm wages in Elmira, but even at that higher level, a $677 bounty represented two years wages. [24] And for many potential recruits the $13 a month pay for privates was not all that much less than their civilian pay. "Cash in hand" of $450 was particularly attractive. The cash bounty attracted volunteers, but it also attracted bounty jumpers who would enlist with no intention of actually serving and then bolt at the first opportunity after being paid. [25]

The prospective officers of the 179th New York Volunteers had a professional interest in successful recruiting – their commissions depended on it. There was even something of a going rate for securing a commission based on the number of soldiers recruited. John Andrews arrived at the Elmira Military Barracks in the summer of 1864 with a letter of introduction from a local judge to Capt. Robert Dumars of the 161st New York Volunteers. Dumars offered him a "Sergeantcy" if he could furnish seven or eight men for the 161st. Andrews said he would consider it and then went to the office of Maj. A. S. Diven, the head of the volunteer recruiting service for Western New York. Diven recalled receiving a letter of recommendation for Andrews and initially offered him the possibility of a clerkship, but Andrews wanted a position in the field.

> [Diven] thought a moment and then proposed that I should raise a company and telling me to wait he went out and in a few minutes returned with Col. Gregg, and in a short time I was authorized to raise a company in Schuyler [County] for the 179th N.Y. Vols. and Anson [Andrews' cousin who accompanied him] was to assist. Col. Gregg thought it doubtful about my getting a full company, but assured me if I got 30 men I should have a 2d

Lieutenancy, forty men, a 1st Lieutenancy, and if we raised fifty men, he would give me the 1st and Anson the 2d Lieutenancy. [26]

The increasing burden of quotas on towns and the availability of large bounties led to the rise of a new business – civilian recruiting agents. While prospective officers such as Colonel Gregg, Major Sloan and Lieutenant Andrews had the incentive of recruiting soldiers to fill the ranks of their own units, civilian recruiting agents had no intention of serving in the military themselves. As with any occupation, there were both good and bad recruiting agents. It was not necessary for a recruit to sign up through a recruiting agent, and there were widespread abuses, notably charging recruits exorbitant fees for cashing their bounty scrip. [27] However, many communities came to view recruiting agents as a necessary evil to help fill their quotas. [28] The *Watkins Express* reported that the local recruiting agents – "Messrs. Jamison & VanAllen, Headquarters at Curtis's Hotel; Messrs. White & Ellis, Headquarters at the Jefferson House; Mr. J. T. Hudson, Headquarters at his Market" – offered "every facility ... for obtaining information as to the different Regiments, Bounties, &c." [29] Ontario County found it necessary to appoint five recruiting agents to help fill its quota from the July 18, 1864 call for more troops. [30]

Because civilian recruiting agents were not necessarily recruiting on behalf of any particular regiment, their newspaper advertisements quoted the same bounties, but without reference to a unit. An ad in the March 10, 1864 *Elmira Weekly Gazette* trumpeted trumpeted "Rally Round the Flag Boys!" [31]

While the 179th New York Volunteers was not specifically mentioned in the advertisement, J. A. McWilliams provided a fair number of troops for the 179th New York. In addition to whatever agreements he may have had with Elmira and/or prospective recruits, the federal government paid him $15 per new recruit. [32]

As fewer and fewer men were available to volunteer, a bidding war developed in 1864 among the various communities trying to meet their quotas and avoid the shame of a draft. The *Ontario County Times* reported in February 1864 that communities were prepared to pay recruits "as much as they can get elsewhere." [33] In response to the complaint that few of the men enlisting in Buffalo were actually credited to Buffalo and Erie County, the *Buffalo Morning Express* pointed out in April 1864 that: "Other localities pay larger bounties and it is the undeniable right of every man to enlist wherever he pleases. ... The only way to remedy the matter is to pay a higher bounty." [34] Commenting on the total $677 bounty for a three year volunteer, the *Ontario Times* also stated that: "Those who desire to enlist should remember that never before, and probably never again, will patriotic duty be so liberally rewarded." [35] However, events proved the *Times* wrong on that score as well. By the end of 1864, bounties in New York reached $1000 or more as the Union army's need for new troops to replace losses in the field increased over and over again and competition among communities to fill the resulting quotas intensified. [36]

Thus Supervisor Tuthill did not rely on moral persuasion alone in his address to the men of Jerusalem. In case his emotional appeal did not work, Tuthill also tried economic self-interest:

> look at the splendid bounties she offers you to enlist in her service, ... $677 bounty and advance pay to each new recruit, and $852 to each veteran who will enlist for three years or during the war, besides thirteen dollars per month, with the strongest probability of having it increased to eighteen or twenty dollars, besides board and clothing – a yearly allowance of $433 or $1299 for three years for each new recruit – a sum sufficient to purchase a snug farm – a dependence for life. [37]

The possibility of acquiring enough capital to buy a farm was a powerful incentive for many. At the end of the war, a state census enumerator in Tioga County reported that: "In this district, many Poor families sent their sons to the Army and with their Bounty bought small places with the money other-wise would not haved [sic] owned any property." [38] Commenting more generally, the *Elmira Daily Advertiser* wrote in September 1864 that men:

> are eagerly accepting the high bounties, which will put money in their pockets and leave a large sum for the support of their families. Debts, too, are paid off without feeling it. Mortgages on homesteads and small farms are being cancelled, obligations which have straightened the means of so many are easily met, and ease and comfort and the ready means of support dawn on a multitude of households. The money expended for bounties has thus reverted back to the benefit of our loyal citizens generally... The good accomplished by the use and circulation of so large sums of currency will redound to the growth and prosperity of the business interests of our city and town. [39]

The Enrollment Act included a provision with strong historical precedent in both the United States and Europe that would be unthinkable today – the ability to provide a substitute. (A qualifying substitute could not himself be eligible for the draft, which made immigrants and men under twenty prime candidates.) [40] The practice "was based on an assumption that the talents of men who could afford substitutes might be of more value on the homefront, organizing and producing the materiel of war, than in the army." [41] In August 1864, the *Watkins Express* reported that: "Many of our business men in this County [Schuyler] are making efforts to secure substitutes to release them from liability under the approaching draft." [42] Providing a substitute qualified a man for Elmira's "Roll of Honor" for "greatly aiding in the filling of our quota." Elmira Mayor John Nicks received special mention because he had provided a substitute even though he was above the draft age. [43]

A new feature – also unthinkable today – was the so-called "commutation clause," which allowed a draftee to pay $300 for an exemption. However, the payment was only good for that particular round of the draft and did not buy a permanent exemption. In theory, the commutation clause would limit the going rate for a substitute to $300, thereby making it affordable for more men. In the South, which had no commutation provision, the cost of a substitute reached $6000 by late 1863. [44]

Four months after joining the 179th New York in the field, John Andrews had seen enough of war to write his younger brother, who was still in school:

> Homer, don't you ever let anything induce you to become a soldier. If necessary let father pay out every cent he is worth to exempt you. Homer I would rather hear that your right leg had been taken off than to hear that you had enlisted. [45]

However, the $300 exemption fee was beyond the means of many men, [46] even if they had been inclined to pay it. The substitution/commutation structure led to the criticism in the North (and the South) that the Civil War was a "rich man's war and poor man's fight." [47]

The combination of the commutation clause and the various exemptions limited the yield from the draft. For the June 15, 1863 call for one hundred thousand troops, the town of Barrington in Yates County had 140 men in Class One. The procedure was for the district provost marshal to draw up to twenty percent of the names, although thirty-seven names were drawn for Barrington seeking to reach its quota of twenty-five men. The results were the following:

Paid Commutation	16
Non-resident	4
Physically deficient	6
Only son of aged parents	1
Over 35 and married	4
Only son of widow	1
Failed to report	2
Over age	1
Two brothers in service	1
Served	1

George N. Robertson was the only one whose name was drawn who actually served. Barrington could count toward its quota the sixteen who paid the commutation fee to the federal government, but still fell seven men short. However, there was no provision in the regulations for a second drawing to meet the shortfall, so the deficit was carried forward to the next call. [48] Results like these led Army Chief of Staff Henry W. Halleck to conclude in June 1864 that:

> As nearly all our resources for supplying the losses of the armies in the field
> are now exhausted, I have urged the resort to a new draft. I think one will be
> ordered as soon as Congress repeals the $300 commutation clause. So long
> as that exists we cannot get men, although a draft would bring some money
> into the Treasury. [49]

Of the 207,000 men who were drafted by the Union during the war, 87,000 paid the commutation fee – $26 million at $300 per exemption. [50] The commutation clause not only provided revenue for the Union war effort, it also created opportunity for the private sector. George R. Youngs and James Burns from Penn Yan in Yates County offered insurance against the draft. For a premium of $100, they would pay the $300 or secure a substitute. The deal was not bad for the substitute either. The substitute got the $300 from the insurance brokers plus $677 in state and federal bounties. [51]

However, revenue from the commutation clause was never expected to fund the entire war effort. The federal government had to issue bonds. Marketing the bonds became a major effort. One group of potential purchasers was the very soldiers who had received the bounty payments. The *Elmira Daily Advertiser* advised that the recruits seek "some safe and remunerative investments for their funds" and concluded that: "a soldier can make no better, more patriotic or remunerative disposition of his bounty money than by investing in the new Government 7-30 bonds [three year bonds paying 7.30% interest]." An officer was available at Barracks No. 1 of the Elmira Military Depot to sell the bonds. [52] The federal government sold nearly $800 million of the "seven-thirties". They were marketed in amounts as low as $50 to make them widely affordable. They were widely advertised and were the precursor to the twentieth century "war bonds". [53]

In order to pay the cost of local bounties, cities and towns also had to issue bonds. In August 1864, Elmira issued bonds at 7% interest, each bond in the principal amount of $500. [54] The cost of filling its quota had been $164,000. [55] In the spring of 1864, Company A's Daniel B. Lee and his wife Jane corresponded over whether they should invest his bounty money in bonds or in land. His wife preferred to buy a house and lot in town. Lee preferred the bounty bonds as a way of saving toward buying a farm when he returned home at the end of the war:

> I would not buy anywhere at present. The bounty orders are better than money. There is now ten percent premium on the orders and they are still advancing. Every hundred dollars is now worth a hundred and ten dollars and on interest beside... At present the orders are the best and safest investment we can procure. [56]

As if the draft itself was not complicated enough, the Enrollment Act of 1863 was overlaid on a continuing dispute between the federal government and the states over which would control the raising of troops. The federal government preferred to send new recruits to existing units in the field – many of which were seriously understrength due to battlefield casualties and illness as the war continued. The states preferred to create new regiments. The states' motivation was patronage. The federal government appointed the generals, who commanded brigades and larger units, but the states had the right to appoint the officers in new regiments – a colonel, a lieutenant colonel, and a major at the regimental level and a captain, a first lieutenant, and a second lieutenant for each of the ten companies comprising the standard regiment. [57] The new recruits themselves apparently also preferred serving in units manned and commanded by their neighbors. [58]

The practice of creating new regiments rather than sending replacements to existing units in the field was opposed by the career military. General Sherman said that it took a year to get a new regiment ready for combat, while replacements could be trained by veteran officers and sergeants. [59] This view was not limited to the professional military. In an article titled "The Correct way to raise Recruits Successfully," *The Hornellsville Tribune* had reported in January 1864 that:

> Col. Bentley, of the 63d N.Y.S. Volunteers, writes home that his regiment, whose term of service expires in a few months, has re-enlisted, will come home on a thirty days furlough, and while at home, will fill their regiment with new recruits, and after the respite and filling up, will return full fledged and fresh for service again.
>
> We understand such is also the decision of the 86th. ...
>
> We like the plan of letting the old regiments, whose term of service has nearly expired, come home on furlough, particularly so many of them as are willing to re-enlist, and let them enjoy a brief season of civic life at home – at the same time induce all they can to embark in the patriotic cause with them. Old regiments, even when reduced to a tithe of their original number, may be successfully filled up in this way, and be matured and ready for active service much sooner than where regiments are made up almost entirely from raw recruits. [60]

During 1862, only fifty thousand of the four hundred twenty-one thousand new three year enlistees had been sent to existing regiments. [61] The adoption of the Enrollment Act in 1863 was intended to be a victory for the federal government over the states by giving the federal government control over disposition of the new recruits. [62] And for a short time, it functioned that way. In October 1863, President Lincoln called for three hundred thousand volunteers to be raised by the states, but to be assigned to the states' existing units in the field. The draft would kick in for any state that did not meet its quota. The vast majority of the nearly four hundred thousand troops raised was assigned to existing units. [63]

However, the more powerful states, including New York, objected and pressed for their right to create new regiments. In February 1864, the War Department authorized the governors of New York and several other states to raise infantry troops to be formed into new regiments. [64] On March 22, 1864, the New York Adjutant General's Office – on behalf of "His Excellency Governor Seymour" – "respectfully" requested that the federal provost marshal muster in Albert Terrill, George Carpenter and James Farr as the officers of Company A of the 179th New York Volunteers. [65] Similar exercises of patronage by the state followed for the officers of the other companies of the 179th.

On February 1, 1864, President Lincoln issued an order for five hundred thousand men. The *Ontario County Times* and the *Watkins Express* explained that the number of new soldiers was actually only two hundred thousand because troops raised by the October 1863 call would be credited toward the five hundred thousand number. [66] At the same time, the *Ontario County Times* noted that:

> even this explanation does not prevent the order from being received with some degree of surprise. The hope had been widely entertained among the people that no more men would be needed; that the 300,000 called for in October would enable the government to make short work with the rebellion, and effect an early restoration of peace. [67]

In the end, the *Ontario County Times* trusted in President Lincoln's judgment, concluding that:

> Better to raise 500,000 to ensure victory than 100,000 to encounter defeat. Therefore we say amen to the President's call, feeling sure that it will be responded to with the same noble alacrity and the same persistent devotion to the national cause, that have marked the action of the people on similar occasions before. [68]

Optimistically, the *Watkins Express* commented: "This will perhaps be the last call of the war for volunteers, therefore let the response be hearty, the rally enthusiastic, and the remaining work, as heretofore done, with a will!" [69] But even five hundred thousand was not enough. Only six weeks later, President Lincoln called for an additional two hundred thousand troops, with the draft to start on April 15, 1864. [70]

In the meantime, on February 8, 1864, William M. Gregg of Elmira had been authorized by New York State and the federal government to raise a regiment of infantry in Western New York State. That regiment became the 179th New York Volunteers.

Maj. William Gregg, 23rd New York Volunteers

CHAPTER TWO

Motivations

A number of historians – and many of the veterans who enlisted in 1861 and 1862 – have questioned the patriotism of the men who did not come to the defense of the Union until after the draft and the high bounties came into play in 1864 and 1865. The most extreme adherents of this view have referred to the men receiving the high bounties as mercenaries. [1] However, this criticism is misdirected for four reasons.

First

> from the Army's perspective, the relevant consideration was not the degree of the men's patriotism, but rather whether they made good soldiers. While many claimed that the high-bounty men made poor soldiers, the evidence is to the contrary for the men of the 179th as a group.

Second

> human motivations are generally more complex than the lack of patriotism/ high bounty criticism implies. For example, a man who placed his obligation to family above his obligation to help preserve the Union was not necessarily a man lacking in the values that bind a society together. Moreover, a person's balancing of considerations can change over time. A man who felt in 1861 that the Union would survive the anticipated short war without him may have felt by 1864 that the prolonged war required him as a citizen to step up and

enlist independent of monetary considerations. (There is also the practical consideration that the government did not have the logistical capability in 1861 to handle the numbers if every able-bodied man had enlisted then.)

Third

the roughly eight hundred to a thousand men comprising a high-number regiment came from a variety of circumstances that undercuts the lack of patriotism/high bounty criticism. Thus some of the men of the 179th had just turned eighteen in 1864 and were therefore underage at the beginning of the war. Moreover, some of the men of the 179th had in fact enlisted in 1861 or 1862 and chose to serve again after their original enlistments had been completed.

Fourth

the fact that the men took the bounties offered in 1864 does not mean *ipso facto* that that was their driving motivation. One would have expected that a man driven by financial considerations would have gone to great lengths to keep out of harm's way at all times. The casualty numbers for the 179th demonstrate that that was generally not the case. An extreme case to the contrary was Company I's John Cook, an eighteen-year-old farmer from Tompkins County. He was captured at the battle of Poplar Spring Church. After being paroled from Salisbury Military Prison, Cook was furloughed to recover at home. Notwithstanding the hardship he had endured, he returned to the field, but almost immediately became sick again and died in a military hospital far from home. Company F's Ezra Northup, a nineteen-year-old farmer from Yates County, enlisted in the 179th with the understanding that he would serve as a musician, but when the 179th reached Virginia the regimental band had not been organized. As Northup's first sergeant recalled, Northup "willingly buckled on the armor of a private soldier." Northup was wounded in the June 17, 1864 assault "on a part of the field where there were no cowards." [2]

That was not the conduct of men just in it for the money.

The best answer to the question of motivation would come from the individual men of the 179th New York. Unfortunately, that answer will almost never be found. Bell Irvin Wiley, the author of *The Life of Billy Yank: The Common Soldier of the Union*, who probably read the correspondence of more Union soldiers than any other historian, cautioned against expecting an easy answer:

It seems clear...that the great bulk of volunteers responded to mixed motives, none of which was deeply felt.

One searches most letters and diaries in vain for soldiers' comment on why they were in the war or for what they were fighting. [3]

One soldier from the 179th who did discuss his motivations in writing was John T. Andrews, who joined the 179th as a second lieutenant in the fall of 1864. As a recent college graduate from a prominent family, his socio-economic status was not typical of the soldiers of the 179th, but his agonizing over whether to enlist or not at the beginning of the war is interesting to consider. [4] After a month in the field, Andrews recalled the carefree days of college after war broke out.

John Andrews

And yet, during all this time – during my whole college course at Alfred and at Union – I felt as though I was not doing my duty. When the first blast of the war trumpet rang throughout the whole North, calling patriots to their country's rescue I felt that I ought to respond; but a dear mother lay at death's door patiently awaiting the summons of her Lord, and I could not darken her last hours by expressing a wish to go. She died. I quietly pursued my studies till Fall and then another call for more men came and I spoke of going. Uncle John [T.?] said (not to me but in his own family circle) that if I went he would get a commission for me. All my friends and acquaintances told me I was foolish to think of going so long as my health remained as poor as it then was; father urged me not to go; my sisters were in tears every time I came into their presence; and I yielded. I would not, had I not felt that they were right – my health was too poor to endure a soldier's hardships and exposures.

For three years I continued my studies, yet I could not but ask myself the question, at times, who will be to blame if our Union is destroyed? and the answer invariably came. Those young men who, like myself, remain at home while the great struggle is going on. During my last term I made up my mind that after my graduation I would even with my poor health give my services to the government till rebellion was crushed or my life ended. [5]

Beyond John Andrews, I have found no other individual statements of motivation. For the rest of the men of the 179th, identification of general themes is the best that I can achieve.

Many of the men in the 179th New York were actually serving their second tour of duty. Almost all of the officers recruited in the spring of 1864 had enlisted in 1861 or 1862, but their original terms of enlistment had expired or they had otherwise left the service. In many cases, their original units had been deactivated. Major A. S. Diven, the provost marshal and head of the Volunteer Recruiting Service for the Western Division of New York, stated that the 179th "is to be officered by good men who have seen service." This cadre of veteran officers provided a critical source of experienced leadership for the 179th. As Company F's Newton Spencer recalled after the war, the 179th New York when initially organized was "seasoned with a thick sprinkling of tried and true veterans – staff and line officers mostly 'vets'." [6]

Moreover, approximately 11 percent of the enlisted men joining the 179th in the spring of 1864 had also enlisted in 1861 or 1862, but their original terms of enlistment had also expired and in most cases their original units had been deactivated. The following are the percentages of enlisted men in the 179th volunteering for their second or third enlistment [7]:

Company A	nine of 80	11%
Company B	ten out of 81	12%
Company C	thirteen out of 80	16%
Company D	ten out of 80	12%
Company E	nine out of 80	11%
Company F	ten out of 80	12%
Company G	three out of 81	4%

These veterans also provided an important source of experienced leadership for the 179th. Many of them became sergeants and corporals in the initial organization of their companies. Martin Doty – a twenty-eight-year-old druggist when the war broke out – and Levi Force – a twenty-year-old student – rose through the ranks to captain by the end of the war, commanding Companies B and C respectively. Charles Carr (21/shoemaker), Charles Lockwood (22/clerk), Henry Mapes (20/farmer), and Samuel G.H. Musgrave (23/cabinet-maker) rose to lieutenant. [8]

The prior service by these officers and enlisted men suggests yet another question. Having already loyally served their country, why did they choose to put their lives in danger again? Without questioning their patriotism and commitment to seeing the war through to the end, some may have also found the return to civilian life too tame after the heightened emotions caused by war. As described by nineteenth century journalist Ida Tarbell:

> [Y]ears of fighting, of defeat and victory, had hardened many of them into warriors, and they loved their trade. They might grumble at times, but the passion for danger and adventure had its hold on them, and no man who has once learned to love war steps back to a civilian's life with a whole heart. [9]

Similarly, James Marten wrote about the special status of being a soldier in *Sing Not War: The Lives of Union & Confederate Veterans in Gilded Age America*. He noted that veterans:

> rarely suggested that they loved war or killing, enjoyed camp life, or welcomed forced marches. But they almost universally expressed appreciation, their love for having been soldiers. Their service defined them, made them different, provided unique rewards and self-esteem beyond anything most Gilded Age Americans could muster. [10]

For veterans "reupping" as enlisted men there was the even higher bounty for veterans. Other veterans may have been motivated by the prospect for advancement to higher rank. The creation of a new regiment offered new officer and non-commissioned officer positions to be filled.

In addition to continuing patriotism, both the lure of military service and the prospect of advancement may have motivated the 179th's three most senior officers: William Gregg, Franklin B. Doty and J. Barnett Sloan.

When Gregg died in 1881, the *Corning Journal* described his character as follows:

> He was a rare organizer; shrewd, sagacious and persevering. He was ambitious, and this aroused hostility which was not mollified by his plain mode of speaking. He was true to his friends...

We have said that he was ambitious. It was a laudable desire and warranted by
his intellectual qualities and patriotic services. [11]

Gregg was born in Elmira in 1823 and learned the trade of a saddler. He was financially
successful, reporting real property valued at $12,290 and personal property valued at
$4,350 in the 1860 census. [12] He was elected sheriff as a Democrat in 1856. He was reputed
to be among the first men in Elmira to enlist in 1861. He served as major in the 23rd New
York Volunteers until 1863 when his term of enlistment expired and the 23rd
New York disbanded.

His command of a regiment offered Gregg promotion two higher ranks to full colonel. Gregg
seemed to like having responsibility for a large body of men. The regimental history of the 23rd
New York twice recounted the solicitude of Gregg (and Lieutenant Colonel Crane) for their men
during hard marches.

[W]ith their usual kind-heartedness, [they] relieved many a poor fellow of
his load long enough to get rested, so as to continue the march and keep
up... [T]hey were continually aiding these men by cheering words,
carrying their guns, and even dismounting, compelling the weary fellows
to ride. Such kindness is not soon forgotten by the soldier. [13]

Gregg was also willing to use his authority to do the right thing. When a Union artillery
battery commandeered a widow's horse, Gregg interceded on her behalf to secure the return of
her horse. [14]

Because of shortfalls in recruiting, the 179th took the field without him as a battalion in
the spring of 1864 under the command of Lieutenant Colonel Doty. Colonel Gregg remained
in Elmira through the summer recruiting to complete the 179th's complement of ten companies.
That task was accomplished by early fall and he joined the 179th in the field in October 1864. While
recruiting, Colonel Gregg also remained politically active. At the end of August 1864, he served as
a delegate from Elmira's 4th Ward at the county convention of the Union [Republican] party. [15]

In the 179th's last battle, Gregg was wounded leading the charge and was brevetted brigadier
general. Gregg's military ambitions may well have been satisfied thereby, but after the war he
unsuccessfully pursued the Republican nomination for a seat in Congress. [16]

While Colonel Gregg remained in Elmira recruiting, Lt. Col. Franklin B. Doty commanded the
179th in the field in the spring and early summer of 1864. Doty was an able, battle-tested officer,
having served in the 23rd New York Volunteers as a company commander. He was thirty-one
when he enlisted in 1861. When then Captain Doty returned home with the 23rd New York in
mid-1863 upon the expiration of his two year enlistment, a local newspaper provided the following
complimentary history of his service:

Capt. Doty is the son of the old hotel keeper of that name, well-known to
the older citizens of Hornellsville and Steuben county. At the time of
the breaking out of the rebellion he was at Fort Pickens near Mobile. He
hastened home and joined the first Hornellsville company, then being
organized by Lieut. Col. Crane, as a private. When Mr. Crane was made
Lieut. Col. at the organization of the 23d Regiment, Mr. Doty was
selected as the most suitable person to take command of the company;
and he was promoted to Captain. Without any ostentation or noise,
he brought his company to a State of discipline and perfection in drill,
scarcely excelled by any in the Regiment. – His quiet, unassuming

disposition as a man, and his firmness as an officer, have made him beloved by both officers and men. His company have made no march without him at their head. He fought at their head at Rappahannock Crossing, Sulphur Springs, Gainesville, Bull Run, South Mountain, Antietam, and Fredericksburg... Lieut. Bennett informs us that at Antietam he saw Capt. Doty take and disarm a secesh with his own hands. [17]

When Doty requested a ten day leave of absence in 1863, the commanding officer of the 23rd New York, Col. Henry Hoffman, stated that: "Capt. Doty has by his ability and fidelity to duty earned any favour consistent with existing orders." [18]

Doty was an adventurous spirit, as evidenced by the fact that as a young man before the war he had left landlocked Hornell to go to sea on a whaler. Doty knew the risks of war, having been in a number of battles with the 23rd New York, including Antietam and Fredericksburg. [19]

Doty had seemed destined for leadership since childhood. At the end of the war, a childhood schoolmate recalled a George Washington-like incident involving Doty.

[H]e was then the soul of truth and of integrity. Of great personal bravery among the boys, never flinching from the most severe and arduous play, always leading the troop of schoolboys in their more vigorous sports....

I well remember an event that tested his truthfulness. It was during the rule of Samuel Street as school teacher. ... [A]n excellent well meaning man [who] had no other idea of governing a school except by birch whips ... He was a terror to us little fellows. One summer day the odor of burning matches filled the school room: – who was the guilty party? No flame could be seen, and it was impossible to discover whence the smell emanated. ... [Mr. Street] began ... with the question "did you strike a match in the schoolroom?" All answered "No:" finally it came to Frank – "no" was his reply – then paused a moment ..." but," said he, "I reached my hand out of the window and struck some matches on the side of the house." How his outspoken truthfulness filled us all with a boy's worship of a noble trait. [20]

While there is no basis to suggest that Doty's strong patriotism had waned since 1861, the prospect of promotion from a company commander to a field grade officer as second in command may have heightened his motivation to return to war.

John Barnett Sloan was twenty-three-years old and living in New York City when the war broke out. He enlisted for a two year term in the 31st New York Volunteers and was made a first lieutenant. Contemporary lore provides the following account from Sloan's early service. When the 31st was ordered to Washington, a number of recruits refused to go, and Lieutenant Sloan's forceful handling of the situation created some ill will toward him in the regiment. Shortly after they arrived in Washington, a soldier attacked Sloan and Sloan killed him with his sword. Several days later another soldier attacked Sloan and Sloan killed him with his pistol. Sloan surrendered himself and requested an investigation. He was exonerated by a court-martial. The sentence was submitted to General McClellan for his review. McClellan reputedly was so impressed by Sloan's actions that he called Sloan in to meet him. McClellan is reported to have told him: "Lieutenant, you are acquitted:

you were born to be a soldier. I see that you have but one bar upon your shoulder; you are worthy to wear two." [21]

Sloan served in McClellan's Peninsula campaign, where he was wounded in two separate incidents of hand-to-hand combat. He was furloughed to recover from those wounds and then served as a recruiting officer for several months. He returned to the front in time for the battle of Fredericksburg where he was wounded again. He was mustered out in May 1863 when his term of enlistment expired, but was also given a promotion to major for meritorious service effective January 1863. [22] Sloan would have been the lieutenant colonel in a reorganized 31st New York, but there were insufficient reenlistments to continue the regiment. [23]

Sloan was certainly a hardened military man of action. While the possibility of immediately holding higher rank may have influenced Gregg and Doty, Sloan entered the 179th with his prior rank of major. Perhaps he hoped for another chance at promotion to lieutenant colonel which had eluded him in the 31st New York.

Although the prospect of commanding a company as a captain may have motivated Robert Stewart, John Barton and Daniel Blachford, who had served as lieutenants during their first tours

William Bird, Jr.

of duty [24], promotion does not appear to have motivated William Bird, Jr., who would command Company D of the 179th. Bird had been mustered out of the 37th New York as a captain, but was initially to be mustered into the 179th as only a first lieutenant. [25] He became captain of Company D only when the man initially slated for the position withdrew. Bird, a farmer, may well have been one of those citizen-soldiers who could not give up war.

Bird's mother and father brought him to the United States from Scotland in 1834 at the age of four. Bird's father pursued his trade as a granite cutter and stone mason in New York City, Upstate New York, Connecticut, and Massachusetts for fifteen years as the family grew, and then purchased a 120 acre farm in Ellicottville, Cattaraugus County in 1849. In the 1860 Census, Bird, Sr. was recorded as a mason with real property valued at $1800 and personal property at $800. William Bird, Jr., then thirty, and his younger brothers were running the farm. [26]

Bird enlisted in Company I of the 37th New York in May 1861 and initially served as an enlisted man. He became orderly sergeant in the initial organization of Company I shortly after his company reached Virginia. [27] Bird seemed to like the responsibility of command. He took great pride in his responsibility as orderly sergeant:

> I have been doing two men's duty for the last two weeks since [?] went home and I have been drove to death but I am tough and hearty. ... The Orderly has the whole charge of the company in active service. I call the men up at four in the morn and am busy until I order the lights out at half past ten at night. I have to draw all the rations and see that the cooks have them cooked at the proper time and see to things generally. [28]

Bird described the excitement of his first sight of the enemy in an August 1861 letter to his father. He was in command as orderly sergeant of a party of skirmishers.

> I was in the road with two men with me. The rest were in the woods on both sides of the road when just as we got on top of the hill we come on a party of the enemy's cavalry pickets about 25 rods off. They fired a

pistol on us and then turned tail and went off like the devil down the road. We fired four shots on them and dropped one of them off from his horse. ... We returned to camp in the evening and were highly complimented by the Colonel and myself in particular for my coolness and courage. [29]

Bird was promoted to second lieutenant in May 1862 for gallantry at the battle of Williamsburg during McClellan's Peninsula campaign. A month later, he suffered a bayonet wound in the leg and a bullet wound in the shoulder at the battle of Fair Oaks. He returned to duty after several months and was promoted to first lieutenant and then captain. He served as a company commander in the battles of Fredericksburg and Chancellorsville. [30]

War took its toll on Bird. After the battle of Chancellorsville, in which his company suffered twenty casualties and his regiment over two hundred, he wrote home that:

The army is badly used up and will take some time to get fixed up again. I don't think any thing more can be done before our time is up which is only three weeks now and I am glad of it for I have had enough of the war. [31]

Notwithstanding his discouragement in May of 1863, Bird enlisted in the 179th nine months later in February 1864. Why did he re-enlist? If Bird gave an explicit answer to the question, I have not found it. Some possible insight is provided in his post-war recollections. In 1883, Bird wrote the Pension Bureau, that when he was mustered out in 1863, "My occupation being that of a farmer I returned to my farm but finding myself unfitted for manual farm labour (by reason of my wound) after remaining at home about two months I recruited a new Company." Why he felt that his wounds rendered him unfit for farm labor but not for the rigors of war is not apparent. It would seem that he missed the military life. [32]

Similar considerations may apply to the veterans who reenlisted in the 179th New York as enlisted men. However, they – as opposed to the officers – were eligible for bounties. Moreover, veterans received higher bounties than new recruits.

However, the fact remains that the vast majority of the men of the 179th had not enlisted earlier in the war. Before dismissing them as unpatriotic, other factors need to be considered.

Some of the men who enlisted in the 179th in 1864 had been too young to enlist in 1861. Roughly a sixth of those enlisting in the 179th in the spring of 1864 were only eighteen years old, which means they would have been underage in 1861, 1862 and much if not all of 1863. Another six percent were nineteen. This does not necessarily mean that these eighteen and nineteen-year-olds enlisted in 1864 with the same patriotic enthusiasm that their older brothers, cousins, fathers and uncles did in 1861. While these eighteen and nineteen-year-olds were not imminently subject to the draft in the spring of 1864, they were eligible for the bounties being paid at that time. However, enlistment by eighteen and nineteen-year-olds in the spring of 1864 at least suggests the need for caution in assuming that soldiers in the high-number regiments lacked devotion to the Union cause. For example, when nineteen-year-old Charles Baker reached the front in Virginia and wrote his mother, he did not speak of money: "I enjoy myself here because I believe that I am doing my douty." [33]

The percentages of eighteen and nineteen year olds for the individual companies are the following [34]:

	18 years old	19 years old	Total
Company A	26%	5%	31%
Company B	16%	10%	26%
Company C	25%	6%	31%
Company D	27%	5%	32%
Company E	6%	5%	11%
Company F	6%	6%	12%
Company G	6%	10%	16%

Another consideration that some men who joined the 179th in 1864 would have faced in 1861 was family obligations. As Steven Ramold noted in *Across the Divide*:

> leaving their families for war caused a moral and economic quandary. Men were absenting themselves not only from their roles as fathers and husbands, but also from their responsibility to provide for the care and comfort of their wives and children. [35]

A man who placed his obligation to his family above his obligation to his country did not necessarily fail to do the right thing. For example, in 1861, Marshall Phillips and his wife had five children under the age of fifteen. Leaving his wife to manage a farm and raise five children would not have been an easy choice. However, by 1864, the draft effectively mandated that choice. There was no exemption for fathers of large families. [36] When his eldest son, Newton, enlisted in the 179th just shy of eighteen years old in February 1864, Marshall enlisted the following day. Marshall Phillips was mortally wounded in the 179th's first battle. Daniel Ormsby was also mortally wounded in the June 17 assault. He had six young children in 1861. [37] Similarly, Timothy Buckland had seven children under the age of sixteen (all daughters) in 1861. He was taken prisoner at the Battle of the Crater and died in Salisbury Prison. Moses Brown had five children under the age of fourteen in 1861. He died of lung congestion in January 1865. [38] Men supporting elderly parents would have faced similar concerns in 1861 about abandoning their family obligations. [39]

The 179th had one documented case of a conscientious objector: Roswell H. Davis, who lived in Volney, New York. He was drafted in August 1863, declared fit for service, and ultimately assigned to the 179th New York. He told the Provost Marshal's Office that: "it was against my principles to take arms against my fellow man. I belong to an Association entitled "The Children of God" one of the tenets of which is that we will harm no man." On that basis, Davis refused to report despite the Provost Marshal's direction to do so, and went home. [40]

Finally, it should be recognized that the physical danger and hardship of fighting in the army dissuaded many men from serving. Despite the threat of the draft and the lure of bounties, roughly half of the men of military age in the North never did answer their country's call. [41] However, the men of the 179th did serve their country.

The element of personal risk undertaken by the men of the 179th should not be overlooked. In 1861, there was little if any understanding in the general population of the grim reality that war meant death and injury. The limited casualties in the Mexican War had barely touched the general population and had occurred fifteen years before at that. [42] As James McPherson notes, "In 1861 many Americans had a romantic, glorious idea of war." [43] In 1861, the possibility of death in battle was discussed, if at all, in heroic terms, as exemplified by the death of Col. Ephraim Elmer

Ellsworth, the Union's first war hero. Ellsworth was shot after taking down a Confederate flag that had flown on the top of a hotel in Alexandria. He was lionized in the newspapers. [44] [Sketch: Ellsworth's death]

By the beginning of 1864, the reality of massive casualties without individual glory in battles such as Antietam, Fredericksburg, and Gettysburg had hit home. And photographs provided a new visual reality for death on the battlefield. [45] *The New York Times* wrote of Matthew Brady's first exhibition after the Battle of Antietam in 1862: "Mr. BRADY has done something to bring home to us the terrible reality and earnestness of war. If he has not brought bodies and laid them in our door-yards and along the streets, he has done something very like it." [46] [Photo: Antietan dead] For family men, the widely reported story of Sgt. Amos Humiston dying at Gettysburg with a photo of his three children in his hand added a personal element to the risk. [47]

In the end, the question of motivation is not only multi-faceted, but ultimately irrelevant. The real question is whether the men who enlisted in the 179th New York in 1864 made good soldiers, regardless of their motivation for enlisting. Many veterans and historians have criticized the men in the high-number regiments not only for being unpatriotic, but also for being bad soldiers. [48] As we will see, that criticism was wide of the mark for the vast majority of the men of the 179th New York.

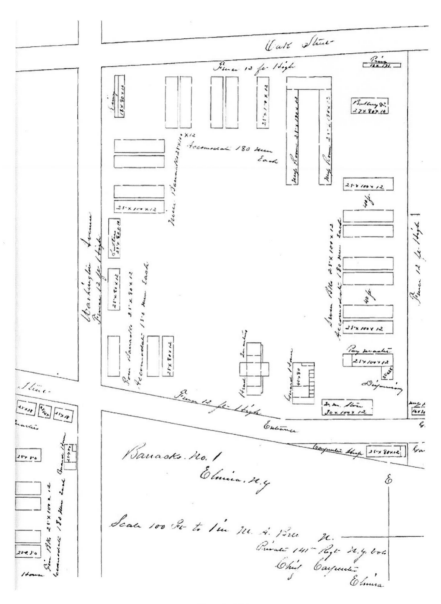

Barracks Map

Arnot Barracks, Elmira, 1864

CHAPTER THREE

Raising the 179th

Three days after President Lincoln issued a call for another five hundred thousand troops in February 1864, the Provost Marshal General's Office authorized the Governor of New York to raise forty new companies of infantry "to be combined into regiments as fast as companies are completed." These units were to be assigned to the Ninth Corps of the Army of the Potomac. [1] Two divisions of the Ninth Corps had been detached from the Army of the Potomac in the fall of 1863 and sent west to support the Army of the Tennessee, but were ordered back east in early 1864. At that point, the Ninth Corps had approximately six thousand veteran troops, but ultimately began the spring 1864 campaign with a strength of twenty-four thousand troops, augmented by the new recruits. [2]

On February 8, 1864, Secretary of War Edwin Stanton authorized William Gregg to raise a regiment in Western New York. Governor Horatio Seymour also authorized Gregg to proceed. The resulting new regiment was the 179th New York Volunteers. [3] On February 13, 1864 and again on February 22, the Headquarters of the Volunteer Recruiting Service for the Western District of New York advised the federal provost marshals of the various congressional districts in the area that "it is very desirable that [the 179th] Regiment be filled as soon as possible" and that bounties could be paid to recruits for the new regiment on the same basis as recruits for existing units in the field. The district provost marshals were authorized to grant short furloughs to "reliable men." On February 29, the provost marshal for the Elmira area was directed to furlough all men mustered for the 179th

New York Volunteers. [4]

The creation of the 179th was reported – or advertised – throughout Western New York. Two weeks after the call for five hundred thousand men, *The Havana Journal* reported that "Major Gregg of the old 'Southern Tier' 23rd NYSV is actively engaged in getting up a new regiment to be designated the 179th NYSV." [5] The *Owego Gazette* reported on February 18 that "already six skeleton companies are in progress." [6] The *Yates County Chronicle* reported the same day that Capt. Rodgers and A. T. Farwell were recruiting for the 179th and on March 10, 1864 that Sloan had begun recruiting for the 179th and was authorized to pay the usual bounty, including "the County, State and National." [7] A handbill distributed by Sloan offered a bounty of $677 for new recruits and $832 for veterans to join the 179th New York Volunteers. *The Hornellsville Tribune* reported that: "Lieut. Barton, late of the 141st, and Lieut. Prentiss of the 23rd, have been authorized to raise a company for this regiment in the 3rd Assembly District" (and incorrectly stated that the 179th New York was the only new regiment authorized to be raised in New York State). [8]

Giles Holden

Giles Holden, a newspaperman with the *Niagara Falls Gazette*, opened offices in Lockport and Suspension Bridge to recruit a company for the 179th New York. [9] Holden took a different tack in his recruiting ads for "Capt. Holden's company" in the [Batavia] *Spirit of the Times* and *The* [Warsaw] *Western New Yorker*. He led with money – $700 to new recruits, but then claimed that the 179th was being recruited "For Railroad Service" and repeated that at the end of the ad. He also described the 179th as "The only New Regiment for which Local Bounties are still paid. The only one where Good Men have a chance of promotion." [10]

Voluntary enlistment called for a written contract setting forth the terms of service agreed to. By signing the standard Volunteer Enlistment form, the recruit acknowledged that he had "volunteered ... to serve as a *Soldier* in the *Army of the United States of America*, for the period of THREE YEARS, unless sooner discharged by proper authority" and that he agreed to accept "such bounty, pay, rations, and clothing, as are, or may be, established by law for volunteers." He also solemnly swore "that I will bear true faith and allegiance to the *United States of America*, and that I will serve them honestly and faithfully against all their enemies or opposers whomsoever; and that I will observe and obey the orders of the President of the United States, and the orders of the officers appointed over me, according to the Rules and Articles of War." (emphasis in original)[11]

On the back side of the form, the recruit declared that he had never been "discharged from the United States service on account of disability or by sentence of a court martial, or by order before the expiration of a term of enlistment" and that he knew "of no impediment to my serving honestly and faithfully as a soldier for three years."

The form also included a section for "Consent In Case of Minor" and a section for the details of any prior service. Among the enlistees in the 179th New York was Newton Phillips, who was not yet eighteen. He enlisted on February 12, 1864 with the written consent of his father, Marshall Phillips, who then himself enlisted the following day. [12]

The section on prior service was relevant because a veteran was entitled to a higher bounty. Approximately ten percent of the men enlisting in the 179th New York in the spring of 1864 had previously served in other units. [13]

The new recruit was examined and accepted by the surgeon of the district's enrollment board. The surgeon would certify that the recruit was "free from all bodily defects and mental infirmity, which would in any way disqualify him from performing the duties of a soldier." [14] However, medical examinations generally were superficial and it has been estimated that a quarter of the recruits should have been rejected for medical reasons. [15] The army's need for more troops prevailed over sound medical practice. And some men may have preferred the bounty payment to a medical disqualification.

The captain and provost marshal, signing as "Recruiting Officer", certified that he had "minutely inspected the Volunteer" and that "he was entirely sober when enlisted." The recruit's height, eye and hair color, and complexion were also described. [16]

Individual soldiers for the 179th New York were recruited in towns throughout western New York State. After being mustered in individually in the various provost marshal districts – and paid their local bounty, the recruits for the 179th were forwarded to the Elmira Military Depot for the formation of the companies that would comprise the 179th New York. The commander of the depot certified on the enlistment form that the recruit had been turned over to him. Depending on the location where the recruit started the process, it was possible to complete the paperwork in a single day, although there frequently were delays in forwarding the recruits from the local provost marshal's office to Elmira. [17]

Elmira had been selected by Governor Edwin Morgan as one of New York State's three military depots in 1861, along with New York City and Albany, because of its transportation connections. [18] Elmira was located at the intersection of two railroads – the Erie Railroad, which ran east-west, and the Williamsport & Elmira (subsequently the North Central Railroad and ultimately the Pennsylvania Railroad), which ran north-south. Elmira was also located on the Chemung Canal, which offered a connection north to the Erie Canal. All tolled, 20,796 Union soldiers were enrolled, equipped and at least partially trained in Elmira during the course of the war. [19]

Four barracks were built around Elmira: Arnot Barracks, later referred to as Barracks #1, which was located a mile north of town (and housed the 179th New York in the spring and summer of 1864); Camp Rathbun, later referred to as Barracks #3, which was located a mile west of town (and also housed troops from the 179th before becoming a prisoner of war camp in August 1864); the Post Barracks, located a mile west of town; and #4, Camp Robinson, located a mile and a half southwest of town on the other side of the Chemung River. Two military hospitals were established as well as other military support facilities. [20]

By the end of June of 1861, 9,500 soldiers had already gone through the Elmira Depot on their way to war. [21] However, things slowed down considerably for the next two years. The Post Barracks and Camp Robinson were deactivated in 1863, although some new facilities were added at Camp Rathbun and the Arnot Barracks.

When the draft began in July 1863, Elmira also served as the draft rendezvous for Western New York. The Elmira depot began filling up again at the end of 1863 after the draft in July and the call for three hundred thousand more troops in October. By February 1864, when President Lincoln announced a call for another two hundred thousand troops, the Elmira barracks facilities were overcrowded. On January 31, 1864, Lt. Col. Seth Eastman, the commander of the Elmira Depot, reported to Brig. General Lorenzo Thomas, the Adjutant General of the War Department, that the troops were "very badly crowded in Barracks that were intended for about half the men in them." A week later, Eastman reported that there were 4300 men at Elmira, but quarters for only 3560. In addition, "[T]here are now several thousand recruits in the hands of the Provost Marshal [who was responsible for enlistments] ready to be sent here as soon as there is room for them." [22] The *Yates County Chronicle* reported that: "Elmira is said to be overflowing with soldiers. They are sent forward from all parts of the State faster than the officers there are able to perform the red tape exercises required to send them forward to the field." [23]

Eastman subsequently received authorization for additional disbursing agents to increase the number of soldiers who could be processed for forwarding to five hundred per day. (For the last two weeks of January 1864, the average had been less than 140 per day.) He also drew upon the troops at the depot to serve as clerks. [24] Eastman also received authorization to build new housing in Barracks #1 and Barracks #3, but that authorization came just as Eastman reported that "the number of recruits has been reduced to suit the capacity of the quarters." Still, to maintain that balance, the Provost Marshal's Bureau had been "directed to order in but three hundred [recruits] daily for the present." [25]

The recruits for the 179th began arriving in Elmira in March 1864. [26] Those enlisting in February had benefited from the crowded conditions at Elmira. As noted, on February 29, 1864, the provost marshals had been directed to furlough all soldiers mustered in for the 179th, rather than forwarding them to Elmira. As a result, the February enlistees got to remain home after enlisting for several weeks longer than their comrades who enlisted in March and April. [27]

The recruits for the 179th were housed in Barracks #1. [28] It was bounded on the north by Washington Avenue, on the east by Oak Street, and on the south by the canal yards. The entrance was on the west side where Lake Street and Conongue Streets intersected at an angle. [29]

The setting of Barracks #1 was:

> quite as high as the surrounding country, on firm, hard, gravelly soil, covered with greeensward, which does not become soft even during very wet periods, though the drainage is not good. The form of the ground is nearly a square, whose side is about 300 yards. There is not in its vicinity either marsh, standing water, or dense forest, or any locus of malaria or disease. [30]

As for the individual barracks buildings,

> The height of the buildings on the inside is about 8 feet to the eaves and 15 feet to the ridge pole. They are quite well ventilated by means of windows and doors. The quarters of the men comprise ten buildings [88 by 18 feet each with wooden bunks placed end to end on each of the long sides of the building, arranged in two tiers, 12 sets of 2 double bunks, one above the other] and are designed for 100 men each, though 150 can readily be accommodated and comfortably. [31]

The kitchen and the mess hall were in the same building. The mess hall "is completely furnished with tables and benches and will seat 1,000 men, while the kitchen is abundantly supplied to cook for that number." [32]

Barracks #1 was reported in January 1864 as being "in good condition, having been little used." [33] However, the status of the latrines which had been described in 1862 as "wretchedly deficient and in bad order," may have been questionable. Similarly, the mess hall may have had "a terrible stench" from "soups which have been spilt on the floor." [34]

Prior to 1864, meals at the depot had been furnished by a contractor at a cost of 28 cents per ration. Starting in January 1864, the meals were cooked by soldiers. There were two meals a day – at nine in the morning and three thirty in the afternoon. Meat was served at both meals along with coffee. An inspecting officer reported that: "It is cooked by soldiers and *well* cooked" (emphasis in original) He further reported that: "Every man I asked said he was satisfied," although he acknowledged that "the bread furnished is only of fair quality." [35] In May 1864, Eastman reported to Thomas that: "The police of the Barracks, Mess Rooms and Grounds is excellent. The rations [are] good and vegetables are bountifully supplied the troops." [36]

However, Company A's Daniel Lee did not see it that way. Lee wrote his father that he had already lost sixteen pounds in the first two weeks and was "in a fair way" to lose sixteen more "if I don't get used to the fare faster than I have." Company C's George Hickey was only slightly more complimentary in a letter to his father: "We have enough to eat such as it is." [37]

Lee also described barracks life at Elmira, hopefully with some exaggeration:

> If you was here you wood think it was as a compleat a hog pen as evere you did see. Are hog pens is about 80[?] feet long by sixteene and when we com to our eating room to smell the ritch perfume it wood give a most any men an apetite for there fodder. [38]

Major Sloan's promise in his recruiting advertisement that the men would be provided a "New Clean Camp" at Elmira may have been only a reference to the new barracks then to be constructed, but it may also have reflected a reputation for conditions that were not as good as officially reported. [39]

The minimum number of enlisted men required to muster in a new infantry company was eighty. By the beginning of April, the number of enlisted recruits designated for Company A had reached eighty and Company A was formally mustered in on April 5, 1864. [40] Captain Albert Terrill began organizing Company A. In Order No. 1, dated April 7, 1864, he appointed Company A's non-commissioned officers: five sergeants and eight corporals. Terrill directed that the newly appointed non-commissioned officers "will be obeyed and respected accordingly." [41]

The ever present concern about alcohol was addressed by Captain Terrill in Order No. 2: "Any non-commissioned officer of Co. A ... being found under the influence of liquor while on duty will be reduced to the ranks and his position filled by a more worthy soldier." [42]

The district provost marshals continued forwarding recruits for Companies B and C. The pace was slow at the end of March, but then quickened in April. The provost marshal for the 27th District (Chemung, Steuben and Alleghany Counties) forwarded five recruits on March 31, two on April 2, three on April 8, seventy-five on April 11, nine on April 14, and at least twenty-one on April 16. [43] Upon also reaching eighty enlisted men, Companies B and C were mustered in on April 13 and April 23 respectively. [44]

The formation of the 179th New York had to contend not only with the ups and downs of recruiting, but also with the problem of bounty jumpers. Shortly after President Lincoln's February 1864 call for troops, the *Elmira Press* observed that:

> We have heard it stated that if one will start out in almost any direction from Elmira, by looking over the fences and into the corners, he will hardly fail to find one or more suits of soldiers' clothes. Last Saturday, a gentleman in Southport found three suits in his garden lot, and we heard of two suits being picked up just outside of town yesterday. These are in every case entirely new, and are cast off by men who have enlisted for the sake of getting the bounties, and have deserted as soon as they received the greenbacks. [45]

This was a colorful exaggeration, but the problem of desertion – discussed further in Chapters 5, 14 and 19 – was real. In the leading study of desertion during the Civil War, Ella Lonn concluded that the "large and numerous bounties given to volunteers proved undoubtedly an inducement to desert for the purpose of reenlisting, or to enlist when the recruit knew that he had no intention of remaining in the field." [46] The 179th New York saw both the "one time" bounty jumper and the professional recidivist as the individual companies were organized in Elmira and then sent to the front.

Bounty jumping was an attractive proposition for an unscrupulous individual. The reward was high and the risk of getting caught was low. While the amount of the bounty – $677 in New York the spring of 1864– does not seem large, it was by Civil War era standards when a farm laborer earned only $13 to $30 a month depending on the season.

Once payment was received, there were many opportunities to escape before a recruit would find himself in the trenches. [47] First, there was the trip from the local provost marshal's office to Elmira. Then there was the stay at the Elmira Military Depot – which could be several months long – while recruits were accumulated to form companies and then regiments. And then there was the trip to the front. The cash that bounty jumpers received was not only their incentive to desert, but also an important means of escape. Many bounty jumpers bolted at an opportune moment, but others simply bribed the guards to escape. [48]

It was nearly impossible to deny a determined bounty jumper all opportunity to escape. According to Ella Lonn, once the bounty jumper escaped, "The vast size of the country, the feverish zeal of each town and city district to fill its quota, rendered it hard to detect the miserable bounty-jumpers." [49]

The provost marshal's office actively pursued deserters. A $30 bounty for the return of deserters incented private citizens to become involved as well. The provost marshals did have some success. The provost marshal for the 27th District reported the arrest of twenty-seven deserters during the first ten days of March 1864 and another twenty-six by March 21. [50] At the end of April 1864, there were about two hundred deserters in the guardhouse at Elmira. [51]

Sometimes the bounty jumper did not get very far before being arrested. John Henry Newman deserted from Barracks #3 around eleven the night of June 18, 1864 and walked to Corning where he was arrested in civilian clothes the next day. [52] Company D's John McNulty (alias John McInnerney) deserted from Barracks #1 on July 7, 1864, but was still in Elmira when he was arrested two days later. [53] Some bounty jumpers were not particularly creative. Abel Webb bought his way out of Barracks #1 and then went home to Bolivar, New York where he was arrested a month later. [54] Family members were not always loyal to their bounty jumper. Steven Hungerford deserted from Barracks #1 on February 18, 1864. He was arrested in Troy, Pennsylvania on June 13, 1864, wearing civilian clothes and working on a farm. He claimed his name was Stephen Hanford. His mother and father confirmed that he was Stephen Hungerford. [55]

It was not unusual for a successful bounty jumper to try again. At a time when there were no social security numbers, picture ID's or fingerprint identification, it was very easy for a recruit to enlist under one name, desert, and then enlist in a different unit under a different name. Personal recognition was the only effective means of detecting such a bounty jumper, [56] but that means was more successful than might at first seem. Because all recruits from western New York were funneled through Elmira, bounty jumpers ran the risk of being recognized there by their former comrades if they enlisted a second time.

There were a number of men in the 179th New York who deserted and tried to enlist in another unit to receive another bounty. For example, James Scott enlisted in the 179th at Buffalo and deserted from Barracks #1 at Elmira in April 1864. He then went back to Dunkirk and enlisted in the 15th Engineers under the name of John McKenn. However, he was recognized and arrested when he returned to Elmira with the 15th Engineers in May. Similarly, William Dunn enlisted in the 180th New York in Buffalo and deserted. He then enlisted in the 179th at Elmira, but was recognized in the barracks by recruits from the 180th. [57] John Sullivan (alias Michael Wallen) and John McKee (alias Francis Reilly) enlisted in the 180th New York in Buffalo, where they each received a $200 bounty. They deserted on the way to Auburn, went to Dunkirk and enlisted in the 179th New York, receiving another $200 bounty, but also were recognized. [58]

When caught, a bribe was also a last resort. James Scott offered Company E's Sgt. Charles Lockwood $100 and then $200 to let him go. [59] When Franklin Wilkins was arrested a day after he deserted from Barracks #1, he unsuccessfully offered the officer $100 to let him go. (Wilkins was mortally wounded in the final assault at Petersburg.) [60]

Still, the great majority of bounty jumpers evaded capture. [61]

The Elmira Military Depot served not only as the place for organizing the 179th New York, but also as the place for conducting initial training. The purpose of what we refer to today as "basic training" is to turn a civilian into a soldier and prepare him for battle. James McPherson wrote in *For Cause and Comrades* that:

> The traditional means of motivating soldiers to fight are training, discipline and leadership. Civil War volunteer regiments were notoriously deficient in the first, weak in the second and initially shaky in the third. [62]

According to McPherson, "Infantry training consisted mainly of the manual of arms and close-order drill, with a little bayonet exercise and target practice thrown in when time and equipment were available." [63] They would have been trained based on William Hardeee's or Silas Casey's *Tactics* both of which taught doctrines "that had not changed much for a century or more." [64]

While the purpose of "close-order drill" in today's military is to inculcate discipline, Richard Slotkin notes that: "In 1864 it was training for combat. The infantry was armed with single-shot rifle-muskets, and the only way to deliver significant firepower was by massing them shoulder-to-shoulder to deliver their fire." The complex maneuvers were necessary to move troops quickly from one point to another and then reform them in the lines that would bring their firepower to bear. [65] The specific responsibilities for the individual officers and non-commissioned officers to make that happen were detailed in the manuals. The roles of the five sergeants – first, second, third, fourth and fifth – were as much functional as hierarchical. [66]

Given the complexity of the subject matter, Hardee provided the following guidance for teaching in the *School of the Soldier*:

> 48. Individual instruction being the basis of the instruction of the companies, on which that of the regiment depends, and the first principles having the greatest influence upon this individual instruction, classes of recruits should be watched with the greatest care.

> 49. Instructors will explain, in a few clear and precise words, the movements to be executed; and not to overburden the memory of the men, they will always use the same terms to explain the same principles.

> 50. They should often join example to precept, should keep up the attention of the men by an animated tone, and pass rapidly from one movement to another, as soon as that which they command has been executed in a satisfactory manner. [67]

The first companies of the 179th had but a month or less of training in Elmira. There was little if any time at Elmira for target practice by the soldiers of the 179th because they did not receive their weapons until just before they left. Companies A, B and C had another month of training on Arlington Heights across the Potomac from Washington before the 179th headed to the front in Virginia. Companies D, E and F had an additional two weeks at Arlington Heights, while Companies F and G went directly to the front from Elmira. This was actually more training than many Civil War regiments received. [68]

However, the 179th New York did have one important advantage. At the beginning of the war, the newly forming regiments did not have veterans available to train them. [69] The 179th New York was very fortunate to have a core of seasoned officers and non-commissioned officers to direct the training.

Captain Albert Terrill, the commander of Company A, had previously served with the 38th New York Volunteers for two years. First Lt. George D. Carpenter had served for a year in the 126th New York, but Second Lt. James Farr had no prior service. [70]

In Company B, Capt. Robert Stewart had served as a second lieutenant in the 141st Infantry, one of Elmira's other "home" regiments. First Lt. George Cook had no prior service, but Second Lt. James Bowker, who also initially served as the acting regimental adjutant, had served in the 23rd New York as a second lieutenant. [71]

In Company C, Capt. John Barton had been a first lieutenant in the 141st New York Volunteers and First Lt. John Prentiss had been a second lieutenant in the 23rd New York. Second Lt. Nathaniel P. T. Finch, a surveyor and budding lawyer by profession, had no prior service. [72]

In Company D, Capt. William Bird had been a captain in the 37th New York as noted. First Lt. Baker Saxton had been a captain in the 154th New York. Second Lt. Jeffrey Wisner had served as an enlisted man in the 107th New York. [73]

In Company E, Capt. Daniel Blachford had been a second lieutenant in the 21st Infantry. First Lt. John Hoy had served as a sergeant in the 21st New York and had been wounded at the Second Battle of Bull Run. Second Lt. Louis J. Ottenot had served as a private in the same company of the 21st New York as Blachford. [74]

In contrast to the first six companies, none of the officers of Company F had seen prior service – Capt. Allen Farwell, a hotel-keeper turned blacksmith in his mid-thirties; First Lt. David A. Bradley, a twenty-two year-old house painter and bartender (and Sloan's brother-in-law); and Second Lt. Giles Holden, a thirty-five year-old newspaperman. However, Company F did have two sergeants who were veterans – William Norton from the 23rd New York and John W. Durham from the 33rd New York. Twenty years after the war, Norton recalled that "the officers were as green as the raw recruits" and that Durham and he "performed substantially all the duties of officers & non-commissioned officers, and most of those duties, and all of the responsibilities, fell upon me." [75]

Four of Company C's five sergeants had prior service – three in the 23rd New York. Company A had three sergeants who were veterans. Companies B, D, and E each had two. [76]

The Civil War sergeants undoubtedly played the same role as the sergeants in the army of my day – they were the backbone of the unit, the ones who got things done. The 179th was fortunate to have had these experienced sergeants in its ranks. The combination of officers and non-commissioned officers with combat experience throughout the 179th probably significantly reduced the training deficit feared by those who opposed the creation of new regiments rather than refilling existing regiments.

During the recruits' stay at Elmira, training had to compete with the needs of running the depot. Soldiers of the 179th were detached for a variety of post duties. Company A's James C. Rutan was detailed "to act as sergeant major of the post, Barracks No. 1" on April 13. The following day Company A's Daniel Lowell was detailed "to write for Captain Menger at post headquarters." On April 20, Company A's Henry Kingsley, Company B's H. F. Beebe and Chester Hill, Company C's A. P. Benjamin, and Company F's Newton Spencer were detailed as clerks. [77] The new barracks were built by soldiers, and the 179th's William Shipman, Daniel M. Searles, Joel Bostwick, and Edwin Atkins were among those detailed as carpenters. [78] James Vangelder, David Shepard, William Jackson, William Zimmer, Henry Newell, and John Alcott were detailed as bakers. [79]

Because of the risk of desertion, guards were detailed to accompany small detachments of troops forwarded from Elmira. Company A's Lt. George Carpenter was detailed, along with three enlisted men, to escort fourteen recruits, ten colored troops and two deserters from Elmira to New York City. Company A's Daniel B. Lee was sent as a guard with a squad on an eight day trip to Washington in mid-April. [80]

In order to increase recruiting efforts, Company B's First Lt. George Cook was temporarily assigned to Major Diven for recruiting service on April 18. Company B's John Kerrick and Company C's Martin Doty were also assigned to temporary duty with Major Diven at the same time. [81]

Furloughs were also granted to a number of soldiers in the 179th during this period. [82] Company A's James Rutan, who lived in nearby Horseheads, was given a pass from "5 o' clock P.M. until 7 A.M. daily" to enable him "to remain with his family nights". [83] This authorized him to miss the 6 a.m. and 9 p.m. (and possibly the 5 p.m.) daily roll calls that were established by Captain Terrill. Rutan's only child, two-year-old Ida, had died just after he had enlisted and the opportunity to be with his wife undoubtedly provided great comfort to both of them.

However, the real obstacle to effective training was the immense pressure to forward troops to the front, not detached duty assignments or furloughs. At the end of January 1864, the War Department directed the commanders of each draft rendezvous that: "every effort must be made to dispatch troops as fast as they receive their bounties." [84] On March 11, 1864, Major Diven directed the district provost marshals to "immediately" send to the Rendezvous all men enlisted and mustered. "[A]n energetic movement on the part of the respective Provost Marshals of this Division will aid much in securing an increased number of men in the field." [85] Shortly after taking command of all the Union armies in the spring of 1864, newly promoted Lieutenant General Ulysses S. Grant directed that "active measures be taken to get into the field all recruits, New Organizations and all old troops that can be spared." [86]

In response to a request for information on delays in forwarding troops, Colonel Eastman, commander of the Elmira depot, replied on April 10, that of the 1,404 recruits then at the depot, 186 belonged to the 179th New York, but that they "can not be forwarded until the Regt is completed" and only one company (A) had been mustered in at that point. [87] However, that practice soon changed. Three weeks later, the 179th followed the new practice that troops "are forwarded to Washington as sufficient numbers of recruits are received to form a Company to its minimum number." [88]

On April 25, Eastman advised Thomas that there were 1029 recruits at Elmira, including 397 from the 179th New York and 23 from the 180th New York which was also organizing in the spring of 1864. Eastman reported that: "Two companies of the 179th Regt have been mustered in and they could be sent to the front at any moment that instructions are given." [89]

Not surprisingly, the orders for Company A and Company B to move south came the next day. The soldiers were paid at 1 p.m. on April 26 and left Elmira on April 27. [90] Their pay was comprised of one month's advance pay ($13 for a private) and an advance of $60 on their $300 federal bounty. [91] (Their local bounty – around $300 at this time – would have been paid before they reached Elmira.) Army pay of $13 per month was less than the pay for farm laborers – $13 per month in 1860, but $18 per month ($25 in summer) by 1865 in Horseheads, New York. [92] As for Union soldiers generally, pay for the 179th was irregular after that.

Company C was completed and ordered south several days after Companies A and B. Companies D and E were filled by the middle of May, but after that the supply of voluntary recruits for the 179th slowed to a trickle. [93] After Company F was mustered in on May 25, 1864, there were only between fifteen and thirty recruits left for a seventh company. [94] On May 2, the War Department had ordered that drafted men and substitutes be assigned to the 179th New York to speed up the process, but this did not result in substantial numbers (although seven drafted men had been assigned to Company D). [95]

Drafted men John Kennedy and Charles Flint and substitute Stephen Green were assigned to the 179th New York on June 10. [96] The War Department repeated its instructions on June 24. Roswell H. Davis and Thomas H. Graham were assigned to the 179th on July 8; George Kiefer and Abram Rose on July 23, and Jay Cole on August 11. [97] Green was subsequently mustered in with Company B of the 179th, Graham in Company E, Kennedy in Company F and Flint in Company H, but there is no record of the others actually being mustered into the 179th. [98]

At this point, the 179th New York Volunteers was four companies short of a full regiment. It was proceeding south in piecemeal fashion as a mere battalion.

William Hemstreet

Another new regiment was also recruiting. Lewis T. Barney had been authorized to raise the 180th New York Volunteers as its colonel. [99] Henry Messing and William Hemstreet had also been authorized to recruit for the 180th New York. [100] Progress for the 180th New York Volunteers was even worse than for the 179th. On May 2, Eastman reported to Thomas that none of the companies of the 180th had yet been mustered, "there not being a sufficient number belonging to the same company to muster." [101] By May 22, the number of recruits belonging to the various companies of the 180th had increased to about 130, still only the equivalent of a company and a half. [102] On June 20, Eastman noted that: "the 180th Regt NY Vols ... has been several months organizing and not one Company up to this date has been completed, so that it can be mustered and forwarded.... If it can be done I should recommend that the recruits be assigned to the 179th Regt N.Y.V." [103]

On July 20, the recruits for the 180th were finally consolidated into Company A, which was ordered to proceed to Washington two days later. [104] On July 23, the War Department, noting that the 180th had "failed to organize within a reasonable time," transferred Company A to the 179th New York and also directed that all enlisted men in the Western Division of New York not yet mustered in be forwarded to the 179th New York. [105] Thus Company A of the 180th became Company G of the 179th. Company G, under the command of Capt. James Day, joined the 179th in the trenches at Petersburg the day before the Battle of the Crater. [106]

Demographically, the 179th New York Volunteers was a little more native born, a little more farmer by occupation, and a little younger than the average Union regiment. The men were also more likely to be married.

More than three-quarters of Union soldiers were native born. [107] That was true for Companies A (83%); B (94%); C (77%); D (80%); and F (77%), but a majority of the men in Companies E

(53%) and G(57%), which were recruited primarily in Buffalo, were foreign- born. Eight different countries were represented in Company G and six different countries in Company E. [108] While roughly 15 percent of the soldiers from New York State were born in Ireland, [109] only 11 percent of the soldiers in the first seven companies were born in Ireland. Company E had a strong Irish contingent (23%), as did Company G (17%). Ethnic differences proved to be divisive in a number of Union regiments, but I have found no evidence one way or the other for the 179th New York. [110]

In terms of occupation, nearly half of Union soldiers had been farmers before the war. More than ten percent had been common laborers. [111] A majority of the men were farmers in Companies A (54%); B (65%); C (51%); and D (58%), but only 42 percent in Company F. Again Company E and Company G were different from the Union army demographic with only 13 percent and 26 percent farmers respectively. [112]

In terms of age, the men of the first seven companies on average (twenty-five years and three months) were about five months younger than the Union army as a whole, not a significant difference. [113]

With respect to marital status, almost half of the men of the 179th New York were married, compared to roughly thirty percent of the men in the Union army overall. [114] The difference is substantial, but I have been unable to determine whether it had any impact. Being married gave a man an additional tie to his community, which may have made him more susceptible to community pressure to enlist. However, at the same time, family obligations may have discouraged him from doing so. [115]

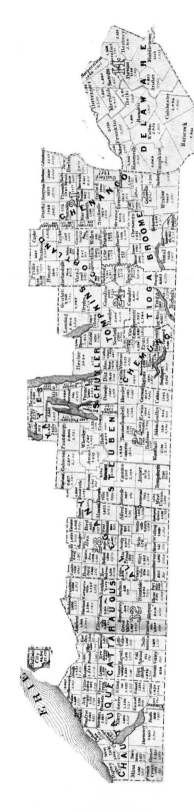

Southern Tier Counties, Courtesy New York State Library, Manuscripts and Special Collections, Albany, New York

Main Street, Penn Yan, New York, Courtesy of Yates County History Center

CHAPTER FOUR

Home Towns

The 179th New York Volunteers was principally recruited in counties in New York's Southern Tier (the area bordering Pennsylvania) [1]. However, approximately a quarter of the men came from the Buffalo area (Erie County). About five percent came from nearby Bradford County in Pennsylvania. [2] With such a broad recruiting area, the 179th New York Volunteers was more geographically diverse than the typical Union regiment. [3] However, I found no indication that that geographic diversity adversely affected the performance of the 179th New York.

Some companies were nicknamed for particular towns. Company A was sometimes known as the "Horseheads Company" [Chemung County]; Company C as the "Hornellsville Company" [Steuben County]; Company D as the "Dunkirk Company" [Chautauqua County] and Company F as the "Penn Yan Company" [Yates County]. However, the nicknames imply more homogeneity than in fact was the case. Generally it took recruits from quite a few towns to make up a company of eighty men. Company A seems to have been called the "Horseheads Company" because that is where most of its officers and non-commissioned officers were from. Only a handful of its men in the ranks hailed from Horseheads – most were from Elmira, Lockport and Buffalo. Companies C and F did have a fair number of enlisted men as well as officers from Hornellsville and Penn Yan, but the majority still came from other towns. The fact that many of the out-of-towners had enlisted in Hornellsville and been credited against its draft quota may also have influenced the choice of nickname. Company D seems to have been called the "Dunkirk Company" because that is where the men came to enlist from surrounding areas. [4]

Nor were the recruits from a particular town limited to a particular company. Significant numbers of residents from Hornellsville were found not only in Company C, but also in Companies F, G, and H, for example. A recruit's sense of community also was not limited by company boundaries. Company B's William Lamont referred to the men of the "Dryden Company" in a letter home, by which he seemed to mean the men from Dryden who had enlisted in the 179th regardless of the company they were assigned to. [5]

Companies B, E, G, H, I and K did not have "town nicknames." Company B was recruited primarily in the Elmira area; Companies E and G in the Buffalo area; Company H in the Elmira and Niagara areas; Company I in Danby and Newfield (Tompkins County); and Company K in Broome and Tioga Counties. [6] (There was no Company J.) [7]

Buffalo and some of the Southern Tier towns shared in varying degrees the economic and social impacts of New York State's canal system. The impact of the Erie Canal on Western New York cities like Rochester, which led the nation in population growth for the decade of the 1820's, and Buffalo, which took the lead for the 1830's, is well known. However, the Chemung Canal and the Crooked Lake Canal (Keuka Lake Canal today) also made "canal towns" out of Elmira, Horseheads, and Penn Yan. The main toll house on the Chemung Canal was located in Horseheads and can be seen in the center of this 1860 photo of Hanover Square in Horseheads. [8]

The Southern Tier was part of a larger area of New York State known as the "Burned-over District," the area west of the Adirondack and Catskill Mountains which underwent intense religious, social and intellectual ferment during the first half of the nineteenth century. As Whitney Cross, the leading historian of the "Burned-over District" has observed:

> This section was the storm center, and religious forces were the driving propellants of social movements important for the whole country in that generation. ... Neither the causes of the Civil War nor the origins of national prohibition, to cite only two prominent examples, can be thoroughly understood without reference to the Burned-over District. [9]

Abolition of slavery and temperance were closely linked with the religious revivalism of the day. [10] "No other section of the country would throughout the years before the Civil War prove to be so thoroughly and constantly sensitive to antislavery agitations." [11]

However, the experience was not uniform throughout the area. "Yankee" heritage, a key indicator of intensity, was relatively high (more than eighty percent) in Cattaraugus and Chautauqua Counties, while it was relatively low (less than sixty percent) in Steuben (Hornellsville), Chemung (Elmira and Horseheads), Yates (Penn Yan), and Tompkins (Ithaca) Counties. [12] The "enthusiasms" that occurred in the Burned-over District were also "chiefly rural". While some of the developing cities and towns in Western New York State "reflected the rural mind" in this regard, such as Rochester and Lockport, Buffalo, Elmira and Binghamton (Broome County) did not. [13]

Brief histories of Elmira in Chemung County, Buffalo in Erie County, and Danby and Newfield in Tompkins County during the pre-Civil War and Civil War eras follow.

ELMIRA

The 179th New York Volunteers has been referred to as one of Elmira's four "home" regiments. [14] However, the association seems to be based more on the facts that the 179th's commander, William M. Gregg, was a prominent citizen of Elmira; that the 179th was organized in Elmira; that many men enlisted for the 179th in Elmira; and that the 179th's post-war reunions were held in Elmira, than the actual number of Elmirans in the ranks.

Walling's *1867 Route and City Guide for the Erie Railroad* described Elmira as "one of those cities whose growth seems almost like magic, having grown up almost entirely within the last thirty years." The magic was what George Rogers Taylor has called the "Transportation Revolution," sparked by canals and then by railroads. [15]

Lake Street, Elmira

The economic impact of the Chemung Canal on New York's Southern Tier was much less dramatic than the impact of the Erie Canal on the villages to the North, but still significant. Construction of the Chemung Canal began in 1830 and was completed in 1833 at a cost of $344,000. Running twenty-three miles long, the canal connected the Chemung River at Elmira to the southern end of Seneca Lake at Watkins Glen. Steamboats towed the canal boats north across Seneca Lake to Geneva where the Cayuga and Seneca Canal headed north for a connection to the Erie Canal. [16]

The Chemung Canal brought great economic and social change to Elmira and the other Southern Tier towns along its route.

The canal gave local areas access to markets that had been inaccessible. Communities along the Chemung Canal sent coal, lumber, plaster, salt, and agricultural products to Buffalo, Rochester, Albany, and New York and received manufactured goods in return. The populations in Elmira, Corning, Havana (Montour Falls), and Watkins Glen grew as business boomed. Sawmills, gristmills, groceries, pottery works, banks, boatyards, and foundries were among the businesses spawned locally by the canal. The economy, land values, and even land use changed due to the Chemung Canal.

While the groundbreaking celebrants eagerly anticipated the future economic benefits the canal would bring, they failed to anticipate the social effects. Increased contact with distant areas brought diseases to their doorstep. The need to build and maintain the canal brought an influx of workers, mainly immigrants from Ireland. The canal laborers and the workers in the newly created industries combined to create a wage-earning working class dependent on their jobs and their employers. The poverty, working conditions, and drinking habits that characterized the workers contributed to greater crime and social tensions. Middle- and upper-class citizens worried about the habits that characterized the working poor. Foul language, intemperance, crime, and failure to observe the Sabbath were among the complaints lodged against the workers as communities discovered that not all progress was positive in nature. [17]

The railroads began to impact the Chemung Canal in the 1850's. The impact initially was complimentary as the railroads brought goods to the canals for delivery to areas not served by the railroads. The Chemung Canal hit its prewar peak in tonnage and tolls in 1854 at 270,000 tons and $21,000. The long term decline of the Chemung Canal began as the railroad network expanded and transportation by rail became more reliable. The Civil War brought a temporary surge in canal traffic, but by 1870, tonnage had fallen to 206,000 tons and revenues even more dramatically to $4800 due to price competition from the railroads. The State closed the canal in 1878. Over its nearly fifty year life, the Chemung Canal generated $525,000 in tolls, but the cumulative cost of construction, operation and maintenance was almost $3.5 million. [18]

Frank Leslie's Illustrated Weekly glowingly reported in 1857 on the prosperity brought to Elmira by the Chemung Canal and the railroads. Elmira's "streets are handsomely laid out, churches and schools are numerous; it possesses enterprising business men, an energetic press, [and] banks that pay specie on the strength of their promises" and that, located amidst "an agricultural country that has no superior in the world," Elmira "has surpassed all its competitors in the race for improvements."[19]

Boosted by the Chemung Canal and the railroads, the population of Elmira increased from 3879 in 1835 to 4791 in 1840 (a 24% increase) to 5898 in 1845 (23% increase) to 8166 in 1850 (38% increase). However, population growth had slowed considerably after 1850, with Elmira reaching 8496 in 1855 (4% increase) and 8683 in 1860 (2% increase). [20] Elmira's growth did lead the State Legislature to reclassify Elmira as a city from a village in April 1864. [21] In 1865, the legislative map for New York State showed the total population of the five wards to be 13,128.

That same year, Thomas Maxwell, the first toll collector at Horseheads, noted that:

We have lived to see Elmira, which thirty years ago numbered but her hundreds, and everyone well known, now roll up her ten or twelve thousand, and many of us scarcely know our next neighbor. [22]

Elmira was not entirely free from the influence of the enthusiasms that flourished in the

Burned-over District. "Elmira was one of the canal towns that fire-and-brimstone ministers thought was in need of salvation." [23] Michael Horigan has observed that: "If there were a boilerplate issue in Elmira, it was temperance." [24] The influence of the temperance movement on the soldiers of the 179th was felt not only during the Civil War, but was reflected many years later when one of their reunions was held at the rooms of the Women's Christian Temperance Union.

Abolitionism made a strong run in Elmira, but fell short of becoming the prevailing view. A major anti-slavery meeting was held in Elmira as early as 1837. The trustees of the Presbyterian Church dismissed their minister because he had attended the meeting. [25] In 1845, forty some members of the Presbyterian Church were dismissed because of their support for the abolition of slavery. They then formed the Independent Congregational Church. In 1854, the Reverend Thomas K. Beecher – son of the Reverend Lyman Beecher, one of the foremost abolitionists of the day, and half-brother of the Reverend Henry Ward Beecher, a well-known abolitionist in his own right and of Harriet Beecher Stowe – became pastor of the Independent Congregational Church. The following year, a preacher who was a former slave delivered guest sermons against slavery at the Independent Congregational Church and the First Methodist Episcopal Church. In 1861, another schism over abolition in the Presbyterian Church led to the formation of the Second Presbyterian Church. [26]

Elmira was an active "station" on the Underground Railroad going back to 1840. As many as 800 slaves passed through Elmira on their way to freedom. One of the early arrivals was John W. Jones, who escaped from a plantation near Leesburg, Virginia. He became the sexton of the First Baptist Church and later became responsible for burying the dead Confederate soldiers from Elmira Military Prison. Through his diligence, all but a handful of the Confederate dead were buried with their names on their headstones. Ironically, he arranged to send back to Virginia the body of a son of the overseer at the plantation he had escaped from. [27]

Still, despite the support of Rev. Beecher and Elmira's most prominent businessman, Jervis Langdon, the future father-in-law of Samuel Clemens, abolitionism remained the minority viewpoint in Elmira as the war approached. [28] As one abolitionist observed, it was "a time when opposition to slavery was costly, when it ruled a man, not only out of his political party, but out of his church and good society, and caused his children to be pointed at with a sneer." [29] Even the *Elmira Daily Advertiser,* which had supported Lincoln in 1860, felt constrained in 1861 to disclaim its support for abolitionism. In the 1860 Election, 56% of Elmira voters had voted for Lincoln. [30]

When the Civil War began in 1861, Elmira was selected as one of New York State's three military depots, as discussed in the preceding chapter. As important as Elmira was to the Union war effort, Elmira's Civil War reputation is invariably linked to the Confederate prisoner of war camp which opened in the summer of 1864. Many Southerners referred to Elmira as the "Andersonville of the North". One historian has noted that the departure of the first six companies of the 179th for the front contributed to the slack period at Elmira that led to its selection as a new location for housing Confederate prisoners. About seventy-five soldiers of the 179th New York – one of Elmira's "home" regiments – would later find themselves in Confederate military prisons. [31]

As the home to a major military depot, Elmira changed a good deal during the Civil War. In response to the 1865 New York State census question about the impact of the war, the enumerator for Elmira's Second Ward observed:

> A great desire to become quickly Rich out of the Government by fat contracts [and] high office. Stealing from Government. Selling whiskey. Bounty Brokerage Bounty jumping Speculating in petroleum lands and stocks "Style"

in houses, Carriages & Dress a great dread of assessors and tax collectors being Religious [only] on Sunday. [32]

A similar impact from government spending was noted by the census enumerator for Elmira's First Ward:

An increasing tendency to extravagance and display. The large Government expenditures at this post with the large number of officials & troops stationed here have doubtless greatly fostered this tendency at this point. The same causes have led to a largely increased consumption of intoxicating drinks & the consequent increase of vice & crime. [33]

Saloons had sprung up next to Barracks #1 and Barracks #3. By 1865, Elmira had sixty licensed premises for the consumption of alcohol. A Utica newspaper observed that "there is not a city or town in the state where so much liquor is used in proportion to its size and population" as Elmira. [34]

The *Elmira Daily Advertiser* noted that Elmira was in a very prosperous condition as a result of the war, but lamented Elmira's moral condition:

Brazen and licentious women never flowed in our streets, at all times of the day and night, more than at the present times. Female purity and modesty is everywhere shocked by them. Our liquor saloons never flourished in such numbers and with such pecuniary success; the proprietors of these, in many instances counting their yearly gains by the thousands. The growing and tender youth of our city are allowed to literally run wild, specimens of whom can be found waiting upon and obtaining entrance at our theaters night after night; by their lawless condition receiving the fruitful seeds that in a few years will yield the harvest of polluting sin. [35]

A local newspaper editor recorded in his diary (surely with some degree of exaggeration) that "More than one of the officers of the post assured me that there were one thousand prostitutes in Elmira, ... and from more than one surgeon I heard statements of the proportion of their soldiers who suffered from venereal taint, which surpassed anything in the recorded military statistic of the world." [36]

The census enumerator for Elmira's First Ward felt that the war had "greatly increased [crime] in this city." The *Watkins Express* noted at the end of the war that: "Elmira is fast earning an unenviable reputation for crime of almost every description known to the laws." And while the war brought money to Elmira, the new wealth was not evenly distributed. The First Ward enumerator estimated an increase of 10% in pauperism, while the enumerator for the Second Ward simply saw an increase. [37]

Thus in the Civil War era, Elmira was a city undergoing significant economic growth, moral concern and social fervor.

BUFFALO

"... And every inch of the way we know,
From Albany to Buffalo."
Traditional Erie Canal Song

The Erie Canal made Buffalo. Located at the western terminus of the Erie Canal where it joined Lake Erie, Buffalo became the commercial gateway to the west. Buffalo became America's greatest inland port and the largest grain transfer point in the world before the Civil War. Buffalo's location on the Erie Canal and Lake Erie and its relative proximity to New York, Chicago and Boston, also led to Buffalo's development as a manufacturing center. By the end of the nineteenth century, Buffalo rivaled Pittsburgh as a steel producer. [38]

Buffalo circa 1860

Peter Bernstein described the impact of the Erie Canal on the towns along its route in *Wedding of the Waters: The Erie Canal and the Making of A Great Nation:*

> In all the towns and cities that boomed once the canal opened, a striking improvement in real wages and living standards accompanied the brisk growth in manufacturing and the accompanying improvement in labor productivity. For the first time, luxury articles were available to people in the working class. Clothes and even furniture were no longer homemade items but something to be bought in the stores, often mimicking the high fashion of the wealthy. One historian describes the pattern of social change as the "democracy of expectant capitalists." [39]

Shortly after the Civil War began, a long-time Buffalo resident, Guy H. Salisbury, looked back over the previous twenty-five years of Buffalo's development. Buffalo had become a real city. Salisbury wrote that:

> In 1836 we had less than 16,000 inhabitants. [19,715 in 1835] Now we may in round numbers count 100,000. [81,129 in 1860] We had then but a single street paved, for one-fifth of a mile in length – now we have fifty-two miles of superior pavement in one hundred and thirty-seven streets or two hundred and fifty-nine times as much as in 1836. Then we had but one mile of imperfectly constructed sewers, in three streets – now we have an extensive and connected system of sewerage, of which fifty-two miles have already been built in the most substantial manner, in one hundred and twenty-four streets, the benefits of which to the public health, cleanliness and comfort will be incalculable.

We had then but the dim lamps of oyster cellars to light the steps of benighted aldermen and drowsy watchmen – now we have one of the best gas works in the Union... Then we obtained the indispensable element of water from public and private wells, often at inconvenient distances... Now, we have the current of the Niagara river flowing in large iron pipes through every section of the city...

Our harbor was in 1836 of such limited capacity as to present a seeming barrier to the increase of our commercial business. Now, by an enlarged and liberal system of improvement we have in all, some thirteen miles of waterfront, for lake and canal craft – enough to answer all the wants of our commerce for an indefinite period. [40]

As early as 1845, the Buffalo Board of Trade was forward-looking enough to have held its first meeting on "change." [41] In 1853, *Harper's New Monthly Magazine* featured Brooklyn, Rochester and Buffalo in an article about the "Growth of Cities in the United States."

The wonderful vitality which has stimulated the growth of each has been drawn from separate and distinct sources: Brooklyn from its proximity to a great and increasing commercial city; Rochester from the inherent energy, industry, and enterprise of its aggregating population; and Buffalo from its eligible position in the great pathway of commerce between the Atlantic and the States along the Lakes and the Father of Waters... Buffalo is like a publican and toll-gatherer upon the highway, growing rich and lusty upon the spendings of troops of wayfarers, who eat, drink, and are merry, pay tribute and pass on.

Buffalo was referred to as the "Child of Traffic." The prior year nearly one thousand sailing ships had brought imports valued at $35 million to Buffalo. Imports to Buffalo on the Erie Canal were valued at $42 million and exports at $21 million. [42] By the Civil War, Buffalo would also have extensive railroad links to the East through Rochester and Albany and Elmira. [43]

Buffalo's transportation-based economy: "created a large number of semiskilled and unskilled jobs in Buffalo. Indeed, with its grain mills, canal traffic, and railroads Buffalo offered opportunity to unskilled workers that few cities could rival." [44]

Rapid population growth reflected Buffalo's economic development. From 1824, the year before the Erie Canal opened, to 1860, Buffalo's population increased thirty-fold – from 2,600 to 81,000. [45]

"Most people in Buffalo were newcomers." [46] Economic growth attracted not only the native born from other parts of New York State, but also immigrants. By 1850, forty-two percent of Buffalo's population was foreign-born. German immigrants slightly outnumbered the Irish with each at sixteen percent of the total population. In terms of heads of household (which more closely approaches men eligible for military service), immigrants outnumbered the native born by a ratio of four to one – only slightly more than twenty percent were native born, while nearly forty percent had been born in Germany and seventeen percent in Ireland. Only two percent of the heads of household in Buffalo had been born in Buffalo or other parts of Erie County. Other nationalities included English at four percent of the total population, Canadians at three percent, and French and Scot, each at a little over one percent. [47] Moreover, there was movement amongst

Buffalo's own residents. Half of Buffalo's residents in 1845 had moved on by 1855. [48]

Thus Civil War-era Buffalo was an ethnically diverse city undergoing significant economic and social change. Its men generally did not form the ties of social permanence with Buffalo that men generally did in New York's smaller, mature communities.

NEWFIELD, DANBY AND THE OTHER HOME TOWNS

Perhaps forty percent of the men who joined the 179th New York came from home towns with a population of 3000 or less – often considerably less. After Buffalo and Elmira, the Town of Newfield in Tompkins County sent the largest number of its residents to the 179th New York – over fifty. Nearby Danby sent thirty. These numbers were unusually high for an individual town. A couple of other towns in Western New York each sent a dozen or so men to the 179th New York, but most sent only a handful. Most of the men from Newfield and Danby had been born there. And that was often the case with the other towns.

While it may be that by the Civil War many people in Elmira "scarcely knew our next neighbor," that would not have been the case in Danby and Newfield in Tompkins County. They were both relatively mature small towns in a rural area.

Newfield, N.Y.

Settlement of Danby had begun shortly before 1800, Newfield shortly after 1800. [49] Danby and Newfield grew annually by 11% and 15% respectively from 1814 to 1820, but after 1820 growth declined to the low single digits. The population of Danby peaked in 1840 at just under 2600 and slowly declined through the Civil War. The population of Newfield peaked just before the Civil War at just under three thousand and then began declining. [50]

In 1855, sixty-six percent of Danby's acreage and sixty percent of Newfield's acreage had been improved. [51] An historian writing in 1894 said that Danby "has always been chiefly a grain and stock growing district." Newfield did have several mills that produced 70,000 barrels of flour a year. [52]

Tompkins County was strong territory for the Republican Party. John Fremont received nearly sixty percent of the vote for President in 1856. Lincoln received fifty nine percent in 1860 and sixty percent in 1864. [53] In the 1830's, Danby and Tompkins County as a whole were evenly split on the Anti-Masonic Party, but only about a third of Newfield supported the Anti-Masonic Party. [54] The Temperance movement was quite strong in Tompkins County. [55]

Unlike Buffalo or Elmira, Danby and Newfield experienced few economic or social changes during the Civil War. In response to the question in the 1865 New York Census "What other changes [in addition to changes in farm wages, real estate prices, poverty and crime] in the social condition of the people have you observed since 1860?' the enumerator for Danby responded: "Not any of importance." The enumerator for Newfield responded at some length in terms of the "bitterness of party spirit," but also did not identify any additional significant social or economic changes in the community during the war. [56]

The census enumerators for the other towns sending men to the 179th New York also general-

Library of Congress

Danby Federated Church

ly did not note other significant change caused by the Civil War. The enumerator for Ithaca's Third Election District (Tompkins County) reported that: "This is a well-established town, & but little change has been made either in the farming or social condition of the people." The enumerator for Union (Broome County), reported that "The poor people in the town are generally in a better condition than before the war," but saw "No material changes in morals & c." The report for Port Crane (Broome County) was "no material difference" and for Groton (Tompkins County) "no perceptible change." The report for Owego Town (Tioga County) was: "None. A man that was a man before enlisting has remained a man." [57]

Thus, a significant proportion of the men of the 179th New York came from smaller towns that had not undergone the rapid economic and social development that Buffalo and Elmira had up to and during the Civil War. Ties to the community were stronger there than in Buffalo and even Elmira. Differing degrees of strength of community ties are a significant factor in explaining differing rates of desertion among the various companies of the 179th New York, as discussed in Chapters 5, 14 and 19 below. However, apart from differences in desertion rates, I found no indication that the "rural" companies of the 179th New York performed better in battle than the "urban" companies or vice versa.

Soldiers Rest, Washington City

CHAPTER FIVE

The Battalion Moves South

As noted, Elmira was chosen as a military depot because of its railroad connections – east-west along the Erie Railroad and north-south along the Northern Central Railway. The individual companies of the 179th New York Volunteers were ordered to Washington, D.C. from Elmira and used both railroads to go to war.

On April 26, 1864, Lt. Col. Seth Eastman, the Commander of the Elmira Military Depot, ordered Companies A and B to proceed to Washington the following day. [1] The news had not been expected by the soldiers. Daniel B. Lee wrote his wife that they "must pack up and be ready to start in one hour for Washington on so short notice." Company B's Henry F. Beebe was "rather in a Flutter." [2] Eight men from Company B promptly deserted. [3]

Companies A and B already had their weapons and were issued two days of cooked rations. [4] They were paid on April 26. [5] They were not necessarily paid entirely in cash. When the 107th New York left Elmira in August 1862, they were paid with drafts for their state bounty of $50. A local citizen, Tracy Beadle, cashed the drafts for the soldiers so that they did not have to send them to Albany. [6] The soldiers of the 179th New York may have been similarly accommodated. If they had the same options as the soldiers of the 107th, they would have been able to allot a portion of their monthly pay to their families. [7]

Companies A and B left Elmira for Jersey City around eleven thirty at night on April 27, 1864 under the command of Captains Albert Terrill and Robert Stewart with roughly 150 men. [8] They took the Erie Railroad. It is possible that they traveled by second class passenger train rather than freight car or open troop transport. [9]

[Map: New York Railroads]

They started out east toward Deposit, New York and then proceeded southeast along the Delaware River to Port Jervis. From Port Jervis, they jogged northeast to Middletown and then southeast to Suffern into New Jersey, passing through Paterson to Jersey City, a distance of 273 miles. They arrived in Jersey City around three in the afternoon. They averaged just under eighteen miles an hour for the fifteen hour trip. [10]

Jersey City was an important port in that day. Near the Erie Railroad terminus was the Cunard wharf for steamers to Liverpool. Ships for Bremen and Hamburg left from nearby Hoboken. [11] It must have been an impressive sight for someone who grew up in the small towns of Upstate New York.

[Map: New Jersey Railroads]

During the Civil War, it was not possible to travel from New York City to Washington, D.C. on a single railroad, much less without changing cars. After changing trains, Companies A and B left Jersey City at five in the evening and proceeded to Baltimore, a distance of 188 miles. They would have proceeded from Jersey City to New Brunswick on the New Jersey Railroad; thence to Trenton on the Camden & Amboy Railroad; and thence to Philadelphia on the Philadelphia & Trenton Railroad. They arrived in Philadelphia around daylight on April 30. They may have been routed through Philadelphia on a combination of the Reading, Junction, Pennsylvania and West Chester Railroads. The Philadelphia, Wilmington & Baltimore would then have carried them to Baltimore, crossing the Susquehanna River by ferry between Havre de Grace and Perryville, Maryland. [12] They stayed overnight in Baltimore before heading to Washington. [13] A first class passenger fare for New York to Washington was $8.25, but the government was charged only $5.00 for troops. [14]

[Map: Philadelphia to Washington]

Company C — eighty-one men strong under Capt. John Barton — left Elmira at 3:30 a.m. on April 29, taking the more direct route south on the Northern Central Railroad through Harrisburg, and joined Companies A and B in Baltimore. [15] From there the three companies — with a combined strength of roughly 230 — left for Washington at 11 a.m. on April 30 on the Washington Branch of the Baltimore & Ohio. [16]

The New York to Washington rail corridor was extremely important to the Union war effort. The demands of the government for the transport of troops and supplies strained the capacity of the railroads in the corridor (although troop transport may have accounted for only ten percent of total passenger traffic during the Civil War). The possibility of constructing a special government line between New York and Washington was considered, but strongly opposed by the existing railroads because of fear of post-war competition. As Army Quartermaster Meigs wrote in January 1864, "the question of taking actual and entire military possession of these railroads has been discussed more than once." [17]

While the privately-owned railroads played a behind the scenes role in the Petersburg campaign in 1864 and 1865, the military railroad that the Union army built to extend the captured City Point Railroad from the docks on the James River to the troops in the field was the "foundation of the [Union army's] logistical effort at Petersburg." [18] Railroads played a huge role in the ultimate Union victory in the East and West. Carl R. Fish has written that "It is arguable that without the railroad the South would have proved unconquerable." [19] Two different business journals wrote in 1862 that "the successful prosecution of the war becomes almost solely a question of transportation" and that "War is now dependant for its successes on railroads and Telegraphs." [20] Indeed, Grant chose Petersburg as a strategic objective in the summer of 1864 in significant measure because it was a critical rail center for the supply of Richmond and Lee's Army. [21]

On May 1 and May 2, the three companies were at Soldiers Rest in Washington. [22] "Soldiers' Rests" were facilities operated by the U.S. Sanitary Commission to ease the difficulty of travel for the soldiers. Margaret Leech described the operation of the Soldiers' Rest in Washington in her Pulitzer Prize winning *Reveille in Washington, 1861-1865*:

> [T]he men were well fed and lodged, efficiently policed and forwarded. As the
> troop trains neared the capital, the Commissary Department was notified, and
> gangs set to work cutting meat, cooking, and laying the tables. Promptly on
> their arrival, the men sat down to a hot meal. [23]

Company B's Henry F. Beebe, a twenty-one-year-old farmer, was less complimentary. "Sitting on the back steps of what is called the Soldiers Rest," he wrote his parents that it is "rather a poor rest I think." [24]

Captain John Barton wrote home that they had arrived in Washington "all right." While in Washington, Barton saw several officers from the 141st New York Volunteers, in which he had previously served. [25] There was also time for sightseeing. Henry Beebe walked around the Capitol building with its newly completed dome and nearly completed expanded wings. He wrote his parents that "I have seen considerable since I left home …, but I have not seen any place that looks any better to me than old Alleghany Co." [26] Company C's Abner Roberts, an eighteen-year-old farmer from Avoca in Steuben County, was more impressed. "I took a walk around the Capitol. I never had any idea before what it was. It almost paid me for three years fighting." (Thomas Crawford's statute of Freedom had been installed on the top of the Capitol dome in December 1863.) [27] Roberts also saw some rebel prisoners at the old Capitol building.

At 2 p.m. on May 3, the 179th began their march to the western shore of the Potomac, crossing at the Long Bridge. [28] [Photo: Long Bridge] They marched about four miles and then "put up our tents." [29] The arrival of the three companies at Arlington Heights on May 3 completed a six day trip for Companies A and B, and five days for Company C.

The 179th was assigned initially to the Twenty-Second Corps in May 1864 for the defense of Washington. [30] On May 3, 1864, the 179th established its regimental headquarters at Arlington Heights, Virginia between Fort Runyon and Fort Albany. [31]

Fort Runyon was situated to defend the southern approach to Long Bridge (located where the 14th Street Bridge is today). It was one of the first – and also the largest – of the forts built in 1861 as part of the defense of Washington. As hostilities threatened, the Union command was concerned that Confederate troops could occupy the heights on the west side of the Potomac and bombard the Capitol and other government buildings. Construction of Fort Runyon and several other forts began the very same day – May 24, 1861 – that the first Union troops occupied Alexandria County in Northern Virginia. [32] Several weeks later, Fort Albany was commenced two miles to the west on the higher elevation of the Arlington Heights ridge to provide greater protection.

Despite its size as the largest of the forts defending Washington, Fort Runyon's tactical significance was short-lived. When General George McClellan took command of the Army of the Potomac in July 1861 after the first battle of Bull Run, he focused on the Arlington Heights line of fortifications and new construction rendered Fort Runyon obsolete. The 179th New York Volunteers reached Fort Runyon in May 1864 just as the Union army's artillery inspector issued a report that it was "out of repair and is at present unoccupied." [33] [Map: Fort Runyan]

One of the prominent features on the west side of the Potomac River prior to the Civil War was Arlington House, the ancestral home of Mary Custis, who was the wife of Col. Robert E. Lee. [Photo: Arlington House] Arlington House had been built in Greek Revival style on an 1100 acre plantation by George Washington Parke Custis, President Washington's adopted son. Lee was one of the preeminent officers of the Federal army prior to the Civil War. A distinguished graduate of West Point and a Mexican War hero, he had been offered command of the Union troops being raised at the beginning of the war. However, Lee declined, remaining loyal to his native State of Virginia, and entered Confederate service. He left Arlington House in April 1861, never to return. Union troops took over Arlington House as a headquarters in May 1861. The Union army also began using the grounds of Arlington House as a cemetery – the forerunner of Arlington National Cemetery. [34]

Company A (and probably other companies) camped on the grounds of Robert E. Lee's mansion. [35] Daniel B. Lee wrote his wife that General Lee's "house" was as beautiful a place "as I did ever see." [36] Lee also wrote his wife about Freedman's Village, which Congress established on the Arlington estate in 1863 to house slaves who had escaped to the North.

> [There are] some 12 hundred negrows rite here with in one half mile of our tents and there is such a [illegible] in the morning that I can't tell wheater it is lit or not for the blacks do look so much like a cloud arising that they do shade the whole sun and the niger stink is so strong that we can't hardly bare it. [Sketch: Freedmans Village]

Lee further observed that "it is just for slavery that does keep this thing [illegible]. If it wasn't for that we wood all be to home about our domestic business in peas." [37]

Morale apparently was high. Company A's Hosea Fish, a forty-four-year-old farmer, sent home a cheerful report just after the 179th arrived on Arlington Heights: "My health is firstrate and I feel quite contented. We draw our rations and do our own cooking. We are in Virginia and can see a good way around us. The country is nice and pleasant to look at." [38] Company B's Homer Olcott, a twenty-year-old farmer, wrote: "I am quite comfortable here... I am [in] good spirits." Company C's George Hickey, a twenty-year-old carpenter from Hornellsville, wrote his father that: "I like it firstrate. Uncle Sam gives us enough to eat and good tents to sleep in." [39]

Training apparently became more serious when the 179th reached Arlington Heights. Company C's scribe reported on May 6 "commenced drilling in earnest" and on May 7 "Company drilling twice each day." [40] The 179th apparently did some training with live ammunition during this period. On May 4, Company B's Sergeant Daniel Compton "received accidental gunshot wound in the hip." [41] It was "feard he will not live," but Compton survived and was later promoted to first sergeant and then to second lieutenant at the end of the war. [42]

Hopeful rumors are a part of every soldier's war. On May 13, Daniel Lee wrote his wife that "the news has come here that we have taken richman. I hope that it is true. If so you may look for me home agane in a short time." [43] The rumor of course was not true. Perhaps the rumor was based on Grant's comment to a newspaper reporter after the Army of the Potomac crossed the Rapidan River on May 4 that it should take only four days to get to Richmond – if Lee cooperated. [44] By May 13, the Army of the Potomac in fact was progressing toward Richmond, but Lee definitely was not cooperating. The Union troops suffered heavy losses at the Battle of the Wilderness (May 5 to May 7) and the initial days of the Spotsylvania campaign. [45]

The other companies of the 179th were directed by the Headquarters of the Department of the East in early May to join Companies A, B and C in Washington "as soon as organized, armed and equipped". [46] Company D – eighty-three men under Capt. William Bird, Jr. – arrived at Arlington Heights the evening of May 16. [47] Company E – eighty-four men under Capt. Daniel Blachford – left Elmira on May 18 and arrived at Arlington Heights only two days later on May 20 – another clear demonstration of the strategic value of the Union railroads. [48] Lieutenant Colonel Doty, whose muster had been authorized by the raising of the fourth company [49], left Elmira on May 19 and took command of the five companies, then still only at battalion strength, on May 22, 1864. [50]

Captain Bird wrote his father at the end of May that "we have got a very good camp in a fine orchard the apples are as large as plums good dry ground and good water." [51] Daniel Lee agreed that they were in a "beautiful place," but complained to his wife that "it is so hot here that I can't hardly stand the weather. I have just come off from a drill with my shirt sweet with sweat." [52] Four months and three battles later, a soldier from the 179th recalled "how we enjoyed camp life [on the Heights of the Potomac]; how we laughed and eat and grew fat." [53]

Bird recounted that "we don't have much to do here but drill, but we keep pretty busy at that." Apparently his new recruits were testing his leadership skills: "I have had a pretty tough time getting my company broke in for I have got some of the greatest villains [illegible] but I am getting them pretty well subdued now." [54]

Whether the 179th New York was headed for combat or not was unclear. Bird expected that the 179th would stay at Arlington Heights until the remaining companies of the regiment had arrived and wrote his father that "when we are full we will probably be sent to guard some Rail Road or fort." [55] Even when the 179th left Arlington Heights for the front in Virginia, Daniel Lee wrote his wife that he thought they would be sent to guard prisoners. [56] Whether Bird and Lee honestly believed that or were trying to avoid worrying their families, neither guard duty nor garrison duty became the long term mission of the 179th New York Volunteers. Hosea Fish's letter to his family when the 179th first arrived on Arlington Heights proved more prophetic: "We can't tell anything about how long we shall stay here. It may be from 2 to 4 or 6 weeks. The capt. [Terrill] said if our men at the front were successful we would stay here a good while but if they get whipt we will be thrown forward." [57]

As the 179th moved into the Washington defenses on May 3, General Grant had a conversation with President Lincoln that directly affected the 179th's next deployment. A great number of Union troops had been committed to the defense of Washington, D.C. and the Northern states from invasion by Lee's army. Grant explained to Lincoln that:

> These troops could perform this service just as well by advancing as by remaining still; and by advancing they would compel the enemy to keep his detachments to hold them back, or else lay his own territory open to invasion. His answer was: "Oh, yes! I see that. As we say out West, if a man can't skin he must hold a leg while somebody else does." [58]

On May 30, the five companies of the 179th left the Washington defenses for the front. Daniel Lee wrote home with the news: "I must march today to the front which makes sad feeling here

Quartermaster's Wharf

now." [59] The 179th marched the short distance to Alexandria in two hours and pitched their tents. [Lithograph: Alexandria] After a day's stay in Alexandria – Abner Roberts had time for a swim in the Potomac and a visit to the hotel where Colonel Ellsworth, the North's first war hero, was killed in 1861 – the 179th boarded the military transport *John Brooks* the evening of June 1. (Veterans of the 23rd New York would have remembered the *John Brooks* from the first leg of their trip home the year before.) The port sidewheel and smokestack of the *John Brooks* are barely visible in the center of a photo of the Quartermaster's Wharf in Alexandria taken in the spring of 1864. [60]

The 179th "anchored untill morning," starting out around four in the morning. They were traveling with one or more other units because twelve hundred troops were on board. A picture taken in 1890 gives an indication of what the *John Brooks* would have looked like with twelve hundred soldiers aboard. [61]

The *John Brooks* proceeded south down the Potomac River into the Chesapeake Bay. Passing Mt. Vernon, the *John Brooks* presumably followed the custom of the day by tolling the ship's bell as a salute to George Washington. [62] Further south, they approached the Yorktown Peninsula where Lord Cornwallis and his British soldiers had surrendered eighty years earlier to General Washington and the Colonial army supported by the French navy under Admiral DeGrasse.

[Map: To White House Landing]

The 179th then headed west, up the York River. At West Point, they took the left fork, which is the Pamunkey River. They continued west up the Pamunkey River, passing Cumberland Landing, which had been a Union supply depot during McClellan's unsuccessful Peninsula campaign in 1862. A few miles past Cumberland Landing, they disembarked on June 3 at White House Landing, which had also been a supply base for McClellan in 1862 and was now serving as a base for Grant's current campaign. [63] Daniel Lee said that he had had a "hard time of it" during the two day and two night voyage. [64]

[Photo: White House Landing]

As the 179th went ashore on June 3, the fighting was still heavy at Cold Harbor fifteen miles to the west and the soldiers of the 179th could hear "the cannon firing faster than one can count." [65] Abner Roberts wrote his sister:

> I don't know how soon we shall have to go to the front. Grant says he is a going to have two hundred thousand troops in the field by the fifteenth of this month. Well if I have got to go and fight I am willing to go.

(Roberts was captured two weeks later in the 179th New York's first battle and died at Andersonville in September 1864.) [66]

The battalion's first assignments upon arrival were to guard approximately seven hundred Confederate prisoners and to assist in the hospital. [67] Roberts described the Confederate prisoners:

> they were the worst looking fellows that I ever saw. They were dirty and ragged. There was some lieutenants and other officers and there was one woman with them. She is orderly sergeant. They behaved themselves very good.... The rebels are so lousy that they have to hold their shirts over the fire to burn the lice off. [68]

It would not be long before the soldiers of the 179th themselves would encounter lice.

Hospital duty gave a harsh introduction to the reality of war. Daniel Lee, who had been detailed to help move the wounded in the hospital, wrote his wife "if you cood just see the wounded that is here coming every our it would scare you. Some with one arm off and some with part of there head off and in all shape." "I must confes it a grate deal wors than I did think it cood be." Company A's Private Henry Kingsley wrote his parents in similar words: "It is offal to see the wounded men. There is some with their legs shot off. Both legs." [69] Company C's George Hickey was detailed "to help to load wounded on the boats to go to Washington." Ironically, he would die of typhoid fever while being transported on one of those boats six weeks later. [70]

Against that horror, thoughts of home were a necessary escape. Lee wrote: "I do dreeme of home most every night and of coming home fast." [71] Kingsley, who was sick with typhoid fever that would take his life two weeks later and who had also seen the wounded in the hospital, wrote his parents: "I would give my bounty if I was back in that old blacksmith shop. I could iron lumber wagons forever if I could get home again." [72]

Company F, under Capt. Allen Farwell, along with Maj. J. Barnett Sloan (whose muster was authorized by the raising of the sixth company), left Elmira on June 1 at five in the evening. Like Company C, Company F took the Harrisburg route and arrived in Baltimore the following morning at nine o'clock. [73] George White, a farmer, described the trip in a letter to his mother. Perhaps hoping to comfort his mother (and/or himself), he spoke of farming rather than going to war: "We had a splendid ride... There was a great difference between the looks of crops in New York and the south part of P[ennsylvania]. They were planting corn in N.Y. and in P[ennsylvania] they were a hoeing it." They had a breakfast which White described as consisting of "stinking beef and bread and coffee. I did not eat much, especially of beef." Company F left for Washington at noon by train, arriving at three that afternoon. Although they traveled in baggage cars, White "had a good chance for viewing" the Maryland countryside. "Every thing shows sines of poor farming." [74]

Company F stayed in Washington for three days and left for White House Landing on the mail steamer *Highland Light* on June 5. After a "good journey" of two hundred forty miles in twenty-four hours, Company F arrived at White House Landing on June 6 and camped about a mile from the river. [75] Once again, Union transportation logistics had brought troops to the front quickly.

With only six companies, the 179th still was not yet at full regimental strength of ten companies. Two weeks later, the War Department directed the Elmira Draft Rendezvous that any unassigned men from the 1863 draft be assigned to the 179th and forwarded "without delay." The War Department had already assigned ten draftees to the 179th in May. [76]

A June 15, 1864 "Memorandum of Troops forwarded from Department of Washington to Army of the Potomac since May 1, 1864" showed two entries for the 179th New York – 357 and 85 for a total of 442. [77] The number 357 presumably refers to Companies A through E, which had been together since May 20 at Arlington Heights, while the number 85 presumably refers to Company F, which had arrived at White House Landing on June 6.

The 179th's last infusion of troops until the fall of 1864 came with the arrival of Company G. (As discussed in Chapter 3, Company G had started out as Company A of the 180th New York Volunteers.) Company G joined the 179th at Petersburg on July 29, 1864 – the day before the Battle of the Crater. Thus for two of its three major battles, the 179th fought at only battalion strength.

BOUNTY JUMPERS

Not only was the 179th New York still three companies short of a regiment, but "bounty jumping" took its toll in the move south from Elmira. Numerous stops and changes of train cars along the way offered bounty jumpers ample opportunity to bolt. [78] For example, in Company E, five soldiers deserted on May 18 when Company E left Elmira; one in Harrisburg on May 19; ten in Washington on May 20; four at Camp Casey on May 21; two at Camp Casey on May 22; one at Camp Casey on May 23; two at Camp Casey and two at Alexandria on June 2; three at Camp Casey and one at Alexandria on June 3; and three at White House Landing by June 9. [79]

Overall, fifteen percent of the men in the first seven companies deserted between the time their companies were mustered in and the time their companies arrived at the front. The men from the 179th who deserted on the way to the front were more likely to be foreign-born than native-born. Twenty-eight percent of the foreign-born men deserted, while only eight percent of the men born in New York and sixteen percent of the men born in other states deserted. Laborers were much more likely than farmers to desert. A third of the laborers deserted, while only seven percent of the farmers deserted. The deserters were also two years younger on average. [80]

Desertion en route to the front was not uniform among the companies. The rate among Companies A, C, and G was about four percent, but forty-four percent of the men in Company E and twenty-one percent of the men in Company F deserted on the way to the front. [81]

The high desertion rate in Company E, which was raised from the Buffalo area, reflects the high percentage of foreign born-men (53%), the relatively high percentage of laborers (31%) and the relatively low percentage of farmers (13%). Company E also had the highest percentage of boatmen/sailors (18%)– a group that deserted as often as laborers. [82] Foreign-born men and laborers and boatmen/sailors would be expected to have weaker ties with their local communities than native-born men and men with higher-paying jobs.

There is an interesting subset of five men in Company E who were born in Buffalo, who lived in Buffalo at the time of the Civil War and who enlisted in Buffalo with their enlistments being credited to Buffalo. None of the five–which included two laborers–deserted on the way to the front (although one did desert in early July). These men had strong ties to Buffalo, making them more receptive to community pressure to volunteer to avoid a draft. [83]

In contrast to Company E, Company A had less than twenty percent foreign-born men and only nine percent laborers, but fifty-four percent farmers. Only five percent of the men in Company A deserted before reaching the front. The numbers for Company C, which also only lost five percent to desertion, are similar–twenty-three percent foreign-born, fifty-one percent farmers and nine percent laborers. [84]

Company G, which lost only four percent of its men en route to the front, is more difficult to explain. Company G was recruited in Buffalo around the same time as Company E, which lost forty-four percent to desertion. Company G had the highest percentage of foreign born men–fifty-seven percent, which would suggest a much higher desertion rate than four percent. [85]

At least part of the explanation for the lower desertion rate lies in differences in the nationalities, occupations and ages of the foreign-born men in Company E and Company G. [86] For the 179th New York overall, thirty-seven percent of the foreign-born men were Irish and only seventeen percent were German. Company E closely mirrored that at forty percent Irish and seventeen percent German. However, in Company G the two nationalities were evenly split at just under thirty percent each. The German-born men in the 179th New York deserted before reaching the front far less frequently (7.4%) than the Irish-born men (40%). [87]

Company E had seventeen Irish-born recruits – three-quarters deserted. Company G had fourteen Irish-born recruits, but only one deserted. Probably the most critical difference between the Irish-born men in the two companies was the mix of occupations. Forty percent of the Irish-born recruits in Company E were laborers, while less than thirty percent of the Irish-born recruits in Company G were laborers. Forty percent of the Irish-born recruits in Company G came from "skilled" trades (cooper, carpenter, baker, butcher, tailor), while only ten percent did in Company E (tinsmith, painter). [88] The Irish-born recruits in Company G were also on average two years older than the Irish-born recruits in Company E, allowing more time for assimilation in America. [89]

CUMBERLAND HEIGHTS DETACHMENT

Before the the 179th was formally transferred to the Ninth Corps on June 11, a detachment of about one hundred men under the command of Capt. Albert Terrill was sent back down river five miles to Cumberland Landing. Homer Olcott wrote his father that they were sent there "to guard the river from guerillas which troubled our boats." [90] Although Captain Terrill commanded Company A, the bulk of the detachment came from Companies C and D. [91] The defenses at Cumberland Landing consisted of two small works about five miles downriver from White House Landing. [92]

The following encounter with the 179th on June 6 was prosaically reported by the acting master of the United States Steamer *Shokokon*, which had taken position off of Cumberland Heights to protect Union military transport ships:

> Nothing occurred of note until the 6th of June, when a small force of the One hundred and seventy-ninth New York Volunteers came down to occupy the heights. I gave them all assistance they required in landing and getting their stores ashore. Everything remained quiet until the morning of the 21st instant, when a party of about 150 rebel cavalry (dismounted) came down to Cumberland Point– during a thick fog – and fired from the bank of the river at one of the transports passing that point – details as per the report of that day. On the evening of the 22nd, the force occupying the heights evacuated and passed down the river. I rendered them all assistance possible in getting on board the transport. [93]

It does not appear that the 179th engaged the rebel cavalry on June 21 from its position on Cumberland Heights. The *Shokokon* was able to disperse the Confederates by shelling the shore and the woods. [94] Although the 179th did not suffer any casualties from hostile fire while at Cumberland Heights, two soldiers from Company A suffered accidental gunshot wounds on June 11. Jesse Cornell was wounded in the fingers of his right hand, while Stephen DeKay was wounded in the right foot. DeKay's wound was the more serious, requiring amputation of a part of his foot on June 30. It was reported on July 5 that "everything [is] proceeding satisfactory," but DeKay died on July 29 from "excessive supperation." [95] Company A's Lewis Kellogg suffered a more mundane back injury and hernia when he slipped while assisting in carrying a barrel of pork up to the heights. [96]

ASSIGNMENT TO THE NINTH CORPS AT COLD HARBOR
[Illustration: Ninth Corps Badges]

The men in the 179th New York not detached to Cumberland Landing moved from White House Landing to Cold Harbor on June 10, [97] and the 179th was assigned to Ambrose Burnside's Ninth Corps, as contemplated back in February. [Photo: Burnside] A graduate of West Point in 1847, Burnside had a mixed record during his ten years in the army before returning to civilian life. As a young lieutenant in the Mexican War, he was a gambling man and unlucky, a man who "became known by his dangerous penchant for increasing the stakes whenever the cards went against him: he would wager again and again, until his last dollar had gone across the table. When the war officially ended ... he owed six months' pay." [98] Burnside rejoined the army at the beginning of the Civil War. He was alternately brilliant and obtuse. His amphibious expedition in North Carolina during the first half of 1862 was a success. The troops he had raised became the Ninth Corps, with its descriptive uniform badge. He could have been a hero at Antietam, but was too slow to adapt to field conditions, failed miserably at Fredericksburg as commander of the Army of the Potomac and both liberated Knoxville and was besieged there at the end of 1863. Because Burnside ranked Meade, the Ninth Corps reported directly to Grant until May 24, 1864, when it was formally assigned to the Army of the Potomac. There had been some misgivings about Burnside's performance throughout the Overland campaign– he was too deliberate, i.e., late, in getting his men into action and often failed to give adequate support when needed. [99]

If Burnside's weaknesses did not present a danger foreboding enough, the 179th was assigned to the First Division, commanded by James Ledlie. Ledlie had only been division commander since June 7, but was already known as reckless, a drunkard in battle and hard to find in the fog of battle. [100] For reasons soon to be seen, Ledlie has been referred to as the Union's worst general, a superlative not without serious competition. [101] [Photo: Ledlie]

The 179th's Regimental History includes "Cold Harbor, June 11 and 12, 1864" as one of the 179th's engagements. However, there were no significant combat operations on either of those days, and the 179th's service at Cold Harbor (spelled "Coal Harbor" in Company E's Morning Report and many contemporary accounts) was limited to picket duty. [102]

Around ten o'clock the night of June 11, the 179th went on picket duty on the extreme left of the Union lines. [103] The next day the 179th saw its first hostile fire – artillery shells that "burst in plain view," but fortunately "short of our target," in the words of William Larzelere. [104]

Grant and Cincinnati

CHAPTER SIX

Grand Strategy ... Constant Battle

In February 1864 Congress passed a bill reviving the rank of lieutenant general – last held by George Washington – with the object of promoting Ulysses S. Grant to command all Union armies. President Lincoln signed the bill into law on February 29, nominated Grant that same day, and the Senate confirmed him two days later. [1] At that time recruiting for the 179th New York was well under way.

Putting Grant in overall command was intended to be a decisive move. As Bruce Catton wrote in *Grant Takes Command*:

> The point here was that by creating a new higher rank and giving it to General Grant the administration was pointedly serving notice on every officer in the army that Grant was going to be the boss to the end of the war... In effect the government was staking everything on the bet that Grant was going to win the war. [2]

Grant arrived in Washington on March 8 [3] and wasted no time planning the spring offensive. His initial idea was to move Union armies to Norfolk, Virginia and then toward Raleigh, North Carolina, forcing Lee to respond by abandoning the Confederate capitol in Richmond. However, General Halleck timely warned Grant that Lincoln's primary objective was the destruction of the Army of Northern Virginia, not the capture of Richmond. [4]

Grant then developed a strategy that for the first time coordinated the Union's military efforts across half a continent, in both the Eastern and Western theaters of operations. By simultaneously moving against the Confederate forces on five different fronts, Grant would take full advantage of the North's superior numbers. Grant laid out the components of the strategy in an April 4 letter to William Tecumseh Sherman, whom he had appointed to succeed him in the West.

> It is my design, if the enemy keep quiet and allow me to take the initiative in the spring campaign, to work all parts of the army together, and somewhat toward a common centre. [5]

Grant's approach reflected President Lincoln's thinking. As early as January 1862 Lincoln had understood the central strategic challenge facing the Union armies:

> I state my general idea of this war to be that we have the **greater** numbers, and the enemy has the **greater** facility of concentrating forces upon points of collision; that we must fail, unless we can find some way of making **our** advantage an over-match for **his**; and that this can only be done by menacing him with superior forces at **different** points, at the **same** time; so that we can safely attack one, or both, if he makes no change; and if he **weakens** one to **strengthen** the other, forbear to attack the strengthened one, but seize and hold the weakened one, gaining so much. (emphasis in original) [6]

[Map: Grand Strategy]

Grant established his headquarters in the field, with the Army of the Potomac and away from the grinding political machinery of Washington. For the next year Grant was seldom out of sight of George Meade's Army of the Potomac, then located in winter camp in the vicinity of Culpeper Court House, seventy miles northwest of Richmond.

Grant envisioned five prongs of attack. Meade and the Army of the Potomac, "increased by Burnside's corps of not less than twenty-five thousand effective men," would "operate directly against Lee's Army, wherever it may be found." [7]

Benjamin Butler, commanding the Army of the James in Eastern Virginia, was to approach Richmond from the south side of the James River.

Nathaniel Banks, after completing his assignment from Halleck to move up the Red River, would attack Mobile, Alabama.

Franz Sigel would take ten thousand men into the Shenandoah Valley to interrupt the rich flow of food and other supplies meant for Lee in Richmond. [8]

Grant proposed that Sherman "move against Johnston's Army, to break it up and to get into the interior of the enemy's country as far as you can, inflicting all the damage you can against their war resources." [9] He trusted his friend to work out the details – "I do not propose to lay down for you a plan of campaign, but simply lay down the work it is desirable to have done and leave you free to execute it in your own way." [10]

Public expectations were high on the results to be achieved by Grant. *The Hornellsville Tribune* ran a piece from Rochester's *Monroe Democrat*:

> Nothing has given greater satisfaction to the public recently than the announcement by Gen. Grant of his purpose to establish his headquarters with the army of the Potomac; and, according to our advices, the soldiers of that army, and at least a portion of the officers, share in the feeling. The

belief is universal that he will vindicate in Virginia the fame which he has acquired through his successes in the southwest. [11]

On May 4, the Army of the Potomac crossed the Rapidan River to begin the Overland campaign. Sherman started for Atlanta the next day.

[Map: Overland to Richmond]

Recently reorganized, leaving old camps behind, moving with large numbers and vulnerable miles-long wagon trains, the Army of the Potomac did not travel far enough its first day's march. Cautious Union corps commanders were intercepted as they marched through the Wilderness and sharp close-in fighting began on May 5. Three fierce days of bloody battle were followed by almost continuous combat and marching during the next month – Spotsylvania Court House, North Ana, and Cold Harbor (only eight miles from Richmond) – as Grant maneuvered inexorably to the southeast, trying to turn Lee's flank and destroy the Army of Northern Virginia as a fighting force. Lee successfully parried each of these thrusts, but at a huge cost to his officers and men. More importantly the Army of Northern Virginia was forced onto the strategic defensive for the balance of the war. [12] From May 4 through June 12 at Cold Harbor both sides suffered casualties so extensive that the armies were essentially used up – fifty-five thousand killed, wounded and missing for the North and thirty-three thousand for the South. [13]

BREAKING CONTACT WITH LEE'S ARMY

For more than a week after the battle of Cold Harbor the two armies settled into a deadlock that saw no major offensive action while they began to collect their wounded and bury their dead. It was clear to Grant that he could not stay and hammer away at Lee's defensive fortifications – the price was too high – and there was little room for maneuver so near Richmond. Undaunted, Grant conceived of a bold, and quite risky, maneuver to disengage from Lee, move east a few miles toward White House Landing under cover of darkness and then south across the James River. Grant recalled in his *Memoirs* that:

> The move was a hazardous one to make: the Chickahominy River, with its marshy and heavily timbered approaches, had to be crossed; all the bridges over it east of Lee were destroyed; the enemy had a shorter line and better roads to travel on to confront me in crossing; more than fifty miles intervened between me and Butler, by the roads I should have to travel, with both the James and the Chickahominy unbridged to cross; and last, the Army of the Potomac had to be got out of a position but a few hundred yards from the enemy at the widest places. [14]

The strategic impact of crossing the James River would be huge. Lee had earlier advised the Confederate President, Jefferson Davis, that: "We must destroy this army of Grant's before he gets to the James River. If he gets there it will become a siege, and then it will be a mere question of time." [15] The significance of the maneuver was recognized even in the enlisted ranks of the 179th. Newton Spencer wrote *The Hornellsvile Tribune* that the Army of the Potomac had accomplished "one of the most brilliant and successful change of base known in our military annuals." [16]

As was the case throughout the Overland campaign and until the end of the war, Grant's general vision was implemented by Meade and his chief of staff, General Andrew A. Humphreys. "How skillfully all the logistics were surmounted" can be credited to Humphreys' clear marching orders and mastery of detail. [17]

Grant's objective was Petersburg, a rail center located twenty-three miles south of Richmond on the south side of the Appomattox River. Petersburg was a key source of supply for both the Confederate capital and the Army of Northern Virginia. Five railroads comprised the Petersburg hub, and six major wagon roads also ran into Petersburg. [18] Two toll roads on the southern side of town would become important objectives for the Union army – Jerusalem Plank Road initially and later Boydton Plank Road. [19]

JUNE 12 - GRANT'S "HAZARDOUS" MOVE SOUTH BEGINS
[Map: North of James]

After dark on June 12, the Army of the Potomac began the change of front to Petersburg planned by Grant. The Eighteenth Corps marched back to White House Landing and boarded transports. They proceeded down the Pamunkey River to the Cheasapeake, up the James River to City Point, and then west to Point of Rocks on the Appomattox River, eight miles north of Petersburg. [20]

Later that night, after the Eighteenth Corps left the Cold Harbor positions, the Sixth Corps and the Ninth Corps headed toward Jones Bridge on the Chickahominy River. It was a "black and starry" night "with a waning moon." [21] Ledlie's division arrived at Tunstall's Station on the Richmond and York River Railroad – about eleven miles away – at daybreak on June 13. [22] The 179th was assigned to "cover the rear" and regimental lore has it that the 179th was the last Union unit to leave the Cold Harbor positions. Regardless of whether the 179th was actually the last, their departure at two in the morning on June 13 certainly put them among the last. [23] Burnside reported to Meade that: "our command and pickets were withdrawn without the knowledge of the enemy. The last reports make the enemy firing at one of our battery epaulements after our pickets were a mile off." [24] Thus, the 179th can claim credit for participating in the initial deception of Lee and the Army of Northern Virginia that was critical to the success of Grant's strategy.

There was one casualty for the 179th. When the soldiers of the 179th had been quietly called in from their positions on the picket line, Company A's Henry Menhenitt was either overlooked or could not be found and remained in his vedette post. He was captured the next morning and sent to Andersonville, but survived. [25]

Ledlie's division resumed the march on June 13 around eleven that morning and halted for the night near Jones' Bridge over the Chickahominy River – another march of about eleven miles. [26] The "traffic" was heavy – Company F's William Larzelere estimated that they were among twenty thousand troops – and the road was "extremely dusty." [27]

Menhenitt

[Sketch: To the James]

On June 14, Ledlie's division and the 179th New York Volunteers started at eight o'clock on the march to the James River, not quite fifteen miles away. [28] That same day, a dispatch from Lee's headquarters stated: "Grant's exact whereabouts and intentions still undetermined." [29] Ledlie's division set up camp about two miles below the pontoon bridge that had been built for the Army of the Potomac's supply wagons to cross the James River. [30]

The pontoon bridge, the longest of the Civil War at twenty-two hundred feet, was constructed near Fort Powhatan. It had been built in just seven hours on June 14 – an extraordinary engineering feat in any era. The pontoon bridge had to be anchored in both directions against a four foot tide. The Fifth Corps' artillery chief described it as "really a wonderful piece of pontooning, equal I suspect to anything of the sort ever before done." [31] The 179th and Ledlie's division remained there for the rest of the day through the next night of June 15. [32]

[Map: Fort Powhatan June 1864]

Company C's John McGrath (alias John Brown) described the march–with some exaggeration–in a letter to his mother: "We marched ... in a burning sun for three days. We had not bit to eat nor water to drink." Fifteen years later, Company C's John Ludlum recalled that: "our march was very rapid. Belts buckled tight with 40 rounds of cartridges & all of our equipments & the day was exceptionally warm." [33]

Pontoon over the James

EIGHTEENTH CORPS ON JUNE 15

The Union had a rare opportunity to hamstring Confederate supply logistics in the east. Not only did Lee not know where the Army of the Potomac was headed, but Petersburg was lightly defended. The Confederate troops under the command of P. G. T. Beauregard numbered only twenty-two hundred while the Eighteenth Corps had upwards of sixteen thousand troops. Beauregard immediately asked Richmond and Lee for reinforcements, but he was not taken seriously because nobody believed that the Army of the Potomac could have moved in force so quickly from Cold Harbor. [34]

The Eighteenth Corps, commanded by William F. "Baldy" Smith, began the attack on Petersburg on June 15 as the other units of the Army of the Potomac were marching overland toward Petersburg. [35] When the Eighteenth Corps attacked Petersburg, Lee still did not know exactly where the full Army of the Potomac was to be found. The Eighteenth, after all, was on loan from the Army of the James.

After Cold Harbor, Smith was more than usually cautious and made slow progress against limited Confederate resistance leading into Petersburg during the day of June 15. The main works around Petersburg, known as the Dimmock Line, were begun in the summer of 1862 but not completed until the spring of 1864. The works appeared formidable.[36] The Eighteenth Corps began its attack on the Dimmock Line at seven the evening of June 15 and breached the northern half of the line with "astonishing ease," capturing Batteries No. 3 through No. 11.[37]

[Map: Dimmock Line]

Smith reported that "Unless I misapprehend the topography, I hold the key to Petersburg."[38] Moreover, Hancock's Second Corps had just arrived, bringing the Union strength to more than thirty thousand. The Union troops could have walked into Petersburg that night, but did not due to ineffectual communication and decision-making by the two corps commanders.[39]

[Photo: Beauregard]

Grant wrote in his memoirs that "I believed then, and still believe, that Petersburg could have been easily captured at that time."[40] Beauregard gave the same assessment after the war, writing that "Petersburg at that hour was clearly at the mercy of the Federal commander, who had all but captured it, and only failed of final success because he could not realize the fact of the unparalleled disparity between the two contending forces."[41]

During the night of June 15, Confederate reinforcements arrived, bringing their strength to about ten thousand and narrowing the Union's advantage. Weighing the risks, Beauregard had dangerously moved a division from his nearby defensive positions at Bermuda Hundred. A breakthrough there by Butler's Army of the James also would have threatened Richmond. Petersburg's defenders quickly built more earthworks during the night of June 15 on the west side of Harrison's Creek. These Confederate positions are referred to as the Hagood Line after the Confederate brigade commander whose South Carolina troops manned the position.[42]

Despite the lack of quick victory, the Union still had a preponderance of troops on the battlefield. With two corps in place and three more on the road it was still possible to take the vital rail center. For the men of the 179th, the next few days would be their first bloody test.

[Sketch: Crossing the James]

Soon after dark on June 15, Ledlie's division and the 179th New York began what Ledlie described as a "long and tedious march," crossing the James River and heading toward Petersburg as they marched through the night.[43] The Ninth Corps proceeded toward Petersburg with Willcox's division in the lead, followed by Ledlie's division and then Potter's division. The 179th may have sung the same popular Union marching song that other units of Ledlie's division did en route that day.[44] Sung to the same tune as "John Brown's Body" and the "Battle Hymn of the Republic," the lyrics were:

We 'll hang Jeff Davis on a sour apple tree!
We 'll hang Jeff Davis on a sour apple tree!
We 'll hang Jeff Davis on a sour apple tree!
As we go marching on![45]

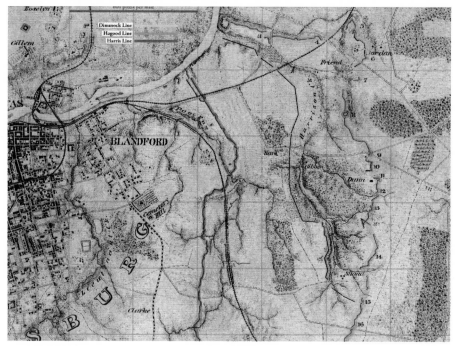

Mid-June 1864

CHAPTER SEVEN

First Charge of Ours

Shortly after daylight on June 16, the Ninth Corps broke for an hour's rest near Prince George Courthouse. The sound of the battle could be heard in the distance.[1] Advance elements of Willcox's division reached the outer defenses of Petersburg around ten o'clock, with the remainder of the Ninth Corps arriving by one that afternoon.[2] The Ninth Corps had covered about fifteen miles at roughly a mile an hour.

[Map: June 16]

The arrival of the Ninth Corps (including the 179th New York) on June 16 increased the Union strength to fifty thousand troops, but they were facing strong Confederate positions by that time. The first elements of the Ninth Corps took position to the left of the Second Corps. Shortly thereafter, Ledlie's division was ordered to proceed down Prince George Court House Road to a road about half a mile east of the Dimmock Line and then turn south through a woods for about a mile. Ledlie's division took position behind Potter's division across from Confederate Batteries No. 15 and 16 of the Dimmock Line.[3]

Ledlie's division arrived at that location around five the evening of June 16.[4] Ledlie's division took positions at right angles to the Baxter Road, covering a wood in front of the main Confederate line.[5] Confederates had cut the trees and then sharpened the branches where they lay. The church belfries in Petersburg could be seen in the distance. The troops began digging breastworks, continuing the work into the night. [6] The 179th was under Confederate artillery fire that night. [7]

[Map: June 16, 6 p.m.]

Also around six o'clock, two brigades from the Ninth Corps participated in an attack led by the Second Corps, but the 179th was not involved. [8] The Union forces suffered heavy casualties, but achieved only limited gains by the end of the day on June 16. However, they did capture Batteries No. 12, 13 and 14 of the original Dimmock Line. [9] As the Confederate forces fell back, Beauregard became concerned that the Hagood Line also could not be held and ordered that a new line closer to Petersburg on more advantageous ground be started. This line became known as the Harris Line. [10]

The (Petersburg) *Daily Register* reported that as of the end of the day on June 16:

> The utmost confidence reigns throughout all classes of our citizens. Petersburg is safe from the fiercest assault of the enemy. It is unnecessary to make any further allusion to our means of defense, which are simply sufficient for all emergencies ...

> The enemy have suffered fearfully, and on our side the loss has not been small, but all is guess work at present. [11]

Unfortunately for the city, by the morning of June 17 Grant had one hundred thousand men on the south side of the James River. [12] The strategic significance was huge. As noted, Lee had said that: "We must destroy this army of Grant's before he gets to the James River. If he gets there it will become a siege, and then it will be a mere question of time." [13] Grant was across the James and it was now just a question of time. Despite their early confidence, the citizens of Petersburg were within the range of Union artillery during the ensuing nine months. They suffered a great deal. [14]

The Ninth Corps prepared for its own attack on the Dimmock Line the morning of June 17. The Ninth Corps maneuvered that day around and through a series of ravines formed by the branches of Harrison's Creek. Movement in the ravines was complicated by both constricted lines of sight and obstacles placed by the Confederate soldiers. The central landmark in the immediate area was the Shand House (also spelled Shind), which was located above the ravines. [15]

[Sketch: Burnside's Charge]

Potter's division began the day with a stealthy attack at 3 a.m. on Battery 15 of the Dimmock Line and the Shand House that surprised the Confederates, who gave up roughly six hundred prisoners and strategic position on the high ground at Shand's. [16] Potter's division kept advancing until they were stopped by stiff resistance at the next Confederate line – the Hagood Line on the other side of Harrison's Creek.

Ledlie's division had been ordered to support Potter, but a combination of factors prevented that.

First, the order was delivered late to Ledlie and his division had been asleep. Sunrise on June 17 was at 4:48 a.m. [17]

Second, as Ledlie's division began the move toward Batteries No. 15 and No. 16, which had been taken by Potter's division early in their assault, they had to maneuver in the dark through the quarter to half a mile of tree stumps left by the Confederates to both hamper the movement of an advancing force and to provide a more open field of fire from Batteries 11 through 16 of the Dimmock Line. The advance was slow-going.

> The pines were cut about three feet from the ground, toppled so that a soldier would have difficulty either climbing over or crawling under the trees. Rebel soldiers had trimmed the branches so that sharp points faced the Yankee line. [18]

A soldier in the 2nd Pennsylvania Heavy Artillery (Third Brigade of Ledlie's division) recalled the ordeal: "we were ragged enough before we struck that, but when we finally got through that slashing our clothing was hanging in tatters." [19]

Third, when moving from Batteries No. 15 and 16 toward the Shand House, Ledlie's division proceeded down the wrong ravine. [20] The division remained in the Battery No. 15 and 16 positions until about four in the afternoon. [21]

As these attacks were developing, General Lee was still uncertain as to Grant's intentions and whereabouts. At 6 a.m. on June 17, Lee then at Drewry's Bluff on the James River, not quite halfway from Richmond to Petersburg, sent a message to Beauregard: "Can you ascertain anything of Grant's movements? I am cut off now from all information." [22]

Beauregard replied at 9 a.m.:

> Enemy has two corps in my front [it was actually three – the Eighteenth, Second and Ninth], with advantage of position [confirming General Smith's assessment]. Impossible to recover with my means part of lines lost. Present lines entirely too long for my available forces. I will be compelled to adopt shorter lines. Could I not be sufficiently re-enforced to take the offensive [and] thus get rid of the enemy here? Nothing positive yet known of Grant's movements. [23]

Shortly thereafter Beauregard gave Lee a further update:

> The enemy carried this morning another of the weak points in the old lines [Potter's attack]. He appears to be concentrating toward our right center for another attack. I am collecting all available troops to resist until night, when I hope to be able to occupy new lines. We greatly need re-enforcements to resist such large odds against us. The enemy must be dislodged or the city will fall. [24]

At 11:15 a.m. Beauregard speculated, incorrectly, that Warren's Fifth Corps had been deployed to respond to Confederate General Early's movements in the Shenandoah. Beauregard again asked for immediate reinforcements "to crush the enemy in our immediate front." [25]

At noon, Lee replied to Beauregard's 9 a.m. dispatch: "Until I can get more definite information of Grant's movements I do not think it prudent to draw more troops to this side of the river." [26] Grant's strategy still had a chance to succeed as long as Lee did not deploy troops to counter the increasing numbers of Union troops arriving at Petersburg.

At 4:00 p.m., Ledlie's division was ordered to support an attack by Willcox's division on the Hagood Line, just north and across Harrison Creek from Shand's House. Ledlie's division took positions in a ravine in front of and to the right of Shand's House, about 300 yards in front of the Confederate positions. [27] Willcox's division charged across the open field. Although the Confederate trenches were only waist deep and had no ditch in front of them, [28] Willcox's division was repulsed with hundreds of dead and wounded. [29]

At 5:30 p.m., Ledlie's division received orders to prepare for its own attack around sundown against the same Confederate positions where Willcox's division had just been repulsed with heavy losses and Potter's division had ultimately stalled earlier in the day. [30]

Half an hour before Ledlie received orders to attack, Beauregard had sent Lee a report on intelligence obtained from Union prisoners. Finally, an accurate picture of the Union movements was beginning to emerge for Lee.

> Prisoners just taken report themselves as belonging to the Second, Ninth and Eighteenth Corps. They state that the Fifth and Sixth Corps are coming on. Those from Second and Eighteenth came here by transports and arrived first; others marched night and day from Gaines' Mill and arrived yesterday evening. The Ninth crossed at Turkey Bend where they have a pontoon bridge. They say Grant commanded on the field yesterday. [31]

The section of the Hagood Line that Ledlie's division was about to attack was quite formidable, although hastily prepared. As noted, the Confederate trenches were only waist deep, but they occupied the crest of a ridge above Harrison Creek. Between the ridge and the ravine of Harrison Creek was a field with corn then ten inches high. The distance from the ravine over the cornfield to the Confederate trenches was about three hundred yards. This section of the Confederate line was in the form of a broad "V" with the base of the "V" facing toward Harrison's Creek. Two artillery positions on the Confederate left and one on the Confederate right could provide enfilading fire on an attack across the cornfield. [32]

The Confederate positions immediately in front of Ledlie's division were manned by the 34th and 46th Virginia of Wise's brigade and the 23rd South Carolina of Elliott's brigade (both brigades of Bushrod Johnson's division). [33]

The 179th was not in the best of shape for the upcoming battle. Company A's Daniel Lee described the soldiers of the 179th as "completely tired out" after their hard march from Cold Harbor. [34] The rest of the Army of the Potomac was tired as well. General Meade, reporting to General Grant on the Second Corps' attacks on June 16, noted on the morning of June 17 that "Our men are tired and the attacks have not been made with the vigor and force which characterized our fighting in the Wilderness." [35] As Thomas Howe wrote in his history of the fighting at Petersburg from June 15 to 18, 1864, "The average Union soldier was just too tired to fight well." [36]

The 179th was also only about 230 strong for the assault, [37] well below the paper strength of a standard regiment of ten companies of eighty to one hundred men each. Not only was the 179th comprised of only six companies at that time, but one hundred soldiers were still on detached duty at Cumberland Heights. Companies E and F had also lost nearly seventy men to desertion since they left Elmira. [38] However, there were other, older regiments that were even weaker. The 29th Massachusetts went into battle that day with only five officers and seventy enlisted men. [39] The 21st Massachusetts had only between 130 and 140. [40]

Ledlie's division moved into position for the attack under cover of the Harrison Creek ravine. They lay prone on the western slope of the ravine for about an hour. [41] The incline from the ravine was steep enough to protect the Union soldiers from the direct fire of the Confederate artillery, but not steep enough to protect them from Confederate ingenuity. The Confederate artillerymen employed "ricochet firing with solid shot," described by Capt. John Anderson of the 57th Massachusetts as follows:

> Ricochet is where the artillery is fired with a small charge at a small angle of elevation. The projectile soon strikes the ground and continues in a straight line, rebounding every few yards until its force is spent. It is very destructive

as it passes, with each rebound rising but little above the ground. It cannot be used to advantage except in an open country where there are no objects to cause a deflection. In this case it was across a level cornfield. After the second rebound the direction of the projectile can be obtained, which gives one an opportunity of dodging them, if he is quick enough. We were kept dodging most of the time. [42]

Ledlie's division suffered casualties of thirty-two soldiers killed and wounded from artillery fire before the attack even began. [43] Company F's Corp. John H. Carley had his arm shot away from the shoulder and died two days later. Sgt. John W. Durham was severely wounded by grapeshot in the shoulder, but survived. [44]

[Map: June 17, 6 p.m.]

Ledlie's division began its attack up from the ravine around six in the evening. The division was deployed in three lines. The first line was comprised of the First Brigade (Colonel Gould) on the right (56th, 57th and 59th Massachusetts) and the Second Brigade (Lieutenant Colonel Barnes) on the left (29th Massachusetts, 3rd Maryland and 179th New York Volunteers). The Second Brigade's 100th Pennsylvania Volunteers were deployed as skirmishers across the entire line. The Second Brigade's 21st Massachusetts was deployed on the First Brigade's right at a forty-five degree angle to protect against a flank attack by the Confederates. The division's second and third lines were comprised of the Third Brigade's (Lieut. Col. Barney) two regiments – the 14th New York Heavy Artillery and the 2nd Pennsylvania Provisional Heavy Artillery, both deployed as infantry. The second line advanced about one hundred paces after the first. [45]

Ledlie's division advanced at a southwestern angle from the ravine. [46] The Regimental Chaplain of the 125th New York Volunteers (Barlow's division of the Second Corps) observed the attack from their position on higher ground:

> The dark mass then moved along, slowly at first; but gradually the pace was quickened until it reached the brow of the hill, when, with a deafening cheer and guns at a 'charge,' the men broke into the double quick. But they were met with a murderous fire – such a fire as seemed impossible to withstand. Solid shot, shell and bullets soon wrought great havoc in the column. The men broke, and then reformed; and at last gained the victory. [47]

Ledlie described the assault in his report to General Burnside:

> I gave the order for the charge, with directions to my command not to fire a shot until reaching the enemy's lines. The line was then moved forward with bayonets fixed, charging at a run over the entire distance [300 to 500 yards] with steadiness and bravery. ... The men charged the works fiercely and bravely, mounting the parapet and leaping quite over the ditch into the enemy's lines where the fight became a hand-to hand conflict, my men using the bayonet and breech, and succeeded in carrying the works in handsome style. The troops pressed forward and also succeeded in taking another line of the enemy's works. [48]

An officer of the 46th Virginia described their fire at the first wave of attacking federal troops:

> when [the enemy was] within 200 yards of our works the rear rank of the left

wing was ordered to open fire upon him, which they did with great precision, that not only checked his advance but literally mowed them down, ... and when the smoke rose only a few could be seen straggling to the rear and right oblique. [49]

Captain Bird, commander of the 179th's Company D, wrote his father that: "Our Regt was on the left of the first line exposed to the flank fire of a battery... [The Confederate breastwork] was taken with the bayonet. We did not fire a shot until we were across it." [50] Company F's William Larzalere wrote in his diary that the attack "was done under a mushroom fire of grape canisters shells and musketry. [51]

The 23rd South Carolina was the first Confederate regiment to be overrun. The 46th Virginia, having been flanked by the rout of the 23rd Carolina, fell back about one hundred yards to an artillery position. The 46th Virginia quickly counterattacked, but was repulsed, losing its commanding officer and "many others." [52] Three Confederate regiments were driven from the field and approximately one-quarter mile of the Hagood Line taken in the attack. The rebel troops on both ends of the breach had to refuse (reverse) their lines. [53]

Ledlie's division remained in the captured Confederate works for several hours under what Ledlie described as "desultory fire". [54] However, "desultory" is likely an understatement. Several Confederate counterattacks in the early evening were repulsed.

At this point in the battle, the Union Fifth Corps was available to coordinate an attack on Ledlie's left, but no decisive action was taken. Both General Meade and the Fifth Corps Commander, General Warren, had become aware from reconnaissance earlier in the day that there was little visible Confederate presence to the southeast of the Ninth Corps' operations. [55] However, news of Ledlie's success did not immediately reach Meade. At 7:30 p.m. the Fifth Corps assistant adjutant general reported to his counterpart on Meade's staff that "[s]ome prisoners just sent in say that General Burnside's troops are over the works [and] that we can easily capture Petersburg if we push right ahead." [56] At eight that evening, Meade responded to Warren that he had heard no report from Burnside, but "[i]f Burnside has gained any great success which can be followed up I desire you to move forward with your whole corps." [57] Given the apparent lack of reliable information on Ledlie's success, that was a very big "if."

Shortly thereafter, Meade became even more cautious: "unless the advance now being made promises decisive results, you had better hold on to what you have, and postpone any further attack until to-morrow morning, as the men were up all last night." [58] General Warren took the cautious approach, responding at 9 p.m. that:

> Owing to the difficulty of the ground and darkness General Crawford's troops have not yet got into position. I had designed making an independent assault with his division. Nothing decisive can probably be done to-night, and General Crawford is directed to take position on the left of General Burnside's line, and in support of it. This will enable General Burnside to get his command better in order and refill ammunition, &c. [59]

The fatigue of the Union soldiers after the hard march from Cold Harbor was certainly a factor to be considered. Still, just as General Smith had missed a golden opportunity at the end of the day on June 15 by waiting to follow up until "tomorrow morning," so too may Meade and Warren have missed a golden opportunity at the end of the day on June 17. [60]

Around ten o'clock that night, Ledlie's division repulsed a Confederate attack, capturing five officers, seventy-one men and the colors of the 35th North Carolina. However, between eleven o'clock and midnight, Ransom's and Gracie's brigades of Confederate troops attacked again, and this time Ledlie's division fell back because it had been flanked on the left and was running low on ammunition. [61]

The Union troops retreated in confusion back to the ravine from which they had started. [62] Ten soldiers from the 179th were reported as missing in action. Of these ten, four can be documented as having been taken as prisoners. [63] The entire 57th Massachusetts was almost captured, losing only nine men in the end. [64] The missing in action numbers were heaviest in the Third Brigade, with the 14th New York Heavy Artillery suffering the loss of fifty-three soldiers captured or missing and the 2d Pennsylvania Provisional Heavy Artillery twelve. [65]

As the Confederates troops at Petersburg were mounting these counterattacks, Lee advised Beauregard that General Kershaw's division was on its way to Petersburg. [66] At the same hour, Confederate cavalryman W. H. F. "Rooney" Lee, on reconnaissance near the pontoon bridge that the Ninth Corps and others had used to cross the James River, reported that "Grant's entire army is across the river" – a fact by now obvious to General Lee and General Beauregard. [67] However, the Army of the Potomac was rapidly losing the last benefits of its strategic surprise.

With the action on June 17 ending for the day, General Meade ordered "a vigorous assault" at 4 a.m. the following morning "by the whole force of the Fifth, Ninth, and Second Corps." [68] However, during the night of June 17, the Confederate forces fell back from the Hagood Line to the Harris Line. The trenches of the Harris Line had not yet been completed and the Confederate troops continued the work through the night. [69]

[Map: Ninth Corps, June 18]

When the Union forces advanced early in the morning of June 18, they found that the Hagood Line had been abandoned. [70] During the rest of the day they advanced toward the Harris Line, pushing back the Confederate skirmishers. The Ninth Corps advanced with a one division front led by Willcox's division, followed by Potter's division and then Ledlie's division. [71] Willcox was heavily engaged, but the day was a relatively quiet one for Ledlie's division and the 179th New York Volunteers. [72]

The Harris Line became the main Confederate line in that sector for the rest of the Petersburg campaign. [73] The Ninth Corps had advanced the closest to the Harris Line on June 18 and as it dug in remained the closest for the next six weeks as the siege of Petersburg began. [74] The close proximity of the Ninth Corps to the Confederate lines would lead to the Battle of the Crater six weeks later on July 30, 1864.

Like the reports of many generals "fighting" from the rear, Ledlie's report gave no sense of the casualties that accompanied the "bravery," "steadiness," and "handsome style" that he lauded. The 179th lost heavily in the June 17 attack – two officers and nine enlisted men killed; and three officers and sixty-seven enlisted men wounded (ten fatally) in addition to the ten enlisted men missing in action, for total casualties of ninety-one. [75] The 179th fielded only about 230 soldiers on June 17, so overall nearly forty percent of them became casualties. Company D suffered nearly seventy-five percent casualties. Of the twenty-three men in Company D, only six "came out safe" in the words of Captain Bird. [76]

William Larzalere wrote in his diary simply that "our regt was mostly destroyed." [77] Captain Bird used almost the exact words in a letter to his father: "we were almost destroyed." [78] Company A's Daniel Lee wrote his wife that he had survived the battle "threw my good luck because all of the regiment is cut to pieces... It has bin one of the worst battles ever." [79] Company B's Homer Olcott similarly wrote that the 179th "in charging got badly cut up." [80] Company C's John McGrath (alias John Brown) wrote his mother that: "Manny went in that never came out." He described his own injury–"a little scratch on the hand"–in less solemn terms: "I was getting up on the breastworks when some fellow I suppose thought I had no right there so he made a prod at me but only took the skin of my finger." McGrath did not say what had happened to the Confederate soldier. [81]

The other regiments in Ledlie's division suffered heavy losses as well. The 29th Massachusetts also lost forty percent of its men engaged. [82] Burnside reported to Meade after the attack that "there is scarcely anything left" of Ledlie's division.[83] A day later, the 1st Maine Heavy Artillery, also in its first battle, was deployed as infantry and lost more than two-thirds of its men in a frontal assault nearby – the heaviest loss by a Union regiment in a single engagement during the Civil War. [84]

Lieutenat Colonel Doty and Major Sloan, leading the attack for the 179th, were among those wounded. Sloan is reputed to have called out to Doty "*I am mortally wounded!*" As a combat veteran who had been wounded earlier in the war, he had a sound basis to know that. This time, he had been wounded in the lower body and the bullet had not exited. He was taken to the hospital where he died the following day. [85]

Doty was hit in the shoulder by a shell fragment during the initial assault, but carried on, shifting his sword to his left hand as he rallied the 179th for the successful assault. As Doty mounted the Confederate works, he was wounded again in the leg. [86] Company D's Captain Bird was wounded in the knee by a shell fragment just in front of the breastwork. His wound was painful, but ultimately not disabling. He wrote his father that "I am very lucky to get out so cheap." A Confederate shell broke his sword in his hand, but he found a rebel sword as a souvenir. [87]

The 179th's loss of leadership that day was particularly serious. Of the seven officers of the 179th who were engaged, five became casualties. Lieutenant Colonel Doty's wounds took him out of action for two months. [88] Major Sloan, the second in command, was mortally wounded as noted. At the company level, Capt. Daniel Blachford of Company E was killed; Capt. Robert Stewart of Company B was wounded and had his leg amputated in the field hospital that night; and Bird's wounds were serious enough to send him to hospital in Washington and he never returned to the field. [89]

Such a heavy loss of officers was not unusual. In Ledlie's division, the 2d Pennsylvania Provisional Heavy Artillery lost seven officers, the 14th New York Heavy Artillery lost six, and the 57th Massachusetts lost five that day. [90] The day before, the 57th New York (Third Brigade of Barlow's division, Second Corps) had lost ten of their twelve officers in a charge. [91] Burnside reported that "our losses in the engagements of the 16th, 17th, and 18th [of June] were very severe, among which were many of our best commanding officers of brigades and regiments." [92] As James McPherson notes, Civil War officers "led by example, not prescript. And in combat they led from the front, not the rear." As a result, an officer's chances of being killed in battle were fifteen percent higher than an enlisted man's chances of being killed. [93] A New Jersey officer, Maj. Thomas J. Halsey, wrote his wife on June 18, 1864:

> I am still alive to date. Lib, this is a fearful fight we are in & the prospect of
> getting out unharmed is slim. Our officers have to expose themselves and a
> great many of them get killed & wounded. I hope and trust I may get out all
> right. [94]

Casualties among the officers of the 179th necessitated some reassignments. Captain John Barton from Company C was promoted to major on July 13 and took command of the 179th.

(Company A's Capt. Albert Terrill was acting commander in the meantime.) First Lt. John Hoy became acting commander of Company E and Second Lt. Louis Ottenot from Company E may have moved over to take command of Company B. First Lt. Baker Saxton took command of Company D. [95]

In the enlisted ranks, it was a tragic day for the Phillips Family in Company A. Father Marshall was mortally wounded, while his eighteen-year-old son Newton was wounded and lost the use of his arm. [96]

Levi J. Rowley, a forty-three-year-old mechanic, was among those who demonstrated their bravery. He was recommended for the Medal of Honor for conspicuous gallantry. The recommendation gave the following details:

> in the battle of the 17th June 1864, before Petersburg, Va. Private Rowley did, in advance of his company, encounter six rebels, and ordered them to lay down their arms; five of them did so, but one would not surrender, whereupon Rowley bayoneted him, and brought the five into our lines; afterwards brought in a number of his own company, who were severely wounded. [97]

There is no way of accurately gauging the psychological impact on the enlisted men in the 179th of the first battle casualties, but the day after on June 18 there were at least two cases of possibly self-inflicted wounds in Company F – George W. West shot a finger and Daniel R. Bacon shot his big toe. Company E's William Spaulding shot off a finger on June 26. [98] Company F's Tuthill Dence shot his hand on an unspecified date in June "and died in consequence." [99]

There seems to have been enough doubt about whether Bacon's or West's wounds were self-inflicted that they were not disciplined. However, Spaulding's wound while on picket duty on June 26 was suspicious enough that he was court-martialed. The regimental surgeon, Lt. Col. Joseph Robinson, and the surgeon at City Point both provided "expert" forensic opinion that the injury had been inflicted by a pistol at close range as evidenced by powder burns. Spaulding was sentenced to hard labor for five years in the Dry Tortugas as well as forfeiture of pay. [100]

The men of the 179th had finally "seen the elephant" – the colloquial phrase of the day for being in combat. [101] They performed well in their first battle despite their small numbers, limited training and the hard march from Cold Harbor. The 179th attacked entrenched positions – albeit hastily prepared – that were well-supported by artillery, but still had the discipline to successfully attack after being initially repulsed. Much of the credit must go to the officers.

The 179th's heavy loss was reported in contemporary newspaper accounts, although the number killed was significantly overstated, and became part of regimental lore. Actual casualties were ninety-one, somewhat less than forty percent of those engaged. *The Hornellsville Tribune* reported on June 23, 1864 that the 179th's losses had been "very heavy" – forty-three killed and sixty-seven wounded among the roughly two hundred engaged. The *Buffalo Daily Courier* carried a July 8, 1864 letter from its correspondent: "[The 179th] was engaged in a most desperate and bloody charge ... and succeeded in carrying that part of the line, but at a fearful sacrifice, losing full one half of the men engaged." [102] On July 17, Spencer wrote from Petersburg that the 179th "participated in the memorable and bloody charge here, losing over half of those actually engaged." [103] This must have been chilling news on the home front as families waited for the names to match the numbers of casualties.

In a summary of the regiment's service written near the end of the war in April 1865, *The Hornellsville Tribune* stated that "the 179th went into the fight with 230 men, and, lost 120 killed and wounded." [104] In an article on the 179th's first reunion in 1880, the *Elmira Daily Advertiser* wrote that "a detachment of four companies suffered severely" in the battle.[105] The 179th was described as having been "greatly decimated" in the newspaper report on the 1894 reunion.[106] Forty years after the war, Company F's Charles B. Baker recalled (incorrectly) that only sixty men of the 179th had survived the June 17 battle.[107]

Larzalere recorded in his diary that the day after the battle was "passed in sorrow & care of the wounded." The night of June 18 they slept in the cornfield where they had attacked the day before. The next day, a Sunday, they rested.[108]

On June 20, the men of Company E gathered to honor the fallen Captain Blachford. Reflecting their background as "citizen" soldiers, they held a "meeting" "in the rifle pits before Petersburg" and unanimously adopted the following resolutions:

> Whereas, It has pleased Almighty God to remove from our midst in the fierce conflict of battle, our late friend and brother officer, Capt. Daniel Blatchford, who was slain in the bloody charge of the evening of June 17, 1864, and

> Whereas, We deem it our binding duty to express, in words of earnest sympathy, our sincere grief at the great loss which not only our company and regiment, but also our suffering country has sustained; and it is therefore

> Resolved, That in the loss of our late brother officer and companion in arms, the regiment has lost a most efficient and earnest member, who was ever prompt and zealous in the discharge of his arduous duties, and who never hesitated to render brave and diligent service when called upon to render aid in suppressing the atrocious rebellion aimed at the life of government.

> Resolved, That to the family of the deceased we tender our most heartfelt sympathies, and we offer our most earnest condolence to his bereaved and widowed wife and orphaned children, whom this sudden fate of war has smitten with grief and sad affliction.[109]

Back in Penn Yan, New York, a meeting of citizens honored Major Sloan on June 25 with similar resolutions:

> Whereas, Our esteemed friend, Major J. Barnet Sloan, of the 179th Regiment, Vol Infantry, while gallantly leading his Regiment in the attack against Petersburg, on the 17th June inst, –
> Resolved, That we bow in humble submission to the will of "Him who doeth all things well," deeply lamenting the untimely death of our generous and brave fellow citizen, by whose removal, in the morning of his fame, our imperiled country is deprived of the services of a true and tried soldier and officer, and his afflicted wife and little ones of a husband and father.

A committee was appointed to receive his remains and make arrangements for his funeral.[110]

Despite the heavy losses, Newton Spencer remained resolute. He wrote his old newspaper, the *Penn Yan Democrat*, that:

> To see stalwart men mowed down by irresistible lead and iron, is grievous. But this campaign must be pushed to its consummation, though thousands more may fall. The nation cannot recede now.[111]

John B. Sloan

CHAPTER EIGHT

The Good Death and the Loyal Soldier

News of Major Sloan's death must have come as a horrible shock to the Penn Yan community. Sloan had left Penn Yan for Elmira only the month before. On June 4, a large number of citizens had gathered at Benham House for the presentation of "a beautiful Sword, Pistols and Belt" as a testimonial to Major Sloan's "services rendered in defence of our imperiled country and his energy in raising the 179th Regt., N.Y.S.V." So many people attended, that the meeting was held outside. With Major Sloan absent in the field, the Hon. D. A. Ogden directed his remarks to Sloan's father, John Sloan, a justice of the peace.

> We have watched, sir, the military career of your son, with much interest, and have marked with much pleasure his conduct as a soldier. Early in the field – for he was among the first to volunteer – he was early distinguished as an honest, skillful officer; cool under fire, prompt in action and determined, he passed through many hotly contested fields, and in no instance shirked duty or avoided danger where duty called him or his superiors commanded him to go.

> Men thus active, men thus obedient, men thus brave deserve honor and the commendation of their countrymen and should receive the gratitude and support of their neighbors. [1]

After honoring the service of other regiments and soldiers from Yates County, Ogden returned at the end of his lengthy remarks to Major Sloan:

> That he will wear and use these weapons of war worthily we have no doubt, and God grant that he may be saved from harm and in the end and return long to enjoy in the quiet of his home and his beloved family the peace which he fights to secure and the liberties for which he imperils his life. [2]

J. D. Wolcott accepted the gift on behalf of Sloan's father and continued in the same spirit: "when this cruel war is over may it be truly said of the recipient 'God blessed him with length of days to survive it, and he filled them with deeds of valor and glory.'" [3] And now two weeks later this son of Penn Yan was dead.

Death on a battlefield hundreds of miles from family and friends presented a cultural challenge for Civil War era Americans – it was not consistent with the way people were supposed to die. As Drew Gilpin Faust wrote in *This Republic of Suffering: Death and the American Civil War*:

> The concept of the Good Death was central to mid-nineteenth-century America, as it had long been at the core of Christian practice. Dying was an art, and the tradition of *ars moriendi* had provided rules of conduct for the moribund and their attendants since at least the fifteenth century: how to give up one's soul "gladly and willfully"; how to meet the devil's temptations of unbelief, despair, impatience, and worldly attachment; how to pattern one's dying on that of Christ; how to pray. [4]

Family played a critical role in the art of dying:

> Family was central to the *ars moriendi* tradition, for kin performed its essential rituals. Victorian ideals of domesticity further reinforced these assumptions about death's appropriate familial setting. One should die among family assembled around the deathbed. Relatives would of course be most likely to show concern about the comfort and needs of their dying loved one, but this was ultimately a secondary consideration. Far more important, family members needed to witness a death in order to assess the state of the dying person's soul, for these critical last moments of life would epitomize his or her spiritual condition. The dying were not losing their essential selves, but rather defining them for eternity. Kin would use their observations of the deathbed to evaluate the family's chances for a reunion in heaven. A life was a narrative that could only be incomplete without this final chapter, without the life-defining last words. [5]

Deprived of the deathbed, Civil War families had to make adjustments to assure themselves that their father, son or brother had died a "good death." When Company I's Charles S. Baker, a nineteen-year-old farmer from Tompkins County, died of typhoid fever at McDougall General Hospital, the ward master was sensitive to the needs of the family.

> I assume the painful duty of announcing to you the death of Charles S. Baker, which occurred this morning at a 1/4 past two o'clock.
>
> As I attended and administered to his wants during his brief sojourn and sickness here, therefore can truly particularize of his last moments.
>
> He arrived ... greatly reduced and prostrated by the malignant typhoid

fever, he was very delirious and continually talked in wild, incoherent ramblings, occasionally being rational, so that he imparted parting words. He said that he was fully sensible of death impending over him, and spoke in a very calm and cheerful spirit of his approaching *death*, saying that I should write his parents and tell them "that I died happy"– "only regretting that I could not see them."

He said that he was struck with death a Friday night (whilst on the hospital transport) to use his own words "the night was beautiful, beautiful, beautiful."

During Saturday night, we understood him to repeatedly say "drive that team this way;" and frequently calling the name of "Em and Emeline."

We endeavored to administer to his every comfort, and also to restore him, but our efforts were defied by the fatal fever. He was unconscious from 3 o'clock yesterday afternoon; the spirit battling long and persistently in wresting itself from the material form, but trust that he is now painless and happy in the presence of dear departed friends that have gone before to the "Summerland." ...

He died an enviable and honorable death – a glorious self-sacrifice, serving gallantly for his country. [6]

If Ward Master William Dewhurst wrote a letter like this to the family of each of his patients who died, he truly performed a great service.

There was also the public dimension of recognizing the soldier's death in the service of his community. Sloan's funeral was held in Penn Yan on June 27. His brother, Dr. Alexander B. Sloan, had gone to Virginia to bring his body home. "Officers and Soldiers who now are, or have been in the U.S. service, and citizens generally" were invited to attend the funeral. The procession formed at Washington Hall at 1:00 p.m., moved on to Sloan's father's home and then to the First Presbyterian Church. The procession was lead by the Penn Yan Coronet Band followed by Company C of the 59th Regiment of the New York State National Guard. Next came the hearse with the pall bearers. The remainder of the procession was made up of "Horse, with Equipments of Deceased, led by Groom;" "Family of Deceased and Relatives;" "The Clergy;" "Veteran and Disabled Soldiers;" "Public Officers;" "Fire Department;" and "Citizens." [7]

The Reverend Frederick Starr, Jr. officiated. Several weeks later, the Committee on Arrangements asked Rev. Starr for a copy of his remarks for publication. He replied that "a part of the discourse was not fully written out," but he "supplied that portion, in words used at the time, as nearly as I can recall them." His sermon was subsequently published in November 1864 as *The Loyal Soldier. A Discourse Delivered in the First Presbyterian Church of Penn Yan, New York, at the Funeral of Major John Barnett Sloan, of the 179th Regiment, N.Y.V. Infantry.* [8]

Publication of Rev. Starr's sermon was not unusual. Faust notes that:

> In both North and South many of these wartime sermons, as well as funeral biographies and memorials that grew out of them, appeared in print, ranging in size from a pamphlet of a few pages to full-sized octavios designed to serve as monuments to the dead and exhortations to the living. ...

More considered, more polished than condolence letters written from the front, the published funeral sermon was intended for distribution to a wider audience than simply next of kin or even those who might be able to attend a funeral service. The lost life, the soldier's death no longer belonged just to that individual and his family but was also to be understood and possessed by the community – even the nation – at large. [9]

As an officer recently commended by his community and the son of a justice of the peace, Sloan fit the usual profile for a published funeral sermon. [10]

Reverend Starr's funeral sermon was long on "exhortation to the living" on the sins of America and the ultimate righteousness of the Union cause. He was largely preaching to the choir. The towns of Yates County that comprised Penn Yan had given Lincoln a 60% majority in 1860 and would again in November 1864. [11]

He began with Jeremiah 50:28 – "A sound of battle is in the land, and of great destruction." He spoke of the calamity of war.

> War is the symbol of everything fearful, destructive and sorrowful; it is both the stimulant, and the outlet, of the most fiery, excited and revengeful passions; it burdens hearts with loads of unbearable anxieties; causes cruel, sudden, and ofttimes perpetual separations; it leaves the helpless, young and feeble, to want and suffering; exposes the bravest and strongest to hardships, toils and dangers, unknown in any other calling... It reduces the average of national, physical health, height, strength and beauty; it fills homes of happiness with desolation, and hearts of love with unutterable woe – and the flower of the age, the strength and the hope of the nation, it consigns to an untimely and bloody grave. [12]

He then spoke of the sacrifices required by just wars, with a veiled reference to the American Revolution:

> Among the holiest, the most just and profitable wars of history, have been those fought by the people against their own tyrants, or the uprisings of conquered nations to cast off their oppressors; for, in such wars, have gains been made for self-government, and freedom, personal, mental and moral, for the whole man. But no *such* war has been waged, much less carried to a successful termination, without a vast and fearful sacrifice of money, love and life, to achieve the blessings. [13](italics in original)

In contrast,

> There have been wars, undertaken in the behalf of wrong, which have been successful; wherein the weaker party, in the right, has gone down before the stronger party in the wrong. Shall any man say it was well? ...I tell you, NEVER! Unroll the chart of history, and show me the nation that has willfully waged wicked, unscrupulous wars, for conquest, plunder, glory, that *has not*, in herself, according to her intelligence and her sin, *sunk*, correspondingly, in conscience, in true principle, and ultimately, in national grandeur and power. [14] (emphasis in original)

He gave England as an example, pointing to the subjugation of India and China, and concluding that "Her honor is dead, her principles she has abandoned." [15]

Starr then turned to the United States, speaking not only about slavery, but also about the displacement of Native Americans and the invasion of Mexico:

> So, too, in reference to our own land. The red man has been trampled down, and we have, though with great trouble, taken him from his country, and his father's graves. We have conquered, for a paltry debt, the distracted, bankrupt republic of Mexico, and *set an example to imperious France*, which she is following, to reap, *as we did in our day*, the scorn, contempt and condemnation of every other nation. Yea, we have held *for two centuries* a portion of our own nation in barbaric slavery. [16](italics in original)

As to "the war in our land, and its objects," he stated "simply this":

> 1. It was commenced against a government which *could not be, and had not been, unkind, unjust, or oppressive*, towards those who rebelled against it. It was largely in the hands of the rebels themselves. *No right* was denied to the rebelling men, which was not withheld equally from every other citizen. The rebellion was made by the admission of their ablest men, *without any grievance*.

> 2. The rebellion was conceived, planned and advanced to a state of actual war, by its authors, without any opposition, violence or aggravation, on the part of the loyal citizens; *it was arranged and perpetrated in cold blood*.

> 3. *The avowed purpose* of this war was to *divide* the wealth, the territory, the population of this nation, and, with the Southern part, *to set up a new Government*, of a monarchical form, whose leading feature, or, in their words, whose "corner-stone" should be the *conservation and perpetuation of American Slavery.* [17] (italics in original)

With this lengthy introduction, Starr got to his main theme – the "Loyal Soldier".

> I would then speak to you for a few moments –

> I. Upon the *character* of the loyal soldier in this war.
> II. Upon the *blessings* he bestows upon his country.
> III. Upon the *duties* he imposes upon his country.

> First – The Character of the Loyal Soldier.

> 1. *He is brave. ...*

> 2. The loyal soldiers of our army are intelligent, and have been *influenced by noble motives*. It is true that the Government and the local authorities have given bounties, large and liberal, to our soldiers; but in very many instances it will be found that these monies were applied to pay debts, or remove incumbrances which stood in the way of the individuals' leaving home at all. In a land of such wealth as ours, and where labor is so well renumerated [sic], the bounties offered by the Government are a small temptation to any one to expose his life, and endure the hardships of war, and the separation from friends. *The love of country, the love of principle, and the sense of duty*, are the actuating

motives which have filled the Union army. [Starr's perceived need to justify the payment of bounties to recruit soldiers to fight a just war is noteworthy.]

3. The Union soldier is a useful man... To the great and glorious ends for which he fights, he labors faithfully. Oh, it is this sense of usefulness, that is laid upon him of God as his share to perform or bear, that causes thousands to lie without a murmur, far from friends, fevered, wounded, dying, and say – if God will only prosper the right, and bless my country, I can suffer and die for it!

4. He is a man enobled by his calling. …He has a deep and noble exercise of soul; and when clearly perceiving the principles for which he contends, he stands in the charge and carnage of battle, he shall not come forth from that baptism of fire and blood but he comes forth *a nobler man.*

5. He is self-immolated for principle. …

6. The Union soldier who falls fighting in this war *is a martyr.* … [18](italics in original)

Starr then turned to the question "What does the Union Martyr or Soldier Confer on his Country?"

1. *He ennobles its character and its name.* …

2. This country shall be prized by the relatives, and especially by the children and descendants of these martyrs. …

3. This country shall, by what they have done, go down to the future *firm and immovable.* …

4. *Humanity, and good will to men everywhere, has the aid of the Union soldier.* [19](italics in original)

Starr closed the section of his discourse on the "Loyal Soldier" by asking: "And What Ought the Nation and its People to do in Return for the Soldier?"

1. *His memory shall be embalmed in our hearts.* …

2. *The nation should cherish and care for those dependent upon the soldier, left in want by his death.* …

3. *The nation is bound to preserve and cultivate liberty!.* …

4. *It is the duty of this government to expiate the blood of her martyred soldiers, by execution of the decrees of the courts of justice*

5. *The country owes it to the Union soldiers, dead and living, to prosecute this war with all energy to a speedy, glorious and victorious termination.* Leaving out every moral question, *this war cannot be settled except by victory.* The nation, by the audacity and violence of traitors, was put on the defensive in every particular; and whatever victories it may achieve – as long as one State, one county, or one rebel soldier, stands in a state of armed hostility, so long is the nation threatened and kept on the defensive. ... [20] (italics in original)

Without mentioning Sloan by name up to this point in his sermon, Starr was assuring that everyone was firmly "in the choir" on unflagging support for successful prosecution of the war, regardless of the cost. [21]

Starr finally reached the circumstances of Sloan's death, an equally important part of the sermon. Starr told of Sloan's death in a way that would have given comfort to his family and friends.

The Major was leading the Regiment in the charge, when he was shot in the lower portion of the body; the ball remained lodged in his person. He called Col. Doty and remarked – "*I am mortally wounded!*" He was carried to the hospital, where he received the kindest attention from the surgeon, the chaplain, and his brother-in-law [Company F's Lt. David Bradley]; he was cheerful, and sent kind and tender messages to his home and family. He lived from Thursday P.M. six o'clock, when wounded, until Friday P.M., at five and one-half o'clock, when another of the mighty host of martyrs for freedom slept in death. [22] (italics in original)

Starr reassured Sloan's family and the audience that Sloan had died a good death by referring to Sloan's awareness and acceptance of his impending death, the presence of a chaplain and his brother-in law at his bedside, and his "tender messages to his home and family."

Sloan's successor as the 179th's major, John Barton from Company C, died a month later at the Battle of the Crater. His hometown newspaper, *The Hornellsville Tribune*, reported that "a very appropriate discourse was delivered by Rev. Mr. Windsor," but did not quote from it. Barton was buried with Masonic honors with the accompaniment of the Dunkirk Band. The *Tribune* noted that "the gathering was one of the largest ever witnessed in this locality on a funeral occasion." [23]

Lieutenant Colonel Franklin B. Doty, who was also from Hornellsville, was mortally wounded in the last major battle at Petersburg in April 1865. His brother, Lt. Martin V. Doty of Company C, accompanied his body home. For his funeral, three companies from the Veteran Reserve Corps in Elmira and a brass band were detailed to accompany his body on the procession from his house through the streets of Hornellsville to the Presbyterian Church. As with Barton, the *Tribune* reported that "an appropriate sermon was preached," this time by Rev. Mr. Waldo. A group of citizens who had heard Rev. Waldo's discourse asked him to provide a copy to the *Tribune* for publication. Waldo declined because "much of it being delivered *extempore*; it could not go into the hands of the printer without being rewritten entire – This and many other duties forbid my doing at present." However, Waldo did provide the biographical sketch of Doty that he had read during the service, and the *Tribune* printed it – three page-length columns. [24] The *Tribune* also ran a remembrance of Doty written by a schoolmate who remembered Doty as "the soul of truth and integrity." [25]

Two years after the war, the citizens of Hornellsville again gathered to honor Lientenant Colonel Doty, this time to dedicate a stone monument in Hope Cemetery. Horace Bemis, a prominent Hornellsville attorney, began:

We come now in a mass, his old companions in arms, his family, his aged

mother, his brothers, his sisters, the community that loved and honored him…
We could add nothing to the glory that that man has carved with his own
sword, and won by his own pure life. If we were to pour out tears upon that
grave it would not benefit him, or much increase the honor the world will pay
him. Where he has gone the world's praise can never change the record. He has
made the record for himself, and stamped it with the red seal of his life blood.
It is not for us to add to his honors, but there is still reason why we come. His
life was precious, his death was sacred. He gave it for us and for all men who
have an interest in the stability of free government. We acknowledge ourselves
his debtors. [26]

While Rev. Waldo's sermon in 1865 had not been reported, some of his words this day were:
A good name is better than precious ointment. The perfume of his [sic] man's
name is most graceful to the family of which he was a prominent member, and
to us, his fellow townsmen, and to all the lovers of patriotism and purity. [27]

[Photo: Henry Hoffman]

Doty's regimental commander in the 23rd New York, Col. Henry C. Hoffman, noted that it
was particularly sad that Doty had died so close to the end of the war:
While I rejoiced at the downfall of Richmond and the rebellion with it, I could
not help mourning the fall of Colonel Doty. It seemed too bad that a man like
him should not live to enjoy the victory. It seemed sad that a man who had
done so much as he should not survive to enjoy the peace that followed. [28]

Bemis repeated Doty's purported last words, spoken in a passionless voice from his deathbed:
"It is all right. Tell them I died fighting for the old flag." [29] Bemis thus reassured the audience that
Doty had also died a Good Death.

The death of a field grade officer was significant news. Not only were the deaths of Lieutenant
Colonel Doty and Majors Sloan and Barton covered in their hometown newspapers, but Sloan's
death was also reported in the *Geneva Courier* and Barton's death in the *Yates County Chronicle*. [30] At
the company level, the uncertainty over whether Capt. Allen Farwell had been killed or captured at
the Battle of the Crater was reported in three successive issues of his weekly hometown paper. [31]

Not surprisingly, coverage of the deaths of enlisted men was more sporadic and more limited
in space. In addition to Major Sloan, five enlisted men from Yates County died in the June 17
assault. Of the five, Company F's Pvt. John H. Carley was the only one whose death was reported
in the *Yates County Chronicle*. The *Chronicle*'s "Jottings" column briefly noted that his funeral would
be held at the Methodist Episcopal Church, but did not report on the sermon. (Carley's body had
been buried on the battlefield.) [32]

When Company F's Pvt. William Clark died in August 1864, the *Chronicle* noted that Rev. Starr
would deliver a "discourse" at his funeral, but his remarks were not reported. [33] After the Battle of
the Crater, the *Chronicle* reported that: "Sergeant Jeremiah Sprague, who was of the 179th Regt and
formerly of the 33rd, was one of the killed at the last fight before Petersburg.
He was a good soldier, and a son of widow Sprague of this village." (Actually he survived, but was
taken prisoner. He also was in the 14th New York Heavy Artillery, which was in the same brigade
as the 179th.) [34] Even more cryptic was the report that: "George W. Green, of the 179th Regiment
and Ansen A. Raplee of the 148th, died in Hospital last week at New York. Both were soldiers from

Yates County." [35] The *Dryden Weekly News* reported that the funeral sermon for Company A's Moses Brown would be given by Rev. A. McDougell at the Presbyterian Church. [36]

When the death of Company H's Charles Flint was briefly reported in the *Lockport Journal & Courier* in July 1865, his comrade Harry Ap Rees thought he deserved better, and the *Courier* printed Ap Rees' letter to the editor.

> Will you kindly permit me to correct a few slight errors. The name of the deceased soldier ... was Charles Edwin Flint, and not Flinn; his age was twenty-nine, and not thirty. The fever which caused his death may without doubt be attributed to the bursting of a shell near his head, during the last fearful assault upon Petersburg ... I can speak of his merit as a soldier and a man. That he ever did his duty faithfully none can deny. [37]

Soldiers who died from disease were also separated from the support of family and friends. Company I's John W. Cook was taken prisoner near Pegram House on September 30, 1864. He survived four grueling months in Salisbury Military Prison and had a brief furlough home after being paroled in February 1865, only to fall ill when he rejoined the 179th in the field. Cook was admitted to Sickel U.S.A. General Hospital in Alexandria on May 8. [38]

Cook's spirits rose and fell along with his medical condition. He was too sick to be able to write on May 11, but "a lady that is hear" in the hospital took his dictation for a letter to his mother and father that he was "quite sick I am in fever suffering greatly." He asked his parents to write soon, " for I am quite lonely." [39]

On May 28, he was:

> very sick but getting better. I have been sick abed two weeks... [I] have the Inflammatory Rheumatism, and Remittent fever... I do not know if I will ever get home again or not. I would like to see my dear little Frankie and brothers and sisters again. [40]

Three weeks later, Cook felt "worse than when last he wrote and is very poor and entirely helpless and suffers a good deal of pain in his right leg. The right hand is also helpless and useless." Cook told his parents: "I wish you would come and see me as I feel very low." [41]

A letter from home cheered him up at the end of June. He wrote: "I received your kind and welcome letter, so I thought I would write you a few lines to let you know how I am getting along. I am a little better thank God." Feeling better, this time he told his parents not to come because "it will cost you too much." He told his parents not to worry about him, "for I keep up good courage and I hope I will be able to go home soon." [42]

However, by July 20, Cook was "not quite so well as I was when I last wrote." Cook felt "very anxious to hear from you all as I have not heard from you in a long time, and Dear Father if you want to see me I want you to come here right a way as I don't think I can stand it long." Cook suggested to his father two people that he could borrow money from if he needed money for the $25 train fare. (The average monthly wage for a farm laborer in the summer in Upstate New York was about $25 at this time.) [43]

By August, his condition had worsened. On August 8, 1865, he was:

> not as well as usual. I am failing all the time. Father I want you to come and see me. Right off I have got $35.00 Dollars that is enough to pay the expenses and I want to see you before I leave this world. [44]

A friend of Cook's at the hospital, John B. Temple, added a note to the letter: "Mr. Cook, if you want to see your son you had better come as soon as possible. ... N.B. He is very low. I assure you he has the money to my knowledge." [45]

Cook died of remittent fever on August 18, 1865. [46] There is no indication that his father was able to make it to the hospital before he died. Cook suffered greatly in loyally serving his country. Sadly his was not a Good Death.

Company A's Daniel B. Lee also did not die a Good Death. He was captured in July 1864 while going to find water in no man's land. The Confederates first took Lee to Castle Thunder in Richmond. He was then sent to Salisbury Prison in North Carolina, but escaped en route. He began making his way north, but contracted diarrhea. He made it as far as Washington County in the western toe of Virginia, where a sympathetic Southerner took him in on October 14, 1864. Lee died there on November 3, 1864, almost four months after he was captured. [47] Dying in the home of a stranger was not a Good Death.

The antithesis of a Good Death in all respects was suffered by an unknown Union soldier whose body Company D's Lt. John Andrews encountered:

> Saw ... one of the hardest sights of my life. Perceiving a bad odor and enquiring what it was, one of the pickets took us a little beyond the picket line into a low wet piece of ground, densely covered with trees and bushes, through which a small stream was running, and there at the foot of a large tree lay a Union soldier, his legs in the stream – the water of which our men were using – his face alone covered with a few shovel-fulls of dirt. There he lay an offering on the altar of our country – a patriot soldier, food for worms, thousands of which were feasting upon his flesh. [48]

Such an anonymous, abandoned death was all too common during the Civil War. Roughly forty percent of the Union soldiers who died in combat lay in their final resting places as "Unknown Soldiers." [49] The percentage for the 179th New York is in that range. [50] Company B's Leonard Morris recalled the unsuccessful effort to find the body of his comrade John Hannon after the Battle of Poplar Spring Church:

> Three days elapsed before we again got possession of the place where we believed he was killed and by that time our dead had been completely stripped of all clothing and the bodies were so much bloated and decayed that it was impossible to recognize our dead. [51]

In many cases, the dead soldier was buried on the battlefield (if his body was even recovered) or near the hospital. In such cases, the absence of his body was an impediment to the family's experience of the Good Death. Even when the body could be recovered, decomposition would generally have prevented sending the body long distances to home. However, advances in technology combined with the large number of deaths far from home led to widespread use of embalming during the Civil War. Embalming helped maintain at least a semblance of the Good Death. As Faust concluded: "Families sought to see their lost loved ones in as lifelike a state as possible, not just to be certain of their identity but also to bid them farewell." [52]

Believing it would be "a humane act to let the friends of the soldiers know that bodies could be embalmed, coffined and sent home and the cost," the Chaplain of the 89th New York Volunteers sent the *Broome Republican* a list of prices from the Petersburg area in July 1864, noting that "the price of embalming is regulated by Government." The price for embalming varied by rank, ranging from $30 for a private and $35 for a sergeant to $65 for a colonel. A government-provided coffin was free, while a mahogany coffin cost $60, with others available at prices up to $300. Transportation to Binghamton cost $35 "so that the price of sending a private home in a Government coffin would be $65." [53] (Again, this would have been several months pay for the typical farm laborer.)

Embalming at government expense may have become routine. In August 1864, Maria Soles received a form letter from the Surgeon in Charge of Armory Square Hospital with the blanks filled in appropriately:

> It becomes my duty to inform you of the decease of Henry Soles Co. B 179th
> N.Y. Vols. who dies at this Hospital on [August 19, 1864] by reason of Diarrhea.
>
> The body has been embalmed, and the grave registered, so as to enable the
> friends to disinter the remains for transportation, on and after Oct. 1st, should
> they desire to do so. [54]

The family of the fallen soldier would have to go on without him. John Barnett Sloan left a wife and two daughters born in 1861 and 1863. Rev. Starr had spoken of the Nation's duty to "cherish and care for those dependent upon the soldier, left in want by his death." [55] The *Elmira Daily Press* reported on "The New Pension Law" in 1862 that:

> The public are not generally informed of the very liberal provisions made by
> our Government for those disabled in the service, and for the families of those
> who die in the service of the United States. The want of such information may
> deter some from enlisting on account of the claims a helpless family have upon
> them... The benificence of the Government is extended to all the different
> members of the family who had claims on the deceased, and for whom a good
> man would wish to have. [56]

Two officers and nineteen enlisted men were killed or mortally wounded in the June 17 assault. Another ten were missing in action. [57] Their families would be the first to test the government's performance. By and large the government took care of their families, although not necessarily promptly.

Mary Ann Bradley Sloan filed for a widow's pension on July 25, 1864. Lieutenant Colonel Doty, while recovering at home from his own wounds, submitted a statement certifying Sloan's death in action. Because there was no church or town record of their marriage, Mary Sloan submitted the affidavit of three people who were present for the ceremony. On February 14, 1865, the Pension Bureau issued her a pension of $25 per month plus $2 per month for each of her minor children retroactive to the date of Sloan's death. [58] While the seven months processing time may not seem particularly quick, in fairness to the Pension Bureau, the heavy casualties from Grant's Overland campaign in May 1864 created a good deal of work.

The other officer of the 179th New York who died in the June 17 assault was Capt. Daniel Blachford. He left a wife and son. Carrie E. Blachford apparently did not file for a widow's pension until 1869. She was required to submit affidavits from witnesses of her wedding and the birth of her son, but she was awarded a pension of $20 a month with an additional $2 per month for her minor child. [59]

Company A's Marshall Phillips died on June 21, 1864 after being wounded in the head in the charge on June 17. In addition to his son Newton, who was also wounded on June 17, Phillips left behind a wife and five children under the age of sixteen. His widow Sarah filed a pension application in July 1864, but an award of $8 per month was not granted until April 1865 (retroactive to June 21, 1864). An additional $2 per month for each of the minor children apparently was granted in 1867. [60]

Company B's Henry F. Beebe, a farmer, was only twenty-one years old and unmarried when he died. Beebe's father filed a claim with the Treasury Department's Second Auditor's Office on October 10, 1865 for his son's back pay and remaining bounty. That claim apparently was paid within a year. However, his mother, Harriet F. Beebe, did not file for a mother's pension until 1879. As the mother, she had to prove financial dependence on her son at the time he was killed. She submitted an affidavit from an older son who had employed Henry and stated that his brother "contributed his wages toward the support and maintenance" of his parents. She also submitted an April 1864 letter from Henry to his parents as he was leaving Elmira saying that he was sending them $100, as well as the actual receipt from the United States Express Company. Five years after she applied, she was granted an $8 a month pension retroactive to the day Henry died. That had been increased to $12 a month by the time she died in 1910. [61]

Ezra Edmonds was also single when he died. His mother had predeceased him, so his father was the only possible claimant. Bradley Edmonds did not apply until twenty years after his son's death, but he was granted a parent's pension. [62]

The mother of George Morgan, a nineteen-year-old clerk who was also single, did not apply for a mother's pension until 1891 when she was seventy-one. For unknown reasons, she abandoned her application. [63]

Charles Sickler, Lucius Kinnon and Isiah Wiley all left behind minor children. When their wives remarried, support was still continued. [64]

The most troubling case in this group was Company F's Varnum Northrop, a twenty-three-year-old farmer who was missing in action on June 17, 1864. His widow filled her application in July 1865 stating that he had died at Andersonville. However, there is no "Prisoner of War Memorandum" in Northrop's Compiled Military Service Record, which indicates there was no supporting documentation. She found herself in the awkward position of having to prove that her husband had in fact died. An unidentified officer of the 179th apparently was willing to provide an affidavit that Northrop had died on the battlefield, but no affidavit was submitted. Northrop's

Varnum Northup

widow ultimately abandoned her application. [65]

No pension application was ever filed in connection with the death of six of the June 17 casualties – John Carley (age 20), William F. Clark (age 21), John Hancock (age 21), Edwin Livermore (age 18), John McManus (age 22), and Michael Shanahan (age 35). [66] I have confirmed that Shanahan and Clark were single and the other four were young enough that they may not have been married. The absence of a filing by a parent may be due to any number of reasons: the parents had predeceased the soldier, lack of knowledge about the availability of a pension, inability to prove financial dependence, and pride – among other things.

Thus, it appears that the Government generally – but not universally – at least kept the faith with the men of the 179th New York who fell in the June 17 assault. [67]

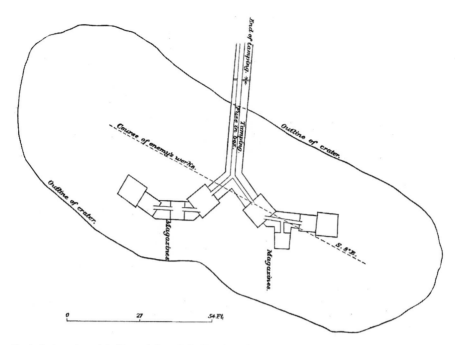

Sketch of mine in front of 2nd Div. 9th Corps, Before Petersburg, drawn by Henry Pleasants, Lieut. Col., 48 Regt Pa Vet. Vols. (Extract), National Archives

CHAPTER NINE

The Siege Begins

On June 18, the day after the battle, the 179th was reassigned to the First Brigade of the First Division of the Ninth Corps, but on July 21 it was assigned back to the Second Brigade. [1] This reassignment back to the Second Brigade meant that the 179th would be in the first wave of the assault at the Battle of the Crater on July 30.

On June 19, Lt. Col. Henry Pleasants of the 48th Pennsylvania was looking from the Union positions across to the Confederate lines, at that point only one hundred and thirty yards away, and in particular at Elliott's Salient, a fort which was about one hundred yards away. Pleasants was an engineer who had pioneered the development of deep shaft coal mining before the Civil War. The 48th Pennsylvania had been recruited in coal mining country. Pleasants proposed to General Robert Potter, commander of the Ninth Corps' Second Division, that a tunnel be dug under no-man's land, filled with powder under Elliott's Salient, and exploded to create a large gap in the Confederate lines. [2] It was not just the short distance that made a tunnel a possibility. The Union lines at that point fell off into a deep hollow and tunneling operations would therefore be below the Confederate line of sight. [3]

Potter forwarded the idea to Burnside, who initially did not respond. However, a more detailed proposal did catch his interest, and he met with Potter and Pleasants on June 24. Burnside gave the go-ahead and Pleasants and the 48th Pennsylvania starting digging the tunnel on June 25, even though General Meade had not yet approved. The plan was to cover twenty-five to fifty feet per day,

Mine Sketch

which would mean that it would take two to three weeks to complete the tunnel. [4]

Burnside forwarded the mine proposal to Meade and Maj. James C. Duane, the Army of the Potomac's Chief Engineer, who had written a West Point manual on military tunnels, on June 25 (the same day that the Cumberland Heights detachment rejoined the 179th at Petersburg). [5] Meade, who was also trained as an army engineer, and Duane were both dismissive. A military tunnel that long had never been constructed and they believed that it would be impossible to ventilate. Meade did not stop the project, but he never fully supported it either. [6]

Pleasants and the coal miners of the 48th Pennsylvania proceeded with their work. Pleasants, Potter and Burnside had recognized ventilation as a challenge, but felt they could solve it as they ultimately did. [7] Pleasants' cross section drawing shows how both the entrance to the mine and the exit point of the ventilation shaft were well below the line of sight from the Confederate lines.

The soldiers of the 48th Pennsylvania dealt with equipment shortages in creative ways. They used empty cracker boxes to carry the dirt out of the mine and placed the dirt in low areas and covered it with branches. They made timber supports from wood from bridges on the Norfolk and Petersburg Railroad. The nailed the supports together in the rear areas to reduce the noise and then brought the supports up to the mine for installation. The handpicked miners from the 48th Pennsylvania who worked two and a half hour shifts were rewarded with a gill of whiskey for each shift. [8]

Great pains were taken to conceal the work, but Confederate General E. P. Alexander, also a West Point-trained engineer, suspected as early as June 30 that a mine was being dug in the area. However, he was wounded and furloughed and did not report his suspicion to General Lee personally. Lee's staff officers were skeptical, but when Alexander's report finally made it to Lee, he authorized efforts to locate a possible Union mine shaft. However, the ensuing Confederate digging and drilling efforts failed to locate the Union tunnel because they were too shallow. Rumors of a Union mine circulated among the Confederate troops and even reached the citizens of Petersburg, but the rumors died out as June turned to July without anything happening. [9]

[Sketch: Petersburg Front]

Meanwhile, Ledlie's division had remained in reserve until June 20 when it relieved General Barlow's division of the Second Corps in the trenches. Ledlie's division was positioned between Potter's division of the Ninth Corps on the left and Turner's division of the Tenth Corps on the right.

That same day, President Lincoln traveled from Washington to City Point, and on June 21 Lincoln and Grant visited the troops at the front. [10] However, the men of the 179th did not see the President because the 179th was in the very front of the trenches that day. [11] At the end of June, Lincoln wrote that "As God is my judge I shall be satisfied if we are over with the fight in Virginia within a year." [12] Within ten months, the Petersburg campaign and the war in Virginia were over, but Lincoln had been assassinated. (The various phases of the Petersburg campaign are described in Appendix C to provide the context for the 179th New York's involvement in the campaign.)

Units of Ledlie's division rotated in and out of the front line trenches until the Battle of the Crater on July 30.[13] Regiments were relieved every four days. The 179th New York began its stint in the front trenches the night of June 20. They "removed to the rear in the 2d line of works" the night of June 23. They were back in the front line the night of June 28 and "moved 20 rods to rear & lay behind breastworks" the night of July 2. They came back to the front lines on July 5 until the night of July 8. On July 10 and 11, they were on picket duty. From July 13 to July 16, they were in the front trenches "under fire of shells." As usual they rotated to the rear on July 17, but on July 19, they moved even further to the rear – about a mile. They returned to the front trenches the night of July 20 and again moved a mile to the rear the night of July 23. They remained in the rear, drilling, until the Battle of the Crater.[14]

Toward the end of June, reports reached the troops that England, France and the Confederacy had sent delegates to Washington to discuss peace. This generated some guarded optimism in the 179th New York.[15] There was also talk that the regiment might be sent to North Carolina to be "recreate[d]" from its losses.[16] A similar rumor in early July was that the 179th would be sent back to Elmira for additional recruiting to be organized into a regiment. Company A's Jacob Graves wrote his father that if that was true, he would be glad – "I have sene ennuf for a spell."[17] (There would be further hardship ahead for the eighteen-year-old farmer to endure. Graves was captured at the Battle of the Crater three weeks later and taken to Danville Military Prison, where he later died.)

The Army of the Potomac's Provost Marshal General described the duty of Ledlie's division during the period July 1 through July 29 as follows:

> Remained in trenches in front of Petersburg, Virginia, with constant sharpshooting and artillery practice, strengthening the works and erecting new ones, especially a mortar battery near the left of the line held by the division.[18]

The *Buffalo Daily Courier*'s unnamed correspondent from the 179th New York reported on July 8 that the 179th "is at present in the front line of our works, only two hundred yards from the enemy's works, giving the 'Johny Rebs' a fair opportunity to pick off our men with their sharp shooters."[19] While home on furlough, Company C's Lieutenant Nathaniel P. T. Finch gave *The Hornellsville Tribune* a similar report about the danger the 179th faced:

> Since the charge on June 17th, the boys have been doing duty in the trenches at the extreme front. The sharp shooters are more vigilant and active before the 9th Army Corps – of which the 179th forms a part – than any other corps in the army.– This is probably owing to the proximity of this corps to the rebel line.[20]

The enlisted men provided more colorful descriptions. Daniel Lee referred to being "in the breastworks under a heavy fire of lead. I have bin under fire now one week ago today where the bulits falls like hale." Even though the 179th had moved back a short distance, on June 25, Lee wrote that "the rebels is in site and a shooting at me."[21] Jacob Graves used similar words in the letter to his father in early July: "we are in the rifel pits. The rebel balls fly very thick. Nite before last the rebs charged our pickets. The bulits flew like hale stones." William Larzelere wrote in his diary on June 21 that the 179th had remained in the front breastworks "all day under fire from reb sharpshooters." Homer Olcott wrote his father that:

> The sharpshooters is firing all the while. We have to lay close. Even while I am writing, the balls is flying over our heads about six feet and lodging in the woods beyond. There has four boys of different Regts been shot today one

through the head in looking over the works but you best to believe I take good care of my head as I can." [22]

The day to day pressure was intense. During the siege, the Ninth Corps:

was positioned closer to the Confederate line than any other corps. This put IX Corps men under constant sniper fire, a situation that took a toll on nerves even more than on bodies. The terms "shell shock" and "battle fatigue," much less "post-traumatic stress disorder," were altogether unknown in 1864, but the more perspicacious military surgeons had already begun to identify something they called "nostalgia," a complex of depression, anxiety, and general nervous exhaustion brought on by continuous combat. [23]

Military commanders said that such troops lacked "vim." [24] Still, Newton Spencer saw the change to picket duty as providing "some respite after their tedious marching and fierce charging and fighting." [25]

The soldiers of the 179th were aware that their corps was in a more dangerous position than the others at Petersburg. [26] Company D's Corp. Oscar Fisk, "a handsome, bright and highly esteemed comrade" from Hornellsville was killed by a sharpshooter on July 2. Fisk was walking through a zigzag traverse heading for a spring in the rear of the Union trenches to get water. As he turned a corner, he was shot in the heart. Spencer was with Fisk when he died, and "That night with a squad of men, I masked that exposed point with pine brush – and piled it so high that no spiteful rebel marksman ever sighted a victim there again." [27]

Other soldiers from the 179th had been wounded in the trenches or on picket: Company B's Charles Wheeler on June 23; Company E's William Spaulding on June 28; Company D's John Martin on July 4; and Company C's John W. Rowley and Company D's Filmore Horth on July 10. [28]

The *Buffalo Daily Courier*'s correspondent in the 179th also described the developing siege:

Affairs here at the front begin to assume the aspect of a regular artillery "siege" of Petersburg, after the fashion of Gen. Grant's Vicksburg siege, and it will require certainly six or eight weeks to accomplish this successfully. Say what they may about "Little Mac" as a "digger," we must state as truth that picks and shovels have been found extremely necessary here to hold our lines against the enemy, who dig as fast as we do! [29]

The six to eight week estimate for success turned out to be hopelessly optimistic. The siege of Petersburg would continue for nearly another nine months.

From the end of June through the end of July, the soldiers of the 179th would regularly put down their rifles for shovels. The "strengthening the works and erecting new ones" reported by the Provost Marshal General was important duty. Field fortifications provided cover for soldiers defending a position by a trench dug for the soldier to stand in or a wall of piled up material that a soldier could stand behind, or a combination of both. Speed and available materials were key. Permanence was generally a secondary consideration because troops expected to move on fairly quickly. However, as Petersburg became a siege, the durability of the fortifications became a much more important concern.

The lay-out of fortifications was a well-developed part of military science. Many of the senior officers on both sides had had the same teacher – West Point's Professor Dennis Hart Mahan, the author of *Treatise on Field Fortifications* (1836). Mahan had graduated first in his class at West Point in 1824 and taught at West Point thereafter until his death in 1871. [30]

Field fortification engineers had their own vocabulary to describe the various elements. Many of the words were French, reflecting the influence of French military theorists: abatis (cut trees and branches placed in front of the fortification to slow down the attackers' advance) and chevaux de frise (sharpened stakes set into a log both along the length and around the circumference for the same purpose); "revetment" (a wall shoring up a mound of dirt); and "gabion" (a cylinder of interwoven sticks and twigs filled with dirt and used as a revetment). [31] The placement of abatis and chevaux de frise is shown in Lieutenat Colonel Pleasants' sketch of the Union and Confederate fortifications above the mine shaft. [see page 82]

Common soldiers used fortification terminology much less precisely than the engineers. Earl Hess notes that while the term "rifle pit" might be understood to mean a foxhole for one or two soldiers, Civil War soldiers used the term much more broadly to refer to any kind of infantry earthworks, whether they be "breastworks" (material such as logs or stones placed on the ground to raise a wall without digging) or a long trench. [32] Spencer described the Union positions in this sector as follows: "Our picket line of rifle pits is within hailing distance of the rebel works; while our two main lines of breastworks are but a few rods in rear of the pickets, and of each other." [33]

A term that would become important for the 179th at the Battle of the Crater is "covered way." "Covered" means protected from direct enemy fire by earthworks or protected from enemy line of sight by geographic position. A "covered way" did not have a roof on it. Covered ways provided safe access to the fortifications from the rear or safe movement between fortifications. [34]

The Fourth of July was a day of national celebration, but July 4, 1864 was not a day off for the 179th New York Volunteers. They were under orders that day "to dig the trenches deep so that the men could walk in them without being seen." (At that point the 179th was in the "rear trenches.") [35] Daniel Lee did find time to write his wife, recalling the Fourth of July that they had spent together two years before and "pray[ing] god to grant the wishes of us both to meet on this globe [again]." Unfortunately, the most noticeable event of the day for the 179th was a raucous incident of drunkenness involving Lt. John Hoy, the acting commander of Company E, and several enlisted men. [36]

The day started off routinely enough. Captain Terrill, then the acting commander of the 179th as the senior captain in the field, woke up Hoy for the trench work. Hoy's tent mate, Company E's Second Lt. Louis Ottenot, also got up and as Ottenot was walking to the trenches, Terrill said to him: "I wish Lieut. Saxton [from Company D] would have command [of Company E]."

Some time later, Hoy returned to the tent with two enlisted men from Company C, Daniel Smith and Edward Rowe. Hoy asked Ottenot if he had any whiskey. Ottenot gave him a canteen and Hoy gave a drink to Smith and Rowe, who already were pretty intoxicated. While the men were drinking and talking and singing loudly, the subject of promotion to fill Captain Blachford's position as commander of Company E came up. Ottenot said word was that the promotion was going to be made "according to seniority" and that Lieutenant Saxton would be promoted. (Saxton's date of rank as a first lieutenant was May 11, 1864. Hoy's apparently was May 16, 1864.) Hoy got up and left the tent, stating "damned if I'm going to stand that."

Later in the morning, Terrill observed Hoy rolling on the ground in the rifle pits, referring to his men as his gorillas. Hoy told Terrill that he was going to get drunk because it was the Fourth of July, but that at midnight he was going to march his gorillas. Hoy told Terrill that he could take his sword as soon as he pleased, but Terrill took no action at that point. Hoy went back to his tent, boasting to Ottenot that he could "whip any son-of-a-bitch of an officer in this regiment." Terrill then placed Hoy in arrest after other officers had protested his initial failure to do so.

Ottenot later went to the regimental headquarters to mail a letter where he coincidentally ran into Saxton. Saxton said that he understood that "Lieut. Hoy is going to whip me and the adjutant before night." Just then, Hoy–having left his tent where he was under arrest– came into the headquarters tent and confronted Saxton–"you're going to be captain of my company." Saxton claimed to know nothing of it. Hoy started at Saxton with the words "You son-of-a-bitch, I can whip you." Saxton threw up his arms in defense, while Ottenot grabbed Hoy and pulled him away. As Ottenot took him out of the tent, Hoy said "that damned dirty son-of-a-bitch wants to be captain of my company." (Hoy and Ottenot had assisted Blachford in recruiting Company E, which may explain Hoy's proprietary temperament.) [37]

Hoy was charged with drunkenness on duty, conduct unbecoming an officer and a gentleman, breach of arrest, conduct prejudicial to good order and military discipline, and striking his superior officer. He pled guilty to the first and third charges and not guilty to the rest. The charges were heard on July 15 and July 16. The court found Hoy guilty of all charges and sentenced him to be "cashiered," i.e. dismissed from the service. General Ledlie approved Hoy's sentence on July 20, as did General Burnside on July 23. [38]

Events overtook Hoy's quarrel with Saxton. Saxton continued serving as the acting commander of Company D and was killed at the Battle of the Crater two weeks after the hearing. The promotion to captain in Company E ultimately went to Ottenot, but not until August 17. [39]

With the wounding of Lieutenant Colonel Doty and the death of Major Sloan in the attack on June 17, Company A's Capt. Albert Terrill had been the acting commander in the field of the 179th. Later, on July 13, Company C's Capt. John Barton was promoted to major, placing him in command. [40] Barton's promotion apparently was well-received by the troops. Newton Spencer wrote *The Hornellsville Tribune* (Barton's home town newspaper) on July 17 that:

> Capt. John Barton, of your place, succeeds the lamented Sloan as Major of the 179th. The news of his appointment reached the regiment a few days ago, and occasioned great satisfaction. He immediately assumed command. I only reiterate what you Hornellsvillains already know when I say that the new Major is an excellent officer – prompt, energetic and thorough, and by previous experience well versed in military affairs. Though not a "new broom" in the service, he "sweeps clean," and we especially like him because he regards a private's rights and interests as worthy of attention and respect. His is a deserved promotion. [41]

For an army of citizen-soldiers, respect for "a private's rights and interests" was important indeed.

Lieutenant Finch similarly told the *Tribune* that: "There is not in the Regiment a better military man, one who understands the tactics more thoroughly, and can execute and explain them on drill more accurately than the Major." [42]

Barton had been sick, although he had not been hospitalized. Finch reported that Barton "has partly recovered from a severe attack of fever and is in the trenches" and expressed the hope that while "his health is rather poor," "he will be enabled to stand the rough usage." [43]

Barton was not the only soldier in the 179th suffering from poor health. Spencer reported that:

> Our present effective force (that is *for duty*) is but 150, out of 450 men who came out with us. These figures are significant of the calamities of war and the unusually rough campaign in which the army has thus far been engaged – although a portion of our losses is due to desertions. – Ninety four men were

wounded and killed in the charge; and a large portion of those remaining are sick. [44]

Notwithstanding these losses, Spencer was confident: "We know that Grant leads us, and this gives us confidence." [45]

On July 24, Spencer wrote his own hometown newspaper, the *Penn-Yan Democrat*, a lengthy letter describing the 179th's experience in the field. At that point, the 179th was about a mile to the rear, drilling. [46]

> The siege of Petersburg has now been in formal operation since the 11th [of July] or just thirteen days. It continues to 'drag its slow length along,' without as yet, any visible effect upon the enemy, and no decisive results at any portion of our line to gladden the hearts of the besiegers or lead us to expect a speedy and victorious termination. Gen. Grant, may, however, be able quite clearly to see his way through what seems to nearly everybody else inscrutable; but it is physically impossible that with our present force the army of Lee can be absolutely and totally cut off from the vast supplies in the Southern interior, and thus be so hemmed in as to be forced to choose between starvation and submission. [47]

Spencer reported that "Our forces lie in the trenches during these long and sultry days, alternately doing picket duty in the extreme front line (only a stone's throw from the rebel works) [s]peculating upon the military prospect, discussing a little politics, reading and writing and dreaming of home." [48]

"Sultry" was a good choice of words to describe the weather. "The summer of 1864 was one of the hottest and driest in memory." [49] A resident of Petersburg reported the temperature on June 26 as "105 in the shade" and added that "the whole town is enveloped in dust." He even hoped that "the searing summer heat" would "weaken Grant's armies and reduce them through disease." [50] A. Wilson Greene referred to a "stifling June [that] gave way to an even more oppressive July." [51] Attorney General Bates wrote at the end of June that in Washington "even the trees in the streets are wilting." [52] The complaint that it is "so hot here" was a recurring theme in Daniel Lee's letters home. [53] *Harper's Weekly* reported that the Union soldiers stretched their tents and blankets across their trenches "like an awning in picturesque confusion, keeping as cool as the torrid climate – aggravated in the pits by the glare from the white sandy soil – and the rebel mortar shells will let them." [54]

Lieutenat Finch told the *Tribune* that: "Water is poor and fast becoming scarce. A drought of nearly two months duration prevails." [55] The drought did finally break with a heavy rain on July 19. Another heavy rain fell during the night of July 24 and some of the trenches were flooded. However, the relief was only temporary and the stifling conditions "returned with a vengeance." [56]

Still, despite all the hardships, Spencer reported that "Since the siege began, the 179th Regiment has been in somewhat better health [notwithstanding his statement the week before]" and that "the rations of food issued are pronounced by veteran soldiers of better quality and more variety than ever before issued to the army of the Potomac while in the field." [57]

The same could hardly be said about the Confederate troops one hundred yards away. Rations were "scanty" and the Confederate troops raided local gardens. Some Confederate soldiers were reduced to selling their shoes to raise money to buy food. [58]

In his memoirs, General Grant explained that: "There never was a corps better organized than was the quartermaster's corps with the Army of the Potomac in 1864." [59] By the time of Spencer's letter home, the Union soldiers in the trenches in front of Petersburg were being supplied from the depot at nearby City Point on the James River. [60] The Union's railroad construction crews had moved quickly. On June 18, they had started rebuilding the now abandoned City Point branch of Petersburg's South Side Line. The Army of the Potomac soon had seven miles of railroad running parallel to its lines to distribute supplies brought to City Point by river. [61]

As of 1864, the official daily "camp" ration (as opposed to "marching" ration) was "20 ounces of fresh or salt beef or 12 ounces salt pork; 18 ounces of flour or 22 ounces of soft bread, or 1 pound of hardtack, or 20 ounces of corn meal; 2 ½ ounces dry beans or peas; 1.6 ounces coffee; 2.4 ounces sugar; 6/10 ounce salt; 4/100 ounce black pepper; 45/100 ounce yeast powder; 1/3 gill vinegar; and 64/100 ounce soap and 24/100 ounce candle." [62] Homer Olcott wrote his father in early July that: "I have coffee and meat for breakfast, meat and potatoes or bean soup for dinner and coffee and applesauce for supper so you see I do not live very bad." [63]

And then there was the ubiquitous "hardtack" – a half inch thick plain flour and water biscuit about 3 1/8 by 2 7/8 inches.

> There were a number of ways of consuming this item. It could be eaten as it was if you had strong teeth – at night they said you couldn't tell whether or not it had weevils. It could be crumbled in coffee, soup, stew, or fried in some meat fat. Hardtack could be toasted on a stick or spread with sugar or soaked and fried. How it was served depended on the amount of time available to prepare it and the imagination of the individual. [64]

Meanwhile, work on the mine was progressing. The 48th Pennsylvania had completed the main tunnel under no-man's land – over five hundred feet long – on July 17. Perpendicular galleries to the right and left for the placement of black powder under Elliot's Salient were completed on July 23. [65] [see page 81] The 179th was in the front trenches that day. [66]

The *Elmira Daily Advertiser* carried a July 25 report that:

> The shelling and picket firing between the 9th Corps and the enemy was more brisk than usual and was kept up all night. During the afternoon a shell from one of our guns struck one of the enemy's caissons, which exploded with a loud noise. Very few casualties occurred considering the large quantities of powder spent by both parties. No exchanges of papers have been made between the pickets for some days, the rebel commander having strictly prohibited it. [67]

On July 27, the 48th Pennsylvania started moving four tons of powder into the galleries under Elliott's Salient. Burnside had requested six tons, but Meade would only provide four tons. [68] The following day at 6 p.m., Pleasants reported that everything was ready to go. [69] The 179th remained a mile to the rear, drilling. [70]

The *Elmira Daily Advertiser* reported the following from the front for the next day:

> Passengers by the mail boat report that on Thursday P.M. [July 28], the rebels in front of Petersburg opened a fire on our forces from our batteries. The batteries on our side replied and soon silenced those of the rebels. Our mortars also opened fire on the city and continued to throw shells into it until a late hour in the night. Several houses were set on fire which must have caused no little consternation in Petersburg, as the alarm bells could be heard ringing in an animated style for a considerable time." [71]

Perhaps the soldiers of the 179th heard these alarm bells. In any event, the reports reaching

New York's Southern Tier by newspaper gave no warning of what was to come on July 30. People back home in New York may well have been more concerned about the Confederate raiding party that had entered southern Pennsylvania. (Chambersburg was burned on July 30.) [72] Or they may have been more concerned about the rumors circulating that Confederate prisoners at Elmira Military Prison were planning a break. [73]

The night of July 28, the 179th moved forward again. [74] Company G joined the rest of the 179th at Petersburg the afternoon of July 29. Company G had initially been mustered in as Company A of the 180th New York Volunteers on July 20, but was immediately transferred to the 179th as Company G when the 180th showed no signs of raising more companies. [75] Company G obviously had had little time for training.

The last report on the "Military Situation" in *Harper's Weekly* before news of the Battle of the Crater was received stated that "the siege of Petersburg assumes no new phase worthy of record." Instead, "the main interest as regards military operations is now transferred to General Sherman's advance on Atlanta." [76]

Ninth Corps into the Crater

CHAPTER TEN

The Battle of the Crater (July 30, 1864)

We often think of war as the ultimate risk of being in the wrong place at the wrong time, with soldiers being at the total mercy of events over which they have no control whatsoever, but we do not usually think of battle as a literal game of chance. However, that is actually how the "place" and "time" were determined at the Battle of the Crater for the soldiers of the First Division of the Ninth Corps, including the 179th New York Volunteers.

General Burnside had originally planned to deploy the Ninth Corps' Fourth Division, commanded by General Ferrero, for the initial assault because these troops were the most rested, having been primarily used for garrison duty up to that point. The First, Second and Third divisions had suffered heavy losses since the beginning of the offensive in May. From June 20 through July 30, these divisions had suffered 12 percent casualties in the trenches at Petersburg from picket and shell fire. Burnside was concerned about their morale.

> they were very much wearied, had contracted a habit of covering themselves by every method within their reach, ... I was satisfied they were not in a condition to make anything like as much of a dash upon the enemy's line as General Ferrero's division, which had not been under any considerable fire from the time of its arrival at this place. [1]

The Fourth Division began training for the assault. [2] However, the Fourth Division was comprised entirely of "colored" troops (except for their officers who were all white) – nine regiments of

"United States Colored Troops." The soldiers in the Fourth Division had never seen action. At the last minute, because of concern about the Fourth Division's lack of combat experience and the public relations implications if the colored troops suffered heavy casualties, Meade countermanded Burnside's decision with Grant's approval. [3]

That left Burnside to choose quickly among Ledlie's (First) division, Potter's (Second) division and Willcox' (Third) division. Because all three divisions were tired from recent action in Burnside's view, he could not decide which to pick and left the decision to his three division commanders drawing lots from a hat. Ledlie drew the proverbial "short straw." While Burnside believed in "trust[ing] to luck," contemporaries and historians have justly castigated him for leaving such an important decision to chance. Nor was the decision a closely guarded secret. Two weeks after the battle, Spencer wrote the *Penn Yan Democrat* that the decision had been made "by lot". [4]

How General Ledlie chose the order of deployment of the two brigades in his division is unknown, but the Second Brigade, commanded by Col. Elisha Marshall, led the First Division into battle. [5]

[Photo: Elisha Marshall]

As previously noted, Ledlie has been referred to as the Union's worst general. [6] The troops of the 179th, like many others in the Army of the Potomac after the Overland campaign, also had another leadership problem to deal with – their regimental and company leadership had been hard hit by battle and disease. [7]

Because the 179th was officially only at battalion strength, Colonel Gregg was still back in Elmira recruiting. Lieutenat Colonel Doty was recuperating at home from his wounds suffered in the June 17 assault and Major Sloan had been mortally wounded. Captain Barton had been promoted to major only two weeks before the Battle of the Crater and took the field that day despite lingering illness. At the company level, Company E's Captain Blachford had been killed on June 17 and Company B's Captain Stewart and Company D's Captain Bird were in the hospital with their wounds from June 17, never to return to the field. In Company A, Capt. Albert Terrill was present for duty, but First Lt. George Carpenter, Second Lt. James Farr and First Sgt. Stephen Compton were all sick in the hospital. [8] The other companies of the 179th had suffered similar losses.

The experience of the men of the 179th on the battlefield on July 30, 1864 was determined by six overriding circumstances.

First, for roughly two-thirds of the men of the 179th New York Volunteers, this was their first battle. The approximately one hundred men who had been on detached duty at Cumberland Heights had missed the June 17 assault. Company G (seventy-eight men) arrived at the front just twelve hours before the battle with hardly any training. The Battle of the Crater was absolutely horrifying for the new soldiers. Roughly one hundred surviving "veterans" of the June 17 assault were present for the 179th New York, but the Battle of the Crater tested even the most seasoned combat veteran. [9]

Second, once the mine exploded, there was an almost constant din of artillery and musket fire in a relatively small area – less than half a mile long and several hundred yards deep on both sides of the lines. The noise was deafening. [10]

Third, July 30 was no cooler than the preceding days. Company G's Lt. William Hemstreet described the day as "excessively hot," and was among those overcome by the heat during the battle. [11] The temperature hit 80 degrees by six in the morning and 99 degrees by noon. The temperatures would have been even higher in the crater and the trenches. Nor had the night ever really cooled down from the day before. As a result, the Union soldiers' canteens were quickly emptied, and the lack of water became a serious hardship. [12]

Fourth, during much of the battle, the soldiers of the 179th New York Volunteers and many other units on both sides were in trenches that were six feet or more deep. Keeping one's head down in a trench could provide a soldier with a degree of safety, but it certainly limited his ability to see what was going on around him. The powder smoke from musket and artillery fire further limited visibility. [13]

Fifth, for much of the battle Union troops were crammed into tight spaces, whether it was the crater itself or the surrounding Confederate works. Conditions only worsened because the initial wave of soldiers failed to advance and more and more Union troops were thrown forward into these constricted spaces. Jammed together, the soldiers had a difficult time wielding their four-and-a-half foot long rifles with bayonets. Union officers had only limited ability in that situation to deploy their men after they first hit the Confederate positions. [14]

Sixth, the ever-present "fog of war" makes it inherently difficult to definitively trace the movements of smaller units like a regiment throughout a battle. Parts of a unit also often get separated from the main body as a battle unfolds. During the Battle of the Crater, the "fog" was particularly thick.

During the night of July 23, the 179th had moved from the front trenches to a position about a mile to the rear and remained there drilling until the night of July 28. That night they moved back toward the front lines, but the precise location they reached that night is unknown. [15]

Company G (originally mustered in as Company A of the 180th New York Volunteers) arrived at the front on July 29. "C.B.C.," the *Buffalo Daily Courier*'s correspondent in the 179th, reported that: "It was hard to take the boys of the 180th with us, but as our numbers were so small it became an actual case of necessity." C.B.C. was right about the numbers. The original six companies had only about 160 men available for the Battle of the Crater. Company E had only ten men available for duty. Company G went into battle with seventy-eight men—roughly 40 percent of the 179th's complement that day. Company G's Lt. William Hemstreet also moved over to command Company B, which had no officers present in the field. [16]

Around nine o'clock the night of July 29, Ledlie's division began moving into place for the attack the next morning. To avoid alerting the Confederate troops, Ledlie's division "marched with the stillness of death; not a word was said above a whisper." They were carrying extra ammunition and three days cooked rations. Company B's Eugene Dunton, an eighteen-year-old farmer, wrote his parents that the 179th "had orders to pack up about 1 o'clock. We marched about a mile to the front where we halted in 10 rods of the enemy where we rested till [4:45 a.m.]." C.B.C. reported that the Second Brigade:

> took their position as first line of battle to the rear of our rifle pits, and were ordered to lie down and keep very quiet. From that time, 1 o'clock, till 4 o'clock, a continual line of troops came up and took their positions to our rear, forming eight lines of battle. Here we awaited the long looked for explosion or "blow up" of the rebel fort, which was only 20 rods from our line. [17]

The Second Brigade, including the 179th, formed in three lines: the 2nd Pennsylvania Provisional Heavy Artillery (deployed as infantry and also known as the 112th Pennsylvania

Regiment); the 14th New York Heavy Artillery (also deployed as infantry); and the 179th New York and the 3rd Maryland Battalion combined. Each line was about 150 yards long and was separated from the others by about five yards. Ledlie's division was in place by two or three o'clock in the morning. The soldiers of the Second Brigade lay on the open ground, but they did not sleep. They were undoubtedly in a "feverish state of expectancy" like the rest of the Ledlie's division. [18]

The plan was to explode the mine at 3:30 a.m. while it was still dark. The hundred yard long fuse was timely lit, but went out before it reached the chamber where the black powder had been concentrated. It took an hour for some intrepid volunteers from the 48th Pennsylvania to enter the mine to figure out what went wrong and then relight the fuse. [19] For those who knew the original schedule, the delay would have added to the tension.

The powder was finally detonated at 4:44 a.m., as daylight was beginning to emerge. Newton Spencer said that "the explosion was the most grand and awful scene I ever witnessed." [20] C.B.C. wrote that: "there was a terrific shock felt by all around, and in one moment the stronghold of the rebels was blown to atoms, carrying with it cannon, bodies and the contents of the fort." [21] William Larzelere simply wrote in his diary that "at daylight a rebel fort was blown up with a loss of 300 Jonnies." [22]

A Union general described the scene in more detail:

Suddenly, the earth trembled beneath our feet. An enormous mass sprang into the air. A mass without form or shape, full of red flames, and carried on a bed of lightning flashes, mounted towards heaven with a detonation of thunder. It spread out like a sheaf, like an immense mushroom whose stem seemed to be of fire and its head of smoke. Then everything appeared to break up and fall in a rain of earth mixed with rocks, with beams, timbers and mangled human bodies. [23]

Charles Houghton from the 14th New York Heavy Artillery, the unit which immediately preceded the 179th in the attack, described the explosion as:

a terrible and magnificent sight. The earth around us trembled and heaved—so violently that I was lifted to my feet. Then the earth along the enemy's lines opened, and fire and smoke shot upward seventy-five or one hundred feet. The air was filled with earth, cannon, caissons, sand-bags and living men, and with everything else within the exploded fort. One large lump of clay as large as a hay-stack or small cottage was thrown out and left on top of the ground toward our own works. [24]

The explosion shook foundations and rattled windows two miles away in Petersburg proper. The explosion was even felt nine miles away on Burgess Farm which would be the scene of fighting in October 1864. [25]

Harper's Weekly's A.H. Waud, a nineteenth century predecessor of today's combat photographers, sketched the explosion of the mine and the beginning of the attack. His vantage point was considerably to the left, from the Fifth Corps' positions to the south of the Ninth Corps. [26] The plume of the explosion is in the distance in his sketch, as are the church spires of Petersburg. The Union front line and the Confederate trenches are not visible.

[Sketch: Duane with Warren, 4:45 a.m.]

The impact of the mine explosion on the Confederate troops above and in the immediate vicinity was absolutely devastating. Roughly 350 Confederate troops in Pegram's (or Elliott's) Salient were killed and Pegram's artillery battery was put out of action.[27] Hardest hit was the 18th South Carolina which was positioned with Pegram's Battery. Three companies of the 22nd South Carolina and one company of the 17th South Carolina were also devastated.[28] A Confederate officer measured the crater the following day at 126 feet long at the surface and 69 feet at the bottom; 87 feet wide at the surface and 38 feet at the bottom; and 25 feet deep.[29] A sketch done by Waud depicting the action around eight that morning shows the debris pile in front of the crater, including the "large clump of clay as large as a hay-stack or small cottage" referred to by Charles Houghton.

[Sketch: Explosion at the Crater]

Frank Leslie's Weekly carried a view of "The Ninth Corps Charging the Enemy's Works After the Explosion of the Mine." [see page 90]

The noise of the explosion was closely followed by the din of the supporting Union artillery barrage – 110 cannon and 54 mortars comprising one of the largest, if not the largest, concentrations of artillery during the war – firing over a two mile front.[30] Spencer described the barrage in heroic terms: "the iron throats of a hundred pieces of Union Artillery belched forth their fiery thunders, dealing havoc and dismay through the rebel ranks."[31] However, as awesome as the barrage was, its impact was not clear. A Confederate soldier in the lines north of the crater wrote his brother that: "We were under the most terrible cannonading I have ever heard, ... The bombardment [illegible] anything I have [ever?] heard but strange, as it is true, very little damage was done to us by these noisy weapons."[32]

[Map: Battle of the Crater, 5 a.m.]

Confederate troops abandoned the trenches for two hundred to three hundred yards on either side immediately after the explosion to seek safety. That gave Burnside a hole in the Confederate line roughly five hundred yards wide.[33] Within five to ten minutes of the mine explosion, Ledlie's division moved forward with the attack.[34] The Union soldiers advanced with little, if any, opposing rifle fire–a situation that existed for roughly fifteen minutes.[35] It would be half an hour before the Confederate forces could bring effective artillery fire to bear.[36] After six weeks of keeping their heads down in the trenches, the lack of fire as they advanced across no man's land probably caused a combination of surprise, relief, and suspicion amongst the attacking troops.

The movement across no man's land was pretty disorganized.[37] The Union attack was to have been made in line in successive waves. However, little advance planning had been done for the Union troops staging behind the front line to get across the eight feet deep Union main trench. The only way across the trench was a "bridge" of sandbags eight to ten feet wide. As a result, the Second Brigade's 150 yard wide battle lines were constricted into two or three man columns to advance.[38] Moreover, the defensive abatis in front of the Union lines had not been removed – negligence by Burnside in Meade's view, but a necessary precaution to avoid alerting the Confederate troops to an impending attack in Burnside's view.[39] The result was that the Union troops could only exit the trenches at improvised points and moved forward in a long series of groups two or three soldiers wide.[40]

The attackers' ears must have been ringing from the explosion and ensuing artillery barrage.

Their hearts must have been racing from the prospect of a frontal assault on the Confederate lines. "The hard fact," as Bruce Catton has observed "was that by 1864 good troops using rifles and standing in well-built trenches, and provided with suitable artillery support, simply could not be dislodged by any frontal assault whatever." [41]

The Confederate troops in front of the 179th had all those advantages. The 179th had learned this lesson with heavy casualties in the assault on June 17 (although they did carry the Confederate lines). Even Grant himself commented that "the enemy's earth-works [at Elliott's Salient] are as strong as they can be made." [42] In Newton Spencer's opinion, without the assurance that the mine would blow up the Confederate fort, "I doubt if a brigade in the entire corps could have been induced by threats or entreaties to make a charge at that point." [43] Still, as carefully planned as the mine explosion seemed to have been, there was no certainty that it would shift the odds in the attackers' favor.

Colonel Marshall reputedly started the advance across no man's land with the command to the officers: "Gentlemen, take command of your lines. 2d Pennsylvania, rise up. Forward, March! By the right flank; march. Over the parapet and swing up your left." Lieutenant Colonel Gilbert Robinson reputedly gave a similar command to the 3rd Maryland and the 179th New York after the 2d Pennsylvania had moved out. [44] However, moving "over the parapet" did not go so smoothly in reality.

The ground in front of the Union troops sloped slightly upward toward the Confederate lines. Lieutenant Colonel Robinson described the advance as follows:

> By keeping a strong right oblique we arrived at the crater formed by the mine, to the right of which the orders for the assault had directed us to form. Through this crater and 150 yards in advance of it the 2d Provisional Heavy Artillery [the first line of attack] charged. The Fourteenth New York [the second line], diverging somewhat to the left, came upon two cannon and their magazine buried in the earth, but not destroyed, which they dug out and prepared for service. The Third Maryland and One hundred and seventy-ninth New York Volunteers proceeded into the second short covered way on the [Union] right, and occupied that position. [45]

Company B's Eugene Dunton described the 179th New York's advance: "We then had the order to charge and away we went over the breastworks, through the fort an[d] in to the rebel works beyond where we halted." Two weeks after the battle, Spencer recalled that:

> The first line of rebel works was reached and carried at the point of the bayonet and many rebels fled in wild consternation before the resistless storm, utterly dismayed and demoralized by the fearful explosion and the fiery and determined assault. That line was magnificently won. The prospect of success was brilliant, and made every Union soldier's heart leap with enthusiastic delight. [46]

However, things were not proceeding as orderly as might be inferred from the accounts of Lieutenant Colonel Robinson and Privates Dunton and Spencer. C.B.C reported that:

> ... all the lines were in a perfect state of disorder, all rushed up, so that one regiment could not be distinguished from another. Then came the order to deploy the regiments and form line to the rear of the captured rebel pits, which was done, but not in good order. Twas here we felt the lack of good generalship. Had our lines been formed properly at this moment our troops

would have had possession of Petersburg. But everything was in disorder. [47]

Lieutenant Colonel Charles Loring, Burnside's assistant inspector general, recalled that when he arrived at the crater shortly after the attack began he found the Second Brigade "crowded together."

> The crater presented an obstacle of fearful magnitude. I suppose it was a hole of about 200 feet in length, by perhaps 50 or 60 feet in width, and nearly 30 feet in depth. The sides of it were composed of jagged masses of clay projecting from loose sand. The upper surface had been of sand, with a lower stratum of clay. It was an obstacle which it was perfectly impossible for any military organization to pass over intact, even if not exposed to fire. The whole brigade was broken up in confusion, and had utterly lost its organization. The officers were endeavoring to reform their men, but it was an exceedingly difficult operation. [48]

One of Ledlie's staff officers, Maj. William Powell, similarly observed that it was:

> as utterly impracticable to re-form a brigade in the crater as it would be to marshal bees into line after upsetting the hive; and equally as impracticable to re-form outside of the crater, under the severe fire in front and rear, as it would be to hold a dress parade in front of a charging enemy. [49]

Loring sent back a dispatch, received by Burnside around 5:45 a.m. reporting that the troops in Ledlie's division would not move forward. [50]

Execution of Meade's plan had gone tragically awry. He had ordered on July 29 that when the mine exploded Burnside's "assaulting columns will immediately move rapidly upon the breach, seize the crest in the rear, and effect a lodgment there." The Eighteenth Corps would support the Ninth Corps on the right and the Fifth Corps would support the Ninth Corps on the left. Meade concluded his order with the admonition that "Promptitude, rapidity of execution, and cordial cooperation, are essential to success." [51] Petersburg would be the Ninth Corps' for the taking. And by blowing out a section of the Confederate lines more than one hundred feet long, the mine explosion had given the Union troops a once in a lifetime opportunity to do just that.

Unfortunately, General Ledlie had communicated a different plan to his two brigade commanders, Brigadier General Bartlett (First Brigade) and Colonel Marshall (Second Brigade). He told them that the First Division's primary duty was to protect the security of the lodgment at the crater and that the hill beyond was a secondary objective. [52] The Fourth Division would attack the hill. [53] Ledlie absented himself from the battle almost immediately after the mine explosion, falling back to the safety of a bomb proof shelter fifty yards to the rear. He spent the remainder of the day drinking, ostensibly for the medicinal purpose of treating a surface wound from a spent bullet. [54] [Photo: Bartlett] C.B.C.'s lament of "the lack of good generalship" was an understatement.

The failure of the Ledlie's division to immediately advance beyond the crater while the Confederate forces were still in a state of shock doomed the attack. Meade had emphasized the need for a rapid advance to Cemetery Hill and events proved him correct. The explosion did totally incapacitate the Confederate troops in the immediate area, but only for fifteen minutes to half an hour. Once the Confederate officers and soldiers recovered from the shock of the explosion, they responded quickly and effectively. In the words of General Robert Potter, commanding the Ninth Corps' Second Division, "the enemy who at first seemed somewhat stunned, was rapidly rallying and beginning to open a brisk fire." [55]

[Photo: Stephen Elliott, Jr.]

The 26th South Carolina and three companies of the 17th South Carolina, roughly three hundred men total, fell back to the ravine 350 yards behind (to the west) of the main Confederate line. [56] The remainder of the 17th South Carolina and the 18th South Carolina held traverses to the north of the crater. The 25th North Carolina fell back to a ravine and covered way several hundred yards to the north of the crater and to the ravine west of the crater occupied by the 17th and 26th South Carolina. The 49th North Carolina had been located four hundred yards north of the crater and moved south toward the crater occupying a covered way perpendicular to the main Confederate lines. [57] From these positions, the Confederate infantry was able to defend with effective musket fire on the north (Union right) side of the crater. Even so, the remnants of the Confederate forces in the vicinity of Elliott's Salient would not have been able to hold against a sustained attack without reinforcements. They were outnumbered at that time by four to one or more. [58]

Another critical response by the Confederates that would ultimately determine the outcome of the battle was also underway. General William Mahone's division of General A. P. Hill's Third Corps was defending the Confederate extreme right, two miles south of the crater. Mahone's division heard the explosion and some soldiers even saw the plume. Following Hill's orders shortly after the explosion, Mahone surreptitiously pulled Wiesiger's Virginia Brigade and Hall's Georgia Brigade out of the lines and sent them to the crater via a circuitous route that successfully masked the movement from Union observers. Mahone himself arrived in the rear of the crater around 8:15 a.m. to reconnoiter, while the two brigades arrived around nine o'clock.

[Photo: William Mahone]

The first Confederate artillery response came from the four cannon of Capt. Samuel Wright's battery located on Cemetery Hill to the north of the Crater. From a range of five hundred yards they fired canister shot down toward the sector where the 179th New York was deployed. [59]

Shortly after the Second Brigade had taken its positions in the Confederate trenches and covered ways, the First Brigade also arrived on the right side of the crater. Brigadier General Bartlett had misunderstood his instruction to deploy on the left of the crater to mean the Confederate's left, with the result that the First Brigade arrived on the Union right – the same side of the crater as the Second Brigade. The troops of the First Brigade were then deployed into the covered ways occupied by the Second Brigade – the 29th, 56th and 57th Massachusetts with the 179th New York and 3rd Maryland and the 21st Massachusetts and the 100th Pennsylania with the 2d Pennsylvania. Part of the 100th Pennsylvania manned the edge of the crater. [60]

Bartlett's error began what became a continuing problem for the Union assault–more and more troops were packed into spaces too tight to maneuver effectively. [61]

Once reorganized, the Second Brigade found it difficult to maneuver in the vicinity of the crater. Lieutenat Colonel Loring explained that:

> The lines of the enemy were found to be of the most intricate nature. There was one uniform front line; then in the rear there were various lines, traverses between them, and bombproofs. It was more like a honeycomb than anything that can be seen in our lines; so that it was exceedingly difficult for troops to spread themselves either way, either to the right or to the left. It had to be done, not by any movement of a mass of troops, but by hand-to-hand

fighting. [62]

The explosion of the mine may have taken out Pegram's Battery and the supporting troops in the immediate vicinity, but it did not solve – and probably complicated – the physical challenges of moving through the "honeycomb" of Confederate works.

Colonel Thomas Clarke, Marshall's assistant adjutant general, described the initial movements by Lieutenat Colonel Robinson, commanding the 3rd Maryland and the 179th New York:

> Robinson ... moved on [northward] in the main [Confederate] line, charging around several traverses, capturing many prisoners and having a continual skirmish with small groups of Confederates across the traverses, conducted mostly by a squad of sharpshooters of his command, armed with Spencers, ... Colonel Robinson and other officers of the 3rd Maryland ... were, more than once, seen leading small squads in charges around these traverses. The distance to the right [north] of the crater, reached by Colonel Robinson's right, was estimated, at that time at over three hundred and fifty yards. [63]

The 179th probably played a supporting role at most in these charges. Robinson, "an experienced and competent soldier" in the view of Capt. John Anderson of the 57th Massachusetts, probably had more confidence in his own 3rd Maryland, a "small veteran organization of prime quality." [64] (The 3rd Maryland fielded only fifty-six soldiers that day.) [65] (Anderson referred to the 179th New York as a battalion of "six companies of a new and incomplete regiment, greatly depleted by the campaign.") [66]

The 2d Pennsylvania had made some progress moving forward (west) of the Confederate line, but had been driven back by heavy fire both from the ravine held by the 17th and 26th South Carolina and Confederate positions in a covered way on their right flank. Bartlett and Marshall decided to try to take the Confederate positions in the covered way. [67]

Colonel Clarke described the planned attack, which occurred shortly after sunrise:

> Colonel Robinson, who had some clear ground before him, was to move out [this time presumably with the 179th as well as the 3rd Maryland] and forward, supported by the 56th, 57th and 29th [Massachusetts regiments] of Bartlett's brigade, who were to form Robinson's second line by moving to the right, along the Confederate front line, and to keep down the flank and

> rear fire. The Provisional 2d Pennsylvania Heavy Artillery, the 21st Massachusetts and the 100th Pennsylvania were to swing up their left and align with Robinson, and the 14th New York Artillery was to file over the traverse at the end of the covered way, and form the second line for this detachment. These four combined movements were attempted, with the result of developing a heavy flank fire from a covered way leading from the hill down toward the destroyed fort. ... The two Pennsylvania regiments lost heavily in officers and men, and Colonel Robinson's command and the 14th Artillery were badly handled by a flank and rear fire. [68]

> C.B.C. described this phase of the battle as follows: "Organizing as well as the occasion would permit, an advance was ordered to an open field and here we had a fair shake at them." C.B.C also reported that: "Here our ammunition gave out," which was certainly possible, but I have not

Edward Gyles   corroborated that. [69]

It may be that Major Barton was mortally wounded and many of the 179th's other casualties, including Company G's Edward Gyles, were incurred during this attack.

Barton was wounded in both legs and evacuated to the rear. Company A's Albert Terrill assumed command as the senior captain in the field. [70]

Bartlett and Marshall had decided to try the same attack again, when the colored troops of Ferrero's division arrived around eight o'clock. Marshall said to Bartlett: "Here is Ferrero. Hadn't we better hold on to what we have got, till we see what the Egyptians can do for us?" The two agreed to suspend their attack. [71]

After an unnerving hour's wait in a covered way, Ferrero's division had begun advancing toward the crater around 7:30 a.m. Lieutenant Colonel Sigfried led the First Brigade past the crater and then to the right (north) along the main Confederate line until they encountered resistance. They then attacked westward, claiming to have captured two hundred fifty Confederate soldiers and two hundred yards of trenches. Colonel Thomas' Second Brigade followed. [72]

Ferrero's division attempted three attacks from the captured Confederate trenches. The first was lead by Colonel Thomas with the Second Brigade's 31st U.S. Colored Troops. They suffered heavy casualties from the fire of the South Carolina regiments in the ravine to the west and fell back. [73] Colonel Bates then organized another attack with the First Brigade's 30th U.S. Colored Troops, but this attack was also repulsed. [74]

The First Brigade then prepared for the third assault with the 23rd, 28th, and 29th U.S. Colored Troops. However, the Confederates were quicker to the mark. Weisiger's Virginia Brigade arrived in time to attack from the ravine 350 yards away just as the 29th U.S.C.T.'s Lt. Col. John Bross was giving the order for the Union attack. Bross was killed in the Confederate's first volley and the colored troops fell back into the captured Confederate trenches, recreating the crowding problem for the Union troops. [75]

As the Confederate troops hit the Union positions, a panicked retreat of Union troops, primarily amongst the black troops, began. Some Union soldiers remained in place, preventing the rout from becoming even worse, but they were overrun in ten or fifteen minutes. [76]

Robinson reported that:

> the enemy made an attack and all the black troops crushed back into the works occupied by [the Second Brigade of the First Division], throwing it into inextricable confusion, and forcing it back upon the troops in the crater. Our men then fell back and were reorganized. [77]

Colonel Clarke similarly reported encountering "an irresistible mass of retreating men" and being "swept back into the field half way to our works." [78]

Company A's Solomon Leonard probably suffered his bayonet wound to the face as the colored troops clambered back into the crowded trenches. Company A's Sergeant Rutan was among the soldiers "crushed ... in rifle pits" when the colored troops retreated. [79] He was carried to the rear back across no man's land by William Wines of Company A – no mean feat at this point in the battle because the Confederate forces were counterattacking with everything they could muster. As a soldier from the 21st Massachusetts (First Brigade, First Division) observed: "it was more dangerous to retreat over the ground between the rebel and Union lines, swept by the concentrated fire of the enemy, than to stay where they were, and the main body of the troops remained in the crater." [80] Captain John Anderson of the 57th Massachusetts Volunteers (also First Brigade, First Division) was more blunt – "It seemed almost sure death to undertake it." [81]

Still, the Union forces tried to facilitate retreat. Robinson described the protective fire provided for the retreating troops. The troops who had preceded them back to the Union lines:

> were therefore retained within the line of works, and directed to cover the
> retreat of those in the fort by a right and left oblique fire, leaving the fort
> blown up by us in the axis of a section without fire. Through the road thus
> opened in the enemy's fire many escaped. [82]

Company F's Capt. Allen Farwell was probably killed as the Union troops were falling back in the face of Mahone's attack. He had been wounded in the side or hip and Sergeant Norton and three or four others were trying to carry him to the rear when he was shot in the head. Norton and the others were subsequently captured – "amidst terrible slaughter" in Norton's words. [83]

Marshall and Robinson did attempt to make one more attack. [84] Most of the First and Second Brigades fell back "to the lines". Marshall told Robinson to reform and recommended to Ledlie that they attack further to the right. Robinson was able to regroup approximately 450 men from the Second Brigade, which probably had started out with over one thousand men, but then received orders to withdraw to the Union lines. [85]

By 9:30 a.m., Grant and Meade had concluded that the attack was a failure and ordered Burnside to withdraw his troops remaining in the Confederate lines. [86]

At this point, the troops of the 179th New York Volunteers were quite disorganized, spread out across no man's land and in the crater itself. For those retreating across no man's land, the day's fighting was over. For those in the crater, it would be several more hours before their day would come to a horrifying end.

The counterattack by Weisiger's Virginia Brigade had essentially driven all the Union forces from the Confederate trenches to the north into the crater itself or back across no man's land. While the crater would ultimately prove to be a trap for the Union soldiers who remained and conditions were so cramped that it was difficult for Union soldiers to move around, they were not defenseless, nor were they prepared yet to surrender.

Around ten that morning, the second of Mahone's transferred brigades, Hall's Georgia Brigade, attacked the crater, from the ravine to the west. The Union soldiers were able to mount heavy musket fire from the lip of the crater and the 14th New York Heavy Artillery even returned canister fire with the two cannon from Pegram's battery that they had retrieved from the debris. This time, the Confederate counterattack was "nearly a complete failure." [87]

However, the reprieve for the Union troops in the crater was only temporary. The Union forces were in a tight space subject to a 270 degree Confederate field of fire. The Confederates had had time to move mortars into position which delivered particularly devastating fire. Dead and wounded soldiers lay throughout the crater. The temperature in the crater probably exceeded one hundred degrees. There was little air circulation and water was running out. The morale of the Union soldiers in the crater was rapidly declining. [88]

As the battle was progressing, Mahone had pulled yet another brigade out of his lines–the Alabama Brigade commanded by Col. John Sanders. Sanders' troops left their positions around eleven and were in position to attack from the ravine west of the crater by one o'clock. [89]

When Sander's brigade began its attack, it was immediately apparent to the senior Union officer in the crater that defeat was imminent and he ordered a retreat. The Union soldiers remaining in the crater held their own for a short time, but were ultimately overwhelmed in hand-to-hand fighting. An oft-quoted exchange led to the Union surrender. A Confederate officer yelled out: "Why in hell don't you fellows surrender? You will all be killed if you do not." He received an immediate response: "Why in the hell don't you let us?" [90]

The Union surrender was not accomplished without further loss. Historians universally agree that many Confederate soldiers brutally murdered black soldiers who were attempting to surrender. [91] The appellation the "Horrid Pit" only begins to describe the experience of the Union soldiers during the last several hours in the crater. [92]

Company D's Sgt. James Spencer was among those who surrendered in the crater. Amidst the chaos he found himself six feet away from an old friend – Lt. James Grierson of the 14th New York Heavy Artillery (also in the Second Brigade). Twenty-five years later, Spencer recalled that after they had been taken prisoner:

> "the Rebels took [Grierson] to be an officer of a Negro Company as there was many Negroes taken prisoner at the same time.... [A] Rebel officer walked up to him and said I will kill you you dam Yankeee Son of a Bitch – at that he took a gun from a Rebel Soldier and aimed the gun at [Grierson's] head. [Grierson] throwed up his left arm and struck the bayonet of said gun throwing the gun up a little... the ball passing his head and struck in the bank behind him."
> [Grierson survived] [93]

Colonel Marshall, the commander of the Second Brigade, was among those captured in the crater and Lieutenant Colonel Robinson took command. The Second Brigade was ordered to return to its camp of July 29 and arrived there at six o'clock. [94]

Robinson's report succinctly summed up the disaster:

> I attribute the abandonment of our lodgment to the excessive massing of troops in the line captured by the First and Second Brigades of the First Division in the morning, into which all the other troops crowded and beyond which none of them advanced. [95]

Although the Battle of the Crater was an utter and complete disaster for the Union forces, the 179th New York Volunteers suffered fewer casualties than it had in the June 17 assault – fifty-six total versus ninety-one. Moreover, a slightly larger number of soldiers was engaged in the Battle of the Crater – approximately 240 versus approximately 230 – resulting in a significantly lower percentage of casualties – roughly twenty-three percent versus roughly forty percent.

As on June 17, the 179th lost key officers. In addition to Major Barton and Captain Farwell, First Lt. Baker L. Saxton (commanding Company D) was killed and Capt. James Day (commanding Company G) was wounded.

The Hornellsville Tribune, a weekly, reported on different pages of the same edition John Barton's promotion to major to command the 179th and his death at the Battle of the Crater on July 30. Barton's ability to relate to the troops was noted by the 179th's pseudonymous correspondent Ord., who wrote the Tribune that:

> His untimely death was mourned, not only by his old company, but by men all throughout the Regiment. I can say without the usual after death exaggeration, that no officer in the Regiment, was so unanimously loved by the men as Major Barton. He had a way of securing the personal attachment of the men that was irresisiable. [96]

The confusion during the battle is illustrated by the uncertainty over the fate of Captain Farwell in a series of contradictory reports in the Yates County Chronicle, his home town newspaper. While enlisted men frequently become separated from their unit during a battle with the result that their fate is unknown, that is a less common occurrence for a company commander. The Chronicle initially reported Farwell as killed in the August 4, 1864 edition. On August 11, 1864, the Chronicle wrote that "other and later reports throw doubt upon the matter and it is claimed he was wounded and taken prisoner." The *Chronicle* assured its readers that "there is no doubt he was doing his whole duty as a soldier whatever else may appear." A week later the *Chronicle* referred to a letter from Newton Spencer stating that Farwell had been wounded below the knee and taken prisoner. [97]

In the August 25 edition, the *Chronicle* expressed fear that Farwell had been killed, and grieved mightily for his loss:

> The Captain was as brave a man as ever wielded a sword; and he enjoyed the unanimous confidence of his entire company. Of all the heroes in this army, none would go more fearlessly or further than he in the line of duty. If he is really lost to us and his afflicted family, it is not their loss alone; for the country has lost one of its finest and most patriotic defenders. [98]

The Penn Yan community would not know the details of Farwell's fate until Sgt. Jeremiah Sprague of the 14th New York Heavy Artillery returned home from Salisbury Prison. Sprague, who had known Farwell before the war, had seen Farwell killed. [99]

In the enlisted ranks, eight soldiers were killed and two mortally wounded. Another sixteen soldiers were wounded, but recovered, including Newton Spencer. Twenty-six enlisted men were missing, sixteen of whom can be confirmed as having been taken prisoner. [100] Thirty years after the Battle of the Crater, Spencer recalled being hit:

> a singing and stinging 'Minie' struck and knocked me down – ploughing its way through a thickly padded (and 'nobby') jacket, and skinning my right ribs. Both wind and grit were promptly knocked out of me and I felt as a very lightweight might feel if Corbett should thump him in the side.
>
> A man who could even pretend to feel brave at just such a moment must have extraordinary 'sand,' and if he should say he experienced no fear, he's probably a reckless and proficient liar! [101]

It is impossible to determine how many soldiers from the 179th actually entered the crater, either in the confusion of the initial assault and/or the retreat into the crater after the Confederate counterattack. The large number of Union prisoners taken by the Confederates in the crater could suggest that most of the missing soldiers from the 179th were captured in the crater. However, Union prisoners were also taken and casualties incurred in the Confederate counterattack in the rifle pits north of the crater where the 179th had initially formed. For example, Company G's Dennis DeFord was taken prisoner in the works north of the crater after being struck by shrapnel rendering him unable to walk. [102] Units known to have had a heavier presence in the crater also suffered higher numbers of missing than the 179th did. The 14th New York Heavy Artillery lost seventy-five missing and the 2d Pennsylvania sixty-six, although those units were both much larger than the 179th. The 27th and 43rd U.S. Colored Troops each reported over one hundred soldiers missing. [103]

William Larzelere summarized the events of the very bad day in simple terms: "Before daylight we moved front. At daylight a rebel fort was blown up with a loss of 300 Johnies. Then the 9th and 18th Corps made the charge and were finally repulsed." Eugene Dunton wrote his parents that: "I have just passed through another 17th of June." [104]

News of the battle was reported in the *Elmira Daily Advertiser* on August 2 under "Latest News By Telegraph – Evening Report."

The very first sentence of the article summed up the battle very well – "After the explosion at an early hour this morning everything betokened a brilliant victory, but soon after matters assumed a different aspect." [105] The description of the battle is fairly accurate, although the article overemphasized the retreat of the colored troops. The losses of General Ledlie's division were estimated at one thousand to twelve hundred, "while many make the figure larger." The capture of Colonel Marshall, as well as General Bartlett, was reported. Amongst the other officer casualties, Major Buxton [sic] [Barton], 179th New York "lost a leg." [106]

**THE ASSAULT ON PETERSBURG
DESPERATE FIGHTING**

The Colored Troops Become Demoralized

LOSSES IN THE 9TH CORPS

Gen. Bartlett a Prisoner

**OUR LOSS 4,000 TO 5,000
REBEL LOSS ABOUT THE SAME**

Newspaper: Loss at the Crater

The Battle of the Crater was no story of mere local interest to the families of the Ninth Corps back at home. The August 13, 1864 edition of *Harper's Weekly*, a leading national newspaper of the day published in New York City, but available locally, carried only a matter of fact account of the battle and the maneuvers that preceded it. [107] However, the front page of the August 20, 1864 edition featured sketches of soldiers carrying powder into the mine. A two page sketch by A.H. Waud depicted the explosion of the mine and the assault. [108] Another sketch of the assault by Waud appeared the following week in the August 27 edition. [109]

Harper's Weekly joined the debate about the performance of the colored troops in the battle, commenting that "[t]here can be nothing more pitiful than the malevolent eagerness with which certain newspapers deride the colored troops for being no braver than the white troops at Petersburg." [110] The editorial position of *Harper's Weekly* was clear:

> We have always insisted that colored men should have the same chance of
> fighting in this war that white men have; and we have always believed that,
> battle for battle, they would show the same spirit and pluck. [111]

Ferrero's division was in fact routed by Weisiger's assault, but Earl Hess has concluded that "[t]he black troops made more strenuous efforts to expand out of the captured works than any other Federal soldiers that morning." [112]

The Battle of the Crater was immediately recognized as an unmitigated disaster for the Union. Even before the end of the day, Grant had telegraphed General Halleck in Washington that the Battle of the Crater "was the saddest affair I have witnessed in the war. Such opportunity for carrying fortifications I have never seen and do not expect again to have." [113] In his *Memoirs* Grant simply stated that "The effort was a stupendous failure." [114]

A disaster this great and this public inevitably resulted in a need to assess blame. At the request of General Meade, forwarded by Grant, President Lincoln ordered that a Court of Inquiry be convened at Petersburg on August 5, 1864. [115] The composition of the court did not bode well for Burnside. The officers appointed by Meade all reported directly or indirectly to him. [116] Burnside protested the composition of the court to President Lincoln in vain. [117]

After sixteen days of testimony from numerous officers present at the battle, the Court of Inquiry reached its conclusions that the "causes of the failure" were: (1) the "injudicious formation of the troops going forward" – "mainly by flank instead of extended front;" (2) "the halting of the troops in the crater instead of going forward to the crest when there was no fire of any consequence from the enemy;" (3) improper employment of engineer officers and working parties in the Ninth Corps; (4) improper leadership of some parts of the assaulting column; and (5) "the want of a competent common head at the scene of the assault to direct affairs as occurrences should demand." [118]

The Court of inquiry also noted the reasons why "the attack ought to have been successful:"

(1) "evident surprise of the enemy" when the mine exploded and for some time thereafter; (2) "[t]he comparatively small force in the enemy's works;" (3) ineffective and limited artillery and musketry fire by the Confederate defenders during the first thirty minutes after the explosion; and (4) some of the initial attacking troops were able to penetrate two hundred yards beyond the crater, but then could proceed no further for lack of support. [119]

Not surprisingly given its composition, the Court found fault with General Burnside for failing to follow the orders of General Meade, including the order to prepare the parapets and clear the abatis for the passage of the troops, and for failure "to apply proper military principles." [120] However, the Court of Inquiry also concluded that Burnside "believed the measures taken by him would insure success." [121]

General Ledlie was faulted for "having failed to push forward his division promptly according to orders and thereby blocking up the avenue which was designed for the passage of troops ordered to follow and support his in the assault." [122]

> Instead of being with his division during this difficulty in the crater, and by his personal efforts endeavoring to lead his troops forward, he was most of the time in a bomb-proof ten rods in the rear of the main line of the Ninth Corps works, where it was impossible for him to see anything of the movement of troops that was going on. [123]

Grant was more blunt in his judgment of Ledlie in his Memoirs, although still in an indirect way:

> In fact, Potter and Willcox were the only division commanders Burnside had who were equal to the occasion. Ledlie besides being otherwise inefficient, proved also to possess disqualification less common among soldiers. [124]

While the Court of Inquiry's judgment sealed Burnside's fate–he had been relieved from command of the Ninth Corps by Meade on August 2, the Court of Inquiry did not have the last word. In December 1864, the Joint Committee on the Conduct of the War decided to conduct its own inquiry. James McPherson notes that the Joint Committee was "Damned by its critics as a 'Jacobin' conspiracy to guillotine Democratic generals and praised by its defenders as a foe of inefficiency and corruption in the army." He concludes that it was "a bit of both." [125]

The Joint Committee proved to be more critical of Meade and more forgiving toward Burnside. In the view of the Joint Committee, the cause of the disaster was:

> mainly attributable to the fact that the plans and suggestions of the general who had devoted his attention for so long a time to the subject, who had carried out to a successful completion the project of mining the enemy's works, and who had carefully selected and drilled his troops for the purposes of securing whatever advantages might be attainable from the explosion of the mine [i.e. General Burnside], should have been so entirely disregarded by a general who had evinced no faith in the successful prosecution of that work, had aided it by no countenance or open approval, and had assumed the entire direction and control only when it was completed, and the time had come for reaping any advantages that might be derived from it [i.e. General Meade] [126]

Thus, a combination of mistakes–large and small–led to the Union defeat. The most significant mistake was Burnside's allowing Ledlie to lead the first wave of the assault. Leaving the "choice" of commander to chance was an abdication of responsibility. Letting the result stand was inexcusable.

As a corps commander, Burnside was responsible to know about Ledlie's drinking problem. Once in charge of the initial wave, Ledlie's own mistakes doomed the assault.

As both Meade and Burnside had recognized, the success of the assault depended on quick exploitation of the element of surprise that necessarily could only be temporary. The plans of both called for sending the first wave of troops beyond the crater to the high ground in the rear. Inexplicably, Ledlie instructed his two brigade commanders that their objective was to stop and hold the Confederate positions around the crater so that later waves of the assault could proceed through and seize the high ground. This miscommunication all but guaranteed the loss of the element of surprise. When Marshall and Bartlett saw the opportunity to move forward and sought Ledlie's permission to advance, he was nowhere to be found.

Ledlie must also share the blame with Bartlett for Bartlett's misunderstanding that his brigade was to attack on the Confederate left instead of the Union left of the crater. The result was that both brigades wound up on the right of the crater at first, increasing the crowding problem.

Meade was very critical of Burnside for not removing the defensive abbatis in front of the Union lines before the attack as he had explicitly ordered. Burnside's defense was that removing the abbatis would have alerted the Confederates to an impending attack. While the abbatis did slow down the Union attack somewhat, the delay does not appear to have been critical and if the Confederates had been tipped off, their response would have been even quicker.

No arrangements were made for ladders or steps for the soldiers to exit the eight foot deep Union trenches. Yankee ingenuity jumped in at the last minute and the troops used muskets with bayonets to help their comrades over the top. The delay caused does not seem to have been critical.

Assessing the significance of Grant's and Meade's decision to overrule Burnside's original decision that Ferrero's division would lead the assault is a challenge. Burnside had initially chosen Ferrero's division to lead the assault because they were relatively fresh. His other three divisions had seen hard duty since the beginning of the campaign, including a month in the trenches constantly under the fire of Confederate artillery and sharpshooters. Ferrero's division began training to lead the assault. Grant and Meade were concerned that if the assault was a failure and casualties among the black troops were heavy, they would be criticized for sacrificing black troops over white troops. In the political climate of the day, that concern was well-based. However, in the end, the actual result was no better—and perhaps worse given the criticism of the black troops for their retreat. Ferrero's division did achieve initial success in the attack. Had they been allowed to perform the mission they had been training for, their performance likely would have been better. Burnside told the Court of Inquiry that: "I am forced to believe that the Fourth Division (the colored division) would have made a more impetuous and successful assault than the leading division." Colonel Henry Thomas, a white officer commanding the Second Brigade of Ferrero's division, agreed with Burnside's decision: "It is an axiom in military art that there are times when the ardor, hopefulness and enthusiasm of new troops, not yet rendered doubtful by reverses or chilled by defeat, more than compensate, in a dash, for training and experience." [127]

Court-martial Transcript

CHAPTER ELEVEN

Court-Martial of a Citizen-Soldier

Blame for the Union's disaster at the Battle of the Crater was assessed not just by those at the highest levels in Washington. At a much lower level, Company F's Newton B. Spencer made his own findings of responsibility and sent them to his hometown newspaper, the *Penn Yan Democrat*. Publication of the letter led to his court-martial. Given the harsh and personal tone of the letter, as well as the sensitivity of its timing, the response of the army is not surprising.[1] The letter is well worth quoting at some length.

> Army Correspondence of the Democrat
>
> The 179th in the Assault
>
> 9th Corps Field Hospital
>
> Near Petersburg Va, August 12, 1864
>
> Dear Democrat,
>
> At the earliest good opportunity, I send you a few particulars of the part taken by the unfortunate 179th Regiment in the murderous assault and humiliating and discouraging repulse of our forces at this point on Saturday July 30th.
>
> You have doubtless laid before your readers the general details

of that sanguinary and disastrous battle and it only remains for me to record the mournful story of our losses as a regiment and a company...

It seemed that nothing short of the interposition of Divine Providence, could check our advance this side of the interior of Petersburg, or even the exterior line of the Richmond defences. Glorious and thorough victory was almost within our grasp, – and yet it eluded us – and only the sad story of the bloody repulse and fearful slaughter of our forces remains to complete the history of a day that dawned in grand triumph for us, and closed upon a scene of heart-sickening disaster & defeat.

You know the cause of that defeat by this time the civilized world must have heard it. The abolition mania for employing "nigger" [2] soldiers has culminated in the worst disaster of the whole campaign and discouraged and nearly demoralized a whole army. It was to glorify the sooty abolition idol that upon a division of raw and worthless black poltroons was devolved the most important task of the whole conflict – in the hope evidently, that they would crown our temporary success with decisive victory, and bear off the hard won laurels of the white fighting men of the gallant old 9th corps. To the eternal credit of Gen. Burnside be it said that he strenuously protested to Gen. Meade against using the negroes at all in the fight; but he was rudely overruled by that unpopular nonentity (of whom you occasionally hear as the nominal commander of the Potomac Army).

To Gen. Burnside should not be attributed *the* failure of that day. The whole project of undermining the rebel works were [sic] his and the original plan of assault – and nothing could have hindered his thorough success but the very measure against which he protested. Meade is the most complete military charlatan that has won a Maj. General's stars, and this army has no confidence in him, nor any respect for him. But for Gen. Grant's personal presence and supervision over him at all times, he would have "swamped" the entire army at the "Wilderness".

"The newspapers" variously estimate our aggregate of losses in the corps at from 2,500 to 4,000. I do not doubt that the official figures (whenever they are allowed to come to light), will show 5,000 in killed, wounded and missing. We have lost enormously in killed and prisoners, and our wounded are legion.

The poor 179th has suffered again fearfully. Our total loss is 70, in a force of 160 engaged. [3] On the 17th of June the loss was nearly 100...

The company [F] went into the fight with 18 men and lost 8, 2 killed, 3 taken prisoners, and 3 lightly wounded.[4] Your correspondent received a slight admonition from a rebel bullet ("Copperhead" though he is) that he was obnoxious to the Confederacy. Perhaps I should not grumble as I "still live."

May I be as fortunate all the way through, only a little more so.... [5]

Only ten men left for duty [in Company F] since June 1st, a period of less than ten weeks hard campaigning. And this is a fair proportion for other companies. Speedy peace is all that can save this forlorn remnant of the "Penn Yan Company."

In Heaven's name you people of the North, come down to the rescue of this army at once, or else baffled and beaten, a peace may be forced upon us by Southern dictators. Do this, or else effect an honorable peace by negotiations, if within the bounds of human possibility. Give up your vain and murderous grip upon the theory of "the last man and the last dollar" for the sake of the negro only, or driven to exhaustion & despair the shattered ranks of this army may yet do their own work of negotiation upon this soil, regardless of your dictation, your whims or political prejudices. Human life is too precious to be longer trifled with merely to satiate political ambition or the sordid contractor's love of gain. "Down with every obstacle to reasonable peace by arbitrament if you will not give us reinforcements," begins to be the cry of the Army of the Potomac.

SPENCER

Spencer's letter was clearly written for the presidential campaign. Spencer was an avowed "copperhead" and the *Penn Yan Democrat* wore its politics on its masthead. [6] A similar critique of the colored troops was written by "C.B.C." from the 179th for the *Buffalo Daily Courier*, another Democratic newspaper. [7] Antiwar sentiment in the North was on the rise. At the end of August, the "Peace" Democrats carried the day on the party platform with a plank declaring the war to restore the Union a failure and "demand[ing] that immediate efforts be made for a cessation of hostilities." [8] (However, the "War" Democrats won on the party's standard-bearer–General George B. McClellan.)

The use of black troops is a key theme of the article and a hot political issue of the day, but Spencer got Burnside's and Meade's positions on the use of black troops reversed. Burnside not only proposed to use Ferrero's Fourth Division of the Ninth Corps– nine regiments of United States Colored Troops – in the assault, but Burnside proposed that the black troops would lead the assault. It was Meade, along with Grant, who countermanded that proposal out of a concern for the political consequences of heavy black casualties if the assault failed. [9]

Spencer apparently was unaware of Burnside's evolving views on the use of blacks as soldiers. Before the war, Burnside was a Democrat and had a "definite distaste" for the abolitionists. He respected the laws treating slaves as property. During his successful campaign in North Carolina in 1862 he had returned fugitive slaves to owners who had remained loyal to the Union. In 1863, he had opposed enrolling blacks and raising black regiments. However, he did not believe that blacks were naturally inferior as many did in that era and he came to believe that the Union could not be restored without the elimination of slavery. By 1864 he had come to "champion the use of the U.S. Colored troops." [10]

There is no apparent political reason why Spencer would have attacked Meade and spared

Burnside. Indeed, Meade was criticized by the Abolitionist press in the Fall of 1864.[11]

As to Spencer's criticism of the performance of the black troops in the Ninth Corps, he either did not know about–or chose not to remember–the performance of the black division in Smith's Corps which captured one of the Dimmock Line batteries at Petersburg on June 15, the day before the 179th arrived.[12] Spencer's assessment of the strategic opportunity that the Union had was spot on, but his accusation that the black troops were responsible for the disaster was not even close to the mark.

Spencer and the *Penn Yan Democrat* were hardly alone in their criticism of the black troops at the Battle of the Crater. Although without the venom Spencer employed, even the pro-Union Party *Elmira Daily Advertiser* reported in one of the subheads for the article on the battle that: "The Colored Troops Became Demoralized."[13]

Surprisingly, Spencer was aware of the fact that Burnside had chosen Ledlie's division to lead the assault by lot. Burnside's tactical plan was sound–putting Ledlie in charge of the first wave was inexcusable. Criticizing Burnside for leaving such an important decision to chance and/or putting Ledlie in charge of the first wave would have been totally justified, but Spencer was silent on that point.

Given the almost universal criticism of Ledlie's performance that day, the absence of any criticism of Ledlie by Spencer is surprising. The possibility that Spencer believed Ledlie to be a Democrat comes quickly to mind, but Ledlie's military advancement came in part through the active involvement of Lincoln and Seward.[14] It may simply be that Ledlie was politically irrelevant in the larger issues of the day.

Having called the commander of the Army of the Potomac "the most complete military charlatan that has worn a Maj. General's stars" and claiming that the soldiers had no confidence in or respect for him, let alone advocating controversial political positions, Spencer left the army's top brass no choice but to discipline him. The army moved quickly. The ink was barely dry in the *Penn Yan Democrat* when the court-martial began on August 27, 1864, two days before the Democratic Convention convened.[15] Spencer was charged with contempt and disrespect of a commanding officer; giving aid and comfort to the enemy; conduct to the prejudice of good order and military discipline; and with violating Article 57 of the Articles of War. Article 57 provided that:

> Whosoever shall be convicted of holding correspondence with, or giving intelligence to, the enemy, either directly or indirectly, shall suffer death, or such other punishment as shall be ordered by the sentence of a court-martial.[16]

Having survived Confederate gunfire in two heated battles with just a slight wound in the second, Spencer was at risk of being killed by "friendly fire" in a courtroom. Not surprisingly, Spencer pled not guilty. He did admit that he had written the letter. His primary defense was that he had never been read the Articles of War– a violation of Article 101, which provides that "The foregoing articles are to be read and published once in every six months, to every garrison, regiment, troop, or company, mustered, or to be mustered, in the service of the United States."[17] Lieutenant Levi Force, Sgt. Edward S. Dunn and Pvt. James Dicker all testified in Spencer's defense that in fact the Articles of War had not been read to Company F.

Dunn and Dicker were both from Company F, so they were logical witnesses as to whether the Articles of War had been read to Company F. However, Lieutenant Force was from Company C. There were no officers in Company F at this time, following the death of Captain Farwell and the assignments of Lieutenants Bradley and Holden on detached duty, but the reason for the presence of Lieutenant Force as opposed to any other officer is not apparent.[18]

When the Judge Advocate asked Force whether the Articles of War had ever been read to the regiment, he responded "They have been read to my company, but not to that of the accused." There was no follow up question on how Force would know that they had not been read to Spencer's company. [19]

But politics was the underlying issue. Before asking about the Articles of War, the Judge Advocate had begun his examination of Force as follows:

> Q. How long have you been acquainted with the accused?
> A. Six months.
>
> Q. Have you had any political discussions with him
> A. No.
>
> Q. Do you know what his political sentiments are?
> A. I always considered him a loyal man.
>
> Q. Have you ever heard him utter expressions detrimental to the government?
> A. No.
>
> Q. Did you ever hear him say any thing that would tend to discourage his comrades?
> A. No.

After the Judge Advocate asked about the reading of the Articles of War, Spencer then followed by questioning Force himself:

> Q. What have been your own political sentiments?
> A. Republican and black abolitionist.

The Judge Advocate then continued with Force:

> Q. Did the principles of the accused differ much from yours?
> A. He is a war democrat, but sound on most issues.

Spencer then returned:

> Q. What has been my general character?
> A. Good. You have always been a good soldier, and ready to do your duty. [20]

The Judge Advocate asked Private Dicker, a native of Penn Yan, what newspapers were printed there and their "political sentiments." Dicker identified the "[Penn Yan] Democrat" as "Democrat" and the "[Yates County] Chronicle" as "Republican." [21]

Spencer also submitted a written statement in his defense. In addition to denying that the Articles of War had been read to him, he also claimed that the casualty numbers that he had given were no different from those in other newspapers and that if he had really intended to give aid and comfort to the enemy with those numbers he hardly would have published them in a "humble and uninfluential country journal, circulating less than a thousand copies weekly." and would hardly have identified himself and his regiment by name and number.

Indeed, Spencer's July 17 letter to *The Hornellsville Tribune* described the losses in the June 17 assault, but occasioned no reprisal, perhaps because the *Tribune* was a pro-

Lincoln newspaper [23]

> The regiment has encountered rough and disasterous usage from the war
> officers [i.e. the officers above the regiment's own officers] and the rebels
> here… Our present effective force (that is, *for duty* is but 150, out of 450 men
> who came out with us. These figures are significant of the calamities of war and
> the unusually rough campaign in which this army has thus far been engaged–
> although a portion of our losses is due to desertions. – Ninety four men were
> wounded and killed in the charge; and a large portion of those remaining are
> sick. [24]

In addition, two days after Spencer wrote his letter to the *Penn Yan Democrat*, Ord. wrote a letter
that the *The Hornellsville Tribune* published on August 25, 1864, just four days before Spencer's court-
martial began. The tone of Ord.'s letter was also strongly critical, but perhaps Ord.'s pseudonym
and/or the *Tribune*'s political position saved him because no charges were brought against him. [25]

Spencer stated that the "main intention" of his concluding paragraph was not to give "aid and
comfort to the enemy," but to "impress upon the minds of loyal people the urgent necessity of
sending speedy reinforcements to the Army of the Potomac to save the Army and the cause from
disaster." [26]

While not a lawyer, Spencer responded to the charge of contempt and disrespect for his
commanding officer with a lawyer's technical argument made in the spirit of a "citizen" soldier:

> while I *supposed* it illegal to employ language towards a commanding officer
> like that quoted anywhere within the Department, I did not know (being totally
> ignorant of the Articles of War) that a soldier in the Department was prohibited
> [from] writing criticisms upon the official acts and standing of such officers to
> be sent or printed outside of such Department. [27] (emphasis in original)

Speaking inside the "Department," Spencer was a "soldier." Publishing outside the
"Department," he was a "citizen."

"For a final answer and defense to all of the charges and specifications against me," Spencer
stated that the letter had been "hurriedly written" under "the spur of impulse and deep chagrin at
the unfortunate disaster … without due deliberation as to its full import" and that he would not
have "sent it at all if retained long enough for a second perusal." [28]

Spencer also introduced in his defense the July 7, 1864 article from the pro "Union" *Yates
County Chronicle* that had lauded his "genuine patriotism" and the concurring article from the
Democrat.

The court found on September 12 that Spencer was guilty on the first charge of "conduct to
the prejudice of good order and military discipline" by writing the article; and guilty on the second
charge of "contempt and disrespect to his commanding officer," Gen. Meade. The court found
Spencer guilty of the third charge of "giving aid and comfort to the enemy," but not guilty of the
"specification" by providing casualty numbers in the article. By far the most important to Spencer
was that the court found him not guilty on the critical fourth charge of "violation of the 57th
Article of War" for which he could have been executed. [29]

Spencer was sentenced to be returned to routine duty, reprimanded in front of his company
and fined $8 per month of his $13 salary for six months. [30]

Spencer's new division commander, General Robert Potter, [31] was incensed and disapproved
the verdict on review. Potter was himself a lawyer and a citizen-soldier who had enlisted in 1861
as a private and risen quickly through the ranks to general. [32] In Potter's view, "The whole tenor

Robert Potter

of the letter shows the intentions of the prisoner to have been to represent the condition of this Army in the worst possible light – to discourage the friends of this Army and comfort its enemies." [33]

With respect to the capital charge, Potter fumed: "the finding of the court is wholly inexplicable, except on the supposition that they are lamentably ignorant." Potter also found the sentence "entirely inadequate to the gravity of the offense of which the Court have convicted him." Potter pointed out that:

> The prisoner is a man evidently of more than average education and intelligence (shown by his *artful and ingenious defence* [to which Spencer inserted the handwritten note on his copy: "It was sufficiently ingenious to beat *you*, General Bob Potter! -N.B.S." [34]] as well as by his letter) and of experience in the world.

His plea of ignorance of martial law seems rather assumed than real; the statement that the letter was hurriedly written … and 'would not have been sent if retained long enough for a second perusal' seems most improbable – the letter is dated thirteen days after the main event of which it treats.

The superiority of the prisoner in education and intelligence renders his offense the more serious. [35]

[Photo: George Meade]

Notwithstanding having been called a "charlatan" by Spencer, General Meade denied General Potter's request that Spencer be retried by a higher level court and returned the matter to Potter. Meade specifically pointed out that "It was not for any personal reasons that this case was sent down to the Div. for trial" (to which Spencer added the marginal notation "Bosh!" on his copy). [36] Potter returned the case to the same officers for reconsideration on the third and fourth charges. After "maturely considering the evidence adduced," they found Spencer "not guilty" on both. The company-level officers who predominated on the court-martial panel may well have been more in touch with the morale of the troops than General Potter. [37] Spencer may have been a hostile critic, but he was no "shirker." Execution of an apparently wounded soldier for expressing sentiments undoubtedly held by many other soldiers probably would not have set well with the soldiers of the Army of the Potomac right then.

So "citizen-soldier" Newton B. Spencer dodged the bullet. However, due to illness, Spencer sat out the rest of the war in a hospital, [38] and he does not appear to have sent any further letters to hometown newspapers. In the end, General Potter's objective of silencing Spencer was achieved, just not by Potter's hand. And Ord.'s exercise of his free speech rights may have been chilled. His only other letter to the *Tribune* after that stayed away from controversy, thanking the ladies of Hornellsville for the mittens they had sent to the 179th, providing an updated roster of the officers, and praising Colonels Gregg and Doty as "the two best men in the army of the Potomac." [39]

Newton Spencer was caught between the differing civilian and military views of the value of free speech.[40] Company D's Lt. John Andrews and Company K's James Vandemark got caught between the differing civilian and military views on access to information. For a citizen, the right to be informed about the government's doings is sacred. Access to newspapers is presumed. For the military, a well-informed soldier is not necessarily considered an asset. Senior commanders on both sides became concerned about the discussions of the war between the line soldiers during informal truces and the regular practice of exchanging northern and southern newspapers.

General Meade issued Army of the Potomac Special Orders No. 157 on June 9, 1864:

> No communication will be had with the enemy unless especially authorized from these or superior headquarters, or except so far as may be necessary to properly receive a flag of truce coming from the enemy's lines. All other communication is strictly prohibited, whether by means of conversation, signals, or otherwise, or by interchange of newspapers or commodities. Corps commanders will see that the unauthorized intercourse with the enemy, which it is known has from time to time taken place, notwithstanding the reiterated orders on the subject, is no longer tolerated.[41]

However, the men in the field demonstrated both before and after S.O. No. 157 was issued that a citizen-soldier will have his newspaper. As a war correspondent for *The New York Times* wrote after the Battle of Fredericksburg, the soldiers in the Army of the Potomac "feel that things are at loose ends – in fact they know it for our army is one that reads and thinks."[42]

It is doubtful that S.O. 157 was ever consistently enforced, but Andrews and Vandemark had the misfortune to be involved with the purchase of Confederate newspapers at a particularly sensitive time.

On January 29, 1865, the picket line of the Ninth Corps' Third Division had been approached by a representative of Confederate diplomats Alexander Stephens, R. M. T. Hunter and J. A. Campbell who desired to cross the line "in accordance with an understanding claimed to exist with Lieutenant General Grant, on their way to Washington as peace commissioners."[43] This request was sent up the chain of command to Secretary of War Stanton, and rumors undoubtedly quickly passed through the ranks. This contact was the beginning of what subsequently became known as the Hampton Roads Conference held with President Lincoln and General Grant on February 3 on Grant's flagship, the *River Queen*. The lead-up to the conference generated a good deal of press coverage.[44]

Andrews went on picket the evening of January 29. The night was quiet, but cold. There was "but little firing. Our men fired less than usual – only two or three rebel shots came over." A close call did occur towards morning when a Union soldier carelessly fired into Andrews' pit, "very nearly hitting one of the men near me." Shortly thereafter, Andrews:

> went along the line under my charge and gave orders that there be no exchanging papers with the rebels. I had received no orders from the Captain of the picket, but I knew that there was a general order to that effect (but I did not know that that same order forbid any communication whatever with the enemy, and from that ignorance I got into trouble.[45]

Andrews took a short nap from around eleven o'clock to noon – definitely not permitted for the Lieutenant of the Picket, and while he was asleep, Company A's Pvt. George Cross bought a newspaper from some nearby Confederates.

Around one o'clock, the brigade officer of the day, Maj. Lyman Knapp of the 17th Vermont, came along and asked if any papers had been exchanged. He likely had heard rumors about the Confederate peace commission and was interested to see what he could find out.

Major Knapp was given the newspaper that Private Cross had bought. After reading it, Major Knapp said that he would like to see a later paper, but that they should buy it rather than exchanging a Northern newspaper for it. Shortly after Knapp left, "a couple of Rebs showed themselves in the woods with papers." Andrews took off his sword and approached them, along with Company A's Pvt. James Wattleworth. Andrews bought that morning's *Richmond Examiner* for 75 cents. Andrews barely had time to read it before it was sent for by Brigade Headquarters, "but I had it long enough to read that Vice President Stevens [sic], Asst. Sec. of War Campbell and Senator Hunter left Richmond the morning before on a peace mission to Washington." [46]

Andrews and Wattleworth, along with another lieutenant from another unit who was angry that one of his men had been taken prisoner earlier in the day, took the two Confederate soldiers prisoner. Andrews recounted that they told him that there was:

> no need to have taken them for in a few days they would all come in. They
> acknowledged they were fighting in a bad cause, were whipped, and thought
> peace would soon be made. [They] were rather pleased with being captured,
> but thought they would be accounted for as deserters and that they didn't like.
> [They] were comfortably dressed, but not as well as our soldiers are; their
> clothes were not alike, one being a "butternut" and the other a dirty "grayback."
> (Their shoes were nearly worn out.) (emphasis in original) [47]

After being relieved from the picket line and returning to camp, Andrews found a brigade staff officer waiting for him. Anderson was taken to brigade headquarters to be interviewed by Colonel Titus, the acting brigade commander, about the "affair." At General Potter's direction, Andrews was to be placed in "close arrest" back at the 179th's camp.

Colonel Gregg "was very much excited" when Andrews returned – "My God, Andrews, what have you been doing!" However, after a full explanation from Andrews, Gregg was satisfied that Andrews was not to blame and headed to brigade headquarters to see what he could do. Not finding immediate success, Gregg asked Andrews to write a statement for General Potter. Gregg then forwarded the letter to the brigade commander, Brigadier General Simon Griffin, with the statements that Andrews had "labored by 'duty and study' to fit [him]self for [his] position" since being mustered in as an officer in mid-December and "bid fair to make a `good officer'" and that Gregg thought that "the present trouble arose from a want of experience and not from any evil intent." General Griffin forwarded the statements to General Potter, adding his own view that: "Lieut. Andrews' statements are corroborated by other evidence." [48]

Potter, however, was unforgiving and ordered Gregg to prefer charges. The charge was disobedience of orders and the specification was "hold[ing] communication with the enemy by meeting one or more of the rebel pickets outside the vidette line and exchanging or buying newspapers" while officer of the picket in violation of S.O. No. 157. [49]

Andrews acted as his own counsel and declared: "I think I managed it as well as a lawyer could." [50] Andrews had been under close arrest prior to the trial, but Colonel Gregg had allowed him freedom of movement within the camp to find his witnesses. The prosecution called George Cook, the regimental adjutant, and Privates Edward Allwood, James Wattleworth and George Cross from Company A. Andrews also called Company I's Pvt. Hugh Brown.

Once again, the court-martial court, which included the 179th's Major Terrill and Company A's Captain Carpenter, was more lenient than General Potter. The court found Andrews guilty of the specification "but attach[ed] no criminality thereto" and not guilty of the charge. This time General Potter approved the proceedings. [51]

Sergeant Vandemark was sergeant of the picket the day after Andrews had returned to camp. There was no question that Vandemark had obtained a newspaper from Confederate soldiers, [52] so the key issue in the trial was the orders given by the officer of the picket to Vandemark. Lieutenant Frost of the 11th New Hampshire testified that his "instructions were to allow no wood cut in front, to allow no men to go in front of the picket post, also to allow no communication with the enemy whatever." Company A's Pvt. Waterman Giles; Company K's Pvt. Beniah Vandemark (possibly a relative); Company D's Corp. John Lawrence; Company B's Corp. John Kerrick; Company A's Sgt. Adam Cortwright; and Company K's Pvt. Roswell Wright were called by the prosecution, but all denied that Sergeant Vandemark had been given orders by Lieutenant Frost not to communicate with the enemy. Sergeant Cartwright testified that they were told not to go beyond the vedette posts; Private Vandemark testified that Lieutenant Frost had told Vandemark "to keep the men all awake, to fire once in ten minutes and not in volleys – this is all I heard;" and Private Wright testified that Frost had told Vandemark "to keep his men awake and not to let them lay down and to keep firing." [53]

Sergeant Vandemark did not testify, but submitted a written statement. He denied receiving any orders from the officer in charge of the picket that day against communicating with the enemy. He also stated that "it is untrue that I ever knowingly, willfully disobeyed an order. I never have and I never will." He also described the "practice" with respect to exchanging newspapers:

> I knew there was an order against exchanging newspapers on the picket lines but for some time before the day on which I am charged with disobeying orders papers were bought or exchanged daily and conversation carried on by the pickets of the two sides. I consequently supposed the orders were revoked. Men exchanged papers daily and were not punished or even reproved. Was it not natural to think that there was nothing forbidding such transactions. [54]

Notwithstanding the consistent testimony by the witnesses other than Lieutenant Frost that Frost had not given an order against communicating with the enemy, Vandemark had admitted that he had guilty knowledge of S.O. No. 157. The nine judges of the panel (all of whom had served on the court hearing Andrews' case) found Vandemark guilty and sentenced him to be reduced to the ranks. It seems unlikely that Vandemark was impressed by military "justice." [55]

Blick's Station

CHAPTER TWELVE

Low Point (August 1864)

The 179th had been hurt badly in the Battle of the Crater. Not only were the casualties heavy, but there was the demoralization of defeat. On June 17, they had at least captured the rebel positions, even if they ultimately retreated. The Battle of the Crater was a rout. To make matters worse, disease continued to spread through the ranks. [1] At the Battle of Weldon Railroad in mid-August the 179th could field only one officer and eighty-one enlisted men. [2]

The mixture of pride and defensiveness in Ord.'s August 14, 1864 letter to *The Hornellsville Tribune* was probably typical of the state of mind in the 179th at that time:

> on the 30th, the boys were thrown into that strong line of the rebels. No one can, with justice, blame the 179th, or the 1st Division of the 9th Corps for their part of that disastrous day's work. They gained rather than lost laurels there. They left half their number behind, killed, wounded or missing. [actually around 20%] Well may it be said that the 179th has been baptized in blood...
>
> The history of the service will not show an instance where a detachment of six companies without colors, without knowledge of Battalion drill, without a Regimental organization, has been shoved into active campaigning as the 179th has been; and we hope for the good of the country it never will. Our regiment

should have – if it had been drilled and disciplined as Regiments invariably have been – about 400 men for duty; it has less than 100. It is as bad as murder to send new men from the North into an active campaign in this climate without a preparatory hardening process.[3]

Ord.'s complaint about a lack of training was certainly legitimate, but it was hardly unique. Union regiments were not "invariably" well drilled.[4]

As for the present, Ord. reported that:

The regiment is constantly in danger – We lose a man nearly every day. The utmost care is required to avoid the storm of shot and shell from the rebel lines; but sickness is thinning our ranks faster than rebel bullets... If we ever reach winter quarters, most of those will return, but some I fear, are so broken down that they will never be mustered out by mortal hands.[5]

Two days before Ord.'s letter, Spencer had sent the letter to the *Penn Yan Democrat* that led to his court-martial. He accounted for the losses in the enlisted ranks in his own Company F since leaving Elmira with eighty "able bodied" men on June 1 as follows[6]:

Total wounded and in hospitals	18
Died from wounds	4
Killed in action	4
Missing in action	2
Sick in hospital	22
Deserted (tough bounty jumpers)	12
On detached service (field artillery)	8
Present on duty	10
Total	**80**

The dozen desertions had been a big loss for Company F. Desertion was also a continuing problem in August. Another ten men deserted, including six from Company G.[7]

The Regimental Surgeon, Dr. Joseph Robinson, wrote a friend whose son had died in the 179th in mid-August that: "Our regiment has suffered terribly. We have not over 40 men for duty of the 580 that came out with us & are losing more every day."[8] Casualties had particularly thinned the officer corps in the 179th. As Ord. noted in mid-August, "very few of the original officers are left." He recounted that:

Capt. Terrill of Co. 'A' is in command of the Regiment; Capt. Stewart of Co. 'B' lost a leg on the 17th, and is in the Hospital at Washington; Capt. Barton of Co. 'C' was killed on the 30th; Capt. Bird of Co. 'D' was struck by a piece of shell upon the knee in the charge of the 17th, and is home, but will save his leg; Capt. Blachford of Co. 'E' was killed on the 17th; Capt. Farwell [Co. F] was killed or taken prisoner on the 30th, and Capt. Day of Co. 'G' was wounded on the 30th, and is at home.[9]

[Photo: John Parke]

At a higher level, General Burnside and General Ledlie became casualties of their own incompetence. Burnside was replaced by General John Parke, his chief of staff, as commander of the Ninth Corps. Ledlie was replaced by General Julius White as commander of the First Division.[10]

August began with a return to trench warfare. The day after the Battle of the Crater, the First Division and the 179th remained in the rear. [11] However, after dark that day, they returned to their previous position in the trenches, relieving Carr's division of the Second Corps.[12]

The night of August 8, the 179th New York and the 3rd Maryland relieved the 14th New York Heavy Artillery in the Second Brigade's position in the trenches on the First Division's right. General White ordered that troops in the trenches would be relieved every two days, but that each of the First Division's two brigades were to maintain 450 men "constantly in the front line." [13]

July's oppressive heat had continued into August. The temperature at City Point at six in the morning on August 9, 1864 was 98 degrees. [14] Ord. referred to "mercury at 100 degrees" in his August 14 letter. [15]

[Illustration: City Point Explosion]

On August 9, a Confederate saboteur placed a time bomb on an ammunition barge moored at City Point. Union casualties from the ensuing explosion were forty-three dead and 126 injured. [16] Company G's Solomon Leonard, a twenty-nine-year-old farmer, was at the wrong place at the wrong time. He had suffered a bayonet wound in the mouth at the Battle of the Crater and been sent to the hospital at City Point. Having recuperated, he was ready to return to the 179th and was boarding a train at City Point when the explosion occurred. He was struck in the head by a piece of timber and died instantly. [17]

[Photos: Aiken House and Weldon Picket Lines]

The Battle of Weldon Railroad began on August 19. The Ninth Corps' First Division (General White) and Third Division (General Willcox) were ordered to support the Fifth Corps. White's division was relieved from the lines by a brigade from the Second Corps and started moving west around three in the afternoon. The Second Brigade (including the 179th) followed the First Brigade. The roads "owing to the rain, were exceedingly bad" and it took two hours to march the roughly two miles to Aiken House. Musket fire was heard to the right and front. [18]

[Photo: Colquitt]

White's Division formed with the First Brigade on the left, initially connecting with Willcox's division, and the Second Brigade on the right. The 179th was deployed as skirmishers on the far right in anticipation of the arrival of the Ninth Corps' Second Division (General Potter). The First Division advanced and soon encountered Colquitt's Brigade of Mahone's Division, shortly after entering the nearby woods. White reported that "after a sharp engagement of about half an hour," the Confederates "were driven from the field in disorder ["utterly routed" in the words of Lieutenat Colonel Robinson], leaving their dead, a considerable number of wounded, and many small arms." Robinson estimated that the Confederates had been pushed back a mile. The First Division also reported capturing roughly sixty prisoners. [19]

[Photo: Blick's Station, see page 116]

On August 20, the 179th established new headquarters near Blick's Station and remained in that vicinity until the end of September. [20]

[Photo: Weldon Railroad]

Lieutenant Colonel Doty, who had been wounded in the assault on Petersburg on June 17 and placed on leave to recover, returned to duty on August 23. He took over command of the 179th from Captain Terrill. (On August 27, Terrill was promoted to major, confirming him as second in command in the field to Doty.) A childhood friend who had seen Doty at home recuperating saw him as "almost helpless from his wounds," concluding that "his days of active fighting were over." [21] Nonetheless, Doty had recovered and was back at the front.

On August 31, the 179th New York was occupying the far left of the First Division's lines when General Hartranft removed the 179th to occupy the part of the line vacated by the removal of the 2nd Pennsylvania. [22]

At the end of August, the 179th was still in sad shape. Overall, there were only seven officers and 128 enlisted men available for duty. Even at that, forty of the enlisted men were on detached duty, including nineteen with the 27th Artillery Battery. Two hundred fifty-two enlisted men and eight officers were reported sick – two-thirds of the 179th's paper strength. [23]

At the Company level, Company A, for example, had only twenty-seven enlisted men available for duty. Both of its officers and thirty-one of its enlisted men were sick. Neither First Lieutenant Carpenter nor Second Lieutenant Farr was even nearby. Carpenter was on furlough from Volunteer Officers' Hospital in Washington, D.C. and Farr was in hospital. The situation was only slightly better by the end of September. Carpenter had returned to duty, but there were still twenty-eight enlisted men sick. [24]

The weakness of the 179th New York was reflected in Lieutenant Colonel Doty's ratings of the companies at the end of August: "Fair" in Discipline; "Good" in Instruction; "Fair" in Military Appearance; "Good" in Arms and Accoutrements; and "Poor" in Clothing. [25]

As of September 1, the companies of the 179th New York were commanded as follows [26]:

A	1st Lt. George Carpenter	E	Capt. Louis Ottenot
B	Capt. Robert Stewart	F	(1st Lt. George Carpenter)
C	1st Lt. John Prentiss	G	Capt. James Day
D	2d Lt. Jeffrey Wisner		

However, Carpenter, Stewart, Prentiss, Day and possibly Ottenot were all sick or wounded in military hospitals, and Wisner was on recruiting duty in Elmira. [27]

The First Division was temporarily discontinued on September 1, 1864, and the 179th New York was transferred to the Third Division. The very next day, the 179th was reassigned to the Second Division (General Potter). [28] The 179th would remain in Potter's division for the rest of the war.

The 179th New York's duty during the first part of September was routine. Assignments included fatigue duty chopping trees on September 7 and 17 and building a fort on September 23. They did battalion or brigade drill or inspection on September 14, 19, and 20. Most of the time they were in camp, sometimes "doing nothing." [29]

As September progressed, the numbers in the 179th increased. The less seriously wounded men from the June 17 assault and the Battle of the Crater began returning – a dozen by the end of the month. Men taken sick were also beginning to return to the field –eight in September. [30] The first seven companies began receiving replacements for men lost during the summer. Nearly seventy new recruits arrived at the 179th's camp the morning of September 30. [31] But the most important event was the arrival of Companies H, I and K in mid-September, bringing the 179th to the ten companies of a regiment.

Joesph W. Robinson

CHAPTER THIRTEEN

Threats of Disease and Infection

While home on leave of absence in July 1864, Lt. Nathaniel Finch told *The Hornellsville Tribune* that:

> The hardest working officer in the regiment is Dr. Joe Robinson. Surgeons have poor assistants, but Joe has been without aid of any kind. One half of the Regiment has some complaint that requires prescriptions. Diarhea prevails, with quite a number of cases of fever. Joe is required to stay within 300 yds of the front line which brings him within range of "minnies," shell and other deadly missiles. He has erected, in common with other Surgeons, a small fort. It is known as Fort Robinson. This protects from "minnies" and most of the shell. It is nothing unusual to hear such missiles very close to the fort. [Finch] was in there one day when a solid, Whitworth, steel shot, weighing about 20 lbs came over and struck the earth about ten rods from Fort Robinson. [1]

Lieutenant Colonel Joseph W. Robinson was assigned to the 179th on May 16, 1864. Four days later, he was sent to Albany "for the purpose of procuring medical stores." He then joined the 179th in Washington and served with the 179th through the end of the war. [2] After the war, until his death in 1886, Robinson wrote supporting affidavits for the pension applications of countless veterans from the 179th.

After attending Alfred University and Oberlin College, Robinson returned home to Hornellsville to study medicine with his father, a prominent physician. Robinson then attended Buffalo Medical College, graduating in 1860. He completed his medical education with post graduate work at Bellevue Medical College. Before joining the 179th New York, Robinson had served as the Surgeon for the 141st New York Volunteers during the Peninsula campaign.[3] Ord. noted that that experience "gives him a great advantage over many Surgeons in the care of our men."[4] Robinson had briefly been a prisoner of war during the Peninsula campaign. He had resigned from the army in May 1863 because "the condition of my parents' health and the business affairs of the family imperatively demand my presence at home."[5]

While Dr. Robinson had no assistant when Lieutenant Finch was writing in July 1864, he did have an assistant surgeon for a brief period in the Fall of 1864. William C. Bailey served as Assistant Surgeon from September 1 to October 13, 1864, when he was promoted to Surgeon for the 186th New York. Phineas E. Rose served as Assistant Surgeon for less than a week. He was mustered

in on November 1, 1864, but on November 5, 1864 he was sent on detached duty with three artillery batteries and never returned to the 179th. A. H. Brundage, a doctor before the war, enlisted in Company I in September 1864, but apparently did not serve in a medical capacity. He was allowed to resign in January 1865 to accept a commission as assistant surgeon in the 6th New York Cavalry.[6]

Dr. Robinson had the apparently very capable assistance of Martin V. Doty as hospital steward. Doty, nicknamed "Dave" or "Davy" by the troops, was the younger brother of Lieutenant Colonel Doty. Like his older brother, Dave Doty had served for two years in the 23rd New York. Doty was appointed as hospital steward on April 23, 1864. Doty returned to the combat arm in January 1865

Martin V. Doty

when he was promoted to first lieutenant in Company C. He was promoted to captain in Company B in April 1865 after the end of hostilities and was brevetted major. After the war, when Dr. Robinson had returned to civilian practice, Doty worked in the early 1880's as Robinson's bookkeeper.[7]

Colonel Gregg, who was a friend of Dr. Robinson's father, described Dr. Robinson as "a good man."[8] "Fort Robinson" apparently was a popular gathering place. On July 18, Major Barton ordered that "[h]ereafter any enlisted man found at the Surgeon's Quarters without a proper *Pass* will be arrested and sent to the Picket-Line."[9]

However, Dr. Robinson was not universally liked among the soldiers. Company B's William Lamont wrote his sister that in comparison to the surgeon in the 185th New York, whom Lamont apparently knew, "the only thing good about our Dr. is his name, that is Dr. Robinson." (Apparently Lamont's doctor at home was a Robinson.)[10] James Rutan wrote his wife that he didn't like Dr. Robinson "mutch". Still, twenty years later, Dr. Robinson wrote a letter supporting Rutan's pension application.[11]

Dr. Robinson's battlefield experience notwithstanding, his effectiveness in treating the soldiers of the 179th was limited by the state of medical knowledge of the day. According to Jeffrey Sartin, the Civil War:

> was the last great armed conflict in the world fought without knowledge of the germ theory of disease. Within a few short years, brilliant men such as Pasteur, Lister, and Koch would illuminate the nature of microbial illness and antisepsis.

For the hapless participants in the Civil War, however, sickness and death remained a mystery ...

Therefore, the unfortunate participants in the Civil War fought too soon: only ten years later, the death toll from disease might have been a mere fraction of what it was. [12]

Disease was actually the most serious threat for the Civil War soldier – twice as many died from disease as from battle. [13] In the middle of August 1864, Ord. observed that "sickness is thinning our ranks faster than rebel bullets." [14] In the 179th New York, 109 men died from disease, while only 72 died from combat (a ratio of 1.5:1). [15] Thus, of the 1080 men who served in the regiment, one out of ten died from disease. Moreover, even those soldiers who recovered from their illnesses during the war were more likely than their disease-free comrades to suffer chronic conditions in later life. [16]

Death from disease was no less final, but as an Iowa soldier noted, it brought "none of [the] honors" of death on the battlefield. [17] Company B's Eugene Dunton survived both the June 17 assault and the Battle of the Crater only to die of disease on a hospital ship between City Point and Washington on August 28, 1864. [18] When Company I's Charles S. Baker died of typhoid fever, Lieutenant Edward Lounsbery wrote Baker's father and was sure to state that Baker "was brave and fought manfuly in the battle of the 30th Sept." as well as praising Baker as "a good soldier beloved and respected by all of the members of the Company ... [and] always ready to do his duty." [19]

While epidemics of measles, mumps and smallpox were the primary threat at the beginning of the war, by the time the 179th was raised in 1864 the threat had shifted to what Drew Gilpin Faust referred to as "the intractable camp illnesses: diarrhea and dysentery, typhoid and malaria." Throughout the Civil War, nearly three-quarters of Union soldiers suffered from "serious bowel complaints." [20]

Contaminated water was the most serious threat to the health of the Civil War soldier. There was little if any understanding among the officers or the surgeons - -much less the enlisted men- of the importance of distancing the latrines from the water supply. [21] Lieutenant Finch told *The Hornellsville Tribune* in July 1864 that: "Water is poor and fast becoming scarce. A drought of nearly two months duration prevails." [22]

Typhoid fever caused about two-thirds of the disease related deaths in the 179th New York. [23] In November 1864, the Army of the Potomac's medical director had conducted an investigation into an outbreak of "typho-malarial fever" in the 179th New York and two other regiments in the Ninth Corps. His investigation:

> developed the fact that the men "burrowed" to some extent, their camps were on low ground near a swamp, and the issue of vegetables had been neglected. In order to secure vegetables in that corps two pounds of coffee in each 100 rations were dropped, and in lieu of this sixty pounds of potatoes and seventeen pounds onions were furnished. [2]

George Worthington Adams wrote in *Doctors in Blue* that: "The only serious rival of camp filth as a health menace was poor and unbalanced diet. ... Whatever the official ration table might say, active armies sometimes went without vegetable issues for weeks or months." [25]

Today, we think of diarrhea as nothing more than an unpleasant inconvenience, but during the Civil War, it was a potential killer. In the 179th New York, it caused about a quarter of the disease-related deaths. [26]

Disease was so prevalent that the soldiers took it as a fact of military life. Company K's Abner Welch, a twenty-five-year-old farmer, wrote his parents in October 1864 that: "I am as well as common for here, but at home I should call myself unwell." [27] (If Welch got better it was not for long. He was admitted to the Ninth Corps Hospital with typhoid fever on December 11, 1864 and died four days later.) [28] Sickness was so much a fact of everyday life in the 179th that its absence was noteworthy. Company C recorded in its Morning Report for November 11, 1864: "No one sick this morning." [29]

Treatment for disease was primitive. Blackberry roots were considered by the soldiers to be the best remedy for diarrhea. [30] James C. Rutan recalled that after being stricken with diarrhea during the move south from Alexandria he had tried to remain with the 179th and not go to the hospital by "administering remedies to himself such as steeping blackberry leaves and roots and taking opiates, & etc. & etc." [31] Opiates in fact had a constipating effect. [32]

Company B's John H. Kerrick, a twenty-one-year-old teacher from Bradford County, Pennsylvania, received the following treatment for chronic diarrhea: "The Diarrhea being of a common inflammatory type was arrested by Pills of Opium & Camphor or Pills of Opium and Accetas Humbic [?] whilst [illeg.] was administered to build up strength and appetite." The treatment for Company A's Levi Jones was "Astringent & Tonics, Stimulant. Careful Diet." Company D's Francis Harvey received "Opiates. Alteratives [?], Tonic, Astrygens [?] Careful Diet." [33]

The letters of Company I's John Cook, an eighteen-year-old farmer from Newfield, to his parents described his suffering in varying levels of detail:

> I am in a fever suffering greatly. ... I am not abel to rite. (May 11, 1865)

> I have the Inflamatory Rheumatism and Remittent fever. My right foot & hand was swelled up like cushions, the Doctor lanced them and there run a half pint of blood and matter from them. I have flax seed meal poultice on them now. ... I get good food, but have no appetite to eat except milk porridge. I am to sick to write, so I asked a comrade to write for me. (May 28, 1865)

> I am requested by your son to write you ... He says he feels worse than when last he wrote and is very poor and entirely helpless and suffers a good deal of pain in his right leg the right hand is also helpless and useless. ... I am so poor and sore that it hurts me to be lifted in bed, but I must lay and suffer all. ... I have the dysentery very bad and it runs me down very low and makes me weak. (June 20, 1865)

> I am a little better thank God. I had my foot lanced eight times, my hand three and my right thumb once. ... Mother, I don't want you and father to worry about me for I keep up good courage and I hope I will be able to go home soon. (June 30, 1865)

> I am not quite so well as I was when I last rote .... I don't think I can stand it long. [T]ell [my brothers and sisters] that I don't know as I ever will get home to see them and Father I want you to come as quick as you get this letter. (July 20, 1865)

I am not as well as usual. I am failing all the time. (August 8, 1865)

Cook died of remittent fever on August 18, 1865.[34]

Company B's Paulding Vincent, a twenty-three-year-old laborer from Alfred, also suffered, as described by his doctor:

> This patient transferred from... [on August 2, 1864] in a perfectly delerious condition profuse diarrhea... Pulse ... very feeble. Stimulants with Brandy were freely employed but evidently to no purpose. I kept a nurse sitting by him constantly to observe and meet every emergency with the appropriate prescription. He continued to sink until 7 o'clock P.M. August 4th when he died [of typhoid fever and chronic diarrhea].[35]

Even if the men were not sick enough to go to hospital and remained in camp, they still suffered. John Andrews wrote in November 1864 that: "Night after night I hear the groans of the sick as they sit shivering around the campfires, or as they go moaning along by on their way to the sink [latrine]."[36]

We are still trying to understand the mental health problems caused by war as we have seen the effects of traumatic brain injury and post-traumatic stress disorder resulting from the wars in Vietnam, Iraq and Afghanistan. Eric Dean, Jr. demonstrated that these problems existed during the Civil War in *Shook Over Hell: Post-Traumatic Stress, Vietnam, and the Civil War*, despite the long held view to the contrary.[37]

The army was not completely oblivious to mental health concerns during the Civil War. There did seem to be some recognition of the stress caused by duty in the trenches. In a December 26, 1864 report, the medical director of the Army of the Potomac observed that:

> The position occupied by the Ninth Corps at the front was exposed to continual picket-firing (often kept up in the night) and to sharpshooters, whose skill and vigilence severely taxed the energies and health of the men at the midsummer season.[38]

When John Andrews arrived at the front in October 1864, he heard that sector referred to as "Hell' as all our boys call it who have been there all Summer. For three months they lay there and during the whole time were constantly under the fire of the rebel batteries and exposed to rebel sharpshooters."[39]

The problem was that the Army did not know how to deal with mental illness and tended to dismiss its various manifestations under the rubric "nostalgia." Soldiers with mental health problems were generally seen as malingerers.[40] Mental health counseling was not available.

The Army did have a special hospital in Washington for "Insane Soldiers." Company F's Carl Frederick, a fifty-six-year-old farmer born in Denmark, was wounded in the June 17 assault. He was admitted to the general hospital in Annapolis on June 20, 1864. A military surgeon later certified that Frederick was "suffering from insanity symptoms of which were observed immediately after admission and have increased to the present time." Frederick was admitted to the "Government Hospital for the Insane" on October 1, 1864. He was discharged on June 5, 1865 "because of having recovered his reason."[41]

Company B's Samuel Champlin, a thirty-four-year-old farmer from Alfred, was admitted to the First Division hospital with acute diarrhea on July 2, 1864. He was transferred to general hospital and given a furlough on September 8, 1864. For the next several months his personal physician filed the standard letters that he was still sick and unable to travel. Champlin returned to Slough

General Hospital in Alexandria. Apparently there was a change in Champlin's behavior that came to the attention of his family and/or friends. (He was diagnosed as suffering from "chronic eczema.") In May 1865, Champlin's personal physician traveled to Alexandria to examine him. While stating that he had treated Champlin for chronic diarrhea while he was on furlough, Champlain was now "afflicted with mental aberration or derangement which is liable to terminate in general and perhaps incurable insanity." (Because the war was all but over, it seems unlikely that Champlin was feigning mental illness.) Champlin's doctor proposed that Champlin be released to his care and that he would "exonerate and indemnify the U. S. Government from all responsibility." The proposal became moot with Champlin's discharge on May 25. [42]

However, Champlin's mental health problems continued after the war. He entered the Government Hospital for the Insane in 1868 with "chronic mania." In 1871, a surgeon concluded that: "the disease has gradually developed into demenia" and that it was "of a permanent character." [43]

While John Andrews does not appear to have been incapacitated at any time by the "blue devils," he was willing to acknowledge their existence. In December, he wrote his brother that: "I am troubled tremendously with the blue devils." On March 3, 1865, he recorded in his journal: "Have felt quite down-hearted today. Had company all the time nearly. Still I had the 'blues'". The next day he did not finish a letter because of the "blues". On March 6, he recorded: "Owing to the 'blues' have done nothing today." [44]

The Army also did not know how to deal with traumatic brain injury. The cases of Company H's Charles Flint, a twenty-eight-year-old boatman, and Company G's Casper Notter, a twenty-eight-year-old farmer, are interesting to consider as possible examples of traumatic brain injury, albeit without a proper diagnosis.

In the final assault at Petersburg on April 2, 1865, an artillery shell burst near Flint's head. He was not reported as wounded, nor was he admitted to hospital. However, after the battle Flint complained of severe head pain and his sergeant, Harry Ap Rees, thought "his manner thereafter [was] strange and his mind seeming to be affected." When the 179th New York was discharged in June, Flint requested Ap Rees to accompany him home to Lockport. One of Flint's sisters recalled that: "all the while he was in Lockport he suffered intensely with his head. He had such a fever a great deal of pain & he could take no nourishment." His family did what they could for him, "rubbing his head with ammonia & camphor, he was almost crazed with pain." After three days, Flint decided to go visit his brother in Titusville, Pennsylvania. Several days after arriving in Titusville, Flint died. The diagnosis was brain fever. [45]

Notter suffered a "concussion of the brain" at the Battle of the Crater caused by an artillery shell. He was returned to the 179th New York on August 1. On August 5, he shot himself in the hand and had two fingers amputated. Shortly thereafter, he suffered from a loss of speech and hearing. He was furloughed from the Alexandria General Hospital in November, but overstayed his furlough before returning. He was finally discharged from the Army in March 1865. The charge of desertion for overstaying the furlough was removed in January 1865. [46] The fact that Notter was not court-martialed for his self-inflicted wound suggests that the Army understood that extenuating circumstances were involved.

The venereal disease rate for the Union army overall was about eight percent. The dozen or so cases documented in the Carded Medical Records suggest a much lower incidence of venereal disease in the 179th New York Volunteers than in the Union army overall. However, the Carded Medical Records undoubtedly understate the incidence of venereal disease in the 179th New York.

The multiple records for these thirteen indicate that some clerks were more sympathetic than others, sometimes recording only "sick" rather than "syphilis" or "gonorrhea" or simply leaving the "Diagnosis" or "Complaint" line blank. [47]

The state of medical knowledge with respect to surgery was no better than it was with respect to physical and mental illness. As one surgeon recalled in 1918,

> It can easily be understood how and why we surgeons in 1861-65, utterly unaware of bacteria and their dangers, in our ignorant innocence committed grievous mistakes, which nearly always imperiled life and often actually caused death. ... We operated in old, blood-stained and often pus-stained coats ... We operated with clean hands in the social sense, but they were undisinfected hands. ... We used undisinfected instruments from undisinfected plush-lined cases, and still worse, used marine sponges which had been used in prior pus cases and had been only washed in tap water. If a sponge or an instrument fell on the floor it was washed and squeezed in a basin of tap water and used as if it were clean. [48]

Edgar Lattin

Therefore, wounds from enemy bullets and artillery shells presented a two-fold threat to the soldier – physical damage to his body and the possibility of fatal infection. The soft minie ball used by both sides shattered the bones it struck. Amputation was the best way to limit serious infection. The operation was generally performed in the field hospital the day of the battle or soon thereafter. Company B's Capt. Robert Stewart had the lower third of his leg amputated the night of June 17. Company D's Edgar Lattin had part of his arm amputated right after the Battle of the Crater. [49] Contrary to popular myth, both Union and Confederate surgeons generally had chloroform available as an anesthetic. [50]

However, amputation was not without risk. Of the nearly 30,000 Union soldiers undergoing amputation, more than a quarter died. [51] Adjutant James Bowker and Company D's Lucius Kinnon were among those who died following amputation. The medical chart for Kinnon recorded that:

> Supporting treatment and poultices to stump which did not [mend?] properly.
> The patient seemed in good condition–appetite good and very little pain. On Saturday morning was as well as usual. On Ev'ng of Saturday June 25th/64 Died of Asthenia [loss of strength]. [5]

When Lt. Jeffrey Wisner was wounded in the arm in October 1864 while on picket, Dr. Robinson recommended amputation, but Wisner declined and survived. [53] Similarly, Company B's Samuel Coon recalled that when he arrived at Fairfax Seminary Hospital after being wounded in the calf: "The assistant Surgeon was going to take my leg off but I begged & scolded & took on so that finally the Surgeon in charge came in... He examined my leg and said it could and should be saved." [54]

Even when there was no bone damage, infection could still be fatal. The Surgeon at the Buffalo General Hospital wrote the following report on Company B's Israel Graves, a nineteen-year-old farmer from Aleghany County:

> suffering from Gun Shot Wound of middle posterior part of right Thigh without injury to the bones, July 28th. The wound became gangreneous and gradually extended, producing a great deal of constitutional sympathy, had

considerable Diarrhea at times, which yielded readily to treatment, on the morning of August 27th Hemorrhage from the Femoral Artery took place, lost considerable blood. Tourniquet was applied immediately, lived about two hours. [55]

Soldiers suffering from infected wounds had a surprising ally. After serving on hospital duty at White House Landing, Daniel Lee wrote his wife that: "the wounded men is got magets in their sores and does stink so bad." [56] Disgusting as that sounds, the maggots actually helped recovery by eating the diseased flesh. [57]

The enormous number of casualties–sick and wounded–required the Army to reorganize how it provided medical care. By the time the 179th New York Volunteers reached the field in the summer of 1864, the Army of the Potomac had replaced reliance on the regimental field hospital with a system of "depot" hospitals at the division, corps and army levels. [58]

After the Battle of Cold Harbor, the Army of the Potomac moved its depot hospital from White House Landing, where a number of soldiers from the 179th New York had been temporarily detailed, to City Point in conjunction with the change of front to Petersburg. [5]

[Sketch: City Point Depot Hospital]

The City Point facility was an impressive complex, temporary though it was. It covered 200 acres on a broad plain on the south side of the James River about a mile from City Point heading toward Petersburg. (Today, the John Randolph Medical Center occupies the site.) Twelve hundred tents "abutt[ing] on streets sixty feet wide" with a main avenue 180 feet wide provided a capacity of 10,000 patients. From May 16 through the end of October 1864, the Army of the Potomac Depot Hospital handled nearly 70,000 patients. [60]

[Photo: City Point Hospital Wharf]

Supplies were ample for the depot hospital at City Point. The Army of the Potomac's Chief Medical Officer, Edward B. Dalton, reported in December, 1864:

> The purveying department met all necessary demands with promptness and liberality. Nothing really essential to the care of the wounded was wanting. Bedsacks and blankets were supplied without stint, although for a time bedsacks were dispensed with, except in the severer cases, a large proportion of the patients being placed upon sacks amply filled with straw and arranged upon the ground beneath the tents. None were without shelter. Drugs and dressings in abundance, hospital stores, ice and even delicacies were constantly issued; cooking stoves, caldrons and portable ovens were on hand in sufficient quantity for any emergency. [61]

Because of this logistical support, the City Point Depot Hospital became the outstanding field hospital of the war. [62]

However, the depot hospitals near the field were not intended to provide long-term care. Hospitals in the rear were necessary. [63] The Chief Medical Officer of the Army of the Potomac's Depot Field Hospital at City Point described the Army's practice at the end of 1864 as follows: "[the wounded], especially the severely hurt, were sent north as rapidly as possible, while the sick, as a general rule, were removed only when the character of the case rendered a change of climate essential to recovery." [64]

A system of general hospitals – so-called because their patients were not limited to soldiers from particular units – had been built since the beginning of the war. [65] Medical facilities to treat wounded and sick soldiers was one of the many areas where the federal army was woefully unprepared for war. Before the Civil War, the federal army had only one military hospital – a forty bed facility at Fort Leavenworth. Soldiers were generally sent home for medical treatment in the peacetime army. [66]

The need for additional facilities to treat soldiers after the first level of care in the field became quickly apparent. By June 30, 1864, the Union had built 190 general hospitals with 120,000 beds, and by the end of the war, 204 hospitals with 137,000 beds. [67] The new hospitals generally used the "pavilion" design originated by Florence Nightingale to provide more ventilation. Pavilion hospitals could be constructed fairly quickly. Saterlee General Hospital with a capacity of 2,500 beds was built in forty days. [68]

[Lithograph: Mower Hospital]

Mower Hospital in Philadelphia, with a staff of 622, was the largest hospital in the world at the time. (At least thirty men from the 179th New York were patients at Mower.) [69] During the course of the war over one million Union soldiers were treated in these general hospitals. [70]

The effectiveness of this hospital system was not only important to the soldiers who were patients. It had strategic implications as well. Margaret Humphreys concluded in *Marrow of Tragedy: The Health Crisis of the American Civil War* that:

> The Union ... created a more effective system to put [its] men back in the ranks after they became sick or wounded. Armies were central to the war, and health care was central to the armies' numbers and effectiveness. There can be no doubt that the Union marshaled and employed the tools available in mid-nineteenth century medicine to greater advantage than did the Confederacy. [71]

The men of the 179th New York had a direct interest in these general hospitals. Nearly five hundred men from the 179th – nearly half of those who passed through its ranks–spent time in one or more of these general hospitals. Ord. was not exaggerating about the 179th being "represented in many a Hospital" when he described the impact of sickness on the 179th in August 1864. As of August 14, 1864, sixty-eight men from the 179th were sick in twenty-nine different general hospitals. [72]

Martin Wilkin

Ward K at Armory Square Hospital in Washington (see photo in the endnote) is often presented to show what a typical ward looked like. The 179th New York's Adjutant, James Bowker, was a patient in Ward K, and another dozen soldiers from the 179th, including Company F's Martin Wilkens, were patients at Armory Square. [73]

The treatment of Co. K's Orrin Hawkins, a thirty-eight-year-old farmer from Candor in Tioga County, illustrates the hierarchy of treatment facilities. Hawkins suffered a gunshot wound to the thigh on October 28, 1864 while on picket duty. He was wounded around 8 a.m. and carried back to camp by two soldiers. He was then carried to an ambulance which took him to the field hospital where his wound was dressed. The regimental surgeon then directed that Hawkins be taken to the Ninth Corps Hospital at City Point. Hawkins was first taken by ambulance to the Weldon Railroad junction with the U.S. Military Railroad and then by train to City Point, about fifteen miles away. He arrived at City Point that same evening. On November 6, 1864, he was transported from City Point to Washington on the U.S.A. Hospital Steamer Connecticut. He was admitted to Mt. Pleasant U.S.A. General Hospital the following day. He was furloughed for a month on January 3, 1865 and ultimately returned to duty on February 9, 1865. [74]

[Sketch: Ninth Corps Hospital]

Although the improved facilities and system of care were superior to the medical care provided to soldiers in past wars, the soldiers of the 179th New York still had a generally low opinion of it. Company D's William Tuck, was wounded in the hand on April 2, 1865 and taken to the field hospital. He later called it "the Slaughter House." [75]

After returning from a hospital, Company B's William Lamont wrote his sister that: "I was very sick when I went there but came out alive, but there was a great many died when I was there most of them for want of care. ... They do not give a man long to decide which way he will go." [76] Lamont remained skeptical about the quality of hospital care. In January 1865, he wrote that: "Moses Brown has gone to hospital. I think the next we hear from him he will be dead." [77] Brown in fact died of acute bronchitus/congestion of the lungs on January 19, 1865 in the Ninth Corps Hospital at City Point. [78] Still, despite his skepticism, Lamont also survived a second hospital stay at the end of the war for "general debility." [79]

Separate hospitals were built for officers. Captain Bird had a higher opinion of his medical care at the Officers Hospital in Annapolis, Maryland.

> This is a very fine place here the Hosp is on the grounds of the Naval School in a lot of fine brick buildings on the shore of the Chesapike Bay. I have a good room well furnished and good board and attendance for which I have to pay $1.00 per day.

> We get plenty of fresh fish and oysters here and there is a fine chance of bathing and boating and plenty of peaches and melons very cheap so I don't care how long they keep me here.

> There is about 400 wounded officers here and we are not allowed to leave the ground without a pass but we have everything we need inside. [80]

The general hospitals were located far from the front. The first general hospitals were concentrated in the Washington and Philadelphia areas. At end of 1862, "a host of politicians, benevolent ladies and state agents began lobbying to have general hospitals established in their home states and to have as many as possible of the wounded sent to them." [81] One of the hospitals that lobbied to receive more soldiers was St. Mary's Hospital in Rochester, New York and soldiers of the 179th New York were among the beneficiaries. [82]

[Sketch: St. Mary's Hospital]

St. Mary's had been officially contracted as a military hospital in March 1863. The hospital was paid $5.50 per week for each military patient, although no payment was made for periods when the patient was on furlough granted by the hospital. Relatively few patients were received during the first year. Only twenty-four soldiers were under the hospital's care in April 1863. The hospital had originally expected to receive approximately one hundred soldiers from the Rochester area who had been furloughed from other hospitals. However, when their furloughs ended, the soldiers were ordered back to those other hospitals. In May 1864, a delegation including the Mayor of Rochester traveled to Washington and successfully argued to the Surgeon General that sick soldiers from Western New York would be better off "quartered" in hospitals located in Western New York. In short order, St. Mary's Hospital began to prepare for the arrival of upwards of three hundred sick and wounded soldiers. Dr. Azel Backus, the surgeon at St. Mary's Hospital, went to New York City to accompany the wounded back to Rochester. [83]

On June 7, 1864, 375 soldiers arrived in Rochester, via the Erie Railroad. They were met at the depot by a group of ladies who provided lunch and "other luxuries and necessities." There were no ambulances at the hospital in those days and the soldiers were accordingly transported from the station to St. Mary's Hospital (and Rochester City Hospital) by "hackmen" offering their services for free and by street car, courtesy of the street railway company. Another seventy-five soldiers arrived nine days later. By the time the first soldiers from the 179th New York arrived on August 9, this new phase was well underway. The soldiers from the 179th, with their residences if known, were the following: D.H. Sheppard (Van Etten, Chemung County); James C. Rutan (Horseheads, Chemung County); William Gibson; Abram O. Gray; William T. Wise (Elmira, Chemung County); William W. Arnold; and Alexander Gardner. [84]

No civilian patients were treated at St. Mary's at this time. The number of soldiers under care apparently varied from 400 to as many as 700 at a time. At times, patient beds were placed in the corridors and even in tents on the hospital grounds. [85]

Individual soldiers, as well as their friends and families, also lobbied for their transfer to hospitals closer to home, albeit with mixed success. Company A's William Chamberlain was transferred to Elmira in October 1864 on the recommendation of the surgeons in Alexandria. [86] Also from Company A, Eleazer Baldwin's request to be transferred from Washington to Rochester was granted. [87]

However, the request by Company F's Sgt. John Durham, who was wounded on June 17, to be transferred to Elmira was denied despite his pointing out that he was serving his second tour of duty. However, he did later receive a furlough to recuperate at home. [88] The brother of Company I's Nicoll Jones, who was wounded in the Battle of Poplar Spring Church, unsuccessfully tried to pull political strings to have him transferred to Elmira "where he will be near home." The military surgeon concluded that Jones was unable to travel because of his wound. Jones remained in Alexandria until he was discharged in June 1865. [89]

Even better than a transfer to a nearer hospital was a furlough to home. Of the approximately five hundred men of the 179th New York who were patients at a general hospital, about one-third received furloughs of varying lengths. [90] Among those receiving a furlough was Company D's Jacob Hausner. Harewood Hospital attached his photo to his furlough paper, thus making it one of the first "Photo ID's." [91]

The standard for sick leave was that the soldier would not be fit for duty within thirty days, but was still able to travel. No more than twenty percent of the patients could be on furlough at any one time from a particular hospital. [92]

The fact that a soldier was able to travel did not necessarily mean that he was in good health. In some cases, the medical officers may have recommended that a leave of absence be granted because of concerns that the soldier was likely to die. When James Bowker, the 179th's adjutant, applied for a thirty day leave of absence following amputation of his arm, the surgeon in charge of the Ninth Corps field hospital at City Point recommended that Bowker's request be granted "inasmuch as his recovery will be remote and uncertain." While Bowker's request apparently was granted, he did not make it home and died in Armory Square Hospital October 26, 1864. Soldiers from the 179th who were able to make it home from the hospital for the opportunity to die a "good death" in the presence of their families included Company A's David Leonard; Company B's Samuel H. Lane and Homer Olcott; and Company K's Arthur Carmen. [93]

Hausner Furlough

Col. William Gregg, 179th New York Volunteers

CHAPTER FOURTEEN

A Regiment at Last!

As noted, a standard regiment during the Civil War was comprised of ten companies. Anything less was referred to as a battalion or a detachment. [1] A regiment was entitled to its own flag. A battalion or detachment was not. The 179th New York Volunteers had come south in the Spring of 1864 with only six companies joined by a seventh just before the Battle of the Crater and thus was not a full-fledged regiment entitled to a flag. As John Andrews noted, "The regiment not being a regiment has been all through the summer campaign without colors." (emphasis in original)[2] Indeed, the 179th was referred to as a battalion in the Army of the Potomac's June 30, 1864 Table of Organization. [3]

The symbolic importance to the Civil War soldier of his regiment's flag as the personification of his regiment cannot be overestimated. Countless soldiers died for the honor of carrying the regimental flag to glory at the head of a charge. The 179th's color sergeant, Charles E. Hogan, was shot dead planting the 179th's colors on the Confederate fortifications near Fort Mahone on April 2, 1865. [4] Ord.'s lament in August 1864 that the 179th was "a detachment of six companies without colors" [seven companies counting Company G] reflects a clear sense of lesser status being in a unit without a flag. [5]

In mid-September, the 179th's final three companies – H, I and K – arrived in the field. When the 179th was presented with its colors at a dress parade on October 13, 1864, the soldiers of the 179th received the flag "with hearty cheers." [6] The "national colors" of the 179th would ultimately be inscribed with the following battles: "Petersburg, June 17th and July 30th, 1864; Weldon Railroad; Poplar Spring Church; Hatcher's Run; Petersburg, April 1st and 2nd, 1865."[7]

Regimental Guidon

A full complement of ten companies also meant that the 179th was authorized a full colonel. Having completed recruitment of the 179th in September, Colonel Gregg left Elmira and assumed command in the field the evening of October 8. "The boys went out in front of his tent and gave him twice six rousing cheers – they appeared pleased at the idea of having a colonel at last."[8]

The fact that the 179th had arrived at the front four companies short of a full regiment had not gone unnoticed in the field. After the 179th was reassigned to the First Division's Second Brigade, Col. Elisha Marshall, the brigade commander, wrote to Major A.S. Divan, the Assistant Provost Marshal in Elmira on July 24, 1864, beseeching him: "Cannot you assist in filling up & completing the 179 NY Vols?"[9]

The day before, the War Department had reassigned Company A of the 180th New York Volunteers as Company G of the 179th. Company G had arrived just in time for the Battle of the Crater. And recruiting had been given high priority back north. Two weeks before Marshall sent his letter, Captain Terrill, then acting commander of the 179th, wrote Major Diven on behalf of the 179th's officers in the field, who "were becoming worn out ... owing to the severe duties imposed upon them" and "unofficially" requested Divan to return Lieuts. Holden and Wisner to the field to "share the duties." Diven's answer has not been located, but the immediate answer apparently was negative because Holden and Wisner remained on recruiting duty for another two months until the last three companies of the 179th were filled.[10]

The 179th faced a difficult recruiting challenge. Not only did the 179th have to recruit three more companies to complete its organization as a regiment, but the 179th also had to recruit men to replace the soldiers in the first seven companies lost to battle and disease. Recruiting in the summer of 1864 was even harder than it had been in the spring. Fewer men were available to recruit and local governments had to increase their bounties, which set off a competition among them with spiraling bounties. The 179th also had to compete with other units seeking to replace their losses in the field. For example, Capt. Harry Shipman enlisted 101 recruits for the 137th New York.[11] Moreover, the 179th New York was not just competing with other infantry regiments. Other branches of the military competed on the basis of less hazardous duty. "If you wish to avoid carrying a Musket ... and from up to [illegible] pounds on your back and avoid doing picket duty, enlist in the 16th Independent [Artillery] Battery."[12] The navy also presented a safer alternative for potential recruits.[13]

Recruiting had continued after the first companies of the 179th had left for Virginia at the end of April, but the results had not been fruitful. Giles Holden reported from Rochester on July 5, 1864 that he had not been able to secure any additional men for the 179th. He complained that "it seems almost impossible to get a man accepted by the examining surgeon" in Rochester, Dr. Azel Backus (who was also the Chief Surgeon at St. Mary's Hospital, one of the U.S.A. General Hospitals). He expressed the frustration that "quite a number of men that I have had rejected have fallen into the hands of brokers [and] run off to other Districts and accepted." He planned to go to Lockport where the local authorities offered a bounty that was $100 more than in Rochester. He also noted that Rochester's Bounty Committee was considering raising its local bounty to $400.[14]

By the end of July, Holden was back in Rochester and briefly optimistic: "I am doing very well now considering everything. Am getting about five men per week." He was encouraged that "the people seem to be waking up to the necessity of putting their [illegible] to the work and will try hard to fill the quota." Half of those he was recruiting went as substitutes, half as volunteers. He hoped to "fill an entire company before the 5th of September." [15]

However, by mid-August, Holden had become pessimistic. He had no new recruits to report from Rochester, explaining that "But few volunteers are offering, and those for regiments originally raised here." Once again, the grass seemed greener in Lockport. "I think if I were transferred to Lockport (29th Dist) I should do far better, as these recruits are offering more freely." [16]

At that time, the 179th still had only about forty recruits in Elmira for the eighth company (H). The 180th had only twelve recruits in Elmira and once again it was recommended that they be reassigned to the 179th New York. [17]

Later in August, Holden did report two new recruits from Rochester, but he apparently was branching out his efforts. He said that he had the "promise" of ten men from nearby Livonia in Livingston County and hoped for ten to twenty-five men from Yates County and Orleans County. [18]

However, when it came to converting these volunteers into soldiers, Holden encountered problems from the provost marshal's office. In response to a district inquiry about whether volunteers could be mustered for the 179th and 180th New York Volunteers, Major Diven immediately responded:

> Your attention is called to repeated printed circulars sent to your office and to at least two written circulars from this office issued within a few weeks wherein it explicitly states Provost Marshals can not muster for regiments whose organization have not been once completed. The 179th has only six companies. The 180th has no companies at all. When you can muster for them you shall be advised. [19]

Fortunately for the 179th New York, this prohibition was rescinded soon thereafter. [20]

Company D's Lt. J. Amherst Wisner had a fair amount of increasing success in Elmira in August and September 1864, recruiting one man during the week ending August 6, three the week ending August 13, seven the week ending August 20, two the week ending August 27, five men the week ending September 3, five men the week ending September 10 and twelve men the week ending September 17. [21] Once the original companies had been refilled and the new Companies H, I and K left for the front, the need for heavy recruiting ended. Wisner left Elmira to rejoin the 179th in Virginia on September 21. The *Elmira Daily Advertiser* proudly announced:

> Lieut. Wisner is Elmira born and has grown to youthful manhood in our midst and the wishes of a multi[tude] will desire his safety and success amid the perils to which he will soon be exposed. It is hoped that he will return home when the war is over, laden with a warrior's full fame and glory. [22]

As noted, local government bounties had had to be increased. The *Elmira Daily Advertiser* had worried at the end of July 1864 that the Board of Supervisors had not set the bounties high enough:

> Men are daily examining where they can obtain the largest pay, and are governed entirely in their preference of the town or city that pays the largest bounties. If some town in Washington or Yates county offers a larger bounty than can be obtained here, then all the volunteers enlisting here will be secured for those towns rather than for us. ... While waiting for the action of the Board of Supervisors, we lost several recruits who were residents of our own city, whose enlistment was credited to towns in distant counties. [23]

The General Recruiting Office in Elmira advertised in August 1864 the "Highest Bounties Yet." [24] The local bounty of $400 and national bounty of $300 for a three year enlistment may have been the highest paid up to that point, but that total would soon prove uncompetitive.

The *Yates County Chronicle* reported at the beginning of September that:

> The Board of Supervisors assembled again on Monday last, and immediately raised the Bounties to $650 for one year; $750 for two years; and $850 for three years. This was deemed sufficient and satisfactory, but citizens of the town of Torrey, assuming to act for the town, immediately offered $250 higher and enlisted a dozen of more men in this village, in time to be sent to Avon the next morning. This action on the part of that town, induced the citizens of Milo to hold a public meeting, (elsewhere noticed) and resolve to raise a Town Bounty of $300. Other towns adopted like measures, and the whole matter seems to be growing into one of reckless competition. [25]

In Watkins (Schuyler County), John Andrews also encountered free-market competition:

> Starkey [Yates County] raised the bounty to $1400 for one year recruits, and for two or three days there was a great rush through Watkins to Starkey, and I could do nothing at recruiting – I only got one man, James A. Haddock. Our bounties then were but $600 for one year and a hundred additional for two, and two hundred additional for three years. [26]

The Schuyler County Board of Supervisors subsequently raised the bounty to $800 for one year and $900 and $1000 for two and three years. Nearby Reading raised an additional $100 and Dix an additional $200 per recruit by private subscriptions. (Andrews' father apparently was among the contributors.) [27]

Within the space of a week or so, Andrews raised twenty-five new soldiers, a little short of the thirty that Colonel Gregg expected for a second lieutenant, but Gregg still offered that rank to Andrews.

In September 1864, A. B. Galatian had traveled to Tennessee to try to find volunteers there to fill Elmira's quota. He was not alone. One hundred forty-five recruiting agents from other parts of the North were also there. They all returned home without success when General Sherman forbade recruiting in Tennessee. [28] Broome, Schuyler and Yates Counties' recruiting agents were equally unsuccessful in their forays down south. [29]

While efforts to complete Company H and replenish the prior seven companies continued across much of the Southern Tier, recruiting for Companies I and K was much more focused. Edwin Bowen from Newfield in Tompkins County had been authorized by Governor Seymour to raise a company and he filled most of what became Company I with recruits from four towns in the county – Danby, Newfield, Ithaca and Caroline. Similarly, Company K under Moses Van Benschoten, a veteran of the 23rd New York, was filled primarily from towns in Broome County and to a lesser extent from towns in adjacent Tioga County. Ten or so volunteers came from nearby Bradford County in Pennsylvania – presumably attracted by the high New York bounties. [30]

That does not mean that recruiting in Tompkins County and Broome County was at all easy.

Bowen was a thirty-three year old farmer, married with two young children. His real property was valued at $1000 in the 1860 census. [31] His August 17, 1864 advertisement in the *Ithaca Journal* presented a supposed simple choice: "$592 for one year, and No Draft! or a Draft and No Pay! Which will you choose?" Bowen also promoted "the opportunity for the men of Newfield and Tompkins County, to go all together, and have an opportunity to chose their own officers, while drafted men are sent anywhere at the pleasure of the Government." [32]

The $592 number advertised by Bowen was comprised of a $300 county bounty, a $100 federal government bounty and a year's pay of $192 at $16 per month. (It did not include a component for the town bounty.) A week later, the *Ithaca Journal* reported that Bowen was "progressing well." [33] However, progress toward filling all the town quotas for Tompkins County to avoid a draft on September 5 must not have looked very encouraging because on August 27, the Board of Supervisors doubled the bounty to $600 for one year and $800 for two years. [34]

The *Ithaca Journal*, a pro-Lincoln paper, pushed hard for voluntary enlistments, highlighting the money and downplaying the risk of harm:

> Men of Tompkins County; the Board of Supervisors have acted nobly, patriotically, generously! They have placed within the reach of any one who chooses to accept it means sufficient to buy a farm, and require in return only a single year's service in behalf of your country!
>
> The war is near its close. It cannot possibly last another year. It will probably not last another six months. Should the new call be substantially filled during the next few weeks, by volunteers before the 5th, or by draft immediately thereafter, it is doubtful if another battle will have to be fought to finish the rebellion. ... the overwhelming force which our Government is about to send against them, and the very fact of our overpowering numbers will of itself be likely to render any further fighting unnecessary.
>
> Here is a chance to lay by more clear money in one year, than many men can hope to save in several long years of hard patient toil and the closest economy. Many men in the county have labored hard for ten, fifteen and twenty years, and pinched and save, and yet not worth today $700. *Seven Hundred Dollars* can be put at interest at once, out of this enterprise, and still leave the wages untouched. Or $1000 can be put at interest for two years service. Will not patriotism and a commendable love of gain prompt an immediate response? (Italics in original) [35]

The citizens of Dryden held a special meeting on August 8 to support recruiting efforts. Their resolutions included requesting the Town's Supervisor and War Committee "to make use of all necessary means to maintain the high patriotic character of the Town, and save it, if possible from the necessity of a draft." [36] Five war meetings were held in Danby the last two weeks in August – Supervisor Curtis was present to "receive recruits, pay all the bounties ... and furnish transportation to Owego [where the district provost marshal's office was located]." [37] In Ithaca, stores were closed at 4 p.m. "to give opportunity for all to unite in war meetings." [38] News of the fall of Atlanta to General Sherman reached Ithaca on September 3, which may have helped stir patriotic fervor. [39]

At the end of August, the pro-McClellan (Ithaca) *Citizen & Democrat* confidently predicted that a draft would be necessary. [40] However, in the end, not only did Bowen recruit a full company, but the towns of Tompkins County met their quotas and avoided a draft. [41]

In Broome County, where Company K of the 179th was principally recruited, the *Broome Weekly Republican* sarcastically reported on August 31, 1864 that: "There is an admirable good prospect for a draft here on the 5th of September, which should be very consoling these hot days." [42] Broome County had raised only ninety soldiers for its quota of 429. Recruiting agent

George Bartlett had advertised earlier in the month a "National Bounty" of $100 and a "County Bounty" of $300 for one year enlistments. [43] The ad did not refer to a town bounty, but there was developing competition among the towns of Broome County. [44]

Binghamton initially adopted a town bounty of $200, but when "the towns surrounding Binghamton had voted to pay $600, [it] became necessary for this place to compete with the other towns on the bounty basis" and Binghamton went to $600 as well the next week. [45] Following a rally at Brigham Hall "filled to overflowing," Binghamton saw some success – "the recruiting office ... has been thronged by volunteers." [46] For the last week before the scheduled draft, businesses in Binghamton closed every afternoon at 4 p.m. [47] Chenango and Vestal also paid a $600 bounty and reported that their quotas had been filled. [48] The *Binghamton Standard* reported that "probably all towns in the county, now pay a town bounty of $600. If any now do not, they probably will before the close of the week." [49]

New recruits for the 179th New York did not come only from New York. Bounties in New York State were considerably higher than in Pennsylvania in the late summer of 1864 and approximately twenty-five men from nearby Bradford County came across the border to volunteer in Owego (Tioga County). The towns of Bradford County did not aggressively utilize local bounties. [50] Immediately after President Lincoln announced the July 18, 1864 call for 500,000 men, Towanda adopted a local bounty of $200 for one year men, but none of the other towns in Bradford had acted by the end of July. (*Bradford Argus*, July 21 and July 28, 1864) The Bradford County men were credited primarily to Dryden in Tompkins County (ten, which apparently helped Dryden meet its quota); and Union in Broome County. About half of the Bradford County men were assigned to Company E as new recruits and nearly half to new Company K. [51]

The demographics for Companies I and K were very similar. Both companies had very high percentages of recruits born in New York and in the United States – 89% and 95% respectively for Company I and 79% and 97.5% respectively for Company K. Company I had only four foreign-born recruits and Company K only two. [52] This made Companies I and K more "native New York" than any of the companies recruited for the 179th in the spring. [53]

Companies I and K were also similarly dominated by farmers – 84% in both companies. Company I's William Howell was an eighteen-year-old farmer from Danby. That percentage far exceeds the percentage for farmers in the first seven companies. (Company B did have 65%.) There were only three laborers in Company K and none in Company I. Company I had three teachers and a student. After farmers, the next most common occupation in Company I was carpenter at four. Company K had two musicians. [54]

William Howell

The makeup of Company I is particularly striking because of the link of its soldiers to the local communities credited for their enlistments. Company I was also the most geographically concentrated of the 179th's companies. Of the eighty-six original recruits in Company I, sixty-three were from Newfield and Danby. Of the sixty-three, thirty-six were farmers who had been born in Newfield or Danby. Another seven had been born in Newfield or Danby and were pursuing other occupations. [55]

Of the other twenty-five of the original eighty-six, another five enlisted in Newfield or Danby, but were born in another part of Tompkins County. Another seven were born in and enlisted from other towns in Tompkins County. [56]

In contrast, Company H turned out to be the 179th's third most diverse company. Relatively low percentages for Company H were born in New York (54%) and the United States (60%). A quarter of the men in Company H were born in Ireland and 7.5% in Canada, with the total foreign-born at 42%. Only Company G at 57% and Company E at 43% had higher percentages of foreign born recruits. [57]

Only forty percent of the men in Company H were farmers – half the percentage for Companies I and K. Thirty-one percent of the men in Company H were laborers. Fifteen different professions made up the remaining thirty percent of Company H. [58]

With respect to age, the average for the first seven companies had been just over twenty-five. Company I was similar with an average of just under twenty-five and a half. However, the men of Company K on average were two years older at just over twenty-seven and the men of Company H were a year older at twenty-six and a half. Fifteen percent of the men in Companies H and K were forty or older, twice the average for the first seven companies. However, the percentage of eighteen-year-olds in Companies H and K was only slightly lower than in the original seven companies. This suggests that Upstate New York still had a strong pool of eligible men in the Fall of 1864. [59]

As opposed to the first seven companies of the 179th, the last three were led by officers and non-commissioned officers with limited prior service.

Company H was led by Capt. Giles Holden, who had been previously promoted to second lieutenant in Company F of the 179th in May. However, he had been on recruiting service and had not been in the field during the 179th's earlier battles. First Lieutenant Fitz Culver had briefly served as an enlisted man in the 44th Infantry. Second Lieutenant Samuel G. Hathaway Musgrave had been promoted from First Sergeant of Company B of the 179th and had originally served as a private in the 23rd New York. He had been wounded in the June 17 assault. [60] Two of Company H's five sergeants had prior service.

"Fitz" Culver

Captain Edwin C. Bowen led Company I, but had not previously served. First Lieutenant Davis C. Marshall and Second Lt. William B. Kinney also had not previously served. [61] None of Company I's five sergeants had prior service.

In Company K, Capt. Moses Van Benschoten had served as a captain in the 23rd New York. However, neither First Lt. Robert Hooper, nor Second Lt. William C. Foster had previously served. [62] One of Company K's sergeants had prior service.

Company H and Company I were mustered into service in Elmira on September 13, 1864. They left Elmira that day and joined the 179th in the field around September 18. [63] Company K was mustered in on September 15 in Elmira, left the following day and arrived in the field on September 20. [64] That the three companies could reach the field from Elmira in five days is an impressive statement of the Union's logistical capability.

The compressed schedule between recruitment of the three companies and their delivery to the field provided even less time for training than had been available to the original companies of the 179th New York.

Company H suffered a similar problem with desertion en route as Company E and Company F had experienced. Five recruits deserted at Elmira on September 13, 1864, the day that Company H was ordered south. Another six deserted from Elmira the following day when Company H departed. Later that day, Company H stopped in Williamsport and another seven soldiers deserted.

When Company H stopped in Harrisburg, one more soldier deserted. [65] Of the nineteen who deserted, ten had said they were born in Ireland and two in Canada. Six had said they were laborers, four farmers and two boatman. [66]

Desertion among the Irish-born and Canadian-born men in Company H was proportionately higher than among the other men. Sixty percent of the Irish-born men in Company H deserted (eleven of eighteen), all but one en route. Two-thirds of the Canadian-born men in Company H deserted (four of six), two en route. [67] Interestingly, fewer Irish-born laborers deserted (about half) than for the Irish-born generally. Because the numbers are so small, it is difficult to draw conclusions about the two other Irish-born men in Company H who did not desert, but one was a farmer and one was a printer.

In striking contrast to Company H, Company I and Company K had no desertions en route. The absence of desertions en route in Companies I and K reflects the close ties of the soldiers to their home towns where they were recruited and enlisted. Morale also seems to have been strong. Company I's John Patterson, a twenty-eight-year-old farmer, wrote his father on September 12 that: "The boys is well and in good spirits." (Patterson died from typhoid fever a month later.) [68]

With respect to nationality, Company I had only two Irish-born soldiers, William Taggert (age thirty-four) and James Cook (age twenty-four) both of whom were farmers who enlisted in Danby. (The 1860 Census records Taggert in Danby, while I could not identify Cook's residence in 1860.) [69] Company K had one Canadian-born soldier – David Russell, a forty-two year old boat caulker. (Company K had no Irish-born men and Company I had no Canadian-born men.)

The performance of the men from Bradford County, Pennsylvania men is also noteworthy. They were enticed across the border by the higher New York bounties. They had passed on the entreaties of the 141st Pennsylvania which was recruiting in August 1864 and advertised itself as "mainly composed of men from Bradford County," but referred only to the $100 federal bounty for one year enlistments. [70] They had no ties with the New York towns where their enlistments were credited. And by enlisting in New York, they were not helping their home towns in Pennsylvania avoid the draft. Thus the Bradford County men enlisting in the 179th New York in the late summer of 1864 would seem to have presented a risk of bounty jumping. [71]

However, none of the men from Bradford County who enlisted in the 179th New York deserted, either en route to the front or from the field. The reasons for this loyalty to duty are not readily apparent. Bradford County was strongly pro-Lincoln, but so were most of the Southern Tier counties in New York. The answer seems to be once again rooted in the ties to the local communities that the Bradford County men would return to after the war. While the *Bradford Argus* and *The Bradford Reporter* had not heavily pushed the duty to the local communities to help avoid a draft, they had promoted the duty to the nation to serve in the army. Thus *The Bradford Reporter* had written that:

> Every citizen ought to be in some way represented in the army; either by personal service or by sending his son or brother, or by furnishing some other at his expense... [W]hoever stands idle now does less than his duty to his country.

> The whole country ought to be divided into but two classes – those who are in the field and those who by their labor at home maintain the families of the absent. [72]

While these Bradford County men were not serving in a Pennsylvania unit, they were still serving their country in the 179th New York.

Support for the elimination of slavery was also stronger in Bradford County than in many areas of the North. David Wilmot, author of the Wilmot Provisio, which would have prohibited slavery in the territory acquired from Mexico, represented Bradford County in Congress from 1845 until 1850 as a Free Soil Democrat. While Bradford County continued to support Wilmot, he did not run for re-election when he lost the support of Tioga and Susquehanna Counties. He later became one of the leaders in the founding of the Republican Party in Pennsylvania and became Pennsylvania's member on the Republican National Executive Committee in 1856. [73]

George Pratt

The first seven companies also began receiving new recruits. Company A received twenty-nine replacement troops who entered the service in August and September 1864, including George Pratt. Sixty percent were farmers, thirty percent were laborers, and ten percent were craftsmen or clerks. [74] Sixty percent had also been born in New York State, while eighteen percent were foreign-born, all but one in Ireland. Their average age was just under twenty-three, but the average was skewed by two men in their forties. Half the new recruits were between the ages of eighteen and twenty. Compared to the original complement of Company A, roughly the same percentage of new recruits was foreign-born, but the percentage of Irish was much higher. [75]

At a time when the 179th was filling its remaining three companies and refilling its original companies with volunteers to become a full regiment, many existing regiments were being replenished from Elmira with draftees and substitutes. On August 11, 1864, a detachment of one hundred drafted men and substitutes was forwarded from Elmira to the 61st New York Volunteers in the Army of the Potomac; one hundred and two to the 104th New York on August 13; and seventy-three to the 104th New York on August 15. Similarly, 198 substitutes were sent to the 86th New York Volunteers and 97 to the 43rd New York Volunteers on October 1. [76] Thus, the 179th New York had a much lower percentage of draftees and substitutes than many other regiments at this time.

The influx of new recruits for the 179th New York created the potential for divides between the new companies and the old companies and within the old companies between the lower bounty veterans and the higher bounty new recruits. The new companies and the new recruits had not endured the June 17 assault and the Battle of the Crater and the new recruits had received bounties that were hundreds of dollars more than the men who enlisted in the original seven companies had received. Potentially even more significant was the fact that the new recruits had been required to enlist for a term of only one year, compared to the three year term for the men enlisting earlier in 1864. [77]

I have not located any express statements by men of the 179th discussing these possible divides in any significant way. The veterans of Company C called themselves the "Old Guard," a reference to Napoleon's Old Guard. However, in the same sentence that Ord. used that phrase, he referred to new recruits bringing Company C "to nearly its former strength" without suggesting that the new recruits were inferior. [78] John Andrews occasionally used the phrase "old soldiers," but it was in deference to the value of their experience without reference to bounties. He did write his brother in January 1865 that: "I am down on these high bounties. A very large number of these high bounty men are of no use to the Army – they are rather a detriment to it." He made the comment shortly after the execution of Waterman Thornton, so he may have been referring to the higher bounty recruits who came into the 179th in the Fall as a group. But otherwise his criticism of high bounty men was limited to those who actually deserted. [79] The tone of one of the letters of William Lamont, who arrived as a new recruit for Company B in Fall 1864, suggests that he was unhappy with the 179th New York and not just the Army in general, but he definitely felt like one of "the Boys" by the end of the war. [80]

However, there is some interesting indirect evidence that the 179th's original volunteers did not view the later recruits as their equals. When the regimental history was published in 1900, the descriptions of the individual companies made it very clear which were comprised of three years men – Companies A, B, C, D, E, F, and G; which companies were comprised of one year men – Companies I and K; and which company was comprised of a mix of both – Company H. In addition, the lists of soldiers for Companies A, C, D, E, F and G included only the original complement. Only the list for Company B included the later recruits – who were by and large one year men – and even then as a separately identified list. This may reflect a view by the compilers of the regimental history that their comrades who enlisted later in 1864 and in 1865 were less worthy of recognition. [81] One can imagine how the later recruits in these companies felt when they picked up a copy of the history of their regiment only to discover that their names were not included.

Poplar Spring Church

CHAPTER FIFTEEN

September 30, 1864

Company I's John W. Cook, a twenty-three-year-old farmer from Newfield, expressed his anticipation of upcoming battle in a September 19, 1864 letter to his parents from "Camp near Petersburg":

> We came here on Saturday last. We have been very near to the lines. We can hear the firing. Every day we are under marching orders Every moment and don't know how soon we shall start for the front...

> Their is from 1 to 2 hundred thousand men here and they keep coming. Every day we expect a battle any minute and it will be a big one. To the ground for 25 miles [illegible] is all soldiers and horses and waggons and is all alive and in motion. Our line of works reaches 24 miles long. It would be a big sight for you father to see. It would think that their is not men on Earth Enough to whip them, but we can not tell [illegible] can't go in battle to quick to suit me. I am ready for the Jonnys [1]

Most Civil War units in the Union armies had little training before they went into battle, but even by that low standard, the men of Companies H, I and K were poorly prepared for what lay so soon before them. They went into battle at Poplar Spring Church less than two weeks after they arrived at the front and a month or less after they had enlisted. Company K's Charles Johnson, a twenty-four-year-old farmer from Broome County, recalled that: "We had our guns for a period of three to four days, when we were put right into the firing line. Some of us had never handled a gun before." [2]

[Map: Major Roads and Rail Lines]

By the end of August the Army of the Potomac was holding a one mile section of the Weldon Railroad in the vicinity of Globe Tavern. That forced the Confederate troops to off-load supplies coming up the Weldon Railroad from North Carolina and move them by wagon around the Union forces into Petersburg. Two other critical Confederate supply routes lay to the west of the Weldon Railroad – the Boydton Plank Road and the South Side Railroad. These two supply routes became the target of the Union's next offensive undertaken by the Fifth and Ninth Corps with Gregg's cavalry division supporting. [3]

General Parke, commanding the Ninth Corps, received the following orders for the offensive from General Humphreys, the Army of the Potomac's Chief of Staff:

> General Warren is ordered to move out the Poplar Spring Church road and endeavor to secure the intersection of the Squirrel Level Road. The commanding general directs that you move out after and co-operate with him in endeavoring to secure a position on the right of the enemy's position. Try to open a route across the swamp to vicinity of Miss Pegram's, below Poplar Spring Church, and take post on Warren's left. Gregg will be directed to move out to Wilkinson's. [4]

[Photo: Willcox Staff]

Parke proceeded with the reconstituted divisions of General Willcox and General Potter (whose division now included the 179th New York Volunteers). [5] Potter's division had been "massed preparatory to a movement" on September 28. [6] The 179th broke camp on September 25 and marched to a new location, but then returned on September 28. [7] Orders were given on September 29 to be ready to move out at seven thirty the following day. [8]

The 179th New York had approximately four hundred soldiers present for duty on September 30. However, nearly 60 percent were the newly arrived recruits in Companies H, I and K – approximately 220 soldiers. Another 15 percent or so were unassigned replacements for the original seven companies who had arrived just that morning – nearly seventy men. Before those replacements arrived, the original seven companies had been reduced to mere shadows of their original complements as shown in the following table:

Company	Officers	Sergeants	Corporals	Privates
A	1	1	1	19
B	1	0	2	11
C	1	2	3	15
D	1	1	3	4
E	1	4	3	21

Information is not available for Company F and Company G. The twenty-one privates in

Company E included sixteen new recruits received in mid-September. Only Company E was commanded by a captain. The 179th was hardly in top condition as it entered the battle.[9]

[Photo: Simon Griffin]

The 179th was in the Second Brigade, commanded by General Simon Griffin. The Second Brigade moved out at nine o'clock the morning of September 30, passing through Fort Dushane and then linking up with the First Brigade. With the First Brigade in the lead, the two brigades marched along Poplar Spring Church Road, passing the church.[10] They then "took position in line of battle to the left of a line of the enemy's works near the Peebles House, which General Warren had previously carried."[11]

Newly arrived recruit George Hemingway described this movement:

> We came to one little Fort that our boys had taken. Their was ded men and wounded all around which made things look very bad to me but we soon came to another. A long line it was to and their was dead men on a large scale. Went up to it marched along the whole length was about half a mile in length and went into the woods and lay down. We lay their for some time and then went on after the Rebs again.[12]

Around three o'clock that afternoon, General Griffin moved the Second Brigade from the Peebles House past the Pegram House on to a large open field on Pegram's Farm. The Boydton Plank Road was their objective. The 2nd New York Mounted Rifles (not yet provided with horses) were deployed as skirmishers, followed by the 6th and the 11th New Hampshire. About 400 yards past Pegram House, they encountered Confederate resistance. The Second Brigade then formed in two lines of battle: the 6th, 9th and 11th New Hampshire and the 2nd Maryland in the first (with the 2nd New York as skirmishers) and the 17th Vermont, the 31st and 32nd Maine, the 56th Massachusetts and the 179th New York in the second.[13] After marching down a lane, the 179th came to a halt to form in line of battle. Just as they were about to move forward, a Confederate volley "pounded into" them, wounding Company I's Charles Barnard, an eighteen-year-old blacksmith, in the head, but he survived.[14]

The Second Brigade then moved forward into the woods past the Pegram Farm. George Hemingway recounted that: "We advanced into the woods and the Rebs threw over the shells at us. One struck about a rod from me and then glanced over my head. Another struck a tree a little to the left and splinters flew as I never saw them before."[15] Thirty years after the war, Charles Johnson recalled being in the woods under fire: "For a time we lay in the woods, but not long before the rebels began firing upon us, letting the shot and shell into the woods until it was just about torn to pieces. We could see our comrades killed and dying all about us."[16] Company A's Sgt. Arthur Beebe was struck by a large tree limb severed by an artillery shell. He suffered several broken ribs and shortly thereafter was hit by a minie ball in the left hip.[17]

[Map: Poplar Spring, 5 p.m.]

The 179th then "advanced about half way through the woods and then lay down in line of battle and several Regs formed in front of us and advanced on the Rebs again."[18] The Second Brigade's skirmishers reached and took the Jones House and the first line reached the edge of the woods in front of the Jones House. The First Brigade moved up on the left.[19]

Around five o'clock, Potter ordered his two brigades to advance past the Jones House toward the Boydton Plank Road. However, having been ordered to advance "as rapidly as practicable, without reference to any one else," Potter's Second Division had no support on either its right or left. [20] The Second Division ran into trouble almost immediately, as recounted by Potter.

> As soon as we had got well out into the open ground we found the enemy advancing in a southwesterly direction from the woods and low ground to the front and on my right ... The enemy were in such large force and so far overlapped my right, that I apprehended they would get on the road by which I had advanced and cut me off. ... [T]he right began to give way, and the enemy pressing vigorously, and having got nearly behind my right, and penetrating also between the two brigades, the lines commenced falling back in considerable confusion. [21]

General Griffin similarly reported that the Confederates had "a line of battle stronger than our own, and overlapping us on both flanks." Griffin sent all the regiments of his second line forward "to sustain the first line" – except for the 179th. His decision to hold back the 179th may have been based on the fact that three-fourths of its soldiers were very raw recruits or he may have intended the 179th to protect his right flank and rear. Even with reinforcements from the second line, the situation deteriorated rapidly. "[B]eing furiously attacked on three sides by superior numbers [the Second Brigade was] compelled to abandon the place, losing heavily." Griffin reported that: "Forced to retire in haste, they did so in some disorder, and being closely followed by the enemy in force the whole line was carried away." [22] After falling back, the Second Division was able to rally at the Pegram House and "checked and repulsed" the Confederate attack. The Second Brigade lost nearly five hundred soldiers as captured or missing. For the Second Division as a whole, the number was over twelve hundred. [23]

[Map: Poplar Spring, 7 p.m.]

Located not far behind the rest of the Second Brigade, the 179th was quickly struck by the Confederate onslaught. Hemingway described the situation: "The ground was a knoll and the Rebs came onto us from the other side. The Colonel [Lieutenant Colonel Doty] ordered us to retreat but before we could get away the Rebs shot and wounded a good many of the 179 boys and took a few prisoners." [24] Company I's Ambrose Worden recalled that it was after sundown and:

> first we knew the Johnnys swung around in our rear. ... [Our regiment was being surrounded rapidly by the "Johnnies".] As soon as the Col. [Lt. Col. Doty] of the Regt saw this he ordered us to fall back & we did fall back every man doing the best he could. [25]

Referring to himself as "a new recruit" carrying a full knapsack, Worden tripped in a post hole. He had to cut the strap to get the knapsack off and continue his retreat. [26] First Lt. Robert Hooper, commanding Company K that day, recalled that they had retreated "in confusion." [27] Some of the soldiers of the 179th – Hemingway among them – may have begun to retreat even before Lieutenant Colonel Doty gave the order. When the Confederates were charging, Hemingway is reported to have said "Let's [get] out of here!" When last seen by his friends, Hemingway was "running beside some woods, the Rebs was close behind." Close enough behind that Hemingway was wounded and captured. [28] Worden avoided capture, but Alfred Worden, a possible relation from Newfield, did not. [29] Company A's Peter Patric was a stretcher bearer and recalled that he was "knocked down and run over by the men retreating from the field." [30] Company I's Charles W. Blackmer recalled that the "command was very much scattered." [31]

Major John Hudson of the 35th Massachusetts Infantry, which was positioned about fifty yards in front of the 179th New York, observed the Confederate attack developing on the 179th as follows:

> I noticed two or three scattering shots, apparently far off on our right or a little in rear of it. Believing that it was only what naturally would happen between our skirmishers and the enemy's, I thought nothing of it; ... Presently as I stood behind a pine tree near out line, I saw the small regiment in our rear rise up and stand in a line a moment, then look to their right uneasily and waver, and then break by individuals from the right to the rear with considerable animation at the reception of a shot or two upon its flank. It might have appeared then as if this regiment were in undue haste to retire, for no effort whatever was made to change front or direction. It would appear now that, standing on ground lower than that which I stood on, it was able to see beneath the branches the array that was coming upon its flank so unexpectedly, though I could not see it, and so, wisely, made no attempt at resistance. [32]

Richard Sommers wrote in *Richmond Redeemed: The Siege at Petersburg* that "Spotting the legs of an onrushing battle line greatly disquieted the New Yorkers – all the more so because most of the regiment was unarmed." [33] However, while the 179th certainly retreated in confusion, Sommer's conclusion that most of the regiment was unarmed seems incorrect. Nearly three-quarters of the 179th's troops on the field that day were new recruits, but Charles Johnson's statement indicates that Company K was armed. Similarly, Company I's Charles S. Baker wrote home on September 19, 1864 that "We have received our guns and equipage." Waterman Thornton, a new recruit in Company E referred to "halt[ing] in the woods to load our pieces." There is also no reason to believe that the veterans in the original companies were not armed. However, only some of the new recruits in Company B were armed. [34]

Company E's Sgt. Charles Hogan estimated that the 179th fell back about three-quarters of a mile to Confederate trenches that had been taken earlier in the day. [35] Company F's William Larzelere also estimated the retreat at three-quarters of a mile. [36] That suggests that the 179th fell back all the way to the Peebles House rather than to the Pegram Farm, where other elements of the Ninth Corps successfully regrouped and stemmed the Confederate advance. [37]

On a day when things were going badly for the 179th, at least Company F's Charles B. Baker, a nineteen- year-old laborer, had a stroke of luck. His musket was shattered in his hand, but he was not injured. Forty years after the war, he proudly recalled that he had been "continuously with his company in every engagement in which they took part" and that he had missed only six days of duty during his service. [38]

[Sketch: New Picket Line]

The night of September 30, the Second Division left a picket line at the Pegram House and withdrew to the former Confederate positions at the Peebles House which they had left earlier in the day. [39]

On October 1, the 179th spent a "cold and rainy" day and night in the trenches near the

Peebles House. [40]

[Sketch: Looking Left on the Weldon Railroad]

On October 2, the Second Brigade and 179th "advanced again in strong force" to the positions at the Pegram House. That night, "fearing an attack from the enemy every moment, every man and most of the officers assisted in building breastworks," as Company A's Lt. Farr recalled twelve years later. Farr and Company I's William Howland and David Nicols suffered ruptures from lifting heavy logs. [41] The 179th remained in that vicinity for the next two months. [42]

Elihu Linkletter

[Map: Poplar Spring, October 1]

In his report to General Parke, Potter observed that: "The majority of the troops behaved well, but the recruits (mostly substitutes, and many unable to speak English) behaved badly." However, the "greatest inconvenience and serious trouble resulted from the scarcity of officers, large numbers of both field and line officers having been recently mustered out of service." [43] Having advanced without support on the right or left, albeit under orders, into an overwhelming Confederate counterattack, Potter may have unfairly singled out the new recruits. Nor were the new recruits in the 179th mostly substitutes or unable to speak English.

The 179th's officially reported casualties on September 30 were one officer mortally wounded, one enlisted man killed, twenty-three enlisted men wounded and thirty-three enlisted men missing. [44] The Carded Medical Records for the 179th indicate substantially more wounded – close to forty. [45] Among the wounded was Company A's Elihu Linkletter, an eighteen-year-old farmer. His left hand was amputated. [46]

Second Lt. James Bowker was mortally wounded. Colonel Gregg thought highly of Bowker, who had also served in the 23rd New York. Shortly after Bowker's death, Gregg wrote his friend Judge Ariel Thurston that Bowker "was a gallant officer and was well entitled to the promotion to which I recommended him." [47]

Considering the number of men engaged, casualties were proportionately heavier in the "veteran" companies than the three new companies. Company A suffered six casualties (three killed/ no wounded/three missing) out of twenty-two men engaged and Company B suffered five casualties (one officer killed/no wounded/four missing) out of fourteen engaged – roughly a third of those engaged. In contrast, Company I suffered sixteen casualties (one killed/five wounded/ ten missing) out of seventy-seven engaged – about one-fifth. Company K with seventeen casualties (two killed/two wounded/thirteen missing) was similar. [48] Whether the proportionately higher casualties meant that the veteran companies resisted the attack more vigorously is hard to say.

Almost all of the soldiers reported as missing in fact were captured and were ultimately sent to Salisbury Military Prison in North Carolina. Privates Charles Johnson and George Hemingway were among those captured.

In addition to the casualties, the rout on September 30 had two longer term impacts on the 179th. First, there was the loss of equipment. Two weeks after the battle, there were soldiers sleeping by fires without the blankets and overcoats they had lost when they retreated.[49] Second, there was the impact on the morale of the new recruits of having "skeddadled".[50] The soldiers from the original six companies at least had the attack on June 17 to fall back on for positive reinforcement or even the Battle of the Crater or Weldon Railroad, but for the soldiers in the three new companies September 30 was their only significant combat action for another six months. Noting that they had "broke and run in every direction," Company B's William Lamont, a newly arrived recruit, wrote a friend that: "we are in hopes to do better next time."[51]

The battle of Poplar Spring Church was the 179th New York's worst performance in the field. The secondary role given to the 179th as the Second Brigade advanced toward Jones House during the early evening of September 30 probably reflected an assessment by General Griffin that the 179th had only limited capability at that time. The 179th was deployed in line of battle facing toward Jones Farm and apparently had no pickets on its right flank where the Confederate attack came from. The 179th was caught by surprise and apparently was unable to even fire an organized volley or two before retreating. While Lieutenant Colonel Doty did order the retreat, there are indications that some soldiers broke and ran before the order.

Should Doty have attempted a stand to try to buy time for the rest of the Second Brigade and Potter's division? Under the circumstances, quickly changing front would have been a difficult maneuver for even a veteran regiment. For a regiment three-quarters of whose soldiers had been in the army for thirty days or less it simply wasn't feasible. The cost of resistance surely would have been the capture of most of the 179th New York–perhaps two or three hundred prisoners instead of thirty on a day when Potter's division had over twelve hundred men captured. Retreat may well have been the correct decision, but there was little that was orderly in its execution.

While September 30 did not end well for the Ninth Corps, the Union army nonetheless was able to extend its lines further to the west. A map of the forts constructed shortly after the battle gives a picture of the progress by the Army of the Potomac.[52]

[Map: Poplar Spring Forts]

Salisbury Prison

CHAPTER SIXTEEN

Prisoners of War

In each of its major engagements, the 179th reported men missing in action – ten on June 17 at Petersburg; thirty-one at the Battle of the Crater; thirty-three at Poplar Spring Church; and eight in the final assault at Petersburg.[1] The majority of the missing in these battles had been captured and became prisoners of war. Union soldiers captured in 1864 had the misfortune to become prisoners of war at a time when the exchange/parole cartel agreed to by the Union and Confederacy in 1862 had broken down and the Confederate capability to provision its own troops, much less prisoners of war, was severely strained. As a result they were subjected to extreme hardship in terms of both living conditions and food, particularly during the winter of 1864 - 1865.

Prisoners of war did not present much of a problem early in the war for the simple reason that neither side was capturing many enemy soldiers. As the number of prisoners began to increase, the Confederacy initiated discussion of exchanges in order to avoid having to feed them. The Lincoln Administration initially was reluctant to take any action that might be viewed as recognizing the legitimacy of the Confederate States of America, but in July 1862 agreement was reached on an exchange/parole cartel. Prisoners were to be exchanged on a one for one basis within ten days of their capture. The side holding a greater number of prisoners would parole them, allowing them to return home with the understanding that they could not be reassigned to duty until the other side had enough soldiers to exchange against the parole debit. Sick and wounded prisoners generally were given priority.[2] In theory neither side would hold significant numbers of prisoners of war for a prolonged period of time.

However, the cartel arrangement broke down in 1863 and by the time of the Battle of Poplar Spring Church in Ocober 1864 was "almost completely inoperative."[3] The initial cause was the controversy over the Union's use of freed slaves as troops. In response, the Confederacy stated that "all negro slaves captured in arms [would] be at once delivered over to the executive authorities of the respective States to which they belong to be dealt with according to the laws of said States" and that the captured white officers who commanded them would be treated in the same manner, which included potential prosecution under laws against inciting slave insurrection.[4] Union Secretary of War Stanton, with President Lincoln's support, suspended the cartel agreement, taking the position that there would be no further exchanges until the Confederacy agreed to treat all Union prisoners – black or white – equally.[5]

Late in 1863, the Confederacy softened its position somewhat and proposed to exchange black soldiers who were legally free at the time they enlisted in the Union army, but Stanton continued to insist on equal treatment for all black soldiers.[6]

When Grant became General-in-Chief in March 1864, he supported the policy that there would be no exchanges until the Confederacy agreed to treat all black prisoners equally with whites. However, he also came to recognize that the no-exchange policy had a military benefit to the Union, albeit at a heavy cost to the prisoners themselves. In August 1864, Grant wrote to General Butler, the Union's Commissioner of Exchange (and also commander of the Army of the James), that:

> It is hard on our men held in Southern prisons not to exchange them, but it is humanity to those left in the ranks to fight our battles. Every man we hold, when released on parole or otherwise, becomes an active soldier against us at once either directly or indirectly. If we commence a system of exchange which liberates all prisoners taken, we will have to fight on until the whole South is exterminated. If we hold those caught they amount to no more than dead men. At this particular time to release all rebel prisoners ... would insure Sherman's defeat and would compromise our safety here.[7]

Two days later, Grant expressed the same sentiment to Secretary of State Seward:

> We ought not to make a single exchange nor release a prisoner on any pretext whatever until the war closes.

> We have got to fight until the military power of the South is exhausted, and if we release or exchange prisoners captured it simply becomes a war of extermination.[8]

Earlier in August 1864, Robert Ould, the Confederate Agent of Exchange, had written the War Department proposing that "in view ... of the very large number of prisoners now held by each party and the suffering consequent upon their continuing confinement" the Confederacy would change its position and accept man for man exchange without parole of the excess remaining on one side.[9] Ould's letter was referred to General Butler who responded in a strongly worded five page letter on August 27. Butler began by expressing his skepticism because Ould had not expressly confirmed that black soldiers would be treated equally.

> To avoid all possible misapprehension or mistake hereafter as to your offer now, will you say now whether you mean by "prisoners held in captivity" colored men, duly enrolled and mustered into the service of the United States, who have been captured by the Confederate forces, and if your authorities

are willing to exchange all soldiers so mustered into the U.S. Army, whether colored or otherwise. [10]

Butler passionately stated the basis for the Union position that black soldiers receive equal treatment:

> it is neither consistent with the policy, dignity, nor honor of the United States, upon any consideration, to allow those who, by our laws solemnly enacted, are made soldiers of the Union, and who have been duly enlisted, enrolled, and mustered as such soldiers – who have borne arms in behalf of this country, and who have been captured while fighting in vindication of the rights of that country – not to be treated as prisoners of war, and remain unexchanged and in the service of those who claim them as masters; and I cannot believe that the Government of the United States will ever be found to consent to so gross a wrong. [11]

No agreement was reached at that time.

Soldiers captured by both sides in the early fall action around Petersburg – especially in the Battle of Poplar Spring Church – led Lee to propose to Grant on October 1, 1864 an exchange between the Army of Northern Virginia and the Army of the Potomac "man for man, or upon the basis established by the cartel." [12] In response, Grant noted that the Union troops recently captured included a number of "colored troops" and specifically asked Lee whether he "propos[ed to] deliver these men the same as white soldiers." [13] When Lee responded that "negroes belonging to our citizens are not considered subjects of exchange and were not included in my proposition," Grant declined the proposal on October 3. [14] Thus, the fate of the soldiers of the 179th captured on September 30, like that of thousands of other Union prisoners of war, was sealed for the upcoming winter. [15]

However, in January 1865, the Confederacy finally agreed to exchange all black prisoners on the same basis as white prisoners. [16] The change in position may have been motivated by the fact that the Confederacy was then itself considering enlisting black soldiers in its ranks, but the change may also have been motivated by humanitarian concerns for the prisoners. Significant exchanges and paroles of Union prisoners took place in February and March 1865, which included prisoners from the 179th.

SALISBURY MILITARY PRISON

The majority of the soldiers from the 179th who became prisoners of war were ultimately sent to Salisbury Military Prison in North Carolina. While not as notorious as Andersonville, Salisbury was no less harsh. Of the nearly thirty soldiers from the 179th who can be documented as having been taken sent to Salisbury, fourteen died there and another four died shortly after returning to the Union lines when the exchange/parole system was resumed in February 1865. [17]

The soldiers of the 179th taken prisoner on September 30, 1864 wound up at Salisbury Prison. Most of them were new recruits. Company B's George Hemingway had enlisted on August 18, left Elmira on September 17; arrived at the 179th's

Charles Johnson

camp at Petersburg on September 29; and was captured the next day. Hemingway wrote his cousin that "When I left you at Elmira little did I think that I would meet the Rebs so soon and fall a prisoner into their hands." [18]

Not all of the prisoners from the 179th were taken directly to Salisbury. One group, including Charles Johnson of Company K, was taken first to Belle Island in the James River near Richmond where they stayed one night. They were then taken across the river to Libby Prison in Richmond, where they stayed for about three weeks. Relatively speaking, Johnson "found the rations and water to be of better quality than any other place" they were imprisoned. From Libby Prison, they were taken back to Petersburg, where they spent two weeks "liv[ing] under an old tobacco factory." They were then transferred to Salisbury Prison in North Carolina. [19]

Another group, including Company K's Theodore McDonald, may have gone directly to Libby and Salisbury Prisons without the stops at Belle Island and Petersburg. At a reunion after the war, McDonald said that he had been taken to Libby Prison and then to Salisbury Prison in a group of about fifty prisoners. [20]

George B. Hemingway undoubtedly did not think so at the time, but the gunshot wound in the left thigh that he suffered on September 30 in the Battle of Poplar Spring Church may have saved his life. He was captured, but because of his wound he was exchanged and avoided Salisbury Prison. Hemingway was initially taken to Richmond, but quickly paroled after four days on October 8 at Varina, Virginia, the original exchange point under the cartel. He was admitted to a Union hospital in Maryland the following day. Although it was a flesh wound, it never healed properly. He never returned to duty and was discharged at the end of the war with a one-half disability pension of $4 per month. [21]

A common first experience for Union prisoners was the confiscation of their valuables. The prisoners would often try to hide what they could. Charles Johnson had the benefit of being at the end of a group of prisoners being searched "so as I watched them performing their work of robbing our men, I had it all studied out." He was among the successful.

> My fortune consisted of a $10 bill, one $2 and one $1 bill, along with some currency [coins?]. The bills I saved by folding very tightly and placing them between my teeth next to my cheeks. When it was my turn to be searched, I was leisurely eating Johnnie cake. I afterward had occasion to be thankful that I had saved this money. [22]

The dominant physical feature of Salisbury Military Prison was an empty cotton factory, a three story plus attic brick building that was about twenty years old. The Confederate government had purchased it for $15,000 in 1861. The prison had opened in December 1861 and by the middle of 1862 there were 1,400 prisoners there. However, up until October 1864, the majority of the prisoners were disloyal Confederates, Union and Confederate deserters, and Confederate criminals.

[Diagram: Salisbury Prison]

When the Union decided to stop exchanging prisoners, the number of Union prisoners at Salisbury greatly increased. A total of 10,321 Union prisoners were received between October 5, 1864 and February 1, 1865. Although the prison was only equipped for 2500 prisoners, the prison population peaked at 8740 on November 6, 1864. [23] By the Fall of 1864, the old cotton factory building was used as a hospital and the prisoners were kept in the open on grounds of sixteen acres, surrounded by a wooden stockade fence twelve feet tall. Guards "were looking down upon us all the time," according to Johnson. [24]

Johnson recalled that:

> For the first few weeks of our stay [at Salisbury], we had but little shelter. And the nights by this time [early to mid-October] were becoming very cold and rainy most of the time. We would sleep in piles, about a hundred in a pile. Some would sleep under for a while, then those on top of the pile would root down so as to take their turn at getting warm. This went on for some time, until they took mercy and gave us a few of their condemned tents. Although these were not very good, and far from enough, still we considered them better than nothing. We made the best of them by sleeping with our feet to the center of the tent and our heads to the outside, in this way we were enabled to get a larger number in the tents. Those of us who were less fortunate dug holes underground where we spent the winter. It was not long, however, before we had plenty of room in our tents, our comrades were dying off by the hundreds. [25]

The report for the Confederate army's Inspector General on the conditions at Salisbury confirms Johnson's account, as do the recollections of prisoners from other units. [26]

Among the less fortunate prisoners were Company C's Sgt. John Price and Company F's Sgt. William Norton. Price and Norton had not known each other very well before becoming prisoners of war, but became close friends at Salisbury. Norton had been captured at the Battle of the Crater and initially sent to Danville Prison. Because he had been wounded, he was sent to Richmond to be exchanged. However, the Confederate surgeon who examined him found him to be in too good condition to be exchanged and he was sent to Salisbury Prison, where he encountered Price, who had just been captured at Poplar Spring Church.

Thirty-five years after the war, Price recalled that Norton's "clothing was thin and scanty and well worn. The seat was out of his trousers and his bare bottom was well exposed to the autumn breezes." For the first several weeks, Price and Norton had no shelter, but they, along with a soldier from a Vermont regiment, built what Price referred to as an "underground residence." Norton recalled it in more detail.

> [We] constructed a home for ourselves under ground, without nails and almost without tools, the overhanging earth being supported by timbers furnished, and sorely needed, for fuel. In this hole I and my companions *resided* for nearly four months without furniture and without straw, though each of us had a blanket. [27] (emphasis in original)

Conditions worsened as the prison population increased in the Fall of 1864. Food and medicine were in short supply. Rations were passed out once a day. Johnson recalled that:

> Usually this was only a very small piece of Johnny cake and sometimes soup, made of peas or beans, ... Many times the rations would run out before the lines had received their rations, so we would have to go without that day and many others. Some would go for three days without a thing to eat. [28]

However, Johnson always seemed to be able to find a little extra, using the money he had hidden to buy provisions from the prison sutler or from local peddlers when he was on detail outside the prison. The quality of these extra rations was not necessarily the best. Johnson bought a meat pie "which was almost my undoing. I always thought it was made of horse meat. I surely was never able to finish that pie, the piece I ate made me deathly sick." [29]

For water, the prisoners initially were sent in two man details to a nearby creek to bring back water in barrels, but later dug a sixteen foot deep hole within the prison grounds to collect surface water. "To get the water [Johnson] took a regular army cup and put a bail in it. The bail being made from a strip of leather cut from an old boot leg. Each morning, early, before the water was riled, I would go and draw water." [30]

Death was an everyday reality at Salisbury. Johnson recalled that:

[Sketch: Salisbury Hospital]

> When our men died during the night the other men in the tent would take anything which they could wear from the dead men. They did this because they were nearly naked themselves and suffering from cold and exposure. The dead were taken to the deadhouse, being thrown any way into the wagon. ... I shall never forget the ghastly sight of men's hands and heads dragging over the wheels of the wagon as they were being conveyed from the deadhouse to their graves. [31]

The prisoners from the 179th made it through October, but they began succumbing to the harsh conditions in November. The nights were getting very cold by the middle of November. [32] By December, "diarrhea [was] raging to an alarming extent" and scurvy was "fast spreading" in the prison. [33] William Norton recalled that: "During our sojourn in Salisbury we were all more or less afflicted with scurvy." [34] Theodore McDonald recalled that: "During January and February 1865 the weather was very severe and the prisoners exposed to the weather and a large number were frost bitten." [35]

Company A's Timothy Buckland succumbed on November 11, making him the first of the 179th's prisoners to die. He was the father of eight children, five of them under the age of sixteen, including a baby daughter he had never seen. [36] The pace of death quickened in December. Company A's Anthony Tobias died on December 3 of diarrhea. Company K's Thomas Johnson and Company G's Henry Miller died on December 9. They were shortly followed by Company I's Ira Stoddard, who died of chronic diarrhea on December 19; Company K's William Lewis, who died on December 29, also of chronic diarrhea; and Company I's Alfred Worden who died on December 30 of starvation. [37]

News of the fate of these soldiers was slow to reach home. Anthony Tobias' family had initially been told by comrades from the 179th that he had been killed on September 30. Then they learned from the Soldiers' Aid Society in Washington that he had been taken prisoner. On December 20, Tobias' daughter Maggie – not knowing that her father was already dead – wrote the "Commissary General of Prisoners" asking for "all the particulars ... concerning my dear Pa."

> I have a great desire to write to my loved father, but don't know whether I shall be permitted to do so until I hear from you. Please ans[wer] without a moments delay and you will oblige the praying daughter of Anthony Tobias. I feel that all Daughters, Sisters & Mothers should pray unceasingly for their Dear Soldier Friends. [38]

January 1865 was nearly as bad as December had been, with another three dying – Company I's John Drake on January 5 (starvation and inflammation of the brain); Company I's Bradford Hallett on January 11 (debility); and Company K's Isaac Hill on January 16 (chronic diarrhea). Company I's Hurlbert Reed (starvation and rheumatism), Company B's Thomas Chapman (diarrhea), and

Company K's William Newman (diarrhea) died in early February before the paroles began. [39]

Tobias, Hill, Lewis, Newman and Chapman died in the prison hospital. Johnson was dismissive of the quality of care in the hospital: "The water and food of this hospital caused practically all who ever reached there to die of chronic diarrhea." [40] However, Company H's William Patterson, Company I's Elijah Smith and Company K's Joseph Prentice did survive the hospital and were paroled. [41]

For the prisoners from the 179th at Salisbury, the death rate was roughly 40 percent. For Salisbury prisoners overall during the period October 1864 to February 1865 it was about 28 percent. This compares to 29 percent for Andersonville overall and 15.5 percent for Confederate prisons in general. [42]

As in all the military prisons, there were a number of escape attempts, and as many as three hundred Salisbury prisoners did succeed. The most dramatic attempt began at 2 p.m. on November 25 when a cry from the leader for "those that are for liberty follow me" led a mass charge toward the main gate. The attempt was timed for the changing of the guard. [43]

Charles Johnson recalled the plan nearly fifty years later:

[Sketch: Escape Attempt]

> Our plan was to seize the arms from the guards, who were guarding the well, cookhouse and gate, and were about 30 in number. We could get their arms and cartridges and then fire on the outside guards and get out through the gates. Well, the plan sounded good, but when it came to getting the cartridges there was but one. Of course, after the first shot was fired we did not get much farther. [44]

The Union prisoners had the misfortune that a Confederate unit boarding a train at the nearby depot had not yet departed. [45] Johnson recalled that the Confederate guards:

> were frightened so they rushed this regiment upon us. They set cannons in the stockade and made a cross-fire upon us. Of course we couldn't do anything. That really was the worst moment of my life. There we were, huddled like a lot of sheep, with them firing incessantly upon us. We had absolutely nothing to defend ourselves with, so had to take it. [46]

After the firing ended, the Union prisoners were ordered back to the tents. Sporadic firing by the Confederate guards continued and Johnson was wounded in the back of the head by a "charge of buckshot." Johnson went to the prison hospital where "a great many" wounded had already been taken and "placed on benches or tables with a strong guard around them." Johnson recalled that:

> It was certainly pitiful to see these comrades suffer and even worse when the young doctors began hacking off their arms and legs. Such screaming and screeching and untold misery, I thought I could never stand it. The rebels had absolutely no mercy with the men because we had tried to break out. [47]

The Confederate commandant at Salisbury reported the casualties as "2 of the guards killed, 1 mortally wounded, and some 8 to 10 slightly wounded. The prisoners had 13 killed, 3 mortally wounded, and 60 others wounded." [48]

A number of tunneling efforts were made. The most successful involved the escape of approximately one hundred prisoners in January 1865. [49] Company G's James Williams is the only prisoner from the 179th said to have escaped, but the details are unknown. [50]

Conditions were so harsh that as many as two thousand of the roughly ten thousand Union prisoners at Salisbury enlisted in the Confederate army in order to be released. As early as November 5, 1864, the Confederate army attempted to recruit Union prisoners at Salisbury to garrison forts further south, thereby freeing up able-bodied Southern soldiers to serve at the front. In return for enlisting in the Confederate army, a Union prisoner of war would receive $100 in Confederate script, $20 a month, full rations, and new clothes. Wagon-makers and blacksmiths were particularly sought after. [51]

Three of the 179th's soldiers were among the Salisbury prisoners who did enlist in the Confederate army – Company D's John Gay, Company F's John Hall, (January 1865)[not to be confused with Company A's John Hall who also was a prisoner of war]; and Company K's Will H. Barber (January 16, 1865). Hall (a laborer) had been captured at the Battle of the Crater, while Barber, (a farmer) had been captured at Poplar Spring Church. [52]

Jerry Daniels of the 22nd Iowa Infantry reputedly gave the following explanation to a sick comrade why he accepted the offer:

> I can't do you any good if I stay, and I will desert and make for our lines at the first opportunity. If I live this way much longer, I shall die. I am already on the verge of insanity, and before I get too weak to travel I will try to escape. To stay here is certain death. I will lose nothing by leaving, and here, now comrade, I leave you my piece of blanket. That is all of the world's goods I have. It will do you more good than I can if I stay, and with my blessing, I bid you farewell, hoping to meet you again on earth; if not, I hope to meet you on the sunny banks of Eternal Deliverance, where there will be no rebel prisons and bloodhounds. [53]

However, while the prisoners who stayed probably did not disagree with Daniels' statement of the underlying facts, they had little sympathy for those who joined the Confederacy and ran them through a gauntlet of epithets and whatever missiles might be at hand. [54]

In February 1865, the prisoner exchange program was resumed and the decision was made to return the Union prisoners at Salisbury. There had been no shortage of rumors of exchange in past months. Johnson recalled that: "We were somewhat gladdened at times only to have it sink into disappointment. A report would come every week to the effect that we were to be paroled or exchanged. At last the time came." [55]

[Map: Railroads of North Carolina]

The healthier prisoners, nearly three thousand, were taken to Wilmington, North Carolina, a major port. The soldiers paroled at that time included Company B's Jarvis Kenyon; Company C's John H. Price; Company F's William L. Norton; Company I's Nelson Beadell; and Company K's Theodore F. McDonald, Horace Cornelius, Abram Lane and Joseph J. Prentice. [56]

Those headed for Wilmington left on February 22 with three days rations. [57] They started off by foot in a column two to three miles long. They reached Greensborough – approximately fifty miles away – the afternoon of February 25. For soldiers who had been in a military prison for four and a half months marching sixteen miles a day for three days straight was quite an ordeal. Sergeant Norton, "troubled with boils and show[ing] unmistakable signs of weakness," gave out the morning of the second day. Fortunately, a sympathetic Confederate surgeon gave him a pass to ride the train and Sergeant Price was allowed to accompany him "as a sort of attending nurse." [58]

At Greensborough, the soldiers were then put on flatcars and left by train for Raleigh around nine o'clock that night, arriving there the following morning around eight o'clock. They were welcomed by some pro-Union residents. They continued on to Goldsborough, arriving there at dark that same day. In Goldsborough, the local people "thronged around to give them food," notwithstanding Confederate army orders to stay away from the prisoners. The parole process for the Salisbury prisoners began on February 28 in Goldsborough and continued over the next several days. [59] Their spirits were cheered as they approached the Union lines and they were greeted by a banner proclaiming: "We welcome you home, our brothers" and a band playing "Home Sweet Home." [60]

Company F's William Norton was paroled at N. E. Ferry on February 28, 1865. He was initially sent to "CPW" on March 11 and reported to Camp Parole, Maryland on March 12 where he was assigned to the 2nd Battalion, Paroled Prisoners. On March 17, he received a thirty day furlough and returned to Reading. He was suffering from typhoid fever and his doctor submitted an affidavit that Norton would not be able to report back to Camp Parole on April 17 because he was unable to travel. [61]

Roughly fourteen hundred sick prisoners from Salisbury were sent by rail to Richmond by way of Danville. [62] Charles Johnson was in this group. The trip got off to a bad start. They were given three days rations, but their train was late and by the time it arrived, their rations had been consumed. The trip was too much for many of the sick prisoners. Johnson recalled that:

All along the way the train stopped at most every station to throw off the dead bodies of those who died on the way.

We were riding in box cars on this trip and the conditions were absolutely filthy. Many of us who were stronger made our quarters on top of the cars and rode in this measure. It was raining so much that we were chilled through most of the time. [63]

Their ordeal did not end when they reached Richmond. "The rivers were so swollen that it was impossible for us to get across. The boats were not able to run for two weeks after we had arrived at Richmond." [64] The formal transfer of these prisoners took place at Aiken's Landing, below Dutch Gap on the James River. On the Union side of the point of exchange, "a great string of ambulances were bearing the wounded and sick who were unable to help themselves." Johnson recalled that a group from the Christian Ladies Commission "served us with a few cookies and coffee. These proved to be a life saver." [65] From Aiken's Landing, the newly freed prisoners were taken by boat down the James River and then up the Chesapeake Bay to Annapolis Junction.

In order to provide a holding point for paroled soldiers awaiting confirmation of exchange under the cartel, the Union had built special facilities such as Camp Parole, located in Annapolis, Maryland. As Union prisoners were held for longer periods and under more dire circumstances, medical facilities to treat the returned prisoners, who generally were in much weakened health, were necessary as well. Camp Parole was originally located on the campus of St. John's College in Annapolis, Maryland, but in May 1863, the government leased a nearby 250 acre farm and moved the camp there. The camp population varied from two thousand to ten thousand paroled prisoners at a time. [66]

Johnson recalled that on arrival at Camp Parole: "we were given a good scrubbing, shaved and new uniforms, making us quite like humans again." He then spent two weeks in the hospital. [67] Once the prisoners had regained a degree of health, they were generally furloughed for a month or more to their homes. In the spring of 1865, it was the exception rather than the rule for an exchanged Union prisoner to return to his regiment in the field. In recognition of the hardships they endured, the War Department directed that they be promptly discharged after Lee surrendered in April. They were also to be given an extra three months of pay. [68]

The survivors of Salisbury were physically broken. When Charles A. Beckwith saw his comrade John Price in Elmira three months after Price had been released from Salisbury:

> I did not know him at first. He was very poor and his complexion was very yellow and was weak. I assisted him to the train on that day as he could scarcely walk. He was so weak in his limbs. I asked to see [his] legs and arms as I had never seen scurvy the disease [he] said he had. He showed them to me ... They were all sores or yellow spots looked like scales. He had lost most of his teeth. [69]

Price himself simply stated that he had "lost his health" at Salisbury. [70]

A number of the soldiers of the 179th died shortly after being returned to the Union lines – William Ostrander on April 24, Reuben Lewis on July 25, and John W. Cook in August 1865 among them. [71]

Company K's Abram Lane was furloughed and died on April 4, 1865 shortly after arriving home. A family friend, George Tuthill, had brought Lane home from Camp Parole in Maryland. The family physician, Dr. Eli Beers, promptly attended to Lane, finding him suffering from chronic diarrhea and general debility and "very ill and weak, & unable to sit up." Dr. Beers rendered Lane "such aid as was in his power as a Physician," but Lane "rapidly declined." At least Lane may have died a "good death" in the presence of his wife Mary, son Charlie and other family and friends. [72]

Having only recently been released from the horror of Confederate Prisons, Company K's Horace Cornelius suffered the indignity of incarceration in a Union prison. After arriving at Camp Parole, Cornelius had been furloughed for thirty days on March 14. While returning a little late, Cornelius was arrested on the train at Havre de Grace, Maryland on April 17 because he was not carrying a pass or a furlough paper. He was first confined at Fort McHenry in Baltimore and then at the Prince Street Military Prison in Alexandria. [73]

After the Union prisoners were paroled, Salisbury Prison was closed and the facility served as a supply depot until the end of the war. When Union troops entered the former prison on April 12, 1865, they burned it. One of the Salisbury Prison commandants, Maj. John Henry Gee, and the commandant of Andersonville, Capt. Henry Wirz, were the only Confederate prison commandants to be tried for war crimes. While Wirz was found guilty and hanged, Gee was acquitted. [74]

ANDERSONVILLE

For the 179th's soldiers captured on June 17 and at the Battle of the Crater, their experience generally was no better than those captured at Poplar Spring Church – just two to three months longer. Of the ten soldiers missing in action after the June 17, 1864 assault, six can be confirmed as having been taken prisoner. They were sent to Andersonville. Five died there – Company A's Hosea Fish, Company C's Abner Roberts and Emmons Morgan, Company D's Bryant Dains and Company F's Charles Relyea. Company A's John Hall survived, as did Henry Menhuitt, who had been captured at Cold Harbor when he was left behind on picket during the change of front. Hall was exchanged in December 1864 and back in the field with the 179th in January. [75]

Hosea Fish wrote his wife from Petersburg two days after the battle:

> I am a prisoner of war and am not verry badly used. In a day or two I expect to be taken further south. 150 others were taken at the same time. We have

had hard tack and bakon which is very good. I am in a more comfortable situation than I expected to find. Be cheerful and not at all uneasy about me. I dare not write much because both governments will read what I write but remember I could write much that would be pleasing to you. Therefore be contented with respect to me. [76]

[Photo: Andersonville]

Unfortunately for Fish and his fellow prisoners, "further south" meant Andersonville. Hosea Fish died of dysentery on July 31, 1864. Fellow prisoner John Hall was with Fish when he died. "[Fish] had not eaten anything for a day or two and [Hall] cooked some rice for him and he eat a little of it and then turned over and died." [77] Company D's Bryant Dains had been wounded before being captured, but it was diarrhea that took his life on August 1. After a month in the Andersonville Hospital, Company C's Emmons Morgan died of dysentery on September 2. Company C's Abner Roberts died the next day and Company F's Charles Relyea died on October 31. [78]

When John Hall returned to Company A in January 1865 after having been exchanged he looked very healthy. [79] However, when Hall arrived at the Union lines on December 1, 1864, he was suffering from scurvy. [80] He had been paroled at Savannah, Georgia on November 28, 1864, part of a group of ten thousand sick and wounded soldiers exchanged on both sides. [81] Three days later he reported at Camp "CGB" in Maryland and the following day at Camp Parole. Hall was then given a thirty day furlough and rejoined the 179th shortly after returning in January. [82]

Company A's Henry Menhuitt recalled forty years after the war that he:

> was compelled to live without shelter from heat, cold & storms and to lay upon the bare ground... was given but little food and that which was given him was poor and unpalatable... was obliged to drink very impure water and was soon prostrated with a painful violent diarrhea. [83]

After the fall of Atlanta, Menhenitt was one of the Union prisoners transferred to Florence, South Carolina in November 1864. When he was paroled in March 1865, a Union doctor told him that he could not live. His weight had dropped from 170 pounds to ninety pounds while he was a prisoner of war. Nonetheless, Menhenitt recovered and lived to at least the age of sixty-eight. [84]

DANVILLE AND LIBBY PRISONS

[Lithograph: Danville Prison]

Of the thirty-one soldiers missing in action at the Battle of the Crater, at least twenty can be confirmed as having been taken prisoner. [85] They presumably were among the roughly fifteen hundred Union prisoners, including about five hundred colored troops, who were subjected to a humiliating march through the streets of Petersburg, "much after the style of a circus." [86] The Union prisoners were taunted by the citizenry, with much of the invective being directed at the Union's use of black troops. [87] Almost all of the prisoners from the 179th New York were sent to Danville Military Prison in Virginia. Eight were fortunate enough to be paroled or exchanged in September and October 1864 – Robert O. Crawford (September 1), William Crawford (October 17), Dennis DeFord (September 12), David Sherman (September 12), Benjamin Hays (September 24), David Meirthew (September 24), and Nathaniel Reed (October 16). [88]

James Spencer recalled that after he was taken prisoner:

> the Union forces commenced shelling Petersburg and the rebels marched us

around Petersburg three days in the hot sun thinking of course that the Union Army would stop shelling when they found out they were killing their own men. [89]

When Spencer was taken prisoner, a rebel soldier took his hat. Spencer "was compelled to march in the hot sun with nothing to cover my head," other than a handkerchief, and suffered sunstroke. [90]

Spencer spent the first five months of captivity at Libby Prison and was then transferred to Danville. [91] While he presumably did not know it at the time, he was reduced to the ranks on January 1, 1865. [92] Heartless though it might seem, Company D needed to fill his sergeant's slot. (The Regimental History noted that he "[w]as reduced to the ranks while in prison without fault on his part.") [93]

[Lithograph: Libby Prison]

Libby Prison in Richmond was comprised of three connected warehouses making it a total of three hundred feet long. During the course of the war, Libby Prison held approximately one hundred twenty-five thousand Union Prisoners – forty thousand to fifty thousand for an extended period. By the time that the prisoners from the 179th arrived, Libby Prison had transitioned to a holding depot for prisoners being processed through Richmond for other prisons. [94]

A relative of Robert Crawford recalled that when Crawford was captured he "was kept two days without food & then given a full ration of cob-meal corn bread half baked, which brought on diarrhea & a continuation of same food made it chronic." [95] However, that attack of diarrhea brought him an early release from captivity. He was sent to the hospital in Danville Prison on August 14, 1864 and then to Richmond on August 30. As noted, he was paroled at Varina, Virginia on September 1, 1864 and went into the hospital at Annapolis two days later. [96]

Some of the prisoners from the 179th at Danville were later sent to Salisbury for unknown reasons. Co. F's Sergeant William Norton was sent to Salisbury on October 9, around the same time as the soldiers from the 179th captured at Poplar Spring Church began arriving. For Norton to be able to say that he survived Danville and Salisbury was quite an accomplishment.

[Sketch: Aiken's Landing]

The prisoners from Danville – Company C's Daniel Hazelton among them – were also paroled at Aiken's Landing. With an earlier start and a shorter distance to travel, they were paroled

Daniel Hazelton

on February 22 – ten days or so before their comrades from Salisbury. [97] *Harper's Weekly* ran a sketch of Union prisoners being paroled at Aiken's Landing the day before. The magazine reported that: "The work of exchange is now going on as rapidly as possible." [98]

James Spencer arrived at Camp Parole on February 25 and was furloughed on March 5. He remained at home on extended furlough until he was discharged in June 1865. [99]

Eight soldiers from the 179th died at Danville – Company A's Jacob Graves, Company B's George M. Lattin, Company C's John Taylor and William Walker, Company D's Edson

A. Andrews and Howland Washburn, and Company G's Andrew Huston and J. Smith. Diarrhea was generally the cause of death. [100]

Thirty years after the war, one of the eight, Edson Andrews, was remembered poetically in a history of Cattaraugus County:

> He heard his country's call and gave his life,
> Just wed; from nuptial joys he went where grim
> Death grinned o'er Petersburg;-
> Ta'en in that strife
> He died - sad prison death - far, far from
> Home, and friends, and wife. [101]

Howland Washburn

Because the exchange/parole cartel was not in effect in 1864, the men of the 179th New York who were taken prisoner suffered extreme hardship, including a higher mortality rate than their comrades who remained in the field. But that hardship could have been prevented only if the Union had acquiesced in the Confederate insistence that black prisoners would not be exchanged. Harsh as the consequences were for the white prisoners, the Union was right to stand by the principal of equality.

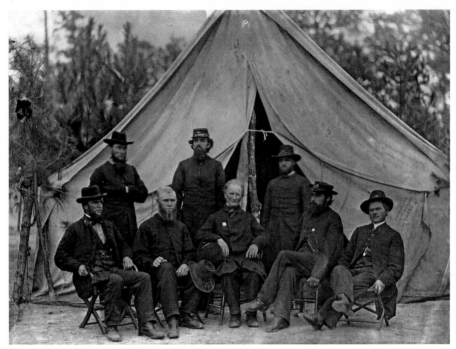

Ninth Corps Chaplains

CHAPTER SEVENTEEN

Religious Faith

"Civil War armies were, arguably, the most religious in American history," according to James McPherson. "Union and Confederate soldiers were products of the Second Great Awakening, that wave of evangelical revivals which swept the United States in the first half of the nineteenth century." [1]

Taking that observation to the level of the individual soldier is problematic because "both 'religion' and 'faith' may be possessed in differing degrees and varying levels of personal commitment." [2] Stephen Woodworth has estimated that "somewhat under half [of the soldiers]" "openly profess[ed] and live[d] the Christian faith." [3] That estimate seems plausible for the soldiers of the 179th. (I also did not find any evidence that there were Jews or other non-Christians in the 179th.)

Completion of the regiment in September meant that the 179th New York was also entitled to a regimental chaplain. The 179th's officially designated regimental chaplain, Edwin A. Taft – a Baptist, arrived in camp a week after the Battle of Poplar Spring Church.

Chaplains in American armies originated in the colonial days, and Congress has authorized a chaplain for each regiment since the national army was formed in 1783. [4] When the War Department issued the plan of organization for the volunteer force called forth by President Lincoln in the spring of 1861, it provided that:

> There will be allowed to each regiment one chaplain, who will be appointed by

the regimental commander on the vote of the field officers and company commanders on duty with the regiment at the time the appointment is to be made. The chaplain so appointed must be a regularly ordained minister of some Christian denomination, and will receive the pay and allowances of captain of cavalry [$145 per month].[5]

Approval by the governor and by the religious denomination were also required.[6]

The status of the chaplain in a military organization was somewhat vague – they held unspecified officer's rank "without command." They did not wear an officer's uniform, but their dress was officially prescribed:

> Plain black frock-coat, with standing collar, one row of nine black buttons on the breast, with "herring bone" of black braid around the buttons and button holes. Plain black pantaloons. Black felt hat, or army forage cap, with a gold embroidered wreath in front, on black velvet ground, encircling the letters U.S. in silver, old English characters.[7]

The fact that the 179th did not have a regimental chaplain when it moved to the front in the spring of 1864 did not prevent the soldiers from practicing their religious faith. When the 179th arrived at Arlington Heights, Company A's Hosea Fish was one of a group of soldiers who held their own service that night: "one of the boys red a chapter in the testament. Then we kneeled down and I prayed."[8] Shortly after the 179th arrived in Virginia, Company A's Corporal Daniel D. Lowell was unofficially appointed as "pastor" for the 179th. He was also detailed as "postman to carry mail to and from Washington." Before the War, Lowell "taught school and preached the Gospel."[9]

The religious content of Lowell's sermons is not clear. His fellow townsman from West Almond, Daniel Lee, wrote his wife that Lowell "has turned to be a good democrat sins he came here... [L]ast Sunday he did preach to us here and did preach against republickens ism." Lowell apparently was assigned a "house" of unknown size for religious purposes.[10]

Nor is it clear how long Lowell served as unofficial chaplain for the 179th. However, it could not have been longer than August 24, 1864, when he was admitted to the First Division, Ninth Corps Hospital with jaundice. He was transferred to the Depot Field Hospital at City Point three days later and then to Willets Point Hospital in New York Harbor. He received a brief furlough and then was transferred to the U.S.A. General Hospital in Elmira where he spent the rest of the war.[11]

Company I's Davis C. Marshall was a Baptist minister, but he had enlisted in August 1864 as a private. He was promoted to First Lieutenant in September 1864. At the end of the war, Marshall was brevetted captain for his service.[12] I don't know if he served the regiment in an informal religious role. Company B's Lieutenant William Bogart and Company I's Lieutenant William Kinney were also ministers before the war, but again I don't know if they played any informal role in the religious life of the soldiers. Company A's Elihu Linkletter, Company D's Ezra Tinker, and Company I's Francis King became ministers after the war.[13]

Before Taft arrived in the field, the *Elmira Daily Advertiser* announced on September 17, 1864 that the Rev. Mr. Taft, Chaplain of the 179th New York Volunteers, would be preaching that Sunday at the First Baptist Church. Taft had studied at Madison University,

Ezra Tinker

which had been founded by the Baptist Education Society. (It is Colgate University today.) [14] Despite the War Department's authorization, chaplains were in short supply and the 179th New York was fortunate to have Chaplain Taft. In June 1862, only sixty percent of Union regiments had a chaplain. [15] (I don't know if Taft is one of the Ninth Corps chaplains in the October 1864 photo at the beginning of this chapter.)

Taft and a friend, soon to be Lieutenant John Andrews, left Elmira for the front in Virginia on October 3 and arrived at City Point two days later. They stayed the night with the agent of the Christian Commission, C. J. Nicholson, who was a friend of Taft's from Madison University. They attended an evening prayer meeting for the soldiers in the Christian Commission's "chapel" – a large cloth tent. The soldiers sang traditional Methodist hymns – "We're Homeward Bound," "Shining Shore," "How Sweet the Name of Jesus Sounds," and "Jesus, Lover of My Soul." Nicholson read the 107th Psalm: "O give thanks unto the Lord, for he is good; for his mercy endureth for ever." The soldiers were "praying with trembling voices, the tears streaming down their bronzed cheeks, praying to be restored to their loved ones at home." [16]

Later that night, Andrews attended a nearby "negro prayer meeting."

> It was comprised of negro soldiers, and men, women and children from the negro camp. There were several hundred present. A negro preacher conducted it. It was to me a solemn and impressive sight–that black preacher, impassioned, illiterate praying to the same God we all worship, praying for the same country we are now fighting for–that dusky crowd swaying to and fro, following with murmurs of approval the wild, weird strain of their preacher. [17]

Joseph Becker sketched a negro prayer meeting at City Point the month before:

[Sketch: Prayer Meeting]

The next day Taft and Andrews took the U.S. Military Railroad from City Point to what was then the end of the line roughly sixteen miles away – Warren Station at the junction with the captured Weldon Railroad. Travel was rough – they rode on bales of hay and sacks of grain and had to change cars three times. They had to walk the last three miles to reach the 179th's camp. [18]

When they arrived on October 6, Chaplain Taft got right to work and held his first prayer meeting for the 179th on Sunday evening, October 9. Sunday evening was the regular time for prayer meetings. As with the Christian Commission a week before, the 179th's chapel was a tent. Taft would serve the soldiers of the 179th through the end of the war. [19]

Taft did not formally receive his commission as chaplain until November 13. [20] Even an appointment as chaplain had its complications. Five signatures from members of the denomination were necessary for the petition to the governor. Andrews had gotten the signature of an Elder Taylor for Taft just before they left for the front and another friend in Albany helped speed up the process. [21] To complicate matters further, Taft was a private in the 5th New York Heavy Artillery. He had enlisted in January 1864, but had been on detached duty as a clerk at the Elmira Draft Rendez Vous. He had to go to Harpers Ferry to muster out of the 5th New York Heavy Artillery to take the Chaplain's position in the 179th. Andrews lent him twenty dollars for the trip, which was successful. [22] Fortunately, Taft did have the required support of the officers of the 179th. Shortly after his arrival, all the officers of the 179th in the field had signed a letter to Governor Seymour requesting him to commission Taft as regimental chaplain. [23]

In addition to ministering to the needs of the soldiers, Chaplain Taft also had "the sad duty" to inform family and friends that "those who had just left them had fallen in battle." [24] The duty was no less sad when the soldier had died from disease. In January 1865, Company A's Private Moses Brown died of acute bronchitis. On January 26, Chaplain Taft wrote Mrs. Brown:

> I suppose ere this you have heard of the death of your husband. I was not aware of it myself until the other day. I went to the hospital to see him and take a letter and was surprised to find him gone. The hospital is fifteen miles from the camp and I went down only once a week. A few days before I saw him & he thought he was better.
>
> He died rather suddenly at last. He expressed to me a firm trust in his Saviour...
>
> They said he was very trusting until the last. One month ago at the old camp he consecrated himself anew to his Master. He regretted that he had not lived up to his christian profession but determined to do so in the future. He was always at the meetings & ready to take part afterwards and I believe was ripe for the harvest like a shock of corn.
>
> Trust in your Saviour my Sister. Your husband is not lost but gone before.
>
> The day is not far distant when we shall rest in God with him if faithful to the vows we have taken. Mourn not but look up and feel to say "thy will not mine be done O Lord." ...
>
> Yours in hope & sympathy
>
> E.A. Taft
> Chaplain [25]

Mrs. Brown could not be at her husband's deathbed, but at least she was reassured about the state of his soul. (Rev. A. McDougall preached a funeral sermon for Brown in April 1865 at the Presbyterian Church in Dryden.) [26]

McPherson refers to a study of American enlisted men in World War II that found that prayer was the main factor that kept them going when the going got tough. He concludes that "the same was true of Civil War soldiers." [27] Company F's George B. White asked his mother to remember him in her prayers and in return promised to "try and live right in the sight of the Lord." [28]

When a representative of the U. S. Christian Commission visited Company K's Stephen Ferris, a thirty-nine-year-old farmer from Tioga County who was suffering from chronic diarrhea, at the Slough Barracks Hospital in May 1865, he found Ferris feeling "quite low," "only waiting for the Master's summons." But Ferris' faith was strong – he had been "a professor too long to be enchanted by the devil now." (Ferris recovered.) [29]

Many Civil War soldiers carried their own pocket Bibles to support their faith. The New Testament was the preferred choice for a pocket Bible because the Old Testament was four times as long and the New Testament "contains more direct and open statements of ... doctrine." The goal of the American Bible Society was to distribute Bibles to all soldiers and it printed over five million during the war. [30]

His *New Testament and Psalms* undoubtedly helped sustain Company A's James C. Rutan. The last page of Rutan's *New Testament and Psalms* bears the following pencil notes:

> Red through on the battlefield near Petersburgh 1864
>
> Red through In Ladies Home U.S.A. General Hospital New York March 12, 1865.

[Carte de Visite: Apostles' Creed]

There are also marginal pencil "checks" by numerous passages in the *New Testament and Psalms*, presumably those most meaningful to him. In a letter to his wife about their future, he indicated that he would accept "the Lord's will." Rutan also carried a carte de visite sized rendition of the Apostles Creed in decorative calligraphy – "I believe in God the Father Almighty, maker of heaven and earth, and in Jesus Christ his only son, our Lord." A carte de visite sized print of a painting of a women kneeling in prayer was signed by his wife with "devotion". [31]

[Carte de Visite: Kneeling in Prayer]

Company E's James Van Gilder also read his Bible, although apparently in part due to the lack of other pastimes. "We do not have anything to do but cook and eat our rations and read my Testament. I have read it almost half through." [32]

Daniel Howard of Company H used his pocket Bible for a much more wordly purpose. Very few Civil War soldiers had dogtags, so he wrote the following on the inside cover:

> Should anybody find this and know the fate of the owner they will please forward it with a note stating the facts to Mr. George Hanlon, Elmira, Chemung County, New York [33]

Steven Woodworth concluded that: "It can certainly be said, and accurately, that the imminence of death and maiming, suffering, and hardship concentrated the religious thinking of the Civil War soldiers..." [34] On Sunday, June 19, 1864, two days after the 179th's and his first battle, Rutan took comfort reading the XCI Psalm.

> 1. He that dwelleth in the secret place of the Most High shall abide under the shadow of the Almighty.
>
> 2. I will say of the Lord, He is my refuge and my fortress: my God; in him I will trust.
>
> 3. Surely he shall deliver thee from the snare of the fowler and from the noisome pestilence.
>
> 4. He shall cover thee with his feathers, and under his wings shalt thou trust: his truth shall by thy shield and buckler.
>
> 5. Thou shalt not be afraid for the terror by night; nor for the arrow that flieth by day;
>
> 6. Nor for the pestilence that walketh in darkness; nor for the destruction that wasteth at noonday.
>
> 7. A thousand shall fall at thy side, and ten thousand at thy right hand; but it shall not come nigh thee. ... [35]

The June 17 battle does seem to have "concentrated the religious thinking" of Daniel B. Lee. Before the battle, Lee's comments about his fate were not explicitly linked to God: "It may be my lot to not ever see home again, but all I can do is to hope for the time to com when I can see my family in peas and content." [36] References to God generally were reserved for the sections of his letters addressed to his seven-year-old daughter, Hannah Ann, and were expressed in a general way.

I do feel as that god will spare me to come home and live with you agane.
[circa May 1, 1864]

May god grant that we may meet agane on this globe or earth. [May 28, 1864]

How I do long for the time to com that I can see you and your mother to onse
more, but god only nows when that time will com. [June 6, 1864] [37]

In his first letter after the June 17 battle, Lee spoke of "luck," but made clear that his "luck" was "God's will."

Again I am spared to right you but it is just through my good luck because all
of the regiment is cut to pieces. ... If I can have the luck to get home again how
happy I should be which I really think will be if it is god will for me to. [38]

A week later he wrote that he had been "under fire" since June 17, "and yet I have bin spared and I do hope it will be god's will that I may see you agane." [39] In his last letter to his wife and daughter before he was captured, Lee wrote:

I do think I shall be spared to see you agane... there is men shot all of the time
but the blessed god has seen fit to save me until now and if it is his wishes I
shall be spared to see you agane. [40] (Lee did not return home, dying of disease.)

While Lee does seem to have believed in the doctrine of "divine providence," there is no express reference to prayer (as opposed to hope) in his letters, nor did he speak directly of an afterlife (as opposed to his hope to meet again "on this earth"). [41]

Homer Olcott was quite clear about his belief in an afterlife: "may it be his will to give both of us good health to meet on earth. If not may we so live so as to meet in heaven in one unbroken family where we shall part no more." [42]

When Company B's George Hemingway was captured at the Battle of Poplar Spring the day after he arrived at the front, he viewed it as "the will of Providence and I submitted to my fate as cheerfully thinking that it was for a good cause that I fell bleeding into their hand." [43] Homer Olcott was also comfortable with God's will: "if it is God's will [I] will pass safe through, if not, his will be done, not mine... [M]y mind is at peace on that account for I feel that I have changed since I left Elmira and I feel that God is with me." [44] Stephen Compton wrote in his diary on New Year's Day 1865: "This is Sunday the 1st of the yr 1865. God has spared me to see its entrance. Shall I see its exit. God grant that ere the end of this year peace may bless our land." [45]

The resolutions adopted by the soldiers of Company E to honor Captain Blachford after he was killed in the June 17 assault also reflect a belief in divine providence: "Whereas, It has pleased Almighty God to remove from our midst in the fierce conflict of battle, our late friend and brother officer, Capt. Daniel Blachford." [46]

Of course not all the soldiers in the 179th directly stated religious beliefs in their letters home (which is not to say that they did not have religious beliefs – only that they did not state them in their letters.) Company D's Capt. William Bird also felt lucky to have survived the carnage of the June 17 assault with just a wounded knee, but did not specifically attribute his luck to God. [47] There also are no religious themes in the fourteen surviving letters that Company B's William Lamont wrote to his family. [48]

During his fatal illness in the summer of 1865, Company I's John Cook wrote his parents six letters from the hospital, but strong expressions of faith are absent. On June 30, 1865, he wrote "I am a little better, Thank God" – more a figure of speech than an expression of faith. In his last letter to his parents, Cook wrote that "I am failing all the time" and asked his father to come visit him in the hospital. "I want to see you before I leave this world." [49]

On the other hand, the representative of the Christian Commission who visited Company A's Nathaniel Mabe, an eighteen-year-old laborer, while he was suffering in the hospital from typhoid fever and dysentery described him as "A praying Christian boy. He wept much in talking of his Christian mother." (Mabe returned to duty two months later.) [50]

After attending the soldiers' prayer meeting at City Point, Andrews wrote in his war journal:

> Oh, how much I wished I were a christian then that I might kneel down and
> pray to God for those I loved. "There is rest for you" they sing at the close, but
> I felt as though it were not for me. [51]

However, his views may have changed. Several months later, he noted wistfully on February 19, 1865:

> A quiet pleasant holy Sabbath it has been – but there are no Sabbaths in the
> army. There are occasionally some *almost* and today has been one of them. [52]
> (emphasis in original)

On March 19, 1865, he attended religious services in the chaplain's tent for the first time. [53]

Confronted by the prospect of death or serious injury, the religious beliefs of many of the men in the 179th New York brought them peace of mind.

Working Parties

CHAPTER EIGHTEEN

Fall Camp at Pegram Farm

While the 179th had had to contend with blistering heat during the summer, fall brought the prospect of cold – and rain. The night of October 8, John Andrews slept in Captain Ottenot's tent – "The wind blew hard and the little cloth tent was but a slight protection against its biting cold." [1] After several days of rain in November, Andrews gloomily noted that it: "is raining yet, and the prospect is fair that it will rain – forever." [2]

After the Battle of Poplar Spring Church, the 179th New York camped on Pegram Farm for the next two months. [3] On October 2, the 50th Engineers began constructing what would be named Fort Welch. Three hundred men from the Ninth Corps were detailed to assist in the work, and that included men from the 179th New York. William Larzelere and other troops from the 179th were on fatigue duty the night of October 3 working on the fort. [4] Company K's Abner Welch, a twenty-five-year-old farmer, wrote his family that: "This fort that I worked on day to knight is now named Fort Welch so when you read about it you will know that I have been their." [5]

The 179th had been encamped in the woods just outside the breastworks, but on October 7 moved to an open field inside the works behind Fort Welch and near the remains of the Pegram House. [6] For a period of time, the Army of the Potomac's general headquarters was located only about one hundred yards from the 179th New York's camp. Company B's William Lamont, a twenty-two-year-old farmer from Dryden, wrote his sister on October 24 that "I see Grant and

Meed and Potter every few days." [7] Three days before, Grant and Meade had passed through the 179th's camp on their way to Fort Welch. Andrews "had a good sight at the hero of Shiloh, Donaldson & etc." [8]

The night of October 11, nearly the whole regiment was out on picket under command of Lieutenant Force. [9] As the Petersburg campaign developed into a long siege, going out on picket became the critical part of the soldier's duty. Lamont wrote his sister at the end of October that he was: "on picket 24 hours every third day sometimes not quite so often. We drill the rest of the time." He described picket duty as "lonesome work." [10]

The purpose of the picket line in the Petersburg campaign was "not simply to give an alarm and retire on the main position," but to be "a forward defense capable of 'the most desperate resistance to any line of battle that might be brought against it.'" [11] Conditions on the ground governed the deployment of pickets in any particular location. Typically, the picket line was a series of entrenched positions located about fifty feet apart, each with four to seven men. A vedette line of "gopher holes" was located about fifty yards in front of the picket line. [12]

Lamont described the routine of picket duty:

> We do not fire any on picket in the day time but as soon as it is dark we commence and keep it up until sun rise. We have to keep our heads pretty close to the ground some of the time for the Johneys shoot very careless. They made a break on our picket line a short time ago. They drove the pickets in on our right, but we stuck to our pits and drove them back. [13]

In a later letter, Lamont wrote that: "This is my knight for picket. I have got 75 rounds of cartridges I think that will be as many as I can shoot." [14]

Colonel Gregg described the practical "rules of engagement" for picket duty that had been worked out by the soldiers:

> I was division officer of the day...It was my duty to inspect the picket guards, but at several places where lines are so close we are not required to go as they shoot officers. But privates have an understanding not to fire upon one another when they relieve guard. When they want rest, one or the other side calls out for a truce to make coffee or for any other reason. Then both sides come out of their holes – talk together like old friends, and exchange coffee and tobacco. [15]

This was a change – back in June, Confederate sharpshooters tried to pick off men when picket lines were relieved shortly after dark. [16]

Benjamin Hadley

Casualties on picket duty for the 179th were relatively light during the fall and winter of 1864 to 1865. No one in the 179th died on picket duty after Company C's James Brown died of wounds received on August 6. Second Lt. Jeffrey Wisner was wounded while on picket on November 30, 1864. He returned home to Elmira without the glory that the *Elmira Daily Advertiser* had hoped for. [17] Also wounded while on picket in the fall and winter of 1864 to 1865 were Company K's Orrin Hawkins (October 28), Company G's Levi Walker (December 10), and Company F's Benjamin Hadley (February 2). [18]

While pickets may have fired without taking careful aim, there were still close calls. John Andrews noted on March 22, 1865 that:

"the firing on both sides was considerable and the balls came close. Several came closer to me than was agreeable." [19] The picket lines were often close enough for verbal communication. William Lamont wrote his sister that: " We are not allowed to say much but we sing out to them some times." [20] Rather than exchanging volleys of minie balls, the soldiers occasionally traded pointed words and taunted each other as occurred after the Union failed to take the South Side Railroad at the end of October.

Face-to-face conversations could be more personal. Lieutenant Levi Force talked for an hour in between the picket lines with a Confederate lieutenant and a civilian trying to get back to his farm to retrieve some legal papers. They shook hands and Force shared the whiskey in his canteen, although permission to cross into the Union line was denied to the civilian. Force spoke of what "we would do when this rebellion is put down." The Confederate lieutenant replied that "when the rebellion is put down we (the rebels) will be the worst-whipped nation that was ever heard of." [21]

While some units began to build winter quarters as early as the latter part of September, [22] the 179th New York was not progressing. William Lamont explained to his sister at the end of October that: "We expect to move every day so we do not fix up our tent any." [23] However, by the beginning of November, the soldiers of the 179th were busy chopping down trees in a nearby woods and hewing them to build up their quarters. [24] Andrews observed that: "The most of them now have quite comfortable quarters – a pen built up of logs, about three feet high, the cracks plastered with mud, and over this their shelter tents, – and with a fire place in one end of it they make themselves quite comfortable indeed." [25]

Brick for fireplaces came from the ruins of nearby houses. [26] For his quarters, Andrews had purchased a stove from a sutler for seven dollars. [27] The stove made their tent "a favorite resort of half-frozen officers." [28] Still, in Andrews' view the location in an open field was not good for winter quarters. [29]

Rumors of a new offensive began circulating in the 179th's camp on October 25. A substantial movement seemed afoot based on orders "to deal out sixty rounds of cartridges per man to be carried in their cartridge boxes, and forty rounds in their haversacks; also to deal out three days rations to be carried in their haversacks and three days rations to be carried in their knapsacks, also three days rations of beef to be driven along; and the regiment to get ready to move." [30] The Ninth Corps did not move out as expected on October 26 and the rumor mill started to work overtime:

> Various are the rumors afloat as to where it will strike when it does move. In the morning it seemed to be the general opinion that our Corps was going to "the right" to reinforce Butler and make a heavy strike there; but along in the afternoon the current began to set in the other way, and this evening no one feels the least doubt but that there will be a heavy blow struck on "the left." [31]

Andrews remarked on the prevailing optimism:

> Doubtless another of Grant's "left flank movements" is to be made, and we all feel confident that it will be successful. The whole army is in the best of spirits and feels the greatest confidence of the success of the movement about to be made. With them it is a fixed fact that the South Side Railroad is now to be taken. [32]

The South Side Railroad was indeed the objective of Grant's next offensive, which took place on October 27 and 28. As General Meade's Aide de Camp, Theodore Lyman, put it:

> We must keep at them, that is the only way; no let up, no armistice. They perfectly hate what we are doing now, going a couple of miles and fortifying,

then going two more and fortifying again; then making a sudden rush, taking a position and a lot of cannon, and again fortifying that. All these moves being a part of what we may call a throttling plan. [33] (emphasis in original)

This offensive involved elements of the Second, Fifth and Ninth Corps. The plan was that the Ninth Corp, which was located at the western end of the Union lines, would move due west from Fort Cummings along Hawks Road until it encountered new Confederate entrenchments believed to be still under construction and lightly defended. The Ninth Corps would then move through those positions to the Boydton Plank Road and then on to the South Side Railroad.

The Fifth Corps would also leave the Union lines at Fort Cummings, but would drop below the Ninth Corps and then head west toward the crossing of the Boydton Plank Road over Hatcher's Run and then on to the South Side Railroad. Not only did the Union generals believe that the new Confederate positions in this area were still not completed, they also believed that the new lines ended above the Fifth Corps proposed point of attack.

The Second Corps would drop even further south, cross Hatcher's Run at Cummings Ford, and then proceed west into an area believed to be lightly defended. [34]

However, the plan was based on bad military intelligence. The Confederate entrenchments had in fact been completed several days before and the Confederates were able to bring sufficient forces in line to properly defend them. [35] The new lines also extended further to the east of the Boydton Plank Road crossing. In the event, the Fifth Corps and the Ninth Corps were both unable to find weak spots in the positions in front of them. Because Grant was discouraging any frontal attack against strong positions and the heavy casualties that would bring, the Fifth and the Ninth Corps dug in and waited to see what the Second Corps could accomplish, ultimately retiring to the Union lines the next day.

The Second Corps initially encountered little resistance and was able to move west below Hatcher's Run as far as Burgess' Mill, where it survived a nearly successful Confederate attack. In the end, Grant became concerned that the Second Corps would move too far west and risk being cut off from the Fifth and Ninth Corps if the Confederates attacked across Hatcher's Run. Thus, Grant called off the attack and called what had been conceived of as a major offensive a "reconnaissance." [36] John Andrews noticed the difference, writing in his journal about "our late battle or 'reconnaissance in force' as General Grant calls it." [37]

To begin the offensive, the Ninth Corps broke camp at 3 a.m. on October 27 and headed south within the Union lines to Fort Cummings. It started raining as the Union forces moved out – "old soldiers say it always rains when the Army of the Potomac moves." It "rained by spells all day but by evening it poured down. " (emphasis in original) [38] The Ninth Corps exited Fort Cummings on time with Willcox's First Division in the lead, but the First Division stopped at an abandoned Confederate position nearby (Fort McRae) and did not start up again until five thirty that morning. This delay may have enabled the Confederates to timely bring up troops to fill their new positions before the Fifth and Ninth Corps arrived. [39] Ferrero 's Division came next and Potter's division followed as the reserve, holding at Fort McRae. [40]

[Sketch: Vaughn Road, October 27]

As it became apparent that there was no weak spot to attack, Willcox's division took position opposite the new Confederate lines. Ferrero's division moved into line to the right of Willcox and Potter's division in turn moved into line to the right of Ferrero. Potter's division then extended its lines north then east back to the Union lines near Fort Welch. [41] Potter's division "threw up a good line of breast-works" that afternoon and chopped down the trees in front of the line. [42] The 179th

New York was in the woods about a mile and a half from Fort Cummings and "could see nothing of what was going on, yet the battle was all the while raging." At some point in the afternoon, the 179th New York was "ordered to the breastworks to prepare to receive a charge as it was thought the rebs would soon be upon them, but 'nary' [a] reb came."[43]

It rained even harder during the night. Nonetheless, the 179th New York and the rest of Potter's division worked through the night, slashing more timber in the front of the lines and opening roads in the rear. Company C's Lt. Levi Force commanded the 179th's seventy man detail. He returned in the morning "pretty well soaked." As John Andrews observed, Force was "always called upon whenever there is any duty to be performed."[44]

During the morning of October 28, the Ninth Corps continued cutting down trees for several dozen yards in front of the lines with the tops pointing toward the Confederates.[45] The Ninth Corps, along with the Fifth and Second Corps, was then ordered to return to its original positions. The Ninth Corps started back at 1 p.m. (Potter's division at 3 p.m.) and completed the return to Pegram's Farm by 6 p.m. Confederate cavalry had attempted to cut off Potter's troops, but were blocked by a swamp.[46]

A 179th "Memorandum" briefly summarized its action:

> Left camp near Pegram House Virginia at 3 A.M. moved towards the left on a reconnaissance in force –threw up breastworks and remained until next day about 3 o'clock P.M. when we received orders to return to our old Camp where we arrived about half past four o'clock P.M. Casualties. One man wounded on picket, slightly.[47]

William Lazalere succinctly summarized the action: "made flank move and to the left. Found the enemy too strongly entrenched. Fell back to old camp."[48]

The optimism that Andrews had reported on October 26 disappeared after the battle. On October 29, he recorded in his War Journal that:

> Our men feel very despondent and perhaps think we were more badly whipped than we in reality were. Most all call it the worst failure of the campaign and consequently feel that the war is prolonged indefinitely.[49]

The feelings of "despondency" may well have been aggravated by the Confederate pickets taunting across the lines – "why didn't [you] take the South Side Railroad?" – and the Confederate bands playing the "Rogue's March." (emphasis in original)[50]

The feelings of despondency may have increased on October 31 when the 179th mustered for pay. The muster was not for actually paying the soldiers. The muster was for the purpose of collecting information to prepare the payroll for future payment.[51] While military pay was hardly substantial, the real problem for soldiers was not the amount, but the infrequency with which it was paid. Military regulations required that pay be given every two months, but that simply did not happen.[52] When they were discharged in June 8, 1865, Company A's James Applegate had not been paid since September 9, 1864 and Zavin Carey had not been paid since December 31, 1864.[53]

In mid-November, William Lamont wrote his sister that "I am getting short of money would like 5 dollars by return mail."[54] After frequent requests for money over the succeeding months– never more than $5, Lamont wrote his parents in February 1865:

> You may think that I am very extravagant in using so much money but if it was not for the money I get from home I am afraid I would come out spring poor for my appetite is so good that I can not make nine hard tacks last me twenty four hours.

Lamont said that there was "a report that we are going to draw part of [our pay] next week, but there are so many false reports we haven't much hope of getting it." [55] He was right.

The shortage of cash was not limited to enlisted men. In December 1864, Colonel Gregg thanked his good friend Ariel Thurston for sending him a draft – "the draft enclosed came safe, and in good time, as I was about whipped for money." [56]

In contrast, John Andrews seems to have had a surplus of funds. On a page of his War Journal, he noted the following [57]:

Lent Capt. Force (Paid)	$15.00
Lent Capt. Pierson (Pd.)	$3.00
Lent E.K. Smith (Pd.)	$2.00
Lent Jasper Jayne	$1.00
Lieut. Bogart owes me	$35.00
Lent Doty (probably Martin)	$1.00
Lent Capt. Pierson	$5.00

Andrews seems to have been something of an equal opportunity lender. He made loans not only to his superior officers, but also to enlisted men, albeit in smaller amounts–Corporal Jasper Jayne and Private Eugene K. Smith, both under his command in Company D. There is no indication whether Andrews charged interest.

Not only were the soldiers short on cash, but there had also been a breakdown in the supply chain. In early October, there had been a shortage of rations to the point that some soldiers may have gone without food for several days. [58] And there were complaints about the lack of variety in army fare. Abner Welch began a letter to his parents by complaining that: "I am sick of hardtack and bread." Still, newly arrived recruit James Vangilder wrote on September 26: "We have good pork and good coffee and sugar and hardtack and that is good enough for anybody and we have sweet potatoes and that is not all." [59]

For variety, the soldiers could on occasion turn to the sutlers whom the army allowed to accompany the troops. One of the soldiers' main needs for cash was to buy food and other things from the sutler. Daniel Lee bought cakes and cheese, but also seems to have relied on the sutler more generally as well – he wrote his wife that he bought all his food from the sutler and that it cost $2 per day for one-quarter of what he wanted. [60] William Lamont bought "from the suttlars when I get a chance but that is not very often, they do not come around very often." On one occasion, he bought flour from the sutler and made pancakes. [61]

The sutlers' prices that the men of the 179th paid in the fall of 1864 were the following [62]:

Apples (about the size of an egg)	5 cents
Butter (half a pint)	80 cents
Condensed milk (one pint)	$1.72
Crackers (pound)	50 cents
Pot of cheese	75 cents
Pies	25 cents
Whiskey (pint)	$5

By comparison, market prices in Canandaigua, New York were 75 cents to a dollar for a bushel of apples and 24 to 27 cents for a pound of butter.[63] And an apple purchased in Canandaigua would not be "about the size of an egg"! Still, apples apparently were particularly popular. When the sutler was ordered away in March 1865, Andrews noted that it was "much to the dissatisfaction of the apple hungry ones."[64]

Tobacco was also in demand. For Daniel Lee, the concern about tobacco was over economics rather than health. "Tobacco is so [high?] here I must quit using it." "My tobacco cost me about five dollars a pound here."[65] Company A's Jacob Graves, an eighteen-year-old farmer, asked his father to send him a dollar so he could buy tobacco.[66]

Like Jacob Graves, the soldiers of the 179th were often short on cash, but the sutlers often accommodated them with credit. Sutlers could afford to take the risk because the government allowed them to put a "stoppage" on the soldier's pay.[67] When Timothy Shaw died, his final statement showed that he owed sutler Judd O'Neill $12. When Henry Hauser was discharged he owed O'Neill $3.[68]

After the Boydton Plank Road offensive at the end of October, the 179th New York returned to its regular routine. Lamont described his day in a letter to his sister on November 15:

> I do not no what to write about but I guess I will tell you what I have done today. It is the same most every day only when on picket. The first place the bugal blows at 6 o'clock for roll call. I then go to the spring which is about 40 rods wash fill canteen breakfast 7 the police duty till 8 then wait on how [illegible] till 8:30 fol mail read letters till 9 if you get any. Then co drill till 11. Dinner 12. Battalion drill from 4 till 4:30. Dress parade 5. Super 5:30. Roll call 8. Lights out 8:30.[69]

"On Saturdays," John Andrews recounted, "there is no drill. That day is given the soldiers to do their washing, to clean their arms for Sunday inspection, & etc. The camp is then generally very lively, some washing, some at sports of various kinds, Bands playing, and everyone enjoying himself."[70]

Sundays were different according to Lamont: "I have more to do sundays than any other day. We have inspection in the fore noon and review in the afternoon."[71]

For a brief time there was a new activity – target practice. Target practice was a rare event in the Union army.[72] During the mornings of November 5 and November 7, the 179th did target shooting.[73] Company I's Elias Beach, a twenty-year-old farmer from Newfield, was injured during the exercise – struck in the eye by "a piece of gun cap."[74] Company C and probably other companies did more target practice on November 9.[75]

On November 18 Andrews wrote in his journal:

> Camp full of rumors of a movement. Some say to the Army of the James, around at Dutch Gap where it is one continual battle; others to Covington, Ky.; while some think Burnside is going to take command and take us to Wilmington. That there is to be a movement *somewhere all believe*, and yet we know nothing about it – we have not yet received marching orders.

Elias Beach

We feel in our very bones that there is to be a movement, and all the old soldiers say they can see indications of it, but I can see none. [76] (emphasis in original)

In the end, there was rain – and no movement (if one had been planned). The "old soldiers" "feel very thankful for this rain for they think it has saved them from a battle, perhaps a series of them." [77]

President Lincoln had declared Thanksgiving as an official holiday in 1863 and the government and community organizations undertook extensive efforts to provide a special Thanksgiving for Union troops in the field. Such was the case in 1864, but the results were somewhat disappointing for the 179th New York.

To begin with, the provisions arrived a day late for the 179th. Nonetheless, John Andrews described the dinner as "a pretty good meal of turkey." Each soldier got two apples, but they were "very poor, badly decayed." One pie and ten cakes had to be shared amongst the men of Company C. Andrews acknowledged the gifts from "friends at home," but "the larger part is destroyed or fails to reach its destination." [78]

As enlisted men, William Lamont and William Larzelere had an additional gripe. Lamont wrote his sister: "Our thanksgiving dinner came yesterday. For my share I got a nice piece of turkey, 5 apples, 1/2 turnip, 1/2 of a cookey, 1/2 fried cake. It was surprising to see the load of turkeys, but the shoalder straps got their share first." [79] Larzelere had a similar view:

Our Thanksgiving turkies have just come. A great many wagon loads of them for our Brigade. We get some apples & a few turneps with them. Jars of cranberry sauc, pies, cake & [?] ...do not reach their intended destination, for some of the commissary officers and other officials manage to appropriate them to their own use. It is just so with the sanitary goods sent to hospital, the officials and Doctors at the hospitals manage to get the best part. Now whoever want to send luxuries to their friends in the Army had better direct to their friend personally for it is more safe. [80]

In the army – as opposed to a democratic society, all men are not created equal.

Firing Squad

CHAPTER NINETEEN

Desertion

Desertion and absence without leave were significant problems for the Union army (as they were for the Confederate army) throughout the war. [1] When General Joseph Hooker took command of the Army of the Potomac in January 20, 1863 shortly after the disasterous assault at Fredericksburg, the situation with desertion "seemed almost hopeless." [2] Several hundred soldiers a day were deserting and roughly a quarter of the Army of the Potomac was absent. [3] Hooker made a serious effort to arrest deserters and tighten discipline and for a time desertion in the Army of the Potomac almost ended. [4]

For the Union army overall, desertion was brought down to just over 3,400 soldiers per month by the end of 1863 from over 5,500 per month earlier in the year. [5] However, desertion jumped to nearly seven thousand soldiers in January 1864 and peaked at over ten thousand in October and November 1864. [6] In 1865, when it was increasingly apparent that the Union would soon win the war, between five thousand and seven thousand Union soldiers still deserted every month. [7]

In the leading study of desertion during the Civil War, Ella Lonn grouped the causes of desertion from the Union army into nine "heads":

(1) opposition to "coercion of the South by military force"

(2) the "hardships of war," both in terms of shortages of food and equipment and of exposure to the extremes of weather

(3) extended delays in pay and the consequent inability of the soldiers to support their families at home

(4) "an utter absence of a realization of the obligation incurred by enlistment and failure to impress that obligation on the mind of the soldier by firm discipline."

(5) lax discipline, particularly with respect to sick leave and furloughs

(6) "war weariness and discouragement" with the lack of progress toward Confederate defeat

(7) "Probably the most serious cause producing desertion was the calibre of recruits, noticeably inferior after 1862. Reinforcements were constantly being sent to the armies, but they were for the most part mercenaries, immoral and cowardly"

(8) the "large and numerous bounties given to volunteers proved undoubtedly an inducement to desert for the purpose of reenlisting, or to enlist when the recruit knew that he had no intention of remaining in the field"

(9) "the cowardly or traitorous encouragement of desertion by civilians," which could take forms as different as inciting the draft riots and encouraging soldiers not to return from furlough [8]

Article 20 of *An Act for Establishing Rules and Articles for the Government of the Armies of the United States* (the Articles of War) provided that:

> All officers and soldiers who have received pay, or have been duly enlisted in the service of the United States, and shall be convicted of having deserted the same, shall suffer death, or such other punishment as, by sentence of a court-martial, shall be indicted. [9]

The policy of the Union army and the Lincoln Administration toward punishment for desertion varied over time and with the circumstances. Earlier in the war, punishment for desertion had been less harsh. Rather than death, "such other punishment" as dismissal with loss of pay was the penalty, even for desertion in the face of the enemy. [10] Unless repeated, an attempt to desert, even from the front, did not result in execution. [11]

Executions for desertion became common in the Army of the Potomac in 1863, initially under General Hooker and then under General Meade when he took command after the Battle of Chancellorsville. On March 10, 1863, President Lincoln issued an executive order directing all soldiers "now absent from their respective regiments without leave" to return to their regiments forthwith. He further provided that all absent soldiers who reported by April 1, 1863 would not be punished except for the loss of pay and allowances during their absence. However, those soldiers absent without authorization who did not report by April 1 "shall be arrested as deserters, and punished as the law provides." He also implored the citizenry not to encourage desertion, which was "weakening the strength of the armies and prolonging the war, giving aid and comfort to the enemy, and cruelly exposing the gallant and faithful soldiers remaining in the ranks to increased hardships and danger." [12] Meade reported that when five deserters were shot at once in August 1863 some of his veteran soldiers commented "Why did they not begin this practice long ago?" [13] In Meade's view, the veterans realized that their own security would be thereby enhanced (as Lincoln suggested). [14] The five were "substitute conscripts who enlisted for the purpose of deserting after receiving the bounty." [15] Even President Lincoln, who often commuted death sentences for deserters, viewed these cases as "very flagrant" and rejected the appeals of the five soldiers despite their pleas that they "each have wives & children depending upon us." [16]

On February 26, 1864, the War Department, at the direction of President Lincoln, ordered that "the sentences of all deserters, who have been condemned by Court Martial to death... be mitigated to imprisonment during the war, at the Dry Tortugas, Florida, where they will be sent under suitable guards." [17] However, this demonstration of mercy did not last long. On May 8, 1864, Secretary of War Stanton directed that "all stragglers from the Army of the Potomac ... be at once brought before a drum-head court-martial, and if found to be deserters or stragglers without authority, that they be immediately executed." [18] By the later part of 1864, executions were taking place almost daily in the Army of the Potomac. [19] John Andrews wrote his brother in January 1865 that: "Executions have taken place by the wholesale in the army during the Fall and Winter." [20]

Confederate efforts to encourage desertion by Union soldiers began in mid-1862 on a local basis and became more serious and broader in scope by early 1864. [21] In July 1864, both General Lee and General Beauregard proposed orders that would encourage desertion by facilitating the return of the deserters to the North. Confederate General Orders No. 65 was issued on August 15, 1864:

> It having been represented to the War Department that there are numbers of foreigners entrapped by artifice and fraud into the military and naval service of the United States who would gladly withdraw from further participation in the inhuman warfare waged against a people who have never given them a pretext for hostility; and that there are many inhabitants of the United States now retained in that service against their will who are averse to aiding in the unjust war now being prosecuted against the Confederate States; and it being also known that these men are prevented from abandoning such compulsory service by the difficulty they experience in escaping therefrom; it is ordered that all such persons, coming within the lines of the Confederate armies, shall be received, protected and supplied with means of subsistence, until such of them as desire it can be forwarded to the most convenient points on the border, where all facilities will be afforded them to return to their homes. [22]

The Second Corps' Third Division reported to the Army of the Potomac's Chief of Staff on August 26, 1864 that copies of Order No. 65 are "now being distributed to our pickets wherever circumstances will admit it. Where the pickets are near enough they are thrown over; at other places they are left near springs & c., where the pickets of each army get water." [23]

[Photo: Castle Thunder, April 1865]

Both General Grant and General Lee noted in September 1864 that Order No. 65 was having its intended effect. [24] The Confederates carried out Order No. 65 by gathering the Union deserters in groups of a hundred to a hundred and fifty at Castle Thunder in Richmond and then sending them to Abingdon or Bristol in Southwest Virginia to pass through the Union lines in Kentucky. The provost marshal's office at City Point actually assigned a spy to desert and document the process. The spy's group passed through the Cumberland Mountains at Pound Gap and entered the Union picket lines at Louisa on the Big Sandy River. [25]

The experience of the 179th New York Volunteers during the fall and winter of 1864-1865 illustrates the problem of desertion and how it was handled during that period in the Army of the Potomac.

Ella Lonn noted that "once in camp, or at the front, the most favorable opportunity for taking French leave was from the picket line, preferably of course, at night." [26] During picket duty on the night of October 11, five men deserted from the 179th. John Andrews derisively noted that: "Two were Canadians—three were McClellan Democrats—and all of them traitors." [27] Company

H's Robert Hunt (Ireland) and Francis Lewis (Wales) were foreign-born, but not Canadian-born, although they may have been living in Canada. The other three were born in the United States– Company H's James Cole and Norman Hagadorn in New York and Company G's Noah Leah in Ohio. Apart from Andrews' assertion, their politics are unknown. As a group, their demographics defy generalization. Their ages were twenty-one, thirty-four, thirty-seven, thirty-nine and forty-one. Two were farmers, while the other three were a seaman, a laborer and a lumberman. They enlisted in four different locations. However, four of the five were from Company H. All four made good their escape. [28]

As a deterrent, the practice in the Army of the Potomac was that full units would be assembled to view the execution of deserters who had been caught. [29] On October 14, 1864, the men of the Ninth Corps' Second Division marched by regiment to the field where the execution of Charles Merling, a deserter from the 2nd Maryland Infantry, would take place. They formed a hollow square around the grave that had been dug. In addition to the Second Division, there were thousands of spectators from other units. Andrews described the scene:

> About half past nine the funeral procession marched into the hollow square. First came the officer in charge, then followed the band playing a solemn death march, then four men bearing the coffin, and following the coffin came the unfortunate wretch who had twice deserted his country, once pardoned and afterwards found fighting in the ranks of the rebels. He walked erect and apparently unconcernedly, between the two chaplains who accompanied him. His hands were bound and his coat thrown carelessly over one shoulder. He was followed by the detachment which was to shoot him. All along the lines the procession marched, the band playing that doleful death march, and then to the grave. Gen. Potter commanding the Division and his staff stood near the grave. The officer in charge read the sentence, the chaplain prayed for the unfortunate man, removed his hat, seated him on his coffin, and tied a white handkerchief over his eyes, the detachment of soldiers took their positions. The officer ran his sword into the ground, they raised their pieces, he clapped his hands together, they took aim, he clapped his hands together again, they fired, and the deserter fell back on his coffin, the blood streaming from his head and breast down over the sides of his coffin. Then the whole division turned, marched off by regiments, with colors flying, and the bands playing the liveliest airs. As the armed soldiers marched off, the stragglers broke through the guards and rushed up to look upon the victim – so eager is man to gaze upon scenes of blood. [30]

Andrews observed that "This whole affair passed off with such military precision that there was nothing to shock the feelings of anyone. The old soldiers after it was over with thought nothing further of it, but the new recruits as soon as they reached their tents" wrote letters home. [31] (Andrew McCallum sketched the scene that day.)

[Sketch: Firing Squad see page 177]

At least in this instance, the public execution did not seem to have had its intended effect. The next night, five men deserted from the 179th– three from Company C and two from Company A. [32] Privates Edward Rowe and Daniel C. Smith, who had been involved in the drunken incident with Lieutenant Hoy in July, along with Private Julius Schulenberg, were the three from Company C. They were part of a detail under Company A's Lieutenant Farr who had been sent out around 5 p.m. in groups of three to man nine or ten picket posts. The Union picket posts were only about thirty or forty rods from the Confederate pickets at that point. The three had been discovered missing by Farr around 4 a.m.[33] The two soldiers from Company A, Privates Richard McGregor and Peter Nash, were also on picket duty.[34]

Andrews observed "a general feeling of despondency in our regiment on account of these desertions." That may have been due to the fact that at least Rowe, Smith and Schulenberg were part of the 179th's original complement from the spring, rather than new recruits from the fall who had received even higher bounties. He minimized the loss of these soldiers by rationalizing that the Confederates:

> are welcome to all they can get from us for none but cowards – "dead beats" –
> ever desert a good cause. Those that deserted from our regiment their officers
> said they could never get them into a fight.[35]

The prior behavior of Rowe, a twenty-one-year-old clerk, and Smith, a twenty-one-year-old boatman, certainly indicates that they were not committed to a soldier's life. They had gotten falling down drunk with Lieutenant Hoy on the Fourth of July. They had been arrested, along with Schulenberg, the evening of August 11, 1864 by a Union cavalry patrol guarding the cattle herd near Coggins Point, Virginia a distance of twelve miles from the 179th. They were found "near, though within the outer line of cavalry pickets," and therefore they had been charged then only with "straggling" rather than desertion.[36] They apparently also shirked combat.[37]

The flow of deserters was not one way. "Two Johnnies [came] in" on October 17. Andrews observed that Confederate soldiers "desert to us in larger numbers than our men do to them."[38]

On October 23, a hapless John Smith from Company E was caught trying to desert:

> it being dark and he becoming befogged, [he] followed along a path in the
> woods that brought him back to our lines. He was halted by a picket and
> asked "who goes there" to which he replied "a deserter" and came in, threw
> off his accouterments saying "*There* I am through working for Uncle Sam"
> thinking he had come into the rebel lines.[39](emphasis in original)

Andrews speculated in his diary that Smith "will probably be shot as he has nothing to fall back upon. His character as a soldier was a poor one."[40] William Lamont, who had been one of the two other soldiers on picket with Smith, overheard an officer say that "it would go hard" with Smith because it was his second time deserting.[41] Smith had deserted on June 3 from Camp Casey and gone home.[42] He had been returned to the regiment and fined twelve dollars a month – all but $1 of his monthly pay.[43] The speculation that Smith would be shot proved incorrect. Smith was apparently more adept at escaping than deserting and escaped from the guardhouse.[44]

Andrews also commented that:

> So many of these high-bounty men and substitutes have deserted that the
> pickets have orders to halt any man who gets beyond the line and if he does
> not halt when called to, to shoot him. This has tended greatly to stop
> desertions.[45]

On the night of October 29, Company A's Private William H. Shipman left his picket post without authorization and did not return until morning. When he was court-martialed, Shipman pled guilty, but explained that he "took the Canteens and went into Camp to get them filled." and that he "had always done his duty." Shipman was sentenced to the loss of six months' pay.

(Lieutenant Colonel Doty was president of the court.) [46]

If the threat to shoot soldiers who passed the picket lines deterred desertion as Andrews suggested, the effect was only temporary. On November 17, five men deserted from Company H – Privates Jacob Perry, a twenty-one-year-old New York-born spinner; John McDonald, an eighteen-year-old laborer born in England; Henry Maxwell, an eighteen-year-old teamster born in Canada; and Franklin Wright, an eighteen-year old-laborer born in Iowa; and Corporal Charles Povey, an eighteen-year-old cabinet maker born in Canada. Perry was serving his second tour of duty. [47] They were never apprehended, but Henry Maxwell surrendered on March 24, 1865 to claim the Presidential Pardon (discussed below). [48]

This was, however, the last group desertion in the 179th. There was also only one more individual desertion from the front. Yet another soldier from Company H, Private Michael Ferguson, an eighteen-year-old New York-born laborer, deserted from picket duty on December 10, 1864. [49]

Toward the end of November, the 179th learned that Edward Rowe and Daniel C. Smith, who had deserted on October 16 along with Julius Schulenberg, were in custody at City Point. After they had deserted, they had been taken to Kentucky by the Confederate army and released in accordance with General Orders No. 65. They were in a group of about one hundred Union deserters that had been sent through the lines by the Confederates, but they had been captured by Union cavalry. [50]

Rowe and Smith were court-martialed separately on consecutive days, Rowe going first. The first witness for the prosecution was their company commander, Lieutenant Force. After establishing that Rowe had been assigned to picket duty and that he had last been seen around 4 a.m., the judge advocate asked Force whether Rowe was a "recruit or substitute." Force answered that Rowe was "a recruit, a volunteer," and that Force had seen Rowe receive the local bounty of $300.

The judge advocate then asked if Rowe had "ever been in action with the regiment" and Force answered that Rowe had not. As of the time he allegedly deserted, Rowe could have been in action with the 179th in the June 17 assault, the Battle of the Crater, Weldon Railroad and Poplar Spring Church. While Rowe could have been with the detachment at Cumberland Landing on June 17, Force's testimony suggests that Rowe had been a shirker at least in the other actions. While Force did not mention either the Fourth of July episode of drunkenness or the August charges of straggling in his testimony, neither event would have encouraged Force to give Rowe the benefit of any doubt.

The judge advocate then asked Force whether the men in the 179th were aware of the Confederate War Department's Order No. 65. Force testified that he had discussed Order No. 65 with Rowe, telling Rowe that in his view, "it was very improbable about the Rebel government carrying out said order, and that I thought it was not safe for any one to take advantage of it." Force said that Rowe had agreed with that assessment.

Force's advice proved to be prophetic. A captured Union soldier might well have thought in good faith that the best way to get back to the Union lines was to claim to be a deserter entitled to the benefit of Order No. 65. However, those statements could come back to haunt the soldier if heard by other Union soldiers.

The two key witnesses against Rowe and Smith were Private James M. Hays of the 7th Indiana Volunteer Infantry and Private John W. Booth of the 1st New York Dragoons. Hays had been taken prisoner on August 19 at Weldon Railroad. He had escaped in October by cutting a hole in a railroad car while being transported from Belle Isle to Salisbury Prison. He was recaptured shortly thereafter and then claimed to be a Union deserter. He was then sent to Castle Lightning in Richmond, a holding point for Union deserters. Booth arrived at Castle Lightning after a similar series of events starting with his capture in the Shenandoah Valley.

Hays and Booth saw Rowe and Smith at Castle Lightning and testified that both Rowe and Smith had told the Confederates that they were Union deserters. The challenge for the court was to figure out who really was a deserter and who was posturing as a deserter to get back to the Union lines. When Booth testified that he had claimed to be a deserter to get back to the Union lines, the judge advocate asked him "How do you know the prisoner did not call himself a Yankee deserter for the same purpose?" Booth answered, "I do not know but that he did."

In the end, it was probably their conduct after being released by the Confederates that did Rowe and Smith in. Once in Kentucky, Booth and Hays sought out a Captain Patrick, told him their stories and requested his assistance in getting back to their units. Rowe and Smith made no such effort and instead sought work on a river boat. They had the misfortune to be working on the same boat that Booth and Hays were returning on. Rowe and Smith were arrested and at first claimed to be southern citizens, but ultimately admitted that they were from the 179th.

Smith and Rowe claimed that they had been captured by two Confederate soldiers while filling their canteens. A creek ran between the lines where they were on picket duty, closer to the Confederate side. Pickets were allowed to get water one at a time and Rowe and Smith's story was that the creek in front of them was much closer than the water source within their lines. The story was plausible, but not believed.

Rowe and Smith were sentenced to be hung "in presence of as much of the command to which his regiment belongs as the exigencies of the service will permit" and the sentence was carried out on December 10, 1864. [51] A soldier from the Seventh Rhode Island described the execution as follows:

> At one P.M. Edward Rowe and Daniel C. Smith, two deserters from the One Hundred and Seventy-ninth New York were hung for desertion, just east of Hancock Station. They were comparatively young men, had willfully deserted to the enemy, and a few weeks later, had been recognized among a lot of rebel prisoners captured by their own regiment [not correct as noted above]. Great curiosity was exhibited to see the culprits, and to witness the grim event; so, on this occasion, the voluntary spectators outnumbered those compelled to witness the execution, though generally the reverse obtained. Moreover, death by hanging is considered by many less blood curdling and less revolting than shooting. Two-thirds of our division formed a hollow square around a regularly constructed scaffold. Then the condemned were brought forth from the guardhouse and escorted to their fate in the following manner: A band playing a dirge, two coffins borne by soldiers, the two culprits good-looking and apparently intelligent, with wrists handcuffed behind them, two chaplains, an infantry guard on either hand, and a cavalry guard surrounding all. One of the prisoners had a cousin walking by his side, and the two engaged in conversation as they passed along. The doomed were surprisingly cheerful as they were conducted around three sides of the hollow square, bearing smiling faces, laughing, chatting, and nodding to recognized comrades in the ranks. They ascended the steps of the scaffold without faltering, and one who had been puffing all the while at a cigar [Rowe], continued smoking until it

dropped as the rope tightened with a jerk around his neck. The army overcoats buttoned about their shoulders were not removed, but they could not conceal their violent, though ineffectual efforts to free their hands, the drawing up of the feet, the heaving of their chests, or the spasmodic tremors that frequently darted through their frames, but constantly becoming weaker and more infrequent until they finally ceased. Companions in life, dishonor, treachery, and misfortune, they remain companions in leveled unknown graves. [52]

John Andrews, who had been in Albany at the time, was told (probably by Levi Force) that Rowe and Smith "conducted themselves like heroes even to the scaffold" and that Rowe had "smoked a cigar till he had ascended the steps of the scaffold." [53] Smith reputedly told the chaplain several hours before he was executed that his mother had often told him as a youth that he "would be hanged if he did not mend his ways!" [54]

Neither Rowe nor Smith said anything in their testimony about their fellow deserter Julius Schulenberg. Whether he traveled with them to the Union lines or not is unknown. However, when Schulenberg applied for a pension thirty years after the war, he revealed that he had enlisted in the Union navy under the name of Thomas P. Willson on December 30, 1864, had served on the ironclad *Louisville*, and had been honorably discharged from the Navy in the summer of 1865! Notwithstanding his apparently loyal service as Thomas P. Willson, Schulenberg's pension application ultimately was denied because he had deserted from the 179th and had received a second bounty in excess of what he would have been entitled to had he completed his service with the 179th New York Volunteers. [55]

Waterman Thornton of Company E was hung at noon on January 6 for deserting to the enemy on September 30 during the Battle of Poplar Spring Church. Thornton was a forty-year-old laborer born in Canada who joined Company E in the field as a new recruit on September 2. [56] Like Rowe and Smith, Thornton had been taken by the Confederates from Virginia to Kentucky and released. He had initially told the local Union provost marshal that he was a farmer from Virginia, but subsequently admitted he was from the 179th New York. His change of story may have been motivated by the fact that he saw another Union soldier who had been in Confederate custody with him near Petersburg.

Company E Sergeants Charles Hogan and Charles Lockwood both testified that Thornton, claiming to be lame, had refused to resume marching toward battle after the company had stopped for a rest and that they had not seen him again. Thornton cross-examined both witnesses – a step not always taken by an accused soldier – in an unsuccessful attempt to prove his story that he had dropped back from the march because he was lame, had later attempted to catch up with his company, and had been captured in the process. Thornton's description of events as he was trying to find his unit does have some contemporaneous plausibility. Thornton also made the interesting argument that he had enlisted for one year "with good intentions," receiving a $600 bounty, and that if he had really intended to desert he would have enlisted for three years and received a higher bounty!

As with the courts-martial of Rowe and Smith, a key witness was a fellow union soldier in custody in Virginia. Corporal Levi Heaton of the 1st New Jersey Cavalry testified that Thornton had told his Confederate captors that "he was a drafted man ... and had told his friends at home and had written to them that he intended to desert from the Union army." The prosecution also attempted to establish that "General Order No. 65, Rebel War Dept." was generally known in Thornton's company. Neither Hogan nor Lockwood remembered having heard of the order, but

Heaton testified that he had heard Thornton say that he was familiar with it. The prosecution also asked Lockwood the amount of the bounty that Thornton had received. Lockwood did not know, but said that others enlisting at the same time received one thousand to eleven hundred dollars.[57]

The regimental surgeon, Dr. Joseph Robinson, testified that Thornton had complained about his hip and inability to walk when he joined the 179th in the field, but Robinson "could not discern anything serious" and gave Thornton some liniment. Sergeant Hogan testified that Thornton had been lame and excused from duty by the doctor in the past, but had not been excused from duty that day. (There is no CMR for Thornton indicating admission to a hospital prior to September 30.) On cross-examination by Thornton, Hogan testified that Thornton's eyes had "looked red and bloodshot" that day.

The "character" evidence against Thornton was not particularly compelling. Lieutenant Lockwood testified that: "He did not do much duty. He was never on picket duty to my knowledge. He seemed to be somewhat opposed to doing duty." When Thornton asked Hogan about Thornton's "general character" on cross, Hogan stated that he did not remember "having seen him doing any duty," but that "I never heard anything against his character."

The judges found Thornton guilty and sentenced him to be hanged.[58] Two days before he was executed, he wrote to the Ninth Corps commander, Major General Jonathan G. Parke, that he had been "captured in action" and that:

> After some days retention as a prisoner of war, & changing hands different times, it happened through omission of vigilance on the part of my enemies, that the opportunity of escaping presented itself to me by misrepresenting myself to be a refugee, which I much preferred, rather than linger in the loathsome Prisons of the South.[59]

Thornton said that he was escorted through the lines "after which I reported myself to the Provost Marshal of Post at Louisa, Ky preparatory to being forwarded to my command." However, to his "astonishment," he found himself "confronted and falsely accused before the Prov Mar aforesaid by an escaped prisoner [Heaton] who was captured the same day I was made prisoner ..." (In an earlier note, Thornton apparently had written that at the time he was captured he had told the Confederates that he was a deserter.)[60]

At the time of his execution, Thornton continued to protest his innocence, showing "some considerable emotion while on the scaffold." When the chaplain asked Thornton if he had anything to say as the rope was being put around his neck, he replied "Nothing, only that I am being murdered." John Andrews recorded in his War Journal that a pardon from General Grant arrived two and a half hours after Thornton was executed.[61]

Andrews did not quite have the facts correct. On January 6, President Lincoln had telegraphed Grant, inquiring: "If there is a man at City-Point by the name of Waterman Thornton who is in trouble about desertion, please have his case briefly stated to me & do not let him be executed meantime."[62] More accurately, Grant's messenger would have been bearing a stay of execution for Thornton rather than a pardon, but it was still too late. Grant informed Lincoln on January 7 that Thornton had been executed the day before.[63]

Despite Thornton's possible innocence, Andrews wrote his brother that the three executions were a "black record" for the 179th, but that "we who remain feel that the poor stuff was about weeded out."[64]

William Lamont did not witness Thornton's execution because "I was lucky enough to be on picket and did not have to witness. I could hear the band play the dead march when they were going to the gallows. That is as near as I want to be to any such business." [65]

Shortly thereafter, the 179th saw the execution by firing squad of a deserter named Clements from the 32nd Maine. [66] Andrews was under house arrest following the newspaper incident while on picket duty, and thus was "spared the shocking sight." [67] By this time, Andrews' attitude toward executions had changed considerably.

Not all of the 179th's deserters from the front who were caught were executed. Company H's Private John Bonny, alias Henry Mills, was charged with deserting on September 21, 1864, shortly after Company H arrived at the front. He had been arrested by Union cavalry pickets. When he was tried on December 3, 1864, he pled guilty. He was not sentenced to death. Instead, his sentence was a dishonorable discharge with loss of all pay and confinement at hard labor at Albany State Prison for five years—one year "with ball and chain." [68] Whether his life may have been saved by his guilty plea, by the fact that he had just arrived at the front, or by the fact that Lieutenant Colonel Doty was the senior officer on the court is not apparent.

Company C's Private George W. House, a twenty-one-year-old New York-born laborer, fared even better in his court-martial. He had deserted on August 5, 1864 and had been arrested in Washington on August 15. Like Bonny, House pleaded guilty, but was only sentenced to being returned under guard to the 179th with the loss of pay of $10 per month for two years. [69] The reason for such lenient treatment is not apparent.

The predominance of men from Company H among the men from the 179th New York who deserted from the front in the fall of 1864 is particularly striking. In contrast, there were no desertions from the front in Company I and Company K which had arrived at the front at the same time as Company H. Nor were there desertions from the front among the new recruits who arrived at the front in the fall as replacements for the other seven companies. There was also only a handful of desertions from the front at this time among the "veterans" who had been serving in the field since June.

There is certainly evidence of the factors identified by Ella Lonn. Bounties were even higher in the late summer and fall than they had been in the spring. As evidence of the "hardships of war," cold temperatures and rain came into play with the arrival of fall. This factor would have been aggravated to the extent that soldiers lost their blankets in the retreat at Poplar Spring Church. [70] Rations had been missed in the 179th New York for a brief period in October. The men of the 179th were running short on cash because they had not been paid. The defeat at Poplar Spring Church on September 30 probably contributed to "war weariness and discouragement." However, these factors applied across the entire regiment. They do not explain the differences in desertion from the front between Company H and Companies I and K, for example.

As with "bounty jumping," the primary explanation for differences in desertion from the front seems to be the relative strength of community ties. The men in Company I and Company K had much stronger ties to their communities than the men in Company H. Company H was recruited from many different communities across several counties, while Companies I and K were recruited from just a few in one or two counties. Company H also had a much higher percentage of foreign-born recruits than Company I and Company K. Half of the men in the 179th who deserted from the front in the last three months of 1864 were foreign-born. [71]

The evidence also suggests another factor not directly identified by Ella Lonn—a company history of significant desertion. Nearly a quarter of the men of Company H had deserted en route in September. Another fifteen percent deserted by the end of the year. Company E had seen a similar pattern in the late spring and early summer. Nearly forty-five percent of the men in

Company E had deserted en route to the front at the end of May and the beginning of June. After a month at the front, including the June 17 assault, another fifteen percent of those remaining deserted on July 6 and 7. For the companies that saw fewer of their men desert en route, desertion from the front was not a significant problem.

Desertion from the front by men of the 179th was also usually undertaken in a small group, rather than individually. Five men from Company H deserted on November 17; four from Company H and one from Company G on October 11; and three from Company C and two from Company A on October 15. Individual men deserted on October 23 and December 10.

The passage of time at the front also seems to have allowed the development of unit cohesion that worked against desertion–a "band of brothers" effect. Company B and Company D had no desertions from the front in the fall of 1864. Company G had only one, Company A had only two and Company C only three. Even Company E had only one. [72]

Desertion from military hospitals was treated far less severely than desertion from the front, presumably on the theory that the soldier involved by definition had been either wounded or taken sick in serving his country. Of the nearly five hundred men from the 179th New York admitted to general hospitals, I have identified only a few who deserted from the hospital. [73]

Company A's George Cross, a twenty-seven-year-old mason from Horseheads, deserted from Mower Hospital in Philadelphia in an unsuccessful attempt to visit his sick wife, Mary Ann. He left Mower on August 8 and was arrested in Wellsville, New York on September 1, having walked the last part from Williamsport. He was returned to the hospital. While Cross was still in the hospital, his mother sent him a letter on October 29 to tell him that his wife:

> was taken with the typhoid fever October the 12 and one spell we thought she was getting better and the fever turned and she now by spells is crazy ... [doctors] said they thought she would not get well ... when Mary Ann is in her right mind she says all she wants is to see George...Now George go to your officers and try to get home for a short time. I no they will let you come in case of sickness and death.

Cross applied for a furlough on November 5, but the record does not indicate whether it was granted (or whether his wife recovered). He deserted again on December 2 and again was caught. Cross insisted that he had not intended to desert in August and the Army apparently believed him because he was returned to duty in January 1865 with there being no record of charges for desertion having been brought. [74]

Company D's William Holliday was taken sick with jaundice just before the Battle of the Crater and sent to Harewood U.S.A. General Hospital in Washington. He was granted a thirty day furlough in August and timely returned, but then deserted from the Hospital on October 4. He was arrested in civilian clothing in Annapolis on October 17. He was found guilty in a court-martial on December 19, 1864 and sentenced "to be returned under guard to his company and regiment for duty, with loss of pay and allowances now due, to forfeit ten dollars per month of his monthly pay for the period of eighteen months, and make good all time lost by desertion." (The fact that Holliday had deserted in September 1863 after being drafted and had only been assigned to the 179th after having been arrested in April 1864 apparently did not come up at his trial.) Holliday did return to duty and was killed in the final assault on Petersburg in April 1865. [75]

William H. Dickey was another soldier from Company D who deserted from the hospital. He was taken sick with an unspecified disease in August 1864 and admitted as a convalescent to the General Hospital on Camden Street in Baltimore in September. He deserted from the hospital on February 22, 1865 after procuring civilian clothes, but was arrested in Baltimore the following day. He was not court-martialed until May 1865, and was found guilty of being absent without leave rather than desertion, perhaps because the war was over and it was common practice to grant furloughs from hospital. [76]

The more difficult question to assess is whether a soldier "deserted" from sick leave granted by a hospital. Lonn noted that "[o]ne of the earliest means [of desertion] scarcely deserves designation as a method; it was merely to refrain from returning from sick leave or a furlough." "Sick leave was in one way and another gravely abused." [77] Lonn noted that there was a lax sentiment about sick leave and many soldiers viewed it "equivalent to a discharge from the service." [78]

Of the nearly five hundred men from the 179th New York who were patients in general hospitals, roughly one hundred fifty received sick leave furloughs. [79] The length of the furlough is generally not stated in the Carded Medical Records and furlough documents rarely made it into the soldier's CMSR. As a result, it is not feasible to determine the number of men from the 179th who overstayed their sick leave.

Once a soldier was home on medical leave, the challenge for the Army was how to monitor the progress of his recovery. If the soldier lived in a community close to a military surgeon, the surgeon could examine the soldier, but in most cases, the Army had to rely on the integrity of the soldier's personal physician. The practice was for soldiers to seek to extend their furlough by submitting a letter from their local doctor that they were too sick to travel. [80]

Therein lay the potential for abuse. The letters were required to be under oath, but a sympathetic physician could subjectively conclude that the soldier was not yet up to travel and return to duty. A physician's certificate of inability to return to duty was valid for twenty days at a time. It is not unusual for the CMSR of a soldier from the 179th to contain numerous such certifications (which is NOT to say that they were not medically justified). [81]

If a soldier failed to return by the expiration date of his furlough and had not timely filed a physicians' certificate, he was declared a deserter. However, in most instances a failure of paperwork was at fault and the charge of desertion was cleared up, sometimes during the war, but sometimes not until many years later when a pension application was pending. [82]

Taking physician's letters at face value, I have found only a few soldiers who apparently deserted from hospital furlough. [83]

The 179th New York probably granted in excess of one hundred furloughs during the Fall and Winter of 1864-1865. Desertion from these furloughs was rare, presumably because they were discretionary and furloughs would only be granted to soldiers whom the officers of the 179th considered trustworthy. But the officers' judgment was not perfect. Company G's First Sergeant Archibald McNeil received a ten day furlough at the end of November to visit Washington. A seemingly safe choice given his rank, McNeil never returned and was last seen in Elmira. [84]

Company H's Private George Dudley (aka Lake), a twenty-six-year-old farmer, did not return to duty from Batavia when his furlough expired on February 8, 1865. Lake was reported to the Provost Marshal's Office in nearby Lockport with the request that Lake "be arrested and sent back to his regiment." On March 9, 1865, the provost marshal wrote his counterpart in Springfield, Massachusetts that Lake and his wife had left Batavia and shipped their household effects to Springfield. Lake apparently was not apprehended. In 1888, the War Department denied Lake's request that the charge of desertion be removed and that he be granted an honorable discharge. [85]

On March 11, 1865, President Lincoln issued a proclamation, as authorized by Congress, offering a pardon to all deserters who returned to their units or surrendered to a provost marshal by May 11, 1865. [86] At least seven of the 179th's deserters sought the pardon. Company K's Lyman Perry, a thirty-six-year-old farmer from Candor in Tioga County, who had not returned from furlough in February, turned himself in in Owego on May 2, 1865. Company B's Charles L. Gardiner, a twenty-two-year-old farmer, had not returned from a thirty day furlough granted by David's Island Hospital in September 1864 and surrendered himself in Elmira on May 8, 1865. Company A's Arthur Beebe, a twenty-five-year-old farmer, also had not returned from furlough and surrendered in Elmira on May 10, 1865, the day before the deadline. Company F's Wilbert Simmons, an eighteen- year-old farmer, turned himself in on April 27, 1865. [87]

The fact that these four men were farmers and therefore likely to return home after the war suggests that they may have felt a need to square things in some way with their communities. However, I do not know how communities viewed the pardon.

Company G's William Conroy had been wounded at the Battle of the Crater and had not returned from a furlough granted by Mt. Pleasant Hospital in November 1864. He sought the pardon on April 22, 1865. [88] Company F's George W. West had been wounded in the left hand in the June 17 assault and had two fingers amputated several days later. He was initially sent from the front to Harewood General Hospital in Washington and then Cuyler General Hospital near Philadelphia. He received a furlough in August and returned to Cuyler after having been granted an extension. He was transferred to the Invalid Corps in October, but apparently remained in the hospital. He received another furlough in November, but this time did not return. Instead he went to Canada and stayed with a cousin while learning a new trade – carriage painting. (He had been a clerk before the war.) He returned to Canandaigua, New York on May 8, 1865 to accept the Presidential Pardon. [89]

"Bounty jumping" (desertion en route) hit the 179th New York Volunteers hard, particularly in Companies E and H. However, after the "bounty jumpers" deserted and the companies of the 179th reached the front, desertion became a much less significant problem. Men in the 179th with strong community ties were very unlikely to be "bounty jumpers" and as the men of the 179th served together in the field, unit cohesion developed that further deterred desertion.

MARVELOUS EQUESTRIAN PERFORMANCE ON TWO ANIMALS,
By the celebrated Artist, PROFESSOR GEORGE B. MAC, assisted by the noted Bare-back Rider, GEORGE H. PENDLETON, on his Wonderful
Dunnion Steed, PEACEATANYPRICE.
N. B. The beautiful creature, PEACEATANYPRICE, recently imported from Europe, was sired by JOHN BULL, and dam'd by AMERICA.

Marvelous Equestrian Performance on Two Animals

CHAPTER TWENTY

U.S. Election and Voter Fraud

At a time when the future of the republic was at stake, the problem of how soldiers in the field could vote was particularly critical. While from today's perspective absentee ballots are the obvious solution, at the time of the Civil War, state constitutional and/or statutory provisions required voters – men only in that era – to vote in person in the election district where they were registered. [1]

In addition to the inherent inequity of depriving a man of his right to vote because he was putting his life on the line in distant fields to preserve the Union, there was the practical problem that soldiers made up a significant percentage of the electorate. In New York State, for example, contemporary estimates were that the roughly two hundred thousand soldiers serving out of state represented between one-quarter and one-third of the electorate. [2] As a result, during the early years of the war, the states remaining in the Union amended their constitutions and statutes to provide for soldier voting from the field. [3]

In New York State, the constitution originally provided that a man "shall be entitled to vote in the election district of which he shall at the time be a resident and not elsewhere." [4] Many people questioned the constitutionality of the Legislature's attempt to address the problem by statute, and Governor Horatio Seymour, a Democrat, vetoed the bill passed in 1863. [5] However, Governor Seymour sensed "the increasing pressure in behalf of soldier voting" and proposed a constitutional amendment. The electorate voted on the amendment at a special election in March 1864 as the 179th was being raised. [6]

Almost everyone expected the amendment to pass by a wide margin. *The Hornellsville Tribune*, a Republican paper, observed that:

> no truly loyal, patriotic man, will vote against such a measure. If any one is entitled to such a privilege, it is the man who leaves home with all its endearments, and lays his life upon the altar of his country, enduring hardships and privations in her defence and preservation. [7]

Some Democrats were concerned – in the words of the Republican leaning *Dunkirk Journal* – that: "*Abe Lincoln would make the soldiers vote as he wanted them to*," (italics in original) but *The Hornellsville Tribune* was correct that public opposition was doubtful. The *Penn Yan Democrat* simply reported the upcoming vote and gave the facts relating to the canvas without any editorial comment. [8]

Statewide, the voters approved the amendment by an 84 percent to 16 percent margin. In Democratic New York City, the vote in favor was only 70 percent, as it was in other Democratic areas. In contrast 97.6 percent of the voters in Yates County supported the measure as did 94 percent of the voters in Ontario County. [9]

The states followed one of two different approaches to provide the opportunity for soldiers in the field to vote. The more common approach was simply to bring the ballot box to the field for the soldier to insert his ballot just as he would have done at home. New York and Illinois adopted the more complicated format of proxy voting. The soldier would prepare his ballot in the field and give it to a person he would authorize to take it home and cast it on the soldier's behalf. The complexities of the proxy vote created the opportunity for fraud, for example, by removing the ballot and inserting another or by forging the authorization. [10]

A good deal was at stake in the 1864 election. Popular frustration in the North with the government's inability to subdue the South put Lincoln very much at risk. Republican strength had declined since Lincoln had been elected in 1860. In New York State, Lincoln had received a majority of 50,136 votes (53.7%) in 1860. In 1861, the Republican majority in the secretary of state race had increased to 107,712 votes. However, in 1862, Seymour – the Democrat – was elected governor by 10,752 votes – a drop for the Republicans of 60,000 votes since 1860 and nearly 120,000 since 1861. In 1863, the Republicans held the secretary of state, but with a majority of only 29,405. [11]

The stakes for the Confederacy in the Union presidential election were high as well. In August 1864, General Grant wrote to his political mentor, Congressman E. B. Washburne, that:

> I have no doubt but the enemy are exceedingly anxious to hold until after the Presidential election. They have many hopes from its effects. They hope a counterrevolution. They hope the election of the peace candidate. [12]

In September, the *Ontario Times* quoted an article from the *Richmond Enquirer*:

> *Every defeat of Lincoln's forces*, even holding them steadfastly at bay, INURES TO THE ADVANTAGE OF McCLELLAN...THE INFLUENCE OF THE SOUTH, *more powerful in the shock of battle than when throwing her minority vote in the electoral college*, WILL BE CAST IN FAVOR OF McCLELLAN *by this indirect yet efficacious means*. [13](emphasis in original)

The Republican-leaning *Ontario Times* added the rhetorical question: "Loyal Democrats, do you hear that?"

In mid-nineteenth presidential politics incumbency conferred no apparent advantage. No incumbent president had been renominated since 1840 and no incumbent president had been reelected since 1832. [14] Lincoln was renominated by the Republican Convention in Baltimore on June 7, 1864, but his prospects for reelection were not bright. The heavy casualties suffered by the Union army in Grant's Overland campaign, which had started in May, were well-known to the public. [15] On July 18, 1864, Lincoln's prospects suffered another jolt when he announced a call for five hundred thousand more troops with any shortfall to be filled by a draft that would occur just before the election. [16] The *Broome Weekly Republican* tried to put a brave face on the news:

> The issuing of the Proclamation of the President for another draft at this time shows a moral courage worthy of all admiration. The Country requires it and the President does his duty without regard to the bearing it may have upon his re-election. Like Henry Clay, he had rather be right than be President. [17]

More realistically, Thurlow Weed, the guru of New York politics, believed in August that "Lincoln's reelection [is] an impossibility". The people are wild for peace." [18] A Democratic newspaper editor was, not surprisingly, even more emphatic: "Lincoln is deader than dead." [19] Lincoln himself was pessimistic. On August 23, he wrote that:

> This morning, as for some days past, it seems exceedingly probable that this Administration will not be re-elected. Then it will be my duty to so co-operate with the President elect, as to save the Union between the election and the inauguration; as he will have secured his election on such ground that he can not possibly save it afterwards. [20]

[Cartoon: Old Bulldog]

As difficult as the straits Lincoln faced were, he at least did not face a Democratic Party that was entirely of one mind. When the Democratic Party met for their convention in Chicago at the end of August, War Democrats, who supported continuation of the war until reunion was achieved, but without the abolition of slavery, contended with Peace Democrats, who sought an immediate end to the war. [21] The War Democrats won the nomination battle with the former Army of the Potomac commander George B. McClellan being selected as the nominee, but the Peace Democrats won the platform battle. A key plank in the Democratic platform stated that "after four years of failure to restore the Union by the experiment of war," it was time to "demand that immediate efforts be made for a cessation of hostilities." [22] A pro-Lincoln cartoon portrayed Grant as a bulldog astride the Weldon Railroad looking toward Richmond and saying "I'm bound to take it," while McClellan remonstrated with Lincoln "don't you think you had better call the old dog off now."

Despite the division between the Peace and War Democrats, on August 31 Lincoln reputedly said: "I am a beaten man, unless we can have some great victory." [23] In the end, General Sherman's capture of Atlanta, General Sheridan's success in the Shenandoah Valley, and Admiral Farragut's success in Mobile Bay compensated for the dismal – or at least uninspiring – news coming from the front at Petersburg. [24] The pro-Lincoln *Elmira Daily Advertiser* on October 7, 1864 and *Ontario Times* on October 19, 1864 carried the same map showing the Confederate territory that the Union forces had regained. Union success in Tennessee, along the Mississippi to the Gulf of Mexico, in Florida and in northern Georgia was apparent. The *Advertiser* exclaimed that: "Verily, the Rebellion is being subdued, and the 'Old Flag' is again making glad the eyes of the people all over the Old Union. Let the good work go on until Treason is crushed and Liberty, Law, and Justice are triumphant", and exhorted its readers to "Vote for Lincoln and Liberty, Against McClellan and Slavery." [25]

As election day approached, the election looked like it could be close, and "[i]t was clear to both parties that the absentee vote [of the soldiers] could prove critical in the presidential election." [26] McClellan's past popularity with the Army of the Potomac was well-known. Whether that popularity continued with the current soldiers was unknown. (For example, the vast majority of the soldiers in the 179th New York had joined the Army of the Potomac fifteen months or more after McClellan had left it). [27] Lincoln believed that he was more popular than McClellan with the soldiers. Lincoln had made many trips to the front like the one on June 20 to Petersburg, and it has been estimated that two hundred fifty thousand Union soldiers had personally seen him during those visits. [28] Lincoln's confidence in the soldiers' vote may have been the motivation for the order from the War Department in October 1864 that the furloughs of all disabled soldiers home from hospitals be extended to November 12, 1864. Company A's Daniel Compton, a Pennsylvania resident and voter, was furloughed from hospital for the specific purpose of going home to vote. [29] Interest among the troops of the 179th New York Volunteers in the upcoming presidential election had developed as early as the end of May when the 179th's acting chaplain, Daniel Lowell, a "good democrat", "did preach against Republicanism." [30] In July, Newton Spencer reported (although his objectivity is not beyond question) that:

> a remarkable unanimity of sentiment between professed Republicans (former Lincoln men) and Democrats, – a harmony which increases with each day, and must ultimate in quite complete unity of action when it comes to voting for President. Regardless of all other questions, the prevailing sentiment is, "We must have a change of rulers. We must try new men and new measures. Mr. Lincoln, (say most of his old friends,) is a failure; and mere honesty of purpose is neither vigor, sound judgment or ability. I simply repeat to you what I know and hear daily among the soldiers; and in corroboration of it, I may mention that an informal vote lately taken in two Companies of the 179th Regiment, showed 36 opposed to "Abe's" re-election, and but 9 in favor of it, or 4 to 1, And of those 36, full one-half are Republicans and former "Lincolnites". Of course there isn't much "room for argument" here. [31]

Back home, the developing campaign was so heated that even the traveling circus had become politicized. Wheeler, Hatch & Hitchcock's Circus and Royal Hippodrome, which advertised itself as "The Only Legitimate Circus Now Traveling in the U.S.", arrived in Elmira for two performances on August 18, 1864. [32] The circus clown apparently mocked "young men as fools who enlist for the bounty" and called President Lincoln a clown. The pro-Lincoln *Elmira Daily Advertiser* was incensed, while the pro-McClellan *Elmira Daily Gazette* defended the circus. [33] The *Advertiser* wrote:

> The Circus last evening took occasion to resolve itself into a McClellan mass meeting and a sty of general abuse of the Administration on the part of the speeches of the clown, the miserable tool of the proprietors. About two-thirds of the audience resented this dastardly affront, and we presume a stronger protest would have been entered by the officers and soldiers present, had there been an inkling that Wheeler, Hatch & Hitchcock's Circus was a copperhead campaigning affair exhibiting through the country at the beck of New York unprincipled politicians. We desire to warn the neighboring towns and our contemporaries against the copperhead raid in store for them, wherever this rebel-helping crew may hereafter exhibit. [34]

Three weeks later the Democrats in Ithaca carefully planned to take advantage of the crowds drawn there by the circus to stage a McClellan-Pendleton rally. Things started well with a brass band and three cheers for McClellan and Pendleton, but just as the band was playing its second song, the news arrived that Sherman had taken Atlanta. A Union man stole the stage, read Secretary Stanton's statement to the crowd, and called for three cheers for the Union army. The pro-Lincoln *Ithaca Journal* reported that: "Had a shell from one of Sherman's great guns exploded among [the McClellan supporters], it could not have created greater consternation nor dispersed them more suddenly." [35]

The family and friends of John Andrews kept him well apprised of developments at home in the political campaign. They were all staunch Republicans. His sister Emma and a friend separately wrote about a "great Copperhead mass meeting" in nearby Watkins in mid-October. Emma painfully reported on the long procession all around town and the "hateful banners and McClellan flags," but gleefully reported a Republican prank. They had snuck into the procession "the awfullest looking old cart...[with] Old Jeff Davis dangling from a long pole...and...Little Mac handcuffed and bound for Fort Lafayette. It *was* rich." [36] (emphasis in original)

Both Emma and brother Homer wrote Andrews about a "great Union mass meeting" in Watkins at the end of October attended by an estimated fifteen thousand people – "the largest crowd that ever was seen in Watkins." The speeches by ex-Governor Nobles of Wisconsin and Colonel Jacques "were grand. It did every body good to hear them." [37]

Back in the camp of the 179th, Andrews heard support for Lincoln in October:

> The cooks' fires are surrounded by large groups of humped up shivering men, who are talking in a very subdued way of the situation, the prospects of the war, and of the political campaign now in progress. All seem to concur that Old Abe's chances were the best. [38]

Company E's James Vangilder had written home: "Tell William Henry to be sure and vote for old able for he will split the rails and lay them strait." However, Vangilder apparently was in the minority in Company E. At the end of September, Company E reportedly split thirty-four for McClellan to three for Lincoln in a straw poll. [39] (Company E had been recruited in Buffalo, a Democratic area.)

For Andrews, the upcoming election was the focus of much of his attention. The election featured prominently in his letters to and from his family, and two nights before the election, Martin Doty and he stayed up until midnight talking politics and war measures. [40] But not all the soldiers in the 179th were so preoccupied with the election. In two letters to his family shortly before the election and one shortly after, William Lamont wrote not one word about it. [41]

As serious as the discussions that occurred among the soldiers undoubtedly were, one soldier in the 179th saw an opportunity for humor. Seeing the commissary sergeant approaching on a "very lean, scarecrow of a horse," the soldier said:

> "I could take that horse and ride safely to Richmond and back today." Everyone, of course, denied this and wished to know how he would manage to do it. "Why," said he, "I would tell the rebs that the horse's name was McClellan and then I would not be molested." A laugh greeted this and all assented. [42]

Preparations for voting in the field by New York's soldiers began in September when Secretary of State DePew sent two hundred thousand blank forms and envelopes to the field and hospitals and naval stations. [43] Part of the form was to be filled out locally by the soldier's regiment. Andrews recorded in his diary that he had been filling in voting forms on October 17, 18 and 19. [44] On October 18, the assistant provost marshal from New York's 26th Congressional District came through the 179th's camp "to look after soldiers' votes." [45]

The paperwork was fairly involved. The soldier would begin by filling out a "Soldier's Power of Attorney" form, identifying his regiment and residence and the person he "authoriz[ed] and empower[ed]" to cast his ballot "in my name and stead...the same as if I was personally present at the election." The power of attorney had to be witnessed. The soldier would then designate his choice for president on the separate ballot document.

The power of attorney and the folded ballot were then enclosed in a special envelope with a printed affidavit on the front to be signed and witnessed. The text of the affidavit included a series of representations as to the duration of residence in New York State (one year), the county (four months), and the city or town (thirty days), as well as a representation that "I have not made any bet or wager...depending on the result of said election."

This envelope was sealed and placed in an "outside envelope" which was forwarded to the person designated by the soldier. The soldier's designee then opened the outside envelope and delivered the sealed, unopened inner envelope with the ballot to the polling place. [46] In theory, the soldier's ballot was to be deposited with the regular civilian ballots so there would be no way of knowing who the soldiers voted for. However, that does not seem to have been the case in practice. A friend back home reproached Andrews for putting his name to "five or six democratic votes," but assumed Andrews had not known how they were cast. [47]

The *Yates County Chronicle* complained that while "the copperheads did not dare openly oppose" the soldiers' vote at the polls in March, they had succeeded through the Legislature in adopting "such conditions and restrictions as were well calculated to defeat its effectiveness." [48]

Not all the war news at this time was good for Lincoln. Grant's offensive at the end of October had stalled. Frustration at military defeat spilled over into politics. Andrews told his brother:

> what I hear on all sides here in camp. Gen. Meade is called a "d-ned old
> copperhead" and this movement "an electioneering tour for McClellan." I
> of course do not believe Gen. Meade wished our army to suffer defeat in order
> that McClellan might gain votes by it, but I write this to let you know with how
> little favor Meade is regarded in this part at least of the army. [49]

The soldiers of the 179th were probably repeating what was circulating in the newspapers. Meade had not received a regular army promotion from Lincoln when others had and the *Washington Chronicle* speculated that Meade was supporting the opposition as a result. Another publication reported that Meade "was delivering the army vote to McClellan." However, Meade gave no public indication of supporting either Lincoln or McClellan. [50]

As the election approached, "[p]arty spirit ran very high, and partisans upon either side were prepared to do anything which the law permitted to promote the cause of their party." [51] One of Andrews' female correspondents, Mollie Langworthy, feared even worse:

> The Democrats are becoming recklessly desperate in [New] York state.
> I fear they will succeed in electing Seymour. They will if it can be done by the
> most dishonorable plotting and intriguing which only copper heads ever
> dreamed of – or are capable of executing. [52]

Governor Seymour appointed fifty or sixty agents recommended by the Democratic Party to take only Democratic votes from the soldiers in the field. The New York State Republican Committee followed course. [53]

For some party agents of questionable integrity, the potential for fraud presented by proxy voting proved irresistible. On October 26, four of the agents appointed by Governor Seymour were arrested in Baltimore by military authorities on charges of election fraud. One of the agents (Ferry) confessed and he and another (Donohue) were convicted by a military commission and sentenced to life in prison. Lincoln approved the sentence. [54] On October 27, Col. Samuel North, a member of Governor Seymour's staff heading the vote gathering in Washington, also was arrested. [55]

News of the alleged fraud spread quickly, the *Buffalo Morning Express* and the *Buffalo Daily Courier* reporting it on October 29, the *Elmira Daily Advertiser* on October 31, the weekly *Broome Republican* on November 2, and the weekly *Hornellsville Tribune* on November 3, 1864. [56]

Company E's Capt. Louis Ottenot – a Democrat – had been given a fifteen day leave of absence on October 20 to take soldiers' votes back to Buffalo. [57] The *Buffalo Morning Express* (a pro-Lincoln newspaper) carried the following story on November 5 – three days before the election:

> FRAUDULENT SOLDIER VOTES IN TOWN – Beware of Them !! The Union [Republican] men of this city and County, by some strange oversight, have had no agent at the Army of the Potomac, except to the 187th Regiment, to take the votes of the Union soldiers for this locality. The result is that George Talbot, Henry P. Clinton and Capt. Ottenot, who was arrested on Thursday and taken to Washington, had the handling of all the votes for Erie County, Union as well as Democratic, except such as have been sent by mail. So far as Ottenot is concerned, he has been detected and is on his way to punishment...
>
> We now caution all Union men against votes which they have received from Democratic Head-quarters by private hands, for all such, though they started from the army enclosing the name of Lincoln, now contain that of McClellan and Seymour [the Democratic candidate for governor]. Of this there will be abundant proof when it is needed. The envelopes of these votes have been opened, after the manner of Ferry and Donohue [reported in the November 2, 1864 edition to have confessed to being agents of Governor Seymour], and Union soldiers have been defrauded of their suffrages. We yesterday saw one of these proxies, from a Union soldier to his Union friend, which was taken from Talbot's budget and delivered to him by the hands of an individual, who we will not name as he may be wanted in another quarter. That was one of the votes bearing the signature of Ottenot.
>
> The inner envelope had been opened – the Lincoln vote had been abstracted, and a McClellan vote had been substituted therefor. This is made apparent by the fact that in the haste of the depredator, the proxy was left outside the wrapper, and hence by holding the wrapper up to the light the McClellan and Seymour votes are clearly distinguishable. [58]

This timeless plea to get out the vote followed the story of fraud:

> To Union Voters – Give One Day to the Cause.
>
> Union men cannot too clearly understand that all the labor and expense of the campaign now drawing to a close will have been WASTED AND USELESS if a FULL VOTE be not secured! [59] (emphasis in original)

The allegations against Captain Ottenot were also reported in the *New York Times*, which also supported President Lincoln: "Inspectors, Take Notice, That all soldiers' votes purporting to be sworn to before the following persons are fraudulent: ... Louis J. Ottenot Capt. Co. E, 179th N.Y. Vols." [60] The *Times* reported that Ottenot had admitted that he had "signed his name to a large number of blanks, affidavits and powers of attorney in Col. North's office [in Washington]" and that Ottenot "seems quite penitent." [61]

Just before the election, William Larzelere's wife, Sarah, wrote him about the vote fraud. "There has been quite a time about the soldiers votes being changed. Lincoln taken out of the envelope and Little Mac put in place. Two men have been caught and sentenced to state Prison for life for the rascally act." She told him that his vote had been received in Penn Yan, but "[w]e do not know though but what it has been changed." [62] Andrews received a similar letter from his brother Homer relating that "[t]he Copper Heads are raising the devil in this State with the soldiers votes forging them, but as good luck will have it they have been discovered." [63] The *New York Tribune* estimated that Lincoln had been "cheated" out of thirty thousand votes. [64]

On Election Day, Andrews reflected in his War Journal that:

> the fate of our nation is this day being decided. "Lincoln and Johnson" is Union, Universal Freedom, Success; but "McClellan and Pendleton" means Disunion, and success and slavery for one Confederacy and humiliation and ruin for the other. But the result of today's election is not doubtful. Lincoln *will be* reelected; we shall yet have Union – although my bones may be bleaching before the joyous time comes to gladden the heart of our nation. [65]
> (emphasis in original)

Lincoln barely carried New York with a narrow 50.5 percent to 49.5 percent margin. [66] Of the counties where the 179th was recruited, only Erie (Buffalo) gave McClellan a majority, although he came within 174 votes in Chemung County (51.4% to 48.6%). [67]

Did the soldiers' vote affect the outcome in New York State? The actual impact will never be known with certainty because the soldiers' votes were not separately tabulated in the local voting places in New York. [68] Twelve of the states allowing soldiers to vote from the field did separately tabulate them, and in those states Lincoln received a 70 percent majority from the Army of the Potomac soldiers compared to the 53 percent majority he received from civilian voters in those states. [69]

Given the close outcome, James McPherson has concluded that the soldiers' vote may have made the difference in New York State. [70] On the other hand, Josiah Benton, writing in 1915, had concluded that the soldiers' votes were "of little consequence" except in Maryland. [71] All things considered, McPherson's conclusion seems the more reasonable because the race was so close, soldiers represented as much as a quarter or more of the potential electorate and soldiers in other states voted heavily in favor of Lincoln. [72] Additional supporting evidence – albeit of unknown reliability – may be found in contemporary newspaper reports of New York regiments voting heavily in Lincoln's favor. [73]

After being arrested in Buffalo on November 3 and taken to Washington, Ottenot was kept in custody for three months in Capitol Prison. [74] When he expressed concern about being absent from his company, Col. John Foster from the judge advocate's office told him: "You need not trouble yourself about your company; you will never see it again." Ottenot was first told that he would be tried himself; then that he would be called to testify against Colonel North; then he would be called to testify against Lieutenant Lockwood from Company E, who had also been arrested; and ultimately that he would not be needed. In the end, Ottenot was never charged and he was never tried. [75]

Ottenot was kept in solitary confinement for the first thirty days, subsisting on prison fare. Conditions improved somewhat for the remaining two months, but the the *Buffalo Daily Courier* report that he had been confined for three months "in one of the Administration's Bastille's" seems not far off the mark. [76]

Ottenot's congressman, Democrat John Ganson, intervened on Ottenot's behalf with Secretary of War Stanton, who ultimately ordered Ottenot's release. Ottenot was ordered to return to his regiment, but because he did not believe he deserved "the treatment I had received I did not feel it my duty to return to the field." He accordingly tendered his resignation, which Stanton initially declined, but ultimately accepted on March 6, 1865. [77]

Allegations of voter fraud in the 179th were not limited to Captain Ottenot. Lieutenant Charles Lockwood, also from Company E, was arrested on December 26, 1864 while officer of the guard. Lockwood may have suspected that he was under investigation. On December 15, he had tendered his resignation "unconditional and immediate on account of Private and important Family affairs and Sickness which requires my Immediate attention at home." [78] Like Ottenot, he was held in old Capitol Prison without any charges being preferred and was subsequently released and returned to the 179th in the field on February 24. [79] However, Colonel Gregg placed Lockwood under arrest the following day because Gregg apparently had good evidence that Lockwood had in fact sent fraudulent votes forward. [80] Lockwood was found guilty by court-martial on the charge of conduct prejudicial to good order and military discipline and cashiered effective April 16, 1865. [81]

A month after the election, Colonel Gregg, a Democrat before the war, wrote his friend Judge Ariel Thurston, a Democrat turned Republican, on the state of the "Democracy" (i.e., the Democratic Party).

> I see the World made a suggestion the other day to the Democracy which it would be well for them to adopt, viz, to give up slavery. It has served their purpose for a long time but it is played out. It can never be made to pay either to grow cotton or Democracy. Gabriel with his great bugle could not blow it into power again if he should try.

> But the Democracy can restore the Union and themselves to power by standing squarely up to the old landmarks. Let them get back upon the Buffalo platform, slough off such rotten material as Seymour [defeated Governor of New York], Wood, Vallandigham [one of the leading Peace Democrats], Brooks & Co. and power will surely come to them. Aint it plain for H. [who?] to see that it was not the greatness of Lincoln, Weed & Co. that gave the government to the Republicans but the very weakness of the Democratic leaders? The fact is the old party has been sick for the last ten years and instead of calling in such doctors as William Cullen Bryant, David Wilmot, and others who understand the old man's case, they have quacked the old patient almost to death with such physicians as old Filmore, C. Chauncey Burr, and Booby Brooks. How long do you think an old line Doctor like Dr. Hart would live if you should call in some Indian quack to administer to him if he was sick? The sight of the physician would almost kill him. It would at least come as near to it as these gentlemen have to killing this grand old Democratic party. [82]

However, as events unfolded, it was the Republicans that became the "Grand Old Party", and Democrats would not elect another president until Grover Cleveland in 1884.

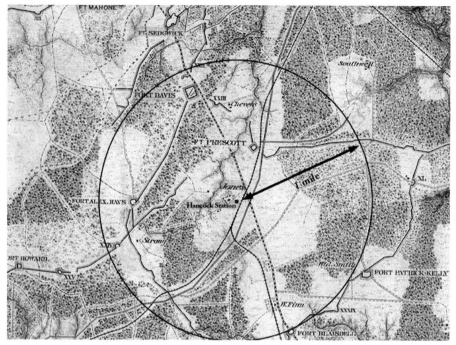

Hancock Station Vicinity

CHAPTER TWENTY-ONE

Winter Camp Near Hancock Station

On November 29, 1864, the 179th New York left their camp near Pegram House around one in the afternoon and marched four miles to the right to older Union positions to establish a new camp in the vicinity of Hancock Station and Jones House. The move was part of an exchange of positions by the Second and Ninth Corps.[1] The opposing lines were much closer in that sector and the 179th had seen hard duty there during the summer. John Andrews noted that: "the old men (in distinction from the new ones) say they would much prefer going in to battle, to going back there again." (emphasis in original)[2] The 179th New York and the 186th New York were deployed in the Union lines between Fort Davis and Fort Hays. Together their forces totaled 965 men, theoretically the number for one regiment, not two. The 179th went out on picket duty that night, and Company D's Lt. J.A. Wisner was wounded in the arm.[3]

Hancock Station Sketch

Hancock Station was located just west of where the U. S. Military Railroad crossed Jerusalem Plank Road, about three-quarters of a mile in the rear of Fort Davis and a mile and a quarter in the rear of Fort Sedgwick.[4] The U.S. Military Railroad, built to supply the Army of the Potomac from City Point as the Union lines extended increasingly westward, was an impressive accomplishment. But its stations were hardly imposing presences. They were little more than a railroad siding with or without a platform for unloading freight. Hancock Station was no exception. Jones House was a farmer's house nearby built around 1810 (and is today known as Walker House).

The 179th began building winter quarters at their new camp on December 3. In a December 5 letter home to his old friend Judge Ariel Thurston, Colonel Gregg reported that he had just established his new headquarters, but expected only a short stay of a few days "from present indications."

> I think Grant is preparing to strike for Richmond. Whether he will make a
> flank movement or strike from the shoulder remains to be seen. From our
> camp it is only about one and a half miles to Petersburg, but from the looks
> of the rebel works between this and that city, I think it is a rough road to
> travel. I believe that I had rather go around.[5]

Gregg's assessment was incorrect in one respect, but correct in another. Rather than remaining near Hancock Station for only a few days, the 179th would remain camped there until the end of the Petersburg campaign. But something was afoot.

[Map: Warren's Raid]

On December 7, General Warren and the Fifth Corps began a raid that would reach thirty miles south of Petersburg to destroy track on the Weldon Railroad. While the Union forces had captured in August the section of the Weldon Railroad as it entered Petersburg, the Confederates were still bringing supplies up from North Carolina on the Weldon Railroad, transferring them to wagon at Stony Creek Station and ultimately bringing them into Petersburg along the Boydton Plank Road.[6] Operating in Confederate territory far from the main body of Union troops, Warren was out of touch with Meade for several days. Concern arose that Warren might need help to return to the Union lines. General Potter was put in command of a body of troops (including the 179th New York Volunteers) that was placed on standby to be ready to assist Warren and the Fifth Corps if needed.[7]

Still without word from Warren on the afternoon of December 10, Meade ordered Potter to:

> immediately move with your command down the Jerusalem plank road to
> the support of Major-General Warren....You will march without intermission
> to the Nottoway River and across that stream to Sussex Court-House, from
> which point you will ... endeavor to ascertain General Warren's position and
> communicate with him.... The great object is to assist General Warren, but in
> attempting this you must be careful not to place your command in a position
> to have it isolated, but must keep open your line of retreat toward the James
> River and this army.[8]

Potter's command was to take four days' rations, "sixty rounds of ammunition on the person," another fifteen rounds on pack mules, "a few ambulances, and the minimum allowance of hospital stores; [but] no baggage wagons on any pretext."[9]

Having witnessed the execution of Rowe and Smith earlier in the day, the 179th New York left camp around five o'clock that evening and headed south along the Jerusalem Plank Road, leaving their knapsacks behind.[10] After marching twenty miles through the night "without intermission," Potter's command reached Freeman's Bridge on the Nottoway River by five in the morning on December 11. Potter described it as "a very good march to this point, indeed. No straggling."[11]

However, it turned out that the Fifth Corps was not in trouble after all. Upon learning of Potter's arrival at the Nottoway River, Warren sent him a dispatch from Sussex Court-House that:

"We shall not need your assistance further, and if your men are not too fatigued I wish you would march back at once, as you may be needed with your corps." [12]

At six in the morning, the 179th "camped in a cotton field, cooked coffee, and rested till the 5th Corps passed us." [13] After resting for six to eight hours, the 179th started back and reached camp back near Hancock Station around ten or eleven o'clock that night. They had marched roughly forty miles in just over twenty-four hours. [14]

At the same time that the 179th New York and the other troops under Potter's command reached Hancock Station, Meade received Warren's report on his mission: "I have completely destroyed the railroad track from the Nottoway [River] to Hicksford... I have met but trifling opposition or annoyance." [15]

The 179th's scribe succinctly summarized the mission from their perspective: "Roads very muddy, hard march. Nothing of importance occurring. Supposed object of march to aid 5th Corps." [16] The dubious tone of the 179th's scribe is not surprising. Old Vets in the 179th said that it was "the hardest march they had ever made." [17] Company I's Abram Meyers recalled that: "it snowed, rained and hailed all night the first night. The next day it was cold and the snow was about three inches deep." Company H's Denton Dexter recalled that: "The regiment was hurried all night and the strain was more than men could endure. I carried a gun, haversack, a double round of cartridges, a blanket and several days' provisions." Company H's Harry Ap Rees later claimed: "that trip alone was worth a pension." [18]

One of the soldiers of the 179th dropped dead in camp when they returned. Others were sent to the hospital. [19] Company C reported that its men were "very tired from the effects of our march. All complaining of sore feet." [20] Company C's Lt. Levi Force was so exhausted that he laid down and fell asleep without his blankets despite the cold. [21]

While Potter's report of "no straggling" may not have been accurate with respect to some regiments, [22] it does appear to be essentially accurate with respect to the 179th. Company I's John Van Riper, who did not return to camp until December 13, was the only one officially reported as a straggler. [23]

The 179th remained in camp on December 12 and 13 under orders to be ready to move again, but nothing came of it. [24] The 179th returned to regular duty.

In his letter to Judge Thurston, Colonel Gregg described the location of the 179th's new camp.

> "Fort Hell" [Fort Sedgwick] is about half a mile to our right; it is a hot place. Our division extends about two and a half miles, commencing at Fort Rice on our right, our left resting on the Weldon road. In many places the pickets are not more than one hundred feet apart. A constant firing is kept up during the night with musketry. Artillery and mortars join in occasionally. Drums, bands, and bugles altogether make so much confusion that I find it quite difficult to keep an idea in my head long enough to write it out. [25]

The 179th's camp was behind the main lines, but still within the range of Confederate fire. Colonel Gregg noted that:

> The bullets from the rebel line come into our camp very often, but as of yet none of my men have been injured. The camp next to mine has lost five men since we came here. Two of them have died. Our men have all got barricades in front of their tents. [26]

John Andrews similarly noted: "Occasionally a shot comes over into camp, but no one as yet has been injured. Yesterday morning a shot came into Lt. Bogart's tent. It struck a log over the Lieutenant's head, bounded over him, and brushed by Lieut. Tinker's shoulder." [27]

However, things were apparently quiet enough along the front that Gregg invited Judge Thurston to visit.

> If you and [John Arnot, former Mayor of Elmira] were here at this time I could entertain you elegantly. My new house is well calculated to accommodate visitors, why don't you come? I tell you you would be well paid. The weather is delightful. Why do you stay home shivering and pinching yourselves when a few dollars in money and a few days time can be so well and so profitably spent in a visit to your old friend who will take great pleasure in showing you all that can be seen upon our side of the lines? I promise you that if you do not see Petersburg you shall hear her church bells ring. [28]

Dr. Robinson, the father of the 179th's regimental surgeon, had already been visiting Gregg for several days from Hornellsville. [29]

However, Colonel Gregg's view of his living conditions in early December 1864 was the exception. Progress in building a new camp was slow. Building a camp had to defer to the demands of picket duty and other military operations. Company C reported on December 20 that they had cleared their company street and begun working on their tents, but the next day the tents were flooded. They continued working on the tents and moved into their new quarters on December 30. [30]

The physical location of the camp was a problem. A week after the 179th arrived, William Lamont wrote home that: "We are in the swamp yet near Hancock Station but I think we will not stay here much longer. If we do, the Regt will all be in the hospital. It looks more like a Co than a Regt." [31]

John Andrews had a similar assessment at the end of December:

> We are encamped in a miserable swamp hole, where we are obliged to wade around in mud and water ankle deep. To be on duty one night and stumble around over stumps and into holes full of water of course is enough to disgust any new recruit with soldiering. [32]

Things apparently were not any better in January. After a hard rain the night of January 9 into the following morning, Stephen Compton wrote in his diary: "Our camp is nearly under water." [33] And William Lamont would still write at the end of February that: "I would like to traid this camp for a better one." [34]

Ord. put a better face on it for the people back home, describing the 179th's quarters as "the best along these lines in our opinion" in a letter to *The Hornellsville Tribune*. [35] Ord. reported about five hundred men in camp. He described it as "a model camp" and he also invited readers to come visit: "Beyond a salute for victories won on other fields, or a little squabbling among the uneasy pickets, nothing in the pyrotechnic line shall disturb your equanimity."

Winter inactivity provided the opportunity for 179th to fill officer and non-commissioned officer vacancies resulting from combat and disease going back to June. Going into fall and winter camp, only Company E of the first seven companies had a captain in the field (and he – Captain Ottenot – had been arrested in November on voter fraud allegations). First Lieutenant George Carpenter had commanded Company A since Albert Terrill had been promoted to major in August. Carpenter was also informally commanding Company F at Colonel Gregg's request after Captain Farwell had been killed at the Battle of the Crater and Lieutenant Bradley had been sent on detached duty. Company B's Capt. Robert Stewart had had his leg amputated in June, but did not leave the service until January 1865. Lieutenant James Bowker had been mortally wounded at Poplar Spring Church. John Prentiss had been promoted to captain in Company C after the death of John Barton, but Prentiss had been sick ever since and was ultimately discharged for disability in December. Lieutenant Jeffrey Wisner had been in command of Company D after Baker Saxton had died at the Battle of the Crater (Captain Bird had been wounded in the June 17 assault and discharged in August.) However, Wisner had been wounded in November and left the service. Company G's Capt. James Day had been wounded at the Battle of the Crater, but was not discharged for disability until January 1865. [36]

In many instances, the candidates for promotion were logical successors. For example, in Company A, the vacancy created by Captain Terrill's promotion to major was filled by First Lieutenant Carpenter on December 23. Second Lieutenant Farr in turn was promoted to first lieutenant and Orderly Sergeant Compton to second lieutenant. In Company C, Levi Force had been promoted to second lieutenant in August and had been in de facto command during Captain Prentiss' illness. Force was promoted to captain at the end of December when Prentiss resigned.

However, at least one officer appointment was controversial.

[Photo: Gov. Seymour (D)]

John Andrews had come south with only a promise of a commission from Colonel Gregg. He spent October and November in the camp of the 179th New York waiting for Governor Seymour to act on Colonel Gregg's recommendation. On October 25, frustrated that he had not yet received his commission from Albany, Andrews had written in his journal that: "Gov. Seymour is granting commissions for this regiment to some of his Copperhead friends that have never been heard of before in this regiment. The Col. feels very indignant at this, the more because the Gov. is entirely disregarding his appointments." [37]

The issue of Governor Seymour appointing officers that "have never been heard of before" in a regiment had gone public in another of Elmira's home regiments in early 1864. Seymour appointed an outsider – A. J. McNett – to the vacant lieutenant colonel position in the 141st New York. All the officers of the 141st New York went public with resolutions and a letter to the governor opposing McNett's appointment: "[W]e consider the policy of filling vacancies with men outside the regiment, who have never shared its hardships, know nothing of its desires, and can not be presumed to care for its interests, highly injurious to the service." [38] However, Seymour stood firm and the appointment went through. (McNett served through the end of the war and was brevetted brigadier general.) [39]

To Andrews' dismay, Sgt. Maj. Thomas Smith was appointed first lieutenat of Company D by Governor Seymour. Andrews claimed that Smith "[o]btained it by political influence. Paid a Dr. Ward of Hornellsville, a particular friend of Gov. Seymour's, to obtain it for him. The Colonel is justly indignant about it, and refuses to let him muster on it." [40]

Gregg complained to his friend Judge Ariel Thurston that Lt. James Bowker had not been promoted to captain, despite Gregg's recommendation, before Bowker was mortally wounded at Poplar Spring Church.

> [Bowker] was a gallant officer and was well entitled to the promotion to which I recommended him, and which he would have received but for the malignity of copperhead democracy. Gov. Seymour has done his widow great

injustice by allowing himself to be controlled by a miserable politician of Hornellsville. I have sent the Governor the proof that he has been selling commissions. Any man would get a commission by paying this scab $150. I know by his own letters. The Governor knows it by this time, and I have no doubt despises him as heartily as I do, and as all other men do who know him as well as I do. [41]

[Photo: Gov. Fenton (R)]

On November 28, Andrews – with Gregg's support – left the camp of the 179th New York for Albany to "obtain from Copperhead Seymour a commission if I could." [42] On the way, Andrews stopped in Elmira to meet with A. S. Diven "inasmuch as he had been instrumental in getting me into this box I was in." Diven advised Andrews "to wait till January when the semi-rebel Seymour had given way to the patriotic Fenton and then he would do what he could for me." [43] (Seymour had just been defeated for reelection by Reuben Fenton.) Andrews nonetheless decided to proceed and after stopping off at home, where he received some letters of recommendation from local influentials, he headed to Albany.

When Andrews arrived in Albany, he fortuitously ran into Sgt. Charles Hager from Company E, who was also seeking a commission from Governor Seymour. They decided to approach the governor together. It turned out that the only slot available was a "Second Lieutenancy" in Company D created by Jeffrey Wisner's resignation. Despite Gregg's recommendation, Seymour had given the available "First Lieutenancy" in Company D to Sergeant Major Smith. [44] The New York Adjutant General privately told Andrews that it was a "damned shame" that Andrews had not gotten the first lieutenant slot, "but that it was 'some of that damned Ward's doings.' (Dr. Ward of Hornellsville had been paid $150 by some of Smith's friends to procure the commission for him.)" [45] Governor Seymour gave the second lieutenant commission to Andrews telling him that he had "better accept a 2d Lieutenancy as it is all you can get." [46] Andrews accepted the commission as a second lieutenant and was formally mustered in on December 18, 1864. He eventually was promoted to first lieutenant on March 25, 1865. [47]

Colonel Gregg won the battle of wills with Sergeant Major Smith. Smith ultimately declined the promotion to first lieutenant in Company D. However, he was later promoted to second lieutenant in Company C. [48]

Whether James Griswold's appointment as captain of Company F in December 1864 was controversial is not apparent. Griswold definitely was an outsider. He had enlisted in the 50th Engineers, which became the mainstay of Meade's engineer forces at Petersburg, in September 1861 and had been promoted to sergeant. He had been recommended for promotion to second lieutenant in the 50th Engineers, but never heard from Governor Seymour. In July 1864, he attempted to retain a lawyer to pursue the matter. How a commission as second lieutenant in the 50th Engineers became a commission as captain in the 179th New York is not apparent, but Griswold served as captain of Company F until the end of the war. [49]

In the enlisted ranks, a number of sergeants were absent because they were prisoners of war or in hospital. In order to be able to fill these important positions, it was necessary to demote the absent incumbents to create a vacancy, unfair as that might seem. Orderly Sergeant James Spencer, who had been in command of Company D at the Battle of the Crater when he was captured, was at Salisbury Military Prison when he was demoted to private – "without fault on his part" in the words of the 179th New York's Regimental History. [50] Company A's Sgt. James C. Rutan was reduced to the ranks after he had been in the hospital for five months. [51]

During January and February 1865, the individual companies described their duties in similar terms in their Morning Reports. Company A and Company D reported "doing picket duty & drilling". Company B, Company C, Company E, Company F, Company G, Company H, Company I and Company K reported doing the same while within range of enemy fire. [52] William Lamont wrote his sister that "We do not drill any now but our duty is very heavy I am on duty every other day mostly picket." [53] Company D's Ezra Tinker wrote the *Dundee Record* that: "Our regiment during the entire winter, lay a little to the left of Fort Steadman doing picket duty, occasionally going out on raiding excursion, to the great annoyance of the Johnnies." [54]

The relative inactivity over several months apparently caused a fall off in the level of attentiveness by the guards. Lieutenant Colonel Doty :

> noticed with regret the loose manner in which guard duty has been performed in this command. The attention of Officers is called to the Regulations and to previous orders issued from these HdQrs in relation to this duty.

> Hereafter the Officer of the guard will be *required* to visit every post of his guard frequently during the day and at least three times during the night, once before midnight, and twice after midnight, for the purpose of instructing the Sentinels in their duties and to see that they perform them properly. [55](emphasis in original)

Still, Colonel Gregg rated the 179th "Good" on "Discipline" at the end of February – an improvement over the "Fair" rating he had given at the end of October and the end of December. [56]

The health of the 179th was also improving. In December, Stephen Compton wrote his wife that: "The health of the regiment is quite good. The men are generally fleshy and hearty." [57] While Compton overstated the status of the regiment as of December, the trend was positive. Company A had had thirty-one men "Absent-Sick" at the end of August 1864, but only sixteen at the end of February 1865. Company B had forty-seven "Absent-Sick" at the end of August, but only twenty-seven at the end of February. The number dropped from forty-nine to twenty-nine for Company D. This improvement in health probably put an additional one hundred or more soldiers on the ground for the 179th New York. [58]

Some of the soldiers wounded in the June 17 assault, the Battle of the Crater and the Battle of Poplar Spring Church were also returning to duty – five in October, four in December, eight in January, none in February and five in March, for a total of twenty-five [59] As of March 15, the 179th was reported as having 440 men present for duty, 508 men present and 726 men in aggregate. [60] That force level was more than the first six companies had had when they arrived at White House Landing in June 1864.

The 179th's improving strength showed. On March 20, General Potter held a brigade review. General Griffin sent an aide to tell Colonel Gregg that General Potter "had praised the appearance of our regt. very much." [61] Two weeks later, General Griffin would select the 179th to lead the Ninth Corps' final assault at Petersburg. [62]

[Photo: Presentation Sword]

The work done by the officers was also recognized within the 179th New York. On March 8, the "boys" of Company B presented Lt. Edward Lounsbery "with a sword worth eighty dollars." Andrews described Lounsbery as "one of the finest officers in the regiment." [63] A week later, the 179th's officers gave Lieutenant Colonel Doty "a nice set of horse equipment." [64] At some point, the men of Company C gave Levi Force a presentation sword. [65]

Cautious optimism about the war's end had been developing in the 179th New York, albeit with the recognition that the end would not come without further loss of life. On Christmas Day Stephen Compton wrote his wife:

> The news from the armies is encouraging. The work goes bravely on and hope springs up anew in our hearts, the hope of a speedy termination of our national contest. O what a day that will be if we are spared to see it. A proud day for Americans, as glorious a day as ever shone upon any nation on the globe. My imagination runs out to grasp the glory of our Country when we shall have conquered rebellion. But it strives in vain. I begin to think that this winter and spring will end the contest. God grant that it may be so. [66]

A day later, John Andrews wrote his father in similar terms: "Well, I hope the slaughter of next Summer's campaign will not be as great as last Summer's was. We all hope to get the 'Johnnies' on the run next Spring and to completely finish them by the 4th of July." [67]

The Union artillery salutes at Petersburg on February 24 to celebrate the fall of Charleston, Savannah and Wilmington harbor "in rapid succession" bolstered that optimism. [68] Continuing Confederate desertion presumably was also taken as encouraging evidence. On February 15, ten Confederate soldiers from Holcombe's South Carolina Legion deserted at the 179th New York's picket line. "They ... were a happy set of fellows to think that they had at last got out of 'the service.' They said they had 'soldiered' nearly four years and deserted now because there was no prospect of peace." [69]

Grant's next offensive from February 5 to 7, 1865 was not as successful as had been hoped, but the Union still gained two crossings over Hatcher's Run for future exploitation. [70] The 179th New York was not directly engaged in that offensive, but had been "ready to move at a moment's notice" if needed. [71]

The winter of 1864-1865 provided the opportunity for the 179th New York to rebuild. There was time to train the new recruits who had arrived in the field in September. Many sick and wounded veterans returned to the ranks from hospital. Officer vacancies were filled. The forced march in December increased the capability of the 179th to maneuver as a unit. Victory was in sight. The 179th New York was ready for the upcoming spring offensive.

James C. and Amelia Breese Rutan

CHAPTER TWENTY-TWO

Ties With Home

Ties with home [1] were very important to the soldiers of the 179th New York. Shortly after arriving in Virginia in October 1864, John Andrews reflected in his War Journal about a soldier's relationship with family and friends:

> Dear ones at home while you are thinking of brothers, sons, husbands, fathers, remember that they on the tented field or on the bloody one of battle, are thinking of you, longing for your sympathy and asking for your words of encouragement and support. Although far from you, our friends, there is a bond of love that still holds us to you and by us will never be severed. [2]

William Lamont spoke for generations of soldiers serving far from home when he wrote his parents that he "could injoy rading a leter from home every day." [3] Stephen Compton wrote his wife: "O how much I prize the letters from home." [4] These letters were treasured. Lamont wrote his sister the very next day after receiving a letter from her, telling her that he had "read it for the third time." [5]

News from home was important – even about mundane things. Henry Beebe wrote his parents: "let me know how you are all getting along. Have you heard from Uncle William Coleman, Aunt Louisa or any of the rest of the folks up west. Which colt did you trade off and what are you doing with the old horse and so on. You see that I want to hear from every thing." [6] Jacob Graves was also explicit: "I want you to rite and tell me how the crops is out there and how the mare gits along. How many cows are you raising this summer and if the mare has got a colt or not." [7]

It especially mattered to the soldier that the family member or friend had taken the time to write. Homer Olcott, a twenty-year-old farmer, wrote his family that: "You can not imagine the pleasure it gave me to get a letter from father in his own handwriting." [8] Andrews wrote in his War Journal that "Father's letter did me good. The simple fact of *his* writing to me is enough to make me feel happier." [9](emphasis in original). Similarly, he noted that "Jose's [Josephine Starkey] letter contained nothing of particular interest. Her letters are *valuable* to me only because they are from *her*." (emphasis in original) [10]

Letters from the soldiers were equally important to their families. One of Andrews' sisters wrote him that:

> [w]e received your letter while at the dinner table today, and of course business was suspended for awhile at least so anxious were we to hear from you. Many tears were shed on hearing of your hardships and privations and at the thought of what you must still endure. [11]

It was not just receiving letters from family and friends that comforted soldiers. Writing letters home also provided an emotional boost. Lamont wrote his sister:

> You must not think me homesick for writing so often. I wrote to Father Saturday but I am on picket now which is lonesome work and it being my birthday I did not no how I would celebrate in any better way than writing home that is if you injoy getting letters from me as well as I do from home. [12]

Correspondence was so important to Andrews that he kept a log of incoming and outgoing letters. From fall 1864 through March 7, 1865, he received seventy-five letters. He was even more diligent, sending out eighty-seven letters during the same time. William Larzelere also kept a log of letters sent and received in his diary. [13]

Andrews corresponded particularly frequently with his younger brother Homer; his younger sisters Mayte and Emma; a potential fiancee, Mollie A. Langworthy; a family friend or relation, Josephine Starkey; and a college friend, Charles Tubbs.

The army wisely recognized the importance of letters to and from home. Mail service was surprisingly quick and reliable. [14] By the spring of 1865, letters mailed from Upstate New York were received by the soldiers at the front in Virginia in as few as four days. Service in the fall of 1864 was only a couple of days slower. The movement of the 179th to the front in the spring illustrated how such rapid delivery was possible—overnight by rail from Elmira to Baltimore; Baltimore to Washington by rail; Washington/Alexandria to City Point by steamer or transport. In May 1865, when the 179th was in camp in Alexandria, Virginia, just across the river from Washington waiting to be discharged, letters arrived in two to three days. [15]

Soldiers were careful to keep a sufficient supply of postage stamps (three cents). Daniel Lee wrote his wife that: "There is one thing I can't get here and that is postage stamps. I haven't got but one more and I do want you should send me five or six at a time." [16] Henry Kingsley wrote about a package from home that he expected to receive that: "most that I care about is them postage stamps." When he died of typhoid fever in June 1864, he had 112 postage stamps in his personal effects. [17] Lamont asked his family to send him "a half dollar wort of stamp." [18]

The periodic movement of units provided a challenge for mail delivery, but simply addressing the letter to the soldier with his regiment and sending it to Washington, D.C. sufficed. The letters were distributed to the field from Washington. [19] Daniel Lee was confident that letters would catch up with him. "I haven't got much letters from you in some time for we have bin on the move so that the male hasn't com to us yet, but if we don't move from here it will be in tomorow." [20] A week later, he received five letters from his wife. [21]

On the other hand, newly arrived recruit James W. Vangilder was not so sure when he wrote home from City Point in September 1864: "Write as soon as you get this. I don't know as I shall get your leter but it wont do no hurt to try one letter but I would not send but one." [22]

Although the soldiers enjoyed receiving letters from home, they could still complain that their families did not write often enough or long enough. William Lamont began a letter to his sister by complaining that: "It has been so long since I have heard from home I thought I would write to find out if the mail had been robbed or not." [23] David June complained shortly after arriving at Arlington Heights: "I want to know what is the matter that you don't write to me. I have wrote several letters and haven't received eny answers." [24] Henry Kingsley scolded his parents: "Why don't you write a longer letters. They are not half long enough." [25]

Of course this criticism could go both ways. John Andrews' sister Emma admonished him that: "I have one fault to find with your letters. They are not half long enough," although she did acknowledge: "yet a half of a loaf of bread is very much better than *none*." [26](emphasis in original) Mollie Langworthy lectured him that he needed to write more often. [27]

Daniel Lee even complained about his wife's handwriting: "right planer if you can for the last letters I did not make out half of them." [28]

Letters home were the only way for families to know that their soldier was all right. Lee wrote his wife and daughter: "I do right to you for I do now that you feel ancious to hear from me every day and so I do right to you so as to let you now that I ain't been yet in the field." After reaching the front in June 1864, Lee wrote them at least ten times over the ensuing month before he was captured. [29] Andrews wrote his brother Homer in the spring of 1865:

Now that the campaign is opened in earnest I shall write you often – even though it be but a few lines at a time – in order that you may not have any unnecessary uneasiness in regard to me. [30]

Lamont wrote his sister "you must worey if you do not hear from me for I do not have time to write." [31]

War news was a prominent feature of the home town newspapers and dispatches from the front appeared within a matter of days. For example, news of the Battle of the Crater was reported in the *Elmira Daily Advertiser* two days later on Tuesday, August 2 under "Latest News By Telegraph–Evening Report" The headline read:

THE ASSAULT ON PETERSBURG
DESPERATE FIGHTING
The Colored Troops Become Demoralized
LOSSES IN THE NINTH CORPS
Gen. Bartlett a Prisoner
OUR LOSS 4,000 to 5,000
REBEL LOSS ABOUT THE SAME

The newspaper article estimated losses in General Ledlie's division at 1,000 to 1,200, perhaps higher. Maj. Barton was listed amongst the officer casualties as having "lost a leg." [32] References to "desperate fighting," overall Union losses of 4,000 to 5,000, loses in Ledlie's division of 1,000 to 1,200, and the wounding of an officer from the 179th surely must have created anxiety among relatives and friends waiting for a post-battle letter.

John Andrews was a fairly regular correspondent with his family, but his younger brother

Homer still wrote him on November 3, 1864 "We saw that your Division had been engaged and are anxious of course to hear from you that all is well." [33] Similarly, Mollie Langworthy wrote: "I read in the paper of the fighting where you were. This news of the battle came the same day of your letter and perhaps you can imagine how anxiously I am looking for another letter." [34]

Three weeks after the Battle of Poplar Spring Church, Asa McDonald wrote Col. William Hoffman, Commissary General of Prisoners in Washington, for news of his son, Company K's Sergeant Theodore McDonald:

> Some of the soldiers write he was wounded By a shell in the head & was in some hospital. Lieut. Hooper writes that Theodore is one of the missing. He was in the Battle of Sept. 30th 1864 on the north side of the James River. I saw in the papers that you was the man to write to for information. My son was 20 years old & was beloved by all that new him. General, I Hope you will let me no where he is as soon as possible. [35]

McDonald had been captured and was sent to Salisbury Military Prison. He was later paroled.

Usually there was little consolation that the officers could offer the anxious family. Company I's Capt. Edwin Bowen answered the family of John W. Cook as follows:

> I am very sorry that I cannot tell you were he is. He went into the fight on 30th of Sept and acted well his part. We were repulsed and ordered to fall back. When we came out of the woods John was not with us. I don't know whether he was wounded and taken prisoner or not. I think he was taken prisoner with ten other men of our co[mpany]. I have not heard anything of them since. Hoping he may come home again. [36]

Cook was taken prisoner and later paroled, but died of disease.

The anxious father of Lt. Henry Mapes wrote the "Captain (or highest ranking officer) of Company D" on April 1, 1865:

> You will confer a great favor by writing me what you may know or can learn in regard to his whereabouts. Is he killed or wounded or a prisoner or is he all right by replying to this immediately you will very much oblige his father. (emphasis in original) [37]

In fact, Mapes was fine.

However, the family's worst fears would often be confirmed. Chaplain Taft told John Andrews about finding a letter from a soldier killed at the battle of Poplar Spring Church to his wife that had not been mailed. Andrews wrote in his War Journal:

> I pity *her* – for he had just left her – and the first news she has of him is that he is dead.; – and yet, we all have friends to mourn for us in case we fall; and terrible indeed is their anxiety while we are thus exposed to danger. *We* endure the hardships; but they suffer more. [38](emphasis in original)

[Photo: Braided Hair]

Photography was still in its infancy, but it offered soldiers a visual connection with their loved ones. Just before the 179th left Alexandria for White House Landing, Abner Roberts wrote his sister that: "I want you to send me one of your photographs and I will get mine taken as soon as I can." [39] James C. Rutan carried three photos – one of his wife and him together taken just before the 179th left for Washington; one of his recently deceased daughter; and one of his two older sisters.

He also carried braided locks of his mother's and a sister's hair. [40] Homer Olcott "put my hand in my pocket and take a look at mother most every day." [41]

Family members also sent packages or "boxes" to their soldiers in the field. "Boxes" from home provided material support. Soldiers asked for a wide variety of things. The length of the request by Abner Welch undoubtedly was unrivaled:

> When I tell you to send me some clothing have the neighbors put in maple sugar and honey and the storekeepers put in candy and raisins and lemons, apples, pears and some chewing gum and [illegible] tobacco, cheese ... put in a johny cake, [illegible], pancakes and puddings and johny cake, butter and all such kind of things. [42]

Eugene Dunton asked his parents for "a good wooll hat and also a shirt." He pointed out that: "You can send it by mail by putting on enough stamps." [43] William Lamont requested "a hat size 6 7/8, a pair of suspenders, one undershirt, a quart cup with handle and burl[?], one pair of socks ... and an almanac." He wrote on January 7, 1865 that he had not received his box because the Potomac was frozen. [44] When the box destined for William Larzelere was delayed, his wife despaired "[f]or I am afraid the things will not taste very good after being so long on the road. And they were so fresh and nice when they were sent." [45] Delivery of the box sent by the family and friends of Homer Olcott was delayed so long that almost everything spoiled, including chicken and apples. "It smelled so bad that it made one of our boys in the tent heave up." Olcott passed along the suggestion of a friend: "when you sends chickens again to leave them alive and put in feed to keep them alive." [46]

Support also came from the community on an organized basis. Ord. wrote in an August 14, 1864 letter to the readers of *The Hornellsville Tribune* that:

> Before I closed my rambling letter I meant to say to the kind folks at home that, next after filling your quota [of troops], you can best help our brave boys lying in the trenches with the mercury at 100 degrees by contributing liberally to the Christian or Sanitary Commission. I cannot in one letter tell how much good these associations do; how much suffering and sickness they prevent by a timely distribution of vegetables, &c., how much pain they alleviate in the Hospitals. It is my experience that the Christian Commission does the most good among the rank and file. Its agents distribute goods personally; a large quanity of Sanitary Goods is drawn by Surgeons and other officers, and does not in every instance reach the men. Send your contributions to the Christian Commissions and send heavy ones, and send them often; and the thanks of the army and the country, and your own conscience shall be your reward. [47]

The United States Sanitary Commission was created by President Lincoln in 1861 – over the objections of the Army Medical Bureau – in response to lobbying by a coalition of prominent doctors, clergymen and women's organizations that sought to improve sanitary conditions for the soldiers in the field. The inspiration was the British Sanitary Commission which had been formed to address the staggering casualties caused by disease during the Crimean War. Lincoln appointed a new surgeon general in 1862 who was supported by the Sanitary Commission. That began "an extraordinarily productive partnership between public and private medical enterprise." By 1863, there were seven thousand local chapters around the North which held "Sanitary Fairs" to raise money. [48]

The Southern Tier Sanitary Fair "in aid of the sick and wounded of our army" opened in Elmira on March 14, 1864 in the First Presbyterian Church as the first troops of the 179th were arriving at the military depot. Preparations had been made throughout the region. *The Hornellsville Tribune* reported that:

> Contributions from any quarter, and of anything that can be converted into money, will be thankfully received...

> We trust that all patriotic men and women, who are reached by this call, will commence immediately the preparation of their contributions for this Fair.

> All the Express and Railroad lines centering in Elmira have offered to carry freight for the Fair, *free of charge*. (emphasis in original)[49]

Tragically, the Fair was cut short by a fire that started when the gas lights were being lit on the fifth day.

> The gas being turned on to a full bead, as the light was applied, it streamed upward and just caught one of the hanging festoons of evergreens. ... every effort was useless, the evergreens having become so dry that the flames went leaping along from festoon to festoon, until, within a few moments, the forest of evergreens and decorations filling the whole interior of the building was one mass of seething flame. [50]

Fortunately, the fire occurred at a slow time and only two people died. The Fair did raise $12,277.81, although the estimated loss to the church and the organizers was between $20,000 and $30,000. [51]

A "Central Fair" had been held in Buffalo in February. A more localized "Canisteo Valley Sanitary Fair" was held in Hornellsville at the same time as the fair in Elmira, reflecting the fact that "the distance and the time and expense of going and returning will prevent many from attending, while such an enterprise got up near by would receive hundreds of dollars that would never be carried or forwarded to other and more distant points." [52]

Similarly, in Ontario County, the Ladies' Hospital Aid group sought donations for their stalls at the Agricultural Fair in September 1864: "The proceeds of the sales are to be appropriated for the relief of our sick and wounded soldiers, and surely all patriotic men and women in the County will find *something* to give in aid of such a cause." [53](emphasis in original)

Even children helped support the troops. In June 1864, a group of five to twelve year old children in a Buffalo neighborhood held a "strawberry fair" (undoubtedly with the help of their parents) and contributed $37.32 to the Ladies' Christian Commission. The *Buffalo Daily Courier* printed their letter:

> The sum is not as large as we could wish, but we hope it may do some good. It is the offering of mere children who love their country, and the soldiers fighting for its cause. In this we have parted with the pocket money usually spent in fireworks and delicacies on the 4th of July; feeling that we shall cheerfully make this small sacrifice for the comfort of those who suffer so much for us. [54]

The Christian Commission was founded in 1861 by leaders of the YMCA to provide material support such as blankets and clothing as well as "spiritual nurture" to Union soldiers. [55]

Both the Christian Commission and the United States Sanitary Commission provided soldiers with stationary. The Christian Commission used the letterhead as an opportunity to present a brief homily for both the soldier writing the letter and his family or friend receiving it. The secular Sanitary Commission simply printed its name with nothing more. The Christian Commission also sent representatives to hospitals to take dictation from soldiers unable to write. [56]

On arriving at the City Point distribution camp in September 1864, William Lamont wrote friends on Christian Commission stationery that bore the phrases that the Commission "sends this as the Soldier's messenger to his Home. Let it hasten to those who wait for tidings." and "Behold! Now is the accepted time; behold, now is the day of salvation." [57] Daniel B. Lee sent a letter to his wife and daughter on similar letterhead with the message "There is a Friend that sticketh closer than a brother." [58] A letter Lamont wrote from Slough Hospital in June 1865 carried the missive "This is a faithful saying, and worthy of all acceptation, that Christ Jesus came into the world to save sinners; of whom I am chief." [59] John Cook used the same letterhead to write his parents in May 1865. [60] A June 1865 letter from Cook to his parents bore the message: "For God so loved the world that he gave his only begotten Son, that whosoever believeth in him should not perish, but have everlasting life". [61]

However, the Christian Commission stationery apparently was not universally available. Nor was it necessarily preferred. Only one of the twenty-five surviving letters from Daniel Lee was on Christian Commission stationary and only three of fourteen from Lamont.

Community support also came on an ad hoc basis. On December 15, 1864, *The Hornellsville Tribune* printed an appeal for "Mittens for the Soldiers":

> Some 250 to 300 pairs of woolen mittens or gloves are wanted immediately for the soldiers of the 179th Regt. N.Y.S. Vols. A call is made upon the ladies throughout this and adjoining towns, to furnish them as soon as possible. Those who have yarn and not the time to knit, are requested to furnish it for those who have. The mittens should have a separate place for the forefinger. Those who can not get yarn may make them of good fulled cloth. Those who respond to this call are requested to send the mittens to M. Aparr's store in this village, when they will be promptly forwarded to the soldiers. This is a work of humanity in which almost every woman can take an active part. The exposure of the soldiers to the cold while on picket, calls loudly for homemade, comfortable mittens, and we trust this call will meet with a hearty response. [62]

It did. A box of mittens arrived at the front on January 22, 1865, and the soldiers of the 179th immediately expressed their gratitude. The following day, Ord. wrote *The Hornellsville Tribune* that he had never experienced "a stormier, more disagreeable day" than January 22:

> The rain froze as it fell; the cold, north wind drove it into every crevice and through the roofs of cloth; mud, deep, unfathomable, was under foot. A box of mittens, the gift of the kind hearted ladies of Hornellsville arrived that night. – Don't you think they were accepted! Did not the forty odd men who went on picket that night have warm hands! And the camp guard, as he paced his beat in the sleety storm, had bright visions of home; he saw familiar faces and his mittens told him that they had not forgotten him. The whole camp was happier for that box of mittens. [63]

Ord. said the soldiers particularly appreciated the personal notes tucked into the mittens – "These were the prizes." He quoted one:

> It's a poor hand I think, that can't shape it's own mitten. You need not laugh at

these odd shaped things, for I doubt not you will sometime receive a worse fitting mitten than either of these, if you have not already. Have you ever? Accept my best wishes. [64]

Ord. concluded that "I cannot sufficiently thank the ladies for this present; but I can wish they were here to see how welcome it was." Individual soldiers were also writing:

And to-day, Sunday, many a hearty fellow, who has faced death and is ready to face it again, is inditing an earnest reply to these welcome notes. Everybody I meet blesses the kind donors. One boy, who received a pair of many colors, says "bully for the girls of Hornellsville." [65]

One of the soldiers who wrote a letter was John Andrews. Quartermaster Nathaniel Finch asked Andrews to write Lizzie Condorman, one of the ladies who had put a note in the mittens she made. "Quartie" assured Andrews, a recent graduate of Union College and eligible bachelor, that he knew Miss Condorman and that "she was highly respectable, *smart, intelligent, good looking*, and – her *parents* were *wealthy*." (emphasis in original) Andrews wrote her and confided in his journal that "I look for a racy reply." [66]

She wrote him back on February 4 and he received the letter just a week later. The style of her opening paragraph reveals much about the social conventions of the day.

Very much to my surprise I was made the Recipient of your letter bearing date January 22nd and as your favor seemed to indicate that even a feeble attempt at answer would be acceptable, I trust to your *forbearance*, as I consign my limited ideas to paper. [67](emphasis in original)

What followed was hardly "racy", but they were the thoughts of a well-spoken and earnest young woman.

We are looking forward with confidence to a speedy termination of this contest. Our Faith has been sorely tried. We have almost despaired at times, but now looking back it seems strange that we have ever, even for a moment doubted our ultimate Victory, for when we trace the growth of our Nation even from the days of the Pilgrims, the struggles and success of Our Fathers when they sought to remove from their necks the Yoke of Tyranny in the grand days of '76 its steady progress onward and upward. We know that Our Glorious Republic has not yet reached the Zenith of her Greatness. [68]

For citizen-soldiers, this kind of recognition of the importance of their service must have been welcome.

[Photo: Cash Home]

The ability of the soldiers in the field to provide reciprocal support to the "Army at Home" was limited. Far from home, the soldiers' traditional roles as breadwinner and head of the family were threatened. In theory, the bounty was intended as a way for the departing soldier to provide for his family while he was away at war. Once in the field, the soldiers were paid in cash, but they could use agencies such as Adams Express or U.S. Express Company to send cash home. George B. White sent his widowed mother $77 when he left for the front in May 1864. "If we are paid soon … what I do not need I can send home next time." [69] Daniel Lee sent his wife $80 of the $100 he received before leaving Elmira. (He added a note to his daughter: "Hannah Ann you must have a new dres out of the mony.") [70] Francis Canfield, who had supported his mother before the war, sent her his $300 bounty order because "he was afraid now that he had to give up work ... that his mother would have to go on the town or be supported by the county." [71] Edwin Williamson sent his widowed mother a check for $200 and $60 in cash. [72]

The real problem for soldiers trying to support their families was not the amount of pay–it was the infrequency with which they were paid.

Often families could not make do back home. The soldiers would give advice on how to reduce costs or what assets to sell to raise cash. Daniel Lee told his wife to: "Sell the sheepe the first opportunity you get and the horses to for it will be hard wintering them I am afraid." [73]

Local government support for impoverished families of soldiers was not widespread. [74] One example of local support was the Buffalo Relief Committee. Their report for December 1864 shows family support payments of between $6 and $8 to Casper Notter, Adam Bierland, Hugh McSarley, John C. Walter, William H. Karl, Adam Becker and Thomas Hennessy from the 179th New York. They were among the roughly six hundred recipients listed. [75]

The soldiers' wives and children had to step up to get the work done on the family farm. The wife of Company C's John Bill wrote him that: "You know how much trouble I have doing the chores and feeding the cattle. Father is not able to do much." [76]

Sometimes the wife had to seek work outside the home. [77] This did not always sit well with the soldier. Daniel Lee admonished his wife "don't work" and when she nonetheless did, he wrote her "I do want you to stop work now." (His concern may have been based on his wife's poor health rather than principle.) [78]

Many of the men of the 179th were married with children. Filling the emotional role of husband and father long distance was particularly trying. William Larzelere's wife wrote him:

> It will be seven years next Friday ... since we were married! It does not seem possible does it? Time flies so fast. Little did I think then that you would ever be obliged to fight for the best interests of your Country. We have seen many dark and Cloudy Days but I pray to God that the bright days will come brighter [than] we have ever seen to us both, and that there is much happiness in store for us yet, for you are so much needed to help bring up your children, that I have faith to believe you will be spared to come home to us yet. [79]

Daniel Lee reserved the last part of most of his letters home for a separate message to his seven-year-old daughter. These notes were usually filled with fatherly advice such as "Hannah Ann you must be a good girl and mind mother." and "You must be a good girl and learn to read so that you can right to me soon." [80]

The cessation of active campaigning during the late fall and winter of 1864-1865 provided the opportunity for some soldiers in the 179th to go home to tend to the needs of their families for a brief time. Some of the soldiers had been away from home since April. Article 12 of the Articles of War authorized the colonel of a regiment to "give furloughs to non-commissioned officers or soldiers, in such numbers and for so long a time, as he shall judge to be most consistent with the good of the service." [81]

Colonel Gregg and Lieutenant Colonel Doty seem to have liberally granted furloughs to non-commissioned officers and enlisted men. For the period January through March 1865, roughly ten to twenty enlisted men were on leave of absence at any one time, generally for fifteen days. [82] That would translate to a total of roughly one hundred enlisted men having been granted leave during that time.

At the end of February 1865, William Lamont noted that "a good many of the boys are home on firloughs." However, he himself did not request a furlough because "I could not stay home more than seven days." [83] For a fifteen day furlough, Lamont was just about right when travel time was subtracted. In addition, the soldier had to pay the cost of transportation home. [84] William Larzelere recorded his furlough to Penn Yan, New York as follows:

> March 1st Left the front. took cars for City Point at City Point took
> the mail steamer City Point... for Washington. distant 390 miles. Time 24
> hours
> [March] 2nd Left Washington for Baltimore 4 1/2 O'clock P.M. distance
> 38 miles Left Baltimore 10:00 P.M. for Elmira by the way of Harrisburgh.
> Arrived
> [March] 3rd at Elmira 2:30 P.M. in Penn Yan at 9:30 P.M. ...
> [March] 4 reached home. found all well...
> March 5 Sunday at home. after an absence of
> nearly 1 year. Spent the week in visiting and receiving calls
> [March] 13th Left home with regret bid "good by" to my wife and friends
> and P. Yan and left for the front.
> [March] 14th Arrived in Washington
> [March] 15th In Washington. Received 4 months pay & 40 dol payment on
> bounty...
> [March] 16th In Washington. at 3 o'clock left on steamer for City Pt.
> [March] 17 Arrived at City Pt. 2 P.M.
> [March] 18 Left for the front. arrived at the reg't at noon

When Larzelere was paid in Washington on March 15, he was charged $14.04 for round trip transportation – roughly a month's pay. [85] Henry Mapes was charged the $18.20 round trip fare to his home in Buffalo, but he was paid the third installment of his bounty and his monthly pay through December 31, 1864. [86]

The vast majority of these men returned on time from their leaves. However, that may have been due to careful selection by Colonel Gregg and Lieutenant Colonel Doty in who they granted leave to. Company G's Archibald McNeil, Company H's George Lake and Company K's Lyman Perry were the only three I have identified who did not. [87]

While the regimental commander could grant furloughs for enlisted men, only the corps commander could grant furloughs for officers. General Parke also seems to have taken a liberal approach to granting furloughs for officers.

Family needs were frequently the basis stated for the furlough requests by officers in the 179th New York. On February 2, 1865, Colonel Gregg requested fifteen days leave to visit his nineteen-year-old daughter. He referred to her with emotionally tinged words as "the sole surviving member of my family, a girl of tender years," and stated his need of "placing her, and the keeping of my home in the hands of other parties." [88]

Lieutenant Colonel Doty requested twenty days leave on January 2, 1865 to visit his home in Hornellsville, New York for the reasons that "I have an aged and infirm Mother dependent on me for support, and my business at home being in such a state as to require my personal attendance." [89] Company K's Capt. Moses Van Benschoeten, Company C's Capt. Levi Force, and Company A's Lt. James Farr also requested furloughs to care for elderly parents who were seriously ill. [90]

Company H's Capt. Giles Holden, whose wife had passed away, requested a twenty day leave because his eight and thirteen-year-old sons "are as I am advised fast acquiring habits that will destroy their future usefulness in life because of the lack of proper care and watchfulness." [91]

The officers of the 179th were often men of some means. A number of the officers requested a furlough to attend to their business interests. Company I's Capt. Edwin Bowen requested a fifteen day furlough because: "I left an unsettled partnership business interest of $5000 ... a large part of which I will lose, unless I am personally present to arrange and settle the issue immediately." [92] Company K's Lt. Robert Hooper, a merchant before the war, also needed to address partnership business interests. [93] Company I's Lt. Davis Marshall had problems with a real property transaction: "Before leaving home I purchased a piece of property which was guaranteed to me to be unencumbered, but I have just received intelligence that the property was mortgaged before I bought it." [94] The Regimental Surgeon, Joseph Robinson requested twenty days not only because his wife was in poor health, but also because he had "left home hurriedly and from necessity left a large amount of unsettled business which demands my personal attention." [95] Company G's Lt. William Hemstreet's wife was not only dangerously ill with diptheria, but she had also purchased a home for $300 while Hemstreet was in the army "and the parties now refuse to give her a deed." There were no other relatives who could help her. [96]

But furloughs were at best a temporary palliative. The only real solution was the end of the war and that was coming soon.

April 2, 1865

CHAPTER TWENTY-THREE

The Final Assault (April 2, 1865)

The approaching inevitability of Union victory was no less apparent to the Army of Northern Virginia than it was to the Army of the Potomac. On March 25, the Confederates attacked the Union lines at Fort Stedman in the Ninth Corps' sector. The attack was Lee's last attempt to break the Union stranglehold at Petersburg. The Confederate attack was initially successful, capturing Fort Stedman and advancing into the Union rear. However, the Union lines ultimately held and the Confederates fell back to their old positions.

The Regimental History of the 179th New York incorrectly reports that the 179th participated in the battle at Fort Stedman.[1] The 179th was poised at the ready in its camp – about three and a half miles from Fort Stedman as the crow flies, but was never called into action.[2]

Firing on the picket lines had been heavier than usual the night of March 24 to 25. At 3 a.m., an officer from General Griffin's staff came to warn the 179th's guards that "it was well ascertained that an attack would be made by the rebels before morning."[3] It is hard to say how seriously this report was taken – most such reports had proven false in the past. Around four in the morning, the 179th's guards heard musket fire that turned out to be the beginning of the battle at Fort Stedman.[4] Andrews recounted in his journal that "we were drawn up in line of battle ready to move at a moment's notice, but it did not become necessary to move us." Similarly, William Larzelere noted "Heavy fight 2 miles on our right. ft. Steadman taken by the rebs at daybreak. 179th fell out to be ready for the fray." By 8 a.m., the battle was over.[5]

Word traveled fast that a Confederate officer had passed himself off as the Union brigade officer of the day, that Confederate soldiers concealing their weapons and posing as deserters had "gobbled" the Union pickets, that the Union garrison had been "caught napping" and that Fort Stedman had been taken without a shot. [6]

As a precaution, the 179th was called to arms at 3:30 a.m. the next two nights. A possible attack on the Confederate positions in front of the 179th at 4 a.m. on March 26 was cancelled. Regular battalion drill continued on the afternoons of March 27 and 28 and company drill the morning of March 28. [7] In the rear of the 179th, "the country back of us is alive with the moving columns" of the troops under General Sheridan moving to the left. Andrews' prediction that "A terrible fight will probably come off in the course of a few days on the left" would prove correct. [8]

At 9 p.m. on March 28, the 179th was ordered to "pack up everything but our tents" and be ready to move at 5 a.m., but nothing came of it. The 179th continued on March 29 with the usual drill as other troops continued moving to the left. Some soldiers of the 179th even attended a concert that evening by the brigade band and the 186th New York's "Glee Club." [9]

At eleven o'clock the night of March 29, the 179th was awakened by a report that the Confederates were attacking. In Company D, "some were terribly frightened, but the most of the men 'fell in' coolly and determinedly." The 179th "double quicked" to the breastworks. How serious the Confederate charge was and how far it advanced are not clear, but the 179th felt that their prompt response had deterred it. [10]

Looking right toward Forts Haskell and Stedman, "there was the heaviest artillery fire" that night that Andrews had ever seen.

> The wind blew the sound from us; but never in my life, have I witnessed another such a beautiful exhibition of fireworks as I then saw. For an hour the air was literally ablaze with shells. I could not but enjoy the sight of those balls of fire following each other so rapidly through the air. [11]

Two nights later, Andrew McCallum sketched the artillery fire over Petersburg.

[Sketch: Night Attack]

The 179th went to sleep when the barrage stopped, but still "slept on our arms." [12]

It rained heavily on March 30 and the 179th remained on alert in their quarters near Hancock Station. In the afternoon, heavy firing could be heard far to the left – Sheridan's offensive. A wagon train of wounded soldiers passed near the 179th at 5 p.m. [13]

At 1 a.m. in the morning of March 31, the 179th received orders to report to Colonel John I. Curtin, commanding Potter's First Brigade at Fort Davis, about three-quarters of a mile away. The night was cold and dark and the march difficult, the soldiers "stumbling over stumps and logs, falling into sinks and mudholes, wading through water and mud." [14] The 179th formed in front of Fort Davis and then in the rear. The planned attack was called off, and the 179th marched back to camp in "a drenching rain." [15] With a mix of soldierly sarcasm and resignation, Andrews wrote in his War Journal the old ditty: "The King of France with forty thousand men marched up the hill and then marched down again." [16] The soldiers of the 179th were "well-pleased" that the attack was called off, [17] but it was to be only a one day reprieve.

Lee's attack at Fort Stedman did not deter Grant from continuing to pressure the Confederate positions. Several days later, General Sheridan led yet another push to turn the Confederate right flank. His victory at Five Forks on April 1 set the stage for the Ninth Corps' final attack the following day. The 179th New York was again in the first wave.

Sheridan's offensive began with battles at Lewis' Farm on March 29 and at White Oak Road and Dinwiddie Court House on March 31. [18] Lee committed his last reserves on March 29. "The Army of Northern Virginia had been stretched as far as it could reach" in the words of A. Wilson Greene. [19] The approach of the Fifth Corps forced General Pickett to withdraw his troops to the Five Forks road junction before dawn on April 1, notwithstanding his success against Sheridan the day before. Lee ordered Pickett to "*Hold Five Forks at all hazards.*" Greatly outnumbered with no reinforcements available, Pickett was unable to do so. Sheridan's attack beginning the afternoon of April 1 had routed the Confederates by the end of the day. The way was open to the long sought after South Side Railroad, which was only several miles away, and the Army of Northern Virginia positions at Petersburg had finally been outflanked. [20]

Following on Sheridan's success on the Union's far left on April 1, Grant that evening ordered an attack on the center of the Confederate positions in front of Petersburg. General Parke ordered Potter's division to attack at 4 a.m. the following morning in conjunction with other divisions on the right and left. Potter's division was to attack along the Jerusalem Plank Road to the left of Fort Sedgwick (often referred to as "Fort Hell" by the troops), with Hartranft's Division on the right. [21]

Greene described the Confederate positions facing the Ninth Corps as follows:

> These works incorporated modified sections of the old Dimmock Line, including Batteries 25-30, where Southern artillery "swept the approaches in every direction." Battery 29, also known as Fort Mahone and nicknamed "Fort Damnation" by the troops, presented a particularly intimidating obstacle. The rambling complex of Rebel entrenchments contained interconnected covered ways, a strong reserve line in the rear, and the usual complement of menacing obstructions in advance of the works... [O]nly inadequate troop strength compromised the otherwise flawless Confederate defense. [22]

[Map: April 1]

However, before that attack occurred, Potter's division was ordered at 10 p.m. on April 1 to attack immediately one mile to the left of Fort Sedgwick and drive in the Confederate pickets. The Second Brigade (including the 179th) under General Simon Griffin was about half a mile to the left of Fort Sedgwick and attacked from there with six regiments. The 179th New York Volunteers were in the first line, along with the 2d Maryland and the 17th Vermont. [23]

The Union had begun an artillery barrage at 10 p.m. to which the Confederates responded. An officer in the 31st Maine recalled that: "I think I never heard such a roar of artillery as this bombardment caused, both sides joining in it." [24] At 11:00 p.m., beneath the artillery fire, and under cover of darkness, the Second Brigade advanced and attacked when the Confederate pickets passed the word "12 o'clock and all is well." [25] The Confederates were caught by surprise and the Second Brigade carried half a mile of the entrenched picket line, capturing eight Confederate officers and 241 men. [26] The 179th claimed credit for between 130 (Company B) and 200 (Companies E and H) of the prisoners taken. [27]

The 179th New York then "lay down behind the picket line for a short time to avoid the shell that they were throwing at us," as Company B's Samuel Coon recalled twenty-five years after the war. However, it was not only Confederate fire that the 179th had to contend with. The 179th New York apparently also came under friendly fire from the 39th New Jersey, which was located in the rear of the 179th. Company E's Peter Florean was probably wounded by the friendly fire. Colonel Gregg sent Lieutenant Musgrave back to stop the friendly fire. [28]

The original 4 a.m. assault was still scheduled to proceed. Despite the successful attack on the picket line west of the planned attack, Parke was concerned about the prospects for success. He telegraphed Army of Potomac Headquarters at 1:45 a.m. that: "Our only hope of success in the assault ordered at 4 o'clock was in a surprise. That is now entirely lost." [29] Headquarters stood by the original order to attack at 4:00 a.m.

[Map: "Hell" and "Damnation," April 2, 4 a.m.]

The Second Brigade hastily withdrew from the Confederate picket lines to form on the Jerusalem Plank Road near Fort Sedgwick for the next attack. The Second Brigade's objective was Battery 28, while the First Brigade's objective was Battery 29 (Fort Mahone). [30] This time the Second Brigade "formed in column by battalion ...with a single regimental front." The 179th was the lead regiment, followed by the 31st Maine, the 6th New Hampshire, the 2nd Maryland, the 17th Vermont and the 186th New York. Leading the attack was a storming party of about one hundred men from Companies C, H, and I of the 31st Maine and a contingent of pioneers to remove the Confederate obstructions. [31]

[Map: April 2, 5:30 a.m.]

At 4:00 a.m., the Union artillery barage began. General John Tidball, the Ninth Corps' artillery commander, reported that: "artillery upon the whole line promptly opened and was immediately replied to in the most vigorous manner by the enemy, and it is probable that never since the invention of gunpowder has such a cannonade taken place." [32] The storming party moved out, passed through the Union picket line, and proceeded in the dark toward the Confederate picket line. When they saw the picket line "not many yards in our front," they attacked at "the double quick" carrying the line, but not before the pickets opened fire, sounding the alarm. The Confederate artillery fired "grape and canister" directed not just at the storming party but at the main column as well. As the storming party approached the obstructions in front of Battery 28, the Confederates added musket fire. By the time the storming party reached the obstructions, "it was [then] so light that concealment was mostly gone" as Capt. Thomas Beals, commander of the storming party, recalled thirty-five years after the war. But the main column had not yet reached the obstructions. [33] Beals correctly surmised that the main column had retreated in the face of the heavy Confederate fire.

[Sketch: Capture of Petersburg]

Regimental lore has it that Colonel Gregg, waving his sword above his head, led with the exhortation "*My brave boys, will you follow me?*" The 179th "charged about sixty rods through an open field, leaping over ditches, stopping to remove Chevaux de-Frise etc., while the minnies, shells, grape, and canister fell in showers upon us," but fell back "before the showers of leaden hail" in the words of Company C's Ezra Tinker, a twenty-two-year-old teacher from Chenango County. Gregg "rallied his shattered columns" for another charge across the field, and apparently linked up with the storming party to remove the chevaux de frises and other obstacles, but they were repulsed again. [34] Gregg was seriously wounded in the head and rendered unconscious by a shell fragment. [35]

After Colonel Gregg was wounded, Lieutenant Colonel Doty took command for a third charge. As the 179th New York and the rest of the main force advanced again, before reaching Battery 28 itself, they encountered "[a] trench [that] had been cut outside the fort many feet deep. The recent rains had partly filled this trench with water. Some of the men fell in as they rushed ahead to climb the high, slanting ascent and were unable to get out and were drowned." [36] Company D's Thomas Townsend was taken prisoner "while in the mud of the ditch surrounding the fort." [37]

Captain Beals recalled that: "[f]inding the direct approach impossible [the storming party and the main body] circled around to the left... and after a sharp struggle ... forced our way inside their works." [38] The 179th "planted our colors on Fort Mahone [Battery 28]." However, Doty was mortally wounded by a shot through the lungs "while waving his sword and leading us on to victory" and the 179th's color sergeant, Charles Hogan was killed by a shot to the head. Company C's Alexander Chandler was wounded twice, first by a bullet that broke his jaw and then in the right shoulder. [39]

General Griffin described the Second Brigade's next movement: "The head of the column, after passing the enemy's main line of works, turned to the left and swept it for about one-fourth of a mile." [40] Beals recalled that: "It was a series of charges and the organizations became intermingled although fighting with a will." [41]

At this point, the 179th New York was commanded by Company I's Capt. Edwin Bowen as the senior captain in the field after Gregg and Doty were wounded. (Major Terrill was on leave.) [42]

The 179th New York may have received friendly fire for a second time during the attack to the left along the Confederate lines. Writing sixty years after the war, Company H's Sgt. Harrry Ap Rees recalled that the Second Maryland (which was in the fourth line of the Second Brigade's attack) had mistaken the 179th New York for Confederate troops and had shot "right into the flanks of the 179th." [43]

At the same time that the Second Brigade was moving left from Battery 28, the First Brigade under Colonel Curtin attacked and took Fort Mahone. However, Griffin reported that:

> [T]he enemy being well posted, and bringing a heavy fire of both artillery and musketry to bear upon our troops, who had unavoidably become somewhat broken and disorganized, our farther advance to the left was checked. ... [T]he enemy was fast bringing up re-enforcements, and kept up a constant and murderous fire on our troops. Many of our commanding officers were killed or wounded, and it was with the greatest difficulty anything could be done toward reorganizing our broken regiments. [44]

Similarly, Curtin concluded that it was not possible to go forward for the second Confederate line "with the disorganized and confused state in which the regiments at that time unavoidably were." [45]

At 5:55 a.m., Parke reported to Meade that: "we have carried lines opposite Fort Sedgwick but the enemy still hold works in the rear." [46] Grant ordered Parke to push on as possible, but at 7:30 Parke responded that the Ninth Corps would not be able to do so. [47] Accordingly, Parke was ordered to hold on to what he had and not to advance unless he saw the way clear. [48]

Parke reported at 7:55 a.m. that: "There are indications of an attempt to retake the line," and again at 11:45 a.m. that: "The enemy does not yet trouble us much but are pressing on our left. They have made unsuccessful attempts to get up a charge. They are placing fresh artillery of the left of the rebel line held by us, and may try to oust us." [49] Forty-five minutes later, Parke reported that:

"The enemy have assaulted in heavy force, and forced back my left. I fear the whole line will have to fall back, and the enemy get between Wright [Sixth Corps] and me. I should have re-enforcements at once." Parke did also report that: "We still hold most of the ground and may repulse his assault." [50]

Parke received his reinforcements in the form of Col. Charles H. T. Collis' Independent Brigade from City Point and Collis' arrival around two o'clock was just in time. His troops were immediately thrown into the breach and helped stop the Confederate attack. It was around this time that Company B's Samuel Coon was wounded in the left leg: "It was while in a charge & the rebel that shot me was so close that when he tried to shoot me through the breast I parried the gun down and sideways." [51]

At 2:20 p.m., Parke reported that with the arrival of Collis' brigade "I feel much more comfortable now." "I feel greatly tempted to make another push." [52]

However, at 3 o'clock, a Confederate counterattack took back much of Fort Mahone and some adjacent positions. A Union counterattack then regained most of the positions east of Fort Mahone. [53] At that point the Confederates were done for the day. At 3:45 p.m., Parke reported that "our men are very weary, but ... we hope to hold without fail." [54]

"As the Battle subsided," the 179th New York was ordered back to camp "for refreshment," as Company D's Jasper Jayne, a twenty-two-year-old laborer from Schuyler County, recalled several years after the war. Around eight o'clock in the evening, the 179th was ordered back from camp to Fort Sedgwick. The soldiers were tired and many of them fell asleep while they waited after arriving at Fort Sedgwick. The 179th was ordered to fall in around nine o'clock, and Jayne was wounded when a rifle accidentally discharged in the flurry. [55]

William Larzelere wrote in his diary with his usual succinctness: "charged & charged again all day." [56] Thirty years after the war, Company D's William Tuck, who had been wounded after the Confederate works were initially taken, recalled the intensity of the day's fighting: "It was no Play Spell to do it, rather those Gray Coats fought like tigers." [57] The 179th New York had been badly scattered by the fighting. Lt. Charles Lockwood wrote the *Buffalo Daily Courier* that two-thirds of Company E had not been heard from at the end of the day. [58] William Lamont wrote that: "There is a good many missing that can't be found." [59]

Confederate losses in other sectors that day made any further Confederate efforts to regain the lost positions around Jerusalem Plank Road pointless. [60] Lee had already concluded by 3 p.m. that the Confederates would have to abandon their Petersburg positions that night. Thus, Confederate troops in this sector were ordered to hold against any further penetrations so that Confederate troops could retreat across the Appomattox River over the bridges at Petersburg during the night. [61]

During the night of April 2, the Union forces saw some indications that the Confederate defenders might be evacuating. [62] When the 179th moved forward the next morning, they – and the other Union troops – discovered that Lee's forces had in fact withdrawn during the night. Larzelere wrote home that:

> after being in a battle which lasted all nigh Staturday nigh all day Sunday and again last night we lay all night upon the battle field to be ready soon as daylight this morning to renew the charge first before daylight this morning. But when we advanced the rebs had fled. We followed in to Petersburg but they were not there. [63]

[Sketch: Race for the City]

The first Union troops – the First Michigan Sharpshooters and the Second Michigan Infantry – entered Petersburg around four in the morning. [64] The 179th arrived shortly after five-thirty. [65] The Company C Morning Report stated directly: "Charged in to the City of Petersburg – it was ours." Larzelere wrote his wife that "all are in high spirits hoping to see the end of rebellion." [66]

The 179th and the other regiments of the Second Brigade formed for a hasty inspection on an elevated green in the city and then stacked arms and marched through town "with columns in perfect order, banners flying, and to the inspiring strains of Faust's quick-step." [67]

Ezra Tinker described the scene in Petersburg:

Men cheered, shouted, yelled, threw their guns and caps into the air. The colored people seemed no less joyous than ourselves. They shouted and blessed the Lord, swinging their hats, caps, bonnets, old towels and table cloths. In short they made all sorts of demonstrations imaginable. The whites on the contrary were very quiet. The ladies seldom favoring us with their presence, and we do not think they were overjoyed at our presence. [68]

Tinker claimed that "the soldiers were orderly, and did not enter the houses or molest personal property save commissary [liquor] and tobacco." [69] In fact, there do seem to have been relatively few incidents of offense to person or individual property of the citizenry of Petersburg. [70] A soldier from the 121st New York did acknowledge that : "At the Commissary we secured some nice hams and some apple jack that was quite smooth, and under its softening influence we forgave a good many of our foes." [71]

The 179th New York Volunteers lost one officer (Doty) and eighteen enlisted men killed or mortally wounded; eight officers and twenty-five enlisted men wounded and eight enlisted men missing, for total casualties of sixty. [72] In addition to Colonel Gregg, the officers wounded on April 2 included Company A's Lt. Stephen Compton, Company D's Capt. Albert Pierson, Company E's Lt. Samuel Musgrave, Company H's Capt. Giles Holden and Company K's Lt. William C. Foster, who also had another ball go through his hat. [73] At the company level, one out of every four officers in the 179th was wounded on April 2.

Gregg and Doty were among the officers mentioned by their acting division commander General Griffin for their "brave and gallant conduct". [74] Colonel Gregg was brevetted brigadier general and Captain Bowen, Captain Force, Captain Holden, First Lieutenant Hooper and Second Lieutenant Musgrave also received brevet promotions for gallant and meritorious conduct in the battle. [75] Company B's First Lt. Edward Lounsbery apparently also acquitted himself well because he was recommended for promotion on April 2. [76]

Company E's Lt. Samuel G. Hathaway Musgrave wrote his mother from the Field Hospital:

My Dear Mother: We had another big battle today. I am wounded in my right side just above the hipbone. Col. Gregg is wounded in the head. Col. Doty is wounded. Capt. Pierson is wounded. Don't be alarmed about me. I ain't bad. [77]

Musgrave's wound was more serious than he acknowledged. Indeed, twenty years later at an annual reunion, Captain Pierson recalled that Musgrave and he had been in hospital together, close to death. [78] Company H's first sergeant, Harry W. Ap. Rees, wrote Musgrave's mother the day of the battle.

My Dear Madam: It is with deep regret that I hasten to inform you of sad news. But also with a fervent hope that God may temper the blow. At eleven o'clock last night we attacked the rebels and have been fighting all day. In a charge on one of the forts, your son Hathaway received a shot in the lower part of the stomach, and fell close to me. We got him placed on an ambulance and taken to Division Hospital, where he now lies. The wound is a severe one, but I trust not mortal. I will see him tomorrow, if possible, and will write again. [79]

Whether Mrs. Musgrave received her son's letter first or Sergeant Ap Rees's letter is not known. Chaplain Taft and Lieutenant Lockwood each at first incorrectly reported that Musgrave had been killed. Over the next several days, Musgrave's mother received reports from Colonel Gregg; a local citizen, Judge Thurston (who had gone to the battlefield from Elmira thinking that his friend Gregg had been killed); and Chaplain Taft that her son was doing well and was in "excellent health and spirit." [80]

Among the enlisted casualties, Company G's Henry Rootkiskie, a twenty-nine-year-old ship's carpenter born in Poland, was wounded for the third time. Rootkiskie had previously been wounded at the Battle of the Crater and at Poplar Spring Church. On May 23, Rootkiskie wrote Captain Messing from Jarvis U.S.A. General Hospital in Baltimore to let him know that: "I am quite well now. I have been a trying to come to my regiment but they would not let me come." [81] Company E's Thomas Connor, a twenty-eight-year-old painter from Canada, and Company D's William Gibson, a twenty-six-year old farmer from Oakfield, were wounded for the second time. Connor had been been wounded in the June 17 assault and Gibson at the Battle of the Crater. Connor's second wound was an inch from the first. Company A's Albert Havens, a thirty-two-year-old farmer was wounded in the left thigh. [82]

One of the soldiers who died in the 179th New York's last battle was Company B's Smith McMaster, a twenty-five-year-old farmer from Tioga County. McMaster was wounded in the abdomen and died on April 3. He left behind a wife, but no children. [83]

Another soldier who died was Company H's George Proper, a forty-three-year-old farmer. Captain Holden, his company commander, wrote Proper's widow:

Albert Havens

> It is my painful duty to inform you that your husband, George Proper, was shot and instantly killed in the assault upon the rebel works before Petersburg on the morning of April 2, 1865. He fell, nobly doing his duty, standing like a man and a soldier against the storm of shot and shell that poured like a hail storm upon us, and although he was not permitted to see the victory we finally won, his honor is none the less. His quiet unassuming ways, the [illegible] and cheerfulness with which he obeyed every order, and performed every duty had won the respect and good wishes of the entire company. Permit me to tender to you my sympathy and join in your sorrow at your great loss. At the same time let us hope that He who "doeth all things well" will so [illegible] that it may prove to be only a blessing in disguise.

Holden also returned to her a letter she had sent to her husband that had arrived after his death. [84]

The 179th had reached its peak combat readiness for the final assault

Smith McMaster

on Petersburg. The three key factors were strong leadership, increased training, and increased numbers with the arrival in the fall of 1864 of the last three companies and replacements for losses in the first seven companies. The 179th's readiness was reflected in the choice of the 179th to lead the Second Brigade's assault.

Leadership succession was critical. When Colonel Gregg was wounded, Lieutenant Colonel Doty was able to step up and regroup the 179th for a successful assault. When Doty was wounded, command passed to Company I's Edwin Bowen as the senior captain in the field. Bowen performed creditably, although it appears that at that point in the battle the various regiments of Potter's division had become interspersed and that the reinforcements under Collis became the effective fighting force.

At the company level, all the original captains of the first seven companies were gone, either dead or wounded in prior battles (or promoted in Terrill's case), but many of their successors had ample experience. Company A's Captain Carpenter had previously served in the 126th New York and had led Company A in the June 17 assault. Lieutenants Farr and Compton had missed both the June 17 assault and the Battle of the Crater due to detached duty and/or sickness, but they had been with Company A since the beginning.

In Company C, Levi Force had been promoted to captain in December 1864 and had commanded Company C since the fall due to Captain Prentiss' illness. A veteran of the 23rd New York, Force had been in all of the 179th's previous battles. In Company G, Captain Messing and First Lieutenant Hemstreet had been in the field at the Battle of the Crater.

However, Company D was led by a newcomer – Capt. Albert Pierson. In Company F, Capt. James Griswold had served as a sergeant in the 50th Engineers before moving over to the 179th New York in December 1864. In Company B, First Lt. Edward Lounsbery had enlisted in September and been promoted from the ranks in October 1864. In Company E, Captain Ottenot had resigned his commission over the voter fraud allegations and Lieutenant Lockwood may have been in custody for the same reason.

The 179th New York had roughly four hundred sixty officers and men available for the battle – its strongest numbers since arriving at White House Landing in June. [85] The fall and winter had provided time for increased training, including some live fire training. While the 179th did not engage in combat during the two day forced march in support of the Fifth Corps in December 1864, the harsh conditions helped build unit discipline and maneuver capability.

Training was particularly important because most of the soldiers in the 179th who took the field on April 2, 1865 were new enough that they had seen little or no combat. Picket duty certainly gave them the experience of being under hostile fire, but it did not give them the experience of maneuvering as a regiment under fire. The men of Companies H, I and K had participated only in the battles of Poplar Spring Church, which provided few if any positive lessons, and Burgess Mill, which involved limited action for the 179th. The same was true for most of the replacements for the first seven companies that arrived in the fall and winter.

Veterans in the 179th New York who had survived the June 17 assault and the Battle of the Crater were few and far between by April 2, 1865. Some were in hospital suffering from subsequent disease. Many of those wounded were still recuperating from their wounds. And some were on parole as former prisoners of war.

Morale was probably fairly high. The 179th was now a full regiment with a full colonel and a regimental flag – both of which seemed to excite the men. The military appearance that so impressed General Griffin and General Potter would reflect strong morale. At least some of the "veterans" of Poplar Spring Church felt that they had something to prove for having "skeddadled."

The success of the 179th in carrying out a night attack on the Confederate picket line on short notice; then moving a mile for an all out attack on heavily fortified positions several hours later; and regrouping for a final successful charge after being repulsed twice speaks well for the leadership and training of the 179th New York at that point in the war.

As Lee's Army of Northern Virginia fled Petersburg in full retreat, Grant wrote Sherman on April 3: "This army has now won a most decisive victory and followed the enemy. This is all that it ever wanted to make it as good an army as ever fought a battle." [86] Sheridan's cavalry divisions, the Army of the Potomac's Second, Fifth and Sixth Corps, and some units from the Army of the James led the direct pursuit of Lee. The Ninth Corps' primary mission was to protect the Army of the Potomac's ever lengthening supply line back to Petersburg and City Point. The Ninth Corps also helped guard the rapidly growing numbers of Confederate prisoners. The 179th New York Volunteers performed both of these assignments, as a unit and in detachments.

[Photo: Confederate Trenches, April 3, 1865]

On April 3, after parading through Petersburg, the 179th returned to camp at Hancock Station to pack up. While they were in brigade formation, they received the news that Richmond had fallen. John Andrews described the troops' reaction as "the wildest excitement I ever witnessed." Colonel Gregg then rejoined the regiment to the cheers of the men after having been wounded in the assault. [87] Still, Gregg was not well enough to take the field, and Captain Bowen remained in command. [88]

WESTWARD FROM PETERSBURG .. COMPLETING THE JOB

The 179th then returned to Petersburg, singing "Rally Round the Flag" as they marched through around noon, and then headed west on the River Road with the Ninth Corps. [89] As the 179th left Petersburg, Company C reported: "Boys feeling good and in good spirits." The 179th marched ten or so miles that first day, halting around eight o'clock that night. [90] They were up early on April 4, "on the march before eight." [91] After marching for only two hours or so, they stopped and stacked arms while they foraged for several hours. After resuming the march in late afternoon, the 179th pitched their tents for the night at sundown, only to be awakened at 10 p.m. and ordered to continue their march until 2 a.m. They finally stopped at Ford Station, having covered only eight miles. "When we were halted we were nearly used up, but still we were put on picket." Approximately one hundred soldiers from the 179th were detailed that night to guard the Sixth Corps' wagon trains. [92]

[Map: Petersburg to Appomattox]

The morning of April 5, the main body of the 179th waited for the Sixth Corps wagon trains to pass. The soldiers of the 179th made good use of the time – "the boys had fine sport this morning shooting hogs, catching chickens & c." Andrews noted that "The inhabitants are Secesh – the men nearly all gone." When they started up, they marched "through a fine country. There were fine residences; beautiful peach orchards in full bloom; farms in a fine state of cultivation apparently." However, this pastoral image did not last. "Quite a number of buildings were burned today and it is said in retaliation for the murder of some of our stragglers last night by guerillas. They cut the throats of some – hung others." A house where "guns, pistols, ammunition, a reb battle flag and a rebel Colonel were found" was also burned, although the Confederate colonel was at least paroled. [93] By the end of the day on April 5, they had covered another eleven miles, stopping at Wellsville Station on the South Side Railroad at 10 p.m. [94]

The 179th had started out from Petersburg thinking they were headed for Lynchburg, Virginia on the North Carolina border, but word was received that Lynchburg had been captured by General George Thomas. Then the word was that the 179th was headed for Danville. That rumor also proved to be false.

The morning of April 6, the 179th was again delayed by passing wagon trains. During most of the day while they were marching they could hear heavy firing up ahead and rumor had it that Lee's baggage train had been taken along with a large number of prisoners. At 5 p.m., they stopped "and the boys raided considerably. Beef cattle, sheep, hogs, chickens made their appearance in camp. Cattle that would weigh [illegible] were shot down and a few pounds cut out of the hind quarters and the remainder left on the ground." [95]

That evening, General Parke ordered the Second Brigade of Potter's division to Nottoway Courthouse. He cautioned that the troops "must look well to the roads leading to the Nottoway River." [96] The 179th was not done for the day after all and they resumed their march at 7 p.m. "The boys started off in the best of spirits singing 'Down with the traitor, up with the stars,'" but as the evening progressed, "swore a great deal at the unmerciful way in which we were put through." [97]. They finally bivouacked at 11 p.m. – "as tired and cross as need be" – near Nottoway Courthouse. [98]

The 179th remained in place on April 7. Andrews noted that: "Boys foraged so extensively that Gen Griffen issued an order forbidding foraging of any kind. It is said the reason he did so was because the boys were destroying property that could be made serviceable to the govt [illegible]." Stephen Compton noted that: "The troops are jubilant" at the news that Sheridan had captured General Richard Ewell "and a whole corps." [99]

On April 8, Grant ordered Parke to send a division to Burkeville "for the purpose of furnishing escorts to prisoners and guards to public property." Parke sent Potter's division. The 179th brought in a detachment of six hundred prisoners. Andrews noted that: "There were quite a number of general officers and officers of high rank in the detachment we guarded. Some negroes and slaves in this detachment cheered loudly as they passed under our flag." The 179th arrived in Burkeville around 10:30 after "a very lively march." [100] Parke reported that the Ninth Corps was "stretched out from Sutherland Station to Burkeville," a distance of roughly thirty miles. [101]

The sad news that Lieutenant Colonel Doty had died caught up with the 179th. "Dave" Doty was given twelve days leave to take his brother's body home. Even though the 179th was on the move, they still received a mail delivery on April 8. [102]

The 179th remained at Burkeville for ten days. Company D described the duty as "guarding the railroad." Company I described it as "Picket and Guard duty." [103] Andrews observed on April 9 that: "Men lay around on the ground lazily sleeping, resting out for whatever awaits them." [104] William Larzelere simply noted "In Camp idle" in his diary for April 12 through 15. [105]

Lee surrendered on April 9 at Appomattox Courthouse, thirty-five miles west of Burkeville, but the news did not reach the 179th until the next day. [106] The official dispatch, which was read to the troops, included Grant's terms of surrender – that the Confederate troops would be paroled and sent home and that officers would be allowed to keep their side arms and baggage. Andrews summarized the reaction as follows: "some are dissatisfied with this, others appear unconcerned in regard to it, but I think all would have been better satisfied if they had been held as prisoners of war." [107] The weather may have put the troops in a less forgiving mood. It had rained most of the night and most of the day. William Lamont at least was in a good mood. He correctly predicted in a letter to his sister that if the news of Lee's surrender was correct, "we will be home to celebrate the fourth [of July] with you." [108]

The one hundred men who had been detached the night of April 4 rejoined the 179th on April 12. [109] They had marched all night on April 4. [110] By April 6, the detachment had reached the junction of the South Side Railroad and the Danville Railroad. When they caught up with Gen. Sheridan's troops, they served for several days as guards for seventeen hundred Confederate prisoners. They headed back on April 9 to rejoin the 179th. It was a difficult march back. They were out of rations and had to take from the locals "which we found very petty – they would holler there goes the damb Yanks and everything else." [111] Confederate partisans were a threat in the area: "It was an every day occurrence to find some of our boys with their throats cut." [112]

On April 11, some of the soldiers of the 179th saw General Grant, General Ord, General Rawlins, General Ingels and their staffs (including President Lincoln's son, who was on Grant's staff) passing through Burkeville on their way to City Point. [113]

Colonel Gregg caught up with the 179th on April 12, as did Captain Holden the following day. Colonel Gregg was accompanied by his close friend, Judge Ariel Thurston, and a cousin. After hearing the initial reports that Gregg had been killed in the final assault, they had come from Elmira to bring his body home. The news that Gregg had in fact survived apparently never caught up with them before they arrived in Virginia, but they undoubtedly never complained. That night, "Garry" of Company C "serenaded the Col. singing the songs of old," and Gregg rewarded him with a drink. [114] The following day Andrews wrote in his journal: "Great rush to Commissary for whisky which has arrived." [115]

Andrews spoke with a number of Confederate prisoners among the roughly twelve hundred being held in Burkeville. He reported that:

> They appeared quite intelligent, said they were aware at the breaking out of the rebellion how it would terminate – were well satisfied with the old government, but were drawn into the whirlpool of secession in spite of themselves; were very anxious that Johnson should surrender; and that they would be very soon permitted to return to their homes. They are overjoyed to think the war is ended. [116]

[Photo: Confederate $100 bill]

Lieutenants Farr and Compton from Company A spoke with prisoners on April 14 and it seems likely that others did as well. Soldiers from the 179th bought Confederate scrip at the rate of twenty-five cents (U.S.) for a ten dollar Confederate "blueback." [117]

Company B's Chester Peckham lost a finger on April 15 when another soldier's rifle accidentally discharged while they were foraging. That made him the 179th's last "battle" casualty. [118]

On Sunday, April 16, a clear and pleasant day, the 179th was inspected at noon by Colonel Titus, its new brigade commander. [119] New rumors were circulating that the Ninth Corps would be sent to Dansville, or to Texas, or to City Point, or to Petersburg or to Richmond. The soldiers even had their own joke. When asked if they had heard the latest news, they would respond "no" because there was always later news not yet heard. The officers' baggage also caught up with them on April 16. [120]

Later in the day, news of President Lincoln's assassination two days before reached the 179th's camp. The 179th took the news hard. Andrews observed:

> The sad news has cast a gloom over the army, and all are clamoring for revenge. Ah! Southern devils ye would fare hard now if the Union army were allowed to take vengeance in their own hands! [121]

Stephen Compton wrote in his diary: "Ah the villiany in the rebel heart. God grant that the report may not be true." [122]

The morning of April 17, the 179th moved camp "from the woods to a beautiful field on the hill just out of the woods," and that evening held their first dress parade since the final assault at Petersburg. During the day, Andrews found time to go into Burkeville Junction.

> Saw there upwards of a hundred rebel cannon which the rebels had buried, marking the places of burial by foot and head boards with the names of Confederate soldiers upon them. ... Small arms are piled up at the Station in cords. [123]

[Sketch: Burkeville Station]

Joseph Becker had sketched the scene at the station the day before.

Rumors circulated that day that the reports of the assassination of President Lincoln were a hoax – that some paroled rebels had cut the telegraph wires and sent the message "to work mischief." However, nobody seemed to believe the rumors and the tragic reality was confirmed. Lincoln's death was observed by the soldiers on April 19. [124] Throughout the Union army the soldiers were formally assembled and read General Orders No. 66 from Secretary of War Stanton:

> The distressing duty has devolved upon the Secretary of War to announce to the Armies of the United States that at 7.22 o'clock on the morning of Saturday, the 15th day of April 1865, Abraham Lincoln, President of the United States, died of a mortal wound, inflicted upon him by an assassin. The Armies of the United States will share with their fellow-citizens the feelings of grief and horror inspired by this most atrocious murder of their great and beloved President and Commander-in- Chief, and with profound sorrow will mourn his death as a national calamity. The headquarters of every department, post, station, fort, and arsenal will be draped in mourning for thirty days, and appropriate funeral honors will be paid by every army, and in every department, and at every military post, and at the Military Academy at West Point, to the memory of the late illustrious Chief Magistrate of the Nation and Commander-in-Chief of its Armies. [125]

The officers of the 179th also took time on April 17 to mourn the death of Lieutenant Colonel Doty. At a meeting chaired by Colonel Gregg, with Adjutant Cook acting as secretary, they voted to appoint a committee of five – Captains Holden, Bowen, and Carpenter; Surgeon Robinson; and Quartermaster Finch – to draft resolutions "expressing our appreciation of Lieut. Col. F. B. Doty." In a formal meeting the following day, the officers adopted the following resolutions drafted by the committee:

> [A]nd whereas Lieut. Col. Doty received his death wound "fighting for the Old Flag," leading his regiment, cheering and encouraging them on to victory, And whereas Lieut. Col. Doty, by his straight forward,

upright career, his gentlemanly conduct, and soldierly bearing, had so endeared himself to the regiment, as to make his loss irreparable, Therefore

Resolved, That in the death of Lieut. Col. Doty, the country loses a true patriot, an able soldier and a devoted servant, his family and his friends a kind, generous, noble hearted gentleman, and the regiment its brightest jewel.

Resolved, That while we bow in humble submission to the fiat of the Divine will, we can but express our great sorrow at his loss, we regret that he was not spared to see the culmination of the great victory he had from the beginning of the rebellion fought to win. [126]

Another committee of officers (Colonel Gregg, Surgeon Robinson, Chaplain Taft and Lieutenant Marshall) was appointed to raise funds for a monument at his grave. [127]

The officers proceeded by motion and second and began the second meeting by reading and approving the minutes of the first. The minutes of these meetings were not official military records and do not appear in the "Regimental Books" for the 179th in the National Archives. The use of meetings according to parliamentary procedure and resolutions to express condolences, as they had done with Captain Blachford, is another demonstration that the officers were "citizen" soldiers.

The officers also extended "to the families and friends of the other officers and men of this regiment who have fallen, our condolences and sympathy." [128] The newspapers of the Western Military District of New York, where the 179th had been recruited, were requested to publish the resolutions, and at least *The Hornellsville Tribune*, Doty's home town newspaper, did so. The *Tribune* had previously written about the high regard the men of the 179th held for Doty:

He was their idol, and well might be. Few regiments had his equal, and none his superior, and having been with them from their organization, while the Colonel had been with them but a few months, their hearts clung with particular fondness to him. [129]

The resolutions were read to the assembled soldiers of the 179th at dress parade on April 19. Captain Holden also read a letter of presentation for a gold watch that had been given to Colonel Gregg at City Point after he was wounded. Notwithstanding the fact that the war was all but over, Colonel Gregg wound up his reply "with a lecture on discipline – mentioning some things he wished corrected." [130]

[Sketch: Black and White Station]

The next day, the 179th New York finally began the journey home. The men rose at daylight and marched fifteen miles back toward City Point. [131] They stopped that night near Black and White Station. [132] Joseph Becker had sketched the station just four days before.

The 179th started out again around seven o'clock the morning of April 21, encountering muddy roads for the first two or three hours, followed by roads "in fine marching condition." They covered fifteen miles or so and camped for the night near Ford Station. They pitched their tents just in time for cover from a heavy rain. [133]

In addition to complaining that they were marched "unmercifully" in the morning, Andrews also criticized Colonel Gregg's decision to demote Company D's cook:

Haddock was returned to the ranks this A.M. by the Col. for being out of the column after having been told to keep at the rear of the regt. The Col. was very unreasonable in this for there were other cooks alongside of the regt at the same time, and have marched where they pleased ever since, without anything being said except occasionally when the Col. felt very cross. [134]

A month later, Company A's Capt. George Carpenter would also complain that Colonel Gregg's discipline at a time when the war was all but over was "very unreasonable."

On April 22, the 179th camped in a cornfield just outside of Petersburg. They had started out at 5 a.m., covering fourteen miles by 11:30 when they stopped for dinner and another six miles in the afternoon, bivouacking "early" at 4 p.m. The 179th marched through Petersburg at eight in the morning on April 23 and reached City Point at two in the afternoon. The 179th arrived at Fort Abbot about two miles from City Point. They remained in camp at City Point on April 24 and 25. [135]

At 5:30 p.m. on April 26, the 179th boarded the steamer *Prince Albert* at City Point and headed down the James River toward Fortress Monroe. [136] Six months earlier, Andrews had come up the James from Fortress Monroe. He had noted:

> One thing that struck me particularly on the voyage up the James was the utter desolation along its banks. Along the whole distance from Fortress Monroe to City Point there is not one village and only occasionally a house. We saw an occasional barn but they were stripped of their boards – the frames and roofs alone remaining. It was a beautiful rolling country, without inhabitants. Where, O where! At the North blessed by free labor, can you find a river whose banks are not thickly dotted with towns, villages, and princely residences? And yet this part of Virginia is the oldest part of the U.S. [137]

[Lithograph: Fortress Monroe]

The men had to sleep on the open deck. The *Prince Albert* passed Fortress Monroe around two fifteen in the morning on April 27; entered the Potomac River around noon; and arrived in Alexandria at ten that night. The men of the 179th slept on board the *Prince Albert* that night. They debarked the next morning and went into camp at Fort Lyon, one mile west of Alexandria. [138] The 179th moved camp about half a mile south on May 8. Even though the war was all but over, the Union's recruiting machine had not yet stopped. The 179th received its last recruit on April 30 – Company H's William Elsbree. [139] At the same time, Stephen Compton wrote his wife that the adjutant general was saying "we will be home by the first of June. Ain't that glorious." [140]

The 179th was well satisfied with this last phase of its service. In the "Record of Events" section of the April 1865 muster roll, Company B wrote: "Of the efficiency and discipline of the Company on the march and in the assault I cannot speak too highly." Company E and Company H each reported: "On picket, in action and on the march the Company have acquitted themselves creditably." [141]

The 179th's final assignment would be to march in the Grand Review.

THE CHANGING FACE IN BATTLE OF THE 179TH NEW YORK VOLUNTEERS

While it bore the designation "179th New York Volunteers" throughout the Civil War, the 179th was in fact a different unit in each battle due to changes in personnel and differences in the level of training and combat experience. Only about one out of eight of the men in the original six companies served throughout the war without being hospitalized (wounded, injured or sick) or captured (or deserting). [142] Companies H, I and K did not arrive in the field until September 1864–after the 179th New York had already fought in three battles. New recruits for the original companies arriving in the Fall of 1864 were in action only for the 179th New York's last two battles. Casualties and disease deprived the 179th New York of much of the increasing combat experience gained as the 179th served in the field.

To recap, the 179th New York Volunteers may be described as follows as it entered each of its battles:

June 17, 1864–A force of approximately 230 men (six companies less the detachment of one hundred men at Cumberland Heights and losses from desertion and disease) comprised of green recruits, but experienced officers.

Battle of the Crater (July 30, 1864)–A force of approximately 240 men (seven companies less the casualties on June 17 and losses from disease and desertion), still comprised largely of green recruits (the one hundred men from the Cumberland Heights detachment and newly arrived Company G). The officer complement had been hard hit on June 17 and the 179th was commanded by a newly promoted major and four of the companies were commanded by lieutenants.

Weldon Railroad (August 19, 1864)–Primarily a force of men with combat experience, but the 179th could field only one officer (a captain) and eighty-one enlisted men. The 179th played a limited role.

Poplar Spring Church (September 30, 1864)–A force of 400 men, but roughly three-quarters of them had been in the army for less than a month (newly arrived Companies H, I and K and new recruits for other seven companies). Lieutenant Colonel Doty was back in the field, but there was little he could do in the face of the overwhelming Confederate counterattack.

Burgess' Mill (October 27-28, 1864)–The approximately 375 men had had an additional month's training since Poplar Spring Church and Colonel Gregg had taken command in the field on October 8, but the Ninth Corps and the 179th New York Volunteers saw only limited action. [143]

April 2, 1865–The 179th New York was at its strongest on April 2, 1865, both in terms of numbers and experience. The 179th New York had built itself into such a state of combat readiness that it was selected to be in the first wave of the Ninth Corps' assault. Gregg and Doty led the charge with roughly four hundred sixty men. While none of the original company commanders remained in the field, there were experienced men such as Levi Force to succeed them. Many of the men wounded in earlier battles or taken sick returned in the spring of 1865. Most of the enlisted men of the 179th present on April 2 had limited combat experience, but they had the benefit of five months training since the Battle of Poplar Spring Church.

Coming Home

Are they coming? Tell – Oh! tell me!
Are our brave boys coming home?
Shall we soon in rapture greet them?
Are they truly free to come?
Are their weary marches ended?
Is their lonely exile o'er?
Will their browned and radiant faces
Brighten lonely homes once more? ...

They are coming! – Yes they're coming,
Soon they'll mingle with us here!
Hear the joyful shouts of triumph –
As they hear our welcoming cheer:
Welcome – welcome! gallant soldiers!
Welcome! brothers brave and true!
Long we've waited for your coming,
We have greetings glad – for you.

Elmira Daily Advertiser, June 10, 1864

Coming Home

CHAPTER TWENTY-FOUR

Basking in the Glory of Victory: The Grand Review and Coming Home

April 1865 had been a whirlwind for the Army of the Potomac and the 179th New York Volunteers. The month began with General Sheridan's decisive victory at Five Forks on April 1. Richmond and Petersburg fell two days later. General Lee and the vaunted Army of Northern Virginia surrendered at Appomattox Court House on April 9. The prospect of the end of the war had barely begun to sink in when President Lincoln was assassinated on April 14. On April 19, John Andrews' sister Emma wrote him that: "This has indeed been so far a month of events. It seems as though we had lived five or six months in less than one." [1] By the end of April, the men of the 179th New York Volunteers were back in Alexandria, waiting to be mustered out.

After a four year roller coaster of accomplishment and frustration, the North was ready for the catharsis of victory. The celebration began in the nation's capital and continued as the Union soldiers returned home.

The war was over, but after arriving in Alexandria at the end of April, the 179th continued the usual regimen of drill with additional brigade reviews. On May 3, the 179th spent one and a half hours in company drill followed by two and a half hours of regimental drill. They spent both the mornings and afternoons of May 4 and May 5 in company drill followed by brigade reviews on May 6 and May 7. New uniforms were issued to many of the officers and enlisted men in the 179th. (At the end of April, Major Terrill had rated the 179th's "clothing" as "Not Good.") [2]

In addition to drill, the 179th had occasional assignments to guard a parole camp. With the cessation of hostilities, the soldiers of the 179th even had some time for tourism. On May 18, many of the men visited Mount Vernon. Some men even had time to receive visits from family members. The wives of Company A's Capt. George Carpenter and Lt. Stephen Compton came down from Horseheads, New York to visit them in the latter part of May.[3]

John Andrews noted a change in attitude of the men of the 179th in a letter to his father: "Before the capture of Petersburg and Richmond and the surrender of Lee, the men were contented. They dreaded battles, but they were here *to do*; now, the work is done, and all want to go home. Hardly anyone is content to 'play soldier'."[4](emphasis in original) Company I's Lt. Davis Marshall felt that his job was done and resigned his commission on May 6. "I am a minister of the Gospel and joined the Army to assist in putting down the Rebellion. I now desire to return to my calling."[5] On the other hand, Company D's Capt. Albert Pierson, who had been wounded in the April 2, 1865 assault, wrote Andrews from the hospital, asking him to "Tell the Col. that I am good for two years service yet if needed for that long."[6]

Stephen Compton wrote his wife on May 7 that: "They are exacting all the extra now in the line of fancy soldiering. The supposition is that they are preparing us for the grand Review."[7] The Grand Review of Meade's Army of the Potomac and Sherman's Army of the Tennessee on May 23 and 24, 1865 in the Nation's Capital was ordered by Secretary of War Edwin Stanton to recognize "the gallant armies now assembling around Washington."[8] The Grand Review celebrated the triumph of American democracy – embodied in the "Union" that the North fought to preserve – and its reliance on the "citizen-soldiers" lauded by General Grant.[9] The journalist Ida Tarbell wrote in 1901 that: "If the belief that a great principle was in danger could raise up such a body of men as this, then government by the people was no longer an experiment. For the North the Grand Review was a benediction on the Civil War."[10]

Twenty years after the Civil War, Grant expressed amazement at the continued energy of the Army of the Potomac and the Army of the Tennessee as they prepared to disband:

> In due time the two armies, one from Burkesville [sic] Junction and the other from the neighborhood of Raleigh, North Carolina, arrived and went into camp near the Capital, as directed. The troops were hardy, being inured to fatigue, and they appeared in their respective camps as ready and fit for duty as they had ever been in their lives. I doubt whether an equal body of men of any nation, take them man for man, officer for officer, was ever gotten together that would have proved their equal in a great battle.[11]

The Grand Review came together fairly quickly and whether it could actually be organized in time was in doubt up to the last minute. On May 12, General Meade wrote his wife that he thought it would fall through. General Grant himself was not sure whether it would occur as late as May 16. General Sherman, who would lead the troops on the second day, read about it in the newspaper on May 19, rather than being informed through official channels.[12]

The citizens of Washington turned out in great numbers to see the review as did between fifty thousand and one hundred thousand visitors from out of town. Elmirans were among those who attended.[13] The 179th New York Volunteers' survivors were among the one hundred fifty thousand Union veterans who participated, triumphantly marching up Pennsylvania Avenue.

[Lithograph: Grand Review]

In preparation for the Grand Review, the 179th had marched the four miles from Alexandria to Washington across the Long Bridge on May 22 and camped about half a mile east of the Capitol. The march had been hard – done at a fast pace in hot weather – and two soldiers in the 179th suffered sun stroke. [14]

At 9:00 a.m. on May 23, 1865, the Army of the Potomac began the Grand Review, with the cavalry coming first. As he approached the reviewing stand, the ever flamboyant General George Armstrong Custer provided an early moment of excitement when his horse bolted and raced ahead. Custer was cheered by the crowd as he brought his horse under control and resumed his place in the procession. [15]

The Ninth Corps followed the cavalry contingent, the Provost Marshal's Brigade, the Engineers and the Signal Corps. [16] The 179th New York Volunteers followed the 11th New Hampshire and the 56th Massachusetts in the Second Brigade of the Second Division. Only sixteen officers and two hundred seven men from the 179th were present. [17]

Harper's Weekly described the spirit of the day:

> In the spring of 1861, there was raised a cry of alarm – 'The Capital is in danger!' and thousands of young men from the store, from the work-shop, and from the farm rushed with muskets in their hands to the rescue. ... Others came – a long train of armed men from every hamlet in the loyal States – and from the streets of that capital these men, and others who have joined their ranks, have for years been marching and fighting until they have reached the victorious end – until they have swept from the field all those who once menaced the safety of the Government... What a record of heroism is compressed within the limits of those years! Too toilsome has the strife been and far too severe for grand military displays during the war. Little attention could be given to dramatic proprieties on the march or on the battle-field...
>
> It was fitting therefore that when the work had all been done, our soldiers who have borne the burden, should, as they returned bringing Peace back with them as a gift to the people, receive in turn some token of the popular appreciation of their services.
>
> It was no ordinary pageant that turned all the people's eyes and so many of their steps toward Washington on the 23rd and 24th of May. It was not the fact that in all probability the privilege would never recur of seeing two hundred thousand soldiers passing in review. It was no mere idle curiosity, but a deep, glorious, solemn sentiment. This sentiment was one of pride mingled with infinite pathos – pride in the youthful strength of a republic tried and found steadfast – pathos from the remembrance of countless heroes who have received their crowns not from mortal hands nor upon mortal brows, who died many of them while the strife seemed yet uncertain.
>
> Only the soldier can appreciate the full meaning of this grand march through Washington. He has been the actor all along while we have been but spectators, even as here. [18]

The route proceeded around the Capitol, down Pennsylvania Avenue to the Aqueduct Bridge.

Library of Congress

Grand Review

The reviewing stand was occupied by newly sworn in President Andrew Johnson, General Grant, cabinet members and senior generals. Secretary of the Navy Gideon Welles noted that Lincoln's absence was felt by all.[19] Public school girls dressed in white and boys dressed in white pants and blue jackets sang as the troops marched past the Capitol. One of the many banners read: "The only national debt we can never pay is the debt we owe to the victorious Union soldiers."[20]

Grant recalled in his memoirs that:

> The sight was varied and grand: nearly all day for two successive days, from the Capitol to the Treasury Building, could be seen a mass of orderly soldiers marching in columns of companies. The National flag was flying from almost every house and store; the windows were filled with spectators; the door-steps and side-walks were crowded with colored people and poor whites who did not succeed in securing better quarters from which to get a view of the grand armies. The city was about as full of strangers who had come to see the sights as it usually is on inauguration day when a new President takes his seat.[21]

Marching twenty abreast, the 179th would have passed by the reviewing stand in but a dozen rows. After passing the reviewing stand, the troops "double-timed" from 18th Street to Washington Circle and then into Georgetown, finally crossing back over the Potomac River on the Aqueduct Bridge and a special pontoon bridge added for the occasion.[22] William Lamont wrote home that: "it was not as hard as we expected for it was a cool nice day." The temperature ranged between a low of 68 degrees at seven in the morning to a high of 75 degrees at two in the afternoon.[23] The next day the 179th was back in camp near Alexandria.

[Photo: Gov. Fenton (R)]

On May 29, the 179th New York was honored by the Governor of New York, Reuben Fenton, who visited the 179th in camp. Fenton made a short speech, complimenting the regiment "highly" for "gallantry, good conduct &c." [24]

June 1 was observed as a day of "mourning & humiliation" for President Lincoln. [25]

At this time, the 179th New York was a small part of the very large challenge facing the War Department and Secretary Stanton – how to demobilize the 1,034,064 men then in the Union army. Assistant Adjutant General Thomas M. Vincent devised the conceptually simple and straightforward plan of reversing the process by which the troops had been mobilized. [26] As Ida Tarbell wrote thirty years after the war,

> the mighty machine that had been devised for getting men into the army from their homes was now to be used for returning them. The officers who had become experts in mustering in men were now to muster them out. The transportation facilities that had taken the men south were to be devoted to taking them north. [27]

The plan was that units would be kept intact as they moved from the field to intermediate rendezvous like Alexandria and then on to the military depots in their home states where they had been mustered in. In order to prevent a mass, chaotic exodus by soldiers wanting to get home as quickly as they could, the decision was made that the soldiers would not be paid until they reached the depots in their home states. [28] For the soldiers in the 179th, this meant that they would be paid and disbursed from Elmira.

The herculean effort required was unprecedented, and the speed with which the Union soldiers were demobilized was impressive. The numbers of men involved dwarfed the numbers involved in the demobilisations in Europe after the Napoleonic Wars. The United States fought the Mexican War with an army only a small fraction of the size of the Union army and many of the Mexican War veterans were regular army and remained in the service. [29] In the East, the first troops headed north from the Washington railroad station on May 29, three days after the surrender of the last significant Confederate force in the field (General Kirby Smith's troops west of the Mississippi). Within the next forty days, two hundred thirty thousand soldiers, including the men of the 179th New York Volunteers, were on their way home from Washington. [30] For the Union army as a whole, nearly six hundred fifty thousand soldiers were mustered out by August 7, 1865. (The federal government did not actually declare the war officially over until August 20, 1865.) Another one hundred thousand soldiers were mustered out by September 14, 1865, and a total of eight hundred thousand by November 15, 1865. [31]

Preparing to demobilize the regiment involved a good deal of very detailed paper work for both the regiment and the individual soldiers. While it was quite time-consuming to compile, all that detail would facilitate administration of the Union army pension system over the next seventy-five years and longer. [32]

The officers of the 179th also took the time to clear up the disciplinary records of some deserving soldiers. On June 3, 1865, Company C's Capt. Levi Force requested the Second Division's Assistant Adjutant General, Maj. Samuel Wright, to remove the charges of desertion against Corp. George Kiefer and Sgt. Beekman King. Kiefer had been drafted in August 1863, but had failed to report and was later forwarded to the 179th from the Elmira draft rendez-vous. Force reported that Kiefer:

> has since joining his command done his duty faithfully in every respect and in the engagement of April 2d before Petersburg Va. was among the first to

enter the enemy works for which he has since been promoted to corporal. [33]

Sergeant King had overstayed his furlough from Harewood Hospital and been arrested. Force pointed out that Sergeant King was also among the first to enter the enemy works on April 2; had been seriously wounded at Antietam; and had previously been honorably discharged in 1863 after his first term of enlistment had expired.

On June 6, 1864, Company G's Capt. Giles Holden sent a similar letter on behalf of Pvts. Isaac Chambers and Peter Simmons. Like King and Kiefer, Chambers was said to have been among the first to enter the enemy works on April 2, 1865. [34]

The 179th New York's anticipated return home was complicated by the fact that the federal government still had a continuing need for troops, albeit in smaller numbers. While the last large Confederate force in the field had surrendered on May 26, 1865, there would still be a need for federal troops to guarantee the return to peace and administer the upcoming reconstruction of the South. Moreover, there were French troops in Mexico under Napoleon III. General Philip Sheridan, one of the North's most celebrated generals, had missed the Grand Review because he had been sent to Texas by General Grant to head a force of fifty thousand troops to keep the French forces in check. [35]

At the end of the war, the 179th New York Volunteers was comprised of two groups of soldiers – those who had enlisted for one year in the late summer and early fall of 1864 and those who had enlisted in the Spring of 1864 for "three years, unless sooner discharged by proper authority." It made no sense to deploy the one year volunteers for garrison duty in the South because they only had three months left to serve. The three years volunteers, on the other hand, were obligated to serve until the spring of 1867.

The risk of transfer to other units was real for the three year enlistees in the 179th. The 48th Ohio Infantry Battalion, for example, was a provisional unit created from three veteran regiments. Seventy-three regiments sent to Texas were not mustered out until the end of 1865. [36]

On May 29, 1865, Col. H. B. Titus, the 179th's brigade commander, noting that the "one year men" were to be mustered out pursuant to Special Order No. 22 of the Ninth Army Corps and the District of Alexandria, initiated an inquiry through division channels to find out if the 179th would be mustered out in its entirety under that order. Titus reported that the 179th had a total of 306 "one year" men and 365 "three years" men. [37] Captain James Casey, the Ninth Corps' Commissary of Musters, advised the Assistant Adjutant General's Office on May 31 that he did not think that the rest of the 179th should be mustered out. However, Colonel Gregg did some lobbying and on May 31, the War Department directed that the 179th "be immediately mustered out of service" under General Order No. 94. [38]

Although the war was over and the 179th was about to be mustered out, Colonel Gregg was still going by the book. On June 3, yet another review of the troops was held. Because Captain Carpenter wished to join his wife, who was visiting, to watch the dress parade, he sent his company forward under the command of Lieutenants Farr and Compton. Colonel Gregg was not pleased. He summoned Carpenter and told him to take command of his company. In the presence of enlisted men and other officers, Carpenter told Gregg that his order was "damned ungenerous and ungentlemanly." Carpenter tried to apologize, but Gregg pressed charges, including contempt and disrespect toward a superior officer. Carpenter pleaded guilty and was sentenced to a reprimand in general orders. [39]

At the June 3 dress parade, the War Department order was read to the 179th and the men were told to be ready to muster out on June 6. [40] Compton wrote his wife that: "The boys are very happy with the prospect of going home & Col. Gregg seems as happy as any of them because he can take them home together. He worked hard at it." [41]

However, as the directive from the War Department made its way back down the chain of command, General Parke raised the question of whether an error had been made, pointing out that "a large number of the men of this Reg't are three years men." On June 6, Assistant Adjutant General Vincent wired Captain Casey that the three years men in the 179th "will not be mustered out, but transferred to some other Regiment." [42] The news traveled quickly and the impact on the 179th was not surprising. Compton wrote the cryptic note in his diary "All sad." [43]

That same day Colonel Gregg went across the river to meet with the War Department again. His mission was successful and demobilization of the 179th was back on track. [44] Colonel Gregg's dedication to the interests of his troops did not go unnoticed. A soldier from the 179th anonymously wrote the *Buffalo Daily Courier* that:

> Being veterans whose term of service did not expire prior to October 1st, 1865, we did not expect this favor at present, yet we gained it through the perseverance and indefatigability of our Colonel, Wm. M. Gregg, an officer whom all of us revere. [45]

While the 179th New York was in limbo, General Grant issued his General Order No. 108 congratulating the citizen-soldiers:

> By your patriotic devotion to your country in the hour of danger and alarm – your magnificent fighting, bravery, and endurance – you have maintained the supremacy of the Union and the Constitution, overthrown all armed opposition to the enforcement of the laws, and of the proclamations forever abolishing slavery – the cause and pretext of the Rebellion – and opened the way to the rightful authorities to restore order and inaugurate peace on a permanent and enduring basis on every foot of American soil....
>
> In obedience to your country's call, you left your homes and families and volunteered in its defense. [Y]ou will soon be permitted to return to your homes and families, conscious of having discharged the highest duty of American citizens. [46]

The 179th New York was mustered out at Alexandria at 11 a.m. on June 8, 1865. Colonel Gregg wired Elmira Mayor Nicks that the 179th was awaiting transportation home. [47] Having received the thanks of their nation, the men of the 179th were about to receive the thanks of their home towns.

At 4 p.m. on June 8, the 179th took a steamer from Alexandria across the Potomac to Washington. They reached Washington at dark and once again stayed at Soldier's Rest. [48] William Lamont had the misfortune to fall ill before the 179th left Alexandria. He wrote his parents on June 9 to tell them that he was in the hospital. He reported that: "I had the pleasure of seeing my Regt. pass last night on its way home. I expect they are most to Elmira by this time." Ten days later he wrote his parents again, asking them to write "as soon as the Boys get home." (Lamont was discharged from the hospital on June 27, 1865.) [49]

On June 9, the regiment boarded freight cars in Washington and headed north for home shortly after noon. [50] The role of the railroads was critical. As William Holberton wrote in *Homeward Bound: The Demobilization of the Union and Confederate Armies, 1865-1866*:

> Railroad transportation, so important in the combat phase of the conflict, both

from strategic and tactical viewpoints, was absolutely necessary to the demobilization of Union forces…. Without railroads, the program would have taken many more months to complete. [51]

The 179th reached Baltimore at four in the afternoon and changed freight cars. They then left for York at six thirty, taking the route through Pennsylvania on the Northern Central Railroad. They reached York that night and Harrisburg at daylight on June 10. Stephen Compton described the train as very slow. They stopped for dinner [lunch] at Sunbury, about forty miles north of Harrisburg. Compton described the people as "very hearty in welcomes." These kinds of "hearty welcomes" at railroad stations for soldiers passing through on their way home occurred throughout the North. [52] The 179th reached Williamsport near the New York border at five thirty that evening.

The 179th finally reached Elmira around four in the morning on Sunday, June 11. Despite the early hour, they were greeted at the depot by a group of prominent citizens and the committee on arrangements and were escorted down Main Street to Church Street and from there to the Williams Street Hospital, where they "found breakfast waiting for us." [53] The *Elmira Daily Advertiser* reported that:

> The boys of the 179th regiment were glad to get the warm coffee so bountifully served up to them…by the ladies, who had labored all night in their behalf. It was the first coffee they had tasted in a long time. [54]

Although the meal was breakfast, the soldiers were served "a large number of huge roasts, more than a tub of butter and a small army of loaves of bread, with pickles and cheese for condiments and plenty of good coffee to wash it down." [55]

After breakfast, the 179th marched to the end of Church Street and camped on a vacant lot on the south side of the street near the Stoneware Factory. Some of the soldiers were allowed to return home. Stephen Compton, who lived in nearby Horseheads, arrived home at six thirty and spent "the Day home happily." [56]

Many people visited the camp during the afternoon and "a great throng of people" was present for the dress parade at six that evening. Although the soldiers of the 179th were living in tents, the *Advertiser* assured that "[o]ur people will see that they need nothing in provision and comfort, until they are discharged from service." [57]

On Monday, June 12, a reception was held for the 179th in Congregational Church Park at 4 p.m. The 179th had marched around the town for the previous two hours. [58] The *Advertiser* had requested that morning that "[t]he ladies who are willing to contribute provisions for the dinner of the 179th Volunteers to-day" deliver them to the basement of the church by 2 p.m. [59] Compton described the event as "splendid refreshments and speeches after." His wife, two children and mother came from Horseheads for the celebration. [60]

The refreshments consisted of "everything in the way of a cold collection …in utmost profusion. Bread and butter, cold meats, pickles, pies, cakes and oranges crowded the boards, flanked with an abundance of cold lemonade." The *Advertiser* reported that:

> The men discussed the meal with excellent appetites, after their long march. – The ladies were everywhere omnipresent dividing and distributing additional provisions here and there and dispensing cool and refreshing liquids. They had arranged their tables most temptingly, and the board was most savory for wearied men. Beauty truly waited upon the brave. [61]

Judge Thurston

The "Address of Welcome" was delivered by Colonel Gregg's friend Ariel Thurston, a prominent Elmira attorney. Thurston had served as a county judge in the 1850's when Gregg was sheriff. Thurston was also a former state assessor and an influential member of the Republican party. [62] He began:

> Veterans of the 179th: – The duty imposed upon me of welcoming you back to your homes is a far more agreeable one than was the duty of putting forth efforts to send you to the war. But far more agreeable is this duty than under other circumstances it might be – If our armies in the field had been defeated we should nevertheless have tendered you a welcome, but not with the joyousness and hilarity that we can, now that you come back after having conquered a pean [sic] and after the suppression of the most gigantic rebellion of which history has given us a record.

Thurston welcomed the return of peace and expressed the hope that there would be no more wars, but made a pointed reference, with the pride of growing American power, to France and England, which had nearly allied with the Confederacy during the war:

> It may be, we cannot tell, that there may be a small account to settle across the water – but we hope for the best. – Now that the Governments of England and France see that we are a Power not to be despised, and that there would be some risk to them, resulting from a hostile collision. It may be and we hope it will, result in permanent peace.
>
> But we will not anticipate difficulty when none at present exists. But merely intimate to them should there be a call to arms, that *we are ready*. (emphasis in original)

The prospect of yet another war so soon after this one likely was not well-received by the citizen-soldiers in the audience.

Thurston had visited the Petersburg battlefield a week after the battle and invoked the "Charge of the Light Brigade" in describing the attack of the 179th on Petersburg:

> Cannon to right of them,
> Cannon to left of them,
> Cannon in front of them,
> Vollied and thundered:
> Stormed at with shot and shell,
> Nobly you fought and fell,
> Gallant Six Hundred!

He paid stirring tribute to the bravery of the soldiers, the loss of life, and what the war had accomplished:

> In doing your duty you have acted nobly. You have shown yourselves the bravest of the brave...
>
> But alas! you are not all here. Doty, Sloan, Barton, Bowker, Blachford, Farwell, and Saxton, commissioned officers, I look in vain for you, and in vain for many missing from the ranks....

Soldiers, you may not all fully appreciate the great work that you have
accomplished. But yet, it doubtless does occur to you, that you have laid
the foundations of this government upon a basis more permanent than that
of any government on the face of the globe. A government which has been
cemented by the blood of thousands slain in its defense, and resting completely
and absolutely in the hands of the people themselves, never can be overthrown.

The result of this war is the actual consummation of a national unity. But,
soldiers, besides all that you have given liberty to the captive and set free
millions of the enslaved and oppressed. Thus have you practically established
the doctrine enunciated in the Declaration of Independence. So that politically
and practically our acts no longer give the lie to the axiom that all men are
created free and equal.

Thurston ended on a note of future pride:

And when in after years you shall hear your prattling descendants reading the
story of the trials and suffering endured by the hearty veterans of this war, may
you thank God that you will be able to say to them *"I was there" "*I too
belonged to the Army of the Potomac.

Thurston was followed by the Hon. Charles Hulett, Chemung County's assemblyman in the
New York State Legislature. He delivered what the *Advertiser* described as "the most thrilling and
fervidly patriotic speech we ever heard from Mr. Hulett." Like Thurston, he applauded the "noble
contribution" of the 179th to the defeat of the "demon of Slavery and Secession."

Colonel Gregg replied by thanking the citizens for the reception they had given the 179th and
said that the occasion "was the most glorious" of his life.

Dr. T. O. Lincoln, the pastor of Elmira's First Baptist Church, then spoke the praises of the
Regimental Chaplain, Edwin A. Taft. [63] Dr. Lincoln "entreated the men to bear in mind the counsels
that their Chaplain had so frequently urged upon them, that they might at last all reach the heavenly
rest, where wars and tumults cease, and peace shall reign forever more."

The last speaker, Elmira Boardman Smith set a less lofty tone. He proposed three cheers –
"not for the Quartermaster's department, not for the Commissary department, but for the *bullet
department*". (emphasis in original) The crowd responded with "a hearty good will and a tiger to
boot."

After the festivities ended, the 179th marched around town until seven that evening,
accompanied by the band of the 1st Regiment, Veterans Reserve Corps. The *Advertiser* reported
that the 179th "finally got back to camp well pleased with the reception it had received on the part
of our citizens, which will be remembered for years to come." [64]

The celebratory tone of the day was marred by the drowning death of Pvt. Russell McKinney,
one of four brothers in Company K. He had survived the war unscathed, but suffered a severe
cramp while swimming at the outlet of Newtown Creek on the Chemung River. Alcohol may have
been involved. [65] His comrades recalled his tragic death as late as their 1907 reunion. [66]

Drowning also claimed the life of Dennis Dempsey of Company G. He had a pass from
Colonel Gregg to visit his home in the Button Woods south of the Chemung River, but had last
been seen in John Brant's store in Elmira with two other soldiers on June 19. He had appeared
to be intoxicated. His body was found on June 25 at the lower point of Big Island. The Coroner's
Inquest concluded that "he probably attempted to make his way to his home in the button woods,

but became bewildered and stumbled into the river, and his condition did not enable him to save himself." He left behind a wife and five children ten and under. [67]

Celebratory drinking by returning soldiers had been a concern for the army. On June 8, the Commander of the Provost Guard in Elmira, implementing a directive from General Grant, issued an order prohibiting hotels and "drinking saloons" from serving intoxicating liquors to "enlisted men actually in the service of the United States, or recently discharged from such service, and waiting at this Rendezvous for their pay or transportation home." [68] All soldiers in uniform were kept off the streets after 7 p.m. on Saturday, June 10. The *Advertiser* noted that they weren't "even allowed to attend Rouse's Theatre" (whose performance the *Advertiser* had favorably reviewed). [69]

On June 17, responding to "frequent complaints" about the sale of intoxicating liquors by unlicensed businesses, Mayor Nicks issued an order calling attention to the City Ordinance adopted on May 9, 1864 that prohibited sale without a license subject to a fine of fifty dollars and also prohibited sale to any "noisy, boisterous or intoxicated persons" with a fine of ten dollars. Mayor Nicks gave notice that "the full penalties of the law and the ordinance will be rigidly and impartially enforced in every case of violation which comes to my attention." [70] (Elmira was in the midst of a mini temperance revival in 1865) The *Advertiser* did note that that the 179th "boasted of only one member who proved himself an habitual drunkard." [71]

There were other regiments "waiting at this Rendezvous for their pay." The 179th had been preceded by the 107th New York Volunteers on June 8 and other units followed. As of June 16, the 109th, the 114th, the 126th, the 137th, the 141st, the 154th, the 167th and the 1st Regiment of Light Artillery, as well as the 179th, were all in Elmira waiting to be paid. [72] More units continued to arrive. The *Advertiser* estimated that there were between three and four thousand troops in Barracks No. 1 and another one thousand camping in other parts of town, like the 179th New York Volunteers. [73] The *Advertiser* further speculated that "there are probably more troops at this rendezvous at the present time, than at any period previous to its formation." Including the Confederate prisoners, the Commissary Department was issuing rations for thirteen thousand men a day. [74]

The soldiers of the 179th were finally paid starting on June 21, ten days after they had arrived. Private Zavin Carey received $236.23 – back pay since December 31, 1864 at $16 per month ($90.66); the remaining installments of his federal bounty ($160); and travel and subsistence ($15.50) less $7.60 for a lost shelter tent half and $22.33 for clothing withdrawn. Private James Applegate received $200.29. Even at the inflated wages caused by the war, the amounts received by Carey and Applegate were the equivalent of more than eight months' wages for a laborer. [75] Sergeant William Larzelere was paid $305. [76]

Flush with cash, the enlisted men contributed to a gift for Colonel Gregg – "an elegant Park Phaeton Double Carriage, with harness and equipments, valued at twelve hundred and fifty dollars." The afternoon of June 21, the regiment assembled at Colonel Gregg's house at the intersection of Sullivan Street and Second Avenue, and Chaplain Taft made the presentation to Gregg:

> Your presence with us as a regiment, has always been cherished, and the same emotions of tender regard felt for you in the past, we deeply feel now. We have loved to follow and obey you. You have been true to us – we have desired to be true to you. Your devotion to us we are unable to reward; but as we are so soon to part, we purpose [sic] at this time, to maker a feeble expression of our regards to you, our Commander, in some tangible form.

Colonel Gregg responded with obligatory humility:

This is more than I merit or deserve. I feel that I am not entitled to this. The laurels that I have won, or that this Regiment has won, is due to your heroism....

I thank you, brave men, for this splendid present, so generously expressive of your respect and love for me. I appreciate your kindness, and shall ever warmly cherish your memories in the future.

He ended his remarks with what the *Gazette* reported as "some very timely and sensible advice to the men to leave for their homes, urging them to beware sharpers, and the various vices, and to be especially jealous of their own reputation and that of the regiment." [77]

The men of the 179th then left Elmira to return to their home towns across Western New York State. The upcoming Fourth of July provided yet another opportunity to celebrate the victory of the citizen-soldiers. On June 15, Governor Fenton issued a letter encouraging local communities to hold Fourth of July festivities "in a manner not only befitting the anniversary of the nation's birth, but also commemorating its recent rescue from imminent peril." [78]

The Hornellsville Tribune announced "a glorious old fashioned fourth of July celebration" and pointed out that: "[i]n addition to the great throng of citizens ... there will be hundreds of war worn soldiers to celebrate with us, and share in our hospitalities." Between five thousand and eight thousand people attended. (The population of Hornellsville was just under five thousand.) Around three hundred soldiers "partook of the rich repast" at the Soldiers' Dinner. The orator of the day, the Rev. Lloyd Windsor, lamented the deaths of Lieutenant Colonel Doty and Major Barton – "worthy and brave soldiers." The *Tribune* concluded that "a more grand and glorious observation of the day, on which people so generally appreciated its true objects and value, probably was never realized before." [79]

Similar festivities occurred in other home towns. The town of Chemung was honored with the attendance of Colonel Gregg at its dinner. The *Yates County Chronicle* reported that: "Penn Yan is making preparations to celebrate the 4th in a manner never before equaled. All the soldiers who went to War from Yates County and have returned are invited, and will be dined on that occasion." The soldiers would also receive a special badge. Between 400 and 500 soldiers were served at that dinner. (Yates County as a whole was credited with providing 2,109 soldiers for the Union army, although they did not all reside in Yates County.) [80]

Local newspapers honored the 179th New York with histories of its service. The *Yates County Chronicle* wrote that "under Col. William Gregg, the gallant Major Sloan and other like officers, [the 179th New York] won an imperishable fame as a fighting regiment." The *Broome Republican* also referred to the 179th New York as a "fighting regiment." [81]

Numerically, the 179th New York Volunteers may have been a "high-number" regiment, but its record in the field – particularly in the June 17, 1864 assault, the Battle of the Crater and the final assault at Petersburg – demonstrated that it was a "fighting" high-number regiment. The 179th New York was justifiably proud of its reputation for its "aggressive work." [82]

Gardner & Compton's Advertisement

CHAPTER TWENTY-FIVE

Citizens Once More

As the Union soldiers were returning home in June 1865, *The Hornellsville Tribune* observed that: "From recruits, new to soldier life, they return hardened veterans, bred in military formulas, and ready with their experience and knowledge to rush again to the aid of the country in any future strait which may overtake it." But having responded to their country's call as soldiers, they were ready to return to their lives as citizens.

> They are longing to return to peaceful pursuits again – to their homes and their firesides, to the loved ones, who have endured the agonies of their absences and dangers, to the bosom of civilized society, from whose privileges they have been too long debarred...

> With the war over, new avenues of industry will be opened up, manufactories, mechanica, arts and agriculture must receive a new impulse, and in those pursuits of peace our discharged soldiers shall prove themselves equally competent as when waging the wars of their country." [1]

Just under half of white men of military age in the North – those born between 1822 and 1847 – had served during the Civil War. For the younger men, the percentages were higher – " 60 for those [born] between 1837 and 1845 and a whopping 81 for those born in 1843 – the boys who turned eighteen in the war's first year." [2] The veterans were proud of their service, many viewing it as the most important part of their lives. However, it was now time to move ahead with the rest of their lives. They "stripped off the blue [and] donned the citizen." [3]

Having just graduated from college when he volunteered, John Andrews had no occupation to return to when the war ended. After he was discharged, he began pursuing a number of business opportunities. In early 1866, he and a friend negotiated the purchase of a five hundred acre farm and mill near Fredericksburg, Virginia. When his late comrade in arms, Levi Force, heard about the venture, he wrote Andrews: "You have really went and gone and done it, bought a farm in Virginia. Ha, ha, why man the rebels will hang you higher than [illegible] immediately our troops are withdrawn." [4] Although Andrews' father was willing to provide him with the necessary capital, the deal fell through when Andrews' friend could not raise his share. Shortly thereafter, Andrews partnered with his brother-in-law to purchase a furniture business in Dundee. Ballard & Andrews proclaimed to the public that: "We have marked our prices *down* and we assure our patrons that we will not be undersold by any dealer in this county or adjoining ones. We shall endeavor by fair dealing, low prices and careful attention to the wants of our customers to give satisfaction to all." (emphasis in original) [5]

After two years, Andrews left the furniture business to read law and he was admitted to the bar in 1869. Combining business and law, Andrews prospered over the years. He had interests in manufacturing linseed oil, butcher's wrapping paper and flour and in real estate lending. [6]

Andrews the eligible bachelor married Arvilla Raplee in July 1866. They had four sons. At the turn of the century, he was practicing law with one of his sons. [7]

Andrews was a lifelong Republican and served in the New York State Assembly in 1882. He also served as postmaster of Penn Yan from 1890 to 1893 and on the Board of Education from 1885 to 1895 and 1902 to at least 1907. Andrews died in 1916 at the age of seventy-four, shortly after completing a trip around the world. [8]

Frederick Bates

Other veterans of the 179th New York who served in public office included Frederic Bates (Company I, mayor of Ithaca and member of State Assembly), William Bird, Jr. (Company D, sheriff of Martin County, Minnesota), Theodore McDonald (Company K, Broome County district attorney) and William L. Norton (Company F, Schuyler County district attorney). As noted, Colonel Gregg unsuccessfully sought the Republican nomination for Congress.

William Norton was first elected district attorney of Schuyler County at the age of twenty-nine in 1870, the same year that he married Emma Robbins. Norton ran as a Republican and was elected by a comfortable margin. He had returned to Starkey Seminary after the war and left there in 1866 for law school in Ann Arbor, Michigan. After a year at law school, he worked at a law firm in Watkins, New York and was admitted to the bar in 1868. [9] He did not run for reelection in 1873, nor did he run in 1876. He did run again in 1879 and was elected to another three year term. However, it took Norton three ballots to get the Republican nomination, only defeating the frontrunner when the two candidates eliminated on the second ballot threw their support to him. [10]

In 1882, he ran for county judge. It took him five ballots to get the Republican nomination. [11] In the election, he was defeated in what was generally a Republican year in Schuyler County, although he lost by less than one hundred votes. The Republicans had viewed Norton's opponent, Martin J. Sunderlin, as a strong candidate, but Norton may also have lost in part because of an allegation by some Democrats that he was "not a member of any Christian Church." [12]

Norton then returned to private practice, although he did later serve on the Watkins Board of Education for several years and as supervisor of the town of Reading in 1884 and 1885. [13] His cases were periodically reported in the press, including one in 1896 when be brought suit against the directors of the First National Bank of Watkins on behalf of the bank's creditors (including himself). [14]

Failing health caused him to retire from the practice of law and he died in 1897 at the age of fifty-seven. He was survived by his wife and two daughters. One of his obituaries referred to his time as a prisoner of war at Salisbury, "where the privations were undergone which undermined his health and have resulted in bringing him to the grave long before the allotted time of man." *The Watkins Express* wrote that:

> We have heard it said that no braver or more conscientious soldier than W. L. Norton ever wore the blue, and we do not find it hard to believe. ... As a citizen Mr. Norton was one of that class of men of which a town can never have too many. He was right-minded, reputable, respected, and a man whose known high character gave his opinions weight in the community. [15]

Among Norton's supporters when he ran for district attorney in 1879 was his comrade from Company F, Newton B. Spencer – an ardent Democrat. Military loyalty won out over political loyalty – as Spencer wrote, "Other things being equal, it is natural that the soldiers of the late Union army should prefer to see old comrades selected for honors in the civil or political field." Spencer wrote a letter endorsing Norton for district attorney. Local Republican papers ran the article again in 1882 when Norton ran for county judge. Spencer played the military card. He wrote that Norton's earlier service as district attorney "reminds me forcibly of another arena, in the exciting and anxious days of 1864, when the same 'Will' Norton did most faithful and efficient service before now historic Petersburg, Virginia as the Orderly Sergeant of Co. F (the Yates company) in the 179th N.Y. Volunteers." He then recounted Norton's "cool determination" in the June 17, 1864 assault. Spencer ended his endorsement of William Norton with the following couplet:

> No knight of old knew less of fear –
> None held his country's weal more dear. [16]

The Watkins Express, a Republican newspaper, also referred to Norton as "a true soldier in the war for the Union." [17]

Spencer had begun his newspaper career with the *Steuben Courier* and worked for a number of New York newspapers before the war. He moved to Wisconsin and founded the *Eau Clair Free Press*, but returned to New York in 1860 to become editor of the *Penn Yan Democrat*. Spencer married Margaret Lyon in Penn Yan on February 6, 1862. They had six children – all sons: Herbert (1862); Martin (1864); Fred (1873); Frank (1876); Ray (1881); and George (1885). (A seventh son died shortly after birth in 1879.) [18]

After the war he worked for many different small town newspapers, primarily in New York, but also in Massachusetts and Ohio. Spencer himself may have run for office right after the war. A Newton B. Spencer lost the race for Yates County Coroner to John Halsted, 1,328 votes to 2,270. [19]

His newspaper colleagues thought highly of his abilities. When Spencer became editor of the *Dundee Observer*, *The Corning Journal* stated that: "He is a 'bright' specimen of a journalist, and in a larger field would make an extended reputation as a first-class editor." At the same time, the *Havana Journal* wrote that Spencer "is one of the most versatile and gifted of country editors. He is a born newspaper man and takes to the making of a lively, spicey and interesting newspaper as naturally as a duck to water." The *Geneva Daily Times* described him as "a graceful writer and his verse and other productions have been widely published, especially his war poems." [20]

Spencer was active in the temperance movement in the late 1870s and early 1880s. He served as President of the Penn Yan Reform Club, represented Yates County at a multi-county Union Gospel Temperance Camp, and spoke frequently in the surrounding area. [21]

In 1885, the newspapers reported on the beginnings of mental health problems for Spencer. *The Watkins Express* wrote that they "were sorry to hear of [his] ill health" and ended on an encouraging note: "'shake'er' if possible, Newton." In February 1886, Spencer was adjudged insane and committed to the Willard Asylum. He returned home in May, reportedly completely cured. At the beginning of 1888, he became editor of the *Dundee Record* and later in the year he was assisting in the editorial work for the *Watkins Democrat*. However, his mental health problems recurred and he returned to Willard Asylum in 1889. He was subsequently confined to Middletown State Hospital from 1891 until his death in 1907. [22] While at Middletown, he wrote two articles on the 179th's war experience for the *Elmira Telegram* – "A War Story" and "First Charge of Ours," the latter of which has not survived. [23] In 1891, he applied for a military pension based on "Disease of the Liver, Melancholia, and General Debility." [24] Whether his mental illness was caused by venereal disease contracted in the summer of 1864, post-traumatic stress from the Battle of the Crater, heredity (his father also died in an asylum), or something else is unknown.

[Photo: Spencer Gravestove]

Spencer's death was widely reported in the New York press, from New York City to Western New York. [25]

The 179th's other occasional newspaper correspondent was the pseudonymous Ord., who was probably Nathaniel P. T. Finch. Finch continued his career as a lawyer after the war in Hornellsville, where he had grown up. He became an assistant general land agent for the Erie Railroad. By 1870, he was prospering, with his real property valued at $6,000 and his personal property at $1,600. He led the effort to establish the Hornell Public Library, raising money through a lecture series that enabled him to meet Henry Ward Beecher, Ralph Waldo Emerson, Horace Greeley and other prominent speakers of the day. In 1873, he married Mary Isabelle Badger. [26]

That same year, Finch changed professions and moved to Georgia where he became an editorial writer for the *Atlanta Constitution*. He acquired a financial interest in the Constitution, which he sold in 1886. While at the *Constitution*, he became a close friend of the author Joel Chandler Harris. [27]

Finch returned north to Plainfield, New Jersey, where he was engaged in business. In 1897, he moved back south to Birmingham, Alabama, where he was an editorial writer for the *Birmingham Age-Herald*. Finch died in Birmingham in 1913 at the age of seventy-four. [28]

[Advertisement: Going West?]

While Finch moved south after the war, about a fifth of the veterans of the 179th New York followed the advice to "Go West, Young Man." [29] Probably the first was Company D's William Bird, Jr.

Immigrants from Scotland in 1834, the Bird family moved from New York City to Upstate New York and then to Connecticut and Massachusetts before purchasing a 120 acre farm in

Ellicottville, Cattaraugus County in 1849. By 1860, the family was considering moving west, but the Civil War put those plans on hold. [30]

Bird received a medical discharge from the service in the fall of 1864 as the result of his wound from the June 17, 1864 assault. Shortly after his discharge, Bird, as the eldest son, went to Missouri to buy land on behalf of the extended family. (One of Bird's younger brothers was serving in a Missouri Union regiment.) However, the family decided that: "On account of feeling endangered by the war, Missouri was not thought to be a desirable place for northerners, so we gave up going there and turned our attention to Minnesota." Bird then went to Martin County toward the end of 1864, purchased farm land and contracted for a log cabin to be completed by May 1, 1865. [31]

The extended Bird Family – William Bird, Sr. and wife Mary; son William Bird, Jr., wife Mary and their two small children; and sons George, Edward and John moved to Minnesota in June 1865 (sons James and Alexander were still in military service). They traveled the fifty miles to Buffalo in two Concord wagons with two full teams of horses. From Buffalo, the wagons were shipped by boat to Milwaukee. Camping along the way, they then proceeded by train and wagon to La Crosse, St. Charles, Geneva, Winnebago and finally Fairmont, Minnesota, two hundred miles west of the Mississippi River near the Iowa border. [32]

By 1870, Bird was farming on his own, reporting real property wealth of $2,500 and personal property of $825. [33] William and Mary's family grew to eight sons and two daughters.

In 1876, Bird was elected sheriff of Martin County, a position he held for eight years. In 1883, Bird explained to the Pension Bureau that: "for the last eight years I have been unfitted for farm labour (by reason of my wounds) & am at present Sheriff of this County." [34] His two teen-aged sons apparently worked the farm. [35]

[Photo: Brothers Bird]

Bird also served on the county commission, the local school board, and the state fish and game commission. He added to the community's social life by founding the *Great Western Band*. He kept his ties with military life by commanding a company in the Minnesota militia from 1882 to 1890. (He had also served in the New York militia as a private for a number of years before the Civil War.) The G.A.R. encampment in Minneapolis in 1906 provided the opportunity for a reunion of the Bird bothers, four of the six having served in the Union army.

When Bird died on his seventy-ninth birthday in 1908, his obituary stated that: "Capt. Bird was a man of grand and sterling qualities of character. His rugged honesty, his plain and unostentatious life, his generous disposition, and kind heart endeared him to all with whom he came in contact." He was viewed as one of Fairmount's pioneers and his funeral was reported as one of the largest ever held in Martin County. [36]

Company G's Chatford Howell, a farm laborer before he enlisted, moved to Bridgeport (Saginaw County), Michigan in the fall of 1865, just a few months after he was mustered out of the 179th New York. He married Mary Brill a year later and they began farming in nearby Merritt Township (Bay County). They had four sons. In 1882, Howell sold the farm and began a general mercantile business. He also later owned a one hundred sixty acre farm. He held a variety of local government positions – supervisor for fifteen years, postmaster for eight years, township clerk,

Chatford Howell

justice of the peace and drain commissioner. Howell died in 1917 at the age of seventy-six. [37]

Levi Force went to California. Force was one of a handful of soldiers in the 179th who were present for every battle. He also participated in six battles with the 23rd New York, including Antietam and Fredericksburg. [38] John Andrews, who had gone to the same high school with Force for a brief time, described him as: "a noble, free hearted, generous fellow, brave as a lion and kind as a woman." Andrews noted that Colonel Gregg was "partial to Force" and that Force was "always called upon whenever there was any duty to be performed." [39] Rising from the rank of private to captain, with a brevet to major for gallantry in the final assault at Petersburg, Force served in the highest tradition of the citizen-soldier.

[Photo: Levi Force Sword]

When the war broke out in 1861, Force left his medical studies and enlisted at the age of twenty in the 23rd New York Volunteers. He completed his medical studies after the war and moved to California. He was physician to the Hoopa Valley Indian Reservation from 1869 to 1872. He then moved to Arcata where he pursued private practice for the rest of his career, except for a brief stint as an acting assistant surgeon in the army and a brief residence in Alameda, California. When he died in 1891 at the untimely age of fifty, the California Commandery of the Military Order Loyal Legion of the United States reported that:

> Death was a relief to him from long and intense suffering; the victim of a disease that no medical or surgical skill could reach, the suffering from which anesthetics alone could alleviate, he passed his last months on earth with the certain knowledge that death was slowly but surely drawing near; he fought his last battle like a Christian soldier and noble gentleman. [40]

William Lamont also went west. His last month in the service was spent in the hospital suffering from "debility from miasmatic disease." [41] He never really regained his health. He was unable to do any kind of manual labor during 1866 and 1867. [42] He moved to Wisconsin in 1867 and lived for a short time with his sister. In the spring of 1868, he moved to Minnesota and purchased a farm outside of Winnebago. However, he was unable to work the farm and moved into town the following year. [43] At some time prior to 1875, he married, but apparently did not have any children. [44] He died in 1888 in Jackson, Minnesota at the age of only forty-six. [45]

William Lamont

Not all the veterans of the 179th New York who went west stayed west.

In 1878, William Larzelere and his family followed the westward migration and moved to Kansas in Oswego, Labette County. Their undoubtedly high hopes were crushed when two daughters died of small pox shortly after the family arrived. A son born a month later lived only a month. Larzelere and his surviving family returned to New York State in 1879. [46] Larzelere died in 1908 at the age of seventy-eight. [47]

In May 1866, James C. Rutan, his wife Amelia and their infant son Frederick moved to Steele County, Minnesota, where Amelia's older sister and brother-in-law had moved before the Civil War. Their second son, Edwin Ellsworth Rutan, was born in Waterford in 1868. However, the Rutans returned to the Elmira area in November 1869 for unknown reasons. [48]

Back east, Rutan transitioned his cabinet-making skills learned before the war to carpentry and home building, working for a number of years with Frederick. The nature of the skilled trades had been evolving rapidly in the second quarter of the nineteenth century as the "transportation revolution" beginning around 1815 fundamentally changed the economy of the United States and spurred economic growth at rates that far outpaced the rest of the world. [49] Woodworking was one of the first sectors to see the introduction of machinery and cabinetmakers were one of the trades to experience the "deskilling" process. [50]

In 1891, the Rutan Family – father, mother, four sons and two daughters – moved to Wilmington, Delaware. One or more of the men in the family were working for the Pullman Palace Car Company, which apparently relocated its Elmira shop to Wilmington. In 1892, Rutan and his three eldest sons were all working for Pullman. During the great strike of 1893 to 1894 at the Pullman plant in Chicago, the Pullman workers in Wilmington stayed on the job, repairing cars sent from the west (although it is not clear how many of the Rutans were still working for Pullman then). [51]

At the time of the 1900 census, James and Amelia Rutan were living in Philadelphia. Rutan, then sixty-two, was still working as a carpenter, but had been unemployed for four months. James and Amelia Rutan died in 1911 on the same day – February 26, she at 1:30 A.M. and he at 4:30 A.M. During the Civil War, Rutan had written his wife that he believed that he would survive the war and spend the rest of his life with her, expressing the desire that: "I want you to be near me if I die first and if it is the Lord's will I will be near you if you go first, and will soon follow you." [52]

As many as three-quarters of the men of the 179th New York remained in their home state. [53]

Most of the men of the 179th had been farmers before the war and they returned home to the land. Daniel Lee did not live to realize his dream of buying a farm with his bounty money, but other veterans of the 179th undoubtedly did so. In November 1865, Huston McKinney purchased a 150 acre farm. He was referred to in 1891 as "one of the leading and prosperous farmers" of Bradford County. McKinney had been born in Bradford County in 1833 and died there in 1935 at the age of 102. [54] Another farmer who stayed put was Ambrose Worden. In 1896, he had been living in the same house in Newfield for twenty-one years. The house was located only three miles from where he had lived when he enlisted in the 179th New York. [55]

Stephen Compton returned to Horseheads after the war and lived there until his death in 1915 at the age of eighty-one. [56] Compton, who enlisted with Rutan, was also a cabinetmaker by training. Compton reported his wealth in the 1860 census as $500 in real estate and $600 in personal property. Around 1860, Compton and his father-in-law, Harry Gardner, began the Gardner & Compton partnership in Horseheads. [57] Gardner and Compton started as cabinetmakers and Rutan was an employee. Their first store was located at Main and Orchard Streets near Hanover Square, the center of town. During the war, Gardner expanded the business into undertaking. In an April 1865 letter to his wife, Compton discussed the advisability of buying a new hearse. He was definitely reentering the business world with the right perspective when he wrote: "Certainly in business we must keep up with the times and the demands of the public." [58] In 1888, Compton described himself as a "merchant in the furniture and undertaker business combined." [59]

Like Rutan, Compton also started building homes. Home building had also undergone significant change prior to the Civil War. New construction techniques significantly lowered the cost and sped up the process. [60] Half a dozen or so of the homes built by Compton or Rutan in the late 1800's are still occupied today.

The shoemakers in the 179th seem to have survived the "deskilling" of their trade, although they did not necessarily prosper. James Wattlesworth, who was born in England, was thirty-nine when he enlisted in 1864. He worked in shops making shoes in Michigan and Indiana after the war.[61] Joseph Potter, born in Ireland, was thirty-five when he enlisted. After the war, he returned to Havana (Schuyler County), where he "managed to do cobbling." In 1890, when he was sixty-two, Potter told the Pension Bureau that he was "very poor."[62]

At least five men of the 179th saw subsequent military service after the Civil War. As noted, Levi Force was a military surgeon for a brief time. Jesse Cornell, a farmer before the war, served in the 42nd U.S. Infantry from 1867 to 1870. Paul Hildreth, also a farmer, served in the 43rd U. S. Infantry as well. Giles Holden served as a Captain and Assistant Quartermaster of Volunteers for ten months during the Spanish American War.[63]

John Hoy's military service was of a different sort. Hoy served the Fenian cause as a regimental commander, leading the Seventh Regiment in the Fenian invasion of Canada from Buffalo in 1866.[64] The Fenian Brotherhood was founded in New York City in 1858 at the same time that the Irish Republican Brotherhood was formed in Ireland. The objective of the Fenian Brotherhood was to free Ireland from British rule.[65]

After the Civil War, the Fenians developed a plan for a three-pronged invasion from Chicago and Detroit in the west, Cleveland in the center and New York and Vermont in the east, with a diversionary attack from Buffalo. However, internal dissension led to one faction pursuing an invasion from Buffalo on short notice. Fenian units from Tennessee, Kentucky, Ohio, Indiana and Louisiana arrived in Buffalo in late May 1866. John Hoy's regiment had an estimated strength of one hundred fifty men and had been largely recruited from veterans of the 155th New York.[66]

[Lithograph: Battle of Ridgeway]

Between one thousand and fifteen hundred Fenian soldiers crossed the Niagara River into Canada in the early hours of June 1, 1866. The following day, the Fenians defeated a quickly deployed force of British regulars and Canadian militia at the Battle of Ridgeway. However, the approach of a British force of five thousand men coupled with the absence of any support from the local population forced the Fenians to withdraw back to the United States. The Fenians were captured mid-river by the United States Navy and charged with violation of the Neutrality Act. Hoy and the other senior officers were kept in custody for several days. Hoy was released on $12,000 bail on June 7, "his friends crowd[ing] around him with their congratulations." In the end, neither Hoy nor any of the other Fenians were ever tried. The federal government even provided transportation home to the Fenians who promised never to attack Canada again.[67]

Rutans Young/Old

Francis Thorne Young/Old

Linkletter Young/Old   *Johnsons Young/Old*   *Elias Beach Young/Old*

The average soldier of the 179th New York who was twenty-five in 1864 was sixty-one in 1900. Even the eighteen-year-olds were in their mid-fifties by 1900. The passage of time is seen in these photos of James and Amelia Rutan; Francis Thorne; Elihu Linkletter; the Charles Johnsons; and Elias Beach.

PENSIONS

While their military careers ended in 1865, the men of the 179th New York still carried with them the effects of their wounds and diseases. The degree of their impairment varied. Some men were able to return to their pre-war professions. Others did so with difficulty. The government's pension program for Union veterans became increasingly important to more and more veterans of the 179th as they aged.

The pension program created for the Union veterans of the Civil War has been referred to as:

[T]he nation's first large-scale social insurance program. It began during the Civil War as a tightly controlled system of war-related disability compensation that, over time, developed into a general disability system and, finally, into a broad-based old-age pension for almost all Union army veterans. Indeed, the Union army pension dominated the federal budget and the political debates of its day to much the same extent as Social Security and Medicare do today. At the program's peak in 1893, 41.6% of all federal budget expenditures were being paid out to military veterans. [68]

Roughly eight hundred veterans of the 179th New York or their next of kin filed for military service pensions – representing roughly three-quarters of the men who served in the 179th. About sixty percent of the applications were filed by the veterans themselves. [69]

Considering that nearly two hundred men of the 179th had been wounded and roughly three hundred men hospitalized for illness during the war, a surprisingly small number applied for a pension during the war or right after it ended – four in 1864, nineteen in 1865, eleven in 1866 and nine in 1867. It is also striking that only one of the veterans of the 179th who applied at this time had been a prisoner of war, considering the hardships suffered in the Confederate prisoner of war camps. [70] Applications by the soldiers themselves dropped off starting in 1868 and averaged only five per year over the next ten years. Applications by widows were much more common during and right after the war than applications by soldiers. [71]

Disability was measured by the degree of impairment to the soldier's ability to earn a living by manual labor. For a private, total disability was compensated at $8 per month. The burden was on the soldier to prove that the disability was service-related. The Pension Bureau took a hard line. The fact that the soldier had passed the military physical before being sworn in was not proof that the claimed disability was not pre-existing. From 1861 through 1865, the Pension Bureau allowed only slightly more than half of the pension claims that had been filed. [72]

All but a few of the applications filed by the men of the 179th from 1864 through 1867 were based on disability caused by wounds rather than illness. In the case of wounds, the medical history was relatively clear, which facilitated processing the claim. Franklin Burton, Bennett Landon, James Lewis, Charles Lounsberry, James B. Luce, Samuel G. H. Musgrave, and Newton Phillips each received their pension awards less than three months after they applied. However, intervals between one and two years were almost as common. Emory Millard had to wait three years and seven months and Ephraim Boughton four years and two months. [73]

The wait was too long for Felix Miller. His thumb had been shot off at the Battle of the Crater and he suffered from a variety of diseases in early 1865 that led to a medical discharge. He applied for a pension in April 1865, but no action had been taken by the time he died in the poor house in 1866. [74]

A veteran's "original" application was rarely his last. As his rated disability worsened or new disabilities developed over time, he filed an "increase" application. An extreme example is Company B's James Fluent, who filed his "original" application in 1866 and "increase" applications in 1875 (granted), 1879 (granted), 1886 (rejected), 1887 (granted), 1888 (rejected), 1889 (rejected), 1890 (rejected), 1892 (granted) and 1896 (granted). [75]

If the veteran applied for a pension within a year of his discharge, the award was retroactive to the date of his discharge. Otherwise the award ran from the filing date. [76]

The Arrears Act of 1879 made a procedural change which created a substantial financial incentive to apply for a pension. By 1879, the award for a new application would run from the date of filing. However, the Arrears Act provided that if a claim was established, the benefit would be retroactive to the date of the soldier's discharge. Thus the soldier would receive a lump sum payment of the amount for the past months going all the way back to June 1865 in the case of veterans of the 179th New York – often $1,000 or more, as well as his regular monthly benefit going forward. [77]

It is dubious that there was any real need for these arrears payments. If the effects of the soldier's wounds or disease had seriously impacted his ability to work after the war, he presumably would have filed for a pension sooner. In fact, the veterans themselves were not the ones who pushed for the adoption of the Arrears Act. Instead, it was the claims agents who saw their livelihood drying up. The lure of a large lump sum payment enabled claims agents to attract new clients who had not previously seen the need to apply for a pension. The claims agents lobbied hard for the passage of the Arrears Act and then after it was passed aggressively advertised its benefits. [78]

Veterans responded as the claims agents had hoped. The number of new claims increased tremendously. [79] Forty-nine men from the 179th applied for a pension in 1879 and another thirty-one in 1880. For the preceding ten years, an average of only five per year had applied. [80]

Not only was there the financial incentive provided by the Arrears Act, but there may also have been an increasing sense of entitlement among the veterans. As Stephen Ramold noted in *Across the Divide: Union Soldiers View the Northern Home Front*:

> Although relatively few men were wholly disabled, increasing numbers came to believe that the war had contributed to minor or even major physical handicaps, and by the end of the century, sympathetic observers estimated that hundreds of thousands of men had eventually lost their vigor as a result of vague wartime maladies and that the life expectancies of tens of thousands had been reduced by a decade or more. [81]

Company B's Edwin Rarrick, a butcher before the war, stated in support of his application that: "Deponent is poor and entirely out of health and verily believes that said diseases were contracted while in discharge of his duties as private in the service of Com. B Regt. 179 N.Y. Vol." [82] Company B's Samuel Coon, a farmer before the war, felt that he was entitled to a larger pension than what he got.

> Now I am no lawyer, but it seems where a man is disabled from Disease & wounds so he can not do manual labor to that extent that he should if dealt with on the square, have more than four Dollars per month. Now all I ask is that you will do by me as you would have me do by you in like condition. [83]

Samuel G. H. Musgrave, who was wounded in the June 17 and April 2 assaults, was in the minority when he criticized pensions for "vague wartime maladies."

> [I] am more particular to help a wounded man than Hospital Suckers as I do not think every body out to have a pension. Only as their wounds and service guarantee... [I]f a man wanted my affidavit for diarrhea, piles, catar &c contracted in the army at this late day he would not get it. Such men I count dead Beats. I am a Republican but would just as leave pension the rebels as dead Beats. [84]

The huge increase in applications caused by the Arrears Act overwhelmed the Pension Bureau staff. The complex process for verifying the applicant's service record and medical history to establish that the claimed disability was service-related and then evaluating his current medical condition and rating his disability was quite laborious in and of itself. (The administrative processing of James C. Rutan's pension claim is described in detail in Appendix H and demonstrates that complexity.) A process that usually had taken between two months and two years right after the war ended now took as long as ten years or more for the men who applied under the Arrears Act.

Of the men from the 179th who initially applied in 1879, Company E's Thomas Gibson and Company F's Benjamin Hadley fared the best – seventeen months from filing to award. Their cases should have been pretty straightforward. The fact that Hadley had been wounded in February 1865 and undergone amputation was documented in contemporary records, as was his discharge for the disability resulting from the wound. The fact that Gibson had been wounded in the June 17, 1864 and April 2, 1865 assaults had also been documented. [85] Giles Holden, who suffered a concussion in the April 2 assault, which was also contemporaneously documented, fared almost as well – eighteen months from filing to award. However, Holden had been an officer and may have received a priority over enlisted men. Company F's Harvey Chapman, who was wounded in the April 2 assault, had to wait three years, even though his wound had been contemporaneously documented. [86]

For men claiming pensions based on disease incurred during the war, the process took much longer – generally ranging from two and a half years to ten years. [87] If the veteran's illness had been documented during the war, a speedier outcome was somewhat more likely, but still not guaranteed. Despite the fact that his illnesses were documented during the war, Company D's Charles Wightman still had to wait ten years for his award.

The increased processing time was not just a function of the increased number of applications. It also reflected increased scrutiny of applications by the Pension Bureau. "[T]he Pension Bureau had considerable discretion … in terms of the speed with which applications were processed … and the rigor of the review (both medical and clerical)." [88] The Pension Bureau was particularly concerned that the lure of a large lump sum payment would increase fraudulent claims and that increased scrutiny therefore was necessary.

After reviewing the claim of Samuel Parsons, who had been discharged from the 179th New York before being mustered into a company, Special Examiner J. H. Jennings concluded that:

> I consider that this claim is one of the most impudent attempts to defraud the Government in procuring a fraudulent pension that has ever come under my observation. There seems to be a general impression that any one can with impunity present any kind of a fraudulent claim, without danger of punishment... His applying for a pension was an after thought, when the Arrears of Pension Bill was passed. [89]

In fact, the evidence was pretty clear that the disabilities claimed by Parsons had originated prior to the war and that he should never have passed the physical. Infuriated by the fraud, Jennings made the "high bounty" argument: "At the time of his enlistment there was a $900 bounty [moving?] in his front and a draft closing up on his rear. He enlisted through a combination of fear and avarice with the intention of never rendering any service." [90]

The Pension Bureau was also concerned that the applicant's fraud would be abetted by untruthful affidavits from his comrades. There is no question that many veterans were quick to support a comrade's application with an affidavit. And for a fair number of claims, the similarity of wording in the affidavits of the applicant and his comrades does raise the question whether the recollections were truly independent. Not only had the men gone through the war together, but sometimes they had grown up together and gone back to the same hometowns. The peer pressure to support a comrade's pension application must have been intense. And there may sometimes have been an understanding that the favor would be returned if needed. [91]

The special examiner reviewing the claim of Company I's Andrew Evarts noted that one of his affiants "is a pensioner ... and appeared to be quite reckless as to what he swore to and strongly biased in favor of all claimants on general principle. I rate him as 'unreliable' because of his utter indifference as to what he says 'So long as it helps a comrade's claim along.'" [92] The special examiner for the claim of Company C's Charles Beckwith reported that: "This claimant belongs to a rather hard set and those who testified in his favor are his companions, and with one or two exceptions are drinking men and would rather shield him than not." [93]

However, it would be incorrect to conclude as a general proposition that the pension filings by the veterans of the 179th were rife with perjury. There certainly were soldiers who took their oath seriously in giving an affidavit. Company D's James Spencer submitted an affidavit for Alvin Kilburn "and went just as far as I could to help him." However, when Kilburn applied for an increase and asked Spencer for another affidavit, Spencer "told him that the Government had done very well for him and he ought to be satisfied and that I could do nothing more for him." [94] (emphasis in original)

As a former officer, Samuel Musgrave received many requests to verify facts. "I am very particular about making affidavits and always word my affidavits to suit my recollection. I have to refuse some as I cannot remember them." [95] William Norton, who was the de facto commanding officer of Company F through the Battle of the Crater, also would not go beyond what he could recall: "I am requested to remember that 22 years ago the fore part of this month the said [Ezra] Northup was excused from duty by me on account of rheumatism; but after considerable reflection I am unable to do so; nor can I deny that I did so – my mind is blank on that subject." [96] As a lawyer, Norton declined to represent Charles Beckwith when he learned that Beckwith's doctor could not testify that Beckwith's rupture had not occurred before the war. [97]

Soldiers who had served hard duty in the field also opposed fraudulent claims as a matter of principle. Company H's George Dudley Lake applied for a pension in 1888, claiming a back injury suffered during the December 1864 forced march. He did not disclose that he had deserted from a furlough home to Batavia in February 1865 and fled to Massachusetts. When the Pension Bureau contacted Giles Holden as his commanding officer, Holden was quick to respond. After doubting that Lake had been on the forced march, Holden stated that: "[Lake] fraudulently procured a furlough of 20 days, deserted from furlough and never returned to service... While willing and anxious to do anything proper to aid any deserving soldier to secure a pension he may be entitled to, I could not in this case even by silence be of such assistance." [98] Alexander Gardiner supported the application by the mother of his deceased comrade with the statement that: "I was a soldier in the army and fought too hard to allow a wrong pension, but Mrs. Canfield deserves and is entitled to hers." [99]

Veterans of the 179th could act based on principle even when their own pensions were involved. Company G's David Meirthew voluntarily surrendered his pension when his eyes got better. [100] Company D's John Lawrence did not object when the Pension Bureau discovered that he had been overpaid due to an error by his claims agent in preparing the filing. "I am only to willing to reimburse the Government for any pension paid to me to which I was not legally entitled to." [101]

Given the intense scrutiny of applications by the Pension Bureau, the best indicator of the integrity of the applications by the men of the 179th would be whether they were granted. [102] All but a handful of the Arrears Act filings by the men of the 179th were in fact ultimately granted. [103]

While increased scrutiny by the Pension Bureau may have been in the public interest, the veterans complained vociferously about the resulting delays. A special congressional committee concluded in 1881 that there had been delays in deciding claims after all necessary information was in the file. Congress later authorized an additional twelve hundred employees for the Pension Bureau. [104] The veterans also complained about the burden of the investigative process. Company I's Frank Tibbets undoubtedly expressed the frustration of many veterans when he responded to an inquiry about the pension application by his comrade Charles Barnard:

> Under the unreasonable rules of your Department and which rules seem to be formulated with the idea that every poor soldier who makes application for a pension is a common enemy of the Government actuated solely by a desire to prey on its wrath, this statement may not be sufficient. It is however the best I can do. [105]

Company C's Thomas Pinch responded to a Pension Bureau inquiry about his comrade John Bills' claim with similar frustration: "When he Enlisted he passed Examination and was Mustered as an Able Bodyed man. And Uncle Sam should take that and his present disability as proof to the Claims. Then give the poor Coffee Coolers what he promised them at the time of Enlistment." (emphasis in original) [106]

The Disability Pension Act of 1890 extended eligibility to non-service related disabilities. [107] This was a huge change. The significance of the change is starkly demonstrated by the experience of Company A's Willard Stevens and Company B's Charles Askay.

In 1888, Stevens was working as a railroad switchman. He was injured in two industrial accidents that year, losing his right arm in one and part of his left hand in the other. When he applied for a military pension in 1890, he was keeping a cigar stand. He was granted a pension of $12 per month. [108] Askay suffered a knee injury in 1888 while being robbed. He applied for a military pension and was awarded $10 a month. [109] Stevens and Askay received a benefit not previously available to Civil War veterans and not available at all to injured civilians.

The 1890 changes also benefitted soldiers who had been unable to convince the Pension Bureau that their disability was service-related. The Pension Bureau had previously rejected Charles Beckwith's claim for a pension because he could not prove that his rupture had occurred during his military service. However, after the 1890 act was passed, the Pension Bureau awarded him a pension of $12 a month for a hernia and disease of the heart. [110]

Eighty-nine men of the 179th applied for a pension for the first time in 1890 and another twenty nine in 1891. The average for the preceding nine years after the Arrears Act window closed had been only fourteen. [111]

While veterans were not behind the Arrears Act of 1879, they clearly were behind the Act of 1890. [112] The Grand Army of the Republic, which was founded in 1866, had become an aggressive and effective lobbying force on behalf of Union veterans. [113] By 1889, the G.A.R. had nearly four hundred thousand members. [114] The pension issue may well have been decisive in Harrison's victory over Cleveland in the 1888 election. The Republican position in favor of pension liberalization was clear. Harrison won by moving New York and Indiana from the Democratic column to the Republican column. New York had forty-five thousand federal pensioners in 1888. Harrison carried New York by 13,000 votes in 1888, while his predecessor had lost New York by 1,047 in 1884. [115]

In theory, the 1907 legislation brought the most sweeping change – a soldier who had served for at least ninety days and been honorably discharged was eligible for a pension when he reached the age of sixty-two, even if he was not suffering from any disability. [116] However, by 1907, most veterans were already receiving a pension under the liberalized provisions of the 1890 act. Only four men from the 179th applied for a pension in 1907, followed by one in 1909 and three in 1910 (the last year a veteran of the 179th applied). In 1915, over ninety percent of the Union veterans then living were receiving a pension. [117]

The real benefit in the 1907 legislation was the increased rates – $12 per month at age sixty-two, $15 at seventy and $20 at seventy-five. For most veterans, this was more than they were receiving under the 1890 law and they were transitioned to the 1907 rates. [118] One hundred ninety-six pensioners from the 179th were transferred to the higher 1907 rates. [119]

Not all veterans of the 179th New York applied for a pension. William Gregg did not, nor did John Andrews. [120] Perhaps they felt that their health and/or financial position did not require it. When William Norton filed for a pension in 1890, he stated that "I have refrained hitherto from making application for pension in part from three reasons, to wit: (1) I have not been a pauper; (2) Pride; (3) The fact that no examining surgeon can know anything about my case except what I tell him; i.e. my trouble is inside and gives no external indications of its existence." (Norton was apparently suffering from stomach cancer.) [121] Joseph Potter did not apply for a pension until 1887 when he was fifty-nine. He told the Pension Bureau that he "is very poor and unable to earn his livelihood and tries very hard to keep off the town" [and] that he "has tried hard to sustain himself for years before he applied for said pension although he was honestly entitled to same." [122]

In addition to the pension system, the federal government also developed a system of "homes" for Civil War veterans who were disabled or were single and just had no other place to go. James Marten observed in *Sing Not War: The Lives of Union & Confederate Veterans in Gilded Age America*, that: "Perhaps no other situation in which a veteran might find himself threatened his manhood more than living in a soldiers' home, where he inhabited the uneasy ground between civilian freedom and military discipline, between dependence and independence." [123]

Company D's Martin Kellsy described his living situation in 1909 when he was seventy-two:

"My wife is dead and I am living with my children (he had eleven children). I go from one to the other. Some of them live in Nebraska, and one in Illinois, one in Texas." [124] By 1917, his children apparently could no longer care for him. He entered the national home in Hot Springs, South Dakota and died there in 1918 at the age of eighty-one. [125]

Other veterans from the 179th New York who died in state or federal soldiers' homes included: Company A's Charles Lawrence (1921), Asa Otterson (1921-Minnesota), and William Walker (1903-Pennsylvania); Company B's James Jarvis (1916-New York); Company F's Henry Schofield (1921-New York); Company G's James Day (Nebraska); and Company H's Elliott Cook (1903-Ohio). [126]

Did the federal government provide fair compensation after the war to the Union veterans and their families? Or was it overly generous?

The original system of a pension based on service-related disability for Civil War veterans followed federal government policy with respect to prior wars and is logically unassailable.

The transition from a disability-based to a service-based structure presents a more difficult issue in the context of the citizen-soldier. [127] There is no question that the Union veterans performed an invaluable service for their country at great personal sacrifice. And there is no question that a majority of the men of military age in the North did not enter the service during the war. Should uninjured citizen-soldiers have been entitled to a special benefit or was the risk of military service which does not incur disability just a cost of receiving the benefits of being a citizen? If citizen-soldiers were entitled to a special benefit, was three months service long enough to justify an old-age pension which could extend for many years? (And hadn't many of the citizen-soldiers already received a special benefit in the form of the high local bounties?)

These questions seem to have been answered with respect to Union veterans more as a question of political power than of political theory, with a strong national economy providing the necessary funding. William Henry Glasson concluded in his 1918 study of federal military pensions that:

> The former [Civil War] soldiers have constantly used their organized strength to secure greater and greater benefits at the expense of the taxpayers of the country. Recurring presidential campaigns have furnished favorable opportunity to make demands for pensions....The satisfaction of such demands has been the price of support at the polls. [128]

The Arrears Act of 1879 clearly was unnecessarily generous. If a soldier's wound or illness had not impacted him enough after the war for him to file for a pension, where was the need for compensation?

Yet the cost to the taxpayer was substantial – probably several hundred million dollars. [129]

During the period that the pension was based on disability, the soldier was required to prove that his disability impaired the performance of manual labor. [130] Thus, a soldier who was able to make a good living by performing white collar work was still able to qualify for a pension. For example, when Company G's William Hemstreet applied for a pension in 1883, he stated that he had worked as a machinist before and just after the war. He reported that: "[B]eing unable to endure manual labor owing to inability to stand continuously on his feet on account of Rheumatic Pains in his Limbs and feet that he has been in the Insurance Business since 1867." [131] However, this disconnect probably reflects more a failure to take account of the changing labor force than a deliberate policy to benefit white collar labor.

The geographic redistribution of wealth effected by the pension system also should not be overlooked. The pension payments were funded by taxes raised throughout the United States, but the Union veterans were not spread uniformly throughout the states. Relatively few Union veterans moved south after the war. Moreover, Confederate army veterans were not eligible for a federal pension. Thus on a per capita basis, the pension dollars received by the Union states far exceeded the dollars received by the former Confederate states. For example, in 1910, New York State received $1.49 per capita and Pennsylvania $1.97, while Virginia received only $.74 and South Carolina $.19. [132] Thus it could be said that the pension system for Union veterans became an exaction of war reparations from the South. [133]

Finally, the amount of the pension was large enough to adequately support the veterans. In 1900, the average annual military pension ($139) was thirty-seven percent of the average annual earnings of all employees ($375). [134] In an era when pensions were otherwise quite rare, a ratio of thirty-seven percent undoubtedly seemed quite generous. Families of the veterans certainly had an obligation to help them. But Civil War veterans without other means of support were hardly living in luxury with their pensions. From today's perspective, when social security is the underlying norm, thirty-seven percent does not seem unreasonable.

Reunion of the 179th, Reg't, N. Y. S. Vol's, Inf,

Sir :

The Ninth Annual Reunion of the 179th, Reg't, N. Y. S. Volunteers, Infantry, will occur at Elmira, N. Y., on Wednesday, Sept. 28, 1887. Headquarters No. 123 West Water St. (Labor Temple.)

Camp-Fire and Sham Battle, Sept. 28 and 29. You are cordially invited to be present and participate in the pleasures of the occasion.

Reduced Fare on all Railroads.

JAS. C. RUTAN, Sec'y.

B. KINNEY, Pres.

Reunion Invitation

CHAPTER TWENTY-SIX

Comrades Forever

The men of the 179th New York Volunteers had only been in uniform for a year or less. But the experience was so intense that it remained with them for the rest of their lives. James Marten wrote in *Sing Not War: The Lives of Union & Confederate Veterans in Gilded Age America* that veterans:

> rarely suggested that they loved war or killing, enjoyed camp life, or welcomed forced marches. But they almost universally expressed their appreciation, their love for having been soldiers. Their service defined them, made them different, provided unique rewards and self-esteem beyond anything most Gilded Age Americans could muster. [1]

To maintain their ties with their military service, veterans joined the Grand Army of the Republic and/or their regimental association.

The G.A.R. was founded in 1866 by Benjamin F. Stephenson in Decatur, Illinois. Membership was limited to honorably discharged veterans of the Union army, Navy, Marine Corps or Revenue Cutter Service who had served at any time from April 12, 1861 to April 9, 1865. [2] G.A.R. Posts were established throughout New York State. Four posts were named after fallen soldiers of the 179th New York Volunteers – Lt. Col. Franklin B. Doty (Post No. 226 in Hornell); Maj. J. Barnett Sloan (Post No. 93 in Penn Yan); Pvt. Marshall Phillips (Post No. 640 in Allentown), and Sgt. Edson Andrews (Post No. 284). A fifth (Post No. 430 in Erin) was named after Colonel Gregg. [3] Veterans of the 179th were active in these chapters and many others around the state, notably Lathrop Baldwin Post No. 6 in Elmira.

The G.A.R. designated May 30, 1869 "for the purpose of strewing with flowers or otherwise decorating the graves of comrades who died in defense of their country during the late rebellion." What started as "Decoration Day" is now observed as "Memorial Day." [4] Elmira observed its first Decoration Day on May 31, 1869. An estimated eight to ten thousand people attended the ceremonies at Woodlawn Cemetery. [5]

Newton Spencer was selected to deliver the Memorial Poem at Penn Yan's first Decoration Day, an honor that was repeated three times over the next ten years. Spencer began his poem:

> Nature's most placid calm is here:
>   Here, too, her bloom is spread,
> To symbolize how well she loves
>   Our mourned and honored dead.
> Her May flowers bright and grasses grow
>   Profusely all around,
> To teach us that she smiles as well
>   As grieves, beside each mound –
> To show that with her tears she blends,
>   In her most kindly way,
> Consoling promise that those gone
>   Shall outlast all decay,
> And not alone in memory live –
>   But, in some coming time,
> Emerge from mouldering cerements
>   To an immortal clime.

He remembered John Barnett Sloan:

> Here lies the brave, intrepid Sloan –
>   At Petersburg shot down:
> Charging the foe he died, and won
>   The patriot-martyr's crown.

And Spencer also remembered the fallen soldiers whose bodies had never been recovered, including Allen Farwell.

> All of our patriotic dead
>   Lie not among these mounds,
> For many sleep within the soil
>   Of distant battle-grounds.
> In conflicts desperate and hot
>   Some comrades fell and died,
> And strangers gave rude burial
>   The rebel foe beside.
> Farwell and Brown, Bell, Wolcott, Beach,
>   And others, sleep to-day
> Where, Southward, armed battalions fought
>   In fierce and bloody fray.
> But Memory reaches out to them,
>   As unto others here
> Guarding their fame with solemn trust,

> And holds them ever dear.

Finally, Spencer made a promise to those who had died.

> In all our annals glorified,
>> Illustriously bright,
> Their laurel wreathes shall never fade
>> In blank Oblivion's night;
> But while Our Banner's stars remain
>> The symbols of our power,
> The fruitage of their daring deeds
>> Will richer grow, each hour.
> In future storm, or while our Peace
>> Glows golden as the sun,
> As sacred as "The Heart of Bruce,"
>> We'll keep what they have won![6]

John Andrews was chosen as the speaker for Decoration Day in Penn Yan the following year. The *Yates County Chronicle* referred to him as "one of the worthiest of the surviving soldiers."[7] Andrews began with a tribute to the fallen soldiers, but also praised the citizen-soldier. By speaking generally, he glossed over the fact that most of the men of the 179th New York had not enlisted until 1864.

> Then my friends what did our soldiers for us? They were not to combat born nor bred amidst alarms. They had been pursuing productive avocations which were fast making our land the envy of the world .... But when the storm burst upon them, they waited not to investigate the cause. Justice marked out for them the golden path, reason led the way and patriotism impelled to action. The garb of the citizen was laid aside, the national blue substituted therefor, and they entered upon a struggle which for four years claimed the attention of the world. They toiled, fought, struggled, suffered and died for your rights – and that of *all* our brethern – for the prosperity we are now enjoying.[8]

He also praised those who "had stood and waited." He recalled:

> those sorrowful days when you fathers, mothers, wives, sisters, brothers and friends of soldiers waited with anxious hearts from day to day for news from the absent... How you labored for them at home preparing and sending to them everything you could that would add to their comfort or happiness or lessen their sufferings – making use of in addition to provide means such efficient agencies as Soldiers Aid Societies, the Sanitary and Christian Commissions which every soldier had reason to bless.

Decoration Day thus became a way to remember not just the fallen, but also the survivors.

In 1880, fifty-five veterans of the 179th reassembled as a unit for the first time since they had been mustered out to determine whether to organize a veterans' association. All of the companies except Company G were represented. [9] Even the youngest of the veterans of the 179th were middle-aged by then.

The *Elmira Daily Advertiser* reported that "the social reunion was of the most enjoyable description, and the comrades talked over old times with a pleasure that was as much food for the listener as it was fascinating to the participants in the scenes that were rehearsed."[10]

[Photo: Elmira Armory]

The meeting was held in the rooms of G.A.R. Baldwin Post No. 6 in the State Armory on Church Street. Except for four meetings held at the W.C.T.U. House in the 1890s, all the meetings of the Association were held there. Dinner was at Wadsworth's Arbour Hotel. [11]

Colonel Gregg was elected President; Company K's Sgt. Theodore F. McDonald (then Broome County District Attorney) was elected Secretary; Company A's Lt. Stephen Compton was elected Treasurer; Company K's Pvt. (then Rev.) Charles Alexander was elected Chaplain; and a vice president was elected for each company (except Company G). An executive committee with Colonel Gregg as chair was elected comprising Company B's Lt. Edward Lounsbery; Company F's Sgt. W. L. Norton; Company K's Corp. James K. Holly; Company E's Sgt. James P. Provost; Regimental Surgeon Col. Joseph Robinson; and Company D's Lt. John T. Andrews. Many of these initial officers would remain active in the association for many years.

The first regular reunion was held in Elmira on February 17, 1881. Attendance dropped to thirty-three, mostly from nearby towns in New York State. The part of the meeting devoted to formal business was limited to taking roll, acknowledging the passing of "comrades," electing the next annual cycle of officers, and confirming the date and place of the next reunion. The heart of the meetings "was spent in telling of war experiences and recalling reminiscences that were enjoyed by all present." [12]

Colonel Gregg was reelected president and Company G was still without representation. Perhaps the soldiers of Company G missed their separate identity as Company A of the stillborn 180th New York Volunteers. Or it may simply have been a question of distance since most of them hailed from the Buffalo area. A committee comprised of Company K's Theodore McDonald; Company I's Frank Tibbets; Company K's James Holly; and Company F's W. F. Norton was appointed "to procure someone to prepare a history of the regiment." [13] A regimental history was ultimately published, but not until 1900 (and it was quite thin at that). [14]

Colonel Gregg died at the age of sixty-one in Elmira on September 2, 1881, shortly before the September 30, 1881 reunion in Candor.

Fifty-five veterans attended the October 11, 1883 reunion in Elmira. W. F. Norton, the chair of the historical committee, was elected president. Norton reported that he had made some progress on the regimental history, but admitted that "he had relied too much on that busy editor, Lieutenant N. B. Spencer of Canandaigua to help him out." At his request, the time to complete the regimental history was extended by a year. The outgoing president, Capt. A. H. Pierson, recalled the time in April 1865 when then Lt. Samuel Musgrave and he had been together in hospital, both close to death. Pierson also recalled that the "boys" had known Musgrave as "the dare-devil." Musgrave himself spoke only briefly, pointing out that "the boys all knew that he was better at fighting with a gun than he was at shooting off his mouth." He said that it "did him good" to be "among the old soldiers again." Judge Thurston was also to have addressed the meeting, but was called out of town at the last minute. [15]

At the 1884 reunion, Norton read the "historical sketch" of the regiment that Spencer and he had prepared. I have not located the text, but the *Ontario Repository and Messenger* reported that: "The sketch showed, among other facts, that the regiment's loss in killed and wounded in a charge at Petersburg, Va., June 17, 1864, was greater in proportion to the number of men engaged, than that of any other regiment belonging to the Army of the Potomac." Heavy casualties were a mark of distinction for Civil War veterans. As Lesley Gordon recently noted, "The higher the casualties, the more proudly heroic the regiment's claim." [16]

The 1886 reunion was attended by fifty veterans, along with a dozen or so family members. Three members from Buffalo–Company G's George C. Hartman; Company E's C. F. Hager; and Company G's George C. Hoas – proposed holding the reunion in Buffalo, but they were voted down. Incoming president Lt. William Kinney proposed his hometown of Binghamton, but that also was voted down, as was Oil City, Pennsylvania. Elmira ultimately became the permanent location and the meeting was scheduled in conjunction with the County Fair, initially the last Thursday in September and later the last Thursday in August. [17]

[Photo: Reunion Invitation see page 262]

The notice for the 1887 meeting promised a "Sham battle" in addition to the "Camp-Fire." Unfortunately, none of the Elmira newspapers for that day are extant, so there is no description of the sham battle.

Attendance probably peaked at seventy-five for the 1889 reunion. This probably represents only about fifteen to twenty percent of the veterans then living, but they were spread across Western New York and the rest of the country. In a pre-automobile age, recreational transportation was more of a problem.

The veterans were aging and the following resolution was passed:

> Again in the yearly cycle of time death has mustered out two more of our comrades, James H. Moulton [Company A] and Bakeman [Beekman] D. King [Company C],
>
> Therefore be it Resolved, That we submissively bow to the Divine decree, realizing that at most it is but a matter of a few short years when we shall all secure our final discharge, to be mustered, as we trust, into the grand army above. [18]

Union veterans "remained very prominent at all levels of politics and society throughout the 1870s and 1880s," with their prominence peaking in the early 1890s according to James Marten. [19] In the 1870s and 1880s there was also a "deluge of personal narratives" written by Union veterans, but I have not located any written by veterans of the 179th (other than the two newspaper articles written by Newton Spencer). [20] It was also during the 1880s that the number of veterans visiting the battlefields in the South increased dramatically. [21] Over a hundred veterans of the 57th Massachusets, which like the 179th had fought at the Battle of the Crater, visited the battlefield in 1887 and even had their picture taken with Confederate General Mahone. [22] The 23rd New York held their 1888 Reunion at Antietam. [23]

Many Union units also placed monuments on the battlefield to mark their accomplishments, sometimes with the financial support of their state governments. [24] For example, the Second Pennsylvania, which was a brother regiment of the 179th in the Second Brigade of Ledlie's division, placed markers to show the high water mark of their advance at the Battle of the Crater. [25] However, I have found no evidence that any of the veterans of the 179th returned to Petersburg, individually or as a group or sought to raise a battlefield monument.

Attendance in the 1890s and early 1900s ranged between thirty and fifty veterans, with some of their spouses and children also attending. It was estimated that there were 250 veterans of the 179th still living in 1894. [26] In 1897, the 179th started awarding a bronze badge to the oldest member in attendance. The first recipient was Company B's Patrick Touhey, who was eighty-one, but he "was far from being the least lively or jolly member present." [27]

[Photo: Gregg Monument]

In 1892, the *Elmira Daily Advertiser* noted that few veterans of the 179th still lived in Elmira and that most came from other places. [28] As part of the 1893 reunion, the veterans visited the grave of Colonel Gregg in Woodlawn Cemetery and proposed adding an inscription to the monument erected by Gregg's family. [29] The simple phrase "Cold Harbor to Appomattox" was added. They again visited Gregg's grave in 1894 to view the addition. [30]

In 1895, the New York State Historian sent out a questionnaire to veterans seeking details about their regiments, such as a list of all battles in which the regiment participated and the names and current addresses of all surviving officers. Apparently only two men from the 179th New York responded and they did not provide any personal recollections of interest. [31]

The Spanish-American War broke out in 1898, and the country called upon the next generation of citizen-soldiers. The veterans of the 179th probably discussed at their 1898 Reunion the fact that their sons were going off to war, although in much smaller numbers and for a much shorter duration. James C. Rutan's son Edwin Ellsworth Rutan was a captain in the Delaware National Guard and his unit was briefly activated, but remained in the United States. [32] After the 1898 meeting, those in attendance had their picture taken in front of the Lake Street entrance to Elmira's City Hall, but I have not located a copy.

[Photo: Title Page]

A regimental history was published in 1900, but there was no mention of it in the newspaper report of that year's reunion. As noted, it is pretty bare bones – thirty-nine pages in a 3 3/4 by 5 1/2 inch format, not much more than a listing of battles and of soldiers' names by company. Twenty years in the making, it could have been so much more than it was. It does not even appear to include material from the "historical sketch" prepared by Norton and Spencer in 1884. [33]

The differences in scope of the listings of names suggests that different people compiled the company lists. Although Companies A through G had numerous new "recruits" after their initial muster-in to compensate for losses from combat and sickness, the names of those recruits are provided only for Company B. The recruits for Companies I and K were included with the names of the original complement. The only recruit included for Company H was Charles Flint, who died shortly after the war, which suggests that his friend Harry Ap Rees may have been the author.

The authors for the individual company listings also varied in the amount and nature of additional detail they provided. For each company, some service detail was provided for the officers and non-commissioned officers (E.g. Company A "Albert A. Terrill, Captain. Had served two years in 38th N.Y.V. Promoted major, Aug. 27, 1864"), but treatment of enlisted men varied. The authors for Companies A, D, G, and H provided no additional detail at all (except the fact that Charles Flint had been promoted to sergeant in Company H). The authors for the other companies provided references to second enlistments, wounds, and being taken prisoner for their enlisted men. Only the author for Company F provided some "human interest" comments – for example, "Chas. was always ready for any duty" (Charles Baker); "Deserved promotion but didn't get it." (George W. Heck); "Enlisted as a musician, but took rifle as private. Was wounded June 17, 1864." (Charles Lounsbury. See also Ezra Northrup); and "He was always ready for duty." (Henry Schofield)

On the assumption that the newspapers wrote the story that the veterans gave them, the report of the 1902 reunion provides an interesting account of how the veterans of the 179th New York wanted to be remembered. The *Elmira Daily Gazette and Free Press* noted that the 179th had not served until 1864, but:

> For the brief period that the regiment was in the field, ... there was crowded into the time a service of hardship and danger that some organizations did not experience during the whole war. The 179th N.Y.V.I. established a reputation for bravery and daring that the descendants of the members may well be proud of while the organization retained the reputation of being fighters that had been fairly earned by the regiments that went out from Elmira earlier in the war. [34]

William Fox's *Three Hundred Fighting Regiments* had been published in 1889. It had become a matter of pride for the veterans of those regiments on the list, and probably a sensitive matter for the veterans of those regiments–like the 179th New York–that were not on the list. [35]

Approximately thirty members attended the 1907 reunion. An estimated two hundred veterans of the 179th were still alive, but at least eleven had died in the last year alone. The veterans of the 179th had moved around the country since the Civil War. The *Chemung Valley Reporter* claimed that "there is not a state in the union that has not some of the old 179th regiment men as citizens," although that was a bit of an exaggeration. Company A's T. C. Smith, then living in Salem, Oregon, was elected president. [36]

The *Chemung Valley Reporter* also recounted the sad story of the one of the four McKinney brothers who had drowned in the Chemung River in 1865 while waiting for his discharge after all four "went through the war safe and sound."

[Photo: Campaign Medal]

In 1907, the War Department authorized the Civil War Campaign Medal to recognize honorable service in the Union army. Company A's Private William Harris was one of only six veterans to receive his medal with the Silver Citation Star for gallantry in action, which was authorized in 1918. [37] Sadly, Harris' citation was awarded posthumously in 1935.

[Photo: 30th Reunion Invitation]

The notice for the thirtieth reunion in 1908 was accompanied by a colorful drawing of soldiers with the American flag captioned: "Nor shall their story be forgot, While fame her record keeps." [38]

[Photo: New England Kitchen]

Attendance fell to twenty-one at the 1911 meeting. Company I's Leander Bowers asked to be relieved after fourteen years service as secretary (and a term as president), but those present insisted that he continue. He relented and was reelected for another nine years until his death. Five deaths were reported. Company E's George Pendleton, aged seventy-seven, received the bronze badge. They dined at the New England Kitchen, their regular venue over the last twenty years of the Association. [39]

In 1912, Company B's Don C. Hanford brought a piece of hardtack that had been issued to him when the 179th was camped at Burkeville Junction at the end of the war in April 1865. That the hardtack had survived nearly fifty years probably did not surprise any of the veterans. Company H's Issac Smith received the bronze badge for the oldest member attending (seventy-eight years old) who had not previously received the badge. [40]

There is a hint in the *Elmira Star Gazette*'s report that those present sensed that this might be their last reunion – "they will endeavor to meet again in Elmira the last Thursday in September, 1913." [41] However, the 1913 meeting was held, and the surviving veterans soldiered on with their reunions until 1925.

During the fiftieth anniversary years of the Civil War, the *Elmira Star Gazette* ran a syndicated series on the daily events of the war. On July 30, 1914, the *Gazette* ran a long story on the Battle of the Crater, but there was no accompanying local story about the veterans of the 179th's memories of the battle. To add insult to injury, the syndicated article in the *Star Gazette* referred to the 179th New York as the 129th New York and said that Bartlett's brigade had preceded Marshall's brigade in the attack. Coverage of the events in Europe leading to the "Guns of August" of World War I was featured in the *Star Gazette* that day. [42]

In 1916, *The (Elmira) Telegram* reported that 126 veterans of the 179th were still living, but only thirteeen were able to attend. At that time even the youngest of the veterans were just shy of seventy years old. Stalwarts E. K. Smith, E. B. Niver, and L. H. Bowers were elected as officers. [43]

In 1917, America entered World War I and the grandsons of the veterans of the 179th were called into service. The *Penn Yan Democrat* ran a story "A Family of Soldiers" recounting that George C. Lockwood had enlisted and was the third generation of his family to serve his country in time of war, following his grandfather, George C. Lockwood of Company D of the 179th and his great-great-grandfather Seymour Lockwood who served in the War of 1812. [44]

Attendance fell to just nine in 1917 and seven in 1920. By 1919, only an estimated eighty veterans of the 179th were still living. When Leander Bowers passed away in 1920, he was succeeded as secretary-treasurer by Nathaniel Reed's wife. In 1921, the eight veterans in attendance expressed the desire that their organization "live on in the minds of their children and their fellow citizens" and opened membership to sons and grandsons. Of the ten veterans attending in 1923, the youngest was seventy-six and the oldest ninety-two. [45]

Leander Bowers

At their Forty-sixth Reunion in 1924 the nine veterans in attendance resolved as usual to meet again the last Thursday in August of 1925 at the Baldwin Post Rooms in the State Armory. However, in the event, only four veterans were present and the 1925 meeting was not held. [46] That apparently was the end of the 179th New York Volunteers Association.

The last veteran of the 179th to pass away was probably Company D's Edwin Morris, who died in 1943 at the age of ninety-six. He had enlisted on January 24, 1865 at the age of eighteen. After arriving at Hancock Station, he was assigned to Company D on February 23. [47]

Morris was also the last surviving Union veteran in Chemung County, as well as the last surviving member of Baldwin Post No. 6 of the Grand Army of the Republic. He had been elected Commander of the New York Department of the G.A.R. in 1941.

When World War II broke out, Morris filled out an enrollment card with the notation "Will gladly cooperate in advisory capacity or shoulder a gun if necessary." One of his last public appearances was at a war bond rally in 1942. [48]

He had been in failing health for a year after suffering a heart attack on Appomattox Day in 1942. He had been encouraged to pass up his customary participation in the Annual Memorial Sunday service at the Centenary Methodist Church for the Baldwin G.A.R. Post because of his health, but he insisted. He said: "It is my duty to my dead comrades to take part in the service. If it causes my death, I will die in the line of duty." [49] He died the following day.

The Elmira *Star Gazette* wrote:

> The last tie is severed; the last link is broken. Hereafter none can say he saw and participated in the great Civil War events; the sons and daughters of the GAR veterans will say, "He told me so and so." [50]

CONCLUSION

Writing a regimental history one hundred and fifty years after the fact, long after all the soldiers and their family members have passed away, it is easy to lose sight of the timeless truth attributed to General William Tecumseh Sherman – "War is Hell." [1] The day before the 179th New York's first battle, President Lincoln addressed the Great Central Fair in Philadelphia: "War, at its best, is terrible, and this war of ours, in its magnitude and its duration, is one of the most terrible." [2]

Seventy-two men of the 179th New York Volunteers were killed or mortally wounded in battle. One hundred nine died of disease, including twenty-one in Confederate military prisons (or soon after their release). Another forty-some survived the ordeal of being a prisoner of war. One hundred eighty-two were wounded, but recovered, although thirty-one suffered amputation. The effects of diseases like diarrhea did not end with the war. Soldiers who were ill during the war were more likely to suffer from chronic conditions in later life than their contemporaries who had not served. An unknown number of soldiers suffered from post-traumatic stress syndrome or traumatic brain injuries that neither they nor the society around them understood. Roughly seventy-five wives became widows and perhaps a hundred and fifty children grew up without their father. The lives of many others were shortchanged by the loss of a son, a brother, or a close friend. [3] As Mark Dunkelman wrote in *War's Relentless Hand, Twelve Tales of Civil War Soldiers*, "The full human cost and grief of the Civil War can never be calculated." [4]

But the Union was preserved. And slavery was ended. Critics of the domestic and/or foreign policies of the United States over the last one hundred fifty years might question whether the Union of 1861 was worth preserving. I do not. And slavery might well have ultimately collapsed of its own weight, but certainly not by 1865.

Like all enlisted men and junior officers, the men of the 179th New York Volunteers endured the consequences of the decisions – good and bad – by a handful of generals. Civil War era military doctrine did not place the value on human life that we do today. The North had a tremendous advantage in numbers over the South and Grant worked that advantage to ultimate victory. But the common soldier paid the price.

By the fall of 1864, Grant had become justifiably wary of frontal assaults, but he still ordered the frontal assaults by the Sixth and Ninth Corps against the heart of the Confederate lines on April 2, 1865. Was that last assault – and the heavy casualties it brought in the 179th New York and other units – necessary? Or could Grant have pursued Sheridan's breakthrough at Five Forks to achieve the same result, albeit not as quickly? [5] Even if the Confederate forces could have been able to fall back from Five Forks to prepared positions closer to Petersburg, they would have been doomed. Not only had the last supply links with North Carolina been lost after Five Forks, but by crossing the Appomattox River west of Petersburg, the Army of the Potomac could have surrounded the Army of Northern Virginia if it remained in Petersburg

The 179th's other battles also raise questions about the impact of decisions by the Army of the Potomac's generals on the men on the ground. A more creative general would have led the Ninth Corps farther to the left to outflank the Confederate forces on June 17 rather than attack them head on. The 179th New York suffered its greatest losses in the June 17 assault – twenty-one men killed or mortally wounded, sixty wounded and ten missing in action. Thomas Howe aptly summed up the initial attacks on Petersburg with the title of his book – *Wasted Valor*. [6]

Although the mine at Petersburg could potentially have produced a decisive victory for the Union, Burnside's and Ledlie's inability to implement the plan of attack caused great loss of life and suffering – thirteen killed or mortally wounded, seventeen wounded and twenty-six missing in action in the case of the 179th New York. The order to Potter at Poplar Spring Church to advance into unreconnoitered territory "as rapidly as practicable, without reference to any one else" put the Second Division (and the 179th New York) at risk of the surprise counterattack that ensued. Was that a wise risk to take? The farther Potter's division got ahead of supporting troops, the lower the likelihood that it could have held any advanced positions that it took.

More generally, did military necessity warrant sending troops into battle before even rudimentary training could be completed? Ord.'s lament that: "It is as bad as murder to send new men from the North into an active campaign in this climate without a preparatory hardening process" gives pause when thinking about how the 179th New York Volunteers was used. [7]

Even more troubling was the Union army's handling of General Ledlie's failure of leadership. While the Court of Inquiry did hold Ledlie, along with Burnside and Ferrero, "answerable for the want of success" of the assault after the mine was exploded, no mention was made of his drunkenness and he was allowed to quietly disappear. [8] That hardly seems sufficient.

Obviously, the Army of the Potomac was not a democratic institution. The common soldier did not elect his army, corps, division or brigade commanders. But the common soldiers did vote to re-elect Abraham Lincoln in 1864. The 1864 election was in effect a referendum on the war and the ability of the soldiers in the field to vote was critical to the concept of the "citizen-soldier."

The role of the citizen who comes to the defense of his country is an underlying theme of this book and was central to American political theory of the era. But the extent of desertion demonstrates that not all men in the North bought into the theory. A young man born in Ireland, newly arrived with employment opportunity limited to the status of a "laborer" might not have thought of himself as a "citizen" and might have viewed the preservation of the Union and/or the ending of slavery as irrelevant. But most of the men of the 179th New York were deeply rooted in their communities. A farmer who owned land in the town where he was born and bred was more likely to feel an obligation to volunteer to help his town meet its quota and avoid the disgrace of a draft. And he was most likely going to return to that town when the war was over. He was serving alongside his neighbors – especially in Companies I and K – and had a stake in performing his duty without disgrace.

Ralph Waldo Emerson spoke at the dedication of a Civil War monument in 1867:

> The obelisk records only the names of the dead. There is something partial in this distribution of honor. Those who went through those dreadful fields and returned not deserve much more than all the honor we can pay. But those also who went through the same fields, and returned alive, put just as much at hazard as those who died, and, in other countries, would wear distinctive badges of honor, as long as they lived. I hope the disuse of such medals or badges in this country only signifies that everybody knows these men, and carries their deeds in such lively remembrance that they require no badge or reminder. I am sure I need not bespeak your gratitude to these fellow citizens and neighbors of ours. [9]

Whether the men of the 179th could have answered their country's call earlier or were motivated by money rather than patriotism may be interesting to contemplate, but in the end what really matters is that as citizen-soldiers they did their duty. Grant wrote in his memoirs that a "truthful history" of the Civil War "will do full credit to the courage, endurance and soldierly ability of the American citizen." [10] I hope that I have done "full credit to the courage, endurance and soldierly ability" of the citizen-soldiers of the 179th New York Volunteers.

ACKNOWLEDGEMENTS

I don't think I'm exaggerating when I say that I have probably spent two thousand hours or more over the past five years bringing this book to completion. I am very much aware that I would still be laboring in the wilderness without the help and encouragement of many people from many places. I want to thank the following people who made it a pleasure for me to research and write this book and, hopefully, a pleasure for you to read it.

This book would not have been possible without the participation of Brian Dawe, a friend and fellow Civil War buff of fifty years standing. During a fortuitous meeting several years ago in the home town we both left long ago, Brian convinced me that electronic publishing was the way to go because of its enhanced capabilities over print publishing for presenting maps and other visual materials. He followed up that advice by creating our website and we were off and running. It is Brian who brought the content, the maps (which he designed from contemporary sources) and the photos and illustrations together as an e-book. But that has not been the limit of his contribution. He regularly provided constructive criticism and in particular helped me think through how to present the experience of the citizen-soldier that is the central theme of this book. He also wrote most of Chapter 6 and provided his field notes and photos from walking the battlefields.

My wife, Lynne, a better writer than I, reviewed drafts of a number of important chapters. There are many things that she helped me say in a better way. Most importantly, she gave me the space to do this project and shares in my sense of accomplishment.

My mother, Helen Hall Rutan, has been a source of great encouragement and support during our many road trips together researching the 179th New York. "Every inch of the way we know, from Albany to Buffalo."

My late mother-in-law, Mary Jane Peck, was always interested in the project and I read an early version of one of the chapters to her shortly before she passed away. Her bequest to me became my research grant and enabled me to make the numerous necessary trips to the National Archives in Washington and New York City, the New York State Library, Elmira, Ithaca, Penn Yan and other places that I otherwise could not have afforded.

My son, Matthew, worked on the index.

Andrew Pace, who recently received his masters degree in history from the University of Chicago, provided valuable editorial support by raising probing questions throughout the text and by assisting with the laborious but necessary process of cite-checking.

I cannot thank Earl Hess enough for his willingness to review first the outline and then the manuscript of a novice historian. His initial comments helped build my confidence that I was heading in good directions and his later comments helped me to better organize and shorten the book.

Glenn LaFantasie provided early encouragement on my approach and pointed me to the John Andrews Papers, far and away my most important source.

Eric Foner, responding to me as a fellow student of the late James P. Shenton, one of Columbia's "Great Teachers," also provided early encouragement on my approach.

Lyn Creswell, a former colleague in the City Attorney's Office, convinced me to write about the home towns of the men of the 179th New York.

Projects such as mine would be impossible without the original source material housed at the

National Archives. That material would be inaccessible without the expertise and professionalism of the National Archives staff. Whether it be in the first floor research center or the second floor reading room in Washington or the Cartographic Section in College Park, Maryland or the branch in New York City, the service provided by the National Archives staff has been invaluable to me.

Equally capable and professional are the National Park Service staff members at the Petersburg National Battlefield. Chris Bryce (Chief of Interpretation), Jimmy Blankenship (then Chief Historian), Julia Steele (Cultural Resources Manager), and Emmanuel Dabney (Park Ranger) were particularly helpful in responding to my inquiries.

For anyone researching New York's Civil War units, the New York State Military Museum's Unit History Project website should be the first stop. Not only is there a good introduction to the unit, but the resources compiled in the "Further Reading" section contain numerous research leads. They kindly added my website and my article in The Chemung Historical Journal to the list for the 179th New York.

Sue and Ed Curtis, the stalwarts of the Salisbury Military Prison Association, provided helpful comments on an early draft of the prisoners of war chapter and gave me a tour of Salisbury and the military cemetery there.

Local historical societies are a valuable community resource. At the Chemung County Historical Society in Elmira, Executive Director Bruce Whitmarsh provided copies of Stephen Compton's letters and diary. Archivist Rachel Dworkin pointed me early on to the New York State Newspaper Project, which has proven to be one of my most important sources. She also found numerous contemporary photos that fit my needs. Kathyrn Whitmarsh, Editor of The Chemung Historical Journal, published my first article as a budding historian. Curator Erin Doane organized the "Civil War in the Attic" exhibition for which my mother and I loaned materials from the family collection. Kelli Huggins organized my talk on the 179th at the Chemung County History Museum.

In an era of microfilm and digital text, I savored the opportunity to read the *Yates County Chronicle* in its original hard copy format at the Yates County History Center. John Potter, Rich Mac Alpine, and Lisa Harper all helped with my research. Ray Copson helped with the arrangements for my presentation on the 179th New York at the center's "History on Tap" series.

The Buffalo newspapers on microfilm at the Buffalo History Center were an important source. The Buffalo History Center also provided the photo of Buffalo for the "Home Towns" chapter. Their collection also includes a number of muster rolls for Company E of the 179th New York.

Donna Eschenbrenner at The History Center in Tompkins County provided both research materials and photos for "The Home Towns" chapter.

I was slow in realizing the important role that the men of Bradford County, Pennsylvania played in the 179th New York. Fortunately, once I did Denise Golden at the Bradford County Historical Society was there to help me.

Lenny Tvdten, Sandy Nuss, and Jim Marushin from the Martin County [Minnesota] Historical Society provided a wealth of information about William Bird, Jr. and his family.

Edward Varno, Executive Director of The Ontario County Historical Society Museum and Research Center, provided extensive information about Newton Spencer and general information about the 179th New York, as well as tracking down a last-minute lead.

Charles Browne and Shirley Spalik from the Broome County Historical Society provided information about some of the Broome County men in the 179th.

Amateur and professional genealogists alike know that the collection of the LDS Church's Family History Museum in Salt Lake City is unmatched anywhere in the world. Included in their collection are New York's 1866 A Record of the Commissioned Officers ..., the 1865 Town Clerk reports on the men who served, many of the older regimental histories and microfilm of the New York State Census records.

A particularly pleasant aspect of the project has been connecting with other descendants of the men of the 179th New York. Particular thanks go to Jeanne Larzelere Bloom, a descendant of Company F's William Larzelere, for her generosity in sharing her research on the 179th New York and transcriptions of his diary and several letters. Bruce Haynes and Maureen Walters (Company G's Chatford Howell) gave me a personal tour of the area around the Cold Harbor battlefield where the 179th New York saw its first picket duty. Donald Tubbs (Company I's Elias Beach), Mary Kay Belland (Company A's Hosea Fish), Corinne DeGraaf and Mary Grindol (Company A's Elihu Linkletter) and David Crance (Company I's James Vangilder) provided letters and/or photos.

Nan Clarke and I have shared the joys and tribulations of writing our first books.

Long time friend John Hendricks gave me good criticism on my first draft of the Preface.

Notwithstanding my frequent travel, I was not able to go everywhere I wanted to. Professional researchers Steve Zerbe, Mary White, and Terry Cook extended my reach, adding further detail to the book.

Michelle Rayner masterfully handled all of my design needs — the cover, interior design, advertisements, the card for selling the e-book, letterhead and business cards.

When it came to self-publishing, I didn't know what I didn't know, but Stacy Dymalski showed me the way and recommended Michelle Rayner.

Joe Frazier in the Summit County, Utah library tracked down limited circulation academic journals that added valuable detail to the book.

As I got more deeply involved in the book, I encountered increasing difficulty balancing the time demands of my job as Salt Lake's city attorney and the 179th New York Volunteers. I greatly appreciate the willingness of Salt Lake City Mayor Ralph Becker to allow me to take additional leave without pay to work on the book during my last two years before retirement.

A final thanks to my friends and colleagues who always remembered to ask – with genuine interest – "how's the book coming?"

APPENDIX ONE

PETERSBURG ENGAGEMENTS

To make study of the military campaign more manageable, Earl Hess, "[i]nspired by an idea proposed by Richard Sommers," has divided the campaign into nine Union offensives, two Union raids to destroy rail lines into Petersburg, and three Confederate offensives.[1] They are briefly summarized below to provide the context for the 179th New York Volunteers' service in the Petersburg campaign.

As a preliminary comment, Grant's underlying strategy as the campaign progressed was to extend the Confederate lines further and further west to their ultimate breaking point, while also regularly testing the Confederate defenses in front of Bermuda Hundred on the east side, north of the Appomattox River, for a direct opportunity at Richmond.

FIRST UNION OFFENSIVE: JUNE 15-18, 1864

This was the initial series of attacks after the Army of the Potomac changed front from Cold Harbor. The Union attacks began against the northeast side of the "Dimmock Line" which had been started in 1862 to defend Petersburg during McClellan's Peninsula campaign. As the Union captured positions on the Dimmock Line, the Confederate troops fell back to the hastily built Hagood Line. The Ninth Corps arrived outside of Petersburg, the afternoon of July 16. In a pre-dawn attack on June 17, Potter's division drove the Confederate troops from Battery 15 of the Dimmock Line back across Harrison's Creek to the newly prepared Hagood Line. Willcox's division was driven back with heavy losses in an afternoon attack against the Hagood Line northwest of Shand's Farm. Around 6 p.m., Ledlie's division successfully breached the Hagood Line in the same sector where Willcox's division had failed, but ultimately was forced back late in the evening. The 179th's first combat action was as part of Ledlie's assault. The 179th suffered roughly forty percent casualties among the roughly two hundred thirty soldiers engaged.[2]

SECOND UNION OFFENSIVE: JUNE 22-23, 1864

This was an unsuccessful attack by the Second and Sixth Corps west of the Jerusalem Plank Road at what was then the far left side of the Union lines. The 179th New York was not involved.[3]

WILSON-KAUTZ RAID: JUNE 22-29, 1864

This was a Union cavalry raid west and southwest of Petersburg that temporarily disabled sections of two of the three railroads supplying Petersburg – the South Side Railroad and the Richmond and Danville Railroad. The 179th was not involved.[4]

FIRST CONFEDERATE OFFENSIVE: JUNE 24, 1864

This was an unsuccessful Confederate attack on the Union's right flank (Eighteenth Corps sector), just south of the Appomattox River. The 179th was not involved.[5]

THIRD UNION OFFENSIVE: JULY 26-30, 1864.

This was comprised of the frontal assault at the Battle of the Crater (referred to as the Mine Explosion in the 179th New York's Regimental History and many Union accounts) led by the Ninth Corps preceded by a maneuver across the James River northeast of Petersburg by the Second Corps. The Battle of the Crater was a disaster for the Union. The 179th New York was in the first wave of the assault and again lost heavily. [6]

FOURTH UNION OFFENSIVE: AUGUST 14-25, 1864.

This consisted of simultaneous Union assaults on both flanks of the lines. On the Union right, the Second Corps unsuccessfully attacked at Deep Bottom, on the north side of the James River. On the Union left, the Fifth Corps, with support from parts of the Second Corps and the Ninth Corps, proceeded against the Weldon Railroad. The most important battles were at Globe Tavern (August 18-21) and Ream's Station (August 25). The 179th was deployed as skirmishers on the far right of the Union lines, east of Globe Tavern, and suffered only one soldier missing in action. The 179th's Regimental History refers to the engagement as Weldon Railroad. The 179th was not involved in Reams Station. While Reams' Station was a defeat for the Union's Second Corps, the seizure of this portion of the Weldon Railroad by the Fifth Corps was a strategic coup for the Union, forcing the Confederates to offload supplies coming by rail from North Carolina and complete the journey into Petersburg by wagon. [7]

FIFTH UNION OFFENSIVE: SEPTEMBER 29-OCTOBER 2, 1864

This was another simultaneous offensive on both flanks. On the left flank, the Union objective was to advance beyond the Boydton Plank Road toward the Appomattox River. The Ninth Corps (including the 179th New York Volunteers) was surprised and overwhelmed as they were approaching the Boydton Plank Road and they retreated in disarray. Most of the 179th's casualties were missing in action. Historians and the 179th's Regimental History refer to this engagement as Poplar Spring Church, although the action occurred on the Peebles and Pegram Farms. [8]

SECOND CONFEDERATE OFFENSIVE: OCTOBER 7, 1864

This was an attack on the Union right flank, north of the James River. Lee unsuccessfully sought to retake Fort Harrrison. The 179th was not involved. [9]

SIXTH UNION OFFENSIVE: OCTOBER 27, 1864

This was to be a coordinated attack on the Boydton Plank Road and the South Side Railroad, led by the Second Corps with support from the Fifth and Ninth Corps. The Ninth Corps advanced on the Confederate positions in front of Boydton Plank Road, but was unable to find a weak spot and withdrew to their original positions after a day. The 179th reported no casualties. The Second Corps had taken a more southerly route around the Boydton Plank Road positions, and had repulsed a Confederate counterattack in the vicinity of Burgess' Mill on Hatcher's Run, but also ultimately withdrew because neither the Fifth nor the Ninth Corps had been able to link up with them. The 179th's Regimental History refers to this engagement as Hatcher's Run, although Hatcher's Run more accurately refers to where the Second Corps was engaged. [10] Today, historians generally refer to this action as Burgess' Mill.

WARREN'S RAID ON THE WELDON AND PETERSBURG RAILROAD: DECEMBER 7-12, 1864

This was a successful effort by the Fifth Corps to tear up more track on the Weldon Railroad. The Fifth Corps withdrew before the Confederates could mount an attack. The 179th was part of the Ninth Corps force that was to provide support for the Fifth Corps that ultimately proved unnecessary. In the end, the 179th's participation was limited to a twenty-five mile forced march out and back on consecutive days and no casualties were suffered. The 179th's Regimental History does not claim this as an engagement. [11]

SEVENTH UNION OFFENSIVE: FEBRUARY 5-7, 1865

This was originally intended as a large-scale raid by the Union cavalry supported by the Fifth Corps on the Weldon and Petersburg Railroad, but at the end of the fighting, the Union still held two crossings of Hatcher's Run south of the Confederate Boydton Plank Road line. This positioned the Union well for future operations against the Weldon Railroad and Lee's right flank. The 179th was not involved. [12]

THIRD CONFEDERATE OFFENSIVE: MARCH 25, 1865

This was a bold – and desperate – attempt by Lee to break the siege and deny Grant his increasingly inevitable success at Petersburg. The attack was concentrated on Fort Stedman. The attack caught the Union defenders by surprise, but the initial Confederate breakthrough was contained and the Confederate troops were forced to retreat to their original lines. The 179th stood at the ready in their camp three miles away, but was not called into action. Nonetheless, the 179th's Regimental History claims this as an engagement. [13]

EIGHTH UNION OFFENSIVE: MARCH 29, APRIL 1, 1865

This was a major offensive on the Union left/Confederate right that led to the Union victory by General Sheridan at Five Forks, often referred to as Lee's Waterloo. The 179th New York was not involved. [14]

NINTH UNION OFFENSIVE: APRIL 2, 1865

This was a frontal assault at the center of the Confederate lines by the Sixth and Ninth Corps following on the Union success at Five Forks. The Ninth Corps attacked from Union Fort Sedgwick ("Fort Hell") toward Confederate Fort Mahone ("Fort Damnation") and the other Confederate positions on either side of the Jerusalem Plank Road. The Sixth Corps attacked from the Union salient at Fort Welch. The 179th was again in the first wave of the Ninth Corps' assault and again suffered significant casualties. The partial breakthroughs by the Sixth and Ninth Corps, following on Sheridan's victory at Five Forks, forced Lee to evacuate Petersburg and Richmond and retreat to the west. [15]

The Ninth Corps and the 179th New York joined in the Union pursuit, but were not in the vanguard. The Ninth Corps and the 179th New York guarded the Union's lengthening supply line. The 179th did not see any further combat. Lee and the Army of Northern Virginia surrendered at Appomattox Court House on April 9, 1865. At that point, the 179th New York was at Burkeville Junction, Virginia, about 45 miles to the east of Appomattox, having marched about fifty miles from Petersburg. [16]

To recapitulate, the 179th New York Volunteers participated in the First, Third, Fourth, Fifth, Sixth, and Ninth Union offensives and was peripherally involved in Warren's Raid on the Weldon and Petersburg Railroad and the Third Confederate Offensive (Fort Stedman). The 179th had only been with the Army of the Potomac for a week when it joined the attack on the Hagood Line on June 17, 1864 as part of the First Offensive. The 179th was in the front lines of the assault at the Crater on July 30, 1864 (the Third Offensive) and on April 2, 1865 (the Ninth Offensive). The 179th lost heavily in these three attacks. Casualties at Poplar Spring Church (the Fifth Union Offensive) were fewer, but still significant. Casualties at Weldon Railroad (the Fourth Union Offensive) and in connection with the Sixth Union Offensive were light. In between battles, the 179th was never far from the range of Confederate guns at Petersburg, manning the trenches, out on picket duty, and the like. Thus, it seems fair to say that the 179th was "forged in the Petersburg campaign."

APPENDIX TWO

———◆———

"Yes, yes, let's talk about the weather…"
(Sir Arthur Sullivan, "The Pirates of Penzance")

Weather

The weather pounded the 179th at both ends of the temperature and precipitation spectrums. Hot and dry in the summer. Cold and wet in the winter. The weather was certainly of interest to the soldiers. Even the most cryptic diary entries for the day often included a reference to the weather. The following are the weather conditions as contemporaneously reported by soldiers of the 179th for the eleven months they were in the field—May 1864 to April 1865.

(For Andrews, Compton and Larzelere, the source is their diary for that date, unless otherwise noted.)

Note: comments in **bold** are from The Reverend C. B. Mackee and his family, living in Georgetown, Washington, D.C. during the four years of war. They have been collected and transcribed by Robert K. Krick in his book *Civil War Weather in Virginia*, University of Alabama Press: Tuscaloosa (2007).

MAY 1864 (Arlington Heights)

6th	Weather very warm	(Co. C Morning Report)
9th	So hot I can hardly stand the weather	(Lee)
	heavy thunder & brilliant lightning at 9 p.m.	
12th	A rainy dull day	(Co. C Morning Report)
	at 4:30 heavy shower, considerable hail	
13th	More rain	(Co. C Morning Report)
	0.74 yesterday and today	
18th	Showers during day	(Co. C Morning Report)
19th	Hot and showery	(Co. C Morning Report)

JUNE 1864 (White House Landing/Petersburg)

6th	Raining	(Lee)
	0.60, heavy rain & high wind at 5 p.m.	
13th	Roads extremely dusty	(Larzelere)
25th	Excessively hot. 90 degrees in the shade	(Buffalo Daily Courier correspondent)
27th	So hot here I feel faint	(Lee)
	very heavy wind 2 p.m.	

JULY 1864 (Petersburg)
[no soldiers' data]

AUGUST 1864 (Petersburg)

14th	Mercury at 100 degrees	("Ord.")

thunder at 2 p.m., heavy shower at 5:30

SEPTEMBER 1864 (Blick's Station)

13th	Cold morning, overcoat used	(Larzelere)

[Graph: Summer 1864 Temperatures]

OCTOBER 1864 (Pegram's Farm)

1st	Cold and rainy	(Larzelere)
6th	Very warm	(Andrews)
7th		
8th	Last night wind blew hard./the little cloth tent was but slight protection against its biting cold.	(Andrews)
9th	Ground white with frost this morning	(Andrews)
10th	Very cold last night	(Andrews)
11th	Cold last night, very warm today	(Andrews)
12th	Started raining at 5 p.m.	Andrews)
13th	Not as cold last night as common /day raw and cold, much the coldest in Virginia thus far	(Andrews)
14th	Last night terrible cold, slept but little/day particularly pleasant	(Andrews)
15th		
16th	Weather warmer than usual, hot today	(Andrews)
17th	Very warm day again following an extremely cold night	(Andrews)
19th	Weather fine, night cold	(Andrews)
22nd	Today is cold and rainy	(Andrews)
24th	Rather cloudy today, but not cold	(Andrews)
26th	Slept but little because of the cold	(Andrews)
27th	Rained by spells all day, but by evening it poured down	(Andrews)
30th	Weather fine	(Andrews)
31st	This morning ground white with frost and blankets wet with dew/weather splendid today	(Andrews)

NOVEMBER 1864 (Pegram's Farm)

2nd	Cold and rainy, fingers numb, difficult to write	(Andrews)
	drizzly from 4 p.m.	
3rd	Rained all day	(Andrews)
	Rainy	(Larzelere)
	drizzled all day, night	
7th	Has rained nearly all day, but weather is warm so men not suffering	(Andrews)
	Rainy day	(Larzelere)
	Rainy, yet warm	(Co. C Morning Report)
	rained all day and night	
8th	The day is beautiful	(Andrews)

	drizzled all day	
9th	Rainy, warm	(Andrews)
10th	weather very warm	(Andrews)
	Rainy, in the afternoon pleasant"	(Co. C Morning Report)
	rained all night	
11th	Weather fine	(Andrews)
	"It is a very pleasant morning."	(Co. C Morning Report)
12th	Weather very pleasant	(Andrews)
	Cloudy and cold	(Co. C Morning Report)
13th	Last night terribly cold, water froze/day fine	(Andrews)
14th	Mild	(Andrews)
15th	Very cold last night, colder than usual today, fire necessary	(Andrews)
16th	Mild and pleasant	(Co. C Morning Report)
17th	Appearance of rain, cloudy with inversion from campfire smoke, but cleared up / day pleasant	(Andrews)
	Mild and pleasant	(Co. C Morning Report)
18th	Day very warm/first night in some time no fire in tent/ raining in the evening	(Andrews)
	Rainy, not very cold	(Co. C Morning Report)
	rained steadily all day	
19th	Rained all night and day, but weather warm	(Andrews)
20th	Rained all last night and today	(Andrews)
	Rainy	(Larzelere)
	Cold and rainy	(Co. C Morning Report)
	drizzled all day	
21st	Rained steadily all day/water stands in deep pools all around	(Andrews)
	Rainy	(Larzelere)
	rained all day	
22nd	Rain has stopped	(Andrews)
	Very cold	(Co. C Morning Report)
23rd	Last night coldest night of the Fall, ground frozen this morning, very cold today	(Andrews)
24th	Last night again very cold, but today rather warmer than yesterday	(Andrews)
25th	Today warmer, last night extremely cold	(Andrews)
	Very pleasant	(Co. C Morning Report)
26th	Weather warm during forenoon	(Andrews)
	Cloudy in the afternoon, rainy this evening.	
	"It is a beautiful sunny morning."	(Larzelere letter)
27th	Cloudy, occasional little sprinkle of rain, but not cold	(Andrews)

DECEMBER 1864 (Hancock Station)

1st	Pleasant as May	(Larzelere)

4th	Warm and fair	(Larzelere)
6th	Warm & fair	(Larzelere)
7th	Rainy	(Larzelere)
	Pleasant day	(Co. C Morning Report)
	Very warm weather, but one cold spell	(Lamont)
	2:00 showery	
8th	Pleasant day	(Co. C Morning Report)
	high wind all night	
9th	Cold	(Larzelere)
	began to snow 8 p.m.	
10th	Snow, rain and hail at night	(Abram Meyers)
	(March to Nottoway River)	
11th	Cold, snow 3 inches deep	(Abram Meyers)
16th	Warm and dry	(Larzelere)
	Very pleasant morning	(Co. C Morning Report)
17th	Warm and dry	(Larzelere)
19th	Warm	(Larzelere)
20th	Colder	(Larzelere)
	As cold as would see in Virginia	(Force/Andrews)
21st	Rainy	(Larzelere)
	Rainy, our tents are flooded	(Co. C Morning Report)
	winter solstice	
22nd	Cold	(Larzelere)
	Bitter cold	(Andrews)
	Rainy and cold	(Co. C Morning Report)
23rd	Cold	(Larzelere)
24th	Cold	(Larzelere)
25th	Quite warm and pleasant	(Compton letter)
26th	Rainy	(Larzelere)
	"The weather is very changeable, sometimes it is very cold, then again warm and rainy."	(Andrews)
28th	Warm and pleasant	(Larzelere)
	0.65 rain yesterday & last night	
29th	Very muddy	(Co. C Morning Report)
	windy all night	
31st	Cold	(Larzelere)

[Graph: Fall 1864 Temperatures]

JANUARY 1865 (Hancock Station)

1st	Bitter cold	(Andrews)
	Cold & clear	(Lazelere)
	"Clear but very cold. Ice made to the thickness of 1 1/2 inches."	(Carpenrer)
2nd	Warmer	(Lazelere)

	Cold this morning but the sun came out fine	(Compton)
3rd	Warmer	(Lazelere)
	It snowed a little, still it is warm. Snows tonight and is colder	(Compton)
	big snow at 3 p.m.	
6th	Raining and very muddy	(Andrews)
	Weather rainy	(Compton)
	rained all day	
7th	Windy with some rain, some sunshine	(Compton)
	0.60 rain	
9th	**Warm and pleasant**	(Lazelere)
	Really poured down during night	(Andrews)
10th	Heavy rain and thunderstorm	(Lazelere)
	Rained hard from about 12:00 last night and rains hard this morning with quite heavy thunder. Our camp is nearly under water. Cleared up just at sunset and weather looked fine.	(Compton)
	rained all last night	
11th	Weather this morning is clear and some colder, but it is not yet froze up. Very muddy.	(Compton)
	high wind all night	
12th	Morning splendid as is also the day	(Compton)
	windy night	
13th	Warm and pleasant	(Larzelere)
	Very fine indeed, seems like June weather	(Compton)
	heavy white frost	
14th	Men ditch our company street to carry off water	(Compton)
15th	Day fine	(Compton)
16th	Warm and pleasant	(Larzelere)
18th	Warm and pleasant	(Larzelere)
21st	Cold and rainy	(Larzelere)
	hailing, rain, sleet, snow all day	
22nd	Cold and rainy	(Larzelere)
	"A stormier, more disagreeable day I never experienced."	("Ord.")
23rd	Rainy	(Larzelere)
	For three days it has rained, ground thoroughly soaked	(Andrews)
	rain thru the day	
24th	Fair weather	(Larzelere)
	Rain stopped/sunshiny and warm/very muddy under foot	(Andrews)
25th	Clear and cold/quite breezy	(Andrews)
27th	Cold	(Larzelere)
28th	Very cold	(Larzelere)
	Clear and warm/muddy under foot	(Andrews)
	quite windy at 4 p.m.	
29th	Day warm and pleasant, night cold	(Andrews)
30th	Day beautiful and pleasant	(Andrews)

FEBRUARY 1865 (Hancock Station)

1st	Day pleasant	(Andrews)
2nd	Warm and inviting	(Andrews)
3rd	Weather fine	(Andrews)
	heavy white frost	
4th	Weather beautiful as May	(Andrews)
	smokey & foggy	
6th	Weather rather cold but pleasant	(Andrews)
7th	Cold	(Larzelere)
	Stormed all day, with a cold sleet	(Andrews)
	snowed 6 inches	
8th	Weather pleasant	(Andrews)
	Cold	(Larzelere)
9th	Pleasant yet rather chilly	(Andrews)
	Cold	(Larzelere)
10th	Weather fine, mud under foot	(Andrews)
11th	Weather fine	(Andrews)
12th	Weather rather chilly, wind blows very hard tonight	(Andrews)
	snowed .5 inch last night	
15th	Rainy day	(Larzelere)
	Raining. "The boys have to wallow around in the mud."	(Andrews letter)
	For several days weather has been rather cold, the nights exceedingly so. It has rained nearly all day	(Andrews)
	rained & sleeted all day & windy	
16th	A little rain and a great deal of mud/warm as a Northern May day	(Andrews)
17th	Warm and rainy	(Andrews)
	heavy fog, rain	
18th	Warm and pleasant	(Andrews)
21st	Weather summerlike	(Andrews)
	"Weather is warm and pleasant and the ground is drying up very fast."	(Lamont)
	heavy white frost	
22nd	Weather beautiful	(Andrews)
	heavy white frost	
24th	Warm, the sky cloudy	(Andrews)
25th	Rain has fallen nearly all day, weather continues warm	(Andrews)
	Rainy	(Larzelere)
	rained all day from 10 a.m.	
26th	Rain has ceased and weather is very pleasant	(Andrews)
27th	Weather fine	(Andrews)
	"The winter weather has passed very quickly."	(Lamont)
28th	Rainy all day	(Andrews)

MARCH 1865 (Hancock Station)

1st	Weather pleasant, though rather cool	(Andrews)
2nd	Rained quite hard nearly all day	(Andrews)
3rd	Rained short time in morning, drizzles a little in evening	(Andrews)
4th	A rainy day	(Andrews)
	rain all night, cleared 10 a.m.	
5th	Pleasant weather today, sun shines a part of the time	(Andrews)
6th	Weather cool, sun shining	(Andrews)
	white frost	
7th	Weather pleasant	(Andrews)
	heavy white frost	
8th	Weather rainy, very warm.	(Andrews)
	began to rain 5 p.m.	
9th	Rained very hard last night, but little today	(Andrews)
	rained all night	
10th	Rained nearly all day, ground very muddy	(Andrews)
11th	Colder than usual last night, ground frozen hard enough this morning to support weight of a man. Pleasant today	(Andrews)
12th	The day is beautiful	(Andrews)
13th	Weather excellent	(Andrews)
14th	Last night rather warmer than usual	(Andrews)
	wild geese passed north	
21st	Commenced raining in the afternoon, rained hard until about midnight	(Andrews)
	began to rain 6 p.m.	
22nd	Day was beautiful, clouds having cleared away sun shone down warm and pleasant	(Andrews)
23rd	Pleasant morning/Heavy wind blew over several trees that demolished several houses, but no one hurt	(Andrews)
	2 p.m. thunder, high wind	
24th	Weather is fine	(Andrews)
	windy all day	
25th	Weather is fine	(Andrews)
	sprinkled all day	
28th	Weather beautiful	(Andrews)
30th	Heavy rain at 3 a.m., rained nearly all day	(Andrews)
	Rainy	(Larzelere)
	drizzle	
31st	Rained nearly all the forenoon/drenching rain at night	(Andrews)
	Rainy	(Larzelere)

APRIL 1865 (Petersburg/Burkeville)

1st	Trees in bloom	(Larzelere)
2nd	Fay fine but windy	(Compton)
6th	Rained a little through the night	(Compton)

7th	Rained slightly this morning	(Compton)
8th	Morning broke very pleasant	(Compton)
9th	Last night cold but today bids fair to be pleasant	(Andrews)
10th	Rained most of the night	(Compton)
	Rained during the night, rained this morning until about 9 A.M. Still continues cloudy	(Andrews)
	rain thru night, drizzly all day	
11th	Still rainy	(Andrews)
	Weather rainy and cool, disagreeable, still cool	(Compton)
12th	Rained at night	(Compton)
	showery all day, heavy 6 p.m.	
14th	Last night rather cooler than usual/today very warm	(Andrews)
15th	Rains hard, stopped toward night	(Compton)
	Rained very hard last night	(Andrews)
	drizzly	
16th	Day is fine and clear	(Compton)
	Clear and pleasant today	(Andrews)
	Easter Sunday	
17th	Day fine	(Compton)
	Weather fine	(Andrews)
18th	Morning fine	(Compton)
	All day it has looked rainy but as yet no rain has fallen	(Andrews)
19th	Morning pleasant	(Compton)
25th	Very warm and dusty	(Compton)
26th	Weather warm	(Compton)

[Graph: Spring 1865 Temperatures]

MAY 1865   (Washington/Alexandria area)

23rd	Cool nice day	(Lamont)
26th	Rainy day	(Larzelere)
27th	Rainy day	(Larzelere)
28th	Weather warm	(Compton)

JUNE 1865   (Washington/Alexandria area and Elmira)

3rd	Very warm	(Compton)
4th	Very hot weather	(Compton)
5th	Morning hot and sultry	(Compton)
6th	Still hot and sultry	(Compton)
8th	Hot	(Compton)
10th	Day cool and pleasant (Harrisburg)	(Compton)
13th	Morning is fine (Elmira)	(Compton)

APPENDIX THREE

Prior Service of the Officers and Enlisted Men of the 179th Regiment New York Volunteer Infantry

Sources:

A Record of the Commissioned Officers, Non-Commissioned Officers, and Privates of the regiments Which Were Organized in the State of New York and Called into the Service of the United States to Assist in Suppressing the Rebellion Caused by the Secession of Some of the Southern States from the Union, A.D. 1861, As Taken from the Muster-In Rolls on File in the Adjutant General's Office, S.N.Y., Weed, Parsons and Company, Printers: Albany (1866), Vol. VI, 107-126.

History of the 179th Regiment N.Y.S.V. – Rebellion of 1861-65, E.D. Norton, Printer: Ithaca, New York (1900).

Graham, Robert H., *Yates County's Boys in Blue, 1861-1865: Who They Were – What They Did*, [self-published]: Penn Yan, New York (1926).

Mills, J., *Chronicles of the Twenty-First Regiment New York State Volunteers*, The 21st Reg't Veteran Association: Buffalo (1887).

Phisterer, Frederick, *New York in the War of the Rebellion 1861 to 1865*, D.B. Lyon Company, State Printers: Albany, New York (Third Ed. 1912).

Phisterer, Vol. V at 4032-4038 unless otherwise noted.

CMSR is the Compiled Military Service Record from the National Archives for the soldier listed.

RH is *History of the 179th Regiment* ...

REC is *A Record of the Commissioned Officers* ..., Vol. VI at 107 et seq.

21NY are the Muster-out Rolls in Mills, *Chronicles* ...

BB is Graham, ... *Boys in Blue*

CWPI is the Civil War Pension Index, accessible on fold3.com.

Regimental Staff		
Colonel William Gregg	Major, 23rd NY	
Lt. Col. Franklin B. Doty	Captain, 23rd NY	
Major John Barnett Sloan	Major, 31st NY	
Surgeon Joseph Robinson	Surgeon, 141st NY	
Company A		
Captain Albert Terrill	Captain, 38th NY	
1st Lt. George Carpenter	2nd Lt., 126th Inf.	
Ezra Beebe (recruit)	24th NY	CWPI
William Beebe	38th NY	(-6/63), CMSR
Asa Otterson	18th Wisc.	CWPI
Corp. Darius Robinson	38th NY	CWPI
Sgt. Ephraim Sherwood	85th NY	CWPI

Sgt. Thomas C. Smith	27th NY	BB, 139; CWPI
Gottlieb Stein		REC
William L. Walker	52nd Pa.	REC
Sgt. James Wattleworth	126th NY	CWPI
Henry Williams	76th NY	CWPI
Company B		
Captain Robert Stewart	2nd Lt., 141st NY	
2nd Lt. James Bowker	2nd Lt., 23rd NY	
2nd Lt. William Bogart	1st Vt. HA, 11th Vt. Inf.	CWPI
William Burke (recruit)	94th NY, 105th NY	CWPI
James Cain	5th Regt., U.S. Cavalry, 34th NY	(-5/63), CMSR; CWPI
Alexander P. Campbell	85th NY and 147th NY	(-1/64), BB at 136, CMSR
Daniel Compton	26th Pa.	CWPI
Alexander Gardiner	136th NY	(-2/63), CMSR
Thomas Hammond (recruit)	109th NY	CWPI
Byron Hodge	16th Pa. Cav.	CWPI
Samuel G.H. Musgrave	Pvt, 23rd NY	(5/61-5/63)
Nathan Osborn	35th NY	CWPI
Nathaniel Reed	171st Pa.	CMSR
Edward White	86th NY	CWPI
William T. White	171st Pa.	CMSR
Stephen Green (recruit)	30th NY	CWPI
Company C		
Captain John Barton	1st Lt, 141st NY	
1st Lt. John Prentiss	2nd Lt., 23rd NY	
Martin Avery	64th NY	CWPI
Alfred Bennett	145th NY	REC, CWPI
Richard Bennett	3rd NY	(-5/63), CMSR, REC
Charles Carr	Pvt, 23rd NY	(5/61-5/63), REC, CWPI
Martin Doty	Sgt, 23rd NY (returned to ranks)	(5/61-5/63), CWPI
Sgt. Levi Force	Sgt, 23rd NY	(5/61 to 5/63)
Nathan Gallett	2d Wisconsin Inf.	BB at 137, CWPI
John Gill		REC
Truman Head	23rd NY	(-5/63), CMSR, CWPI
George Hicks (recruit)	65th NY	CWPI
Paul Hildreth (recruit)	43rd NY	CWPI
Sgt. Beekman King	23rd NY	(-6/63), CMSR
Sgt. John Price	161st NY	RH at 16, REC, CMSR
Orrin Taylor	141st Pa.	CWPI

Robert Wilcox	1st NY Light Artillery	CMSR, CWPI
Company D		
Captain William Bird, Jr.	Captain, 37th NY	
1st Lt. Baker L. Saxton	Captain, 154th NY	
2nd Lt. Jeffrey Wisner	Sgt., 107th NY (returned to ranks)	(7/62-5/64)
Volney Curry (recruit)	9th Mich.	CWPI
Nicholas Dodzell	9th NY Cav.	CWPI
George M. Gregory		REC
Albert Ham (recruit)	107th NY	CWPI
Hiram Hull	37th NY	REC, CWPI
John Jackson	37th NY	REC, CWPI
Martin Kellsy	37th NY	CWPI
Edgar Lattin	154th NY	REC, CWPI
John Lawrence (recruit)	86th NY	CWPI
James Lockie	154th NY, 6th NY Cav.	CWPI
Harvey Luddington	37th NY	CWPI
Schuyler McIntosh (recruit)	23rd NY	CWPI
Andrew Morris (recruit)	7th Pa. Cav.	CWPI
First Sgt. James O. Spencer	37th NY	REC, CWPI
Cyrenian Ulman (recruit)	161st NY	CWPI
Company E		
Elbert Hurlbert	37th NY	CWPI, REC
Captain Daniel Blachford	2nd Lt., 21st NY	(5/61-5/63), 21NY
2nd Lt. Louis Ottenot	Pvt, 21st NY	(7/61-5/63), 21NY
2nd Lt. John Hoy	Sgt., 21st NY	21NY
Seneca Arnold (recruit)	141st Pa	CWPI
Joseph Boughton (recruit)	132nd Pa.	CWPI
Charles Fitts (recruit)	76th NY.	CWPI
James Lewis	50th Pa	CWPI
Sgt. Jacob Langmeyer	Pvt, 21st NY	(9/61- 5/63), CMSR, 21NY
Sgt. Charles E. Lockwood	Pvt, 21st NY	(5/61-5/63), 21NY
Sgt. Henry Mapes	9th NY Cavalry	(-8/63), CMSR
John Munro	74th NY	(-12/63) , CMSR
James P. Provost, Jr.	35th NY	(-6/63), CMSR
Austin Ripley	36th NY	(-7/63), CMSR
Simon Shepard (recruit)	64th NY	CWPI
Charles W. Townsend	25th NJ	(-6/63), CMSR
Company F		
John Brophy (recruit?)	33rd NY	CWPI
Sgt. John Durham	33rd NY	(-6/64), RH at , CMSR

Justus Higby	37th NY, 194th NY	CWPI
Martin Hope	33rd NY	RH at 25, CMSR
Samuel B. Hyatt	30th Indiana Inf.	BB at 137, CMSR
Edwin Knapp	126th NY	BB at 137
First Sgt. William Norton	23rd NY	CWPI
Andrew McConnell	33rd NY	(-6/63), CMSR
John Oakley	13th Illinois Inf.	(-4/63), CMSR
Norton A. Sage	14th U.S. Inf.	CWPI; BB at 138
Francis Tubbs (recruit)	58th Pa.	CWPI
Freeman Warren	50th NY Eng.	CWPI
Austin Whitaker (recruit)	23rd NY	BB at 139
Company G		
Captain James H. Day	Pvt (?), 2d Colo. Cavalry	
1st Lt. William Hemstreet	2nd Lt, 104th NY	
2nd Lt. Henry J. Messing	74th NY	CWPI
George Ganoung (recruit)	32nd NY	CWPI
Conrad Hartman (recruit)	65th NY	CWPI
George Hoas	65th NY	CWPI
Ernest Meisner	49th NY	(-4/63), CMSR
George Wilbur	105th NY	CWPI
Company H		
1st Lt. Fitz Culver	Pvt, 44th NY	(8/61-12/62)
2nd Lt. Samuel G.H. Musgrave	Pvt, 23rd NY	
Lewis Diar	6th U.S. Inf.	CWPI
Elliott Cook	9th NY Cav., 68th NY	CWPI
Henry Foster	141st NY	CWPI
Daniel Howard	108th NY	CWPI
Jacob Perry	34th NY	(-6/63), CMSR
Charles Stevens	5th NY Cav.	CWPI
Albert Tingue	100th NY	CMSR
	7th Independent Battery	
Charles Ostrander	171st Pa.	CWPI
Company I		
Amos Brundage	6th NY Cav.	CWPI
James Cook	3rd Conn.	CWPI
Lant Heverly	56th Pa.	CWPI
Elijah Smith	26th NY	CWPI
Company K		
Capt. Moses Van Benschoten	1st Lt, 23rd NY	

1st Lt. Robert Hooper		RH at 34 states 'was member of military' but I have been unable to confirm
Abram Axtell (recruit)	101st NY	CWPI
John Merithew	23rd NY	CWPI
James Vandemark	171st Pa.	CWPI
David A. Welch	86th NY	CWPI
Edward McKinney	22nd [?] Inf.	CWPI
David Russell	107th NY	CWPI
Starr Wright	37th NY, 101st NY	CWPI
John H. McKinney	171st Pa.	CWPI

APPENDIX FOUR

Table of Organization of the 179th New York Volunteers by Battle

Petersburg
June 17, 1864

Strength: 6 companies, approximately 230 men

Comments: Approximately 100 men, primarily from Companies C and D, were on detached duty at Cumberland Heights under Captain Terrill. In this battle and the April 2, 1865 assault, the 179th had its deepest complement of experienced officers. However, the enlisted men had only limited training and only about 5% had prior combat experience.

Col. (Gregg in Elmira)
Lt. Col. Doty
Major Sloan

Company A

Capt.	(Terrill -- at Cumberland Heights)
1st Lt.	G. Carpenter
2nd Lt.	(Farr -- sick since 6/ 3)
1st Sgt.	(S. Compton -- at Cumberland Heights)
2nd Sgt.	(Wattleworth -- sick)
3rd Sgt.	(Sherwood -- sick)
4th Sgt.	Rutan
5th Sgt.	L. Carpenter -- promoted May 1

Company B

Capt.	Stewart
1st Lt.	(Cook -- on recruiting duty)
2nd Lt.	(Bowker -- Musgrave says not present)
1st Sgt.	Musgrave
2nd Sgt.	D. Compton
3rd Sgt.	Arnold
4th Sgt.	Osborne
5th Sgt.	White

Company C

Capt.	Barton
1st Lt.	Prentiss
2nd Lt.	Finch -- sick?
1st Sgt.	Force
2nd Sgt.	Carr

3rd Sgt.	Pinch
4th Sgt.	King
5th Sgt.	Price

Company D

Capt.	Bird
1st Lt.	Saxton
2nd Lt.	(Vacant)
1st Sgt.	(McLain--deserted 6/3)
2nd Sgt.	J. Spencer
3rd Sgt.	Gregory
4th Sgt.	Crawford
5th Sgt.	Andrews

Company E

Capt.	Blachford
1st Lt.	Hoy
2nd Lt.	Ottenot
1st Sgt.	Lockwood
2nd Sgt.	Langmeyer
3rd Sgt.	Munro
4th Sgt.	Taylor
5th Sgt.	Mapes

Company F

Capt.	Farwell
1st Lt.	David A. Bradley
2nd Lt.	(Holden -- on recruiting duty)
1st Sgt.	Norton
2nd Sgt.	Durham
3rd Sgt.	Dunn
4th Sgt.	Hyatt
5th Sgt.	Loveless

Battle of the Crater
July 30, 1864
Strength: 7 companies, approximately 240 men

Comments: The officer complement of the 179th New York had been hit hard on June 17. At the Battle of the Crater, the 179th was commanded by a newly promoted major and four of the seven companies were commanded by lieutenants. The 179th was still comprised largely of green recruits. The one hundred men who had been at Cumberland Heights on June 17 and newly arrived Company G made up roughly two-thirds of the enlisted men on the field at the Battle of the Crater.

Col.	(Gregg in Elmira)
Lt. Col. Doty	(wounded June 17)
Major Barton	(promoted July 13)

Company A

Capt.	Terrill
1st Lt.	(G. Carpenter -- sick since 7/26/64)
2nd Lt.	(Farr -- sick since 6/3/64)
1st Sgt.	(S. Compton -- sick)
2nd Sgt.	Rutan
3rd Sgt.	L. Carpenter--promoted 7/1
4th Sgt.	Lamberson--promoted 7/1
5th Sgt.	Lewis Kellogg--promoted 7/1

Company B

Capt.	(Stewart -- wounded 6/17)
1st Lt.	(Cook -- on recruiting duty)
2nd Lt.	Bowker -- since 4/22
1st Sgt.	(Musgrave -- wounded 6/17)
2nd Sgt.	D. Compton
3rd Sgt.	Arnold -- sick?
4th Sgt.	Osborn
5th Sgt.	(White--sick)

Company C

Capt.	Prentiss
1st Lt.	Prentiss -- promoted Captain
2nd Lt.	Finch -- sick?
1st Sgt.	Force
2nd Sgt.	Carr
3rd Sgt.	(Pinch--sick)
4th Sgt.	King
5th Sgt.	(Price--sick)

Company D

Capt.	(Bird -- wounded 6/17)
1st Lt.	Saxton -- since 5/11
2nd Lt.	(Wisner -- on recruiting duty)
1st Sgt.	J. Spencer--promoted 6/7
2nd Sgt.	Gregory
3rd Sgt.	Crawford
4th Sgt.	Andrews
5th Sgt.	Baillet--promoted 6/7

Company E

Capt.	(Blachford -- killed 6/17)
1st Lt.	Ottenot
2nd Lt.	(Hoy -- cashiered 7/23)
1st Sgt.	Lockwood

2nd Sgt.	(Taylor--sick)
3rd Sgt.	Sandrock--promoted 7/7/64
4th Sgt.	Provost--promoted 7/8/64
5th Sgt.	Hager--promoted 7/26/64

Company F

Capt.	Farwell
1st Lt.	Bradley -- on detached duty
2nd Lt.	Holden -- on recruiting duty
1st Sgt.	Norton
2nd Sgt.	(Durham--wounded 6/17/64)
3rd Sgt.	Dunn
4th Sgt.	(Hyatt--sick?)
5th Sgt.	Loveless

Company G

Capt.	Day -- since 7/23/64
1st Lt.	Hemstreet -- since 7/23/64
2nd Lt.	Messing -- since 7/23/64
1st Sgt.	McNeil
2nd Sgt.	Lewis
3rd Sgt.	Messner
4th Sgt.	Weston
5th Sgt.	Thompson

Weldon Railroad
August 18-21, 1864

Strength: 7 companies, with only one officer and 81 enlisted men

Comments: Most of the men present in the 179th had been in either the Battle of the Crater or the June 17, assault, but the small number of available troops meant that the 179th played only a limited role

Col.	(Gregg in Elmira)
Lt. Col. Doty	(wounded June 17)
Major Barton	(killed July 30)
Capt. Terrill	(senior captain)

Company A

Capt.	(Terrill -- acting Regt CO)
1st Lt.	(G. Carpenter -- sick since 7/ 26)
2nd Lt.	(Farr -- sick since 6/ 3
1st Sgt.	(Compton -- sick)
2nd Sgt.	(Rutan -- sick)
3rd Sgt.	(L. Carpenter--MIA 7/30)

| 4th Sgt. | Lamberson--promoted 7/1 |
| 5th Sgt. | Lewis Kellogg--promoted 7/1 |

Company B

Capt.	(Stewart -- wounded 6/17)
1st Lt.	(Cook -- on detached duty)
2nd Lt.	Bowker
1st Sgt.	(Musgrave -- wounded 6/17)
2nd Sgt.	D. Compton
3rd Sgt.	(Arnold -- sick)
4th Sgt.	Osborn
5th Sgt.	(White--sick)

Company C

Capt.	Prentiss
1st Lt.	Force -- promoted 8/8
2nd Lt.	(Finch -- promoted Regt Quartermaster 8/8)
1st Sgt.	(Carr--sick)
2nd Sgt.	Pinch
3rd Sgt.	King
4th Sgt.	(Price--sick)
5th Sgt.	

Company D

Capt.	(Bird -- wounded 6/17)
1st Lt.	(Saxton -- killed 7/30)
2nd Lt.	(Wisner -- on recruiting duty)
1st Sgt.	(J. Spencer--7/30 POW)
2nd Sgt.	Gregory
3rd Sgt.	(Crawford--7/30 POW)
4th Sgt.	(Andrews--7/30 POW)
5th Sgt.	(Baillet--sick/promoted 6/7)

Company E

Capt.	Ottenot -- promoted 8/9/64
1st Lt.	Lockwood--promoted 8/9/64
2nd Lt.	Vacant
1st Sgt.	(Taylor--sick?)
2nd Sgt.	Sandrock
3rd Sgt.	Provost
4th Sgt.	Hager
5th Sgt.	(Vacant?)

Company F

| Capt. | (Farwell -- killed 7/30) |

1st Lt.	(Bradley -- on detached duty)
2nd Lt.	(Holden -- on recruiting duty)
1st Sgt.	(Norton--7/30 POW)
2nd Sgt.	(Durham--wounded 6/17)
3rd Sgt.	(Dunn--wounded 7/30/64)
4th Sgt.	(Hyatt--sick?)
5th Sgt.	Loveless

Company G

Capt.	(Day -- wounded 7/30/64)
1st Lt.	Hemstreet
2nd Lt.	(Messing -- sick since 8/19)
1st Sgt.	McNeil
2nd Sgt.	Lewis
3rd Sgt.	(Messner--sick?)
4th Sgt.	(Weston--wounded 7/30/64)
5th Sgt.	Thompson

Poplar Spring Church
September 30, 1864
Strength: 10 companies, approximately 400 men

Comments: At this point most of the men in the original seven companies of the 179th New York had been in one or more battles. However, the original seven companies generally each had fewer than twenty men available. Newly arrived Companies H, I and K, whose men had been in the service for only a month or less, comprised nearly 60% of the force. Roughly another 15% was comprised of new recruits for the original seven companies. Lieutenant Colonel Doty had recovered from his wounds and took command.

Col.	(Gregg in Elmira)
Lt. Col. Doty	(returned August)
Major Terrill	(promoted August)

Company A

Capt.	(Vacant--Terrill promoted to Major)
1st Lt.	(G. Carpenter--sick)
2nd Lt.	Farr
1st Sgt.	(Compton -- sick)
2nd Sgt.	(Rutan -- sick)
3rd Sgt.	(Carpenter--MIA 7/30/64)
4th Sgt.	Lamberson--promoted 7/1/64
5th Sgt.	Lewis Kellogg--promoted 7/1/64

Company B

Capt.	(Stewart -- wounded 6/17)

1st Lt.	(Cook -- on detached duty)
2nd Lt.	Bowker
1st Sgt.	(Musgrave--promoted 2d Lieutenant Co. H 9/12/64)
2nd Sgt.	(D. Compton--sick)
3rd Sgt.	(Arnold -- sick)
4th Sgt.	(Osborn--sick?)
5th Sgt.	(White--sick)

Company C

Capt.	(Prentiss -- sick)
1st Lt.	Force--promoted 9/1/64
2nd Lt.	(Finch -- promoted Quartermaster 8/8/64)
1st Sgt.	(Carr--sick/promoted 9/1/64)
2nd Sgt.	Pinch
3rd Sgt.	King
4th Sgt.	Price
5th Sgt.	Head--promoted 9/1/64

Company D

Capt.	(Bird -- wounded 6/17
1st Lt.	(Saxton -- killed 7/30)
2nd Lt.	Wisner -- returned from recruiting duty
1st Sgt.	(J. Spencer--7/30/64 POW)
2nd Sgt.	(Gregory--died from disease 9/6/64)
3rd Sgt.	(Crawford--7/30 POW)
4th Sgt.	(Andrews--7/30 POW)
5th Sgt.	Baillet--promoted 6/7

Company E

Capt.	(Ottenot -- sick)
1st Lt.	Lockwood--promoted 8/9/64
2nd Lt.	Vacant
1st Sgt.	Taylor
2nd Sgt.	Sandrock
3rd Sgt.	Provost
4th Sgt.	Hager
5th Sgt.	(Vacant?)

Company F

Capt.	(Farwell--killed 7/30)
1st Lt.	(Bradley--on detached duty)
2nd Lt.	(Holden -- promoted Captain Co. H on 9/10
1st Sgt.	(Norton--POW 7/30/64)
2nd Sgt.	(Durham--wounded 6/17/64)
3rd Sgt.	(Dunn--wounded 7/30/64)

| 4th Sgt. | (Hyatt--sick?) |
| 5th Sgt. | Loveless |

Company G

Capt.	(Day -- wounded 7/30/64)
1st Lt.	Hemstreet
2nd Lt.	(Messing -- on leave of absence)
1st Sgt.	McNeil
2nd Sgt.	Lewis
3rd Sgt.	(Messner--sick?)
4th Sgt.	Weston--RTD 8/28/64 --wounded 7/30/64
5th Sgt.	Thompson

Company H

Capt.	Holden -- since 9/10
1st Lt.	Culver -- since 9/13
2nd Lt.	Musgrave -- since 9/12
1st Sgt.	Ap Rees
2nd Sgt.	Tingue (?) or Shackelton (?)
3rd Sgt.	Perry (?)
4th Sgt.	Filmore (?) or Pouey (?)
5th Sgt.	Twitchell(?) to Thomas (?)

Company I

Capt.	Bowen -- since 9/12
1st Lt.	Marshall--since 9/13
2nd Lt.	Kinney--since 9/13
1st Sgt.	Blackmer
2nd Sgt.	Jennings
3rd Sgt.	Brown
4th Sgt.	King
5th Sgt.	McMaster

Company K

Capt.	(Van Benschoten -- sick)
1st Lt.	Hooper -- since 9/15
2nd Lt.	Foster -- since 9/15
1st Sgt.	Crocker
2nd Sgt.	McDonald
3rd Sgt.	Dean
4th Sgt.	Johnson
5th Sgt.	J. Vandemark

Burgess Mill
October 27-28, 1864

10 companies, approximately 375 men

Comments: Both Colonel Gregg and Lieutenant Colonel Doty were in the field and the 179th New York had had an additional month's training since the battle of Poplar Spring Church, but the Ninth Corps and the 179th New York saw only limited action.

Col.	Gregg
Lt. Col.	Doty
Major	Terrill

Company A

Capt.	(Vacant--Terrill promoted to Major)
1st Lt.	G. Carpenter
2nd Lt.	Farr
1st Sgt.	Compton
2nd Sgt.	(Rutan -- sick)
3rd Sgt.	(Carpenter--MIA 7/30/64)
4th Sgt.	Lamberson--promoted 7/1/64
5th Sgt.	Lewis Kellogg--promoted 7/1/64

Company B

Capt.	(Stewart--wounded 6/17)
1st Lt.	Lounsbury -- promoted 10/28
2nd Lt.	(Bowker--mortally wounded 9/30/64)
1st Sgt.	(Musgrave--promoted 2d Lieutenant Co. H 9/12/64)
2nd Sgt.	(D. Compton--sick?)
3rd Sgt.	(Arnold -- sick?)
4th Sgt.	(Osborn--sick)
5th Sgt.	(White--sick)

Company C

Capt.	(Prentiss -- sick)
1st Lt.	Force--promoted 9/1/64
2nd Lt.	
1st Sgt.	Carr--promoted 9/1/64
2nd Sgt.	King
3rd Sgt.	(Price--POW 9/30/64)
4th Sgt.	(Pinch reduced 10/2)
5th Sgt.	Head--promoted 10/24/64

Company D

Capt.	(Vacant-- Bird discharged 8/29/64)
1st Lt.	(Vacant--Saxton killed 7/30/64)
2nd Lt.	Wisner--returned from recruiting duty circa 9/21/64
1st Sgt.	(J. Spencer--7/30/64 POW)

2nd Sgt.	(Vacant--Gregory died 9/6/64)
3rd Sgt.	(Crawford--7/30 POW)
4th Sgt.	(Andrews--7/30 POW)
5th Sgt.	(Baillet--sick/promoted 6/7)

Company E

Capt.	(Ottenot --LOA/ promoted 8/17
1st Lt.	Lockwood--promoted 8/9/64
2nd Lt.	(Vacant)
1st Sgt.	Taylor
2nd Sgt.	Sandrock
3rd Sgt.	Provost
4th Sgt.	Hager
5th Sgt.	(Vacant)

Company F

Capt.	(Vacant--Farwell killed 7/30)
1st Lt.	(Bradley -- on detached duty)
2nd Lt.	(Vacant--Holden promoted to Captain Co. H)
1st Sgt.	(Norton--POW 7/30/64)
2nd Sgt.	(Durham--wounded 6/17/64)
3rd Sgt.	(Dunn--wounded 7/30/64)
4th Sgt.	(Hyatt--sick?)
5th Sgt.	Loveless

Company G

Capt.	(Day -- wounded 7/30/64)
1st Lt.	Hemstreet
2nd Lt.	Messing
1st Sgt.	McNeil
2nd Sgt.	(Lewis--wounded 9/30/64)
3rd Sgt.	(Messner--sick?)
4th Sgt.	Weston
5th Sgt.	Thompson

Company H

Capt.	Holden -- since 9/10
1st Lt.	Culver -- since 9/13/64
2nd Lt.	Musgrave -- since 9/12/64
1st Sgt.	Ap Rees
2nd Sgt.	Tingue (?)
3rd Sgt.	Shackelton (?)
4th Sgt.	Filmore
5th Sgt.	Thomas

Company I

Capt.	Bowen -- since 9/12
1st Lt.	Marshall--since 9/13
2nd Lt.	Kinney--since 9/13
1st Sgt.	Blackmer
2nd Sgt.	Jennings
3rd Sgt.	Brown
4th Sgt.	King
5th Sgt.	McMaster

Company K

Capt.	Van Benschoten--RTD 10/19/64/sick?
1st Lt.	Hooper -- since 9/15
2nd Lt.	Foster -- since 9/15
1st Sgt.	Crocker
2nd Sgt.	(McDonald--POW 9/30/64)
3rd Sgt.	Dean
4th Sgt.	Johnson
5th Sgt.	J. Vandemark

Petersburg
April 2, 1865

Strength: 10 companies, approximately 460 men

Comments: The 179th was at its maximum combat effectiveness for this battle. It reached its maximum number of available soldiers; the fall and winter had provided time for increased training; and most of its officers, non-commissioned officers and enlisted men had had at least some combat experience. Colonels Gregg and Doty were wounded early on in the battle, as were Captains Pierson and Holden, but Capt. Bowen as the senior Captain remaining (Major Terrill was on leave) was able to assume command effectively despite his lack of combat experience.

Col. Gregg
Lt. Col. Doty
Major Terrill -- on leave

Company A

Capt.	Carpenter--promoted 12/23/64
1st Lt.	(Farr -- promoted 12/23/64 -- on leave of absence?)
2nd Lt.	Compton -- promoted 12/23/64
1st Sgt.	Lamberson--promoted 1/1/65
2nd Sgt.	(A. Beebe--promoted 11/1/64: reduced?)
3rd Sgt.	Thorn--promoted 1/1
4th Sgt.	Mills--promoted 1/1
5th Sgt.	Cortright--promoted 1/1

Company B

Capt.	(Vacant-- Stewart discharged 1/7/65/not replaced)
1st Lt.	Lounsbury -- promoted 10/28
2nd Lt.	Bogart -- promoted 12/12/64: sick?
1st Sgt.	D. Compton--promoted 1/1/65
2nd Sgt.	Osborn--RTD 2/23/65
3rd Sgt.	Arnold
4th Sgt.	Morris--promoted 11/2/64
5th Sgt.	Burke--promoted 1/1/65

Company C

Capt.	Force -- promoted 12/22
1st Lt.	M. Doty -- promoted 1/16
2nd Lt.	Smith -- promoted 3/1
1st Sgt.	Carr--promoted 9/1/64
2nd Sgt.	Price
3rd Sgt.	King
4th Sgt.	Head
5th Sgt.	Gallett--promoted 11/15/64

Company D

Capt.	Pierson -- promoted 1/12/65
1st Lt.	Andrews -- promoted 3/25/65
2nd Lt.	Mapes -- promoted 1/1/65
1st Sgt.	Crawford--paroled 2/11/65 from 7/30/64 POW
2nd Sgt.	Baillet--promoted 6/2/64
3rd Sgt.	Hurlburt--promoted11/2/64
4th Sgt.	English--promoted 2/2/65
5th Sgt.	(Vacant?--Andrews dropped 1/1/65: 7/30/64 POW)

Company E

Capt.	(Vacant--Ottenot resigned March 16)
1st Lt.	(Lockwood -- under arrest?)
2nd Lt.	Bogart
1st Sgt.	Provost--prom. 11/2/64
2nd Sgt.	Taylor (?)
3rd Sgt.	Sandrock(?)
4th Sgt.	Hager--promoted 7/26/64
5th Sgt.	Hogan--promoted 11/2/64

Company F

Capt.	Griswold -- since December 25 -- sick?
1st Lt.	Bradley -- on detached duty?
2nd Lt.	(Vacant--Holden promoted to Captain Co. H)
1st Sgt.	(Norton--POW 7/30/64)

2nd Sgt.	(Durham--wounded 6/17)
3rd Sgt.	(Dunn--wounded 7/30/64)
4th Sgt.	Loveless
5th Sgt.	Larzelere--promoted 2/2/65

Company G

Capt.	Messing -- promoted 3/22/65
1st Lt.	(Hemstreet -- sick)
2nd Lt.	Vacant
1st Sgt.	Lewis--prom. 1/26/65
2nd Sgt.	Messner
3rd Sgt.	Weston
4th Sgt.	Thompson--RTD 3/10/65
5th Sgt.	Wilbur--promoted 1/1/65

Company H

Capt.	Holden
1st Lt.	Culver
2nd Lt.	Musgrave
1st Sgt.	Ap Rees
2nd Sgt.	Casey
3rd Sgt.	
4th Sgt.	Thomas
5th Sgt.	Flint

Company I

Capt.	Bowen
1st Lt.	Marshall
2nd Lt.	Blackmer -- promoted 2/1
1st Sgt.	Jennings--promoted 2/1
2nd Sgt.	Brown
3rd Sgt.	King
4th Sgt.	McMaster
5th Sgt.	Landon--promoted 3/25/65

Company I

Capt.	Bowen -- since 9/12
1st Lt.	Marshall--since 9/13
2nd Lt.	Blackmer -- promoted 2/1/65
1st Sgt.	Jennings--promoted 2/1/65
2nd Sgt.	Brown
3rd Sgt.	King
4th Sgt.	McMaster
5th Sgt.	Landon--promoted 3/25/65

Company K

Capt.	(Van Benschoten -- sick)
1st Lt.	Hooper
2nd Lt.	Foster
1st Sgt.	Crocker
2nd Sgt.	(McDonald POW 9/30)
3rd Sgt.	Dean
4th Sgt.	Johnson
5th Sgt.	(J. Vandemark--reduced 1/65)

APPENDIX FIVE

1864 Election Results

Electoral Vote and Popular Vote (%)
234 Total Electoral Votes ==> 118 needed to win

State	Statehood	Lincoln	Percent	Raw Vote Delta	McClellan	Percent
CA	1850	5	59	..	..	..
CT	1788	6	51	2,400	..	..
DE	1787	..	..	..	3	52
IL	1818	16	54	30,800	..	..
IN	1816	13	54	20,200	..	..
IA	1846	8	64	..	..	..
KS	1861	3	79	..	..	..
KY	1792	..	..	..	11	70
ME	1820	7	59	..	..	..
MD	1788	7	55	..	..	..
MA	1788	12	72	..	..	..
MI	1837	8	54	10,600	..	..
MN	1858	4	59	..	..	..
MO	1821	11	70	..	..	..
NV	1864	2	60	..	..	..
NH	1788	5	53	3,600	..	..
NJ	1787	..	..	..	7	53
NY	1788	33	50.5	6,800	..	..
OH	1803	21	56	..	..	..
OR	1859	3	54	1,400	..	..
PA	1787	26	52	20,100	..	..
RI	1790	4	62	..	..	..
VT	1791	5	76	..	..	..
WV	1863	5	68	..	..	..
WI	1848	8	56	..	..	..
Total	..	212	55	..	21	45

NOTE: 1 Nevada elector did not vote.

The total electoral vote for Lincoln and the National Union Party (Republicans, War Democrats and Border Unionists), where the state raw vote was 55% or more, is 102. Four states gave Lincoln/Johnson 54% of the raw vote. Oregon, where the 1400 decisive popular votes easily could have swung to the Democrats, had 4 electoral votes. One would be hard-pressed to think the other three, Michigan (8), Indiana (13) and Illinois (16), would have abandoned Lincoln. All three states had a large enough popular vote that it is unlikely the margins of 11000, 20000 and 31000, respectively, would have swung completely to the Democrats.

Giving all the rest (New York, Pennsylvania, Connecticut and New Hampshire) to the Democrats leaves McClellan still a bit short.

Looking at a map of the outcome, it's hard to visualize a concentration of Democrat victories which would sweep Michigan, Indiana and Illinois:

[Map: Presidential Election 1864]

APPENDIX SIX

Newton Spencer's War Poetry

May 29, 1869
Yates County Chronicle, June 3, 1869

Nature's most placid calm is here:
Here, too, her bloom is spread,
To symbolize how well she loves
Out mourned and honored dead.
Her May flowers bright and grasses grow
Profusely all around,
To teach that she smiles as well
As grieves, beside each mound–
To show that with her tears she blends,
In her most kindly way,
Consoling promise that those gone
Shall outlast all decay,
And not alone in memory live–
But in some coming time,
Emerge from mouldering cerements
To an immortal clime.
Comrades and friends! to consecrate
This day of May we meet:
And the service that we render here
is one both sad and sweet:
For the love we bore the Flag was theirs
Whose last, damp and earthy bed
Is this green hillside–making it
"The Bivouac of the Dead!"
Our dead and yours–our friends and yours–
Loved ones who, yesterday
(So seems the time,) in yonder town
Pursued life's busy way;
Dear ones, whose eyes looked into yours
With soul-lit glances then;
And voices which here cannot thrill
Your hearts with love again;
Familiar faces, pleasantly
Speaking in smiles to you;
And manly forms, erect and strong,
Ready to "dare and do."

These were part of the sacrifice
Upon the altar laid,
In the Nation's dire extremity,
When Treason drew its blade;
And hearts with anguish keen were wrung
When each dread message came,
And in the fearful lists stood out
A fated dear one's name—
Sealed unto death amid the strife's
Terrific crash and roar,
And dying that the Freeman's Flag
Might float forevermore.
Here rests lamented Colonel Lee—
As true as tempered steel—
Who through the conflict faithfully
Strove for his country's weal,
Here lies the brave, intrepid Sloan—
At Petersburg shot down:
Charging the foe he died, and won
The patriot-martyr's crown.
And on the scroll of honed ones
We find sepulchred here
Are other names of those who held
Their country's honor dear—
Aye! dearer far than God's great gifts
Of health and precious life—
Who went forth at the call to arms,
Nor shrank from toil and strife:—
Brown, Hunter, Riker and the young
Lieutenant Lewis, – Gray,
The Pierces two, Murdock and Holmes,
Olmstead, Ingles, Lay,
Clark, Biglow, Oliver, Macacy,
And one whose heart did tend
Toward the wounded and the weak—
Alcock, the soldiers friend.
Upon their graves, in tenderness,
We floral tributes lay—
But no memorial act, howe'er
Heartfelt, can fully say
How much we feel—how much we owe
The brave men who could give
Their all, that Nationality
In this great land may live.
All of our patriotic dead

Lie not among these mounds,
For many sleep within the soil
Of distant battle-grounds.
In conflicts desperate and hot
Some comrades fell and died,
And strangers gave rude burial
The rebel foe beside.
Farwell and Brown, Bell, Wolcott, Beach,
And others, sleep to-day
Where, Southward, armed battalion fought
In fierce and bloody fray.
But Memory reaches out to them,
As unto others here
Guarding their fame with solemn trust,
And holds them ever dear.
In all our annals glorified,
Illustriously bright,
Their laurel wreathes shall never fade
In blank Oblivion's night;
But while Our Banner's stars remain
The symbols of our power,
The fruitage of their daring deeds
Will richer grow, each hour.
In future storm, or while our Peace
Glows golden as the son,
As sacred as the "Heart of Bruce,"
We'll keep what they have won!

The poem delivered by Spencer on Decoration Day in 1878 was printed in the June 6, 1878 edition of the *Yates County Chronicle*.

APPENDIX SEVEN

James C. Rutan's Pension Application

In July 1879, when he was just shy of forty-one-years-old, James C. Rutan wrote a letter to the U.S. Pension Commissioner inquiring: "if I have a sufficient ground for application for Pension. Please inform me and send me the necessary blanks to prosecute my claim. Also if I am entitled to any further Bounty." [1] He enclosed a three page affidavit recounting his work as a cabinet-maker before the war, his military service from enlistment to discharge and his medical treatment during and after the war. [2]

The Pension Bureau sent Rutan "Form A," and on September 18, 1879, he filed a "Declaration for Original Invalid Pension."[3] Rutan stated in his declaration that he:

> was crushed in the rifle Pitts in a charge on the rebel fort after it was blown out and on that occasion received a "sun stroke", ever since which time he has been severely effected with Chronic Diareah and kidney and liver complaint caused thereby. [4]

He did not mention his shell wound received at the Battle of the Crater in either the declaration or the affidavit, perhaps because it had healed long before he was discharged from the service.

Rutan appointed A. B. Gallatian of Elmira as his "true and lawful attorney to prosecute his claim." [5] Galatian had been a recruiting agent during the Civil War. [6] Galatian's fee is not stated, but by law $25 was the maximum permitted and the fee was not payable until after a pension certificate had been issued. [7]

The Pension Bureau requested the Adjutant General's Office to provide Rutan's service history and the Surgeon General's Office to provide his medical history. The dates that the Pension Bureau made those requests are unknown. The Adjutant General's Office replied on March 23, 1881 and the Surgeon General's Office on April 9, 1881. [8] At that point, Rutan's application had been pending for a year and a half.

The report by the Surgeon General's Office stated that:

> James C. Rutan, Sergt, Co A 179 N.Y. Vols was admitted to Depot Field Hosp. 9 A.C. City Point Va Aug 2, 1864, diagnosis, bruised, no disposition Stated that he entered St Mary's G.H. Rochester N.Y. Aug 10, 64 with chronic hepatitis, and was returned to duty Feb 14, 1865, that he entered G.H. Ladies Home Hospital N.Y. City Feb 18, 1865, with pneumonia, and was transferred April 4'65, and that he entered G.H. Elmira N.Y. April 5 '65, with contusion right kidney from wagon wheel, received July 30, 64, and was discharged from service May 18,65. No further record found. There are no records of the Regiment on file. [9]

Rutan had first suffered from diarrhea in June 1864 as the 179th New York left Alexandria for the front. Because he had not been hospitalized at that time and because there were no regimental records on file, there was no documentation on diarrhea.

Rutan was examined by a board of three surgeons in Elmira on June 15, 1881. One of the three was H. C. Chubbuck, who had examined Rutan when he enlisted in 1864. [10] In September 1880, Rutan had moved to Wellsboro, Pennsylvania, the home town of U. S. Senator

Jonathan Mitchell. On January 14, 1882, Mitchell requested the Pension Office to give Rutan's application "special attention … as early as possible". [11] Mitchell also enclosed an affidavit from Rutan's personal physician, Dr. Mary Baldwin. Baldwin stated that Rutan had been under her treatment since December 1881 and that Rutan "has been utterly unable to perform any labor." [12]

The Pension Bureau advised Senator Mitchell that Rutan should submit more information on his medical condition before his enlistment and after his discharge. [13]

Apparently in response to the Pension Bureau's advice to Senator Mitchell, Rutan stated in a new affidavit that he had been in good health until June 1, 1864 when he was "attacked with a severe case of Chronic Diahrea at Alexandria, Virginia." [14]

James A. Christie, an attorney in Horseheads, stated in a July 25, 1882 affidavit that he had known Rutan for twenty–five years and that Rutan "was a sound healthy and vigorous man" when he enlisted in the 179th New York Volunteers based on Christie's observations of Rutan while Rutan was working for Gardner & Compton as a cabinet-maker. [15] Rutan also submitted affidavits from Stephen Compton and Harry Gardner to attest to his good health before enlisting. [16]

Rutan's family physician before the war, Dr. Orlando Groom, recalled treating Rutan only once before his enlistment – for "some slight bowel difficulty." After the war, he treated Rutan for "Rheumatic" in July 1865. Groom noted that Rutan had moved away from Horseheads in 1866 and that he had not treated Rutan again until April 1882. Since then, Groom had treated Rutan for a "severe form of rheumatic neuralgia." Groom attested that Rutan had been unable to perform any manual labor "but has been about on crutches part of the time." [17]

Rutan also submitted an affidavit from former Private William Wines of Company A who had carried him to an ambulance after he had been wounded at the Battle of the Crater. [18]

The Pension Bureau apparently required supporting affidavits from regimental officers. Rutan explained that affidavits "cannot be procured from officers of my regiment" because at the time of the Battle of the Crater "nearly all of my officers were detailed to Cumberland Heights and that at the time of the affidavit "my Captain, Lieutenant Colonel and major are all dead." [19] By 1882, Col. Gregg, Lt. Col Doty, Majors Sloan and Barton, and Captain Terrill in fact were all dead. [20] Company A's First Lieut. George Carpenter and Second Lieut. James Farr were still living, but they had both been sick in the hospital at the time of the Battle of the Crater. [21] Rutan did subsequently submit affidavits from the Regimental Surgeon, Lt. Col. Joseph Robinson and Company A's Lieutenant James Farr. [22]

On October 13, 1882, the Pension Bureau requested the Adjutant General's Office to confirm the presence or absence of Stephen Compton and William Wines on July 30, 1864. [23] The Adjutant General's Office responded three months later that the Company A muster roll for July and August 1864 reported them both to be "absent sick." [24]

The Pension Bureau also asked the Horseheads postmaster for information "as to general reputation for truth and standing in the community" of Christie, Compton and Dr. Groom as well as Dr. Groom's professional standing. [25] The postmaster, L.L. Curtis, promptly responded that the affiants "are all Gentlemen of good standing in this community – their reputation is unquestionable – Doct. Groom stands well in his profession." [26] The postmaster's role in vouching for the honesty of his fellow citizens is an interesting one. There is no reason to doubt the integrity of Messrs. Christie, Compton and Groom, but postmasters in general may well have had conflicting loyalties between their federal employer in Washington and their acquaintances at home.

Rutan was examined again by the same board of three government surgeons in Elmira on October 18, 1882. They concluded that he was entitled to $2 for sunstroke; $2 for liver; $2 for kidney; $4 for chronic diarrhea; $6 for rheumatism; and $2 for the shell wound for a total of $18 per month. [27] However, no pension certificate was issued at that time.

On January 29, 1883, the Adjutant General's Office again confirmed Rutan's service dates. The Ninth Corps' list of casualties confirmed the shell wound in the right side, but the Adjutant General's Office found no record of sunstroke. [28]

In February 1883, Senator Mitchell again inquired about Rutan's case (although Rutan apparently had moved back to New York) and the Pension Bureau again identified more information that Rutan needed to provide, including medical testimony from the doctors who had treated him in Minnesota, where he had lived from 1866 to 1869. [29] Rutan subsequently submitted an "Inability Affidavit" saying that he could not remember their names. [30]

In a March 7, 1883 affidavit, Company A's Sergeant Edwin Lamberson stated that that he saw Rutan every day and that Rutan was stricken with diarrhea in June 1864 and was wounded and suffered sunstroke at the Battle of the Crater. [31] William Wines submitted a second affidavit, but it is not apparent why this was necessary. [32]

Rutan also submitted a September 8, 1883 affidavit from Joel M. Jansen, who was married to a younger sister of Rutan's wife. Jansen apparently had helped care for Rutan in 1865 and 1866. Jansen stated that he "distinctly remember[ed] nursing and caring for him while he was sick on several different occasions during the years 1865 and 1866; and that his disease was chronic diarrhea and disease of the liver and kidneys." Jansen represented that "I have no interest directly or indirectly in the claim for a pension of said James C. Rutan" and did not disclose his relationship to Rutan through marriage. [33]

The Pension Bureau misread the affidavit, assuming that Jansen had served with Rutan in the 179th, and requested the usual confirmation of Jansen's service dates from the Adjutant General's Office. [34] Not surprisingly, the Adjutant General reported no record of service for Jansen. [35] There is no indication in the file whether the Pension Bureau thought that this was a fraudulent affidavit or simply realized their mistake.

In February 1884, Stephen Compton provided another affidavit, but it is not apparent that it filled a gap. [36] Company A's Lieut. James E. Farr, who lived in nearby Big Flats, also submitted an affidavit. Farr had know Rutan before the war and stated that Rutan was sound and healthy at the time of enlistment. He also confirmed Rutan's attack of diarrhea in June 1864. [37] Joseph W. Robinson, the 179th's regimental surgeon, confirmed that he had treated Rutan for acute diarrhea which became chronic in June 1864. Robinson also recalled that Rutan had been injured at the Battle of the Crater, "said injury consisted of a bruised condition of the muscles of the back and [illegible] of the spine." Robinson examined Rutan on February 20, 1884 and concluded that we was "prematurely broken down and destroyed and … totally disabled from [illegible] his subsistence by manual labor." [38]

Even the service dates of the Regimental Surgeon – a lieutenant colonel – had to be confirmed, and the Pension Bureau sent the standard request on Robinson to the War Department. The War Department confirmed his service dates. [39]

On March 24, 1884, Senator Mitchell again called up Rutan's case, even though Rutan had moved back to New York. By 1884, political intervention apparently happened often enough that the Pension Office had a special form for handling it. [40] The Pension Bureau apparently advised Senator Mitchell that Rutan needed to submit better evidence of "continuance." [41] However, as will be seen, the "call up" by Sen. Mitchell may have given the bureaucratic wheels a little push.

In April 1884, James M. Ormiston, of Horseheads and David W. Budd, of Elmira, submitted a joint affidavit stating that they had known Rutan since he was a boy and that they had observed immediately after Rutan's discharge that he "was entirely altered in appearance from the time [illegible] he enlisted, being broken down in health." [42] Ormiston and Budd stated that they had no interest in the case. They did not disclose that Ormiston was married to a sister of Rutan's wife and Budd's brother Joshua was married to Rutan's sister Mary.

The Pension Bureau received this affidavit on April 24, 1884, but in the meantime, Rutan's application was finally starting to move toward approval. His claim was submitted for "admission" on April 8, 1884; passed "legal review" on May 17, 1884; and passed "medical review" on May 22, 1884. A certificate awarding a pension of $2 per month effective May 24, 1865 for "shell wound of right hip" was issued on May 26, 1884 and mailed on June 2, 1884. [43] The retroactive award amounted to roughly $450.

The $450 was undoubtedly welcome, but Rutan probably also was disappointed not to have received any award for his other injuries and illnesses beyond the shell wound. The file does not indicate how it was initiated, but a review of the claim was undertaken. The claim was again submitted for "admission" on July 23, 1884. [44]

On October 13, 1884, a medical referee in the Pension Bureau requested a medical examination of Rutan, specifying in detail the various conditions that were to be examined "with special reference." [45] There is no record of the medical examination in the file.

While the rigor and duration of the Pension Bureau's review of Rutan's claim may have suggested a lack of sympathy, in fact the Pension Bureau proved generous in the end. The Chief of the Board of Review ordered that the certificate be reissued to correct the omission of the other disabilities. [46] On December 11, 1884, Rutan's certificate was reissued to increase his pension to $8 a month retroactive to May 24, 1865 and to $12 a month effective October 22, 1884. [47] The retroactive payment of an additional $6 per month for 233 months amounted to nearly $1400. Combined with the $450 received six months earlier, the total was nearly $2000 – quite a sum in that day. The process had taken more than four years.

Rutan filed for an increase three years later on June 27, 1887. He was again represented by A.B. Galatian. He stated that the disabilities for which he had already been pensioned had increased to the extent that he was "totally incapacitated from any kind of manual labor." [48] He was examined by a medical board on October 12, 1887 and his pension was increased to $16 per month effective that date. [49]

On June 11, 1890, Rutan filed again for an increase. His justification was an:

increase of the disabilities already pensioned – the injury to his hip and spine having progressed to the extent that he is unable to walk or use his limbs except with great difficulty and in a very limited degree – and resulting in a tumour or abcess under, and [?] the main artery and cord of right arm from use of crutches. [50]

Dr. E. Howe Davis submitted an affidavit describing Rutan's health problems since the beginning of the year, concluding that: "his condition is still precarious with no probability that he ever will be able to do but little manual labor." Nonetheless, the request for an increase was denied. [51]

Sometime during 1891, Rutan–then fifty-three-years-old–and family moved to Wilmington, Delaware. Rutan is listed in the 1891 and 1892 Wilmington directories as a carpenter working for the Pullman Palace Car Company. [52]

On November 2, 1897, Rutan filed again for an increase in his pension. He stated that: "he is entirely disabled for all manual labor and as a matter of fact does no labor and can do no labor of any kind." He requested a physical. [53] He was given a physical on October 26, 1898, but his application was denied on December 11, 1899. [54]

In the 1900 federal census, Rutan reported that he was a carpenter, but had been unemployed for four months. The census does not indicate whether his unemployment was caused by medical problems. He apparently stopped working shortly thereafter. [55]

Rutan filed his last declaration for an increase on May 4, 1905, when he was sixty-seven, but it was rejected on November 16, 1905. [56] The last line of the Surgeon's Certificate from his August 17, 1905 physical examination stated "No evidence of venereal disease or vicious habits." [57] The standards had been liberalized in 1890 unless the disability was caused by "vicious habits." [58]

Rutan died in 1911 at the age of seventy-two.

NOTES

Abbreviated Citations

I have used abbreviated citations in the Notes for a number of frequently cited primary sources. Full citation information is provided here. For frequently cited secondary sources, the full citation is provided at the beginning of the notes for each chapter.

Official Records of the War of the Rebellion

I accessed the "OR" on the Cornell University Library "Making of America" website – ebooks. library.cornell.edu/m/moawar/waro.html.

All citations are to Series I unless otherwise noted. The citation to page 110 in Part I of Volume XL of Series I would be: OR (40): 1, 110.

National Archives and Records Administration

The location for all cited records is Washington, D.C., except for the Provost Marshal records which are in the New York City Branch of the National Archives. (The Quartermaster records were in the New York Branch when I reviewed them, but they apparently have been moved.)

(1) Book Records of Volunteer Union Organizations, 179th New York Volunteers, Record Group 94, Records of the Adjutant General's Office, 1780's-1917 (Cited as "Regimental Books").

Vol. 1: Descriptive Book, Companies A-K

Vol. 2: Regimental Consolidated Monthly Report and Order Book

Vol. 3: Order Book, Companies A-K

Vol. 4: Morning Reports, Companies A-K

(2) Muster Rolls, Returns, Regimental Papers, Volunteer Organizations, Civil War, New York, 179th New York Volunteers, Record Group 94, Records of the Adjutant General's Office, 1780's-1917 Box Nos. 3407, 3408 and 3409 (Cited by Box Number).

(3) Compiled Military Service Records, 179th New York Volunteers, Records of the Adjutant General's Office, Record Group 94.12.2 (Cited as "CMSR").

(4) Pension Files, Record Group 15 (Cited by the soldier's name. The file numbers for requesting a soldier's file from the National Archives may be found in the Civil War and Later Veterans Pension Index on fold3.com.)

(5) Carded Medical Records, 179th New York Volunteers , Record Group 94, Records of the Adjutant General's Office, 1780's-1917, entry 534 (Cited as "CMR").

(6) Court Martial Transcripts, RG 153, Records of the Judge Advocate General (Army), Court Martial Case Files, 1809-1894 (The reference number is provided).

(7) Provost Marshal Records (Record Group 94) (the Entry Number is provided)

(8) Quartermaster Records (Record Group 110)(the Entry number is provided)

Soldiers' Letters and Diaries

I have quoted the soldiers' letters and diaries as they wrote them, rather than attempting to correct their grammar, spelling and punctuation, to better reveal their personalities. I agree with the view expressed by Michael Adams in *Living Hell: the Dark Side of the Civil War.*

Because I want them to speak for themselves, I have neither corrected people's grammar nor interrupted their thoughts with that unpleasant expletive, *sic*, supposedly needed to flag linguistic errors. Instead I rely on the reader's common sense to grasp the intended meaning of writings through which our forebears sought to reveal what they experienced. (at ix)

The most frequently cited letters and diaries are from the following soldiers:

(1) John Andrews. Unless otherwise noted, the citation is to the John Tuttle & Arvilla Andrews Papers, Collection #3790, Carl A. Kroch Library, Division of Rare and Manuscript Collections, Cornell University. Andrews' War Journal is cited as "JAWJ."

(2) William Bird, Jr. The letters are in the collection of the Minnesota Historical Society, A/m. B618.

(3) Stephen Compton. Citation is to photocopies provided to me by Bruce Whitmarsh, Executive Director of the Chemung Valley Museum.

(4) William Lamont. The letters are in the collection of the Wisconsin Historical Society.

(5) William Larzelere. Citations are to transcriptions provided to me by Jeanne Larzelere Bloom.

(6) Daniel B. Lee. The letters are in the collection of the U.S. Military History Institute in Carlisle, Pennsylvania, CWMiscColl (Enlisted Man's letters, Jan. 10, 1863-Jan. 14, 1883).

For less frequently cited letters (typically from a pension file in the National Archives), the full citation information is provided in the note.

Newspapers (microfilm unless otherwise noted)

As opposed to soldiers' letters and diaries, I have used "[sic]" as appropriate when quoting newspapers on the assumption that they were generally edited before publication.

NOTES

Preface

———— *History of the 179th Regiment N.Y.S.V. – Rebellion of 1861-65*, E.D. Norton, Printer: Ithaca, New York (1900).

Andrews, John Tuttle and Arvilla Rapleee Andrews Papers, Collection No. 3790, Cornell University, Carl A. Kroch Library, Division of Rare and Manuscript Collections.

Baker, Charles B., "Personal War Sketch of Charles B. Baker," August 25, 1901, J. B. Sloan G.A.R. Post, Yates County Genealogical & Historical Society.

Brandt, Nat, *Mr. Tubbs' Civil War*, Syracuse University Press: Syracuse, New York (1996).

Catton, Bruce, *The Army of the Potomac: A Stillness at Appomattox*, Doubleday & Company: Garden City, New York (1953).

Dean Jr., Eric T., *Shook Over Hell: Post Traumatic Stress, Vietnam and the Civil War*, Harvard University Press: Cambridge (1997).

Dunkelman, Mark H., *Brothers One and All: Esprit de Corps in a Civil War Regiment*, Louisiana State University Press: Baton Rouge (2004).

Dunkelman, Mark H., *The Hardtack Regiment: An Illustrated History of the 154th Regiment, New York State Infantry Volunteers*, Associated University Presses, Inc.: East Brunswick, New Jersey (1981).

Faust, Drew Gilpin, *This Republic of Suffering: Death and the American Civil War*, Alfred A. Knopf: New York (2008).

Foner, Eric, *The Fiery Trial: Abraham Lincoln and American Slavery*, W.W. Norton & Company: New York (2010).

Hess, Earl J., *The Union Soldier in Battle: Enduring the Ordeal of Combat*, University Press of Kansas: Lawrence (1997).

Humphreys, Margaret, *Marrow of Tragedy: The Health Crisis of the American Civil War*, The Johns Hopkins University Press: Baltimore (2013).

Lonn, Ella, *Desertion During the Civil War*, University of North Carolina Press: Lincoln (1998 originally published 1928).

Marten, James, *Sing Not War: The Lives of Union & Confederate Veterans in Gilded Age America*, University of North Carolina Press: Chapel Hill (2011).

McPherson, James, *Battle Cry of Freedom: The Civil War Era*, Oxford University Press: Oxford (1988).

Miller, Richard F., *Harvard's Civil War: A History of the Twentieth Massachusetts Volunteer Infantry*, University Press of New England: Lebanon, New Hampshire (2005).

Moe, Richard, *The Last Full Measure: The Life and Death of the First Minnesota Volunteers*, Minnesota Historical Society Press: St. Paul (1993).

Newsome, Hampton, *Richmond Must Fall: The Richmond-Petersburg campaign, October 1864*, The Kent State University Press: Kent, Ohio (2013).

Phisterer, Frederick, *New York in the War of the Rebellion 1861 to 1865*, D.B. Lyon Company, State Printers: Albany, New York (Third Ed. 1912).

Ramold, Steven J., *Across the Divide: Union Soldiers View the Northern Home Front*, New York University Press: New York (2013).

Sommers, Richard, *Richmond Redeemed: The Siege at Petersburg*, Doubleday & Company, Inc.:

Garden City, New York (1981).

Wiley, Bell Irvin, *The Life of Billy Yank: The Common Soldier of the Union*, Louisiana State University Press: Baton Rouge (1952, 1971).

Wilkenson, Warren, *Mother, May You Never See the Sights I Have Seen: The Fifty-seventh Massachusetts Veteran Volunteers in the Last Year of the Civil War*, Harper & Row, Publishers: New York (1990).

Wolcott, Walter, *The Military History of Yates County, N.Y., Comprising a Record of the Services Rendered by Citizens of This County in the Army and Navy, from the Foundation of the Government to the Present Time*, Express Book and Job Printing House: Penn Yan, New York (1895).

Woodworth, Steven E., *While God Is Marching On: The Religious World of Civil War Soldiers*, University Press of Kansas: Lawrence (2001).

(1) *History of the 179th Regiment N.Y.S.V.* There is actually more information about the service of the 179th in the chapters devoted to individual units in some county military histories than in this regimental history. See, e.g. Wolcott, pages 105-113.

(2) See Lesley J. Gordon, *A Broken Regiment: The 16th Connecticut's Civil War*, Louisiana State University Press: Baton Rouge (2014), 2-3; James I. Robertson, Jr., "Introduction" in Robert Lester, *Civil War Unit Histories: Regimental Histories and Personal Narratives, Part 5, The Union– Higher and Independent Commands and Naval Forces*, University Publications of America: Bethesda, Maryland, v-xii; Michael P. Musick, "The Little Regiment: Civil War Units and Commands," *Prologue*, Vol. 27, No. 2 (Summer 1995), 2-3.

(3) Wilkenson; Moe; Miller. While strictly speaking not a regimental history, Mark Dunkelman's *Brothers One and All* is an exception and does cover many of these subjects in the context of regimental esprit de corps. Dunkelman, *Brothers*. Taken together, Dunkelman's five books about the 154th New York Volunteers provide an unmatched history of a regiment's service. Dunkelman has referred to his first book, *The Hardtack Regiment*, as "a straightforward regimental history, chronicling the 154th's camps, campaigns and battles." *Brothers*, 11. For more on Dunkelman, see Jenny Johnston, "Living History: Witness to the 154th," *The Civil War Monitor*, Vol. 4, No. 4 (Winter 2014), 16. Lesley Gordon states that her recent *A Broken Regiment: the 16th Connecticut's Civil War* is "not meant to be a traditional regimental history" and she covers many of these broader themes, notably the experience of Union prisoners of war. (Gordon, 3-4) Particularly interesting is her discussion of why after the war the men of the 16th Connecticut "chose to commemorate a different past than the one they experienced." (Gordon, 9)

(4) Faust; Dean; Woodworth.

(5) Wiley.

(6) Sommers, 282 & n.14. The quotation was "Let's [get] out of here!" and the soldier who uttered it at the battle of Poplar Spring Church was George Hemingway of Company B. Hemingway was captured and sent to Salisbury Prison. The event was recorded in a letter from his friend Company B's William Lamont to Lamont's sister. See Chapter 15, *infra*.

(7) The phrase "thinking bayonets" is taken from Foner, 208.

(8) Andrews Papers. Andrews kept many of the letters that he received from his family and friends. This is a rare additional resource because the exigencies of war often militated against preservation of the letters that soldiers received in the field. (Ramold, 26; Woodworth, x) Selections from Andrews' diary and correspondence are included in Brandt's *Mr. Tubbs' Civil War*. Tubbs, a college friend of Andrews, did not serve during the war. He completed his education – college followed by law school. However, he corresponded with quite a few friends who did serve, including Andrews, whom he had met at Alfred University.

(9) Catton, 30.

(10) Marten, 260.

(11) *Ibid.*, 206-207. The bias against the "high bounty" men may even be implicit in the

preparation of the regimental history of the 179th New York Volunteers itself, which was basically just a list of names, published in 1900. Each of the original seven companies was comprised of approximately eighty men who signed up for three years and received local, state and federal bounties totaling around $700. In the fall of 1864, each of these companies received twenty to thirty new recruits who had enlisted for only one year, but received bounties in excess of $1000. For Companies A, C, D, E, F and G, the Regimental History lists the names of only the original complement. The new "Recruits" – the "higher bounty" men – are listed only for Company B. The brief descriptions for these companies, including the description for Company B, emphasize that there were comprised of "three years' men". Companies H, I and K (there was no J) were recruited in the fall of 1864 and the Regimental History refers to their recruits as "one year men." (Regimental History, passim) The compilation of names published by the New York State Adjutant General after the war was based on the "muster-in" rolls of the individual companies, which had the same effect of excluding the later recruits. *A Record*, Vol. VI at 107-127.

(12) Lonn, 138. See also Shannon, Vol. II, 49.

(13) McPherson, 606. Hampton Newsome recently wrote that: "[T]he arrival of replacement troops of an indifferent quality had dramatically altered the army [of the Potomac]'s three infantry corps. As a result, the reliability of troops eroded noticeably. In engagements throughout the summer, Union forces reeled back under pressure they might have withstood earlier in the year." (Newsome, 20) (footnote omitted). However, the veterans themselves were not the same soldiers in 1864 that they had earlier been. Newsome himself recognized that "costly assaults" against Confederate fortifications "fostered a heightened sense of caution in the commanders and the soldiers. The [Overland] campaign taught regimental officers that veteran troops would not press their attacks against well-manned field works." (*Ibid.*, 7) Earl Hess stated that: "The Northern war effort was carried by the core of highly motivated men who had enlisted in 1861 and 1862, not by those questionable patriots who were brought in to the army from 1863 through 1865. ..." (Hess, *The Union Soldier in Battle*, 91) Hess is correct in his focus on the absolute necessity of the contribution by the veterans of 1861 and 1862. Even in the 179th New York those veterans provided the leadership the recruits of 1864 needed. However, the Army of the Potomac desperately needed reinforcement in the spring of 1864, see for example Newsome, 6, and the phrase "questionable patriots" distracts attention from the importance of the contribution the new recruits made.

(14) Catton, 30-31.

(15) Company F's Charles Baker did try to establish the 179th's own honorific status. Forty years after the war, Baker recalled that the brigade to which the 179th was assigned "was engaged in so many different charges on the Petersburg front that they were called the 'Charging Brigade'." However, the 179th's brigade assignment changed several times and I have found no corroboration of the nickname. (Personal War Sketch, August 25, 1901, G.A.R. Post No. 93, Yates County History Center)

(16) Phisterer, 4029. The percentages were calculated based on my estimates of the number of soldiers engaged in each battle.

(17) Humphreys, 2. See also Michael C.C. Adams, *Living Hell: The Dark Side of the Civil War*, Johns Hopkins University Press: Baltimore (2014), passim.

Chapter One

Ambrose, Stephen, *Citizen-Soldiers: The U.S. Army from the Normandy Beaches to the Bulge to the Surrender of Germany, June 7, 1944-May 7, 1945*, Simon & Schuster: New York (1997).

Foner, Eric, *The Fiery Trial: Abraham Lincoln and American Slavery*, W.W. Norton & Company: New

York (2010).

Gallagher, Gary W., *The Union War*, Harvard University Press: Cambridge, Massachusetts (2011).

Goodwin, Doris Kearns, *Team of Rivals: The Political Genius of Abraham Lincoln*, Simon & Schuster: New York (2005).

Graham, Robert H., *Yates County's Boys in Blue, 1861-1865: Who They Were – What They Did*, [self-published]: Penn Yan, New York (1926).

Grant, Ulysses S., *Personal Memoirs of U.S. Grant*, Charles L. Webster & Company: New York (1886).

Marten, James, *Sing Not War: The Lives of Union & Confederate Veterans in Gilded Age America*, University of North Carolina Press: Chapel Hill (2011).

McPherson, James, *Battle Cry of Freedom: The Civil War Era*, Oxford University Press: Oxford (1988).

Meier, Michael, T., "Civil War Draft Records: Exemptions and Enrollments", *Prologue*, Winter 1994, Vol. 26 No. 4.

Murdock, Eugene C., "New York's Civil War Bounty Brokers", *The Journal of American History*, Vol. 53, No. 2 (Sept. 1966).

Rappaport, Armin, "The Replacement System During the Civil War," *Military Affairs*, Vol. 15, No. 2 (Summer 1951).

Shannon, Fred A., *The Organization and Administration of the Union army 1861-1865*, The Arthur H. Clark Company: Cleveland (1928).

(1) Gallagher, 27. See also pp. 3, 69, 124, 159; Marten, 22.

(2) The Americans who defended our nation during the war and shaped its character thereafter have been canonized by Tom Brokaw as "America's Greatest Generation." Stephen Ambrose's history of the American army in the European theater is aptly titled.

(3) The phrase "thinking bayonets" comes from Foner, 208.

(4) Grant, Vol. II, 531.

(5) McPherson, 313.

(6) Rappaport, 95.

(7) OR, III(4): 1264. Table with column heading "Call of May 3, 1861 (confirmed by act approved Aug. 6, 1861) and under acts approved July 22 and 25, 1861, for 500,000 men." The table continues for another five pages before summing up to a "Grand aggregate Total" of 2,778,304 men.

(8) McPherson, 600.

(9) *Ibid.*, 430-432, 600-601.

(10) *Ibid.*, 492-93.

(11) Meier, 1.

(12) *Ibid.*

(13) *Havana Journal*, August 16, 1862. The *Journal* expected that localities would want to avoid the "disgrace" of a draft.

(14) *The Hornellsville Tribune*, February 25, 1864.

(15) *Watkins Express*, February 4, 1864 (emphasis in original).

(16) *Dunkirk Journal*, February 5, 1864.

(17) *Ontario County Times*, August 31, 1864. See also *Elmira Daily Advertiser*, July 21, 1864.

(18) *Ontario County Times*, September 14, 1864; *Penn Yan Democrat*, December 4, 1863.

(19) *Yates County Chronicle*, January 7, 1864.

(20) *The Hornellsville Tribune*, December 31, 1863; *Yates County Chronicle*, February 18, 1864.

(21) JAWJ, November 1, 1864.

(22) Shannon, Vol. II, 49-50, 54; See also Starr, 12-13.

(23) *Penn Yan Democrat*, February 26, 1864.

(24) 1865 New York State Census, Chemung County, Elmira, Schedule X, Miscellaneous Statistics. The labor market in upstate New York was hardly uniform. Wages varied from town to town. In Buffalo, the summer farm wage reached $40 per month in 1865. Third District of the Fifth Ward)

(25) See Chapter 5, "Bounty Jumpers".

(26) JAWJ, November 1, 1864.

(27) Letter from A. S. Diven to George Palmer dated January 30, 1864, RG110, Entry 2307, Box 42; Letter from Mary Braithwait to A. S. Diven dated May 19, 1864, RG110, Entry 2023, Box 30. See also Letter from Thomas McElheny to A. S. Diven dated February 22, 1864. (*Ibid.*) McElheny complained that the paymaster in Elmira "had bought in your county bonds at $285 or $15 less than face. This however might not be considered illegitimate as between *sharpers*, but it is *mean* when practiced upon soldiers." (emphasis in original)

(28) Murdock, 261. The town of Cattin gave the firm of Mefors, Cowan, Smith, Haight and McWilliams an exclusive contract and informed the local provost marshal that "we will not hold ourselves responsible to pay any Volunteer any Local Bounty unless they are enlisted through" that office. Letter from Milo P. King to Samuel Harmon (undated circa 1864), RG110, Entry 2222, Box 40.

(29) *Watkins Express*, February 10, 1864.

(30) *Ontario County Times*, August 31, 1864.

(31) *Elmira Weekly Gazette*, March 10, 1864.

(32) Carded Military Service Records, 179th New York Volunteers, *passim*.

(33) *Ontario County Times*, February 3, 1864.

(34) *Buffalo Morning Express*, April 22, 1864. The full quote is the following: "Our afternoon contemporary is considerably exercised because so few of the men enlisted here are credited to Erie county, and hopes the Bounty Committee or some one else will put a stop to what it terms the swindle being practiced on us. The reason why we do not receive the credit demanded, is, that we are not entitled to it. Other localities pay larger bounties and it is the undeniable right of every man to enlist wherever he pleases. But a trifling number of the men enlisted here are citizens of the county, most of them come from Canada, and volunteer for the purpose of making money. We cannot discover then wherein we are swindled in the matter, and should like to be informed what power anybody possesses to secure that for us which we do not buy. The only way to remedy the matter is to pay a higher bounty or for our own citizens to anticipate the draft by volunteering."

(35) *Ontario County Times*, March 9, 1864.

(36) McPherson, 605-606.

(37) *Yates County Chronicle*, January 7, 1864.

(38) 1865 New York State Census, Tioga County, First District of Barton, Schedule X, Miscellaneous Statistics. Without referring explicitly to the bounties, the enumerator for Jerusalem noted that: "There has been a great improvement in the homes of the people many [illegible] have been able to buy farms homesteads and also been able to clothe their families and to improve their education and others have been able to clear their homes from debt." 1865 New York State

Census, Yates County, Jerusalem Second Election District, Section X.

(39) *Elmira Daily Advertiser*, September 14, 1864.

(40) McPherson, 601. See also, *Watkins Express*, August 25, 1864.

(41) McPherson, 431.

(42) *Watkins Express*, August 25, 1864.

(43) *Elmira Daily Advertiser*, September 13, 1864.

(44) McPherson, 432, 602-603; *Elmira Daily Advertiser*, August 25, 1864.

(45) Letter from John T. Andrews to Homer Andrews, December 26, 1864.

(46) McPherson, 602.

(47) *Ibid.*, 431, 601. Future President Grover Cleveland, then a lawyer in Buffalo, New York, and future mega-millionaire John D. Rockefeller, then a merchant in Cleveland, Ohio, were among those who purchased an exemption. (Meier, 1; See also, Marten, 231-232) The fact that Grover Cleveland did not serve in a war to preserve the Union that dominated contemporary consciousness to a degree matched only by World War II does not seem to have harmed his political career. He was elected President twenty years after the Civil War in 1884 and again in 1892 (and also won the popular vote in 1888). However, apart from Cleveland, all the Presidents after the Civil War were Union veterans until 1901 when Theodore Roosevelt, himself a veteran of the Spanish American War, became President following the assassination of President McKinley. Secretary of War Edwin Stanton had presciently predicted at the end of the Civil War that half a dozen future presidents would come from the victorious Union army. (Goodwin, 745-46) This provides an interesting comparison to the twentieth century. World War II veterans Eisenhower, Kennedy, Johnson, Nixon, Ford, Reagan, and George H. W. Bush, along with nuclear submarine veteran Carter, held the Presidency for forty years after the war until Clinton, who did not serve in the military, was elected in 1992. Clinton defeated World War II veterans Bush and Dole to win his two terms.

(48) Graham, 181-91; See also, McPherson, 601.

(49) Official Records, Series I, Vol. XL, Part II, 48. On June 8, 1864, Maj. A.S. Diven, the provost marshal and head of the volunteer recruiting service for the Western District of New York, wrote Brigadier General James Fry, the Provost Marshal General, about the commutation problem: "We are, evidently, to get but few men by drafting. The men left to be drafted will nearly all pay their commutation. A common laborer can get $300 and board. I think if filling the army is the object, the only way is to make another call, place the draft about a month from the call, and invite volunteers. Either this must be done or Congress must amend the law authorizing commutation. Either encourage volunteering and bounties & threaten draft, or make the drafted men serve or find a substitute is the only means of raising any considerable number of troops in this state at least." (RG110, Entry 2020, Vol. 2)

(50) McPherson, 601.

(51) Graham, 191. See also, McPherson, 604-605.

(52) *Elmira Daily Advertiser*, August 25, 1864.

(53) McPherson, 443; *Elmira Daily Advertiser*, August 25, 1864; *Ontario County Times*, August 31, 1864; Michael Lind, *Land of Promise: An Economic History of the United States*, Harper: New York (2013), 137-139.

(54) *Elmira Daily Advertiser*, August 18, 1864.

(55) *Elmira Daily Advertiser*, September 13, 1864.

(56) Letter from Daniel B. Lee dated June 28, 1864.

(57) M. Kreidberg and M. Henry, *History of Military Mobilization in the United States Army 1775-1945*, Department of Defense: Washington (DOD Pamphlet No. 20-212 (1955), 93; McPherson, 326-27; V. Kautz, *The Company Clerk*, J. B. Lippincott & Company: Philadelphia (1864), 132, 134-35.

(58) *Elmira Daily Advertiser*, August 15, 1862. The *Advertiser* did note that volunteers had the option "of going into regiments where they will have the advantage of serving by the side of those who have seen service." (*Ibid.*)

(59) Rappaport, 100; See also, McPherson, 326.

(60) *The Hornellsville Tribune*, January 7, 1864. A week later, the *Tribune* reported that all but fifteen of the soldiers of the 86th New York had re-enlisted, which would go a long way toward meeting the local quotas. The *Tribune* concluded that: "Their home visit, and the flattering inducements in the shape of bounties, will, no doubt, induce many new recruits to come into their ranks." (*The Hornellsville Tribune*, January 14, 1864) The 179th New York actually followed both models. In the spring of 1864, new recruits were sent to the 179th as a "new" regiment. However, in the fall of 1864, new recruits were sent to the 179th as an "old," existing regiment to replace its losses, rather than to another "new" regiment. The "veterans" in the 179th from the spring were able to train the new recruits who arrived in the fall of 1864 in time for the 179th's final battle in April 1865.

(61) McPherson, 326.

(62) Rappaport, 100-101.

(63) *Ibid.*

(64) Official Record, Series III, Vol.IV, at 78-79; Rappaport, 101.

(65) Letter from John Sprague, Adjutant General, to Maj. A.S. Diven, Provost Marshal General and Superintendent of Volunteer Recruiting, Western District of New York, dated March 22, 1864, George Carpenter CMSR.

(66) *Ontario County Times*, February 3, 1864; *Watkins Express*, February 4, 1864.

(67) *Ontario County Times*, February 3, 1864.

(68) *Ibid.*

(69) *Watkins Express*, February 4, 1864.

(70) *Watkins Express*, March 17, 1864.

Chapter Two

Ambrose, Stephen, *Band of Brothers: E Company, 506th Regiment, 101st Airborne, From Normandy to Hitler's Eagle's Nest*, Simon & Schuster: New York (2001).

Brandt, Nat, *Mr. Tubbs' Civil War*, Syracuse University Press: Syracuse, New York (1996).

Faust, Drew Gilpin, *This Republic of Suffering: Death and the American Civil War*, Alfred A. Knopf: New York (2008).

Lonn, Ella, *Desertion During the Civil War*, University of North Carolina Press: Lincoln (1998 originally published 1928).

Marten, James, *Sing Not War: The Lives of Union & Confederate Veterans in Gilded Age America*, University of North Carolina Press: Chapel Hill (2011).

Phisterer, Frederick, *New York in the War of the Rebellion 1861 to 1865*, D.B. Lyon Company, State Printers: Albany, New York (Third Ed. 1912).

Ramold, Steven J., *Across the Divide: Union Soldiers View the Northern Home Front*, New York University Press: New York (2013).

Starr, F., *The Loyal Soldier. A Discourse Delivered in the First Presbyterian Church in Penn Yan, New York, at the Funeral of Major John Barnet Sloan, of the 179th Regiment, N.Y.V. Infantry*, C.D.A. Bridgman, Book and Job Printer: Penn-Yan, New York (1864).

Wiley, Bell Irvin, *The Life of Billy Yank: The Common Soldier of the Union*, Louisiana State University Press: Baton Rouge (1952, 1971).

Wolcott, Walter, *The Military History of Yates County, N.Y., Comprising a Record of the Services Rendered by Citizens of This County in the Army and Navy, from the Foundation of the Government to the Present Time*, Express Book and Job Printing House: Penn Yan, New York (1895).

(1) Perhaps the most blunt was Ella Lonn in her study of desertion from the Union army during the Civil War: "Probably the most serious cause producing desertion was the calibre of the recruits, noticeably inferior after 1862. Reinforcements were constantly being sent to the armies but they were for the most part mercenaries, immoral and cowardly." (Lonn, 138) William Hopkins of the 7th Rhode Island, a veteran regiment which served in the same division as the 179th New York at the end of the war, wrote in 1903 that: "Had the war lasted a year or two longer, and the large bounties continued to increase as they probably would, this buying of men like cattle, would have created so much dishonesty and rascality in and out of the service, that the very foundations of military life and discipline would have been honeycombed, and it would have required one sentinel to keep each new soldier at the front, for desertions were becoming very prevalent among new troops all through our armies in 1865." (W. Hopkins, *The Seventh Regiment Rhode Island Volunteers in the Civil War, 1862-1865*, Nabu Public Domain Reprint (originally published 1903), 243) However, the *Elmira Daily Advertiser* took a different view of the "caliber of recruits" in the fall of 1864 when the bounties in New York were approaching their peak: "Never before, perhaps, was a better class of human material being secured for our armies. The rural districts are sending forth their best developed and most capable young men." (September 14, 1864)

(2) John Cook CMSR; John Cook CMR; Affidavit of William Norton dated June 29, 1886, Ezra Northup Pension File; Ezra Northup CMSR.

(3) Wiley, 39.

(4) Andrews attended Alfred University and Union College. His father, Edwin Andrews, was descended from Aaron Burr and had served a term in Congress. (Brandt, 169). In the 1860 Census, Andrews' father was reported as owning real property valued at $8,550 and personal property at $1,880. (Edwin Andrews, 1860 Census, New York, Ancestry.com)

(5) JAWJ, November 1, 1864.

(6) Letter from A. S. Diven to G. W. Palmer dated February 13, 1864, RG110, Entry 2024, Box 35; Newton Spencer, "A War Story," *Elmira Telegram*, April 28, 1895.

(7) See Appendix C "Prior Service of the Officers and Enlisted Men of the 179th New York Volunteer Infantry" and sources cited therein, including A Record of the Commissioned Officers, Non-Commissioned Officers, and Privates of the Regiments Which Were Organized in the State of New York and Called into the Service of the United States to Assist in Suppressing the Rebellion Caused by the Secession of Some of the Southern States from the Union, A.D. 1861, As Taken from the Muster-In Rolls on File in the Adjutant General's Office, S.N.Y., Weed, Parsons and Company, Printers: Albany (1866), Vol. VI at 107-126. Not all of the enlisted men in Appendix C served the full term of their original enlistment. Some had been discharged on medical grounds. Just over half of the men enlisting in the Union army for three years in the

spring of 1861 did *not* reenlist when their term of service expired in 1864. (Brooks Simpson, "Campaign Promise," *The Civil War Monitor*, Vol 4, No. 4 (Winter 2014), 34. Of the sixty-four enlisted men in the original complement of the 179th New York who had prior service, seven came from the 23rd New York, Colonel Gregg's and Lieutenant Colonel Doty's old regiment. Five of them served in Company C of the 179th. Seven men came from the 37th New York, Captain Bird's old regiment and six of them served with Captain Bird in Company D of the 179th. (Appendix C)

(8) Phisterer, 4032-4038; Regimental History at 8-25.

(9) Tarbell, "How the Union army Was Disbanded," *Civil War Times Illustrated*, December 1967, 6. [Originally published in *McClure's Magazine* in March 1901] While serving as a war correspondent during the Boer War, Winston Churchill came under fire and later recalled that: "There is nothing more exhilarating than to be shot at without result." (William Manchester, *The Last Lion: Winston Spencer Churchill: Visions of Glory, 1874-1932*, Little, Brown and Company: Boston (1983), 228)

(10) Marten, 284.

(11) *Corning Journal*, September 8, 1881.

(12) Ausburn Towner, *Our County and Its People: A History of the Valley and County of Chemung*, D. Mason & Co., Publishers: Syracuse, New York (1892), 245; *The National Tribune*, September 17, 1881, 7; William M. Gregg, 1860 Census, New York, Chemung County, Elmira, Ancestry.com; *The National Tribune*, September 17, 1881, 7.

(13) Pound Sterling (William P. Maxson), *Campfires of the Twenty-Third: Sketches of the Camp Life, Marches, and Battles of the Twenty-Third Regiment, N.Y.V., During the Term of Two Years In the Service of the United States,* Dames & Kent, Printers: New York (1863), 38, 61-62.

(14) *Ibid.*, 59.

(15) *Elmira Daily Advertiser*, August 25, 1864.

(16) *Corning Journal*, September 8, 1881.

(17) *Hornellsville Tribune*, [undated fragment], New York State Military Museum, Unit History Project, 23rd New York Volunteers, Civil War Newspaper Clippings.

(18) F. Doty CMSR, 23rd New York Volunteers.

(19) *The Hornellsville Tribune*, April 20, 1865. John Andrews was among those in the 179th who had listened to Doty's "narration of some of his voyages on the sea." (JAWJ, March 11, 1865, 19)

(20) Letter dated April 23, 1865 from Solon O. Thacher to Philip Van Scoter published in *The Hornellsville Tribune*, June 25, 1865; R. Oakes, "Historically Speaking," *Sunday Spectator*[Wellsville-Hornell, New York], July 8, 1973, 4A.

(21) Starr, 25-26. See also Wolcott, 106-108. I have been able to independently verify only some of these details. On November 15, 1861, a disturbance occurred in Company H while the 31st New York was stationed at Camp Brown near Alexandria. Then First Lt. Sloan of Company I was Officer of the Guard and "was called to quell the same and in attempting to do so, circumstances rendered it necessary for me to use my sword." The next day, Sloan requested his commanding officer to convene a court of inquiry. The enlisted man involved died of the sword wound several days later. That led to an encounter with another enlisted man and Sloan shot and killed him on November 27, 1861. Sloan requested that that incident be included in the court of inquiry. While Sloan's superior officers believed that his actions were justified, they endorsed his request for the court of inquiry because it would provide official vindication. Special Orders No. 158, paragraph 15 of the Army of the Potomac directing that the court of inquiry be convened was signed by an assistant adjutant general "By Command of Maj. Genl. McClellan." However, I have not located

a report or transcript of the outcome of the court of inquiry. Nor have I found any record of personal involvement by McClellan. Sloan was in fact promoted to Captain shortly after these events, but the supporting documentation has been lost. (Sloan CMSR, Robert Scott CMSR, and Francis Killale CMSR, all 31st New York Volunteers) Still, as one of Easy Company's "Band of Brothers" commented about stories about one of his officers during World War II, "We all know war stories seem to have a life of their own. They have a way of growing, of being embellished. Whether the details are precise or not there must be a kernel of truth for such a story to ever have been told the first time." (Ambrose, 206)

(22) Phisterer, 2100; Starr, *Loyal Soldier*, 26-27.

(23) Newspaper fragment on New York State Military Museum Unit History Website, 31st NY.

(24) See Phisterer, 4032-4038. Pay for officers was also substantially higher than for enlisted men. Even after the raise in June 1864, a private was paid only $16 a month, while first and second lieutenants were paid $105.50; captains $115.50; majors $169; lieutenant colonels $181; and colonels $212. (M. Boatner, III, *The Civil War Dictionary*, Vintage Books: New York (Rev. Ed. 1991), 624) However, officers did have to pay for their own food. (See Letter from William Bird, Jr. to Father dated August 20, 1864)

(25) Letters dated April 12, 1864 and April 19, 1864 from Capt. Palmer to Maj. A.S. Diven, Regimental Papers, Box 3408. The 179th probably benefited from the change. The proposed captain, William H. Gibson, had been only a private in the 72nd New York, while Bird had been a captain in the 37th New York.

(26) William Bird, 1860 Census, Ancestry.com; Various documents in William Bird, Jr. File, Martin County Historical Society.

(27) Phisterer, 2164; Bird CMSR, 37th New York Volunteers.

(28) Letter from William Bird to Father dated July 3, 1861.

(29) Letter dated August 1, 1861 from William Bird, Jr. to father. See also letter dated May 10, 1863 from Bird to father.

(30) Phisterer, 2164.

(31) Letter from William Bird dated May 10, 1863.

(32) Letter from William Bird to Dudley dated May 19, 1883, Pension File, National Archives. Bird was wounded in the knee in the 179th's first battle on June 17, 1864 and he never returned to the field. He moved to Minnesota right after the war and resumed farming. However, once again his wounds impeded his ability to farm. He became the Sheriff of Martin County, Minnesota. See Chapter 25 below.

(33) Letter dated September 19, 1864 from Charles S. Baker to Mother, Charles S. Baker Pension File.

(34) Compiled from *Record of the Commissioned Officers*

(35) Ramold, 35. Ramold did note that: "Soldiers could justify doing so if soldiering provided sufficient compensation to replace the wages of male farm labor."

(36) Marshall Phillips, Pension File and CMSR. A man with a large family might have been old enough to fall in class II for the draft (older than thirty-five), but that was not an exemption. Phillips was forty-one years old in 1864.

(37) Newton Phillips CMSR; Marshall Phillips CMSR; Affidavit of Sarah Ormsby dated July 12, 1864, Daniel Ormsby Pension File. Ormsby (age 44) was also in Class II. (Ormsby CMSR) His widow had to endure the further tragedy of the death of three of her children several years later, apparently from disease. (Affidavit of Sarah Ormsby dated March [?], 1867, *Ibid.*)

(38) 1860 U. S. Census, Ancestry.com (Timothy Buckland); Timothy Buckland, CMSR and Pension File; Affidavit of Anne W. Brown, dated April 24, 1865, Moses Brown Pension File. Buckland (age 43) and Brown (age 41) were also in Class II. (Timothy Buckland and Moses Brown CMSRs)

(39) An exemption was available if the man's parents were "infirm" or if he were the only son of a widow.

(40) Roswell H. Davis CMSR; 1860 Census. He was arrested as a deserter in Syracuse, New York on June 7, 1864 while hauling freight on the Erie Canal. He was initially taken to Oswego where he was jailed for three weeks. He was then taken to Elmira in July; then Alexandria where he apparently was court-martialed; and to City Point where he was jailed around October 1. On January 29, 1865, he wrote the Judge Advocate from City Point: "I have passed eight months in prison. I have been greatly injured during that time. I would be pleased to have my case investigated by you at the earliest opportunity." It is not apparent when Davis was released from custody, but in 1871, the Adjutant General's Office issued a "Notation" that Davis was "Honorably discharged to date June 2, 1865." (Davis CMSR) (Davis wrote his letter on Christian Commission letterhead which included the message "Behold! now is the accepted time; behold, now is the day of salvation.")

(41) See Marten, 4.

(42) B. Reid and J. White, "'A Mob of Stragglers and Cowards': Desertion from the Union and Confederate Armies, 1861-65," *The Journal of Strategic Studies*, Vol. 8, Issue 1 (1985), 65; M. Humphreys, *The Marrow of Tragedy: The Health Crisis of the American Civil War*, The Johns Hopkins University Press: Baltimore (2013), 3.

(43) McPherson, *Battle Cry of Freedom: The Civil War Era*, Oxford University Press: New York (1988), 332.

(44) G. Ward, *The Civil War: An Illustrated History*, Alfred A. Knopf: New York (1991), 58. Ellsworth was something of an amateur soldier before the war, having organized a company of elegantly uniformed Zouaves who won drill championships and performed on the White House lawn and before regular army officers at West Point. Ellsworth's parents apparently were close friends of Abraham Lincoln. Ellsworth read law in the offices of Lincoln and Herndon before the Civil War. Ellsworth was close enough to Lincoln that he accompanied the family on the train trip from Springfield to Washington in February 1861. After the inauguration, Lincoln unsuccessfully tried to create–without Congressional approval– a new Bureau of Militia with Ellsworth as the head. (C. Sandburg, *Abraham Lincoln: The Prairie Years and the War Years*, (One Volume Edition), Harcourt, Brace & World, Inc.: New York (1954) at 198, 244; D. Goodwin, *Team of Rivals: The Political Genius of Abraham Lincoln*, Simon & Schuster: New York (2005) at 362-63; D. Donald, *Lincoln*, Jonathan Cape: London (1995) at 254, 273, 285)

(45) Faust, 11.

(46) Jeff Rosenheim, *Photography and the American Civil War*, The Metropolitan Museum of Art, New York: New York (2013), 8-9. Because these photographs were not published in newspapers, it is not clear how widely they were seen. See also Michael Adams, *Living Hell: The Dark Side of the Civil War*, Johns Hopkins University Press: Baltimore (2014), 16-17.

(47) Faust, 11-12. Sergeant Humiston was from the 154th New York which was also recruited in Upstate New York. (Mark Dunkelman, *War's Relentless Hand: Twelve Tales of Civil War Soldiers*, Louisiana State University Press: Baton Rouge (2006), xi)

[Photo: The Children of the Battlefield]

The *Bradford Argus*, in Bradford County, Pennsylvania where a number of recruits in the 179th New York came from, reported a similar story of an ambrotype showing a woman and a little girl which was found on the Wilderness Battlefield. (*Bradford Argus*, July 21, 1864)
(48) See Note 1 above.

Chapter Three

Barber, W. Charles, "Elmira as Civil War Depot and Prison Camp," *The Chemung Historical Journal*, Vol. 6, No. 1 (September 1960).

Byrne, Thomas E., "Elmira 1861-1865; Civil War Rendezvous," *The Chemung Historical Journal*, Vol. 9, No. 4 (June 1964).

Catton, Bruce, *The Army of the Potomac: A Stillness at Appomattox*, Doubleday & Company: Garden City, New York (1953).

Gallagher, Gary W., *The Union War*, Harvard University Press: Cambridge, Massachusetts (2011).

Gray, Michael P., *The Business of Captivity: Elmira and Its Civil War Prison*, The Kent State University Press: Kent, Ohio (2001).

Hallock, Judith Lee, "The Role of the Community in Civil War Desertion," *Civil War History*, Vol. 29, No. 2 (June 1983).

Horigan, Michael, *Elmira: Death Camp of the North*, Stackpole Books: Mechanicsburg, Pennsylvania (2002).

Kautz, August V., *The Company Clerk*, J. B. Lippincott & Co.: Philadelphia (1864).

McPherson, James, *Battle Cry of Freedom: The Civil War Era*, Oxford University Press: Oxford (1988).

McPherson, James, *For Cause and Comrades: Why Men Fought in the Civil War*, Oxford University Press: New York (1997).

Phisterer, Frederick, *New York in the War of the Rebellion 1861 to 1865*, D.B. Lyon Company, State Printers: Albany, New York (Third Ed. 1912).

Wiley, Bell Irvin, *The Life of Billy Yank: The Common Soldier of the Union*, Louisiana State University Press: Baton Rouge (1952, 1971).

(1) Official Records, Series III, Vol. IV, 78.
(2) Catton, 30, 43, 52-53; E. Hess, *The Civil War in the West: Victory and Defeat from the Appalachins to the Mississippi*, The University of North Carolina Press: Chapel Hill (2012), 152, 187; OR, 40(1): 525. Burnside wrote his report for this period in November 1864, after he had been relieved of command. He noted that there was a "preponderance of raw troops" in the 24,000 strength number, but he ultimately concluded that the new recruits "soon became as steady and reliable as the older regiments, displaying a courage which rendered them honorable associates of the veterans." *Ibid.*
(3) Letter from A.S. Diven, A.A. P.M.G. & Supt. V. R. Service to Capt. Samuel M. Harmon, Provost Marshal, 27th District, dated February 13, 1864, Regimental Papers, Box 3408; *Owego Gazette*, February 18, 1864.
(4) Letter from A.S. Diven to Capt. Levi Bowen, Provost Marshal 29th District, dated February 13, 1864; Letter from A.S. Diven to Capt. Edward C. Kattell, Provost Marshal 26th District, dated

February 13, 1864; Letter from Diven to Capt. Edward Kattell, dated February 22, 1864; Letter from Diven to Capt. Samuel Harmon, Provost Marshal 27th District, dated February 29, 1864, all letters Regimental Papers, Box 3408.

(5) *The Havana Journal*, February 20, 1864.

(6) *Owego Gazette*, February 18, 1864.

(7) *Yates County Chronicle*, February 18 and March 10, 1864.

(8) *Penn Yan Democrat*, November 9, 1917, 4; *The Hornellsville Tribune*, February 25, 1864.

(9) *Niagara Falls Gazette*, March 16, 1864; *Niagara Fa;lls Gazette*, [circa] March 16, 1964.

(10) [Batavia] *Spirit of the Times*, March 26, 1864; *The [Warsaw] Western New Yorker*, March 24, 1864.

(11) CMSR, 179th New York Volunteers. The use of the words "them" and "their" in the enlistment form to refer to the "United States of America" in the plural reflects the political theory of the day and is an interesting contrast to our contemporary practice of referring to the United States of America as a singular sovereign entity. ("I pledge allegiance to the flag of the United States of America, and to the REPUBLIC for which it stands. One nation, ...indivisible.") (McPherson, *Battle Cry*, 859) Gary Gallagher downplays the significance of this distinction. (Gallagher, 161) The top of the form included a space for filling in the name of the town that would be credited with the man's enlistment for purposes of the draft quota. Identifying a recruit's actual home town is not as straightforward as it might seem. Because of the draft system, the most important location for administrative purposes was the town to be credited with the soldier's enlistment. That is the "Town of" generally filled in on the top of the enlistment form. Even if a recruit was to be credited to his home town, he didn't necessarily fill out all the paperwork there. Recruits generally went to the town where the provost marshal's office for their district was located to enlist. And then there were the recruits attracted by the higher bounties offered by other towns. For these men, the towns identified on their enlistment papers would bear no relation to their home town. The "place of birth" blank on the enlistment form does provide potentially useful residential information for an era when geographic mobility was much more limited than it is today. The 1860 Census does as well, but for a variety of reasons a person often cannot be definitively identified in the 1860 Census. There are two documents that state a recruit's residence at the time of enlistment (as well as his marital status). If a soldier was hospitalized, the "bed card," which often made it into the soldier's compiled military service record after the war, stated the soldier's residence. Similarly, if the soldier died, the "Record of Death and Internment" also contained that information. The enlistment paperwork for Company A's James C. Rutan and Stephen Compton illustrates the varying data. They both resided in Horseheads, New York. They apparently began the process in Horseheads because the first page of their enlistment forms was witnessed there. That same day they traveled to Elmira (five miles away) which was the location of the provost marshal for the 27th District. By the time they enlisted on February 23, 1864, Horseheads had already filled its quota from the February 2 call. At the top of the enlistment form, "Big Flats" (a town adjacent to Horseheads) was initially filled in, but at some point was crossed out and replaced with "Barrington," the town in nearby Yates County to which their enlistments were ultimately credited. (As a result, these two residents of Chemung County were included in the book *Yates County's Boys in Blue* published in 1926.) For New York State, the form that town clerks were required to file after the war identifying the men who had filled their quotas called for the marital status of the men, but it was not always filled in by the clerks. (Town Clerks' Registers of Men Who Served in the Civil War, ca. 1865-67, New York State Archives and Records Administration, Series 13774, Division of Military and Naval

Affairs)

(12) CMSRs for Newton Phillips and Marshall Phillips.

(13) *A Record of the Commissioned Officers, Non-Commissioned Officers and Privates, of the Regiments Which Were Organized in the State of New York and Called into Service of the United States to Assist in Suppressing the Rebellion*, Weed, Parsons & Company, Printers: Albany (1866) Vol. VI, 107-119.

(14) CMSR.

(15) McPherson, *Battle Cry*, 326.

(16) CMSR. This information could be used to identify deserters in an era when picture IDs did not exist to any significant extent.

(17) Enlistment forms, James C. Rutan and Stephen Compton CMSRs. In the spring of 1864 when men were being recruited for the 179th New York, federal regulations authorized a "premium" of fifteen dollars for recruiting agents. That paperwork was filled out as well. (Letter from A. S. Diven to S. Harmon dated February 29, 1864, RG110, Entry 2222)

(18) Barber, 753; Byrne, 1247.

(19) Barber, 755; Gray, 4.

(20) Horigan, 16; OR, Series II, Vol. IV, 67-76. [Photo: Elmira Prison]

(21) Gray, 4.

(22) Letter from Eastman to Thomas dated February 7, 1864, RG92, Entry 225, Box 561. See also Letter dated August 12, 1864, from Capt. Geo. W. Chester to Maj. General Montgomery Meigs, Quartermaster General, National Archives, RG 92, Entry 225, Box 561; Letter dated January 31, 1864 from Eastman to Thomas, National Archives (New York Branch), RG 110, Entry 2341, Vol. 2, 81.

(23) *Yates County Chronicle*, February 4, 1864. See also *Elmira Weekly Gazette*, January 14, 1864 ("As volunteers are accumulating here at present faster than they can be transported, the business accruing is by no means a light one.")

(24) Letter dated February 4, 1864, from Assistant Adjutant General E.D. Townsend to Eastman, RG 110, Entry 2343.

(25) Letter dated February 23, 1864 from Eastman to Thomas; Letter dated February 15, 1864 from Eastman to Thomas; Letter dated February 4, 1864 from Asst. Adj. General E.D. Townsend to Eastman, RG 92, Entry 2341.

(26) Letter from Daniel B. Lee to his father dated April 5, 1864, U.S. Military History Institute, Carlisle Barracks, PA.; CMSRs for soldiers in Company A.

(27) Letter dated February 29, 1864 from A. S. Diven, A.A. Provost Marshal General and Superintendent of Vol. Recruiting Service, Western Division, State of New York, to Capt. Samuel M. Harmon, Provost Marshal, 27th District, Regimental Papers, Box 3408. The times between enlistment and arrival at Elmira were calculated using the CMSR of individual soldiers.

(28) "Remarks," April 8, 1864, Company A Morning Report, April 1864, Regtal. Books, Vol. 4.

(29) National Archives, Maps Division, RG 92, 1.158-p. The labeling of Lake and Conongue on the drawing does not comport with an 1860 street map of Elmira.

(30) OR, Series II, Vol. IV at 68.

(31) *Ibid.*, 70.

(32) *Ibid.*

(33) Letter (extract) dated January 15, 1864 from Maj. C.T. Christensen to Brig. General Ed. R.L. Canby, National Archives, RG 92, Entry 225, Box 561, Elmira (1864).

(34) *Ibid.*; Letter dated October 4, 1864 from Col. B. F. Tracy to Brig. General L. Thomas, RG 92, Entry 225, Box 561, Elmira (1865). The October 4, 1864 report painted a much more negative picture: The ten original buildings of Barracks No. 1: "were originally of the most temporary character, erected upon the supposition that they were only needed for the first call of 300,000 men. They were placed immediately on the ground and it is almost impossible to keep them clean and pure. The mess house is still worse, it was first built with simply roof and sides, no floor. After it became very muddy they put some scantling down in the mud and on these laid a floor, and in this condition it has been used for three and a half years. During much of this time from 1500 to 3000 men have been fed daily in this building. Much of their food consists of soups which have been spilt on the floor until the room is filled with the most terrible stench. I went through it the other evening while the men were at supper and it made me sick at the stomach, *and this is the place where our Recruits receive their first experience in the service of their country.*" (emphasis added) At the end of the war, while the regiments that had returned to Elmira were waiting for the last paycall before disbanding, Barracks No. 1 held between three and four thousand troops. *(Elmira Daily Advertiser*, June 18, 1865).

(35) Letter dated January 15, 1864 from Maj. C. T. Christensen to Brig. General Ed. R.L. Canby, National Archives RG 92, Entry 225, Box 561, Elmira (1864).

(36) Letter dated May 2, 1864 from Eastman to Thomas, RG110, Entry 2341, Vol. 1.

(37) Letter from Daniel B. Lee to his father dated April 5, 1864; Letter from George Hickey to Father dated April 17, 1864, George Hickey Pension File.

(38) Letter from Daniel B. Lee to Father, April 5, 1864.

(39) On February 17, 1864, nine recruits from "Scotts 900" (Eleventh New York Cavalry/First United States Volunteer Cavalry) signed a letter to the provost marshal for the 27th District complaining about the conditions in Barracks No. 1: "our Barracks is very Cold and Dirty. A few can crowd around the stove and keep from freezing. We suffered severely Last night with the cold and to day it is impossible for men to keep warm." They also complained that they did not have as good fare as state convicts. (Letter to E. C. Kattell dated February 17, 1864, RG110, Entry 2023, Box 30. See also, Phisterer, 943)

(40) Company A Morning Report, April 1864, Regimental Books, Vol. 4. The maximum number of enlisted men for a company was 98, including two musicians and a wagoner, and the minimum was 79. (Kautz, 132)

(41) Company A Morning Report, April 1864, Regimental Books, Vol. 4. Order No. 1 was restated at some point with the April 7 date. An infantry company was authorized one first sergeant, four sergeants, and eight corporals. (Kautz, 132)

(42) Regimental Books, Vol. 3.

(43) Letters dated March 31, 1864; April 2, 1864; April 8, 1864; April 11, 1864; April 14, 1864; and April 16, 1864 from Harmon to Eastman, National Archives, RG 110, Entry 2221, 471, 478, 497, 508, 514, 516.

(44) Regimental History, 11, 16.

(45) *Elmira Press* reprinted in *Watkins Express*, March 3, 1864. Roughly 200 men who had been assigned to the 179th after they had been individually mustered in apparently deserted before they could be "taken up on the muster rolls of regiment" for the companies of the 179th that were being organized. (CMSRs of the men "not taken up") I've drawn a distinction between two kinds of deserters: "bounty jumpers" and men who deserted from the front, hospital, sick leave and furlough because I think that different considerations were in play. "Bounty jumpers," i.e.

men who enlisted simply for the bounty with the intent to desert as soon as possible, had ample opportunity to do so, as the evidence demonstrates. Only the most inartful bounty jumper would wind up in the trenches in Virginia. For someone who did not desert until after reaching the front, more complex considerations likely were involved. (See E. Lonn, *Desertion During the Civil War*, University of Nebraska Press: Lincoln (1998) (originally published 1928), 127-142. See also E. Murdock, *Patriotism Limited–1862-1865–The Civil War Draft and the Bounty System*, The Kent State University Press: Kent, Ohio (1967), 81)

(46) Lonn, 139-142. Provost Marshal James Fry viewed the large bounties as one of the chief causes of desertion. (F. Shannon, *The Organization and Administration of the Union army 1861-1865*, Peter Smith: Gloucester, Massachusetts (1965)(originally published 1928), Vol. II, 71)

(47) The timing and location of bounty payments is illustrated by the experience of Company F's William Larzelere (who was *not* a bounty jumper). He enlisted in Canandaigua and was sworn in there on February 27, 1864. He passed his physical on March 1 and was paid $25 of his federal bounty. On March 11, while still in Canandaigua, he received the Yates County bounty of $300. (He noted in his diary that the "whole amount of bounty, local & [federal] government will be $677.") He was forwarded to Elmira on April 2 and mustered into Company F on May 25. On June 1 he was paid $123 in Elmira and Company F left for Washington that evening. (Larzelere Diary) The federal bounty was paid in five installments, with the recruit receiving only the first installment before heading to the front. (Shannon, Vol. II, 82; James Rutan CMSR) Local bounties were not always paid in cash. (See *Elmira [?]*, August 14, 1862)

(48) *Ibid.* Colonel Eastman was reported to have said that: "the soldiers of the Veteran Reserve Corps employed [in the Elmira Military Depot] have become so corrupted by the appliances of bounty jumpers that they cannot be trusted as guards." Eastman began using "negro recruits" as guards and reputedly found them "entirely reliable." (*Elmira Daily Advertiser*, July 27, 1864)

(49) Lonn, 141.

(50) Letter dated March 26, 1864 from Harman to Fry, RG 110, Entry 2341, 442; Letter dated March 21, 1864 from Harman to Fry, RG110, Entry 2341, 413.

(51) *Watkins Express*, April 28, 1864. The general practice was to return deserters to their units. However, for deserters who had been at large for a number of months this was not always feasible. Company D was the dubious beneficiary of seven drafted men who had deserted in the summer of 1863 and been arrested in the spring of 1864.

(52) Descriptive Book of Arrested Deserters, District 27, RG 110, Entry 2232. Bounty jumpers do not seem to have encountered much difficulty finding civilian clothes. The bounty money certainly provided ample cash. In September 1863, the Army had tried to prosecute a clothier in Elmira who admitted selling civilian clothes to soldiers. (Letter from [Quimby?]to Vincent dated September 7, 1863, RG 110, Entry 2341, Vol. 1)

(53) Descriptive Book of Arrested Deserters, District 27, RG 110, Entry 2232.

(54) *Ibid.*; Abel Webb CMSR.

(55) Descriptive Book of Arrested Deserters, District 27, RG 110, Entry 2232; Letter from [?] to Eastman, July 5, 1865, RG 110, Entry 2221 [?], 693.

(56) The case of William Bird (not to be confused with Capt. William Bird, Jr.) illustrates how the provost marshal's office proceeded in the absence of photo identification. On April 30, 1864 the provost marshal in Rochester wrote the provost marshal in Buffalo that he had in custody "William Tompkins or William Bird Age about 25 dark complexion black eyes dark hair. He is charged with having enlisted in Buffalo. We do not know what regt. Can you give me

any information in regard to this man." The Buffalo provost marshal responded that a William Bird had enlisted in the 180th New York on April 6, 1864 "with the following description: Born: Heath, Mass.; Age: 25; Occup.: Boatman; Eyes: Black; Comp.: Fair; height: 5' 8 1/2." He concluded that "from your description we presume the man you have in custody to be the person." The provost marshal in Auburn added the information that Bird had been forwarded from Buffalo to Auburn on April 6 and had deserted from Auburn on April 21.) (Bird CMSR). The "technology" did exist at the time to use photographic identification, as illustrated by the inclusion of the photo of Company D's Jacob Hauser on the furlough document issued by Harewood Hospital in 1865. (see pages 130-131)

(57) Descriptive Book of Arrested Deserters, District 27, RG 110, Entry 2232; Letter from Samuel Harmon to Seth Eastman dated May 14, 1864, RG 110, Entry 2221, Vol. 1.

(58) *Ibid.* John McKee alias Francis Reilly may have been Joseph W. McKee alias Francis Riley. (See CMSRs) The *Elmira Daily Advertiser* recounted the story of three Canadian substitutes who after leaving Elmira deserted from Camp Distribution near Washington. They then passed themselves off to the Union authorities as Confederate soldiers who had deserted and wished to take an oath of allegiance to the Union. When they were returned to Elmira along with a group of real Confederate prisoners, they were recognized as Union deserters. (July 26, 1864) See also Letter from Frederick Townsend to A. S. Diven dated June 13, 1864, RG 110, Box 40 [?].

(59) Descriptive Book of Arrested Deserters, District 27, National Archives, RG110, Entry 2232.

(60) *Ibid.*; Franklin Wilkins CMSR, CMR.

(61) Company G's William Green, a nineteen-year-old harness maker, was particularly persistent. He enlisted in Buffalo on March 12, 1864 and deserted after Company G reached Elmira. He was arrested by C. H. Dowe and returned to Elmira on May 14, 1864. Green deserted again and was again arrested by Dowe and returned to Elmira on July 23, 1864, just before Company G left for the front. However, the $60 reward paid to Dowe for two arrests, proved to be a bad investment for the Union. Green successfully deserted from his vedette post near Petersburg on August 17, 1864, just before the 179th went into action at Weldon Railroad (William Green CMSR).

(62) McPherson, *For Cause and Comrades*, 46.

(63) *Ibid.*

(64) *Ibid.* John Andrews bought his copy of Hardee's Tactics for $1.50. JAWJ, Vol. 1st, "Expenses," October 1, 1864.

(65) R. Slotkin, *No Quarter: The Battle of the Crater, 1864*, Random House: New York (2009), 97-100.

(66) W. Hardee, *Hardee's Rifle and Light Infantry Tactics, For the Instructions, Exercises and Manoeuvres of Riflemen and Light Infantry*, J. O. Kane, Publisher: New York (1862)(Reprinted by H-Bar Enterprises, Silver Spring, Maryland), 3-5, passim. Hardee laid out the "Posts of the Company Officers, Sergeants and Corporals." For the sergeants: "14. The first sergeant in the rear rank, touching with the left elbow, and covering the captain. In the manoeuvres he will be denominated covering sergeant or right guide of the company. ... 19. The second sergeant, opposite the second file from the left of the company. In the manoeuvres he will be designated the left guide of the company. 20. The third sergeant opposite the second file from the right of the second platoon. 21. The fourth sergeant, opposite the second file from the left of the first platoon. 22. The fifth sergeant, opposite the second file from the right of the first platoon." (*Ibid.*, 4-5)

(67) *Ibid.*, 8.

(68) See McPherson, *For Cause and Comrades*, 46. Company A did not receive their weapons

until April 22. (Letter from Daniel B. Lee dated April 22, 1864) Company C did not receive its weapons until the day before they left. (S.O. No. 191, dated April 26, 1864, RG110, Entry 2351, Vol. 3, 123, para. 2) Company D received its weapons the same day they left Elmira. (Letter dated May 12, 1864 from Eastman to Thomas, RG110, Entry 2341, Vol. 1, 158-159)

(69) King, W. Robertson, and S. Clay, *Staff Ride Handbook for the Overland campaign, Virginia, 4 May to 15 June 1864: A Study in Operational-Level Command*, Combat Studies Institute Press: Fort Leavenworth, Kansas (2d Ed. 2009), 5.

(70) Regimental History, 8; Phisterer, 4032-4038.

(71) Regimental History, 11; Phisterer, 4032-4038.

(72) Regimental History, 16; Phisterer, 4032-4038.

(73) Phisterer, 4032-4038.

(74) Phisterer, 4032-4038; J. Mills, *Chronicles of the Twenty-First Regiment, New York State Volunteers, Embracing a Full History of the Regiment, from the Enrolling of the First Volunteer in Buffalo, April 15, 1861, to the Final Mustering Out, May 18, 1883*, 21st Reg't Veteran Association of Buffalo: Buffalo (1887), Appendix, Muster Out Roll, Company C and Company K. Daniel Blachford's last name is frequently spelled as "Blatchford" in CMSR documents and newspaper reports. Because he used "Blachford" in signing his oath as an officer, I take that as the correct spelling. His wife also used "Blachford" when she filed for a pension.

(75) Phisterer, 4032-4038; Farwell–1860 Census (Allen T. Farwell) and 1863 Draft Registration (Yates County, Ancestry.com; Bradley–Deposition of George Carpenter dated May 9, 1902 (David Bradley Pension File) and 1863 Draft Registration, Ancestry.com; Holden–1880 U.S. Census, Ancestry.com; Affidavit of William Norton dated June 29, 1886, Ezra Northup Pension File. Lieutenat Bradley essentially agreed with Norton's assessment. Bradley recalled after the war that: "Our company, with three or four exceptions, were all green and undrilled, and I was but little better than they." (Affidavit of David Bradley dated March 2, 1878, George White Pension File) In another affidavit, Norton stated that he had been in command of the company on June 17, 1864 as orderly sergeant, which probably was true as a practical matter. (Affidavit of William Norton dated January 16, 1879, George White Pension File)

(76) Regimental History, 8-24, "Prior Service" Appendix.

(77) Company A Morning Report, Remarks for the Month of April 1864, National Archives, Regimental Books, Vol. 4; S.O. No. 185, dated April 20, 1864, RG110, Entry 2351, Vol. 3, 111, para. 2.

(78) S.O. No. 157, Headquarters, Depot for Drafted Men, dated March 21, 1864, and S.O. No. 176, dated April 11, 1864, RG110, Entry 2351, Vol. 3, 45, para. 45 and 91, para. 2.

(79) S.O. No. 186, para. IX, dated April 21,1864, RG110, Entry 2351, Vol. 3, 112.

(80) Letters from Daniel B. Lee dated April 22, 1864 and April 19, 1864.

(81) S.O. No. 183, dated April 18, 1864, RG 110, Entry 2351, Vol. 3, 106, para. 4, 7. Cook was initially sent to Buffalo. (Special Orders No. 338, April 18, 1864, Headquarters A.A. Provost Marshal General, Western Division, State of New York, RG110, Entry) The same day in June that the 179th was attacking the Hagood Line at Petersburg, Cook reported to Major Diven that he had arrived in Rochester. Cook was very optimistic – "every effort is being put forth by the bounty committee to encourage enlistment." The committee was about to raise the local bounty to $300. Cook reported that he had made unspecified "arrangements" with the four members of the bounty committee "to give me their influence." (Cook to Divan, June 17, 1864, Regimental Papers, Box 3408)

(82) Company A's Daniel B. Lee received a brief furlough in early April. (Letters dated April 13, 1864 and April 5, 1864)

(83) Headquarters Depot for Drafted Men, dated April 8, 1864, Rutan Family Collection.

(84) War Departmenr Circular dated January 28, 1864. National Archives, RG 110, Entry 2343.

(85) Letter dated March 11, 1864 from Diven to Harmon, RG 110, Entry 2341. The provost marshals were also directed not to grant any more furloughs.

(86) Letter received April 9, 1864. RG 110, Entry 2222.

(87) Letter dated April 10, 1864 from Eastman to Maj. Louis U. DeLong, RG 110, Entry 2341.

(88) Letter dated May 12, 1864, from Eastman to Thomas, RG 110, Entry 2341.

(89) Letter dated April 25, 1864, Eastman to Thomas, RG 110, Entry 2341.

(90) S.O. No. 191, dated April 26, 1864 and S.O. No. 192, dated April 27, 1864, RG110, Entry 2351, Vol.3, 123, para. 2 and 126, para. 4.

(91) CMSRs for soldiers in Company A.

(92) 1865 New York State Census, First District of Horseheads, Chemung County.

(93) Letter dated May 19, 1864, Eastman to Thomas, RG 110, Entry 2341.

(94) Letter dated May 22, 1864 from Eastman to Thomas, RG 110, Entry 2341.

(95) S.O. No. 201 Headquarters Depot for Drafted Men (Elmira), dated May 6, 1864, Regimental Papers, Box 3408; S.O. No. 232, dated June 10, 1864; S.O. No. 255, dated July 8, 1864, RG110, Entry 2351, Vol. 3; Company D Muster Roll for June 30 to August 1, 1864, John Andrews Papers, Box 5.

(96) S.O. No. 232, dated June 10, 1864, RG110, Entry 2351, Vol. 3, 170-171.

(97) Letter dated June 24, 1864 from Louis H. Delong, Assistant Adjutant General, to Commanding Officer, Draft Rendezvous, Elmira, N.Y., Regimental Papers, Box 3408; S.O. No. 268, dated July 23, 1864, No. 283, dated August 11, 1864; and No. 255, dated July 8, 1864, RG110, Entry 2351, Vol. 3, 197, para. 3, 210, para. 1, and 190, para. 2.

(98) CMSRs; A Record of the Commissioned Officers, Non-Commissioned Officers and Privates of the Regiments Which Were Organized in the State of New York and Called into the Service of the United States, Weed, Parsons and Company, Printers: Albany, New York (1866), Vol. VI, 107-127. John Kenney could be a mispelling. A John Kennedy was mustered into Company F. Jay Cole may have been mustered into Company C, but he may also have been assigned to the 64th New York.(CMSR)

(99) Phisterer, Vol. V, 4038.

(100) S.O. No.175, Headquarters, New York Adjutant General's Office, dated April 30, 1864, Henry Messing CMSR; Affidavit of William Hemstreet, dated April 12, 1883, William Hemstreet Pension File.

(101) Letter dated May 2, 1864 from Eastman to Thomas, RG 110, Entry 2341.

(102) Letter dated May 22, 1864, Eastman to Thomas, RG 110, Entry 2341.

(103) Letter dated June 20, 1864, Eastman to Thomas, RG 110, Entry 2341.

(104) S.O. No. 267, dated July 22, 1864, RG110, Entry 2351; Letter dated July 20, 1864, Eastman to Thomas, RG 110, Entry 2341, 19.

(105) S.O. No. 246, para. 23, dated 1864, RG110, Entry 2351; Phisterer, 4038.

(106) Regimental History, 27. Day had previously served in the 2nd Colorado Volunteer Mounted Cavalry. There is a photo of Day as a captain in the 179th New York Volunteers on the Facebook (R) page for the 2nd Colorado Volunteers Mounted Cavalry.

(107) Wiley, 307. Among the foreign-born in the Union army, Germans were the most numerous.

Men of German, Irish, Canadian and British birth made up five/sixths of the foreign-born. Wiley, 309.

(108) Nationality at Birth, 179th New York Volunteers

Company	N.Y.	U.S.A.	Foreign Born	Number Countries	Highest % Foreign
A	65%	83%	17%	4 England	7%
B	64%	94%	6%	2 Ireland	5%
C	69%	77%	23%	6 Ireland	12%
D	74%	80%	20%	6 Canada	12%
E	37%	47%	53%	6 Ireland	23%
F	67%	77%	23%	4 Ireland	11%
G	27%	43%	57%	8 Germany	14%

Compiled from Descriptive Book, Regimental Books, Vol. I.

(109) Hallock, 129.

(110) The 37th New York, in which William Bird, Jr. had previously served, was raised primarily in New York City. (Phisterer, 2159) Two of the companies had been raised in Cattaraugus County, where Bird lived. Bird wrote that: "We have been expecting our two Cattaraugus companies to be detached from the Regt and ordered to Fort Washington 15 miles down the river as our men are not very well satisfied with the regiment as most of them are Irish and some of the officers are rather rough. We have had Fenton and Rise[?] at work for us very strong and they have had the Secretary of War's promise that it should be done and I think it will." (undated fragment circa July 1861)

(111) Wiley, 304; Hallock, 127.

(112) Occupations for 179th New York Volunteers

Company	Farmers	Laborers	B'keep Clerk	Carpenter	Tailor Shoemaker Cabinetmaker	Blacksmith	Sailor Boatman
A	54%	9%	2%	7%	5%	7%	-
B	65%	14%	1%	1%	2%	-	-
C	51%	9%	4%	4%	3%	1%	6%
D	60%	5%	-	1%	3%	-	5%
E	13%	31%	6%	1%	4%	1%	18%
F	42%	18%	7%	8%	3%	3%	5%
G	26%	22%	5%	9%	7%	4%	5%

Compiled from the 179th New York's Descriptive Book, Regimental Books, Vol. I.

(113) The average age at enlistment for the Union army overall was 25.8. The median was 23.5.

McPherson *Cause and Comrades*, viii. The average age for the companies of the 179th New York is as follows:

Company	Average
A	25.35
B	24.85
C	25.26
D	24.67
E	25.11
F	25.46
G	25.975
7 companies	25.24

(Compiled from the 179th New York's Descriptive Book, Regimental Books, Vol. I.

(114) Based on a sample of 117 hospital cards that indicated that 46 percent of the men of the 179th New York were married. This is much higher than the percentage for the Union army as a whole – 30 percent. McPherson, *For Cause and Comrades*, viii.

(115) See Megan J. McClintock, "The Impact of the Civil War on Nineteenth-Century Marriages," in Paul A. Cimbala and Randall M. Miller (eds.), *Union Soldiers and the Northern Home Front: Wartime Experiences, postwar adjustments*, Fordham University Press: New York (2002), 396 "The evidence suggests that married men experienced the conflict between familial and patriotic duties more acutely than single men.")

Chapter Four

—— *History of the 179th Regiment N.Y.S.V. – Rebellion of 1861-65*, E.D. Norton, Printer: Ithaca, New York (1900).

Barber, W. Charles, "The Civil War Years", *The Chemung Historical Journal*, Vol. 6, No. 1 (September 1960).

Bernstein, Peter L., *Wedding of the Waters: The Erie Canal and the Making of A Great Nation*, W. W. Norton & Company: New York (2005).

Byrne, Thomas E., "Elmira 1861-1865; Civil War Rendezvous," *The Chemung Historical Journal*, Vol. 9, No. 4 (June 1964).

Childs, H., *Gazetteer and Business Directory of Chemung and Schuyler Counties, N.Y., for 1868-69*, Journal Office: Syracuse, New York (1868).

Cross, Whitney R., *The Burned-Over District: The Social and Intellectual History of Enthusiastic Religion in Western New York, 1800-1850*, Cornell University Press: Ithaca New York (1950).

Dieckmann, Jane M., *A Short History of Tompkins County*, DeWitt Historical Society of Tompkins County: Ithaca, New York (1986)

Dunkelman, Mark H., *Brothers One and All: Esprit de Corps in a Civil War Regiment*, Louisiana State University Press: Baton Rouge (2004).

Emerson, Gary, *A Link in the Great Chain: A History of the Chemung Canal*, Purple Mountain Press:

Fleischmanns, New York (2005)

French, John Homer, *Gazetteer of the State of New York: Embracing A Comprehensive View of the Geography, Geology, and General History of the State, and A Complete History and Description of Every County, City, Town, Village, and Locality, With Full Tables of Statistics*, R. Pearsall Smith: Syracuse (1860).

Gray, Michael P., *The Business of Captivity: Elmira and Its Civil War Prison*, The Kent State University Press: Kent, Ohio (2001).

Heverly, Clement Ferdinand, *Our Boys in Blue. Heroic Deeds, Sketches and Reminiscences of Bradford County Soldiers in the Civil War*, The Bradford Star Print., Towanda, Pennsylvania (1898, reprinted 1998, Murrelle Printing Co., Inc., Sayre, Pennsylvania)

Horigan, Michael, "Antebellum Elmira: 1850-1860 (Part One)," *The Chemung Historical Journal*, Vol. 48, No. 1 (September 2002).

Horigan, Michael, "Antebellum Elmira: 1850-1860 (Part Two)," *The Chemung Historical Journal*, Vol. 48, No. 2 (December 2002).

Katz, Michael B., Doucet, Michael J. and Stern, Mark J., "Migration and the Social Order in Erie County, New York: 1855," *Journal of Interdisciplinary History*, Volume 8, Issue 4, Spring 1978.

Kling, Warren, *America's First Boomtown – Rochester, NY: The Early Years and the Notables Who Shaped It*, Rochester History Alive Publications: Rochester (1908).

McKelvey, Blake, *A Panoramic History of Rochester and Monroe County New York*, Windsor Publications: Woodland Hills California (1979).

Phisterer, Frederick, *New York in the War of the Rebellion 1861 to 1865*, D.B. Lyon Company, State Printers: Albany, New York (Third Ed. 1912).

Selkreg, John H.(Ed.), *Landmarks of Tompkins County*, New York, D. Mason & Company, Publishers: Syracuse (1894)

Smith, H. Perry (ed.), *History of the City of Buffalo and Erie County with Illustrations and Biographical Sketches of Some of Its Prominent Men and Pioneers*, D.Mason & Co., Publishers: Syracuse, New York (1884).

Taylor, George Rogers, *The Transportation Revolution, 1815 - 1860*, Holt, Rinehart and Winston: New York (1951, reprinted Harper & Rowe 1968).

Walling, Henry Francis, *Walling's 1867 Guide to The Erie Railway and Its Branches with Descriptive Sketches of the Cities, Villages and Stations and of Scenery and Object of Interest Along the Route*, Taintor Brothers & Co.: New York (1867).

Writers' Group of the Chemung County Historical Society, *Chemung County... its History*, Commercial Press of Elmira, Inc.: Elmira, New York (2d printing 1963).

(1) See en.wikipedia.org/wiki/Southern Tier. Alleghany, Broome, Cattaraugus, Chautauqua, Chemung, Schuyler, Steuben, Tioga, and Yates Counties. I'm using the term "Southern Tier" in its broader sense, which is Alleghany, Broome, Cattaraugus, Chemung, Delaware, Steuben and Tioga Counties plus Chautauqua, Cortland, Schuyler, and Yates Counties

(2) Heverly, Vol. II, 169-413; See also, Note 6, below.

(3) See Dunkelman, 6.

(4) *History of the 179th*, 8, 16, 18, 23; *The Hornellsville Tribune*, February 2, 1865; *Complete Record as Required by Chapter 690, of the Laws of 1865, Relating to the Officers, Soldiers and Seamen Comprising the Quotas of the Troops Furnished to the United States By the Town of [X], County of [Y], State of New York in the War of the Rebellion Covering the Period from the 15th day of April 1861, to the date of the Certificate*

of the Town Clerk, Hornellsville (November 1865) and Horseheads (June 26, 1866), Town Clerks' Registers of Men Who Served in the Civil War ca. 1865-67, New York State Archives, and Family History Museum Microfilm Nos. 1,993,431 and 1,993,407. With respect to Company F and Penn Yan, Lt. David Bradley stated in 1878 that: "I had no acquaintance with more than one quarter of the company before entering the service..." That would imply that he did know three-quarters, but that seems to be an exaggeration. (Affidavit of David A. Bradley dated March 2, 1878, George B. White Pension File)

(5) Complete Record, Hornellsville; Letter from William Lamont to Sister dated November 15, 1864. For example, Lamont was assigned to Company B, but informed his family about the sickness of his fellow townsman Moses Brown in Company A. As discussed above (Chapter 3, note 11), determining a soldier's residence, as opposed to the place he enlisted or the place where his enlistment was credited, is not as easy as it might seem.

(6) *History of the 179th*, 3-4; *The Hornellsville Tribune*, February 2, 1865: Phisterer, Vol. V at 4028-29.

(7) D. Poche, "Ain't No Company 'J' in This Man's Army," 7. www.pochefamily.org/Books/ No Company J.html. Poche notes that neither Union nor Confederate regiments had a Company J. Poche attributes this to the fact that in 18th century English "the capital 'I' and 'J' were interchangeable especially when hand written." He notes that there also is no J Street in Washington, D.C.

(8) Bernstein, 349; McKelvey, 35; Emerson, ix-x. The origin of the town name Horseheads is as grisly as it sounds. During the Revolutionary War, American General John Sullivan led an expedition through this area against the Iroquois Nation, which was allied with the British. On his return through what is now Chemung County, his pack horses were spent, and he put down somewhere between 30 and 300 horses on September 24, 1779. Later, local Native Americans arranged the heads of the horses in rows along an old intersection of paths as a warning to prospective white settlers. The business center of town named Hanover Square arose nearby. (The warning obviously did not have the intended effect.) The horses' heads were still there as late as 1830. Early writers referred to being "at the Horse Heads." (Writers' Group, 84; Childs, "Historical Sketch of Horseheads," 2-3)

(9) Cross, vii.

(10) *Ibid.*, 226.

(11) *Ibid.*

(12) *Ibid.*, 4-6, 68.

(13) *Ibid.*, 75.

(14) Byrne, 1249. Another local historian identified only three home regiments for Elmira and did not include the 179th New York Volunteers. Barber, 754.

(15) Walling, 28; Taylor.

(16) Emerson, ix, 86-87.

(17) *Ibid.*, x. The Junction Canal brought coal to the Chemung Canal from Pennsylvania. (*Ibid.*, 87)

(18) *Ibid.*, 71, 73, 75, 83, 84, 85.

(19) Horigan, Part One, 5255.

(20) Emerson, 61; Letter from County Historian to Mr. Turner dated December 30, 1949 and "County of Chemung–Population, both Chemung County Historical Society vertical files.

(21) Gray, 5, 89.

(22) Emerson, 61.

(23) Horigan, Part Two, 5281.

(24) *Ibid.*, 5282.

(25) *Ibid.*, 5286.

(26) Horigan, Part One, 5252-5253; Part Two, 5288-5289.

(27) Horigan, Part Two, 5290-5291.

(28) Horigan, Part One, 5253; Part Two, 5289.

(29) Horigan, Part Two, 5289.

(30) *Elmira Daily Advertiser,* November 24, 1860.

(31) Gray, 6, 163; *Elmira Daily Advertiser*, July 4, 1864; Phisterer, Vol. I, 302.

(32) 1865 New York State Census, Chemung County, Elmira Second Ward, Section X.

(33) 1865 New York State Census, Chemung County, Elmira First Ward, Section X.

(34) Horigan, Part Two, 5285.

(35) Quoted in *Yates County Chronicle,* April 28, 1864.

(36) Gray, 135-36.

(37) 1865 NYS Census; *Watkins Express*, June 29, 1865.

(38) Bernstein, 361-362; Katz, Doucet and Stern, 672.

(39) Bernstein, 362.

(40) Smith, Vol. I, 122-23.

(41) "Face of Yesterday," *Buffalo Business*, February 1944, Vol. XIX, No. 2, 25, The Buffalo History Museum, Ready Reference File, Buffalo History 1840-1849.

(42) "B.J.L.," "Growth of Cities in the United States," *Harper's New Monthly Magazine*, Vol. VII, No. XXXVIII (July 1853), 171, 174.

(43) Katz, Doucet and Stern, 672.

(44) Katz, Doucet and Stern, 674. In the 1865 New York Census, one of Buffalo's enumerators noted: "A general improvement in [the people's] social and pecuniary condition, especially amongst the laboring class." (First District, Eighth Ward, Section X).

(45) Bernstein, 348-49. A more detailed presentation of the rapidity of Buffalo's (and Erie County's) population growth is the following:

Year	Buffalo	% Annual Increase	Erie County	% Annual Increase of Erie Co.	Buffalo as %
1810	1,508	-	4,667	-	32%
1820	2,095	4%	15,668	24%	13%
1825	5,141	29%	24,316	11%	21%
1830	8,668	14%	35,719	9%	24%
1835	19,715	25%	57,594	12%	34%
1840	18,213	(-2%)	62,465	2%	29%
1845	29,773	10%	78,635	5%	38%
1850	42,261	8%	100,993	6%	42%
1855	74,214	15%	132,331	6%	56%
1860	81,129	2%	141,971	1%	57%
1865	94,210	3%	155,773	2%	60%

(Buffalo History Center, Ready Reference Files, Population: Studies/Articles)

(46) Katz, Doucet and Stern, 677.

(47) S. Gredel, "Immigration of Ethnic Groups to Buffalo, Niagara Frontier, Vol. 10, No. 2 (Summer 1963), Buffalo History Center, Ready Reference Files, "Population figures/tables"; Katz, Doucet and Stern, 674 and Table 2. The foreign-born percentage of Buffalo's total population was also 42% in 1865. (Gredel)

(48) Katz, Doucet and Stern, 678. The percentage moving on varied by age and other factors. For example, over sixty percent of the males aged 20 to 29 in 1845 had left Buffalo by 1855 (Table 4, 679).

(49) Selkreg, 295, 303.

(50) History of Tioga, Chemung, Tompkins and Schuyler Counties, New York, Everts & Ensign: Philadelphia (1879), 392, 531.

Year	Danby	% Annual Increase	Newfield	% Annual Increase
1814	1,200	-	982	-
1820	2,001	11%	1,889	15%
1825	2,372	4%	2,392	5%
1830	2,481	1%	2,664	2%
1835	2,473	-	3,296	5%
1840	2,573	1%	3,567	2%
1845	2,494	(-1%)	3,665	1%
1850	2,411	(-1%)	3,816	1%
1855	2,331	(-1%)	2,800*	-
1860	2,261	(-1%)	2,984	1%
1865	2,140	(-1%)	2,700	(-2%)
1870	2,126	-	2,602	(-1%)
1875	2,161	-	2,528	(-1%)

*Part of Newfield was annexed in 1853 by the town of Catherine's in Schuyler County. Selkreg, 303.

(51) French, 659. In 1875, the percentages were seventy-four percent for Danby and seventy-three percent for Newfield (Selkreg, 466-67, 527).

(52) Selkreg, 299; History, 466-67; Dickman, 81.

(53) Selkreg, 28.

(54) Selkreg, 27.

(55) See Selkerg, 28.

(56) 1865 New York State Census, Tompkins County, Danby, Section X. Miscellaneous Statistics, 110; Newfield [page unnumbered]. The Newfield enumerator's complete statement was the following: "With the breaking out of the Rebellion there was some bitterness of party spirit, which, being fanned & kept alive by the alternate success or defeat of either army in the field, induced such alienation of feeling & personal distrust, as never before existed in this community. All branches of industry was [sic], to a greater or less extent paralyzed save those wherein

immediate returns were to be expected. Men, with compressed but quivering lips would pass each other hurriedly by in their eagerness to obtain the latest dispatches from the field, or gloomily discuss, in groups, the probabilities of the future – but the *Union* still lives, & and with the return to Peace, men naturally fall back to their old channels of thought and action – Of course, nobody here *now*, but strong *Union* men... All branches of industry being revived we'll soon wipe out the National debt & and hand down to generations yet unborn, not only the *freest* but purest & best government the world ever saw. ... In this locality, the returning soldiery nearly without exception, are seeking out new avenues of industry & investment." (emphasis in original)

(57) 1865 New York State Census, Tompkins County, Ithaca, Section X; Broome County, Union, Section X; Broome County, Port Crane, Section X; Tompkins County, Groton, Section X; Tioga County, Owego Town, Section X. However, the response by the census enumerator for Almond (Alleghany County) was similar to the responses by the Elmira enumerators: "The war has evidently increased the spirit of speculation, and love for money. Men do not seem to be satisfied with making money by farming and other enterprises as formerly. [H]ence they are shifting about for an opportunity to embark in some speculation or other business whereby thousands may be realized in a single month or year." (Alleghany County, Almond, Section X).

Chapter Five

——— *Official Records of the Union and Confederate Navies in the War of the Rebellion*, Government Printing Office: Washington, D.C.

Brandt, Nat, *Mr. Tubbs' Civil War*, Syracuse University Press: Syracuse, New York (1996).

Catton, Bruce, *The Army of the Potomac: Glory Road*, Doubleday & Company: Garden City, New York (1952).

Catton, Bruce, *The Army of the Potomac: Mr. Lincoln's Army*, Doubleday & Company, Inc.: Garden City, New York (1951).

Catton, Bruce, *Grant Moves South*, Little Brown & Company: Boston (1960).

Catton, Bruce, *Grant Takes Command*, Little, Brown and Company: Boston (1969).

Foner, Eric, *The Fiery Trial: Abraham Lincoln and American Slavery*, W.W. Norton & Company: New York (2010).

French, John Homer, *Gazetteer of the State of New York: Embracing A Comprehensive View of the Geography, Geology, and General History of the State, and A Complete History and Description of Every County, City, Town, Village, and Locality, With Full Tables of Statistics*, R. Pearsall Smith: Syracuse (1860).

Goodwin, Doris Kearns, *Team of Rivals: The Political Genius of Abraham Lincoln*, Simon & Schuster: New York (2005).

Grant, Ulysses S., *Personal Memoirs of U.S. Grant*, Charles L. Webster & Company: New York (1886).

Gray, Michael P., *The Business of Captivity: Elmira and Its Civil War Prison*, The Kent State University Press: Kent, Ohio (2001).

Greene, A. Wilson, *Civil War Petersburg: Confederate City in the Crucible of War*, University of Virginia Press: Charlottesville (2006).

Hallock, Judith Lee, "The Role of the Community in Civil War Desertion," *Civil War History*, Vol. 29, No. 2 (June 1983).

Hess, Earl J., *In the Trenches at Petersburg: Field Fortifications & Confederate Defeat*, University of

North Carolina Press: Chapel Hill (2009).

Hoffsommer, R., "The Wreck of the Prisoners' Train," *Civil War Times Illustrated*, Vol. 3, No. 2 (May 1964).

Horigan, Michael, "Antebellum Elmira: 1850-1860 (Part Two)," *The Chemung Historical Journal*, Vol. 48, No. 2 (December 2002).

Leech, M., *Reveille in Washington: 1860-1865*, Grosset & Dunlap: New York (1941).

Marvel, William, *Burnside*, The University of North Carolina Press: Chapel Hill (1991).

McPherson, James, *Battle Cry of Freedom: The Civil War Era*, Oxford University Press: Oxford (1988).

McPherson, James, *Tried By War: Abraham Lincoln as Commander in Chief*, The Penguin Press: New York (2008).

Phisterer, Frederick, *New York in the War of the Rebellion 1861 to 1865*, D.B. Lyon Company, State Printers: Albany, New York (Third Ed. 1912).

Ramold, Steven J., *Across the Divide: Union Soldiers View the Northern Home Front*, New York University Press: New York (2013).

Simpson, Brooks D., *Ulysses S. Grant: Triumph Over Adversity, 1822-1865*, Houghton Mifflin Company: Boston (2000).

Walling, Henry Francis, *Walling's 1867 Guide to The Erie Railway and Its Branches with Descriptive Sketches of the Cities, Villages and Stations and of Scenery and Object of Interest Along the Route*, Taintor Brothers & Co.: New York (1867).

Wilkenson, Warren, *Mother, May You Never See the Sights I Have Seen: The Fifty-seventh Massachusetts Veteran Volunteers in the Last Year of the Civil War*, Harper & Row, Publishers: New York (1990).

The title of this chapter comes from Bruce Catton's *Grant Moves South*, a small statement of appreciation for my enjoyment of his books on the Civil War.

(1) S.O. No. 191, Head Quarters Depot for Drafted Men, dated April 26, 1864, Regimental Books, Vol. 2 and RG110, Entry 2351; Company A Misc. Orders, Regimental Books, Vol. 2; Company A Morning Report, April 1864, "Remarks", Regimental Books, Vol. 4.

(2) Letter from Daniel B. Lee dated April 25, 1864; Letter from Henry F. Beebe to His Parents dated April 25, 1864, Henry Beebe Pension File.

(3) Company B, Register of Deserters, Descriptive Book, Regimental Books, Vol. 1.

(4) S.O. No. 191, Headquarters Depot for Drafted Men, dated April 26, 1864, Regimental Books, Vol. 2 and RG 110, Entry 2351; Letter from Daniel B. Lee dated April 25, 1864. .

(5) S.O. No. 191.

(6) *Elmira [?]*, August 14, 1862.

(7) *Ibid.*

(8) Regimental History, 8, 11. Number calculated based on original enrollment–eighty-two for Company A and eighty-three for Company B (*A Record of the Commissioned Officers, Non-Commissioned Officers and Privates...*) less desertions–two from Company A and twelve from Company B (Registers of Deserters, Company A and Company B, Descriptive Book, Regimental Books, Vol. 1)

(9) Gray, 69. In February 1865, the Erie Railroad said that it had a large number of second class passenger cars and could move a detachment of 500 soldiers on just a few hours' notice. (Id.)

(10) Letter from Henry F. Beebe to His Parents, dated April [May] 3, 1864, Henry Beebe Pension

File.

(11) Walling described the route between Jersey City and Elmira – the opposite direction that the 179th traveled – as follows:

"The scenery along the route is eminently grand and imposing. After passing through the picturesque valley of the Passaic, in Northern New Jersey, and the rolling and verdure-clad pastures of Rockland and Orange Counties, where some of the finest dairies in the world are found, the bold and rugged scenery of the Delaware valley engages the attention of the traveler for the next one hundred miles to Deposit Station. From here we cross the country, surmounting a summit, to the Susquehanna valley. The valley of this beautiful river and its tributaries is then followed to Hornellsville." (Walling, 7-8)

The initial part of Company A's and Company B's journey was at night, but they would have passed into New Jersey in daylight. *Ibid.*, 10-12.

(12) Weber, 107, 113, 115.

(13) Beebe April [May] 3, 1864 letter. The 179th's stay in Baltimore was uneventful. At the beginning of the war, the first Union troops passing through Baltimore had been fired on. Shortly after that, when the 23rd New York approached Baltimore, Col. Hoffman ordered the men to load their weapons, which proved unnecessary. (Ramold, 29).

(14) Weber, 118.

(15) Regimental History, 16; See Weber, 109. Abner Roberts said that Company C left Elmira at 4 a.m; arrived in Baltimore at 7 p.m. and stopped for the night; started for Washington the next morning and arrived at 11 a.m. (Letter from Abner Roberts to Sister Mary, dated May 1, 1864, Abner Roberts Pension file) The Company C Morning Report states that they arrived in Baltimore at 5 p.m. and that they left Baltimore for Washington the following day at 11 a.m. (Regimental Books, Vol. 4)

(16) Company C Morning Report, "Remarks," April 1864, Regimental Books, Vol. 4.

(17) OR, Series III, Vol. IV, 49; Weber, 121.

(18) Hess, 203

(19) Hess, 75, 146, 203; Weber, 169.

(20) Weber, 112, 267, n. 19.

(21) Greene, 183; McPherson, 737.

(22) Company A Morning Report, "Remarks," May 1864; Company C Morning Report, "Remarks," May 1864, both Regimental Books, Vol. 4.

[Photo: Soldiers Rest, Washington, D.C.]

(23) Leech, 186; "U.S. Sanitary Commission," Wikipedia. Alexandria Soldier's Rest

[Lithograpgh, Alexandria Soldiers Rest]

A photograph of the same area near the Depot

[Photo: Alexandria View]

(24) Beebe April [May] 3, 1864 letter.

(25) *The Hornellsville Tribune,* May 5, 1864.

[Sketch: Camps at Washington]

(26) Beebe April [May], 3, 1864 letter; Robert Reed, *Old Washington, D.C. in Early Photographs: 1846-1932,* Dover Publications, Inc.: New York (1980), 9-11.

(27) Letter from Abner Roberts to sister dated May 1, 1864, Abner Roberts Pension File; Foner, 271.

(28) Letter from Hosea Fish to wife and children dated May 5, 1864, Loraditch Family Tree, Public Member Trees, Ancestry.com; Company A Morning Report, May 1864 "Remarks"; Company C Morning Report, May 1864 "Remarks", all Regimental Books, Vol. 4. The May 5, 1864 letter from Hosea Fish to his wife and children suggests that it was May 4.

[Photo: Long Bridge, Washington, 1865]

(29) Letter dated May 5, 1864 from Hosea Fish to "Beloved wife and children," Loraditch Family Tree, Public Member Trees, Ancestry.com. There is some question as to whether the 179th New York had an adequate number of tents at this time to cover the entire regiment. In an affidavit in support of his pension application, Egbert Groom stated that when the 179th was on Arlington Heights they had not yet drawn tents and there had been a heavy rain for thirty-six hours. (Affidavit dated April 26, 1886) W. L. Walker filed a supporting affidavit to similar effect. (September 2, 1887) Both Groom and Walker incorrectly recalled that the 179th had been on Arlington Heights in April 1864, rather than May. Albert M. Hall filed a similar affidavit in support of George Woolsey's pension application. (Affidavit of Albert Hall dated August 8, 1888,

[Sketch: Long Bridge]

(30) Phisterer, 4029.

(31) Janet B. Hewett, *Supplement to the Official Records of the Union and Confederate Armies,* Broadfoot Publishing Company: Wilmington, North Carolina (1997),729.

(32) Wikipedia, "Fort Runyon"; National Park Service, Historic Resource Study, Civil War Defenses of Washington, Part I, Chapter IV: The Civil War Years. Fort Runyon was built of earthworks and timber, pentagonal in shape with a perimeter of 1,500 yards and enclosing fourteen acres. (The Pentagon was built nearby eighty years later.) The fort was named after Brigadier General Theodore Runyon, the commander of the New Jersey volunteer troops who did most of the construction work. Fort Runyon housed twenty-one guns manned by more than three hundred artillerymen with a garrison of an additional seventeen hundred soldiers. (*Ibid.*) The *Buffalo Daily Courier* reported in June 1861 that:
The fortifications commanding Arlington Heights are nearly completed. The rapidity with which they were erected is more surprising when their strength and general efficiency are considered. The troops are delighted with their location on the Heights. The view of the city from there is picturesque in the extreme, while there cannot be the least suffering from heat, owing to the luxurious growth of forest and the height of the ground. (*Buffalo Daily Courier,* June 2, 1861)[not cite-checked]
In the spring of 1864, Company A's Daniel B. Lee in fact would complain about the heat. (Letter from Daniel B. Lee, dated May 9, 1864)

(33) OR, 36(2): 883.

(34) E. Thomas, *Robert E. Lee: A Biography,* W.W. Norton & Company: New York (1995), 60, 314; McPherson, 280-281; Kim O'Connell, "Arlington's Enslaved Savior," *Civil War Times,* Vol. 54, No. 1 (February 2015), 34.

(35) Military Collection, Major Edwin P. Rutan, "Miscellaneous", 4. (Rutan Family Collection).

(36) Letter from Daniel Lee to wife dated May 9, 1864.

(37) Letter from Daniel Lee to wife dated May 9, 1864. In his preface to *Mother, May You Never See the Sights I have Seen,* Warren Wilkenson wrote that he wanted to get to know the soldiers of the 57th Massachusetts "who they were, what they did, good or bad or otherwise." (xiv). From today's perspective, it is difficult to confront the racial attitudes of mid-nineteenth Americans – even those of the Northerners. But as painful as they are to read, those attitudes – and the words with which they were expressed – are a historical reality. Bell Wiley observed in *Billy Yank* that: "One who reads the letters and diaries of Union soldiers encounters an enormous amount of antipathy toward Negroes. Expressions of unfriendliness range from blunt statements bespeaking intense hatred to belittling remarks concerning dress and demeanor." (109).

After arriving in Virginia in September 1864, Company K's Warren Newman wrote his father that: "They is plenty of Darkeys hear. I hant seen nothing but niggers sent I left Almira. Tell [Pat?] I have pick him out a wentch." (Letter from Warren Newman to Father dated September 20, 1864, William Newman Pension File). The views of John Andrews are interesting to consider. When John Andrews reached Baltimore on his way to the front in October 1864, he wrote a friend that: "Here we began to see *niggers* and we've seen plenty of them ever since." (emphasis in original) (Brandt, 170. See also Andrews War Journal, October 3, 1864, 29) In January 1865, Andrews tried to discourage his brother Homer from joining the Army – "it is a hard, disagreeable slavish nasty life." A soldier is "not much better than a nigger's dog." (Letter from John Andrews to Homer Andrews dated January 10, 1865, Box 1) Andrews complained in his War Journal in April 1865 that: "My darkey that I impressed into my service yesterday skeddadled last night and I was obligated to carry my own load. " (JAWJ, April 4, 1865) Andrews' politics were strongly anti-slavery. As his college days were coming to a close in June 1864, Andrews expressed sympathy for the "radical anti-slavery" movement that was forming around John Fremont. Fremont had been the Republican Party nominee in its first campaign in 1856 and a group of people who thought that Lincoln was not strong enough in his opposition to slavery were touting Fremont for a third party run. (Goodwin, 624) Andrews wrote in his journal that: "My sympathies are with Fremont and my individual preference would lead me to vote for him but I fear his movement will only tend to defeat the Lincoln Party and yet not succeed itself." (Andrews College Diary, June 8, 1864) Fremont withdrew from the race in September 1864. (Goodwin, 659) Andrews' comments illustrate the tension between theory and reality that we still face today. The black population in the 179th's recruiting areas was sparse. For the counties providing soldiers for the 179th, the black population in 1855 ranged from .2% and .3% in Chautauqua and Alleghany Counties to 1.4% in Broome and Cattaraugus and 1.7% in Chemung Counties. By comparison, the percentage for New York County was 1.9% and for Kings County (Brooklyn) was 2.1%. (French, 150) Even in Elmira, the largest town in Chemung County, there were only 60 black households in 1861. (Horigan, 5290)

(38) Letter dated May 5, 1864, from Hosea Fish to "Beloved wife and children," Loraditch Family Tree, Public Member Trees, Ancestry.com.

(39) Letter from Homer Olcott to Father, Mother and Sister dated May 24, 1864, Homer Olcott

Pension File; Hickey May 4, 1864 letter.

(40) Company C Morning Report, May 1864, "Remarks," Regimental Books, Vol. 4.

(41) Regimental History, 12.

(42) Letter from Hosea Fish to Wife and children dated May 5, 1864.

(43) Letter from Daniel B. Lee, dated May 13, 1864.

(44) Simpson, 293.

(45) Catton, *Grant Takes Command* 204, 220, 221, 223, 229-30, 241-42.

(46) Special Orders No. 107, para. 3, dated May 1, 1864, Headquarters, Department of the East, Regimental Papers, Box 3409[?]. See also letter from Eastman to Thomas dated May 12, 1864, RG110, Series 2351, 158. .

(47) Regimental History, 18, 21; Company C Morning Report, May 1864 "Remarks," Regimental Books, Vol. 4.

(48) Regimental History, 21; Franklin B. Doty, CMSR, 36; S.O. No. 211, Headquarters for Drafted Men dated May 18, 1864, RG 110, Series 2351, para. 2; Return of the Draft Rendezvous, Elmira, N.Y., for the month of May 1864, dated May 31, 1864; Company C Morning Report, May 1864 "Remarks," Regimental Books, Vol. 4.

(49) Regimental History, 18. A. Kautz, *The Company Clerk: Showing How and When to Make Out All the Returns, Reports, Rolls, and Other Papers, And What to Do With Them*, J. B. Lippincott & Co.: Philadelphia (1864), 135.

(50) S.O. No. 212, Headquarters Depot for Drafted Men dated May 19, 1864, RG 110, Series 2351, para. 1; Regimental History, 18.

(51) Letter from William Bird, Jr. dated May 27, 1864.

(52) Letter from Daniel B. Lee dated May 9, 1864.

(53) *The Hornellsville Tribune,* August 25, 1864.

(54) Letter from William Bird Jr. to Father dated May 27, 1864.

(55) Bird May 27, 1864 letter. See also letter from George Hickey to Father dated May 4, 1864, George Hickey Pension File.

(56) Letter from Daniel B. Lee dated May 28, 1864.

(57) Letter dated May 5, 1864 from Hosea Fish to "Beloved wife and children," Loraditch Family Tree, Public Member Trees, Ancestry.com.

(58) Grant, Vol. II, 142-43. Grant's strategy undoubtedly came in for some second guessing in July 1864, when Confederate General Jubal Early's division of 15,000 men had marched undetected through the Shenandoah Valley to the west side of the Potomac. A miscellaneous group of Union troops under General Lew Wallace, who wrote "Ben Hur" after the war, slowed the Confederates down just enough at the Battle of Monocacy River for the Sixth Corps, hurriedly dispatched by Grant from Virginia, to arrive in time to save the Capital. (Goodwin, 641-42)

(59) Letter from Daniel B. Lee dated May 28, 1864.

(60) Letter from Abner Roberts to father dated June 5, 1864; *Campfires of the 23rd*, 130. Plan of the city of Alexandria

[Map: Alexandria Plan]

(61) Letter from Abner Roberts to Father dated June 5, 1864, Abner Roberts Pension File; *The Hornellsville Tribune*, August 25, 1864. A picture taken in 1890 gives a better indication of what the *John Brooks* would have looked like with twelve hundred soldiers aboard.

[Photo: *John Brooks*]

(62) Letter from Homer Olcott to Friends dated June 3, 1864, Homer Olcott Pension File; Goodwin, 513.

(63) Letter from Abner Roberts to Father dated June 5, 1864, Abner Roberts Pension File; Letter from Daniel B. Lee dated June 3, 1864; B. Catton, *Grant Takes Command*, Little, Brown and Company: Boston (1968), 253; B. Catton, *Terrible Swift Sword*, Doubleday & Company, Inc.: Garden City, New York (1963), 288.

(64) Letter from Daniel B. Lee dated June 3, 1864. Company B's Homer Olcott made no mention of hardship in his reference to the voyage. (Letter from Homer Olcott to Friends dated June 3, 1864, Homer Olcott Pension File)

(65) Letter from Daniel B. Lee dated June 3, 1864.

(66) Letter from Abner Roberts to Father dated June 5, 1864, Abner Roberts Pension File; Roberts CMSR.

(67) Letter from Abner Roberts dated June 5, 1864, Abner Roberts Pension File; Affidavit of Jesse Cornell dated October 22, 1888, Egbert Groom Pension File; Letter from Daniel B. Lee dated June 6, 1864; Letter from George Hickey dated June 7, 1864, George Hickey Pension File

(68) Letter from Abner Roberts to Father dated June 5, 1864, Abner Roberts Pension File.

(69) Letters from Daniel B. Lee dated June 6 and June 8, 1864; Letter from Henry Kingsley to Father and Mother dated June 11, 1864 (Kingsley Pension File).

(70) Letter from George Hickey to Father dated June 7, 1864, George Hickey Pension File. Ord. described Hickey as "a good soldier, never avoiding service while he was able to do it." (*The Hornellsville Tribune*, August 25, 1864) Lieutenant Colonel Robinson, a friend of Hickey's father, wrote that Hickey "was one of the best soldiers in the Reg't and we that are left miss him much." (Letter from Joseph Robinson to "Friend Hickey" dated August 18, 1864, George Hickey Pension File).

(71) Letter from Daniel B. Lee dated June 8, 1864.

(72) Letter from Henry Kingsley to father and mother dated June 11, 1864, Henry Kingsley Pension File.

(73) Regimental History, 23; Larzelere, June 1 and June 5, 1864; Kautz, 135.

(74) Letter from George White to Mother, dated June 3, 1864 (White Pension File).

(75) Larzelere Diary, June 5, 1864.

(76) Letter from [illegible name], Assistant Adjutant General, to Commanding Officer, Draft Rendezvous, Elmira, N.Y., dated June 24, 1864; Letter to Commanding Officer Draft Rendezvous, dated May 2, 1864, both Regimental Papers, Box 3408.

(77) OR, 40(2): 48. Other reports provided different numbers, but the numbers can be reconciled depending on whether the Cumberland Point detachment was included. An Inspector General's Report on White House Landing dated June 9, 1864 reported 17 officers and 378 men (total 395) under the command of Lt. Col. Doty as "en route to the army". (OR, 36(3): 724) A "list of troops sent to the front" from White House Landing dated June 10, 1864 reported a detachment of 300 men of the 179th under Lt. Col. Doty as having arrived on June 3 and departing on June 10 for the Army of the Potomac. (OR, 36(3): 738-39)

(78) Brian Holden Reid and John White noted that: "It is amazing to discover how easy it was for soldiers to desert. Union troop trains, for instance, were not provided with water or lavatories. When a train stopped, the men rushed out for what they claimed were necessary purposes and

they simply did not return." B. Reid and J. White, "'A Mob of Stragglers and Cowards': Desertion from the Union and Confederate Armies, 1861-65," *The Journal of Strategic Studies*, Vol. 8, Issue 1 (1985), 68-69.

(79) Company E Register of Deserters, 179th New York Volunteers Descriptive Book, Regimental Books, Vol. 1. Company F suffered a similar pattern of desertions en route when it headed for Virginia at the beginning of June 1864, although the numbers were smaller. Twelve soldiers deserted on June 1 on the way to Washington and another four in Washington for a total of sixteen. This reduced Company F's manpower by twenty percent. (Company F Register of Deserters, Descriptive Book, Regimental Books, Vol. 1) Company B had another four desertions after departing from Elmira. The twelve desertions it had suffered meant that Company B was down nearly fifteen per cent of its authorized strength before arriving at the front. (Company B Register of Deserters) Company D lost eleven soldiers to desertion–two before leaving Elmira and another nine en route to the front,including its first sergeant, Joseph McLain. (Company D Register of Deserters) Company F's Amos J. Bonney, a twenty-nine-year-old laborer, was the 179th's most colorful deserter. Bonney was born in Tioga County, Pennsylvania, but was living in New Orleans when the war broke out. He claimed that he had been compelled to join "the Reblle service" in April 1861, but had deserted from Fort Jackson a year later. He claimed to have received the following recommendation from David D. Porter, commander of the Union naval operations in Florida at the time, to the commander of the U.S. Steamer Rhode Island:

"Will you be kind enough to let Bonney work his way home in your vesle to the United States. He is a Union man and deserted from Fort Jackson, giving us valuable information."

After returning north to Geneva, New York, Bonney was recruited by J. Barnett Sloan, enlisting in March 1864. Apparently not satisfied with being an enlisted man, Bonney secured a series of recommendations from military men and private citizens that he should be an officer. However, he headed south with Company F as a private. He deserted in Washington on June 4 (CMSR). Bonney's travels after deserting in Washington are not clear. He apparently subsequently enlisted in the 12th Iowa Infantry under the name of Andrew Bentley. In November 1865, he was under confinement at Fort Pickens, Florida for unknown reasons. He requested that he be released from confinement to turn himself over to the proper authorities "for trial for the crime of desertion from the 179th New York Volunteers" (*Ibid.*).

(80) Compiled from the Registers of Deserters, Descriptive Book, Regimental Books, Vol. 1 and CMSRs.

(81) *Ibid.*

(82) *Ibid.*; Hallock, 134. Hallock commented that most of the foreign-born recruits "lacked a strong community bond with the United States." See also Reid and White, 75. Reid and White noted that "up to 39% of foreign born recruits deserted in some companies." (*Ibid.*) Because many of the "sailors," and "seamen" were foreign-born, this factor overlaps somewhat with the first. "Sailors/Seamen" born in the United States did desert less frequently than their foreign-born counterparts. About two-thirds of the boatmen were born in the United States. About half of them deserted at some point during the war, compared to all of the foreign-born boatmen. Interestingly, neither of the two boatmen who enlisted in Penn Yan deserted. They had both been born in Yates County and were older (44 and 31) than their counterparts from Buffalo. (CMSRs)

(83) Compiled from the Registers of Deserters, Descriptive Book, Regimental Books, Vol. 1 and CMSRs. While the vast majority of the men recruited for Company E enlisted in Buffalo, only thirty-one percent were actually credited to Buffalo. Buffalo provided the opportunity for towns

falling short in local recruiting to meet their quotas. For example, thirty-three of the men enlisting in Company E in Buffalo were credited to towns in Ontario County. (Compiled from CMSRs)

(84) Compiled from the Registers of Deserters and Descriptive List, Descriptive Book, Regimental Books, Vol. 1 and CMSRs.

(85) Company G was originally Company A of the 180th New York Volunteers. The 180th lost many recruits to desertion from the barracks before Company A was mustered in. The *Elmira Weekly Gazette* reported in June that: "Desertions have been quite common of late, particularly from the 180th." (*Elmira Weekly Gazette,* June 16, 1864) See also CMSRs for men "not taken up" into companies. That could explain part of the lower number for desertion en route to the front.

(86) There may have been differences in discipline/security practices between the two companies that could have impacted desertion rates. Possible differences in recruiting practices might also explain the different desertion rates between Company E and Company G. Different people were doing the recruiting and may have had connections to different segments of the same national communities. Recruiting agents also played a significant role when Companies E and G were recruited. The federal government paid recruiting agents $15 a man at this time. An unscrupulous recruiting agent could have emphasized quantity over quality. Over thirty of Company E's recruits came in through Levi Vallier. Another fourteen came in through an agent named Layton. In Company G, at least a dozen different recruiting agents were involved. Henry Chapman brought in the most men – at least eighteen. (Vallier brought in at least six.) (Compiled from CMSRs) I have not researched the reputations of any of these recruiting agents.

(87) Compiled from the Registers of Deserters, Descriptive Book, Regimental Books, Vol. 1; CMSRs. The percentage for German-born men in the 179th (7.4%) is striking because it is slightly lower than the percentage for New York-born men (8.3%). (*Ibid.*) The lower desertion rate for German-born recruits is not explained by occupation–half of the German-born recruits in Company G were laborers. However, the recruits born in Germany in Companies E and G were about three years older on average (around twenty-nine) than the recruits born in Ireland (around twenty-six). (*Ibid.*) This would have allowed more time for assimilation, assuming arrival in the United States at the same age.

(88) Compiled from CMSRs.

(89) *Ibid.* The other companies, which had smaller numbers of Irish-born recruits, followed this pattern. Only two of Company C's nine Irish-born recruits deserted. Their average age was thirty-one – even higher than Company G's – and only two were laborers. In contrast, all three of Company B's Irish-born recruits deserted – two were laborers and the third a student. The oldest of the three was twenty-four. (Register of Deserters and CMSRs) There is a similar difference in desertion rates between Company E and Company G for other national groups. Two of the five Canadian-born recruits in Company E deserted en route (one a laborer and one a sailor), while none of the eight in Company G deserted en route. Five of the eight English-born recruits in Company E deserted (two laborers, a boatman, a teamster and a spinner), while none of the three in Company G did (a laborer, a carpenter and a tinsmith. In both cases, the men in Company E were actually older than the men in Company G, although the numbers are too small to rely on. (*Ibid.*)

(90) Stephen Compton Affidavit dated December 10, 1890 and Joseph Potter Affidavit dated August 24, 1889, both Joseph Potter Pension File; OR, 36(3): 723; Letter from Homer Olcott to Father dated June 29, 1864, Homer Olcott Pension File.

(91) *The Hornellsville Tribune,* April 20, 1865; Company C Morning Report, June 1864 and

Company D Morning Report, June 1864, both Regimental Books, Vol. 4. *The Hornellsville Tribune* reported on June 23, 1864 that only a portion of Company C had been engaged in the June 17, 1864 attack on Petersburg, which would also confirm that much of Company C was in the detachment at Cumberland Heights.

(92) OR, 36(3): 723.

(93) Official Records of the Union and Confederate Navies in the War of the Rebellion, Series I, Vol. 10, 168. The *Shokoken* was the ship equivalent of a citizen-soldier. It had actually been built as a New York City ferryboat in 1862 for service to Staten Island and was originally named the Clifton. The U.S. Navy purchased the Clifton in 1863 and refitted it, including two thirty pound rifled cannon and four twenty-four pound howitzers. It had a crew of 112 and was capable of a speed of 10 knots. The *Shokokon* had seen more glorious duty in its naval service than ferrying troops. It was initially assigned to the Navy's North Atlantic Blockading Squadron. In August 1863, under the command of the daring, twenty-year-old Lieutenant William B. Cushing, the *Shokokon* had raided the harbor of Wilmington, North Carolina, a key Confederate seaport, and sunk a blocade runner – the Alexander Cooper. The Shokokon subsequently proved unseaworthy and Cushing was assigned a new ship. Cushing, who had been forced to resign from the Naval Academy in 1861 just before graduation for misconduct and poor grades, went on to become one of the best known and most respected officers in the Navy by the end of the Civil War. By May 1864, the *Shokokon* had been relegated to inland waterways. The *Shokokon* and the *Putnam* were ordered on May 8, 1864 to accompany army gunboats in supporting a movement of troops up the Appomattox River. A month later, the *Shokokon* was ferrying the 179th New York Volunteers. (USS Shokokon (1862), Wikipedia; "William B. Cushing," Wikipedia; "Shokokon," Dictionary of American Fighting Ships, Department of the Navy – Naval Historical Center, www.history. navy.mil; "Commander William B. Cushing, USN (1842-1874), Department of the Navy – Naval Historical Center, www.history.navy.mil; L. Zerfas, "Ferryboats Go to War," www.ussforthenry. com.)

(94) OR Navy Series I, Vol. 10, 167-168.

(95) Jesse Cornell CMR; Stephen DeKay CMR.

(96) Affidavit of Edwin Lamberson dated September 8, 1888, Lewis Kellogg Pension File.

(97) Larzelere Diary, June 10, 1864; OR 40(1): 195.

(98) Marvel, 6.

(99) McPherson, *Tried By War*, 8, 74, 143-45, 266; Catton, *Glory Road*, 19; Catton, *Mr. Lincoln's Army*, 254-57, 307-13; Catton, *Grant Takes Command*, 194, 255; Marvel, 355, 359, 361.

(100) OR, 36(1): 916, 917; Wilkenson, 136-141.

(101) McWhiney and Jenkins, 35.

(102) Regimental History, 6; Company E Morning Report, June 1864, Regimental Books, Vol. 1. Both soldiers and reporters had trouble with the name "Cold Harbor." The *Buffalo Daily Courier* ran a letter from "H.W.F." in "Camp Near Petersburg:" "One night we were at Cool Arbour, (not Cold or Coal Harbor, as on the maps and papers, as there isn't a sign of a harbor or an ounce of coal within fifty miles of that base)." (July 12, 1864)

(103) "Remarks," Company E Morning Report, June 1864, Regimental Books, Vol. 4; Larzelere Diary June 11, 1864.

(104) Larzelere Diary, June 12, 1864.

Chapter Six

Catton, Bruce, *Grant Takes Command*, Little, Brown and Company: Boston (1969).

Gallagher, Gary W., *The Union War*, Harvard University Press: Cambridge, Massachusetts (2011).

Grant, Ulysses S., *Personal Memoirs of U.S. Grant*, Charles L. Webster & Company: New York (1886).

McPherson, James, *Battle Cry of Freedom: The Civil War Era*, Oxford University Press: Oxford (1988).

McPherson, James, *Tried By War: Abraham Lincoln as Commander in Chief*, The Penguin Press: New York (2008).

[Photos: Gen. Grant]

(1) http://www.archives.gov/legislative/features/grant/

(2) Catton, 122.

(3) Catton, 124.

(4) McPherson, *Tried By War*, 210-11.

(5) Grant, Vol. II, 130. See generally Ethan Rafuse, "Lincoln, Grant and the Trouble with Robert E. Lee," *America's Civil War*, (September 2014) 61 et seq.

(6) McPherson, *Tried By War*, 70-71; Lincoln to General Buell, copy to General Halleck, January 13, 1862. R. Basler (ed.), *The Collected Works of Abraham Lincoln*, Rutgers University Press: New Brunswick (1953) Vol. V, 98 (emphasis in original).

(7) Grant, 131.

(8) Sigel's role illustrates the interrelationship of the components of Grant's plan. Sigel could either defeat the Confederate troops in the Shenandoah Valley or cause the Confederates to "detach from one of [their] armies a large force to prevent it." Grant used a local saying to describe Sigel's roll that Lincoln himself would use a month later: "In other words, if Sigel can't skin himself he can hold a leg while some one else skins." (Grant, 132)

(9) Grant, 132.

(10) *Ibid.*, 130. Sherman's capture of Atlanta in September 1864 and subsequent March to the Sea, which culminated in the capture of Savannah on Christmas Day, were crippling blows to the Confederacy. Sigel failed at New Market on May 15 and was soon replaced by another political incompetent, Hunter, who eventually yielded the entire Valley and gateway to the North to Jubal Early in July. Butler made too cautious progress and was stopped and reduced to a fixture at Bermuda Hundred by the middle of May. The western campaign was another dismal effort and only Admiral Farragut's intrepid assault in August gave the Union its control over Mobile Bay.

(11) *The Hornellsville Tribune*, April 7, 1864. The public's high expectations proved to be a problem as the Union army's progress in the east was both slow and costly. (Brooks Simpson, "Campaign Promise," *The Civil War Monitor*, Vol. 4, No. 4 (Winter 2014), 33, 36)

(12) Earl J. Hess recently wrote in *In the Trenches at Petersburg: Field Fortifications & Confederate Defeat* that:

"[Lee] had lost the strategic initiative to Lt. Gen. Ulysses S. Grant in the Overland campaign that preceded the confrontation at Petersburg and was fighting to save both his army and the Confederate capital." (Hess, xiii).

(13) Rhea, Cold Harbor, 393.

(14) Grant, 279-80. See also Emmanuel Dabney, "A Federal Opportunity Lost: The Battle of the

Crater," *Blue & Gray*, Vol. XXX, #5 (2014), 7.

(15) Joseph Cullen, "Cold Harbor," *Civil War Times Illustrated*, Vol. 2, No. 7 (November 1963), 17. McPherson states that this was written to Gen. Jubal Early. (At 743)

(16) *The Hornellsville Tribune*, August 4, 1864.

(17) Cullen, 16; Freeman Cleaves, *Meade of Gettysburg*, University of Oklahoma Press: Norman (1960), 234, 259.

(18) Hess, 11. The Petersburg Railroad connected with Weldon, North Carolina, a key Atlantic port for the Confederacy and the supply of Richmond. The Richmond & Petersburg Railroad ran north to the capital. The South Side Railroad ran 124 miles west to Lynchburg, Virginia. The City Point Railroad linked Petersburg by rail to the James River port of the same name. The Norfolk & Petersburg Railroad was completed shortly before the Civil War. (Greene, ix, 4-5; Hess, 10-11)

(19) Greene 5.

(20) Klein, 42-44; Cullen, 15 View from Point of Rocks

[Sketch: Looking South, July 1864]

and the Lookout Tower

[Photo: Weitzel's Tower]

(21) Wilkenson, 161; Cullen, 15-16.

(22) OR, 40(1): 195, 521; Cullen, 15-16.

(23) Larzelere Diary, June 13, 1864; Newton Spencer, "A War Story," *Elmira Telegram*, April 18, 1895; *Elmira Daily Advertiser*, June 12, 1865.

(24) OR 40(2): 9. Nearly thirty years after the war, Newton Spencer gave the following account— which I have been unable to verify – of the 179th New York rejoining the main body of the Army of the Potomac ten hours later. Col. Ely Parker from General Grant's staff asked Lt. Col. Doty: "Is this the new regiment that was left on the picket line at Cold Harbor?" When Doty replied that it was, Parker continued: "Well, we didn't think you would get out of that close corner unscathed or uncaptured; but somebody had to be sacrificed there." Doty proudly reported: "Every man is here, and when the rebs catch the 179th in such a trap, they will catch a weasel asleep! I have been on this ground before – with McClellan – and know the lay of the land." (N. Spencer, "A War Story," *Elmira Telegram*, April 18, 1895) Doty was a veteran of McClellan's Peninsula campaign.

(25) Henry Menhenitt, CMSR; Henry Menhuitt Affidavit, July 18, 1889; Letter, dated November 12, 1886 from J.E. Farr to W.F. Valentine; George D. Carpenter Affidavit, January 14, 1887; James Rutan Affidavit, December 14, 1887; Pension File No. 442,904, National Archives.

(26) OR 40(1): 195, 521-22.

(27) Larzelere Diary, June 13, 1864.

(28) Larzelere Diary, June 14, 1864.

(29) The (Petersburg) Daily Register, June 17, 1864.

(30) Larzelere Diary, June 14, 1864; OR 40(1): 195.

(31) Hess, 9, 17; McPherson, *Battle Cry of Freedom*, 740; Cullen, 16; Klein, 42.

(32) Larzelere Diary, June 15, 1864; OR 40(1): 195, 532.

(33) Letter from John McGrath to Mother dated July 9, 1864, John McGrath Pension File.

(34) Klein, 43.
(35) Hess, 18-19; Klein, 44-45. View on Fort Clifton

[Sketch: Fort Clifton]

(36) Hess, 11; Cullen, 7; Wilkenson, 173; Kevin Levin, *Remembering the Battle of the Crater: War as Murder*, The University Press of Kentucky: Lexington (2012), 9-10.
(37) Hess, 18-19. The XVIII Corps takes Battery 5 at Jordan House

[Sketch: June 15 Assault]

[Sketch: Battery 5]

[Sketch: June 15 Battery]

(38) Klein, 45.
(39) *Ibid.*, 45-47. Charles R. Bowery, Jr. lays the blame on Grant for failing "in the primary responsibility of an army group commander" to assure "the close coordination of the activities of" his units. (*The Richmond-Petersbueg Campaign, 1864-65*, Praeger: Santa Barbara, California (2014), 27) Another illustration of the fact that the public was reasonably well informed of developments is the statement in the *Buffalo Daily Courier* on June 25, 1864 that delay by General Hancock, commander of the Second Corps, had resulted in the failure to capture Petersburg.
(40) Grant, Vol. II, 293-294.
(41) Grant, Vol. II, 293-94; Cullen, 9.
(42) Hess, 19-20; Klein, 47-48.
(43) OR 40(1): 532; Larzelere Diary, June 15, 1864.
(44) Wilkenson, 172.
(45) *The New York Times*, June 7, 1908. The original version was reputedly: "We'll feed old Jeff Davis sour apples 'til he gets the diarhee." (digitalhistory.uh.edu/learning_history/brown/music1.cfm)

Chapter Seven

Anderson, John, *The Fifty-Seventh Regiment of Massachusetts Volunteers in the War of the Rebellion*, E.B. Stillings & Co, Printers: Boston (1896).

Catton, Bruce, *The Army of the Potomac: A Stillness at Appomattox*, Doubleday & Company: Garden City, New York (1953).

Cullen, Joseph P., "The Siege of Petersburg," *Civil War Times Illustrated*, Vol. IX, No. 5 (August 1970).

Gavin, William G., *Campaigning with the Roundheads: The History of the Hundreth Pennsylvania Veteran Volunteer Regiment in the American Civil War 1861-1865*, Morningside House, Inc.: Dayton, Ohio (1989).

Goodwin, Doris Kearns, *Team of Rivals: The Political Genius of Abraham Lincoln*, Simon & Schuster: New York (2005).

Grant, Ulysses S., *Personal Memoirs of U.S. Grant*, Charles L. Webster & Company: New York

(1886).

Greene, A. Wilson, *Civil War Petersburg: Confederate City in the Crucible of War*, University of Virginia Press: Charlottesville (2006).

Hess, Earl J., *In the Trenches at Petersburg: Field Fortifications & Confederate Defeat*, University of North Carolina Press: Chapel Hill (2009).

Howe, Thomas J., *The Petersburg campaign: Wasted Valor, June 15-18, 1864*, H.E. Howard, Inc.: Lynchburg, Virginia (Second Edition 1988).

Klein, Fredic S., " ... Lost Opportunity at Petersburg," *Civil War Times Illustrated*, Vol. V, No. 5 (August 1966).

McPherson, James, *For Cause and Comrades: Why Men Fought in the Civil War*, Oxford University Press: New York (1997).

McPherson, James, *Tried By War: Abraham Lincoln as Commander in Chief*, The Penguin Press: New York (2008).

McWhiney, Grady and Jenkins, Jack Jay, "The Union's Worst General", *Civil War Times Illustrated*, Vol. XIV, No. 3 (June 1975).

Phisterer, Frederick, *New York in the War of the Rebellion 1861 to 1865*, D.B. Lyon Company, State Printers: Albany, New York (Third Ed. 1912).

Simons, Ezra de Freest, *A Regimental History: The One Hundred and Twenty Fifth New York State Volunteers*, Ezra D. Simons: New York (1888).

Starr, F., *The Loyal Soldier. A Discourse Delivered in the First Presbyterian Church in Penn Yan, New York, at the Funeral of Major John Barnet Sloan, of the 179th Regiment, N.Y.V. Infantry*, C.D.A. Bridgman, Book and Job Printer: Penn-Yan, New York (1864).

Walcott, *History of the Twenty-First Regiment Massachusetts Volunteers in the War for Preservation of the Union 1861-1865*, Houghton, Mifflin and Company: Boston (1882).

Wilkenson, Warren, *Mother, May You Never See the Sights I Have Seen: The Fifty-seventh Massachusetts Veteran Volunteers in the Last Year of the Civil War*, Harper & Row, Publishers: New York (1990).

The title for this chapter is taken from the title of an article written by Newton Spencer for the *Elmira Telegram* in April 1892. Unfortunately, the article has not survived. The article is referred to in another article by Spencer (*Elmira Telegram*, April 28, 1895).

(1) Wilkenson, 172; Gavin, 469.

(2) Hess, 24; Wilkenson, 172; OR 40(1): 522.

(3) Wilkenson, 173; OR 40(1): 532; Klein, 48.

(4) OR 40(1): 532. Company F's Josiah Baker recalled the 179th arriving at sundown. ("Personal War Sketch of Josiah Baker," November 11, 1901, Yates County History Center)

(5) The road is referred to by various names. Ledlie referred to it as the Petersburg and Suffolk State Road (*Ibid.*). The contemporary map that I used for general background referred to it as Norfolk Stage Road.

(6) Wilkinson, 172; OR 40(1): 532.

(7) Larzelere Diary, June 16, 1864.

(8) The brigades from the Ninth Corps were Griffin's Brigade of the Second Division and Hartranft's of the Third Division. OR 40(1): 545, 571.

(9) Hess, 24; Howe, 57.

(10) Hess, 23.

(11) The *(Petersburg) Daily Register*, June 17, 1864 (reproduction purchased in Petersburg National Battlefield bookstore).

(12) S. King, W. Robertson, and S. Clay, *Staff Ride Handbook for the Overland campaign, Virginia, 4 May to 15 June, 1864: A Study in Operational-Level Command* 2 ed., (Fort Leavenworth, Kansas: Combat Studies Institute Press, 2009), 89.

(13) Cullen, 17. McPherson states that this was written to General Early. James McPherson, *Battle Cry of Freedom: The Civil War Era*, (New York: Oxford University Press, 1988), 743.

(14) Greene, 190; Charles R. Bowery, Jr., *The Richmond-Petersburg campaign, 1864-65*, Praeger: Santa Barbara, California (2014), 100. The *Bradford Argus* [Towanda, Pennsylvania] reported the following in the same issue that it reported on the Battle of the Crater: "The Petersburg (Va.) papers are full of 'warnings to pedestrians' every day. One of them lately advised – 'all persons, with the least grain of sense in their brains, and not scared out of their breeches, who may be walking along Belinbroke street, to keep as close to the houses on the north side as possible.'" (August 4, 1864).

(15) Howe, 62.

(16) Hess, 25-26; Wilkenson, 174; OR 40(1): 196, 532.

(17) Catton, 195. Solar and lunar calendars give sun/moon rise/set; although the moon was almost full (the 19th), it had set earlier at 2:48 a.m. An idea of the light in the sky at 4 a.m. is shown here (from Starry Night, (c) 2009, Simulation Curriculum Corp.).

[Photo: June 17, 4 a.m.]

and at sunrise

[Photo: Sunrise at 4:48 a.m.]

(18) Howe, 67.

(19) *Ibid.*, 67-68; OR 40(1): 522

(20) Wilkenson, 174; Hess, 26; Anderson, 137. It is not clear when Battery No. 16 fell on June 17. Howe, 172, n. 24.

(21) OR 40(1): 532.

(22) OR 40(2): 664.

(23) OR 51(2): 1079.

(24) *Ibid.*

(25) *Ibid.*, 1079-80.

(26) OR 40(2): 664.

(27) OR 40(1): 532.

(28) Hess, 27.

(29) Wilkenson, 174; Hess, 26.

(30) OR 40(1): 532.

(31) OR 51(2): 1080.

(32) Howe, 75; Anderson, 137; OR 40(1): 533.

(33) Howe, 94.

(34) Letter from Daniel B. Lee dated June 17, 1864.

(35) OR, 40(2): 117.

(36) Howe, 60; Brooks Simpson, "Campaign Promise," *The Civil War Monitor*, Vol. 4, No. 4 (Winter 2014), 35.

(37) *The Hornellsville Tribune*, April 20, 1865.

(38) Register of Deserters, Descriptive Book, Regimental Books, Vol. 1.

(39) OR 40(1): 540.

(40) Walcott, 336.

(41) Anderson, 137.

(42) Anderson, 137-38.

(43) OR 40(1): 533.

(44) Regimental History, 24.

(45) OR 40(1): 532-33; Gavin, 470; Letter from William Bird, Jr. to William Bird, Sr., dated June 21, 1864.

(46) Hess, 27.

(47) Simons, 226-27. Forty years after the war, Company F's Josiah Baker recalled that there had been three charges, not two, and that he had suffered a gunshot wound in his left forearm during the first charge. (Personal War Sketch of Josiah C. Baker, November 11, 1901, J. Barnett Sloan Post No. 93, Grand Army of the Republic (1892), Yates County History Center)

(48) OR, 40(1): 533. While General Ledlie's report is generally accurate, it was not first hand. Ledlie was not present at the point of attack. He was in the rear, drunk, behavior that would be repeated six weeks later at the Battle of the Crater with disastrous consequences for his division. (Wilkenson, 177-79) In Ledlie's absence, the attack was led by Col. Jacob Gould, commander of the First Brigade.

(49) OR, 51(1): 273.

(50) Letter from William Bird, Jr. to William Bird, Sr., dated June 21, 1864. The idea to attack with bayonets may have come from Col. Stephen Weld of the 57th Massachusetts. (Wilkenson, 175) His intention may have been to prevent the soldiers from falling back. Or the idea may have come from General Potter's success in attacking early that morning with the bayonet to keep the element of surprise. (OR, 40(1): 545) In either case, the original inspiration may have been Col. Emory Upton's recent tactical success at the Battle of Spotsylvania Court House. Upton had ordered his troops to attack across two hundred yards of open ground at a run and to not stop to fire until they reached the Confederate trenches. (McPherson, *Battle Cry of Freedom*, 729) Such new tactics were necessitated by the combination of defensive trenches and the increased effective range of the rifled muskets which were commonplace on both sides by 1864. (*Ibid.*, 474-75) In May 1863, while the battle of Chancellorsville was unfolding miles away, Union General John Sedgwick had led a successful bayonet charge at Marye's Heights, the scene of heavy Union casualties at the Battle of Fredericksburg six months before. (*Ibid.*, 642-43)

(51) Larzelere Diary June 17, 1864.

(52) OR, 51(1): 273.

(53) Hess, 27.

(54) OR 40(1): 533.

(55) OR 40(2): 126.

(56) *Ibid.*

(57) *Ibid.*

(58) *Ibid.*, 127.

(59) *Ibid.*, 128.

(60) Thomas Howe also notes the loss of opportunity on June 16. "That Petersburg did not fall on June 16 seems nearly unbelievable. Three Union corps opposed Confederate forces a third of their size...The Union army was unable to capture Petersburg on June 16 in part because of a lack of imaginative leadership. Meade's battle plan called for attack precisely where Beauregard was the strongest. Early in the day Barlow [a division commander in the Second Corps] implied the value of a flank attack on the Confederate right. Beauregard later conceded that a Federal attack along the Jerusalem Plank Road by one corps while another held the Rebel front would have compelled Confederate forces 'to evacuate Petersburg without much resistance.'" Howe, 59 (footnote omitted).

(61) OR, 40(1): 533; Hess, 27; Wilkinson, 179; Howe, 97; Gavin, 473-74.

(62) Walcott, 336.

(63) Phisterer, 4029; Hosea Fish, Emmons Morgan, Byrant Dains, and John Hall CMRs.

(64) Wilkenson, 176.

(65) OR 40(1): 229. See Appendix C.

(66) OR 40(2): 665.

(67) OR 51(2): 1020.

(68) OR 40(2): 120.

(69) Hess, 28.

(70) OR 40(2): 175, 191-92.

(71) Hess, 30.

(72) *Ibid.*, 30-31.

(73) *Ibid.*, 36.

(74) *Ibid.*, 33.

(75) Phisterer, 243.

(76) Letter from William Bird, Jr. to William Bird, Sr. dated June 21, 1864.

(77) Larzelere Diary, June 17, 1864.

(78) Letter from William Bird, Jr. to William Bird, Sr. dated June 21, 1864.

(79) Letter from Daniel B. Lee dated June 17, 1864.

(80) Letter from Homer Olcott dated June 29, 1864, Homer Olcott Pension File.

(81) Letter from John McGrath to Mother dated July 9, 1964, John McGrath Pension File.

(82) OR 40(1): 540.

(83) OR 40(2): 191.

(84) Ron Field, *Petersburg 1864-65: The Longest Siege*, (Oxford: Osprey Publishing, 2009), 26; McPherson, *Battle Cry of Freedom*, 741. William Norton and Newton Spencer argued in a paper that they read at the 179th New York's 1884 reunion that the 179th New York had suffered the highest percentage casualties in the Army of the Potomac on June 17. (*Ontario Repository and Messenger*, September 11, 1884; *Watkins Express*, September 18, 1884)

(85) Starr, 27; *The Hornellsville Tribune*, April 20, 1865.

(86) Franklin B. Doty CMSR at 14; *The Hornellsville Tribune*, April 20, 1865.

(87) Letter from William Bird, Jr. to father dated June 21, 1864.

(88) Franklin B. Doty CMSR, 14, 34.

(89) Phisterer, 509, 4032, 4037; CMRs.

(90) OR 40(1): 228-29.

(91) OR 40(1): 347-48.

(92) *Ibid.*, 523.

(93) McPherson, *Battle Cry of Freedom*, 330.

(94) K. M. Kostyal, *Field of Battle: The Civil War Letters of Major Thomas J. Halsey*, National Geographic Society: Washington, D.C.(1996), 134.

(95) Phisterer, 4030; NYSMI Unit History Project, 179th New York Volunteers Article.

(96) Examining Surgeon's Certificate, December 10, 1864; Officers' Certificate of Disability, signed by First Lieut. George W. Carpenter, December 22, 1864, Newton Phillips Pension File.

(97) Levi Rowley CMSR.

(98) Regimental History, 24, 26; Court-martial Transcript (William Spaulding), Record Group 153, Records of the Office of the Judge Advocate General (Army), Court-martial Case Files, 1809-1894, LL2366-LL2375, Box 716, National Archives. Bacon's and West's carded medical records both say they were wounded.

(99) *Ibid.*, 24.

(100) File LL2375, Record Group 153, Records of the Judge Advocate General (Army), Court Martial Case Files, 1809-1894, LL2366-LL2375, Box 716, National Archives. Spaulding's carded medical records do not refer to the wound being self-inflicted. Spaulding was released in 1866. (S.O. No 27, War Department, Adjutant General's Office, CMSR.)

(101) McPherson, *Battle Cry of Freedom*, 409; Adams, *Living Hell*, 60. Most Union and Confederate soldiers had been raised with the Christian commandment that "thou shalt not kill." How did they deal with that commandment in the heat of battle? Some soldiers dehumanized the soldiers on the other side. Others believed they were fighting a "just war" or that they were following their duty. An Illinois soldier matter of factly explained to his brother and sister the lack of choice as a practical matter: "you would think it was a cruel thing to [shoot] a man at ten [gloss]rod[/gloss] s distance, but just think that your life is at stake if you don't and it will incurige you in this cruel business." (McPherson, *For Cause and Comrades*, 72-73)

(102) *The Hornellsville Tribune*, June 23, 1864; *Buffalo Daily Courier*, July 13, 1864.

(103) *The Hornellsville Tribune*, August 4, 1864.

(104) *The Hornellsville Tribune*, April 20, 1865.

(105) *Elmira Daily Advertiser*, January 23, 1880.

(106) Unsourced September 28, 1894 newspaper clipping in Author's collection .

(107) "Personal War Sketch of Charles B. Baker," August 15, 1901, Yates County History Center.

(108) Larzelere Diary, June 18 and 19, 1864.

(109) New York State Military Museum website, 179th New York Volunteers, Civil War Newspaper Clippings.

(110) Starr, 4-5; *Yates County Chronicle*, June 30, 1864.

(111) *Yates County Chronicle*, July 7, 1864. The *Yates County Chronicle*, the Republican newspaper that quoted Spencer's letter, was even more emphatic:

"That sounds like genuine patriotism. There is sense and pluck and manliness about that. What can we do but push on the war to its just consummation; – the overthrow of the rebellion and the downfall of slavery! That brings us a restored Union and a safe basis for prosperous self-government forevermore. For that consummation we must continue to fight, through all discouragement." (*Ibid.*)

The *Democrat* responded to the *Chronicle*'s salute to Spencer's "genuine patriotism":

"Yes that is so. But where are the Loyal Leaguers, who want the war to continue until the last man is gone and the last drop of blood spilled, who stigmatize men of such principles, as N.B. Spencer as Copperheads and Traitors? Are they to be found in the front with such men as N.B.

Spencer fighting? Never–But they have sense & pluck and manliness enough to accept shoddy contracts and scramble for office." (*Penn Yan Democrat*, unknown date quoted in Transcript of Newton Spencer Court Martial, 20-21)

Chapter Eight

Faust, Drew Gilpin, *This Republic of Suffering: Death and the American Civil War*, Alfred A. Knopf: New York (2008).

Phisterer, Frederick, *New York in the War of the Rebellion 1861 to 1865*, D.B. Lyon Company, State Printers: Albany, New York (Third Ed. 1912).

Starr, F., *The Loyal Soldier. A Discourse Delivered in the First Presbyterian Church in Penn Yan, New York, at the Funeral of Major John Barnet Sloan, of the 179th Regiment, N.Y.V. Infantry*, C.D.A. Bridgman, Book and Job Printer: Penn-Yan, New York (1864).

Wolcott, Walter, *The Military History of Yates County, N.Y., Comprising a Record of the Services Rendered by Citizens of This County in the Army and Navy, from the Foundation of the Government to the Present Time*, Express Book and Job Printing House: Penn Yan, New York (1895).

(1) *Penn Yan Democrat*, June 10, 1864.

(2) *Ibid.*; *Yates County Chronicle*, June 9, 1864.

(3) *Penn Yan Democrat*, June 10, 1864.

(4) Faust, 6.

(5) *Ibid.*, 10.

(6) Letter from William Dewhurst to the Interested Friends of Charles S. Baker, circa October 31, 1864, Charles S. Becker Pension File. The instructions from the U. S. Christian Commission to personnel writing letters for disabled soldiers included the following: "In cases of extreme sickness or death, use great care to get last messages and momentoes, the soldier's testament, diary or hymn book, or a leaf from the tree over his grave., and give full particulars of his last hours and the place of burial." (U.S. Christian Commission form, Henry B. Chapman CMSR).

(7) *Yates County Chronicle*, June 30, 1864.

(8) Starr, 6: *Yates County Chronicle*, December 1, 1864. Notwithstanding the fact that the book was being sold at the offices of its rival, the *Penn Yan Democrat*, the *Chronicle* commented that: "It deserves to be widely circulated."

(9) Faust, 162-63.

(10) *Ibid.*, 164.

(11) *Penn Yan Democrat*, November 7, 1860; *Yates County Chronicle*, November 10, 1864.

(12) Starr, reprinted by Gale Archival Editions as sourced from J. Sabin, Bibliotheca Americana: A Dictionary of Books Relating to America from its Discovery to the Present Time (1868-1936), 7.

(13) *Ibid.*, 8.

(14) *Ibid.*, 8-9.

(15) *Ibid.*, 9.

(16) *Ibid.*

(17) *Ibid.*, 10-11.

(18) *Ibid.*, 12-14.

(19) *Ibid.*, 15-16.

(20) *Ibid.*, 17-22.

(21) The *Penn Yan Democrat* took a harsh view of Rev. Starr's political preaching: "He was a man of good abilities, earnest, zealous and doubtless meant to be a sincere christian, but his indiscreet and often abusive political diatribes from the stump annihilated his influence for good as a christian Pastor." (Quoted in the *Yates County Chronicle*, June 14, 1866)

(22) Starr, 27.

(23) *The Hornellsville Tribune*, August 11, 1864.

(24) *The Hornellsville Tribune*, April 25, 1865.

(25) *The Hornellsville Tribune*, June 22, 1865.

(26) R. Oakes, "Historically Speaking," *The [Hornell] Evening Tribune*, January 23, 1984.

(27) *Ibid.*

(28) *Ibid.*

(29) *Ibid.*

(30) *Geneva Courier*, undated, reprinted in *Yates County Chronicle*, July 7, 1864; *Yates County Chronicle*, August 11, 1864.

(31) *Yates County Chronicle*, August 11, August 18 and August 25, 1864.

(32) *Yates County Chronicle*, July 14, 1864; Wolcott, 106, note *.

(33) *Yates County Chronicle*, September 1, 1864.

(34) *Yates County Chronicle*, August 11, 1864; Affidavit of Jeremiah Sprague, dated March 13, 1865, Allen Farwell Pension File.

(35) *Yates County Chronicle*, September 1, 1864.

(36) *Dryden Weekly News*, April 20, 1865.

(37) Letter from Harry Ap Rees to the Editor dated July 23, 1865, undated clipping, Charles Flint Pension File. The text of the obituary was "Flinn. In Titusville, Pa. Sunday, July 16, 1865 of brain fever. Sergeant Charles Edwin Flinn aged 30 years. Notice of Funeral hereafter." (Charles Flint Pension File, Exhibit B, 7).

(38) CMSR and CMR, John W. Cook.

(39) Letter from John W. Cook to Mother and Father, dated May 11, 1865, John Cook Pension File.

(40) Letter from John W. Cook to Mother and Father, dated May 28, 1865.

(41) Letter from John W. Cook to Mother and Father, dated June 20, 1865.

(42) Letter from John W. Cook to Father and Mother, dated June 30, 1865.

(43) Letter from John W. Cook to Father, dated July 20, 1865; See Note 24, Chapter 1.

(44) Letter from John W. Cook to Father and Mother, dated August 8, 1865.

(45) *Ibid.*

(46) John W. Cook CMR.

(47) Affidavits of Daniel D. Lowell dated September 15, 1866 and January 24, 1876; Affidavit of Abner Hughes dated February 26, 1866, all Daniel Lee Pension File. While he presumably never knew it, Lee was officially reported as a deserter by the 179th New York. Shortly after the war, Jane Lee applied to the Treasury Department for Lee's back pay and to the Pension Bureau for a widow's pension. She submitted affidavits from an Abner Hughes of Washington County, Virginia and from David D. Lowell, the acting chaplain for the 179th in the spring and summer of 1864. Lowell, who was from Lee's home town of West Almond, New York, stated that he "was perhaps better acquainted with Mr. Lee than any other man in the Regiment and I never thought he was a deserter." According to Lowell, Lee had been ordered by one of the officers in Company A "to procure water" for the company and Lee went to "a spring that was in a small

ravine" "some distance off" from where the 179th was located and apparently outside the Union lines. On his way, Lee stopped at Lowell's tent. Lowell saw that Lee had "quite a number of the boys canteens swung acrost his shoulder." Lowell did not remember whether Lee showed him a pass. Abner Hughes was the sympathetic Southerner who cared for Lee. The Second Auditor section of the Treasury Department accepted this evidence and gave Lee's widow his back pay and remaining bounty due. The Pension Bureau, however, was not convinced and denied her pension claim. In August 1866, a William Bingham wrote to the Commissioner of Pensions on Jane Lee's behalf, complaining that the commissioner should not be "any more strict at your Department than at the 2d Auditor's–if one claim is allowed why not allow the other." (Daniel Lee Pension File). Over the next twenty years, a series of unsuccessful efforts was made on Mrs. Lee's behalf to convince the Pension Bureau to reverse its decision. The Pension Bureau considered the desertion charge in Lee's records to be an absolute bar (*Ibid.*). In 1887, the War Department denied the request that the charge of desertion be removed from Lee's records (Daniel Lee CMSR). There is a good deal of indirect evidence in Lee's letters to his wife and daughter indicating that Lee was not a deserter. For example, on June 28, Lee had written his wife about his long-standing desire to purchase a farm and his expectation that he would soon be paid another one hundred dollars. Desertion would have forfeited that payment. In his last letter home, started on July 3 and finished on July 5, he expressed optimism that the war would soon be over. While Lee did not explicitly refer to his "band of brothers," it is clear that the respect of his fellow soldiers and his officers were important to him. Desertion would have forfeited that respect. After returning to camp from a brief furlough in April, Lee wrote his wife that "all of the boys was glad to see me" (April 13, 1864 letter). He took pride in having been chosen for a detail to go to Washington in the middle of April. "When they picked me to go they said that they could trust me to go they thought." (April 22, 1864 letter) As noted above, a fair number of soldiers from Companies B, D and especially E deserted on the way to Washington several weeks later, but Lee did not. When he returned to Elmira, he again wrote his wife that "all of the boys was glad to see me." Particularly noteworthy is his statement that "I have got the good will of all of the boys here now and meant to keep it" (April 22, 1864 letter). Lee also had confidence in his officers: "My captain [Albert Terrill] is a good captain … He don't ask us to go where he won't. I do like all of my officers well. So that is one good thing for us" (Undated fragment, probably mid-June 1864. See also May 28, 1864 letter). Confidence in the officers is a key element of morale in the enlisted ranks. To be sure, Lee complained about the hardships of war and he had seen the 179th New York "cut to pieces" on June 17, 1864, but on balance Lee's state of mind seems to have been that of a homesick soldier who nonetheless intended to stick it out. I think the army got it wrong by refusing to remove the charge of desertion.

(48) JAWJ, October 9, 1864.

(49) Faust, 102.

(50) Taking the number of men missing in action who could not be confirmed as prisoners of war as representing the "unknown soldiers" and assuming that the bodies of all the men reported as killed were recovered, yields a number right at forty percent. See Phisterer, 4029 and the CMRs and CMSRs for the 179th New York.

(51) Affidavit of Leonard Morris, John Hannon Pension File.

(52) Faust, 92-93.

(53) *Broome Republican*, July 13, 1864.

(54) Henry Soles CMSR. I do not know if the Army had a uniform, formal procedure for

notifying next of kin of a soldier's death. It appears that families may first have heard the news from fellow soldiers. Norman Sage wrote the parents of Samuel Hemingway to tell them that their son had died at DeCamp General Hospital. Hemingway's father wrote the hospital: "Can you give me any information in regard to it. Can his burial place be identified" (Letter from Morgan Hemingway dated September 6, 1864, Hemingway Pension File). John Moulton wrote his mother that fellow townsman Hosea Fish had died at Andersonville, and she presumably passed the news along to Fish's family. Moulton in turn had heard the news from paroled prisoner of war John Hall. (Letter from James Moulton to Mother dated January 19, 1865, Hosea Fish Pension File) The regimental chaplain sent Moses Brown's wife a letter when he died. When Company H's George Proper died in the final assault on Petersburg, his company commander, Capt. Giles Holden, sent his wife a letter, but not until five weeks after the battle (Holden himself had been wounded in the battle). William Zimmer's family may have learned of his death by word of mouth after his name was included in a list of deceased prisoners of war published in the *New York Daily Tribune* on December 22, 1864. (Affidavit of Eliza Zimmerman dated March 9, 1865, William Zimmerman Pension File)

(55) Starr, 17. Eight months later, President Lincoln would deliver his famous Second Inaugural Address: "With malice toward none; with charity for all; … let us strive on to finish the work we are in; to bind up the nation's wounds; to care for him who shall have borne the battle, and for his widow, and his orphan..." (Basler, Vol. VIII, 333.

(56) *Elmira Daily Press*, August 14, 1862. See also *Elmira Daily Advertiser*, August 15, 1862 and Brian Jordan, *Marching Home: Union Veterans and Their Unending Civil War*, Liveright Publishing Corporation: Philadelphia (2014), 154.

(57) Phisterer, 4029.

(58) J. B. Sloan Pension File.

(59) Daniel Blachford Pension File.

(60) Marshall Phillips Pension File.

(61) Henry Beebe Pension File.

(62) Ezra Edmonds Pension File.

(63) George Morgan Pension File.

(64) Charles Sickler, Lucius Kinnon and Isiah Wiley Pension Files.

(65) Varnum Northrop CMSR and Pension File.

(66) See Pension Index, 179th New York Volunteers, Fold3.com.

(67) Brian Jordan raises the question of whether the amount of the pension was adequate for a disabled veteran with a family. (*Marching Home: Union Veterans and Their Unending Civil War*, 158) While the widow of a soldier who died received an extra $2 per month for each minor child, a veteran who survived, but was disabled apparently did not. (See Id.)

Chapter Nine

—— *Report of the Joint Committee on the Conduct of the War at the Second Session, Thirty Eighth Congress*, Government Printing Office: Washington, D. C. (1865) (Vol 1).

Axelrod, Alan *The Horrid Pit: The Battle of the Crater. the Civil War's Cruelest Mission*, Carroll & Graf Publishers: New York (2007).

Cavanaugh, Michael A. and Marvel, William, *The Petersburg campaign: The Battle of the Crater 'The Horrid Pit' June 25-August 6, 1864*, H. E. Howard, Inc.: Lynchburg, Virginia (Second Edition 1989).

Goodwin, Doris Kearns, *Team of Rivals: The Political Genius of Abraham Lincoln*, Simon & Schuster: New York (2005).

Grant, Ulysses S., *Personal Memoirs of U.S. Grant*, Charles L. Webster & Company: New York (1886).

Gray, Michael P., *The Business of Captivity: Elmira and Its Civil War Prison*, The Kent State University Press: Kent, Ohio (2001).

Greene, A. Wilson, *Civil War Petersburg: Confederate City in the Crucible of War*, University of Virginia Press: Charlottesville (2006).

Hess, Earl J., *Field Armies and Fortifications in the Civil War: The Eastern Campaigns, 1861-1864*, The University of North Carolina Press: Chapel Hill: (2005).

Hess, Earl J., *Into the Crater: The Mine Attack at Petersburg*, The University of South Carolina Press: Columbia (2010).

Hess, Earl J., *In the Trenches at Petersburg: Field Fortifications & Confederate Defeat*, University of North Carolina Press: Chapel Hill (2009).

Marvel, William, *Burnside*, The University of North Carolina Press: Chapel Hill (1991).

McPherson, James, *Battle Cry of Freedom: The Civil War Era*, Oxford University Press: Oxford (1988).

Phisterer, Frederick, *New York in the War of the Rebellion 1861 to 1865*, D.B. Lyon Company, State Printers: Albany, New York (Third Ed. 1912).

Rolph, Gerald Vern and Clark, Noel, *The Civil War Soldier*, Historical Impressions Co.: Washington (1961).

Schmutz, John F., *The Battle of the Crater: A Complete History*, McFarland & Company, Inc., Publishers: Jefferson, North Carolina (2009).

Sears, Stephen W., *George B. McClellan: The Young Napoleon*, Ticknor & Fields: New York (1988).

Eastern Front from the Confederate point of view

[Map: Petersburg Lines]

(1) Phisterer, 4029; OR 40(1):195, 538.

(2) Axelrod, 34-36; Marvel, 390. Potter claimed to have had the same idea for a mine, but the record indicates that Potter was thinking of a "sap," i.e. an open trench, when Pleasants approached him (See OR, 50(2): 220; See generally Hess: Preface, 1; Axelrod, 36; and Marvel, 390-391).

(3) Hess, *Into the Crater*, 5, 14; *Report of the Joint Committee*, (Vol. I), 112.

(4) Axelrod, 37-46.

(5) Axelrod, 45-46; Hess, *Into the Crater*, 3; Letter from Homer Olcott to Father dated June 29, 1864, Homer Olcott Pension File.

(6) Axelrod, 45-46; Hess, *Into the Crater*, 3; Schmutz, 53.

(7) Axelrod, 42-43. Not all the men of the 48th Pennsylvania were coal miners. (Emmanuel Dabney, "A Federal Opportunity Lost: The Battle of the Crater," *Blue & Gray*, Vol. XXX, no. 5, 2014, 8) After the war, the 48th Pennsylvania's historian explained that the ventilation problem was solved:

"after a method quite common in the anthracite coal mines. A perpendicular shaft or hole was made from the mine to the surface at a point inside of the Union rifle pits. A small furnace, or fire-place, was built at the bottom of this hole, or shaft, for the purpose of heating the air , and the fire was kept constantly burning, thus creating a draft. The door made of canvas was placed in the gallery [i.e. the tunnel], a little outside of this fire-place, thus shutting it in and shielding it from the outside air at the mouth of the mine. Wooden pipes, extending from the outside of this canvas door, along the gallery to the inner end thereof, conducted the fresh air to the point of operations, which, after supplying the miners with pure air, returned along the gallery towards the entrance of the mine, and, being stopped by the canvas door, the vitiated air moved into the furnace and up the shaft to the surface. By this means a constant current of air circulated through the gallery." (Axelrod, 43)

The entrance, from a sketch which accompanied the report to the Joint Committee

[Sketch: Gallery Cross-section]

and a photograph from a field visit in January 2012

[Photo: Gallery Entry]

(8) Axelrod, 56-58; Hess, *In the Trenches*, 45; Cavanaugh and Marvel, 6.

(9) Hess, *Into the Crater*, 18; Greene, 205-206; Dabney, 19. The Confederate division on the Ninth Corps front was commanded by Bushrod Johnson.

[Photo: Bushrod Johnson]

(10) Goodwin, 629.

(11) Larzelere Diary, June 20 and 21, 1864. Larzelere made no mention of President Lincoln.

(12) Goodwin, 631.

(13) OR, 40(1):195; Letter from Homer Olcott to Father dated June 29, 1864, Homer Olcott Pension File.

(14) Letter from Newton Spencer, dated July 17, 1864 in *The Hornellsville Tribune*, August 4, 1864; Diary of William B. Larzelere, June 23 to July 30, 1864.

(15) Letters from Daniel B. Lee dated June 26, 1864 and June 27, 1864. (U.S. Army Military History Institute, Carlisle Barracks, CWMiscColl (Enlisted man's letters, Jan 10, 1863-Jan 14, 1883).

(16) Letter from Daniel B. Lee dated June 27, 1864.

(17) Letter from Jacob Graves to Daniel Graves, July 8, 1864 (National Archives, Pension Files).

(18) OR, 40(1):195. The Second Brigade, which included the 179th New York after July 21, similarly reported "intrenching, picketing, skirmishing, and sharpshooting." *Ibid.*, 196.

(19) *Buffalo Daily Courier*, July 13, 1864.

(20) *The Hornellsvile Tribune*, July 21, 1864.

(21) Daniel B. Lee Letter dated June 26, 1864. He also used the "hail" metaphor in a June 27, 1864 letter.

(22) Letter from Jacob Graves to Daniel Graves, July 8, 1864; Larzelere Diary, June 21, 1864; Letter from Homer Olcott to Father dated June 29, 1864, Homer Olcott Pension File.

(23) Axelrod, 92. Conditions were less dangerous on the Fifth Corps front to the left of the Ninth Corps. *Harper's Weekly* reported that "by common consent among the men on both sides

sharpshooting has been abandoned, and the pickets live amicably near each other, outside their fortified lines." (August 6, 1864, 502). However, after leaving the Fifth Corps' front: "there is no longer any security against being hit, the sharpshooters keeping a bright look-out on both sides, firing at every one who shows himself, and constantly skimming bullets at random, which often take effect upon people unseen by the shooter...All night the firing is kept up with increased vindictiveness, for the purpose of driving in the working parties who come out in the darkness to dig new works..."

(24) Hess, *Into the Crater*, 224.

(25) *The Hornellsville Tribune*, August 4, 1864.

(26) *The Hornellsville Tribune*, July 21, 1864.

(27) N. Spencer, "A War Story," *Elmira Telegram*, April 28, 1895. The facts contradict Lt. Finch's statements to *The Hornellsville Tribune* that: "the 179th has lost but one man since the charge of the 17th of June. They are too sharp for the sharpshooters. Some Regiments lose three or four per day in this way." (July 21, 1864).

(28) CMR, National Archives, RG 94, Entry 534.

(29) *Buffalo Daily Courier*, July 13, 1864. The reference to McClellan as "a digger" is presumably to his caution at the beginning of the Peninsula campaign when he prepared extensive fortifications before eventually attacking.

(30) Sears, 9-10.

(31) Hess, *Field Armies*, 333-339.

(32) Hess, *Field Armies*, 333.

(33) *The Hornellsville Tribune*, August 4, 1864.

(34) Hess, *In the Trenches*, 53, 56.

(35) Transcript of Court-martial of Lt. John Hoy, July 15-16, 1864, 12 (National Archives); Larzelere Diary, July 4, 1864.

(36) Letter from Daniel B. Lee dated July 3, 1864; Hoy Transcript.

(37) Hoy Transcript, 13-14. Hoy may have expected higher rank as a result of the recruiting process. The enlistment forms of at least two recruits bear the handwritten notation "The Recruit selects Capt. John Hoy's Co." (Edgar Maby CMSR; John McDonald CMSR).

(38) Hoy Court Martial Transcript, National Archives. The court found Hoy guilty of the specification that he had struck Saxton. However, because Saxton and Hoy were both first lieutenants, the court apparently found Hoy not guilty of the charge of striking his "superior" officer and found him guilty instead of conduct to the prejudice of good order and military discipline based on that specification. (*Ibid.*) Reflecting the temperance culture of the Burned-over District, the *Yates County Chronicle* ran an article in March 1865 titled "A Terrible Enemy:" "The most terrible enemy that a soldier encounters is liquor drinking. This is not the place for argument on that point. Every great General knows the fact; ... Deeds are daily done under the influence of liquor, which their perpetrators would weep tears of blood to wash out. No man, how ever wide may be the grasp of his intellect, can have an adequate idea of the amount of suffering which would be prevented...by the adoption of the following suggestion, that not one single teaspoon of liquor, wine, beer or brandies be allowed a soldier under any circumstances whatsoever, outside a hospital or sick bed. But let each soldier have an extra allowance of coffee..." (*Yates County Chronicle*, March 30, 1865)

The *Chronicle's* Democratic competitor in Penn Yan was similarly concerned. When the *Penn Yan Democrat* proudly announced the enlistment of its editor, Newton B. Spencer, in the 179th, it also expressed the hope that "he will rely [on] natural courage and bravery rather [than] commissary [liquor]." (*Penn Yan Democrat*, February 26, 1864)

(39) F. Phisterer, New York in the War of the Rebellion 1861 to 1865, D.B. Lyon Company, State Printers (Third. Ed. 1912), Vol. V at 4036. The rumor mill quickly adapted to events. A July 8 letter from the *Buffalo Daily Courier's* correspondent in the 179th New York Volunteers reported that: "Since [Blachford's] death the command of the Company [E] has devolved upon Lieutenant Louis J. Ottenot of Buffalo [the letter ignored Hoy's brief tenure], a thorough, competent and gallant young officer formerly of the 21st Regiment. It is loudly rumored here in camp that he has been recommended to the Captaincy, to which position he is justly and honorably entitled by his gallant military conduct in the past." (*Buffalo Daily Courier*, July 13, 1864)

(40) Phisterer, 4029.

(41) *The Hornellsville Tribune*, August 4, 1864.

(42) *The Hornellsville Tribune*, July 21, 1864.

(43) *Ibid*. There is no carded medical record indicating that Barton was sent to hospital.

(44) *The Hornellsville Tribune*, August 4, 1864.

(45) *Ibid*.

(46) Larzelere Diary, July 23 to July 28, 1864.

(47) Undated newspaper clipping from the *Penn Yan Democrat*, collection of the New York State Military Museum and Veterans Research Center, Unit History Project, 179th New York Volunteers, Civil War Newspaper Clippings.

(48) *Ibid*.

(49) Cavanaugh and Marvel, 6. See also Dabney, 8; Kevin Levin, *Remembering the Battle of the Crater: War as Murder*, (Lexington: The University Press of Kentucky, 2012), 10.

(50) Greene, 203.

(51) Greene, 195.

(52) Goodwin, 637.

(53) Letters from Daniel B. Lee dated May 9, 1864, June 8, 1864, June 27, 1864 and undated.

(54) *Harper's Weekly*, August 6, 1864.

(55) *The Hornellsville Tribune*, July 21, 1864.

(56) Hess, *Into the Crater*, 20, 22, 33; Axelrod, 109.

(57) Undated *Penn Yan Democrat* clipping, New York State Military Museum Unit History website, 179th New York Volunteers.

(58) Greene, 201-202.

(59) Grant, Vol. II, 188. Before Grant began his campaign in May 1864, the Army of the Potomac was supplied by railroad from Alexandria. After crossing the Rapidan, the Army of the Potomac had to be supplied by wagon train. Grant explained that:

"With a wagon-train that would have extended from the Rapidan to Richmond, stretched along in single file and separated as the teams necessarily would be when moving, we could still carry only three days' forage and about ten to twelve days' rations, besides a supply of ammunition. To overcome all difficulties, the chief quartermaster, General Rufus Ingalls, had marked on each wagon the corps badge with the division color and the number of the brigade. At a glance, the particular brigade to which any wagon belonged could be told. The wagons were also marked to note the contents: if ammunition, whether for artillery or infantry; if forage, whether grain or hay; if rations, whether bread, pork, beans, rice, sugar, coffee or whatever it might be. Empty wagons were never allowed to follow the army or stay in camp. As soon as a wagon was empty it would return to the base of supply for a load of precisely the same article that had been taken from it. Empty trains were obliged to leave the road free for loaded ones. Arriving near the army they would be parked in fields nearest to the brigades they belonged to. Issues, except of ammunition, were made at night in all cases." *Ibid.*, 188-90.

(60) Axelrod, 96; Charles W. Bowery, Jr., *The Richmond-Petersburg campaign, 1864-65*, Praeger: Santa Barbara, California (2014), 100-102..

(61) Hess, *In the Trenches*, 75, 203; OR, III(V):69-71.

(62) Rolph and Clark, 14; Sabine, 23.

(63) Letter from Homer Olcott to Father dated July 5, 1864, Homer Olcott Pension File.

(64) Rolph and Clark, 14.

(65) Axelrod, 76.

(66) Larzelere Diary, July 23, 1864.

(67) *Elmira Daily Advertiser*, [circa July 25, 1864]

(68) Axelrod, 77-78; Hess, *Into the Crater*, 50-51.

(69) Axelrod, 83; Hess, *Into the Crater*, 52-53.

(70) Larzelere Diary, July 28, 1864.

(71) *Elmira Daily Advertiser*, [circa July 30, 1864].

(72) McPherson, 757.

(73) Gray, 18.

(74) Larzelere Diary, July 28, 1864.

(75) Regimental History, 27; H. Messing, "Company 'G' – 179th New York Volunteers," (March 30, 1897), Messing Mss., Eli Lilly Library, Indiana University.

(76) *Harper's Weekly*, August 6, 1864, 499.

Chapter Ten

———— "The Court-Martial of Private Spencer," *Civil War Times Illustrated*, Vol. XXVII, No. 10 (February 1989)

Anderson, John, *The Fifty-Seventh Regiment of Massachusetts Volunteers in the War of the Rebellion*, E.B. Stillings & Co, Printers: Boston (1896).

Axelrod, Alan *The Horrid Pit: The Battle of the Crater. the Civil War's Cruelest Mission*, Carroll & Graf Publishers: New York (2007).

Bearss, Edwin C. with Suderow, Bryce A., *The Petersburg campaign, Volume I, The Eastern Front Battles, June-August 1864*, Savas Beatie LLC: El Dorado Hills, California (2012).

Catton, Bruce, *The Army of the Potomac: A Stillness at Appomattox*, Doubleday & Company: Garden City, New York (1953).

Catton, Bruce, *Grant Takes Command*, Little, Brown and Company: Boston (1969).

Cavanaugh, Michael A. and Marvel, William, *The Petersburg campaign: The Battle of the Crater 'The Horrid Pit' June 25-August 6, 1864*, H. E. Howard, Inc.: Lynchburg, Virginia (Second Edition 1989).

Cleaves, Freeman, *Meade of Gettysburg*, University of Oklahoma Press: Norman (1960).

Dabney, Emmanuel, "A Federal Opportunity Lost: The Battle of the Crater," *Blue & Gray*, Vol. XXX, #5 (2014).

Goodwin, Doris Kearns, *Team of Rivals: The Political Genius of Abraham Lincoln*, Simon & Schuster: New York (2005).

Grant, Ulysses S., *Personal Memoirs of U.S. Grant*, Charles L. Webster & Company: New York

(1886).

Greene, A. Wilson, *Civil War Petersburg: Confederate City in the Crucible of War*, University of Virginia Press: Charlottesville (2006).

Hess, Earl J., *Field Armies and Fortifications in the Civil War: The Eastern Campaigns, 1861-1864*, The University of North Carolina Press: Chapel Hill: (2005).

Hess, Earl J., *Into the Crater: The Mine Attack at Petersburg*, The University of South Carolina Press: Columbia (2010).

Hess, Earl J., *In the Trenches at Petersburg: Field Fortifications & Confederate Defeat*, University of North Carolina Press: Chapel Hill (2009).

Newsome, Hampton, *Richmond Must Fall: The Richmond-Petersburg campaign, October 1864*, The Kent State University Press: Kent, Ohio (2013).

McPherson, James, *Battle Cry of Freedom: The Civil War Era*, Oxford University Press: Oxford (1988).

McPherson, James, *Tried By War: Abraham Lincoln as Commander in Chief*, The Penguin Press: New York (2008).

McWhiney, Grady and Jenkins, Jack Jay, "The Union's Worst General", *Civil War Times Illustrated*, Vol. XIV, No. 3 (June 1975).

Reid, Brian Holden and White, John, " 'A Mob of Stragglers and Cowards': Desertion from the Union and Confederate Armies, 1861-65", *The Journal of Strategic Studies*, Vol. 8, Issue 1 (1985).

Schmutz, John F., *The Battle of the Crater: A Complete History*, McFarland & Company, Inc., Publishers: Jefferson, North Carolina (2009).

Slotkin, Richard, *No Quarter: The Battle of the Crater*, 1864, Random House: New York (2009).

Walcott, *History of the Twenty-First Regiment Massachusetts Volunteers in the War for Preservation of the Union 1861-1865*, Houghton, Mifflin and Company: Boston (1882).

Ward, Geoffrey C., *The Civil War: An Illustrated History*, Alfred A. Knopf: New York (1990).

(1) OR, 40(1): 60. Catton, *Stillness at Appomattox*, 225-226.

(2) Bearss, 215-216. It is not clear how much special training the Fourth Division actually did. (Dabney, 19; Hess, *Into the Crater*, 54-55) General Ferrero testified before the Court of Inquiry that "my troops are raw, new troops, and never had been drilled two weeks from the day they entered the service till [the Battle of the Crater]." (OR, 40(1): 93)

(3) OR, 40(1): 60; Slotkin, 145-46; Bearss, 216. Meade is reputed to have said that if the attack failed, "it would then be said, and very properly, that we were shoving these people ahead to get killed because we did not care anything about them. But that could not be said if we put white troops in front." (Cleaves, 277) Cleaves notes that "Meade's position regarding the Negro was similar to that of his own politics – about center." (*Ibid.*, 276) In his memoirs, Grant attributed the decision to Meade. (Grant, Vol. II, 313)

(4) Hess, *Into the Crater*, 57, 51; "The Court Martial of Private Spencer", 36. Although the First, Second and Third Divisions had all seen action, Ledlie's First Division probably was the most rested of the three. (Hess, *Into the Crater*, 57)

(5) Hess, *Into the Crater*, 65-66; OR, 40(1): 541. Newton Spencer said that the 14th New York Heavy Artillery and the 179th were in the first line. "The Court Martial of Private Spencer," 36. Thirty years after the war, Col. Marshall's assistant adjutant general recalled the order with the second and third lines reversed. (Anderson, 205)

(6) McWhiney and Jenkins, 30. "Ledlie's division marched into the crater immediately on the

explosion, but most of the men stopped there in the absence of any one to give directions; their commander having found some safe retreat to get into before they started", Grant, Vol. II, 313-314; "By his conduct and by all accounts, Ledlie was an incompetent, a scoundrel, a drunk, and a coward.", Axelrod, 163; Burnside gave the task to one of the worst division commanders of the war, Hess, *Into the Crater*, 60; Catton, quoting Col. Stephen Weld of the First Brigade's 56th Massachusetts: Ledlie "was a drunkard and an arrant coward...It was wicked to risk the lives of men in such a man's hands.", Catton, *Grant Takes Command*, 321; "Ledlie...was by all evidence both a drunk and a coward.", Bearss, 217.

(7) See Hess, 4.

(8) 179th New York Volunteers, Carded Medical Records, Stephen Compton, Admitted First Division Depot Field Hospital, sick, July 25, 1864, Sent to Emory U.S.A. General Hospital Washington, D.C., July 30, 1864; George Carpenter, Admitted First Division of 9th Army Corps hospital, July 24, 1864, "Feb Inter", Sent to General Hospital, July 30, 1864; James Farr CMSR ("absent sick" June and July 1864).

(9) This is a rough estimate based on the number of troops engaged on June 17, 1864 (approximately 230) less casualties (90) less an estimate for subsequent sickness among the soldiers engaged on June 17.

(10) Hess, 112.

(11) Affidavit of William Hemstreet, April 12, 1883, William Hemstreet Pension File..

(12) Cavanaugh and Marvel, 96; Hess, *Into the Crater*, 112, 180; Hess, *In the Trenches*, 101.

(13) Hess, *Into The Crater*, 87.

(14) *Ibid.*, 97, 135.

(15) Diary of William Larzalere, July 23 to July 30, 1864; Letter of Eugene Dunton to Parents, August 2, 1864, Eugene Dunton Pension File.

(16) *Buffalo Daily Courier*, August 10, 1864.

(17) *Buffalo Daily Courier*, August 10, 1864. Hess, 65-66; OR, 40(1): 535. The *Courier* reported 1 a.m.

(18) Hess, *Into the Crater*, 65-66, 78, 80; OR, 40:1, 541. Historians disagree on the precise location where the Second Brigade formed for the charge. Hess states that: "Marshall's brigade form[ed] three lines of battle on the open ground behind the forward Union line." (*Into the Crater* at 65. In contrast, Slotkin states that: "Marshall's brigade filed into the section of the front line directly opposite Elliott's Salient. ...The trench was packed tight." *No Quarter*, 168-69. Both identify their sources and both interestingly cite Charles Houghton's post-war recollection.

(19) *Ibid.*, 77-78.

(20) *Penn Yan Democrat*, quoted in "The Court Martial of Private Spencer", 34.

(21) *Buffalo Daily Courier*, August 10, 1864. "At fifteen minutes to five the slow match was ignited an[d] in a moment the air was filled with the remnants of canon human bodies an[d] the once rebel fort was no more. It was a complete ruin." (Letter from Eugene Dunton to Parents, August 2, 1864, Eugene Dunton Pension File)

(22) Larzelere Diary, July 30, 1864.

(23) Ward, 312.

(24) Axelrod, 119-20.

(25) Greene, 206-207; Newsome, 104.

(26) Determination of Waud's location is possible, using his notes and contemporary maps. Waud's notes state that "The chief engineer of the A. of P. is standing on the embankment

watching progress." That would be Maj. J.C. Duane. Duane told the Court of Inquiry that at the time of the explosion he "was on the Fifth Corps front, assisting in directing the artillery fire." Although he saw the explosion, he "did not see the assault distinctly; I was too far to the left." (OR, 40(1): 75 - 76) If Waud was viewing the battle from that location, that would account for the lack of detail in his drawing. Waud also refers in his notes to the "magnificent 8 & 10 inch batteries, built and commanded by Col. Abbott" which were depicted "in the middle ground." Abbott was in charge of all siege artillery in the battle area and his heavy artillery and mortars are marked on a plate from the OR Atlas. See Hess, *In the Trenches*, 58 - 59; *Into the Crater*, 64. The full text of Waud's notation is the following:

"Explosion of the mine under the Confederate works at Petersburg July 30th 1864. The spires in the distance mark the location of the city; along the crest, in front of them are the defensive works, it was an angle of these that was blown up, with its guns & defenders. The explosion was the signal for the simultaneous opening of the artillery and musketry of the Union lines. The pickets are seen running in from their pits & shelters on the front, to the outer line of attack. In the middle distance, are the magnificent 8 & 10 inch Mortar batteries, built and commanded by Col. Abbott. Nearer is a line of abandoned rifle pits, and in the foreground is the covered way, a sunken road for communication with the siege works and the conveyance of supplies and ammunition to the forts. The chief Engineer of the A. of P. is standing upon the embankment watching progress throw [sic] a field glass."

[Map: Union artillery positions (Duane with Warren)]

(27) Hess, 85.

(28) Hess, 84.

(29) *Ibid.* It appears that Waud had moved from the Fifth Corps sector to the Ninth Corps sector by 8 a.m. His advantage point would appear to be in front of the covered way from which the Fourth Division advanced.

(30) Cavanaugh and Marvel, 41 - 42; Axelrod, 125; Hess, *Into the Crater*, 87.

[Sketch: Roemer's Battery]

(31) "The Court Martial of Private Spencer," 36.

(32) Letter dated July 31, 1864 to My dear [illegible], Collection Number 643, Martin, John Marshall Papers, 1863 - 1864, MssM3643b, Virginia Historical Society.

(33) Catton, *Grant Takes Command*, 322.

(34) *Ibid.*; Axelrod, 122.

(35) Catton, *Grant Takes Command*, 323-324; Axelrod, 139, 158; Hess, *Into the Crater*, 116.

(36) Hess, *Into the Crater*, 110.

(37) Schmutz, 143-45.

(38) Hess, *Into the Crater*, 64.

(39) Testimony of Ambrose Burnside, December 17, 1864, *Report of the Joint Committee on the Conduct of the War*, Vol. 1, Battle of Petersburg, Government Printing Office: Washington, D.C. (1865), 19.

(40) Axelrod, 128-129; Catton, 321.

(41) Catton, *A Stillness at Appomattox*, 155.

(42) OR, 40(1): 17.

(43) "The Court Martial of Private Spencer," 36.

(44) Anderson, 206.

(45) OR, 40(1): 541. It is not entirely clear which units entered which covered way at which time. Colonel Clarke recalled after the war that it was the 14th New York Heavy Artillery that entered the second covered way and that the 179th had entered the first (nearest to the Union lines) covered way. (Anderson, 207) Robinson did report that after the 3rd Maryland and the 179th New York initially took position in the second covered way Colonel Marshall ordered the entire Second Brigade to form in the first covered way. (OR, 40(1): 541)

(46) Letter from Eugene Dunton to Parents, August 2, 1864, Eugene Dunton Pension File; "The Court Martial of Private Spencer," 36.

(47) *Buffalo Daily Courier*, August 10, 1864.

(48) Joint Committee, 92.

(49) Axelrod, 146.

(50) OR, 40(1): 48, 121.

(51) OR, (40)1: 135, para. 8, 10. Burnside's original plan had called for the assault to clear the Confederate trenches to the right and left of the crater before taking the crest, but had also emphasized the need to move quickly.

(52) Anderson, 204-205; Bearss, 218.

(53) *Ibid.*

(54) Hess, *Into the Crater*, 97-98.

(55) OR Vol. 40, Part I, 547.

(56) Hess, 105.

(57) Hess, 106-107.

(58) Hess, 116

(59) Hess, 110; Cavanaugh and Marvel, 43.

(60) Anderson, 208.

(61) Potter's division was to support Ledlie's division on the right. However, "[t]he smoke and dust were so great at this time that nothing could be seen, and the leading regiments got further to the left than was intended, coming thus in contact with some troops of the First Division and causing some confusion...The movement was further somewhat embarassed by some of the troops of the First Division moving to the right instead of forward." (OR, 40(1): 547)

(62) Joint Committee, 92.

(63) Anderson, 208; *Ibid.* ; OR, 40(1): 114, 541; Hess, *Into the Crater*, 90; Bearss, 221; Slotkin, 198; Schmutz, 150.

(64) Anderson, 204- 205,208, 215.

(65) Hess, *Into the Crater*, 92; OR, 40(1): 114.

(66) Anderson, 205. John Schmutz refers to the 179th as "quite new and untested." It is fair to say that the 179th was "quite new," and a majority of the soldiers of the 179th on the field on July 30 had not been present for the "test" on June 17. (Schmutz, 140)

(67) Anderson, 209-210.

(68) *Ibid.* See also White, "Charging the Crater," *National Tribune*, June 21, 1883; Schmutz, 150.

(69) *Buffalo Daily Courier*, August 10, 1864.

(70) *Buffalo Daily Courier*, August 10, 1864; CMRs. Barton was taken back to the field hospital where he died. Later in the battle the trip across no man's land became extremely difficult due to

Confederate fire.

(71) Anderson, 210-211.

(72) OR, 40(1): 595, 596; Hess, *Into the Crater*, 125.

(73) Hess, *Into the Crater*, 140.

(74) *Ibid.*, 140-41.

(75) Hess *Into the Crater*, 141-42, 155-56.

(76) Hess *Into the Crater*, 157-158; OR, 40(1): 536, 599.

(77) OR, 40(1): 542. See also 9th New Hampshire, 502.

(78) Anderson, 211.

(79) Letter from Lt. William Hemstreet, October 14, 1864, Solomon Leonard CMSR; James C. Rutan Pension File, Examining Surgeon's Certificate, June 15, 1881. During the physical examination, Rutan told the doctor that: "In a charge he was crushed underneath a colored regiment which retreated when his regiment [was] lying in rifle pits in front of Petersburg." See also 9th New Hampshire, 502. The colored troops, who had attacked with fixed bayonets, retreated to the trenches "where we were already as thick as we could stand."

(80) Walcott, 347.

(81) Anderson, 183.

(82) OR, 40(1): 542.

(83) Affidavit of Jeremiah Sprague, March 13, 1865, Farwell Pension File. Sprague said that Farwell had been killed between 9 a.m. and 10 a.m., which would be consistent with Mahone's attack. In a September 30, 1899 letter, Company A's Lt. George Carpenter stated that Farwell had been killed in the rebel lines, but Carpenter was not present that day; see Bradley Pension File. See also Norton Affidavit, February 22, 1890, Norton Pension File.

(84) Anderson, 211.

(85) *Ibid.*; Hess, *Into the Crater*, 158.

(86) Hess, *Into the Crater*, 170.

(87) *Ibid.*, 172-173.

(88) Hess, 178-181.

(89) Hess, 182-83.

(90) Hess, 185; Axelrod, 215.

(91) Hess, *Into the Crater*, 188-89;

(92) Axelrod; Cavanaugh and Marvel.

(93) Affidavit of James Spencer, April 15, 1889, John Grierson Pension File. See also Affidavits of John Grierson, April 2, 1889, Jeremiah Sprague and John Spencer, August 30, 1900, all John Grierson Pension File.

(94) OR, 40(1): 542.

(95) *Ibid.*

(96) *The Hornellsville Tribune*, August 25, 1864.

(97) *Yates County Chronicle*, August 4, 1864, August 11, 1864 and August 18, 1864.

(98) *Yates County Chronicle*, August 25, 1864.

(99) *Yates County Chronicle*, August 11, 1864; Sprague Affidavit, March 13, 1865, Farwell Pension File. The *Yates County Chronicle* had reported on August 11, 1864 that Sprague had been killed. "He was a good soldier and a son of widow Sprague of this village." The *Chronicle* incorrectly reported Sprague as being from the 179th New York Volunteers.

(100) Phisterer, 4029; "Memorandum from Prisoner of War Records" in CMSRs.

(101) N. Spencer, "A War Story," *The Elmira Telegram*, April 28, 1895. "Gentleman Jim" Corbett had defeated John L. Sullivan for the heavyweight championship of the world the year before.

(102) Declaration of Dennis DeFord, July 25, 1887, Dennis DeFord Pension File.

(103) OR, (40)1: 246, 598.

(104) Larzelere Diary, July 30, 1864; Letter from Eugene Dunton to Parents, August 2, 1864, Eugene Dunton Pension File.

(105) *Elmira Daily Advertiser*, August 2, 1864.

(106) *Ibid.*; The *Oswego Daily Palladium*, August 1, 1864, also reported that Major "Buxton" of the 179th had lost a leg. After capture Bartlett was sent to Danville prison where exposure and his wounds led to severe dysentery. He was later transferred to Libby prison and was paroled in September and returned north on the 24th. After a full winter of recovery he rejoined the army in April and was assigned to command of the First Division of the IX Corps. To see the effect of war on General Bartlett, here is a photograph of him and his staff in July 1865, just a month after turning 25 years of age:

[Photo: Gen. Bartlett]

(107) *Harper's Weekly*, August 13, 1864, 515.

(108) *Harper's Weekly*, August 20, 1864, 529, 536-37.

(109) *Harper's Weekly*, August 27, 1864, 548.

(110) *Harper's Weekly*, August 20, 1864, 531. See also Kevin Levin, *Remembering the Battle of the Crater: War as Murder*, (Lexington: The University Press of Kentucky, 2012), 21-22.

(111) *Ibid.*

(112) Hess, *Into the Crater*, 139. See also Kevin Levin, *Remembering the Battle of the Crater: War as Murder*, Lexington: The University Press of Kentucky, 2012, 24.

(113) OR, 40(1): 17; Goodwin, 645-46; McPherson, *Tried By War* at 228.

(114) Grant, Vol. II, 315. The Battle of the Crater is a reminder that the fighting can still be hard for the soldiers on the ground of the victorious side. A Confederate soldier named Younger wrote his brother that "Saturday was the awfullest day I ever saw." (Letter to Brother, August 4, 1864, Collection Number 610, Younger Letters, 1864, MssZL8585b, Virginia Historical Society)

(115) OR, 40(1): 42-43.

(116) Axelrod, viii.

(117) Hess, *Into the Crater*, 221.

(118) OR, 40(1): 127.

(119) *Ibid.*, 127-28.

(120) *Ibid.*, 128.

(121) *Ibid.*

(122) *Ibid.*

(123) *Ibid.* See also, OR, 40(1): 128.

(124) Grant, Vol. II, 313. See also correspondence between Grant and Meade about not giving Ledlie another command. (OR, 42(3): 867, 896)

(125) McPherson, *Battle Cry of Freedom*, 362-63.

(126) Report of the Joint Committee, 11-12.

(127) OR, 40:1, 74; Cleaves, 277. Similarly, General McClellan is reputed to have said in 1862 that: "More than once have battles, nearly lost by veterans, been restored by the intrepid obstinacy of

new soldiers." Reid and White concluded that "this kind of enthusiasm became rarer as the war continued and the novelty of battle wore off." (Reid and White, 75)

[Photo: Looking West]

[Photo: Swale 200 yards west]

[Photo: Swale 200 yards looking east]

[Map: March walks]

[Photo: Tracing Ravine]

[Photo: Confluence Taylor's Creek with north/south ravine]

[Photo: Taylor to Mine]

Chapter Eleven

Cleaves, Freeman, *Meade of Gettysburg*, University of Oklahoma Press: Norman (1960).

Foner, Eric, *The Fiery Trial: Abraham Lincoln and American Slavery*, W.W. Norton & Company: New York (2010).

Goodwin, Doris Kearns, *Team of Rivals: The Political Genius of Abraham Lincoln*, Simon & Schuster: New York (2005).

Hardee, William J., *Hardee's Rifle and Light Infantry Tactics for the Instructions, Exercises and Manoeuvres of Riflemen and Light Infantry, Including School of the Soldier and School of the Company, To Which Is added, Duties of Non-Commissioned Officers, Military Honors to Be Paid By Troops, the Articles of War*, J. O. Kane, Publisher: New York (1862) (reprinted by H-Bar Enterprises: Silver Spring, Maryland).

Hess, Earl J., *Into the Crater: The Mine Attack at Petersburg*, The University of South Carolina Press: Columbia (2010).

Howe, Thomas J., *The Petersburg campaign: Wasted Valor, June 15-18, 1864*, H.E. Howard, Inc.: Lynchburg, Virginia (Second Edition 1988).

Marvel, William, *Burnside*, The University of North Carolina Press: Chapel Hill (1991).

McPherson, James, *Tried By War: Abraham Lincoln as Commander in Chief*, The Penguin Press: New York (2008).

McWhiney, Grady and Jenkins, Jack Jay, "The Union's Worst General", *Civil War Times Illustrated*, Vol. XIV, No. 3 (June 1975).

Phisterer, Frederick, *New York in the War of the Rebellion 1861 to 1865*, D.B. Lyon Company, State Printers: Albany, New York (Third Ed. 1912).

Ramold, Steven J., *Across the Divide: Union Soldiers View the Northern Home Front*, New York University Press: New York (2013).

Wilkenson, Warren, *Mother, May You Never See the Sights I Have Seen: The Fifty-seventh Massachusetts Veteran Volunteers in the Last Year of the Civil War*, Harper & Row, Publishers: New York (1990).

(1) The 1864 issues of the *Penn Yan Democrat* are not extant, except for three issues. The text of the article is taken from the transcript of his court martial. (Transcript, Proceedings of a General

Court Martial, convened at Head Qrs. 2d Div. 9th A.C. by virtue of General Orders No. 36th Para. II, Headquarters 2d Div. 9th A. C. Near Weldon R.R. Va. Aug. 27th 1864. In the case of Private Newton B. Spencer Co F. 179th N.Y. Vols.) A copy of Spencer's personal copy of the transcript with his handwritten marginal notations is in the collection of the U.S. Army Military History Institute, Carlisle Barracks, Spencer, Newton B. - CWTIColl, Pvt's court martial papers, 1864. See also "The Court-Martial of Private Spencer," *Civil War Times Illustrated*, Vol. XXVII, No. 10 (February 1989), 34-40.

(2) While usage of the word is unacceptable to me personally, I have left it in because it is a part of the historical record and conveys the intensity of Spencer's beliefs. As Warren Wilkenson wrote in *Mother, May you Never See the Sights I Have Seen*, my objective has been to present the men of the 179th as they were - "good, bad or otherwise." (Wilkenson, xiv) I have also used the now archaic "negro" and "colored" because those were the phrases of the day.

(3) Phisterer reports the 179th's casualties at the Battle of the Crater as 56–10 killed, 20 wounded and 26 missing. (Phisterer, 4029) My calculation based on the carded medical records for the 179th is 59 - 5 killed, 28 wounded and 26 missing. Spencer's estimate of only 160 soldiers engaged probably does not include the 80 soldiers of Company G that arrived the day before the battle. Because Company G arrived so late and had started out as Company A of the 189th New York Volunteers, being assigned to the 179th only when the 180th failed to organize, Spencer may have felt that Company G really was not a part of the 179th. In a letter written at the same time, "Ord." referred to the 179th as having only six companies, which would not include Company G. (*The Hornellsville Tribune*, August 25, 1864)

(4) Using the carded medical records for the 179th, I calculated Company F's casualties at the Battle of the Crater as six: two killed (Frederick Windangle and Andrew Hurd); one wounded (Edward Dunn); and three missing (Alan Farwell–later confirmed as killed and John Hall and William Norton – later confirmed as prisoners of war).

(5) The carded medical records for the 179th show that Spencer was in fact in the hospital on August 12, 1864, but not because of the "admonition of a rebel bullet." On August 8, 1864, he was admitted to the First Division Hospital with a diagnosis of "primary syphilis." He was sent to the Ninth Corps' Depot Field Hospital on August 14 with a diagnosis of "jaundice" (A "card" also shows him being admitted with diarrhea). On August 29, after the court-martial was completed, Spencer was sent to Washington on the U.S.A. Hospital Steamer Connecticut, with the "complaint" listed as "Paraphymose." He apparently was turned over to the Second Division's Provost Marshal on September 4. He was readmitted to the Ninth Corps Field Hospital on October 4 with "Sec. Syphilis." His problems continued as he was admitted to Ricord (Veneral) U.S.A. Gen'l Hospital in Washington on March 16, 1865 with "tertiary syphilis." Thus it appears that if Spencer was in fact wounded, it was not serious enough to have been recorded. It also appears that Spencer may never have returned to the 179th in the field.

(6) Steven J. Ramold observed in *Across the Divide* that newspapers:
"served as a platform for the soldiers. Writing to their hometown newspapers, soldiers attempted to shape public opinion at home and correct what they determined to be faulty assumptions about the war and its course. Newspapers also served as a place for soldiers to complain beyond any possible repercussion for insubordination. Unable to receive satisfaction, enlisted men often used their hometown newspapers to air their complaints about army life, be it harsh discipline, late pay, or incompetent leadership." (Ramold, 19).

Except for being "beyond any possible repercussion for insubordination," Spencer's letter certainly fits that mold. Spencer's transgression may have been in not writing anonymously as Ord. and C.B.C. did.

(7) C.B.C. described their performance as the "looked for support" in a letter to The *Buffalo Daily Courier*, a week after the battle :

"to the sorrow and dissatisfaction of the boys, it turned out to be our so-called 'Burnside's Pets'; our 'Country's Hopes,' in the shape of a division of *niggers* – curse them. They went forward, made one pretty good charge, but fell back, losing the ground they charged on. They rallied, but poorly, formed line again, and were about to make another charge, when the Johnny's seeing who they had to contend with, gave them a volley, which caused the niggers to fall back, perfectly panic-stricken and in disorder, causing the whole line to fall back to its original position ... Had a good line of white troops been sent instead of niggers, our cause would have had a glorious victory, but as it resulted, it was a most disgraceful defeat." (emphasis in original).

C.B.C. closed his letter hoping that "those who have the 'nigger soldier' and their 'great charges' on the brain, will reform and think that those whom they are to place their dependence upon are their own kindred." (*Buffalo Daily Courier*, August 10, 1864). The identity of "C.B.C." is not readily apparent. While he claimed to be in the 179th New York, he did not specifically claim to be in one of the companies from Buffalo. If "C.B.C." are the author's initials, Company E's Charles Clements is the only possibility, but he had been in hospital suffering from chronic diarrhea since July 24 and was transferred to Harewood Hospital in Washington from City Point on August 1 (CMRs), which would have provided limited opportunity for a visit by a comrade who could have given him the details of the battle for a second hand account. While the letter does contain accurate details specific to the 179th, it is also possible that the *Courier* inserted the comments about the colored troops. The *Courier* followed the letter from the 179th with a letter from another unidentified Buffalonian in the field who was similarly critical of the colored troops (*Ibid*.).

(8) Goodwin, 654.

(9) Hess, 53-56.

(10) Marvel, 20, 90-91, 97,247-248, 268, 349, 422. While in command of the Department of the Ohio, Burnside had overseen the arrest, trial and exile of Clement Vallandigham, a leading "Peace Democrat." (*Ibid.*, 235-237) As a "War Democrat," Spencer apparently was willing to overlook that.

(11) Cleaves, 294-95. Meade, like Grant, was careful not to "give any sign that he favored either candidate." (*Ibid.*, 294). At the same time, there were rumors that Meade felt he had been slighted by Lincoln and as a result was trying "to deliver the army vote to McClellan," but there was no basis for the rumors (*Ibid.*).

(12) Howe, 23-24.

(13) *Elmira Daily Advertiser*, August 2, 1864. See also *The Dunkirk Journal*, "The [colored] troops advanced in good order as far as the first line, where they received a galling fire which checked them, and although quite a number kept on advancing the greater proportion seemed to become utterly demoralized, part of them taking refuge in the fort, and the balance running to the rear as fast as possible." (August [illegible], 1864) *The Dunkirk Journal* was also a pro Union paper. (*The Dunkirk Journal*, September 30, 1864)

(14) McWhiney and Jenkins, 33.

(15) Goodwin, 653.

(16) W. Hardee, *Hardee's Rifle and Light Infantry Tactics for the Instructions, Exercises and Manoeuvres of*

Riflemen and Light Infantry, Including School of the Soldier and School of the Company, To Which Is Added, Duties of Non-Commissioned Officers, Military Honors to Be Paid By Troops, the Articles of War, J.O. Kane, (Publisher: New York, 1862, Reprinted by H-Bar Enterprises: Silver Spring, Maryland), 137.

(17) *Ibid.,* 146.

(18) The answer may simply be that there was a shortage of available officers at that time due to disease and battle.

(19) Transcript, 14.

(20) *Ibid.,* 13-14.

(21) *Ibid.,* 15.

(22) *Ibid.,* 17-18.

(23) The *Tribune* began carrying its endorsement of Lincoln in the June 23 edition shortly after his renomination on June 7. As early as January 7, 1864, the *Tribune's* "editorial" page led with "OUR STANDARD!" followed by a drawing of the waving flag with the phrase "Tis the Star Spangled Banner, O long may it wave. O'er the land of the Free, and the home of the brave!"

(24) *The Hornellsville Tribune,* August 4, 1864.

(25) *The Hornellsville Tribune,* August 25, 1864. "Ord." was probably Lt. Nathaniel P. T. Finch, a native of Hornellsville, who started out in Company C and became the 179th New York's quartermaster (See Chapter 22, Note 67, infra). The *Tribune* had carried an earlier report by Finch that was attributed to him by name (July 21, 1864). As the August 25, 1864 edition of the *Tribune* was going to press, Finch and the editors may have been aware of Spencer's upcoming courtmartial and may have decided to use a pseudonym.

(26) Transcript, 18.

(27) *Ibid.,* 17.

(28) *Ibid.,* 19.

(29) *Ibid.,* 21.

(30) *Ibid.*

(31) The Court issued its decision on September 12 (*Ibid.,* 3), but the 179th had been reassigned to Potter's Second Division on September 2, 1864. (OR, 42(2): 668) Potter reviewed the court-martial verdict on September 14. (Transcript, 22) Whether General Hartranft who was then in command of the First Division would have been any more sympathetic to Spencer is unknown.

(32) "Robert Brown Potter," *Wikipedia.* Potter was born in Schenectady, New York in 1829, making him only 35 in 1864. His father was the bishop of the Protestant Episcopal Church of Pennsylvania. Potter practiced law in New York City before the war.

(33) Transcript, 22.

(34) *Ibid.,* 23.

(35) *Ibid.*

(36) *Ibid.,* 24.

(37) The officers of the court were: Lt. Col. William F. Draper, 36th Mass. Vols.; Capt. Josiah N. Jones, 6th N.H.; Capt. N.H. Joyce, 7th R.I.; Capt. E. F. Austin, 45th Penna.; Lt. Joseph Gottlieb, 35th Mass.; Lt. W.D. Rice, 9th N.H.; and Lt. Newhall Sawyer, 11th N.H. (Transcript, 1) The 9th and 11th New Hampshire, the 35th Massachusetts, and the 45th Penna. were among the regiments that "entered the breach." (Hess, 283, n. 1) The 6th New Hampshire had occupied "no man's land," the 7th Rhode Island had been held in reserve, and the 36th Massachusetts had not received its orders and did not participate in the attack (*Ibid.,* 119, 121, 185).

(38) CMRs, Newton B. Spencer, National Archives; CMSR, Newton B. Spencer.

(39) *The Hornellsville Tribune*, February 2, 1865.

(40) Another example–possibly apocryphal–of the conflict between military authority and the civilian right to speak up for oneself involved William Bird. The incident was recounted by A.H. McCormick, one of the men in the 37th New York. The night before the Second Battle of Bull Run, Bird was in command of the pickets and had just assigned McCormick to a picket post when General Philip Kearny:

"rode up and asked Capt. Bird where the picket was who was supposed to occupy an adjacent post. "No picket there when I took over command, sir" Capt. Bird replied. "You're a – liar," retored [sic] the general. Capt. Bird was a man of some temper himself and countered with "You're a – liar." This of course was the rankest insubordination and in a rage Gen. Kearny ordered Capt. Bird back to his regiment under arrest. The next day the great battle opened. I heard Capt. Bird, saluting Gen. Kearny, say, "Sir, may I command my company in the fight today?" I thought that a good deal of the general's ferocity was pretended as he glared at the captain and replied: "Yes, you're a mutinous little cus but you're a damned good soldier." The captain led his troops into the battle and the charges of insubordination were never pressed, for two days later at Chantilly Gen. Kearny was killed. I fancy they would never have been pressed anyway."

(Undated newspaper clipping from *The Sentinel*, Martin County Historical Society.) I have not confirmed the anecdote, but it has some pausibility. It was not at all unusual for General Kearny to be inspecting positions right at the front, he had an intimidating personality, and he respected good combat leadership. (S. Sears, "Major General Philip Kearny: 'A One-Armed Jersey Son-of-A-Gun,'" *The Civil War Monitor*, Vol. 4, No. 1 (Spring 2014), 33, 37-38)

(41) OR, 36(3): 711.

(42) *The New York Times*, January 16, 1863.

(43) OR, 46(2): 290.

(44) McPherson, 822-824; Goodwin, 691-696; Foner, 315-316.

(45) JAWJ, January 29 and January 30, 1865, 65-66.

(46) JAWJ, January 30, 1865, 68-69. The coverage in the *Examiner* probably was similar to what appeared in the *Richmond Sentinel* that day:

"Messrs. A.H. Stephens, R. M. T. Hunter, and John A. Campbell left Richmond yesterday morning on their way to Washington to confer with President Lincoln on the subject of putting an end to the war, if possible. The circumstances under which these gentlemen have departed on their mission are understood to be as follows: Mr. F. P. Blair, having sought an unofficial and confidential interview with President Davis, departed for Washington with an assurance that our President would be willing at any time, without any obstacle of form, to send agents or commissioners to Washington to confer about terms of peace, if informed in advance that said commissioners would be received. On Mr. Blair's second visit to Richmond he brought the consent of Mr. Lincoln to receive and confer with any agents, informally sent, with a view to restoration of peace. The three gentlemen who left yesterday were thereupon selected by the President, and they have gone without formal credentials, and merely as informal agents, to see whether it be possible to place a conference for peace on any basis which may serve for attempting so desirable a result." (OR Vol 46(2): 303.)

(47) JAWJ, January 30, 1865.

(48) JAWJ, February 2, 1865, 78-79.

(49) *Ibid.*, 79; *Ibid.* February 18, 1865, 108-109.

(50) JAWJ, February 21, 1865. As a lawyer myself, I can say that Andrews established on cross-examination the points that he needed to for his defense.

(51) Proceedings of a General Court Martial convened at Headquarters 2nd Division, 9th A. C. February 16, 1865, Case of John Andrews, 2d Lt D Co. 179th Regft NY Vols, LL3204, National Archives, RG 153, Records of the Office of the Judge Advocate General (Army), Court Martial Case Files, 1809-19894, LL3196-LL3205, Box 880.

(52) Proceedings in the Case of the United States vs. Sergt. James Vandermark, K Co. 179th New York Volunteers, No. L.L. 3204, National Archives, RG 153, Records of the Office of the Judge Advocate General, Court Martial Case Files, 1809-1894, LL3196-LL3205 Box 880.

(53) *Ibid.*

(54) *Ibid.*, Similarly, Andrews wrote his family that: "For a long time this order has been disregarded, and every day the pickets were wont to exchange papers with each other." (Letter from John Andrews to "father, brother and sisters" dated March 8, 1865, Author's Collection donated to Library of Virginia).

(55) *Ibid.*, Company A's George Cross was probably also unhappy with the Army's administration of S. O. 157. In January 1865, Cross was arrested on the order of Colonel Titus, the acting brigade commander, for having communication with the enemy, but the Judge Advocate dismissed the case for lack of evidence. However, the dismissal order apparently did not make it to the right channels and Cross was not released until six weeks later when his company commander, Capt. George Carpenter, complained. (Letter dated March 14, 1865 from George Carpenter, George Cross CMSR.).

Chapter Twelve

Catton, Bruce, *Grant Takes Command*, Little, Brown and Company: Boston (1969).

Foner, Eric, *The Fiery Trial: Abraham Lincoln and American Slavery*, W.W. Norton & Company: New York (2010).

Freeman, Douglas Southall, *R. E. Lee: A Biography*, Charles Scribner's Sons: New York (1935).

McPherson, James, *Battle Cry of Freedom: The Civil War Era*, Oxford University Press: Oxford (1988).

McPherson, James, *Tried By War: Abraham Lincoln as Commander in Chief*, The Penguin Press: New York (2008).

Phisterer, Frederick, *New York in the War of the Rebellion 1861 to 1865*, D.B. Lyon Company, State Printers: Albany, New York (Third Ed. 1912).

Wolcott, Walter, *The Military History of Yates County, N.Y., Comprising a Record of the Services Rendered by Citizens of This County in the Army and Navy, from the Foundation of the Government to the Present Time*, Express Book and Job Printing House: Penn Yan, New York (1895).

(1) Things were not any better on the home front. At the end of July and the beginning of August 1864, civilian morale sank to the lowest levels of the war. (Foner, 304; McPherson, *Tried By War*, 231, 238). The *Dryden Weekly News* tried to boost the spirits of its readers in its August 20, 1864 edition:

"The unlooked-for failure of the assault on Petersburg, July 30th last has cast a feeling of dissatisfaction over the community which circumstances, beyond loss of life and maiming, do not warrant. Our army has as firm a hold on the beleaguered town as it had before the assault, and there is reason to believe that the failure has in no degree interfered with General Grant's original plan of campaign. ... From General Sherman's army we have nothing that is not good. Since the 15th of July to the 1st of the present month one half of the army defending the place have been by death, wounds and prisoners put out of the fight. ... We shall probably hear of the surrender of [Atlanta] before our next issue."

(2) OR 42(1):551. Different numbers of three officers and fifty-six enlisted men are stated in Wolcott, 110. I don't know the source for those numbers, but even if correct, they are directionally consistent with the official report. The 179th New York was not the only regiment reduced to such low numbers. In the Second Brigade, the 3d Maryland took only sixty four men into battle and in the First Brigade, the Fifty Seventh Massachusetts only thirty nine and the 29th Massachusetts only forty. (OR at 551). *The Hornellsville Tribune* (April 20, 1865) reported only "fifty muskets."

(3) *The Hornellsville Tribune*, August 25, 1864. Company B's Eugene Dunton wrote at the beginning of August that: "We have less than 100 men for duty present." (Letter from Eugene Dunton to Parents dated August 2, 1864, Eugene Dunton Pension File). It is not clear whether Ord. and Dunton were including Company G or were treating those men as part of the 180th New York Volunteers. Robert Kellogg of the 16th Connecticut Volunteers used similar language in complaining after the Battle of Antietam about his regiment's lack of training: "'We were murdered,' he angrily charged, reasoning that a green regiment such as the 16th should not have been left 'unsupported in a cornfield in the immediate vicinity of a cunning foe–and, as it were, left to take care of itself.'" (Gordon, 40) The 16th Connecticut had been sent into battle at Antietam only three weeks after it had been mustered in.

(4) McPherson, *Battle Cry of Freedom*, 330.

(5) *The Hornellsville Tribune*, August 25, 1864.

(6) *Penn Yan Democrat*, August 12, 1864, Newton Spencer Court Martial Transcript, U. S. Military History Institute, Carlisle Barracks, CWTIColl.

(7) Company Registers of Deserters, Descriptive Book, Regimental Books, Vol. 1.

(8) Letter from Joseph Robinson to Friend Hickey, August 18, 1864, George Hickey Pension File.

(9) *The Hornellsville Tribune*, August 25, 1864.

(10) OR, 42(2):44, 59, 177-78.

(11) Larzelere Diary, July 31, 1864.

(12) OR 40(1): 196.

(13) OR 42(2): 92.

(14) *The Hornellsville Tribune*, August 25, 1864.

(15) *Ibid.*

(16) Catton, 349-50.

(17) Letter from William Hemstreet to J. H. [Osmer?] dated October 14, 1864, Solomon Leonard CMSR.

(18) OR 42(1):550.

Willcox HQ, August 1864

(19) *Ibid.*, 564.

(20) Field and Staff Muster Roll, for July and August 1864, "Record of Events," Compiled Records Showing Service of Military Units in Volunteer Union Organizations, National Archives Microfim No. 139. *The Hornellsville Tribune*, April 20, 1865 said near Aikens House.

(21) Letter from Solon Thacher to Philip Van Scoter dated April 23, 1865 in *The Hornellsville*

Tribune, June 25, 1865; *The Hornellsville Tribune* said that the 179th New York had only three officers and thirty-eight men when Doty returned. (April 20, 1865)

(22) OR 42(2): 605.

(23) Regimental Return for August 1864, Microfilm No. 139. The outlook on the Confederate side of the lines was not necessarily any brighter. On August 23, 1864, General Lee wrote the Confederate Secretary of War that "without some increase of strength, I can not see how we can escape the natural military consequences of the enemy's numerical superiority." (Freeman, Vol. III, 499)

(24) CMRs; Letter from Stephen Compton, April 5, 1888, George Carpenter Pension File; Company A Morning Report September 1864, Regimental Books, Vol. 4; F. B. Doty, Roster of Absent Commissioned Officers of the 179th Regt. N. Y. Vols., dated September 15, 1864, Regimental Papers, Box 3408.

(25) Company Muster Rolls, August 31, 1864, Regimental Papers, Box 3406.

(26) Phisterer, 4030-4031.

(27) CMRs.

(28) OR 42(2):642-43, 668.

(29) Larzelere Diary, September 24, 1864.

(30) Compiled from CMRs. See also Morning Reports, Regimental Books, Vol. 4.

(31) Morning Report, Regimental Books, Vol. 4. Map of the front August 28, 1864

[Map of Eastern Lines 28 August 1864]

Chapter Thirteen

Adams, George W., *Doctors in Blue: The Medical History of the Union army in the Civil War*, Louisiana State University Press: Baton Rouge (1952).

Bollet, Alfred J., *Civil War Medicine: Challenges and Triumphs*, Galen Press, Ltd.: Tucson, Arizona (2002)

Booth, Benjamin F. and Meyer, Steve, *Dark Days of the Rebellion: Life in Southern Military Prisons*, Meyer Publishing: Garrison, Iowa (1995).

Clayton, Henry, *History of Steuben County, New York*, Lewis Peck & Co.: Philadelphia (1879).

Dean Jr., Eric T., *Shook Over Hell: Post Traumatic Stress, Vietnam and the Civil War*, Harvard University Press: Cambridge (1997).

Faust, Drew Gilpin, *This Republic of Suffering: Death and the American Civil War*, Alfred A. Knopf: New York (2008).

Hess, Earl J., *The Union Soldier in Battle: Enduring the Ordeal of Combat*, University Press of Kansas: Lawrence (1997).

Phisterer, Frederick, *New York in the War of the Rebellion 1861 to 1865*, D.B. Lyon Company, State Printers: Albany, New York (Third Ed. 1912).

Sartin, Jeffrey S., "Infectious Diseases During the Civil War: The Triumph of the 'Third Army'", *Clinical Infectious Diseases*, Vol. 16, No. 4 (April 1993).

Schroeder-Lein, Glenna R., *The Encyclopedia of Civil War Medicine*, M.E. Sharpe: Armonk, New York (2008).

Wilson, Sven Eric, "Prejudice & Policy: Racial Discrimination in the Union army Disability Pension System, 1865-1906", *American Journal of Public Health*, Vol. 0, No. 2010 (February 10,

2010)

(1) *The Hornellsville Tribune*, July 21, 1864.

(2) S. O. No. 213, para. 3, Headquarters, Elmira Depot for Drafted Men dated May 20, 1864, RG110, Series 2351, 156.

(3) Clayton, 337; Phisterer, 4032.

(4) *The Hornellsville Tribune*, August 25, 1864.

(5) Robinson, CMSR, 141st New York Volunteers.

(6) Phisterer, 4032, 4037; Phineas Rose CMSR; A.H. Brundage CMSR.

(7) Phisterer, 4034; Martin Doty CMSR; Affidavit of Martin Doty dated September 7, 1883, Joseph Robinson Pension File.

(8) Letter from William Gregg to Ariel Thurston, December 5, 1864, New York State Military Museum, Unit History Project, 179th Infantry Regiment, Civil War Newspaper Clippings.

(9) General Orders, No. 10 of 1864, Regimental Books, Vol. 2.

(10) Letter from William Lamont to sister dated November 15, 1864, Wisconsin Historical Society. See Affidavit of William Lamont dated December 2, 1878, William Lamont Pension File.

(11) Photograph, Author's Personal Collection; Physician's Affidavit of Joseph W. Robinson dated February 20, 1884, James C. Rutan Pension File.

(12) Sartin, 580, 584. See also E. Hess, 36-37: "Perhaps the most terrible tragedy of the Civil War was that it took place less than two decades before medicine was revolutionized by a series of major biological and technical advances. The use of antiseptics and sterilization and the implementation of higher professional standards for doctors and nurses, would have saved thousands of lives." See also Adams, 228; M. Adams, *Living Hell*, 22.

(13) D. Faust, 4. Still, the 2:1 ratio for the Civil War was a marked improvement over the 8:1 ratio for the British during the Napoleonic wars (circa 1815); the 7:1 ratio for the Mexican War (circa 1845); and the 3:1 ratio for the allies in the Crimean War (1854). Sartin, 580.

(14) *The Hornellsville Tribune*, August 25, 1864.

(15) RH, 5; Phisterer, Vol. 1, 302.

(16) Wilson, 5. See also Adams, 229.

(17) Faust, 4.

(18) Eugene Dunton CMR; Adjutant General report, November 14, 1887, Eugene Dunton Pension File.

(19) Letter from Edward Lounsbery to Mr. Baker, November 6, 1864, Charles S. Baker Pension File.

(20) Faust, 4; Adams, 229.

(21) Sartin, 581.

(22) *Hornellsville Tribune*, July 21, 1864.

(23) Compiled from CMRs.

(24) OR, 42(1): 195.

(25) Adams, 206, 209.

(26) Compiled from CMRs.

(27) Letter from Abner Welch to Parents, October 24, 1864, Abner Welch Pension File.

(28) Abner Welch CMRs.

(29) "Remarks," Company C Morning Report, November 1864 Regimental Books, Vol. 4.

(30) Booth and Meyer, 108, 143.

(31) Affidavit of James C. Rutan, August 9, 1882, James Rutan Pension File. Drug usage had a different social context during the Civil War than it does today.

"[O]pium, rarely mentioned in non-medical literature and records of the Civil War, was [like alcohol] easy to find, pure or in many derivative concoctions: laudanum, paregoric, morphine and several patent medicines. Opiates were freely and legally sold by everyday merchants, and used by anyone who sought relief from most of the common ailments that afflict mankind. And during the 19th Century, there was little stigma attached to using opiates. Certainly, there was no counterpart to today's strong feeling against such use." (James Street, Jr., "Under the Influence: Did Civil War Soldiers Depend on Drugs and Alcohol?" *Civil War Times Illustrated*, Vol. XXVII, No. 3 (May 1988), 31)

See also M. Adams, *Living Hell*, 10. The lack of social stigma is illustrated by the fact that Company A's James C. Rutan freely described in his pension application his use of opiates to treat his diarrhea during the war. (Affidavit of James C. Rutan, dated August 9, 1882, James Rutan Pension File) What Company B's William Lamont referred to as his family physician's "quick step medicine" may have been an example of a patent medicine containing opiates. (Letter from William B. Lamont to Sister, dated February 27, 1865) Even as a prisoner of war, Company K's Charles Johnson was able to obtain "small chunks of something I thought was opium" from the sympathetic head of the Salisbury Prison hospital and made them into pills. (A. B., "Story of A Civil War Veteran," *E. J. Workers Review*, Vol. One, Number 6, August 20, 1919, 21) The Carded Medical Records reveal only one case of drug abuse. Company D's William H. Dickey was admitted to the Post Hospital at Fort Henry from the custody of the provost marshal due to "intemperance from opium." Dickey had been admitted to the Ninth Corps Depot Field Hospital with an unstated malady in August and had been transferred in September to the Camden Street General Hospital in Baltimore, where he was convalescing. He left the hospital without permission on February 22, 1865, but was arrested the following day in civilian clothing and placed in custody at Fort McHenry. The fact that he apparently was able to obtain opium while in custody is consistent with a lack of social stigma. He was court-martialed in May 1865 on a charge of desertion from the hospital, but was found guilty only of being absent without leave and fined just $20. The panel may have shown leniency based on Dickey's prior service from 1861 to 1862 or simply the fact the Lee had surrendered the month before. (William H. Dickey, CMRs; Proceedings of a General Court Martial, The United States v. William H. Dickey, Co. D, 179th N.Y. Vols., National Archives, RG 153, Records of the Office of the Judge Advocate General (Army), Court Martial Case Files, 1809-1894, oo1236-oo1240, Box 2086) Thus experience in the 179th New York seems consistent with James Street, Jr.'s observation that during the Civil War era "Most people using opiates did not become addicted." (Street, 32)

(32) Schroeder-Lein, 240.

(33) "Bed Card," Kerrick, Harvey and Jones CMSRs. See also Robert Mitchell's treatment for chronic diarrhea at hospital in Alexandria: "Cathartics and Aromatics. Sulph Acid and Cinches." "Bed Card," CMSR.

(34) John Cook Pension File; John Cook CMRs.

(35) Medical Descriptive List, Paulding Vincent CMSR.

(36) JAWJ, November 13, 1864.

(37) Dean.

(38) OR, 42(1): 186.

(39) JAWJ, October 23, 1864, 87.

(40) Adams, 228; Schroedere-Lein, 250.

(41) Carl Frederick CMSR and CMRs.

(42) Affidavits of John Slartshorn[?], May 11 and 12, 1865, Samuel Champlin CMSR and CMR.

(43) Examining Surgeon's Certificate by W.W. Potter, March 16, 1871; Affidavit of Jane Champlin, November 22, 1870; Affidavit of Joseph Robinson, May 7, 1870, all Samuel Champlin Pension File; Samuel Champlin CMRs.

(44) JAWJ, March 3, 4 and 6, 1865. Andrews had been acquitted in the court-martial on February 22, but he was not restored to duty until after General Potter approved the verdict on March 4, so that may have been weighing on Andrews.

(45) Affidavit of Harry Ap Rees, August 18, 1890; Deposition of Harry Ap Rees, February 21, 1891; Deposition of Heather A. Shea [?], February 24, 1891; Deposition of Ellen A. Marshall, February 11, 1891, all Charles Flint Pension File. There are no CMRs for Flint.

(46) Casper Notter, Co. G, CMRs and CMSR.

(47) B. Wiley, *The Life of Billy Yank: The Common Soldier of the Union*, Louisiana State University Press: Baton Rouge (1971), 261.

(48) Keen, 14.

(49) Affidavit of Robert Stewart, March 3, 1865, Robert Stewart Pension File; Stewart CMRs; Lattin CMRs. Michael Adams described the impact of a bullet wound in *Living Hell: The Dark Side of the Civil War*:

"Musket balls did massive damage to the body. Unlike a modern high-velocity steelhead bullet in the .30 calibre range, a .57 or .58 lead ball frequently lacked the force to drive through and exit the target, instead staying in the victim, wrecking bone and organs. ... When the rifle fired, the minnie spread out in the barrel, meaning the pliable lead could no longer hold up on impact but became unintentionally a dum-dum or soft-head bullet. Meeting the resistance of flesh and bone, it flattened out further, even assuming the diameter of a half dollar. As it slowed, it travelled the victim, wrecking everything in its way. ... This is also why surgeons amputated so many shattered limbs; physicians lacked the time, tools, operating facilities, or medical knowledge to reconstruct splintered bones. They had to remove the limb before gangrene and peritonitis attacked. ... Minnies inflicted truly horrific damage, their ravaging wounds being excruciatingly painful. " (at 68)

(50) Schroeder-Lein, 17, 21. The author recalls the scene in the movie "The Horse Soldiers" when Union surgeon William Holden had to amputate a scout's foot when gangrene set in. Company A's Jesse Cornell recalled chloroform being used when his fingers were amputated. (Deposition of Jesse Cornell dated May 27, 1904, Cornell Pension File).

(51) Schroeder-Lein, 17, 21. The *Civil War Monitor* states that there were 60,000 amputations with a seventy-five percent survival rate. "Broken Soldiers," *Civil War Monitor*, Vol. IV, No. 2 (Summer 2014), 35. The photographs in the article are particularly striking.

(52) Bowker and Kinnon CMRs; Kinnon Bed Card, Kinnon CMSR.

(53) Affidavit of James Farr, February 28, 1898, Jeffrey Wisner Pension File.

(54) Letter from Samuel Coon to Pension Commissioner, July 15, 1891, Samuel Coon Pension File.

(55) CMSR

(56) Letter from Daniel Lee to Wife, June 8, 1864.

(57) Schroeder-Lien, 121; Bollet, 212.

(58) Adams, 88, 228.

(59) OR 36(3): 723. The Army of the Potomac's depot hospital had been set up at White House Landing only a couple of days before the 179th New York arrived. A number of men from the 179th, including Daniel Lee, were temporarily assigned to the depot hospital. The Army of the Potomac's Chief Medical Officer, Edward B. Dalton, described a huge – and busy – facility. "The hospitals were arranged along the river-bank in double echelon, extending from the former site of the White House some three-fourths of a mile down the river, with a breadth of half a mile. Shelter, supplies, and facilities for cooking were in readiness when the first train reached the landing on the afternoon of the first of June. ... From the first of June to the 13th there were daily and some times hourly arrivals of trains from the front, the number thus received being sufficient to keep the hospitals full in spite of every effort to relieve them." (OR, 36(1):271-2)

A week after the 179th arrived, Edward Schriver, the Inspector General, described the medical facilities at White House Landing as follows:

"The wounded and sick are all in camp. The tents are sufficiently numerous and so pitched as to afford good accommodations. They appear to be doing well, and to receive every attention in the way of medical supplies, diet, nursing & c." (OR, 36(3):723)

Schriver reported that 5,400 patients had been treated on June 7 with seventeen deaths; 5450 patients had been treated on June 8 with twenty-five deaths and 4,006 patients on June 9 with forty-seven deaths. (These would have been casualties from the battle at nearby Cold Harbor that ended on June 3.)

(60) OR, 40(1): 270-71; Adams, 103.

(61) OR, 40(1): 270.

(62) Adams, 103. See also Charles R. Bowery, Jr., *The Richmond-Petersburg campaign, 1864-65*, Praeger: Santa Barbara, California (2014), 102-103.

[Photo: View to Depot Hospital]

(63) Schroeder-Lien, 158.

(64) OR, 40(1): 270.

(65) Adams, 149.

(66) Bollet, 218

(67) *Ibid.*, 221.

(68) *Ibid.*, 219

(69) Adams, 160; Compiled from CMRs.

[Diagram: Mower Hospital Plan]

(70) Bollet, 217; Adams, 150.

(71)) M. Humphreys, *Marrow of Tragedy: The Health Crisis of the American Civil War,* The Johns Hopkins University Press: Baltimore (2013), 9 (footnote omitted).

(72) *The Hornellsville Tribune*, August 25, 1864; Compiled from Carded Medical Records, 179th New York Volunteers.

[Photo: Ward K, Armory Square Hospital]

(73) Compiled from CMRs.

(74) Affidavit of Orin Hawkins, June 2, 1877, Orin Hawkins Pension File; Hawkins CMRs. See also CMRs for Thomas Connor and John Durham.

(75) Affidavit of William Tuck, December 2, 1893, William Tuck Pension File.

(76) Letter from William Lamont to Sister, September 25, 1864.

(77) Letter from William Lamont to Parents, January 7, 1865.

(78) Brown CMR. Dr. Robinson stated after the war that Brown died near Jones House, which probably indicates the location of the Ninth Corps Hospital. (Affidavit of Joseph Robinson dated May 2, 1866, Moses Brown Pension File).

(79) Lamont CMR.

(80) Adams, 172; Letter from William Bird, Jr. to Father, August 20, 1864.

(81) Adams, 157.

(82) Robert F. McNamara, *St. Mary's Hospital and the Civil War*, The Sisters of Charity (circa 1960) 3-4, passim. St. Mary's Hospital was founded in September 1857 by the Daughters of Charity (commonly known as the Sisters of Charity) who had come from Emmitsburg, Maryland. They began the hospital in temporary facilities, initially two adjacent stables, and then opened a new hospital building in 1863 at West Avenue and Genesee Street on the west side of the Genesee River in what is still known as the "Bull's Head" area of the city, named after an old tavern. Over 3000 sick and wounded soldiers were cared for at St. Mary's during the Civil War. (*Ibid.*) The 1864-65 Rochester City Directory listed J.W. Casey as the Resident Physician; Edward M. More as Surgeon; Azel Backus as Military Physician; and Chas. D. McMullen as Reverend. Sister Hieronymo O'Brien was the sister superior of the Sisters of Charity. Sister Hieronymo was a very strong and respected personality. When a young lieutenant tendered his resignation because she had interfered with his cruel punishment of a drunk soldier, hoping that his resignation would be rejected and Sister Hieronymo disciplined, Dr. Backus instead accepted the lieutenant's resignation. (McNamara, 14-15).

(83) McNamara, 6-8, 18; *The [Rochester] Evening Express*, June 4, 1864.

(84) McNamara, 8; *Rochester Democrat*, June 8, 1864; *The [Rochester] Evening Express*, June 7, 1864; St. Mary's Hospital Register, Daughters of Charity Archives, Albany, New York, 134, 136, 168, 170; Shepard, Rutan and Wise CMRs and CMSRs.

(85) McNamara, 8.

(86) Letters from Edwin Bentley to Medical Director, Dept. of Washington, October 16 and 18, 1864, and letter from W. C. May[?] to Maj. Gen'l Joseph Barnes, October 11, 1864, all William Chamberlain CMSR; William Chamberlain CMR.

(87) Eleazer Baldwin CMSR, CMR.

(88) Letter from John Durham to Edwin Stanton, July 7, 1864, John Durham CMSR; John Durham CMR.

(89) Letter from William Jones to Senator Harris, February 8, 1865 and Letter from Edwin Bentley to [?], February [?], 1865, both Nicoll Jones CMSR; Nicoll Jones CMR.

(90) Compiled from CMRs.

(91) Jacob Hauser CMSR.

(92) E.g. U.S.A. Gen. Hospital, "Finley," form, Henry Ellison CMSR.

(93) CMSRs; CMRs. Letter from Noudiah Olcott to [?], September 17, 1864, Homer Olcott CMSR

Chapter Fourteen

Hallock, Judith Lee, "The Role of the Community in Civil War Desertion," *Civil War History*, Vol. 29, No. 2 (June 1983).

Hardee, William J., *Hardee's Rifle and Light Infantry Tactics for the Instructions, Exercises and Manoeuvres of Riflemen and Light Infantry, Including School of the Soldier and School of the Company, To Which Is added, Duties of Non-Commissioned Officers, Military Honors to Be Paid By Troops, the Articles of War*, J. O. Kane, Publisher: New York (1862) (reprinted by H-Bar Enterprises: Silver Spring, Maryland).

Heverly, Clement Ferdinand, *Our Boys in Blue. Heroic Deeds, Sketches and Reminiscences of Bradford County Soldiers in the Civil War*, The Bradford Star Print., Towanda, Pennsylvania (1898, reprinted 1998, Murrelle Printing Co., Inc., Sayre, Pennsylvania)

Phisterer, Frederick, *New York in the War of the Rebellion 1861 to 1865*, D.B. Lyon Company, State Printers: Albany, New York (Third Ed. 1912).

Wiley, Bell Irvin, *The Life of Billy Yank: The Common Soldier of the Union*, Louisiana State University Press: Baton Rouge (1952, 1971).

(1) Hardee, 3; Wiley, 319; Michael P. Musick, "The Little Regiment: Civil War Units and Commands," *Prologue*, Vol. 27, No. 2 (Summer 1995), 2.

(2) JAWJ, October 13, 1864, 57.

(3) OR 40(2): 549.

(4) History of Tioga and Chemung Counties, Chapter XIII, 179th Regiment; Letter from Charles Lockwood, *Buffalo Daily Courier*, April 5, 1865.

(5) *The Hornellsville Tribune*, August 25, 1864.

(6) JAWJ, October 13, 1864. D. Poche, "Ain't No Company 'J' in This Man's Army," www. pochefamily.org. notes that neither Union nor Confederate regiments had a Company J. Poche attributes the reason to the fact that in 18th century English "the capital 'I' and 'J' were interchangeable especially when hand written." (Poche, 7). He notes that there also is no J Street in Washington, D.C.

(7) Phisterer, 140.

(8) JAWJ, October 8, 1864.

(9) Letter from Elisha Marshall to A.S. Diven, July 24, 1864, Regimental Papers, Box 3408.

(10) Letter from A. Terrill to A.S. Diven, July 12, 1864, *Ibid*.

(11) *Binghamton Daily Republican*, October 4, 1864.

(12) *Binghamton Daily Republican*, September 3, 1864. The Ninth Cavalry claimed in February 1864 that the provost marshal for the 31th District had incorrectly told recruits that the Ninth was full and instead induced them to volunteer for the 179th New York. (Letter from Baker Saxton to George Palmer, April 3, 1864, RG110, Entry 2307).

(13) *Binghamton Daily Republican*, September 1, 1864; *Binghamton Standard*, August 31, 1864.

(14) Letters from Giles Holden to A. S. Diven, July 5 and July 28, 1864, Regimental Papers, Box 3408. On the other hand, West Bloomfield's War Committee had complained to Major Diven in February 1864 that: "the Examining and Mustering Board in Rochester are more lenient or less stringent thatn the Board in our own District at Canandaigua. Some who have been rejected by the latter have been accepted by the former." (Letter from Myron Hall to A. S. Diven, February 6, 1864, RG110, Entry 2023, Box 30).

(15) Letter from Giles Holden to A. S. Diven, July 28, 1864, Regimental Papers, Box 3408.

(16) Letter from Giles Holden to A. S. Diven, August 10, 1864, Regimental Papers, Box 3408.

(17) Letter from S. Eastman to L. Thomas, August 17, 1864, Regimental Papers, Box 3408.

(18) Letter from Giles Holden to A. S. Diven, August 22, 1864, Regimental Papers, Box 3408.

(19) Letter from W. W. Hoyt to A. S. Diven and response from A. S. Diven, August 5, 1864, RG110, Entry 2222.

(20) Letter from A. S. Diven to W. W. Hoyt, August 10, 1864, RG110, Entry 2222, Box 40.

(21) Wisner Reports, Regimental Papers, Box 3408.

(22) *Elmira Daily Advertiser*, September 21, 1864.

(23) *Elmira Daily Advertiser*, July 30, 1864.

(24) *Elmira Daily Advertiser*, August 13, 1864. "The following extraordinary inducements are offered to Volunteers who present themselves TO-DAY…

Three Years Volunteers	
Local County	$400.00
Government Bounty	$300.00
Wages at $16 a month for three years	$576.00
Total	$1,276.00
Two Years' Volunteers	
Local Bounty	$300.00
Government Bounty	$200.00
Wages at $16 a month for two years	$384.00
Total	$884.00
One Year's Volunteers	
Local Bounty	$250.00
Government Bounty	$100.00
Wages at $16 a month	$192.00
Total	$542.00
Three Years' Substitutes	
Cash in hand	$900.00

Two Years' Substitutes	
Cash in hand	$600.00
One Year Substitute	
Cash in hand	$500.00

(25) *Yates County Chronicle*, September 1, 1864. See also Graham, 131.

(26) JAWJ, November 1, 1864.

(27) *Ibid.*

(28) *Elmira Daily Advertiser*, August 24, 1864. A.B. Galatian apparently was able to make a career at both sides of soldiers' service. Not only was he a recruiting agent, but twenty years later, he represented veterans in their applications for a military pension. (E.g. James C. Rutan)

(29) *Binghamton Daily Republican*, August 30, 1864; *Binghamton Standard*, August 31, 1864; *Watkins Express*, August 25, 1864; *Yates County Chronicle*, August 25, 1864.

(30) Phisterer, 4029. Company H was principally recruited at Elmira, Horseheads, Niagara, Hornellsville, Ellicottsville, Amity, Chemung, Dansville, Big Flats, and Bradford (Phisterer, 4029). Yates County also attracted many recruits from Bradford County, Pennsylvania, at this time, although they were assigned to other units. (Graham, 131).

(31) Edwin Bowen, Newfield, Tompkins County, New York, 1860 Census, Ancestry.com.

(32) *Ithaca Journal*, August 17, 1864.

(33) *Ithaca Journal*, August 24, 1864.

(34) *Ithaca Journal*, August 31, 1864.

(35) *Ibid.*

(36) *Dryden Weekly News*, August 20, 1864.

(37) *Ithaca Journal*, August 24, 1864.

(38) *Ithaca Journal*, August 31, 1864.

(39) *Ithaca Journal*, September 7, 1864. Recruiting in Broome County and other Southern Tier counties bordering Pennsylvania may have received a slight boost from the Confederate raid at Chambersburg, Pennsylvania, 175 miles away, in late July and early August 1864. The *Binghamton Daily Republican* (August 1 and 26, 1864) and the *Binghamton Daily Democrat* (August 1, 1864) both reported a "Rebel Invasion of Pennsylvania" and that three thousand people had been left homeless. Some men may have feared that the Confederacy could push farther north.

(40) *Ithaca Journal*, August 17, 1864 and September 7, 1864.

(41) Bowen apparently recruited more men than he needed to fill Company I. The enlistment forms for a number of recruits were designated for Captain Bowen's Company, but those men wound up in other companies of the 179th New York. E. g. Simon Shepard (Company E), William McKinney (Company A), Smith McMasters Company B), William Maricle (Company B), and Clement Northrop Company B). (CMSRs).

(42) *Broome Republican*, August 31, 1864; See also *Binghamton Daily Democrat*, August 31, 1864.

(43) *Binghamton Weekly Republican*, August 10 and August 17, 1864; *Binghamton Daily Republican*, August 2, 1864; *Binghamton Daily Democrat*, August 2 and August 11, 1864.

(44) *Binghamton Daily Republican*, September 7, 1864.

(45) *Binghamton Standard*, August 31, 1864.

(46) *Ibid.*; see also *Binghamton Daily Republican*, September 1, 1864.

(47) *Binghamton Daily Republican*, August 29, 1864.

(48) *Ibid.*

(49) *Binghamton Daily Standard*, August 31, 1864.

(50) Heverly, *Our Boys in Blue*. For example, in February 1864, Towanda Borough adopted a $100 bounty "to avoid the approaching draft." (*Bradford Argus*, February 11, 1864) The relatively low bounty notwithstanding, the *Bradford Argus* was able to report on February 18, 1864 that: "It is with unfeigned pride and satisfaction that we announce that the Borough of Towanda has filled her quota, on both calls, and will thus entirely avoid the coming draft." The *Argus* praised Capt. Darling who had recruited men for the 57th Pennsylvania and "permitted them to take the [Towanda] bounty instead of taking them abroad as he might have done. (*Ibid.*) Two men from Bradford County volunteered in Elmira in February when the New York bounties were only somewhat higher and were assigned to Company A – William P. Chamberlain and Asa C. Otterson. (Heverly and CMSRs).

(51) Heverly and CMSRs.

(52) S.O. No. 283, Headquarters, Rendezvous for Drafted Men, August 11, 1864, RG110, Entry 2351, 210, para.8; S.O. No. 285, August 13, 1864, RG110, Entry 2351, 212, para. 3; S.O. No. 287, August 15, 1864, RG110, Entry 2351, 213, para. 3; S.O. No. 296, August 25, 1864, RG110, Entry 2351, 222, para. 6; S.O. 297, August 25, 1864, RG110, Entry 2351, 223, para. 4; S.O. No. 309, September 6, 1864, RG110, Entry 2351, 236, para.5; S.O. No. 310, September 7, 1864, RG110, Entry 2351, 237, para.3; S.O. No. 317, September 14, 1864, RG110, Entry 2351, 246, para. 4; and No. 334, October 1, 1864, RG110, Entry 2351, 283, para. 3. In the foregoing instances, the substitutes and drafted men were designated for specific units. Unless already mustered into a regiment (as in the case of the 179th New York), recruits were sent south for the "Armies in Maryland and Virginia." (See S.O. No. 309, September 6, 1864, RG110, Entry 2351, 236, para.6; S.O. No. 316, September 13, 1864, RG110, Entry 2351, 245, para. 2; and S.O. No. 333, September 30, 1864, RG110, Entry 2351, 282, para. 9).

(53) Descriptive Book, Regimental Books, Vol. 1. Company D had 74% New York-born (80% U.S. born) and Company B had 94% U.S.-born, but only 64% New York-born.

(54) William Howell CMSR; Compiled from Descriptive Book, 179th New York Volunteers.

Occupations

Company	Farmers	Laborers	Barkeep Clerk	Carpenter	Tailor Shoemaker Cabinetmaker	Blacksmith	Sailor Boatman
H	40%	31%	1%	3%	3%		
I	84%						
K	84%						

(55) Compiled from Descriptive Book, Regimental Books, Vol. 1.

(56) Compiled from Descriptive Book, Regimental Books, Vol. 1.

(57) Compiled from Descriptive Book, Regimental Books, Vol. 1. Nationality at Birth Company

Company	N.Y.	U.S.A.	Foreign-Born	Highest% Ireland
H	54%	60%	40%	25%
I	89%	95%	5%	-
K	79%	97%	3%	-

(58) Compiled from Descriptive Book, Regimental Books, Vol. 1.

(59) Compiled from *A Record of the Commissioned Officers, Non-Commissioned Officers and Privates, of the Regiments Organized in the State of New York*, Weed, Parsons and Company, Printers: Albany (1866), Vol. VI, 107 et seq.

(60) Phisterer, 4031, 4033, 4035, 4036; Musgrave CMR.

(61) Phisterer, 4031, 4032-33, 4035, 4036.

(62) Phisterer, 4031, 4034, 4035, 4038. The Regimental History (at 34) suggests that Hooper had prior military service, but I have not been able to confirm that.

(63) *Elmira Daily Advertiser*, September 14, 1864; Regimental History, 31.

(64) *Elmira Daily Advertiser*, September 17, 1864; Regimental History, 34.

(65) Register of Deserters, Company H, Regimental Books, Vol. 1.

(66) Compiled from Descriptive Book, Regimental Books, Vol. 1.

(67) Compiled from Descriptive Book, Regimental Books, Vol. 1.

(68) Danby and Newfield were "cohesive communities". (See Hallock, 126, 130-132). Letter from John Patterson to Father, September 12, 1864, John Patterson Pension File; John Patterson CMR. John Hannon, who would later be assigned to Company B, similarly wrote on September 11, 1864 that: "We came to Elmira Thursday and are having good times... enjoying myself a great dele better than I expected to." (Letter from John Hannon to Mother, September 11, 1864, John Hannon Pension File).

(69) Compiled from Descriptive Book, Regimental Books, Vol. 1.

(70) *Bradford Argus*, August 11, 1864; *Bradford Reporter*, August 3, 1864.

(71) While the *Bradford Reporter* did report on September 1, 1864 that: "volunteering is now going on very briskly at Troy" and that "[m]any of the townships will have their quota filled before the draft," a draft was ultimately necessary in almost all of the Bradford County towns. (The *Bradford Reporter*, October 6, 1864; *Bradford Argus*, October 6, 1864). The *Bradford Argus* did write of the desirability of avoiding a draft, but its rhetoric was not as forceful as that utilized by the New York newspapers. (*Bradford Argus*, February 18, 1864 and August 4, 1864). The *Bradford Reporte* sounded more like the New York newspapers. (*Bradford Reporter*, October 6, 1864: "Let the odium and the responsibility for the draft rest where it belongs [with the Copperheads].").

(72) *Bradford Reporter*, July 14, 1864. The *Reporter* seems to have been more concerned about efforts to demoralize the drafted men, than preventing the need for the draft itself. (*Bradford Reporter*, October 6, 1864).

(73) J. Duff, "David Wilmot, the Statesman and Political Leader," Bradford County Historical Society, 1946.

(74) Compiled from Descriptive Book, Regimental Books Vol. 1. Occupations Co. A Orig. 80: Farmers-54%, Laborers-9%, Clerk-2%, Carpenter-7%, Bookkeeper-5%, Cabinetmaker-7%, Blacksmith - Shoemaker-60%, Boatman-30%, Tailor-4%, Sailor-4%.

(75) Compiled from Descriptive Book. Regimental Books, Vol. I.

Nationality at Birth					
	New York	U.S.A.	Foreign Born	# Countries	Highest % Foreign
Orig. 80	65%	83%	17%	4	England 7%
28 Recruits	60%	81%	18%	2	Ireland 14%

(76) See note 52.

(77) Descriptive Book, Regimental Books, Vol. 1; Regimental History, 29, 31, 34. Company H was comprised of both "three years men" and "one year men." (Descriptive Book; Regimental History, 29) Company H started out with the men recruited in the spring and early summer of 1864 who were left over after Company F was mustered in. There were around thirty "three years men" in Company H or roughly forty percent (Descriptive Book).

(78) *The Hornellsville Tribune*, February 2, 1865.

(79) Letter from John Andrews to Homer Andrews, January 10, 1865.

(80) Letters from William Lamont to Parents, January 7, 1865 and June 1 and 19, 1865.

(81) Regimental History, passim. In 1866, New York State published an official roster which suffered from the same defect. (*A Record of the Commissioned Officers, Non-Commissioned Officers and Privates, of the Regiments Which Were Organized in the State of New York and Called into Service of the United States to Assist in Suppressing the Rebellion*, Weed, Parsons, and Company, Printers: Albany (1866) Vol. VI, 107 et seq.).

Chapter Fifteen

A. B., "Story of A Civil War Veteran," *E. J. Workers Review*, Vol. One, Number 6 (August 20, 1919), George F. Johnson Papers, E - J Workers Review, Aug – Dec, 1919, Syracuse University Library, Special Collections Research Center.

Phisterer, Frederick, *New York in the War of the Rebellion 1861 to 1865*, D.B. Lyon Company, State Printers: Albany, New York (Third Ed. 1912).

Shannon, Fred A., *The Organization and Administration of the Union army 1861-1865*, The Arthur H. Clark Company: Cleveland (1928).

Sommers, Richard, *Richmond Redeemed: The Siege at Petersburg*, Doubleday & Company, Inc.: Garden City, New York (1981).

(1) Letter from John W. Cook to Father and Mother, September 19, 1864, John Cook Pension File. Companies H, I and K came to Petersburg from Washington by water. Company K's Warren Newman wrote his father on September 20 that: "We have been on the water two days and sum of us was sick but we are all well now at preasent." (William Newman Pension File) He also reported that: "The boys ... like it first rate... Tell [Pat?] we have fun down hear...We have got good fare yet mutch better than I expected." (*Ibid.*)

(2) A.B., "Story of A Civil War Veteran," *E-J Workers Review*, Aug. – Dec. 1919, 20, George F. Johnson Papers, Box No. 26, Special Collections Research Center, Syracuse University Library. (Hereafter *E-J Workers Review*) Even in the Civil War era it was not unusual for men to be inexperienced with firearms. (Shannon, Vol. I, 167) John Andrews' sister Emma was incredulous at the lack of training: "Can it be that your company is put right into action? I hardly think that it can for it don't seem possible that you could understand the orders and know how to

execute them without drilling three or four weeks at least." (Letter from Emma Andrews to John Andrews, October 16, 1864).

(3) Sommers, 178-82; Hess, *In the Trenches*, xix.

(4) OR 42(1): 545.

[Photo: David McM. Gregg]

(5) *Ibid.* Because of heavy casualties, Ledlie's old First Division was deactivated at the end of August 1864. Its regiments were transferred to Willcox's Third Division, which was redesignated as the First Division and to Potter's Second Division. Ferrero's Fourth Division was redesignated as the Third Divisipon (OR, 42(1): 545; OR, 42(2): 642-43, 668).

(6) OR, 42(1): 545.

(7) Diary of William B. Larzelere, September 25 to 28, 1864, Private Collection; Letter from John W. Cook to Father and Mother, dated September 29, 1864, John Cook Pension File.

(8) OR 42(1):587.

(9) *The Hornellsville Tribune,* April 20, 1865; Morning Reports, Regimental Books, Vol. 4. The Morning Reports for Company F, Company G, Company H and Company K are not extant for September 1864. The Morning Report for Company I shows three officers and seventy four enlisted men present for duty on September 30, 1864 and Company K probably would be similar. The Morning Report for Company H for October 1, 1864, which would reflect the casualties incurred on September 30, showed two officers and forty-two enlisted men. The history of the 179th New York, published in *The Hornellsville Tribune,* on April 20, 1865, said that the 179th had four hundred men present for duty on September 30, 1864. There was also a detachment of nearly seventy unassigned men who arrived at the 179th's camp before daylight on September 30 and they went into battle with the 179th. (Affidavit of Don Hanford, John Roe and Edward Lousbury, December 26, 1894, John Ault Pension File; Affidavit of John Ault and Joe Roe, January 29, 1884, William Quick Pension File). This detachment had not drawn their tents and was exposed to the "severe storm" which set in for several days (*Ibid.*). (See also Report of Capt. Libbuis Brown, September 23, 1864, RG 110, Entry 2356, Box 44). The Company E Morning Report shows Captain Ottenot as present and Sgt. Charles Hogan so testified in Waterman Thornton's court-martial (LL2924, 5), but he may have been in hospital. (See Ottenot Carded Medical Records)

(10) OR, 42(1): 587.

(11) *Ibid.*

(12) Letter from George Hemingway to Cousin Orry, December 3, 1864, Author's collection.

(13) OR, 42(1): 587.

(14) Letter from Frank Tibbetts to the Hon. J.C. Black, January 21, 1888; Affidavit of Frank Tibbetts, December 8, 1887; Affidavit of Charles Blackmer, November 29, 1887, Charles Barnard Pension File.

(15) Hemingway letter, December 3, 1864.

(16) "A.B.," Story of Charles Johnson.

(17) Affidavit of Arthur Beebe, October 26, 1878; Affidavit of John Creteor, March 10, 1877; Affidavit of Charles Lawrence, October 4, 1897, all Arthur Beebe Pension File.

(18) Hemingway letter, December 3, 1864.

(19) OR 42(1): 578-79, 587-88.

(20) *Ibid.*, 579.

(21) *Ibid.*

(22) *Ibid.*, 588.

(23) *Ibid.*, 142, 508

(24) Hemingway December 3, 1864 letter.

(25) Affidavit of Ambrose Worden, March 21, 1883 and Deposition, April 20, 1896, Ambrose "Worden Pension File. Thirty years after the war, Charles Johnson recalled that:
That night was intensely dark and the rain falling very heavily. In some way or other we became mixed up with some Pennsylvania fellows [45th or 48th Pennsylvania?]. Soon we were unable to distinguish friend from foe. Cavalry was heard coming, in the distance, coming nearer and nearer until we found ourselves surrounded and captured by rebels. About four or five hundred of us were taken." (E-J Workers' Review)
Confederate cavalry also played a role in capturing eight officers and 177 enlisted men of the 45th Pennsylvania (OR 42(1): 585) and 124 soldiers from the 35th Massachusetts. (Sommers, 285).

(26) Worden March 21, 1883 Affidavit and Affidavit of Daniel Crance, April 22, 1896, Ambrose Worden Pension File.

(27) Affidavit of Robert Hooper, August 21, 1881, Charles Baker Pension File.

(28) Letter from William Lamont to Sister, October 2, 1864, William Lamont Papers, Wisconsin Historical Society; George Hemingway Pension File.

(29) Alfred Worden CMSR.

(30) Declaration of Peter Patric, July 8, 1865 and Certificate of Edward Lounsbury, July 8, 1865, both Peter Patric Pension File.

(31) Deposition of Charles W. Blackburn, March 22, 1883, Ambrose Worden Pension File.

(32) OR 42(1): 583-84. The 35th Massachusetts was also routed. As in the 179th, two-thirds of the troops were new recruits who had only arrived in mid-September. Unlike the 179th, though, most of the new recruits in the 35th were German immigrants who did not speak English, making effective communication in the heat of battle that much more difficult. (Sommers, 283) The 6th, 9th and 11th New Hampshire fell back to the Pegram House, concluding that there was no use trying to rally. (Leander Cogswell, *A History of the Eleventh New Hampshire Volunteer Infantry in the Rebellion War 1861-1865,* Republican Press Association: Concord, New Hampshire (1891), 499)

(33) Sommers, 282, 383; Revised Edition (2014), 276-77, 311, 371. See also Charles R. Bowery, *The Richmond-Petersburg campaign, 1864-65*, Praeger: Santa Barbara, California (2014), 83.

(34) E-J Workers' Review; Letter from Charles S. Baker to parents, September 19, 1864, Charles S. Baker Pension File; Statement of Waterman Thornton, Court-martial Transcript LL2924. The October 2, 1864 letter from William Lamont to his sister, which was cited by Sommers, includes the statements: "We was ordered to the rear. I guess they won't put us in the battle until we get our guns." An October 6, 1864 letter includes the statements: "there was but 9 of the boys of our company in the battle. It was all the guns they had." and "our guns are coming tomorrow." Lamont was one of twenty-two new recruits for Company B that arrived at the end of September. A December 3, 1864 letter from George Hemingway, another of Company B's new recruits, makes it clear that Lamont and he were referring only to the new recruits in Company B – the night that the new recruits arrived at the camp of the 179th, they "lay on our arms, that is those that they gave guns, which was 9 and I happen to be one of those..." (Hemingway December 3, 1864). Whereas the practice in the Spring was to arm the companies in Elmira before they were sent south, Companies H, I and K did not receive arms in Elmira before they left. However,

Charles Johnson's statement demonstrates that Company K received arms after arriving in the field and Charles S. Baker's letter demonstrates the same for Company I (Letter from Charles S. Baker to Mother, September 19, 1864, Charles S. Baker Pension File). The men recruited by John Andrews for Company D also did not receive their arms before they left Elmira. They arrived at the front on October 5 and received their arms on October 12. (JAWJ, October 6, October 10 and October 12, 1864)

(35) Hogan Testimony, Thornton Court-martial Transcript, LL2924, 5-6.

(36) Larzelere Diary, September 30, 1864.

(37) OR 42(1): 546, 579; Sommers, 286, 298, 383. Company K's Lt. Hooper estimated that the 179th fell back half a mile. Affidavit of Robert Hooper, August 28, 1881, Charles Baker Pension File.

(38) "Personal War Sketch of Charles W. Baker," August 25, 1901 in *Personal War Sketches*, J. Barnett Sloan Post No. 93, Department of New York, Grand Army of the Republic, Yates County History Center. There is nothing in the 179th's carded medical records that contradicts Baker's claim.

(39) OR, 42(1): 588.

[Sketch: A Cheering Sight-The Arrival of Reinforcements]

(40) OR, 42(1): 579-80, 588; Larzelere Diary, October 1, 1864.

(41) James Farr Declaration, December 16, 1876 and Charles E. Lockwood Affidavit, September 27, 1877, both James Farr Pension File; Larzelere Diary, October 2, 1864; Aaron Bennett Statement, William Howland Pennsion File; Letter from David Nicols to Commissioner of Pensions, July 16, 1886, David Nicols Pension File.

(42) Larzelere Diary, October 2, 1864 to December 1, 1864.

(43) OR, 42(1): 579.

(44) *Ibid.*, 142. The initial report showed forty-four enlisted men missing (*Ibid.*, 588). Phisterer reported eight enlisted men as killed and three as mortally wounded and only twenty wounded and twenty-six missing (Phisterer, 4029). My own review of the carded medical records shows two enlisted men as killed and one as mortally wounded; thirty-eight enlisted men as wounded; and thirty-six enlisted men as missing. The Regimental History (at 10) states that Company A's Anthony Tobias was captured as a result of disobeying an order by Lieutenant Farr, but does not provide any details.

(45) CMRs.

(46) Elihu Linkletter CMR.

(47) Letter from William Gregg to Ariel Thurston, December 5, 1864, New York State Military Museum, Unit History Project, 179th New York Volunteers, Civil War Newspaper Clippings.

(48) Compiled from CMRs.

(49) JAWJ, October 18, 1864, 69.

(50) Andrews referred to the battle on September 30 "when they threw away everything and skedaddled." (October 18, 1864, 70). His account was second hand – he did not arrive at the front until October 6, 1864. In a February 27, 1865 letter to his sister, Lamont wrote that another Union offensive was being planned and that "I hope it will work so they can have one battle without our soldiers running."

(51) Letter from William Lamont to "Friend Daniel," October 6, 1864.

(52) From the OR Atlas, showing positions on October 8, 1864:

[Map: October 8, 1864]

[Map: Western Front]

Chapter Sixteen

—— *History of the 179th Regiment N.Y.S.V. – Rebellion of 1861-65*, E.D. Norton, Printer: Ithaca, New York (1900).

Booth, Benjamin F. and Meyer, Steve, *Dark Days of the Rebellion: Life in Southern Military Prisons*, Meyer Publishing: Garrison, Iowa (1995).

Brown, Louis A., *The Salisbury Prison: A Case Study of Confederate Military Prisons, 1861-1865*, Broadfoot Publishing Company: Wilmington, North Carolina (Revised and Enlarged 1992).

Catton, Bruce, *Grant Takes Command*, Little, Brown and Company: Boston (1969).

Foner, Eric, *The Fiery Trial: Abraham Lincoln and American Slavery*, W.W. Norton & Company: New York (2010).

Gray, Michael P., *The Business of Captivity: Elmira and Its Civil War Prison*, The Kent State University Press: Kent, Ohio (2001).

Greene, A. Wilson, *Civil War Petersburg: Confederate City in the Crucible of War*, University of Virginia Press: Charlottesville (2006).

McPherson, James, *Battle Cry of Freedom: The Civil War Era*, Oxford University Press: Oxford (1988).

Parker, Sandra V., *Richmond's Civil War Prisons*, H.E. Howard, Inc.: Lynchburg, Virginia (1990).

Phisterer, Frederick, *New York in the War of the Rebellion 1861 to 1865*, D.B. Lyon Company, State Printers: Albany, New York (Third Ed. 1912).

Walcott, *History of the Twenty-First Regiment Massachusetts Volunteers in the War for Preservation of the Union 1861-1865*, Houghton, Mifflin and Company: Boston (1882).

(1) Phisterer, Vol. I, 243, 251, 260, 264, 279. These are the numbers in Phisterer's reports by battle. In the summary for the 179th New York as a unit, Phisterer lists only twenty-six missing for the Battle of the Crater and twenty-six for Poplar Spring Church. (Phisterer, 4029)

(2) McPherson, *Battle Cry*, 791; Catton, 370-71; Parker, 16. The full text of the cartel agreement is provided in Brown, 190-92. There were special ratios for exchanging officers for enlisted men – e.g. a colonel for fifteen privates.

(3) Catton, 371. Isolated exchanges did continue to be made, both in individual special cases and for sick and wounded prisoners (Parker, 54-57). In December 1863, Secretary of War Stanton estimated for President Lincoln that approximately 13,000 Union soldiers were being held by the Confederacy as prisoners of war (OR, II(VI): 647).

(4) Catton at 370-71; McPherson, *Tried By War*, 204. See also OR II(VI): 647-48; Proclamation of President Jefferson Davis, December 23, 1862, paras.3,4. OR, II(V): 795. Also provided in Brown, App. D at 193-95.

(5) McPherson, *Battle Cry of Freedom*, 792, 636-37; Catton, 370-72.

(6) McPherson, 792.

(7) OR, II(VII): 606-607. Grant may have had in mind his experience at Vicksburg. He had

taken 30,000 prisoners with the surrender of Vicksburg in July 1863 and General Banks had taken another 7,000 prisoners at Port Hudson. Faced with the practical realities of the field, Grant paroled all of these prisoners and sent them home (OR, 24(3): 470). This did not comply with either the terms of the cartel or Union orders. (OR, II(V): 307, para. 3) General Halleck warned Grant that this "may be construed into an absolute release, and that these men will be immediately placed in the ranks of the enemy. Such has been the case elsewhere." (OR, II(VI): 92-93). While not immediately, that is what happened.

(8) OR, II(VII): 614-615.

(9) OR, II(VII): 578-79.

(10) OR, II(VII): 687.

(11) OR, II(VII): 687-88.

(12) OR, II(VII): 906-907.

(13) *Ibid.*, 909.

(14) *Ibid.*, 914. Notwithstanding his own immediate decision, Grant did state that: "The whole matter, however, will be referred to the proper authority for their decision, and whatever it may be will be adhered to." (*Ibid.*) Given Lincoln's and Stanton's well-known positions, their decision was a foregone conclusion.

(15) Mollie Langworthy wrote John Andrews on November 1, 1864 that: "I get *so impatient* at their keeping our boys in prison or allowing them to be kept and treated so inhumanely – I expect if some of the mothers and sisters were in power, affairs would be arranged about right." (emphasis in original). She followed by asking Andrews: "Are you an advocate for women's rights?"

(16) Foner, 255; Simpson, 403.

(17) Of the seventy-five soldiers from the 179th who can be confirmed as prisoners of war, twenty-one died of disease, one died of wounds and three died of unknown causes (Phisterer, 302, 4029; CMSRs).

(18) Letter from George Hemingway to "Cousin Orry," December 3, 1864, Author's Collection.

(19) *E. J. Workers Review*, 21. Edward Carter from the 35th Massachusetts Volunteer Infantry (1st Brigade, 2nd Division/Ninth Corps) was also captured at Poplar Spring Church and was taken to Petersburg, by train to Richmond (Castle Thunder) and arrived at Salisbury on October 6. *The Prison Exchange* (newsletter of The Salisbury Confederate Prison Association, Inc.), Vol. XII, No. 3 (Winter 2011), 2. In the earlier part of the war, Salisbury was used to show the benign face of Southern prison life ... a scene of baseball in 1862:

[Lithograph: Salisbury Prison, Baseball in 1862]

(20) *Elmira Daily Advertiser*, January 23, 1880. The *Advertiser* incorrectly reported that Company F's Sgt. William Norton had been in the same group with McDonald. While Norton did wind up at Salisbury, he had been captured at the Battle of the Crater, not Poplar Spring Church.

(21) Pension File, George B. Hemingway; CMSR, George B. Hemingway; Letter from Hemingway to "Cousin Orry," December 3, 1864, Author's Collection.

(22) E-J, 20-21. The most famous memoir of Salisbury Prison was written by Benjamin F. Booth of the 22nd Iowa in 1897 from notes on scraps of paper he had kept during his imprisonment. (Booth and Meyer) Booth described an unsuccessful attempt to hide his money (page 59). Private John E. Short of Company B, 21st Massachusetts Volunteers [1st Brigade, 2nd Division/Ninth Corps], was also captured at the Battle of Poplar Spring Church on September 30, 1864. He

described his road to Salisbury Prison as follows:

"We first went to Petersburg, where we were stripped of almost everything. They took away my boots, and gave me a pair of old pointed shoes in exchange. Next we were taken to Richmond, to Libby Prison, where we stayed one day and night, and then started south to Salisbury, N.C. On reaching Salisbury, they put us in a large stockade made of logs, I should think about twenty feet high, inclosing a factory building and some small houses; and divided us up into lots of a hundred each, without reference to regiments." Walcott, 399.

(23) OR, II(VIII): 254; Brown, 23.

(24) E-J, 21; Brown, 17-25.

(25) E-J, 21. On February 10, 1865, the Governor of North Carolina sent the Confederate Secretary of War a letter expressing concern about "the suffering condition of the Federal prisoners" at Salisbury. The Inspector General ordered "an immediate inspection and full report of the subject." The report was submitted on February 17, 1865. (OR, II (VIII: 245) At that time, the Confederate inspectors found "one-third of the [prisoners] burrowing like animals in holes under ground or under the buildings in the inclosure." (OR, II (VIII): 247) Union prisoners also engaged in "burrowing" at Belle Island (Parker, 52,59).

(26) The Inspector General's report included the statement that:

"Three hundred tents and flies of mixed sizes and patterns were issued for the use of the prisoners of war in October ... and constitute the only shelter provided during the winter for a number of prisoners, amounting on the 7th of November to 8,740." (OR, II(VIII): 247)

The citizens of Salisbury also were not indifferent to the hardships of the prisoners. Some took food and clothing to the prisoners. In November 1864, they requested the Confederate States of America's Secretary of War to reduce the number of prisoners because of the overcrowding ("Prison History," Salisbury Confederate Prison Assoc. website).

(27) Affidavit of John Price and Affidavit of William L. Norton, February 22, 1890, both William Norton Pension File.

(28) Private Short's recollection was more detailed:

"For the first four or five days after we got there, they gave us each half a loaf of white bread for a day's ration, and nothing else. After that time, our entire day's ration was one pint of meal (cobs and corn ground together). We cooked the meal as best we could; for fuel we were allowed to go out under guard and get pine wood, and some of us made cakes of the meal and baked them in the ashes; some who had cups boiled it. No salt was given us. Nothing whatever but the meal, except for the first few days." (Walcott, 399-400).

The Confederate Inspector General's Report found that:

"Compared in quantity and kind with the rations issued to our troops in the field, it will be seen that on this score the prisoners have no cause to complain. The rations are cooked before they are issued ... Bread and meat (or sorghum in lieu of meat) are issued every morning, rice or pea soup in the afternoon. The bread which I inspected in the bakery was of average quality and of the average weight of five pounds to the double loaf. A half loaf, therefore, the daily allowance of each prisoner, will average twenty ounces of bread, the equivalent of sixteen ounces of flour." (OR, II(VIII),247)

(29) E-J, 21. Booth noted on December 2, 1864, that: "The sutler is still in business but his trade is not thriving owing to the scarcity of money among the men who would be his patrons if they could. He has to contend against the competition of the citizens who wait along the road to the creek, where we get our water, and among whom a good deal of trafficking is carried on by the

men who go out on the water detail. They prefer to take trade of almost any description rather than Confederate scrip." Booth at 142.

(30) E-J, 21. Private Short similarly recalled that:

"The water was good, but the supply was very short. The only way to get it was by lowering a tin dipper, fastened to a string, into the well. I don't know how many wells there were in all, but we had to go for water at two or three o'clock in the morning, on account of the crowd which were always waiting their turn to get a dipper full." (Walcott, 399-400)

(31) E-J, 22. Booth saw the same occur: "Things have come to such a state with us that it is absolutely necessary to strip the dead to relieve the needs of the living." (117). Private Short similarly recalled that:

"Dead men were always to be seen lying about, although an ox-cart was driven in once, and sometimes twice a day for the dead. They used to pile them in any way. I have often seen men fighting for a dead man's clothes. (Walcott, 400). The scenes in the pen were about the same every day. Many men lost their teeth from scurvy. There was nothing but misery, sickness, and death." (Walcott, 401)

(32) Booth, 121.

(33) Booth, 143.

(34) Affidavit of William L. Norton, February 8, 1886 and Affidavit of John Price, February 24, 1886, both John Price Pension File.

(35) Affidavit of Theodore McDonald dated March 17, 1884 and Affidavit of Charles Baker dated March 17, 1884, both Charles Baker (Co. K) Pension File. The cold weather actually began in December. Booth reported on December 6 that "last night the weather was so cold that it snowed and froze" and on December 8 that twenty some men had died during the night. (Booth, 144, 145) Short recalled that:

"My shoes were all gone in October, and I tied some old rags around my feet, which were very badly frozen during the winter, as were the feet of many others. I saw men with frozen feet, crying like children with pain, as the black flesh was dropping from the bones". (Walcott, 401). The Confederate Inspector General's report concluded that: "More than from any other cause the prisoners have suffered this winter from the want of sufficient and suitable clothing, being generally destitute of blankets and having only such clothes as they wore when captured, which, in the case of many of them, was during warm weather." (OR II(VIII): 247).

(36) Jane Buckland Aff., 3/22/1865, Timothy Buckland Pension File.

(37) "Memorandum from Prisoner of War Records" in CMSRs.

(38) Letter from Maggie E. Tobias to Col. Wm. Hoffman, December 20, 1864, Anthony Tobias, CMSR, National Archives.

(39) CMSRs, PFs. Cause of death was not rigorously determined.

(40) E-J, 21.

(41) Brown, 263. App P [Co. I A.W. Arden to be confirmed]

(42) McPherson, *Battle Cry of Freedom*, 802; Brown, 145; Booth, 88.

(43) Brown, 92.

(44) E-J, 22; Brown, 92. Private Short described the escape attempt as follows:

"Just before Thanksgiving Day, we made a break to escape. Our idea was to get to Newbern, which was supposed to be about a hundred miles away. [in fact 180 miles away] A man they called 'Major,' one of the enlisted men, planned the attack, and notified the men the night before. We attacked the guard about noon, captured several of their guns, and killed three of them. All the prisoners started, and a great many of us got out, myself among the number. Two field-pieces which were on platforms even with the top of the stockade, opened on the prisoners with canister; and the guards mounted the stockade and kept firing in upon them. I have no idea how many were killed, but there must have been a great many. Those of us who got outside were driven back. When we got out we were met by the outside guard of North Carolina militia, all old men; they pitied us, and didn't want to shoot, but begged us to go back. There was a camp rumor that a hundred and fifty of the prisoners got away, but I don't know whether there was any truth in it. I never heard anything of the 'Major' afterwards." (Walcott, 400)

See also Booth, 132-33.

(45) Brown, 92.

(46) E-J, 22.

(47) E-J, 22.

(48) Brown, 94.

(49) Brown, 91, 96-97.

(50) James Williams, CMSR, Company G Muster Role, March and April 1865.

(51) Brown, Appendix N-1. Booth noted in January 1865 that "there has not been a week since we came to this prison" that the rebels have not recruited (173). Booth himself felt that "I would starve to death a dozen times before I would be guilty of such a cowardly and traitorous act – and there were thousands of others of the same mind." (99. See also Booth, 99, 105, 108, 115, 130).

(52) *History of the 179th Regiment N.Y.S.V.*, 25, 35, 37; Brown, Appendix N-1. Barber and Hall are listed in Brown's Appendix N-1. The Regimental History also lists Isaac Hill as having joined the Confederacy on January 15, 1865 (36), but this seems unlikely because Hill apparently died on January 16. The same seems to apply to Company K's Jonas Sweet. (see Jonas Sweet Pension File) Appendix N-1 also lists a John Gage from Company D, a J. Labot from Company K and an I. Saderet from Company K. Gage would be John L. Gay, whose CMSR confirms that he enlisted in the Confederate service. Gay was a drafted man and had deserted from Buffalo in 1863, but had been caught. (CMSR) There is some conflicting evidence in Gay's CMSR suggesting that he was exchanged. See also list of paroled prisoners waiting exchange, December 31, 1864, Camp Parole (John Gui, Private Company D), Andrews Box #3. I found no names in the CMSRs that would appear to correspond to Labot and Saderet.

(53) Booth, 111-12. Daniels is not listed in Brown Appendix N-1. Sergeant Robert Walker of the 189th New York Volunteers, who escaped from Salisbury in February 1865, said that the prisoners from his unit who had enlisted in the Confederate army had been "starved into it." *Elmira Daily Advertiser*, April 16, 1865. James W. Pinch from the 107th New York said that some prisoners "secured better quarters and better food by pretending loyalty to the Confederacy, but sooner than do that I would have suffered starvation." *The Hornellsville Tribune*, March 30, 1865.

(54) Booth, 99, 105-106.

(55) E-J, 22. Booth referred to rumors of parole – positive and negative – on October 29, 1864; November 1, 1864; November 2, 1864; December 5, 1864; January 28, 1865; and February 19, 1865 (Booth, 76, 80, 81, 144, 150, 180, 195). Booth observed that: "The man who allows himself to become depressed and gloomy soon dies." (117).

(56) Brown, 159.

(57) Booth, 203; Brown, 159.

(58) Affidavits of William Norton, February 22, 1890, and John Price, William Norton Pension File; Affidavits of John Price, October 25, 1881 and February 24, 1886, and William Norton,

February 8, 1886, John Price Pension File.

(59) Brown, 160. For example, February 27, 1864 – Company B's Jarvis Kenyon and February 28, 1864 – Company F's William Norton, Company C's John Price and Company I's Nicholas Bedell. CMSRs.

(60) Brown, 159-60; Booth, 206-223. See also Edward Carter, *The Prison Exchange.*

(61) William Norton CMSR; Affidavit of William Norton, February 22, 1890, Norton Pension File. I do not know what location "CPW" is.

(62) Brown, 161.

(63) E-J, 22.

(64) E-J, 23.

(65) E-J, 23.

(66) R. Morris, *A Low, Dirty Place: The Parole Camps of Annapolis, MD 1862-1865*, Ann Arrundell County Historical Society: Linthicum, MD (2012), 53, 67.

(67) E-J, 23.

(68) War Department Directive, May 30, 1865. See., e.g. Charles Barker, John Price, Nathaniel Reed and Lewis Reuben CMSRs.

(69) Affidavit of Charles A. Beckwith, March 2, 1888, John H. Price Pension File.

(70) Affidavit of John Price, February 24, 1886, John Price Pension File.

(71) "Memorandum from Prisoner of War Records" in CMSRs.

(72) Affidavit of Dr. Eli Beers, February 23, 1866, Abram Lane Pension File.

(73) Horace Cornelius CMSR. He was finally discharged.

(74) Brown, 161, 184.

(75) "Memorandum of Prisoner of War Records" in CSMRs. Nearly four hundred men from the 16th Connecticut were sent to Andersonville. Their experience is described in Lesley J. Gordon, *A Broken Regiment: The 16th Connecticut's Civil War*, Louisiana State University Press: Baton Rouge (2014), 145-173.

(76) Letter from Hosea Fish, June 19, 1864, Loraditch Family Tree, Public Member Trees, Ancestry.com.

(77) Letter from James Moulton to Mother, January 19, 1865, Hosea Fish Pension File.

(78) CMSRs.

(79) Compton Diary, January 13, 1865.

(80) CMRs.

(81) OR, II, V: 1120.

(82) John Hall CMSR.

(83) Affidavit of Henry Menhenitt, October 17, 1899, Menhenitt Pension File. Compare the Andersonville photograph from the text with this one of Elmira Prison taken in 1864.

[Photo: Elmira Military Prison]

(84) Affidavit of Henry Menhenitt, July 19, 1889 and Affidavit of George Cross, April 7, 1898, both Menhenitt Pension File; Menhenitt CMSR.

(85) "Memorandum of Prisoner of War Records" in CMSRs.

(86) Greene, 209.

(87) *Ibid.*, 210; Kevin Levin, *Remembering the Battle of the Crater: War as Murder*, The University Press of Kentucky: Lexington (2012), 7-8.

(88) "Memorandum of Prisoner of War Records" in CMSRs.

(89) Affidavit of James Spencer, October 3, 1904, James Spencer Pension File. See also Emmanuel Dabney, "A Federal Opportunity Lost: The Battle of the Crater," *Blue & Gray*, Vol. XXX, #5 (2014), 29-30.

(90) Affidavits of James Spencer, January 17, 1898, June 18, 1898 and October 3, 1904; Affidavit of John Grierson, October 29, 1889, all James Spencer Pension File.

(91) Affidavit of James Spencer, January 17, 1898, Spencer Pension.

(92) CMSR

(93) Regimental History, 19.

(94) Parker, 10, 66.

[Sketch: Libby Prison]

[Photo: Libby Prison, April 1865]

(95) Affidavit of Ira Crawford, January 23, 1895, Robert Crawford Pension File.

(96) "Memorandum of Prisoner of War Records" in CMSR.

(97) Daniel Hazelton, Leander Pierce, Thomas Porter, and Robert Wilkens. "Memorandum of Prisoner of War Records" in CMSRs. Several gunboats and monitors were constantly guarding the river and Aiken's Landing

[Photo: Monitor Onandaga]

(98) CMSRs; *Harper's Weekly*, March 18, 1865, 172. and a contemporary photograph

[Photo: Aiken's Landing]

another view of the Flag of Truce boat "New York"

Photo: Flag of Truce Boat]

(99) CMRs.

(100) CMSRs.

(101) W. Adams (ed.), *Biographical Sketches from Historical Gazeteer and Biography of Men of Cattaraugus County* (1893)

Chapter Seventeen

Armstrong, Warren B., *For Courageous Fighting and Confident Dying: Union Chaplains in the Civil War*, University Press of Kansas: Lawrence (1998).

Cross, Whitney R., *The Burned-Over District: The Social and Intellectual History of Enthusiastic Religion in Western New York, 1800-1850*, Cornell University Press: Ithaca New York (1950).

McPherson, James, *For Cause and Comrades: Why Men Fought in the Civil War*, Oxford University Press: New York (1997).

Miller, Robert J., *Both Prayed to the Same God: Religion and Faith in the Civil War*, Lexington Books:

New York (2007).

Phisterer, Frederick, *New York in the War of the Rebellion 1861 to 1865*, D.B. Lyon Company, State Printers: Albany, New York (Third Ed. 1912).

Wiley, Bell Irvin, *The Life of Billy Yank: The Common Soldier of the Union*, Louisiana State University Press: Baton Rouge (1952, 1971).

Woodworth, Steven E., *While God Is Marching On: The Religious World of Civil War Soldiers*, University Press of Kansas: Lawrence (2001).

[Sketch: Divine Services]

(1) McPherson, 63. See also Woodworth, 8, 26, 231, 253. Many of the recruits in the 179th had grown up in or near the "Burned-over District" of Western New York, an area of particularly intense religious ferment. See generally Cross.

(2) Miller, 11.

(3) Quoted in Miller, 11. See also Miller, xiii.

(4) Woodworth, 145.

(5) War Department, Adjutant General's Office, General Orders No. 15, May 4, 1861, OR III, Vol. 1 ,154; Woodworth, 145.

(6) JAWJ, October 13, 1864, 57; Wiley, 263-64; Woodworth, 149.

(7) Armstrong, 12.

(8) Letter from Hosea Fish to "Beloved wife and children," May 5, 1864, Loraditch Family Tree, Public Member Trees, Ancestry.com.

(9) Letter from Daniel B. Lee to daughter, undated [circa May 1, 1864]p. 6 in my numbered set of copies; Co. A Morning Report, "Remarks," May 4, 1864, Regimental Books, Vol. 4; Affidavit of Daniel D. Lowell, November 14, 1890, Daniel Lowell Pension File. Chaplains commonly served as the "regimental postmaster." Armstrong, 14. Lowell is reported as a farmer in the 1860 Census. Town of Grove, County of Alleghany, Page No. 6, Line 6 (July 25, 1860).

(10) Lee fragments p. 39, p. 6

(11) Lowell CMR, Pension file

(12) CMSR; Phisterer, 4036

(13) Ancestry.com, Public Member Trees (Elihu Linkletter); Declaration for Pension of Ezra Tinker, February 15, 1907, Ezra Tinker Pension File; and *Elmira Star Gazette*, August 31, 1917 (Francis Asberry King).

(14) *Elmira Daily Advertiser*, September 17, 1864; *The First Half Century of Madison University*, 1819-1869, 354, 472.

(15) Woodworth, 148.

(16) JAWJ, October 13, 1864, 34-35. On October 13, Andrews copied into his journal pencil notes he had taken over the preceding days.

(17) *Ibid.*, 36.

(18) JAWJ, October 6, 1864.

(19) JAWJ, October 6, October 9 and October 12, 1864; Compton Diary, January 15, 1865; Phisterer, 4030.

(20) JAWJ, November 13, 1864; Phisterer, 4030.

(21) JAWJ, October 1, 1864 and November 13, 1864.

(22) JAWJ November 14, 1864; Edwin A. Taft CMSR, 5th New York Heavy Artillery; *The First*

Half Century of Madison University, 1819-1869, 163.

(23) Letter to Horatio Seymour, October 9, 1864, Edwin A. Taft CMSR.

(24) JAWJ, October 12, 1864, 55. I don't know whether there was a formal protocol during the Civil War on who was responsible for notifying the next of kin of a deceased soldier – the company commander, the chaplain and/or another person.

(25) Letter from Edwin A. Taft to Mrs. Brown, January 26, 1865, Archives, Hamilton College Library.

(26) *Dryden Weekly*, April 20, 1865.

(27) McPherson, 63.

(28) Letter from George B. White to Mother, June 3, 1864, George White Pension File.

(29) U.S. Christian Commission report, Stephen Ferris CMSR.

(30) Woodworth, 68; Miller, 42; David A. Raney, "In the Lord's Army: The United States Christian Commission, Soldiers, and the Union War Effort," in Paul A. Cimbala and Randall M. Miller (eds.), *Union Soldiers and the Northern Home Front: Wartime Experiences, postwar adjustments*, Fordham University Press: New York (2002), 273-74. Many of the bibles were allowed to be sent to the South under flags of truce (*Ibid.*). It is not apparent how many soldiers in the 179th New York carried pocket bibles. A bible rarely is listed on the official inventories of personal effects prepared for the soldiers in the 179th New York when they died (CMSRs). Exceptions were Company A's Ward Burdick and Henry Kingsley, whose "Book of Psalms" and "Pocket Bible" were listed (CMSRs).

(31) Rutan Family Collection; Undated, unsourced newspaper obituary, Rutan Family Collection. Rutan does not appear to have been dogmatic in his faith. At some point during the war (perhaps when he was a patient at St. Mary's U.S. A. General Hospital in Rochester, New York), he learned about the Book of Ecclesiasticus – one of the books of the "Apocrypha" which appears in the Catholic Vulgate, but not the Protestant Bible. His Baptist faith did not prevent him from making a note in his Bible of verses from Ecclesiasticus relating to knowledge.

(32) Letter from James W. Vangilder to Nancy M. Swansbrow, September 26, 1864, Private Collection.

(33) Chemung County Historical Society. While Howard was in the hospital in November 1864 suffering from fever and diarrhea, a "delegate" from the United States Christian Commission wrote a letter to Hanlon on his behalf. The delegate described Howard as "Rather despondent" at the time (Daniel Howard CMSR).

(34) Woodworth, 104.

(35) Other soldiers also found comfort in the Ninety-first Psalm. William H. Walling quoted it in a letter to his sister in 1862, (Woodworth, 193) and a soldier in the 37th Mississippi referred to it in his diary in 1863 (Miller, ix).

(36) Letter from Daniel B. Lee to William Perry, May 9, 1864.

(37) Letter from Daniel Lee to daughter, undated [circa May 1, 1864] fragment, p. 6; Letter from Daniel Lee to wife, dated May 28, 1864; Letter from Daniel Lee to wife and daughter, dated June 6, 1864.

(38) Letter from Daniel B. Lee to wife, June 17, 1864.

(39) Letter from Daniel B. Lee to wife, June 26, 1864.

(40) Letter from Daniel B. Lee to wife and daughter, July 3, 1864.

(41) Letter from Daniel B. Lee to wife, May 28, 1864. See Woodworth, 27, 35-36, 41, 45.

(42) Letter from Homer Olcott to Father, July 5, 1864, Homer Olcott Pension File.

(43) Letter from George B. Hemingway to Cousin Orry, December 3, 1864, Author's collection.

(44) Letter from Homer Olcott to Friends, June 3, 1864, Homer Olcott Pension File. In a later letter, Olcott wrote that: "I am not afraid. If it is God's will I will come out safe." (Letter from Homer Olcott to Father, June 24, 1864, Homer Olcott Pension File).

(45) Compton Diary, January 1, 1865.

(46) New York State Military Museum, Unit History Project, 179th New York Volunteers, Civil War Newspaper Clippings.

(47) Letter from William Byrd, Jr. to Father, June 21, 1864. This is one of forty-eight letters in the collection, the vast majority of which were written by Bird during his earlier service in the 37th New York. The letters have a secular focus. However, Bird was given a masonic funeral at the local Methodist church when he died in 1908, so religion played some role in his life.

(48) Lamont letters. His June 19, 1865 letter to his parents from Slough Hospital was written on U. S. Christian Commission letterhead, which included the admonition "This is a faithful saying, and worthy of all acceptation, that Christ Jesus came into the world to save sinners; of whom I am chief." There is no way of knowing whether he endorsed the message or appreciated the free stationery and stamp.

(49) Letter from John Cook to Father and Mother, June 30, 1865; Letter from John Cook to Father and Mother, August 8, 1865, John Cook Pension File. Two of Cook's letters were written on Christian Commission letterhead with religious messages, but because he also wrote three letters on secular Sanitary Commission letterhead, it seems likely he was more interested in the free stationary than the message.

(50) Nathaniel Mabee CMSR; CMRs.

(51) JAWJ, October 5, 1864, 34-35.

(52) JAWJ, February 19, 1865.

(53) JAWJ, March 19, 1865.

Chapter Eighteen

Catton, Bruce, *The Army of the Potomac: A Stillness at Appomattox*, Doubleday & Company: Garden City, New York (1953).

Greene, A. Wilson, *Breaking the Backbone of the Rebellion: The Final Battles of the Petersburg campaign*, Savas Publishing Company: Mason City, Iowa (2000).

Hess, Earl J., *In the Trenches at Petersburg: Field Fortifications & Confederate Defeat*, University of North Carolina Press: Chapel Hill (2009).

Newsome, Hampton, *Richmond Must Fall: The Richmond-Petersburg campaign, October 1864*, The Kent State University Press: Kent, Ohio (2013).

Ramold, Steven J., *Across the Divide: Union Soldiers View the Northern Home Front*, New York University Press: New York (2013).

Shannon, Fred A., *The Organization and Administration of the Union army 1861-1865*, The Arthur H. Clark Company: Cleveland (1928).

Wiley, Bell Irvin, *The Life of Billy Yank: The Common Soldier of the Union*, Louisiana State University Press: Baton Rouge (1952, 1971).

Forts on the Western Front
[Map: Forts Near Fort Gregg]

(1) JAWJ, October 8, 1864, 41.

(2) Letter from John Andrews to Sister, November 21, 1864, Library of Virginia.

(3) Letter from John Andrews to Homer Andrews, February, 7, 1865, Library of Virginia; Hornellsville Tribune, April 20, 1865. The proximity of the 179th's camp to Peebles House and Pegram's House as well as Pegram's Farm led to inconsistent references. Andrews humorously illustrated the confusion by beginning one of his letters "Near Pegram House, Va. or Near Peebles House, Va. or Near Patrick Station, Va. or Near Petersburg, Va. or Near Poplar Grove Church, Va." (JAWJ, November 6, 1864, 22).

(4) Hess, 167; Larzelere Diary, October 3, 1864.

(5) Letter from Abner Welch to Father & Mother & Sisters, October 23, 1864, Abner Welch Pension File.

(6) JAWJ, October 7, 1864, 39.

(7) Letter from William Lamont to Sister, October 24, 1864.

(8) JAWJ, October 21, 1864, 84. On November 4 Andrews saw General Parke at Peebles House. "The General is only a First Lieutenant in the Regular Army. He is a young fine looking man, about thirty five years of age, I should judge." (JAWJ, November 4, 1864).

(9) JAWJ October 11, 1864, 52. See also JAWJ, October 23, 1864, 87-88.

(10) Letter from William Lamont to "Sister," October 24, 1864, Wisconsin Historical Society. William Larzelere recorded the 179th's picket duty from October 1864 through March 1865 in his diary as follows (supplemented by JAWJ, Lamont Letters and Andrews and Vandermark court martial transcripts):

10/4/64	At night went on picket
10/5/64	On picket in the woods
10/8/64	Night went on picket
10/9/64	On picket
10/11/64	Andrews: "Nearly the whole regt out on picket duty tonight 240 men"/ Larzelere: "in camp"
10/16/64	On picket line
10/19/64	Night went on picket/Andrews: went out on picket at five - nearly all the regiment went also
10/20/64	On picket
10/23/64	At night went on picket/Andrews: "At five the larger part of the regiment went out on picket"
10/24/64	On picket
10/25/64	In camp
10/26/64	In camp
11/17/64	On picket line
11/25/64	On picket
11/26/64	In camp

11/29/64	Went on picket,
11/30/64	On picket (after march to new camp)
12/5/64	At night went on picket
12/6/64	On picket
12/17/64	At night went on picket
12/18/64	On picket
12/27/64	At night went on picket
12/28/64	On picket
1/4/65	At night went on picket
1/5/65	Returned to camp at night
1/11/65	At night went on picket
1/12/65	On picket
1/14/65	At night went on picket
1/15/65	On picket returned to camp at night
1/17/65	At night went on picket
1/18/65	Returned to camp at dark
1/19/65	At night went on picket
1/20/65	On picket at night returned to camp
1/30/65	Andrews: went on picket
1/31/65	Vandermark: on picket
2/1/65	At night went on picket
2/2/65	On picket. At night to camp.
2/4/65	On picket at night
2/5/65	On picket line
2/6/65	Returned to camp at night
2/18/65	At night went on picket
2/19/65	Sunday at night came off picket
2/21/65	Larzelere: this is my night for picket
2/23/65	At night on picket
2/24/65	On picket returned to camp
(Larzelere on furlough)	
3/19/65	At night on reserve picket

(11) Hess, 238-39.

(12) Greene, 49.

(13) Letter from William Lamont to "Parents," January 7, 1865.

(14) Letter from William Lamont to "Parents," February 21, 1865.

(15) Letter from William Gregg to Ariel Thurston, December 5, 1864, New York State Military Museum, Unit History Project, 179th New York Volunteers, Civil War Newspaper Clippings. See also Catton, 325-26; Charles R. Bowery, Jr., *The Richmond-Petersburg campaign, 1864-65*, Praeger: Santa Barbara, California (2014), 93.

(16) *Buffalo Daily Courier*, June 29, 1864. Bell Wiley cautions that: "one incident of commingling, because of the human interest and drama that it involved, was apt to receive more notice in the records than days of skirmishing and weeks of passive hostility." Wiley, 357.

(17) CMR.

(18) CMR.

(19) JAWJ, March 22, 1865.

(20) JAWJ, October 30, 1864; Letter from Lamont to Sister, October 24, 1864.

(21) JAWJ, October 20, 1864, 80-81.

(22) Hess, 216.

(23) Letter from William Lamont to sister, October 24, 1864.

(24) JAWJ, November 3, 1864.

(25) JAWJ, November 7, 1864.

(26) JAWJ, November 2, 1864.

(27) JAWJ, November 2, 1864. Compared to the $120 to $150 charged for stoves in Arkansas during the winter of 1862-63, $7 seems like a fair price (Shannon, Vol. I, 248).

(28) JAWJ, November 2-3, 1864.

(29) JAWJ, November 7, 1864.

(30) JAWJ, October 25, 1864, 94.

(31) JAWJ, October 26, 1864, 98-99.

(32) JAWJ, October 26, 1864, 99.

(33) Hess, 190.

(34) Hess, 192; Newsome, 133.

(35) Newsome, 135-36.

(36) Newsome, 226, 293.

(37) JAWJ, October 27 & 28, 1864, 100. In a letter to his brother, Andrews questioned how it could be called a reconnaissance when they had been issued six days rations and General Meade had moved his headquarters to Fort Cummings. "I don't know anything about these things, but I simply write what I hear on all sides here in camp." (Letter from John Andrews to Homer Andrews, October 31, 1864).

(38) JAWJ, October 27 & 28, 1864, 106-107.

(39) Newsome, 178.

(40) OR, 42(1): 548, 549, 580; Newsome, 186-187.

(41) Newsome, 186, 191-192; OR, 580.

(42) OR, 42(1): 580.

(43) Letter from John Andrews to Homer Andrews, October 31, 1864 letter, Author's Collection.

(44) JAWJ, October 27 & 28, 1864, 107, October 23, 1864, 88; OR, 580.

(45) Newsome, 228.

(46) OR, 549; 580; Newsome, 287-288.

(47) "Memoranda," Regimental Books, Vol. 2.

(48) Larzelere Diary, October 27 and 28, 1864.

(49) JAWJ, October 29, 1864, 115-16.

(50) Letter from John Andrews to Homer Andrews, October 31, 1864, Author's Collection, donated to Library of Virginia; JAWJ, October 27 & 28, 1864.

(51) Wiley, 48-49; JAWJ, October 31, 1864; Larzelere Diary, October 31, 1864.

(52) Ramold, 42; Wiley, 48-49. While the army provided food and shelter, the rates of pay created a hardship for soldiers with families to support. Even farm laborers were paid better, particularly in the later years of the war when the civilian labor supply was tight. The average monthly wage for a farm laborer in Horseheads, Chemung County, New York increased from $13 in 1860 to $18 ($25 summer) in 1865. Nearby Barton Township in Tioga County saw an even greater increase–from $12.50 ($16 summer) in 1860 to $28 ($35 summer) in 1865. Similar increases occurred in Elmira (1865 New York State Census). The government did increase the monthly pay of a private from $13 to $16 to make up for the loss of purchasing power (Shannon, Vol. I, 246).

(53) Forms No. 5, Author's Collection, donated to Chemurg County Museum. It is not clear that the experience of Applegate and Carey was typical. John Andrews recorded in his journal on March 2, 1865 that: "The Paymaster has been here all day paying the men." (JAWJ, March 2, 1865, 13. See also March 1, 1865, 12–"Regiment Paid"). The CMRs for Applegate suggest that he was at home on that date which would account for his not being paid. However, the CMRs for Carey suggest that he was in camp that day. (CMRs)

(54) Letter from William Lamont to sister, November 15, 1864.

(55) Letter from William Lamont to parents, February 21, 1865.

(56) Letter from William Gregg to Ariel Thurston, December 5, 1864, New York State Military Museum, Unit History Project, 179th New York Volunteers, Civil War Newspaper Clippings.

(57) JAWJ, Vol. 3, 125.

(58) Letter from E. G. Cook to Secretary of War Stanton, December 1, 1864, Elliott Cook CMSR; Letter from Abner Welch to Parents, November 16, 1864, Abner Welch Pension File.

(59) Letter from Abner Welch to parents, November 16, 1864, Abner Welch Pension File; Transcription of letter from James W. Vangilder to Nancy Swansbrow, September 26, 1864, Private Collection.

(60) Letters from Daniel Lee to Wife, June 8, 1864, June 10, 1864 and undated fragment.

(61) Letters from William Lamont to Dear Friends, September 25, 1864, to Friend Daniel, October 6, 1864 and to Sister Bell, December 7, 1864.

(62) Letters from William Lamont. The prices at City Point reported by *Harper's Weekly* on December 10, 1864 were similar. Surprisingly, prices for apples, butter and crackers were still the same in February 1865. (Letter from William Lamont to Parents, February 21, 1865).

(63) *Ontario Times*, June 22, 1864 and December 28, 1864. These are probably wholesale prices.

(64) JAWJ, March 15, 1865.

(65) Letter from Daniel B. Lee to Jane Lee, May 28, 1864; Daniel B. Lee, June 27, 1864.

(66) Letter from Jacob Graves to Father, July 8, 1864, Jacob Graves Pension File.

(67) F. Shannon, *The Organization and Administration of the Union army 1861-1865*, Peter Smith: Gloucester, Massachusetts (1965 originally published 1928) Vol. I, 254-55.

(68) Shaw and Hausner CMSRs.

(69) Letter from William Lamont to Sister, November 15, 1864.

(70) JAWJ, October 22, 1864, 85.

(71) Letter from William Lamont to Sister Bell, November 27, 1864.

(72) Wiley, 26-27, 50.

(73) JAWJ, November 5 and 7, 1864.

(74) Affidavit of Elias Beach [undated], Beach Pension File.

(75) "Remarks," Company C Morning Report, November 1864, Regimental Books, Vol. 4.

(76) JAWJ, November 18, 1864, 32.

(77) Letter from John Andrews to Sister, November 21, 1864, Library of Virginia.

(78) JAWJ, November 26, 1864. Andrews wrote Company C in his journal, but he may have meant his own Company D.

(79) Letter from William Lamont to Sister Bell, November 27, 1864.

(80) Letter from William Larzelere to Sarah Larzelere, November 26, 1864.

Chapter Nineteen

Alotta, Robert I., *Civil War Justice: Union army Executions Under Lincoln*, White Mane Publishing Co., Inc.:Shippensburg, Pennsylvania (1989).

Basler, Roy P. (ed.), *The Collected Works of Abraham Lincoln*, Rutgers University Press: New Brunswick, New Jersey (1953).

Catton, Bruce, *The Army of the Potomac: Glory Road*, Doubleday & Company: Garden City, New York (1952).

Fantina, Robert, *Desertion and the American Soldier, 1776-2006*, Algora Publishing: New York (2006).

Hardee, William J., *Hardee's Rifle and Light Infantry Tactics for the Instructions, Exercises and Manoeuvres of Riflemen and Light Infantry, Including School of the Soldier and School of the Company, To Which Is added, Duties of Non-Commissioned Officers, Military Honors to Be Paid By Troops, the Articles of War*, J. O. Kane, Publisher: New York (1862) (reprinted by H-Bar Enterprises: Silver Spring, Maryland).

Hess, Earl J., *In the Trenches at Petersburg: Field Fortifications & Confederate Defeat*, University of North Carolina Press: Chapel Hill (2009).

Hess, Earl J., *The Union Soldier in Battle: Enduring the Ordeal of Combat*, University Press of Kansas: Lawrence (1997).

Freeman, Douglas Southall, *R. E. Lee: A Biography*, Charles Scribner's Sons: New York (1935).

Lonn, Ella, *Desertion During the Civil War*, University of North Carolina Press: Lincoln (1998 originally published 1928).

McPherson, James, *Tried By War: Abraham Lincoln as Commander in Chief*, The Penguin Press: New York (2008).

Reid, Brian Holden and White, John, " 'A Mob of Stragglers and Cowards': Desertion from the Union and Confederate Armies, 1861-65", *The Journal of Strategic Studies*, Vol. 8, Issue 1 (1985).

Wiley, Bell Irvin, *The Life of Billy Yank: The Common Soldier of the Union*, Louisiana State University Press: Baton Rouge (1952, 1971).

(1) Lonn, 21 et seq., 143 et seq. Freeman, Vol. III, 497, 516-17, 541-42. For Confederate desertion during the Petersburg campaign, see Charles R. Bowery, *The Richmond-Petersburg campaign, 1864-65*, Praeger: Santa Barbara, California (2014), 114-116.

(2) Lonn, 145.

(3) *Ibid.*

(4) *Ibid.*

(5) *Ibid.*, 233 (Table III).

(6) *Ibid.*

(7) *Ibid.*

(8) *Ibid.*, 127-142. See also Fantina, 76.

(9) Hardee, 130.

(10) Lonn, 179-180

(11) *Ibid.*, 181.

(12) Basler, Vol. VI, 132.

(13) Lonn, 181; Catton, 233-34.

(14) Lonn, 181.

(15) OR, 29(2): 102.

(16) *Ibid.*; Basler, Vol. VI, 414-415.

(17) Basler, Vol. VII, 208; Lonn, 169-70.

(18) OR, 37(1): 406.

(19) Lonn, 146, 181-82.

(20) Letter from John Andrews to Homer Andrews, January 10, 1865.

(21) Lonn, 185-186.

(22) OR 42(2): 529; Lonn, 189-90.

(23) OR 42(2): 529.

(24) OR 43(2): 29(Grant); OR, 42(2):1200(Lee).

(25) OR 42(3): 608-609; Lonn, 190-191.

(26) Lonn, 160.

(27) JAWJ, October 12, 1864.

(28) Descriptive Book, Regimental Books, Vol. 1; CMSR.

(29) Lonn, 181-182.

(30) JAWJ, October 14, 1864; See also Larzelere Diary, October 14, 1864; Alotta, 134. Larzelere simply recorded in his diary "saw deserter shot."

(31) JAWJ, October 14, 1864.

(32) *Ibid.*, October 16, 1864; Company A and Company C Register of Deserters, Descriptive Book, Regimental Books, Vol. 1. Bell Wiley notes that there is no evidence that forcing soldiers to view execution of deserts was an effective deterrent (Wiley, 207). Brian Holden Reid and John White concluded that "Executions did not guarantee a deterrent against desertion," giving as an example an incident in which "seven soldiers were paraded and shot before their comrades – but even more desertions followed the same night." (Reid and White, 73).

(33) Court Martial Transcript LL2812 (Case No. 14), 7.

(34) Company A, Register of Deserters, Descriptive Book, Regimental Books, Vol. 1.

(35) JAWJ, October 16, 1864, October 17, 1864, 67-68.

(36) Letter from Capt. Henry Gregg, 13th Regiment, Pa. Cavalry to Brig. General Patrick, Provost Marshal, Army of the Potomac, August 12, 1864, Daniel Smith CMSR.

(37) See text following Endnote 50, infra. Unfortunately, there is no information about McGregor and Nash. Even when the CMSRs were prepared around 1900, there was no record of their enlistment or muster in. However, they were not part of Company A's original complement (CMSRs; Descriptive Book, Regimental Books, Vol. 1).

(38) JAWJ, October 17, 1864.

(39) JAWJ, October 24, 1864, 42.

(40) *Ibid.*

(41) Letter from William Lamont to Sister, October 24, 1864.

(42) *Ibid.*; Register of Deserters, Descriptive Book, Regimental Books, Vol. 1.

(43) CMSR; Court-Martial Transcript.

(44) Smith CMSR. Smith's name is not on the list of Union soldiers who were executed (Alotta, 191-201).

(45) JAWJ, October 24, 1864.

(46) File No. NN 3092, Record Group 153, Records of the Office of the Judge Advocate General (Army), Court Martial Case Files, 1809-1894, NN3087-NN3095, Box 1848, National Archives. Shipman probably was in the June 17 assault, but was sick in hospital during the Battle of the Crater. (CMR) Shipman apparently did not even suffer the loss of pay due to a legal technicality. In December 1864, the Judge Advocate General opined that the proceedings "must be held fatally defective and the sentence inoperative" because he had been charged under Article 99 of the Articles of War rather than Article 46. (File No. NN 3092)

(47) JAWJ, November 18, 1864; Co. H Register of Deserters, Descriptive Book, Regimental Books, Vol. 1; CMSRs. Jacob Perry, who was a veteran of the 34th New York, apparently appeared in New York City at the end of the war as Abraham J. Perry and attempted to be mustered out. It is not clear from his CMSR what happened at that point.

(48) Co. H Morning Report, March 1865, Regimental Books, Vol. 4.

(49) Co. H Morning Report, December 1864, "Remarks," Regimental Books, Vol. 4; Company H Register of Deserters, Descriptive Book, Regimental Papers, Vol. 1.

(50) JAWJ, November 22 and November 26, 1864.

(51) File No. LL 2812, Case No. 14 (Edward Rowe) and Case No. 15 (Daniel Smith), RG 153; Headquarters, Army of the Potomac, General Court Martial Orders No. 49, National Archives; Lazelere Diary, December 10, 1864.

(52) W. Hopkins, 234.

(53) JAWJ, January 24, 1865, 43-44.

(54) *Buffalo Daily Courier*, December 28, 1864.

(55) Declaration of Julius Schulenberg for Invalid Pension dated September 16, 1892, Julius Schulenberg Pension File. Schulenberg's application for the removal of the charge of desertion and for an honorable discharge was denied by the War Department in 1892 (Schulenberg CMSR).

(56) Descriptive Book, Company E, Regimental Books, Vol. 1. In his written statement submitted during his court-martial, Thornton said that "when I entered the army I closed my shop and gave up business for the purpose of enlisting." (Undated "Statement of the Prisoner," court-martial file). This suggests that he was not a laborer.

(57) Thornton stated that he had received a bounty of $600 (Undated statement, Thornton courtmartial file). He argued that he "entered the service with good intentions. If I had intended to desert, I would have enlisted for three years and taken a higher bounty." (Undated "Statement of the Prisoner," court-martial file).

(58) Transcript, No. LL 2924.

(59) Alotta, 151-52.

(60) Letter from Waterman Thornton to Maj. Genl. Parke dated January 4, 1865, No. LL2924.

(61) JAWJ, January 6, 1865, 53; Letter from John Andrews to Homer Andrews, January 10, 1865; Lazelere Diary, January 6, 1865. Other than Andrews' War Journal, I have not seen any reference to a pardon. Alotta makes no reference to a pardon in his discussion of Thornton's case. (At 151-

52).

(62) Basler, Vol. VIII, 203. It was not at all unusual for Lincoln to intervene in this manner in the cases of individual soldiers. (See, e.g. Basler, Vol. VIII, 212 – Henry Stork, 5th Pa. Cavalry; Solomon Spiegel, 9th Mich. Cavalry)

(63) Basler, Vol. VIII, 203. A soldier of the Seventh Rhode Island provided the following account concerning Thornton:

"[January 6, 1865] A member of the One Hundred and Seventy-ninth New York was hung for desertion. He gave his name as Waterman Thornton, which was probably incorrect, as he acknowledged enlisting, receiving bounty and deserting *fourteen* times. He was scarcely thirty years of age, and was destitute of that nerve that had carried his predecessors creditably through the last trying ordeal [presumably a reference to Rowe and Smith]." (Hopkins, 239)(emphasis in original) (See Hess, *In the Trenches at Petersburg*, 228 & n. 55) It is not clear whether the reference to Waterman's being a bounty jumper fourteen times is true. If he were a "professional" bounty jumper, it seems likely that he would have developed the skill to have deserted in Elmira or en route to the front, rather than waiting until a battle. There is also no reference to the fourteen incidents in John Andrews' account in his War Journal or in his January 10, 1865 letter to his brother Homer describing the execution. While trying to convince his brother not to enlist, Andrews complained that "a very large number of these high bounty men are of no use to the Army – they are rather a detriment." It seems likely that he would have included such a fact in the letter or his journal if he had heard it. Unfortunately, Thornton's CMSR is short on details on his service. Lieutenant Lockwood and Sergeant Hogan testified at Thornton's court-martial that Thornton had enlisted in Syracuse as a substitute on August 22 and had joined the 179th in the field around September 1. Thornton gave his age as forty. (Transcript LL2924, 4-5, 12-13) Another soldier who had been in Confederate custody with Thornton testified that Thornton had said he was from Brooklyn (*Ibid.*, 8). In his letter to General Parke, Thornton said that he had a wife and child and had closed his business to enlist (Letter from Thornton to Parke, January 4, 1865, LL2924).

(64) Letter from John Andrews to Homer Andrews, January 10, 1865.

(65) Letter from William Lamont to Parents, January 7, 1865; Larzelere Diary, December 6, 1864.

(66) Larzelere Diary, February 10, 1865.

(67) JAWJ, February 10, 1865.

(68) No. NN 3089, RG 153, Records of the Office of the Judge Advocate General (Army), Court Martial Case Files, 1809-1894, NN 3087-NN3095, Box 1848, National Archives; Bonney CMSR. The representative from the Christian Commission who wrote a letter for Bonney while he was in the 9th Corps Hospital reported that Bonney was "not a Christian," having noted that Bonney was being treated for syphilis. (Bonney CMSR)

(69) File No. nn2645, Record Group 153, Records of the Office of the Judge Advocate General (Army), Court Martial Case Files, 1809-1894, NN2645-NN2658, Box 1800, National Archives; CMSR.

(70) The following are contemporary descriptions of the weather conditions preceding October 11, 1864, when five men from the 179th deserted: (See Appendix D)

October 1.	Cold and rainy
October 2 to 5	No data

October 6	Very warm
October 7	No data
October 8	Last night wind blew hard
October 9	Ground white with frost this morning
October 10	Very cold night
October 11	Cold last night, very warm today

The weather preceding conditions October 15, when five men deserted, were also harsh. Bad weather had continued since the desertions on October 11: (See Appendix D).

October 12	Started raining at 5 p.m.
October 13	Not as cold last night as common /day raw and cold, much the coldest in Virginia thus far
October 14	Last night terrible cold, slept but little/day very warm

The weather conditions preceding November 17, when five men deserted, were not as bad. (See Appendix D)

November 7	Has rained nearly all day, but weather is warm so men not suffering
November 8	The day is beautiful
November 9	Rainy, warm
November 10	Very warm, in the afternoon pleasant
November 11	Weather fine, pleasant morning
November 12	Very pleasant/cloudy and cool
November 13	Last night terribly cold, water froze/day fine
November 14	Mild
November 15	Very cold last night, colder than usual, fire necessary
November 16	Mild and pleasant
November 17	Appearance of rain, cloudy with inversion, but cleared up/pleasant and mild

Except for Henry Maxwell, who had been wounded on September 30, health probably was not a factor (although Francis Lewis had been briefly hospitalized in Elmira with diarrhea back in August). (CMRs) "War weariness and discouragement" may also have been increased among some soldiers by the Army of the Potomac's lack of success at Burgess Mill in October and the re-election of President Lincoln in November, which meant that there would be no quick end to the war. In the cases of John McDonald, Henry Maxwell and Charles Povey, there may have been dismay at having signed up for three years and serving in a company where half of the men were bound only for a year. (CMSRs; Regimental History, 29)

(71) Compiled from Registers of Deserters and Descriptive Lists, Descriptive Book, Regimental

Books, Vol. 1. There does not seem to have been a sense of unit cohesiveness in Company H that would have deterred desertion. (See Hess, *The Union Soldier in Battle*, 111) Hess concluded that: "Much of what kept men going in the challenging environment of the battlefield was the mutually supportive interaction among the members of the small, tight, intimate community of the regiment. Its members often were residents of the same town or county who had joined as a community response to the war effort." (*Ibid.*)

(72) Compiled from Registers of Deserters, Descriptive Book, Regimental Books, Vol. 1.

(73) Compiled from CMSR and CMR. Because the extent of the incapacity of the individual patients is unknown, the universe of potential deserters from hospital cannot be determined.

(74) Letter from [George Cross'] Mother to Son, October 29, 1864, Cross CMSR; Cross CMSR and CMR.

(75) CMSR; CMRs; General Orders No. 56, Headquarters Military Governor, Alexandria, Virginia, January 21, 1865, para. 189 in John Andrews Papers, Cornell University Collection #3790, Box 3.

(76) In his written statement to the court, Dickey stated that after his arrest the local Provost Marshal had sent him to Fort McHenry "as a straggler" and that he had remained there until May 1865. Court Martial File OO1239, Record Group 153, Records of the Office of the Judge Advocate General (ARmy), Court Martial Case File, 1809-1894, 001236-001240, Box 2086). Dickey's carded medical records report that he was admitted to the Post Hospital at Fort McHenry from the prison on April 14, 1865 for "intemperance from opium."

(77) Lonn, 157, 136.

(78) Lonn, 136.

(79) Compiled from CMRs.

(80) The furlough form used by Mt. Pleasant General Hospital included the following "Instructions to Soldiers Unable to Return at the Expiration of Their Furlough:"

"If you are unable to travel at the expiration of your furlough without risk of life or permanent disability, you will forward a certificate stating the number of days you will be unable to travel, not to exceed twenty. This certificate if not given by a Commissioned Medical Officer on duty, must be sworn to before a magistrate, and must have the State, County or other official Seal attached. A Duplicate of this Certificate sho'd [sic] be attached to the furlough. If still unable to travel when the time expires for which the Certificate is given, another should be sent in the same manner. The furlough can not be extended." (Benjamin D. Blair CMSR)

(81) An extreme example is Company B's Henry Carpenter, a forty-two-year-old butcher from Chemung County, who was admitted to Emory U.S.A. General Hospital on August 1, 1864 with a diagnosis of diarrhea. He was furloughed on August 21. He regularly submitted doctor's letters to extend his sick leave – September 20, 1864; October 10, 1864; October 29, 1864; December 3, 1864; December 7, 1864; December 24, 1864; January 13, 1865; February 2, 1865; February 22, 1865; March 13, 1865; and April 21, 1865. He was readmitted to the hospital on May 2, 1865 and discharged from the service on May 19, 1865. (CMSR and CMR)

(82) The following are examples (sources are the CMSRs): *During the War*: Company A's Russell Sisson (December 16, 1864)(later served in the V. R.C.); Company A's Levi Jones (January 3, 1865); Company E's David Simmons (February 3, 1865); Company A's Robert McKinney (March 1, 1865); Company G's Franklin Burton (1865); Company D's William Chichester (February 8, 1865); Company A's Emory Millard (April 22, 1865); Company B's Miles Button (May 20, 1865); Company H's Valentine Smith (1865); *After the War*: Company C's Richard L. Healy (1886);

Company H's Peter Simmons (1886); Company C's Lafayette Hall (1887)(replaced with absent without proper authority); Company A's James C. Rutan (1891)(replaced with absent without leave); Company A's Benjamin Blair (1916). Not all post-war requests to remove charges of desertion were granted. The request by Company B's Alexander Gardiner, who had deserted from hospital in Rochester after being admitted with diarrhea, was implicitly denied in 1891. Gardiner had previously completed a tour of duty in the 136th New York before enlisting in the 179th New York (CMSR).

(83) Company H's Hiram Thomas, a twenty-two-year-old farmer suffering from diarrhea, did not return from a furlough granted by the general hospital in Troy, New York. When Company E's George P. Taylor, a nineteen-year-old hosemaker who also suffered from diarrhea, was arrested four months after his furlough expired, his only excuse was that he had a doctor's letter covering twenty days. Company F's Edwin Knapp, a nineteen-year-old farmer, had been wounded in the June 17 assault and didn't return from his furlough. Company G's James Harrison, a nineteen-year-old boatman, had been admitted to hospital for tuberculosis. He did not return when his furlough expired at the end of February 1865. Company E's J. C. R. Thompson, a thirty-two-year-old clerk, did not return when his furlough expired at the end of October 1864. It is certainly possible that there were extenuating documents that did not make it into these soldiers' files (CMSR and CMR).

(84) McNeil CMSR.

(85) CMSR.

(86) Basler, Vol. VIII, 349-50.

(87) Deserters Who Report Under the Proclamation of the President, RG 110, Entry 2373; CMSR.

(88) Deserters Who Report Under the Proclamation of the President, RG 110, Entry 2373; CMSR and CMR.

(89) CMSR; CMR.

Chapter Twenty

Basler, Roy P. (ed.), *The Collected Works of Abraham Lincoln*, Rutgers University Press: New Brunswick, New Jersey (1953).

Benton, Josiah H., *Voting in the Field: A Forgotten Chapter of the Civil War*, reprinted General Books: Memphis (2010). (originally privately published in 1915).

Casey, John, "Marked by War: Demobilization, Disability and the Trope of the Citizen-Soldier in Miss Ravenel's Conversion", *Civil War History*, Volume 60, Number 2, June 2014. The Kent State University Press.

Cleaves, Freeman, *Meade of Gettysburg*, University of Oklahoma Press: Norman (1960).

Foner, Eric, *The Fiery Trial: Abraham Lincoln and American Slavery*, W.W. Norton & Company: New York (2010).

Gallagher, Gary W., "To love or loathe McClellan?", *Civil War Times*, Vol. 51, No. 2 (April 2012)

Goodwin, Doris Kearns, *Team of Rivals: The Political Genius of Abraham Lincoln*, Simon & Schuster: New York (2005).

McPherson, James, *Battle Cry of Freedom: The Civil War Era*, Oxford University Press: Oxford (1988).

Newsome, Hampton, *Richmond Must Fall: The Richmond-Petersburg campaign, October 1864*, The

Kent State University Press: Kent, Ohio (2013).

Ramold, Steven J., *Across the Divide: Union Soldiers View the Northern Home Front*, New York University Press: New York (2013).

Winther, Oscar O., "The Soldier Vote in the Election of 1864," *New York History*, 25 (1944).

(1) Benton, 2; Winther, 440.

(2) Benton, 67,70. John Casey recently wrote:

"That most states, despite their fears of the soldier vote, sought within the first years of the war to change the election rules so soldiers could vote either in the field or by proxy shows just how important voting was as a marker of social status in the nineteenth century. 'Losing one's vote' was equated with losing one's social caste and brought one dangerously close to the condition of a slave. Therefore, provisions were made to allow Union soldiers to vote." 137.

(3) *Ibid.*, 6.

(4) *Ibid.*, 3.

(5) *Ibid.*, 12, 63.

(6) Winther, 444-45.

(7) *The Hornellsville Tribune*, February 18, 1864. Similarly the *Ontario Times*, another Republican newspaper, emphatically stated that: "None will vote against it but the enemies of our soldiers and the friends of Jeff Davis." (February 17, 1864).

(8) *Dunkirk Journal*, March 11, 1864; *Penn Yan Democrat*, February 26, 1864. The *Troy Press*, also a Democratic newspaper, did speak out against the measure: "This conferring of the right of suffrage on the army in the field is one of the gravest errors yet committed in these times of error, we fully believe." (Quoted in *Ontario Times*, March 16, 1864). Winther concludes that the evidence in support of the assertion that "the boys in blue voted as desired by their superior officers – in other words, for the administration" is "very meagre." (452).

(9) Benton, 73; *Watkins Express*, March 31, 1864; *Yates County Chronicle*, March 17, March 24, and March 31, 1864.

(10) Benton, 7.

(11) *Ibid.*, 9-12.

(12) *Elmira Daily Advertiser*, September 10, 1864.

(13) *Ontario Times*, September 28, 1864 quoting from *Richmond Examiner*, September 8, 1864.

(14) McPherson, 713.

(15) Goodwin, 623; Foner, 302-303.

(16) McPherson, 758.

(17) *Broome Weekly Republican*, July 27, 1864.

(18) McPherson, 761.

(19) McPherson, 758.

(20) Basler, Vol. VII, 514. See also Newsome, 2.

(21) Goodwin, 654.

(22) Goodwin, 654; McPherson, 775-76.

(23) Foner, 308.

(24) Goodwin, 654-55; Newsome, 105; Brooks Simpson, "Campaign Promise," *The Civil War Monitor*, Vol. 4, No. 4 (Winter 2014), 39. Simpson wrote that:

"Make no mistake about it: Ballots and bayonets were intertwined in 1864, with popular support for the war at stake in both the Union and the Confederacy. Grant's assignment was deceptively simple. If he could not defeat the Confederate forces in the field outright, then he needed to at least make enough progress to convince a majority of northern voters to endorse Lincoln's bid for a second term."

(25) *Elmira Daily Advertiser*, October 7, 1864; *Ontario Times*, October 19, 1864.

(26) Goodwin, 663.

(27) Gary Gallagher addresses the "fascinating" question of "why did the officers and men in the Army of the Potomac embrace their young commandeer enthusiastically and maintain their affection for so long?" Gallagher, 18, 20.

(28) Goodwin, 663.

(29) General Orders No. 74, Department of the East, October [?}, 1864, National Archives; Daniel Compton CMSR. In Pennsylvania, the soldiers' votes were separately tabulated, with Lincoln receiving 68% (Benton, 154).

(30) Undated [probably end of May 1864] fragment of letter from Daniel B. Lee to Jane Lee.

(31) Letter, July 24, 1864 in *Penn Yan Democrat*, [undated], New York State Military Museum, Unit History Project, 179th New York Volunteers, Civil War Newspaper Clippings. Presumably Spencer's own Company F, which was raised in the Penn Yan area of Yates County was one of the two companies, but the other is unknown. In 1860, Yates County gave Lincoln a majority of 1,540 votes (67%), a decrease from Fremont's vote in 1856. Lincoln carried every town except Torrey where the vote was exactly evenly split. (*Penn Yan Democrat*, November 7, 1860.) In 1864, Yates County gave Lincoln a slightly smaller majority of 1,342 (64%). The towns comprising Penn Yan went roughly 60% for Lincoln. Torrey went 57% for McClellan. (*Yates County Chronicle*, November 10, 1864) Spencer continued in his letter:

"I remain sincerely firm in the belief that the present Administration is incapable of either successfully conducting the war or of negotiating an honorable peace – that they lack both wisdom and sagacity for either. No true Democrat in the North is so fond of peace as to be willing to sacrifice to it the integrity of the Union, the 'immortality of the Constitution,' and the supremacy of laws. Nor should any Democrat be so pugnacious or blood-thirsty as to insist upon fighting a single moment after those now, unhappily in rebellion, shall have agreed to return to the Constitutional mode of redressing grievances. Upon a platform embracing these dual Democratic ideas, let a statesman and patriot be nominated next month, and two thirds of the army vote will be his. Neither blandishments nor threats can turn the current now steadily setting in against Mr. Lincoln and his wrong-headed, impracticable and intriguing advisers. The president has had enough of the bitter "sweets of office" at an enormous expense of blood and treasure to the country. Let his better judgment outweigh his new-fledged ambition and induce him to retire from the opening contest or the people will surely retire him!"

(32) *Elmira Daily Advertiser*, August 13, 1864.

(33) *Elmira Daily Advertiser*, August 20, 1864. The Wheeler, Hatch & Hitchcock circus had apparently performed without incident in Hornellsville on August 15 (*The Hornellsville Tribune*, August 11, 1864).

(34) *Elmira Daily Advertiser*, August 19, 1864.

(35) *Ithaca Journal*, September 7, 1864.

(36) Letter from Emma Andrews to John Andrews, October 16, 1864; Letter from [?]to John Andrews, October 18, 1864.

(37) Letter from Emma Andrews to John Andrews, October 28, 1864; letter from Homer Andrews to John Andrews, November 3, 1864.

(38) JAWJ, October 22, 1864. During a mid-October visit to the 50th Pennsylvania Volunteers, Andrews learned that they had voted 138 for Lincoln and 12 for McClellan (October 13, 1864). Thirty years after the war, Company E's Charles Carr recalled that the 179th New York "was a strong abolition regiment," but there is no contemporary evidence to confirm that (Deposition of Charles Carr dated December 10, 1897, Charles Lockwood Pension File).

(39) Letter from James W. Vangilder to Nancy M. Swansbrow, December 26, 1864 (Private Collection). As Eric Foner has written, "In this war of 'thinking bayonets,' in which soldiers eagerly debated political issues and wrote numerous letters home, sentiment in the army could not but affect northern politics." Foner, 208. The *Buffalo Daily Courier*, September 26, 1864 and October 5, 1864.

(40) JAWJ, November 6, 1864.

(41) Letters of William Lamont, October 6, October 24 and November 15, 1864.

(42) JAWJ, October 22, 1864.

(43) *Elmira Daily Advertiser*, September 21, 1864.

(44) JAWJ, October 17, October 18, and October 19, 1864, 69, 73, 74.

(45) *Ibid.*, October 18, 1864.

(46) *Ontario Times*, October 5, 1864; *Penn Yan Democrat*, April 29, 1864.

(47) Letter from [illegible] to John Andrews, November 12, 1864.

(48) *Yates County Chronicle*, October 6, 1864. Suspicions of course ran both ways. The *Buffalo Daily Courier*, a Democratic paper, wrote: "We wish we could think we are doing Lincoln and his party injustice when we assert our belief that they intend to rely for success in the coming election, to a great degree, on military interference with the people at the polls." (June 27, 1864)

(49) JAWJ, October 28, 1864, 114.

(50) Cleaves, 294. In fact, Meade apparently went so far as to not even vote at all. (Winther, 456-57) For career military officers, the high rank they held during the Civil War in the much larger wartime army was only temporary. As a result, "regular army" promotions were sought after. Grant had recommended a regular army promotion for Meade in May, but it had not been granted, while Hancock and Sheridan had received promotions in the meantime (Cleaves, 294).

(51) Benton, 77.

(52) Letter from Mollie Langworthy to John Andrews, October 30, 1864.

(53) Benton, 77.

(54) *Ibid.*, 77, 79; McPherson, 804-805, n. 69. In the end, Ferry was released after three years. (Ramold, 163)

(55) Benton, 78.

(56) *Elmira Daily Advertiser*, October 31, 1864; *Buffalo Morning Express*, October 29, 1864; *Buffalo Daily Courier*, October 29, 1864; *Broome Republican*, November 2, 1864; *The Hornellsville Tribune*, November 3, 1864. The fear that fraud would occur had not been limited to the Republicans. On October 8, 1864, The *Binghamton Daily* Democrat wrote that: "It is feared that Democratic voters will be imposed upon with false ballots in the army...All the powers of an imbecile and corrupt administration will be used to force democratic soldiers to vote the abolition ticket." (emphasis in original)

(57) Special Orders No. 284, Headquarters, Army of the Potomac, Regimental Books, Vol. 2.

(58) *Buffalo Morning Express*, November 5, 1864. Company E's Charles Carr recalled in 1897 that Ottenot had submitted votes from dead soldiers in the 179th for Seymour (Deposition of Charles Carr dated December 10, 1897, Charles Lockwood Pension File). Because Ottenot was never

tried, Carr's recollection cannot be verified.

(59) *Ibid.*

(60) *The New York Times*, November 8, 1864.

(61) *Ibid.*, November 6, 1864.

(62) Letter from Sarah Larzalere to William Larzelere, November 4, 1864, Private Collection.

(63) Letter from Homer Andrews to John Andrews, November 3, 1864.

(64) Winther, 451.

(65) JAWJ, November 8, 1864.

(66) United States presidential election, 1864, results by states, Wikipedia.

(67) *Elmira Daily Advertiser*, November 12, 1864; *Broome Republican*, November 16, 1864.

(68) Benton, 81; Winther, 446.

(69) Goodwin, 666; McPherson, 804-805; Benton, 154; Newsome, 303. John Casey recently wrote that: "Recent studies ... have questioned [the] assertion that Union soldiers voted overwhelmingly or voluntarily for Lincoln." (Casey, *Marked by War*, 137, n. 28 and sources cited therein).

(70) McPherson, 805.

(71) Benton, 13.

(72) Although soldiers represented a substantial portion of the potential electorate in New York, it is possible that their voter participation was lower than the participation by civilians. The complexity of the proxy ballot may have discouraged soldiers from voting. Moreover, their proxy votes were not necessarily received on time in their home towns. One of John Andrews' female correspondents wrote that forty soldiers' votes had arrived in her home town the day after the election. (11/12/64) For the states that did separately tabulate soldier and civilian votes, the percentage of votes cast by soldiers typically was less than 10%. For example, the percentages were 9.7% in Ohio, 6.4% in Pennsylvania, 4.1% in Rhode Island, and less than 1% in Vermont (See Winther, 457).

(73) The *Ontario Times* reported that of the 200 officers and men in the 126th New York, only about twenty voted for McClellan, which would be a 90% majority for Lincoln. *Ontario Times*, October 13, 1864. The 126th New York was primarily recruited in Ontario, Seneca and Yates Counties. (Phisterer, 3497) The *Broome Republican* reported results for about a dozen New York units as follows (the area where they were recruited is added from Phisterer):

Vol. Inf. Regiment	Lincoln	McClellan	% Lincoln	Area Recruited
50th Regiment	"almost unaimously for Lincoln"			Elmira area IIPh1669-70
60th Regiment	219	none		Northern NYS IIIPh2539
89th Regiment	"almost unaimously for Lincoln"			Northern NYS IIIPh2539
102nd Regiment	255	75	77%	NYC IVPh3184
107th Regiment	320	80	80%	Elmira, Hornellville IVPh3257
109th Regiment	239	21	92%	Broome/Tioga/Tompkins IVPh3282
112th Regiment	285	9	97%	Chautauqua/Cattaraguas IVPh3320

123rd Regiment	130	20	87%	Washington Co. IVPh3455
137th Regiment	212	9	96%	Western NY IVPh3593
143rd Regiment	275	75	79%	Sullivan Co. VPh3656
149th Regiment	235	15	94%	Syracuse/Onondage Co. VPh3731
189th Regiment	481	77(?)	86%	Western NY VPh4088

Broome Republican, November 2 and November 9, 1864. There is no way of knowing whether these newspaper reports were accurate. Moreover, to the extent they represent actual votes taken, the votes may have been by public display rather than secret ballot. However, they do seem to be at least directionally consistent with the results in other states. The fact that the regiment recruited in New York City (the 102nd), a Democratic stronghold, would be reported as having the lowest percentage for Lincoln also is directionally consistent. Not surprisingly, pro-McClellan newspapers had their own news to trumpet. The *Buffalo Daily Courier* (November 2, 1864) reported that 5th and 14th New York Volunteers had voted 143 for McClellan and only 7 for Lincoln and that the 97th New York had given McClellan a majority of eighty. A significant part of the 5th, a veteran regiment, had been recruited in New York City (Phisterer, 1769), so the McClellan majority is plausible. The reference to the 14th New York is unclear because it had been mustered out in 1863. (Phisterer, 1901) The 97th was recruited as a three year regiment in Oneida County, Herkimer County and surrounding areas. (Phisterer, 3111) On November 2, 1864, the *Buffalo Daily Courier*, a Democratic newspaper, reported majority votes for McClellan in the 147th New York, 95th New York 24th Cavalry, 186th New York (one company), Ames Battery and the 94th New York. Publication of these polls by soldiers was a way to potentially influence the civilian vote back home. (Ramold, 163)

(74) *Buffalo Daily Courier*, February 10, 1865 .

(75) *Buffalo Daily Courier*, February 10, 1865; *Buffalo Daily Courier*, February 6, 1865; *Buffalo Morning Express*, February 6, 1865. Army regulations of the day required charges within eight days and trial within thirty days, but the army did not comply in Ottenot's case. (*Buffalo Daily Courier*, February 10, 1865) Colonel North was acquitted by the military commission when he was tried in January 1865. (Benton, 80).

(76) *Buffalo Daily Courier*, February 10, 1865.

(77) Buffalo *Courier and Republican*, November 1866; Phisterer, Vol. V, 4036. In 1897, Company E's Charles Carr commented that "Influence got Ottenot out" of Capital Prison. (Deposition of Charles Carr dated December 10, 1897)

(78) Letter from Charles E. Lockwood to E.D. Townsend, December 15, 1864, Asst. Adg. General, War Department, CMSR, National Archives. Lockwood was in fact in the Field Hospital at City Point at that time as a result of "being broke down by the hard campaign of last summer." Letter dated December 15, 1864 from Lockwood to General [Townsend]. Lockwood had been admitted to the Field Hospital on November 26 with a diagnosis of "colic." (CMR)

(79) JAWJ, February 24, 1865.

(80) *Ibid.*

(81) General Court Martial Orders, No. 14, para. IV (April 16, 1865), Head-Quarters, Army of the Potomac; Phisterer, Vol. V at 4036. I have been unable to find the transcript of Lockwood's court martial in the National Archives. As a result, I do not know the precise actions that Lockwood

allegedly took. Thirty years after the war, Company E's Charles Carr recalled that Lockwood (and Ottenot) had submitted votes of dead soldiers from the 179th for Seymour. (Deposition of Charles Carr dated December 10, 1897, Charles Lockwood Pension File) Lockwood himself protested his innocence when he applied for a pension. (Deposition of Charles Lockwood, August 2, 1893, Charles Lockwood Pension File)

(82) Letter from William Gregg to Ariel Thurston, December 5, 1864, New York State Military Museum, Unit History Project, 179th New York Volunteers, Civil War Newspaper Clippings.

Chapter Twenty-One

—— *History of the 179th Regiment N.Y.S.V. – Rebellion of 1861-65*, E.D. Norton, Printer: Ithaca, New York (1900).

Greene, A. Wilson, *Breaking the Backbone of the Rebellion: The Final Battles of the Petersburg campaign*, Savas Publishing Company: Mason City, Iowa (2000).

Hess, Earl J., *In the Trenches at Petersburg: Field Fortifications & Confederate Defeat*, University of North Carolina Press: Chapel Hill (2009).

Hopkins, William P., *The Seventh Regiment Rhode Island Volunteers in the Civil War, 1862-1865*.

Petersburg Overview [Map: Entrenched Lines]

(1) Regimental Books, Vol. 2, Memoranda, November 29, 1864; OR 42(3): 757-58; Larzelere Diary, November 29, 1864; JAWJ, January 23, 1865, 42; "Record of Events for One Hundred Seventy-Ninth New York Infantry, April 1864-May 1865," OR Supp. Part II, Vol. 47, 729-739; Hess, 208.

(2) Letter from John Andrews to Sister, dated November 21, 1864.

(3) November 29, 1864 Memorandum, Regimental Books, Vol. 2.

(4) Greene, 478; OR 42(2): 798. US Military RR crossing Jerusalem Plank Road

[Sketch: Crossing Jerusalem Plank Road]

(5) Letter from William Gregg to Ariel Thurston, dated December 5, 1864, New York State Military Museum, Unit History Project, 179th New York Volunteers.

(6) Hess, xix. See also Thomas Grace, "Wreck the Weldon Railroad," *America's Civil War*, Vol. 27, No. 6 (January 2015), 54. Grace incorrectly identifies the Jerusalem Plank Road as the transfer route.

(7) OR 42(3):858, 933.   (8) *Ibid.*, 935.   (9) *Ibid.*, 933, 936.

(10) "Memoranda," December 10, 1864, Regimental Books, Vol. 2.

(11) OR 42(3):967-68.

(12) *Ibid.*, 965.

(13) "Remarks," December 11, 1864, Company C Morning Report, December 1864, Regimental Books, Vol. 4.

(14) "Memoranda," Regimental Books, Vol. 2; Official Records Supplement, II, Vol. 47, 729-30.; JAWJ, January 24, 1865, 44-45.

(15) OR 42(3):951.

(16) "Memoranda," Regimental Books, Vol. 2.

(17) JAWJ, January 23, 1865, 45.

(18) Deposition of Abram Myers dated October 8, 1896 and Deposition of Chauncey Elliott dated December 29, 1896, both Elias Beach Pension File; Affidavit of Denton Dexter dated October 13, 1881 and Letter from Harry Ap Rees to Safford E. North dated November 4, 1881, both Denton Dexter Pension File; Affidavit of Charles Starbird dated December 18, 1879, Charles Starbird Pension File; Letter from Samuel Coon to Commissioner of Pensions dated July 15, 1891, Samuel Coon Pension File; Affidavit of James Provost dated February 14, 1884, William Randall Pension File; New Hampshire Adjutant, 601; Hopkins, 234-235 (refers to rain and freezing cold, but not snow).

(19) JAWJ, January 23, 1865, 45-46. Andrews did not identify the soldier in his journal and I have been unable to do so from the CMRs for the 179th and the individual company "Register of Deaths" in the Descriptive Book. Andrews was on leave of absence at the time of the march, recounting in his journal what he heard when he returned. (Id.) Thus the death may not have occurred.

(20) "Remarks" December 12, 1864, Company C Morning Report December 1864, Regimental Books, Vol. 4.

(21) JAWJ, 45-46.

(22) Hopkins, 235.

(23) "Remarks" December 12 and 13, 1864, Company I Morning Report, December 1864, Regimental Books, Vol. 4. Company H's George Lake stated in his pension application that he had fallen out on the march, but Giles Holden, his company commander stated that he had not been present that day.

(24) Larzelere Diary, December 12 and 13, 1864.

(25) Letter from William Gregg to Ariel Thurston dated December 5, 1864, New York Military Museum, Unit History Project, 179th New York Volunteers, Civil War Newspaper Clippings.

(26) *Ibid.*

(27) Letter from John Andrews to Father dated December 26, 1864, Library of Virginia.

(28) Letter from William Gregg to Ariel Thurston dated December 5, 1864. "I have just completed a house which I find very comfortable." Gregg described his new quarters in verse. "It is a lodge of ample size, Both strong of structure and device, Of such materials, as around, The builder's hand has rarest found."

(29) *Ibid.*

(30) "Remarks," Company C Morning Report, 179th New York Volunteers, Regimental Book Records, Vol. 4.

(31) Letter from William Lamont to Sister Bell, dated December 7, 1864.

(32) Letter from John Andrews to Homer Andrews dated December 26, 1864.

(33) Stephen Compton Diary, January 10, 1865.

(34) Lamont letter to sister, dated February 27, 1865.

(35) *Hornellsville Tribune*, February 2, 1865. The situation may in fact have improved due to drier weather and the digging of a trench to drain the company streets. (See Compton Diary, January 10 to 15, 1865; Appendix D)

(36) Phisterer, 4029 to 4038.

(37) JAWJ, October 25, 1864, 95-96. Andrews did not name names, but he could have had several men in mind. One could have been John J. Swartwout, who was commissioned on September 16, 1864, but was never mustered into the 179th New York. (Phisterer, 4037) Others could have

been Edward Lounsbury who had only enlisted in Company B at the end of August 1864 and was commissioned First Lieutenant effective October 9, 1864 and William Bogart who had enlisted in Company E at the beginning of September 1864 and was also commissioned a second lieutenant as of October 9, 1864. (Phisterer, 4036, 4032. See also JAWJ, October 13, 1864, 38) Andrews had expected to be commissioned in Company E (JAWJ, October 8, 1864, 41), but the commission went to Sgt. Charles Lockwood who was well known to the 179th, having served since Company E was mustered in. (Phisterer, 4036) Sgt. Major Thomas Smith was commissioned on November 23–through political influence in Andrews' view, but he also was well known to the 179th, having enlisted in Company A in February 1864. (JAWJ, November 23, 1864, 35; Phisterer, 4037)

(38) *The Hornellsville Tribune*, February 4, 1864.

(39) Phisterer, 3638-39.

(40) JAWJ, Vol. 2, November 23, 1864, 38.

(41) Letter from William Gregg to Ariel Thurston dated December 5, 1864.

(42) JAWJ, November 28, 1864, 23.

(43) JAWJ, November 29, 1864, 30-31.

(44) JAWJ, November 29, 1864, 35.

(45) *Ibid.*, 35.

(46) *Ibid.*, 34-35. Governor Seymour was unable to find a commission for Hager in another regiment, but promised to put him on the list for the next vacancy in the 179th New York. (*Ibid.*) Hager did subsequently receive a commission on two occasions, but in neither instance was he actually mustered in as an officer. (Phisterer, 4031, 4035)

(47) Phisterer, 4032. Colonel Gregg was "very much enraged" that Andrews only got the second lieutenant commission, and told a friend that as soon as Reuben Fenton became governor, he would make Levi Force, Martin Doty and Andrews captains. (Letter from John Andrews to father dated December 26, 1864, Library of Virginia.) Force was almost immediately promoted to captain of Company C, but Martin Doty was not promoted to captain until April 1865. Andrews received a brevet promotion to captain after the war. (Phisterer, 4030, 4032, 4034)

(48) Phisterer, 4037.

(49) Griswold CMSR, 50th Engineers; Phisterer, 4035 (Griswold, Co. F); Hess, 2. Presumably neither of Company F 's lieutenants would have sought the position after Farwell's death. Giles Holden had become the captain of Company H in September 1864 and David Bradley, the brother-in-law of the deceased Major Sloan was on detached duty, perhaps an assignment intended to protect the family against a second loss. While Company A's First Lt. George Carpenter had also informally acted as the commander of Company F, he was promoted to captain of Company A in December 1864.

(50) Regimental History, 19.

(51) CMSR. Sergeants Sherwood and Wattleworth had been reduced to private within a matter of weeks when they entered the hospital in June 1864. (List of Non-Commissioned Officers, Descriptive Book, Company A, Regimental Books, Vol. 1.)

(52) "Record of Events," Company Muster Rolls, January and February 1865, Compiled Records Showing Service of Military Units in Volunteer Union Organizations, Microfilm Roll 139, National Archives.

(53) Letter from William Lamont to Parents dated January 7, 1865.

(54) *Dundee Record*, April 2, 1865. Clipping in John Andrews Papers.

(55) General Order No. 8, 1865, 179th New York Volunteers, Regimental Books, Vol. 2.

(56) Company Muster Rolls, 179th New York Volunteers, for the periods ending October 31, 1864, December 31, 1864 and February 28, 1865, Regimental Papers, Box 3406.

(57) Letter from Stephen Compton to Wife dated December 25, 1864.

(58) Company Morning Reports, Regimental Books, Vol. 4. There are gaps in the Morning Reports, which were submitted monthly, especially for Companies E, F and G.

(59) Compiled from CMRs.

(60) OR 46(2): 974.

(61) JAWJ, March 20, 1865.

(62) *The Hornellsville Tribune*, April 20, 1865.

(63) Letter from John Andrews to Father, Brother and Sisters dated March 8, 1865, Author's Collection. One dissenter may have been Company B's William Lamont. After the April 2, 1865 attack at Petersburg, in which Colonel Gregg was wounded and Lieutenant Colonel Doty mortally wounded, Lamont wrote his sister that "we haven't any officer left that amounts to anything." (Letter from William Lamont to Sister dated April 11, 1865)

(64) JAWJ, March 15, 1865.

(65) Smithsonian Institution website, Collections Search Center, "Levi Force."

(66) Letter from Stephen Compton to Wife dated December 25, 1864.

(67) Letter from John Andrews to Father, December 26, 1864, Library of Virginia.

(68) JAWJ, February 24, 1865. See also Larzelere Diary, February 21, 1865.

(69) Letter from John Andrews to Sister Etta, dated February 15, 1865.

(70) Hess, xix-xx.

(71) JAWJ, February 5 and 6, 1865.

Chapter Twenty-Two

Giesberg, Judith, *Army at Home: Women and the Civil War on the Northern Home Front*, The University of North Carolina Press: Chapel Hill (2009).

Hardee, William J., *Hardee's Rifle and Light Infantry Tactics for the Instructions, Exercises and Manoeuvres of Riflemen and Light Infantry, Including School of the Soldier and School of the Company, To Which Is added, Duties of Non-Commissioned Officers, Military Honors to Be Paid By Troops, the Articles of War*, J. O. Kane, Publisher: New York (1862) (reprinted by H-Bar Enterprises: Silver Spring, Maryland).

McPherson, James, *Battle Cry of Freedom: The Civil War Era*, Oxford University Press: Oxford (1988).

Ramold, Steven J., *Across the Divide: Union Soldiers View the Northern Home Front*, New York University Press: New York (2013).

Rutan II, Edwin P., "The 179th New York Volunteers," *The Chemung Historical Journal*, Vol. 58, No. 3 (March 2013).

(1) Parts of this chapter appeared in Rutan, 6513.

(2) JAWJ, October 14, 1864, 63.

(3) Letter from William Lamont to "Parents," dated February 21, 1865.

(4) Letter from Stephen Compton to wife dated April 30, 1865.

(5) Letter from William Lamont to "Sister," dated October 24, 1864.

(6) Letter from Henry Beebe to parents dated May 3, 1864, Henry Beebe Pension File.

(7) Letter from Jacob Graves to Daniel Graves, July 8, 1864, Jacob Graves Pension File.

(8) Letter from Homer Olcott to Father, Mother and Sister dated May 24, 1864, Homer Olcott Pension File.

(9) JAWJ, November 12, 1864.

(10) JAWJ, November 19, 1864.

(11) Letter from [?]Andrews to John Andrews, dated October 20, 1864.

(12) Letter from William Lamont to "Sister," dated October 24, 1864.

(13) JAWJ, Vol. III, pages 126 to 131; Larzelere Diary, undated pages at back, Private Collection.

(14) Ramold, 26-27.

(15) Letter from Lamont to "Parents," dated February 21, 1865 (Letter of 2/15/65 received night of 2/20/65; Letter from Lamont to "Sister," dated March 11, 1865 (Letter of 3/5/65 received 3/9/65); Letter from Lamont to "Sister," dated October 24, 1864 (Letter of 10/16/64 received 10/23/64); Letter from Stephen Compton to wife dated May 7, 1865 (letter received within two days). Of course, delivery sometimes took longer. (12/14/64 Letter from Frank Eaton to John Andrews received 1/2/65); (11/28/64 Letter from [Uncle] John Andrews to John Andrews received 12/19/64) For the complete cycle, Mollie Langworthy wrote John Andrews that: "It takes two weeks for my letters to reach you and the answer to return to me." (Letter dated October 30, 1864)

(16) Letter from Daniel Lee to Wife, undated fragment, U. S. Army Military History Institute, CWMiscColl (Enlisted man's letters, January 10, 1863- Jan. 14, 1883). At some point, the Army remedied this oversight. *The New York Times* reported in March 1865 that:
One not in the army can have no adequate conception of the amount of mail matter arriving and departing from City Point. In order to give the general reader some slight idea of the magnitude of the Post Office Department in this army alone, I have but to mention the significant fact that Forty three thousand dollars worth of red [3 cents] postage stamps recently arrived for the use of the soldiers... – stamps enough for one million four hundred thousand letters. (March 16, 1865).

(17) CMSR.

(18) Letter from Henry Kingsley to Father and Mother, dated June 11, 1864, Henry Kingsley Pension File; Receipt dated June 24, 1864, Henry Kingsley CMSR; Letter from William Lamont to "Sister," dated October 24, 1864.

(19) E.g. Letter from Danial Lee to Wife, dated May 9, 1864.

(20) Letter from Daniel Lee to Wife, dated June 17, 1864.

(21) Letter from Daniel Lee to Wife, dated June 26, 1864.

(22) Letter dated September 26, 1864, from James Vangilder to Nancy Swansbrow, Private Collection.

(23) Letter from William Lamont to "Sister," dated December 7, 1864.

(24) Letter from David June to [illegible] dated May 16, 1864, David June Pension File.

(25) Letter from Henry Kingsley to Father and Mother, dated June 11, 1864, Henry Kingsley Pension File.

(26) Letter from Emma Andrews to John Andrews, dated January 30, 1865.

(27) Letter from Mollie Langworthy to John Andrews, dated November 12, 1864.

(28) Letter from Daniel Lee to Wife, dated June 26, 1864. See also undated fragment.

(29) Letter from Daniel Lee to Wife, dated June 7, 1864; Letters from Daniel Lee dated June 3, 1864; June 6, 1864; June 7, 1864; June 8, 1864; June 10, 1864; June 17, 1864; June 26, 1864; June 27, 1864; June 28, 1864; and July 3, 1864.

(30) Letter from John Andrews to Homer Andrews dated March 30, 1865, Author's Collection.

(31) Letter from William Lamont to "Sister," dated October 2, 1864.

(32) *Elmira Daily Advertiser*, August 2, 1864.

(33) Letter from Homer Andrews to John Andrews, dated November 3, 1864.

(34) Letter from Mollie Langworthy to John Andrews, dated November 1, 1864.

(35) Letter from Asa McDonald to Col. William Hoffman, dated October 25, 1864, Theodore McDonald CMSR. McDonald's CMSR indicates that a response was sent to his father on October 31, 1864 (four days after the letter from his father was received), but it is not clear what the response was. McDonald had in fact been taken prisoner and was paroled in February 1865.

(36) Letter from Edwin Bowen to William Cook, dated October 19, 1864, John Cook, CMSR.

(37) Letter from Stephen Mapes to the Captain of Co. D, 179th Regt. N. Y. Vols., dated April 1, 1865, John Andrews Papers, Box #1.

(38) JAWJ, October 12, 1864.

(39) Letter dated May 31, 1864 from Abner Roberts to Sister Kate, Abner Roberts Pension File.

(40) Author's collection; Inventory of Military Collection, Major Edwin P. Rutan, 8.

[Photo: Ida Rutan]

[Photo: Rutan Sisters]

(41) Letter from Homer Olcott to Father, Mother and Sister dated May 24, 1864, Homer Olcott Pension File.

(42) Letter from Abner Welch to Father & Mother & Sisters All, dated October 23, 1864, Abner Welch Pension File.

(43) Letter from Eugene Dunton to Parents dated August 2,1864, Eugene Dunton Pension File.

(44) Letter from William Lamont to Sister Bell, dated December 7, 1864; Letter from William Lamont to Parents, dated January 7, 1865.

(45) Letter from Sarah Larzelere to William Larzelere dated November 4, 1864.

(46) Letter from Homer Olcott to Father, Mother and Sister dated May 24, 1864, Homer Olcott Pension File.

(47) *The Hornellsville Tribune*, August 25, 1864.

(48) McPherson, 480-83.

(49) *The Hornellsville Tribune*, February 11, 1864.

(50) *Elmira Daily Advertiser*, quoted in *The Hornellsville Tribune*, March 24, 1864; 1868 Elmira City Directory at 99.

(51) *Elmira Daily Advertiser*, quoted in *The Hornellsville Tribune*, March 24, 1864.

(52) *The Hornellsville Tribune*, February 25, 1864.

(53) *Ontario Times*, September 21, 1864.

(54) *Buffalo Daily Courier*, July 2, 1864.

(55) McPherson, 483; David A. Raney, "In the Lord's Army: The United States Christian Commission, Soldiers, and the Union War Effort," in Paul A. Cimbala and Randall M. Miller (eds.), *Union Soldiers and the Northern Home Front: Wartime Experiences, postwar adjustments*, Fordham University Press: New York (2002), 263-64.

(56) E. g. Nathaniel Mabey CMSR.

(57) Letter from William Lamont to Friends, dated September 25, 1864.

(58) Letter from Daniel Lee to My dear wife and child, dated June 7, 1864.

(59) Letter from William Lamont to Parents, dated June 19, 1865.

(60) Letter from John Cook to Parents, dated May 28, 1865, John Cook Pension File.

(61) Letter from John Cook to Parents, dated June 30, 1865, John Cook Pension File.

(62) *The Hornellsville Tribune*, December 15, 1864. The appeal for mittens on behalf of the 179th was not unique. The day before the article in *The Hornellsville Tribune*, the commander of the Seventh Rhode Island addressed a letter "To the Ladies of Rhode Island" that was published in the *Providence Press*. He wrote that the soldiers were unprepared for winter and were "suffering from want of mittens, an article which they cannot procure from the government and which most of them are unable to buy." (William Hopkins, *The Seventh Regiment Rhode Island Volunteers in the Civil War, 1862-1865,* (1903), Nabu Public Domain Reprints, 236)

(63) *The Hornellsville Tribune*, February 2, 1865. The Ladies of Rhode Island also responded generously, sending 650 pairs of mittens and gloves to the Fourth and Seventh Rhode Island. (Hopkins, 240) Ord. did not make up the bad weather on January 22 just to make the ladies of Hornellsville feel good. William Larzelere described the day as "cold & rainy." (Larzelere Diary, January 22, 1865)

(64) *The Hornellsville Tribune*, February 2, 1865. The original note is in the John Andrews Papers at Cornell.

(65) *Ibid.*

(66) JAWJ, January 23, 1865 at 18-19.

(67) Letter from Lizzie Condorman to John Andrews, dated February 4, 1865. Andrews probably was a little disappointed by her postscript.

"P.S. They say that a Ladies [sic] letter is never complete without a postscript and as I am no exception to the class, I would like to know the name of Ord of Co. C, the correspondent of *The Hornellsville Tribune*."

So who was Ord.? I believe that Ord. was Lt. Nathaniel P. T. Finch, a native of Hornellsville. *The Hornellsville Tribune* published two letters from Ord. – on August 25, 1864 and February 2, 1865. (Ord. referred in the August letter to an earlier letter to the *Tribune* written in the spring. I have been unable to locate such a letter. If it was published, it would have been published in one of the two issues of the *Tribune* from that period that are not extant – May 26 and June 2, 1864.) The *Tribune* had directly attributed an interview with Finch while he was home on a leave of absence in July, but the impending court-martial of Newton Spencer may have necessitated a pseudonym in August. The lead in the February 2, 1865 article was the delivery of the mittens and it was Finch who had received them as quartermaster – and who had discovered the notes in the mittens. (JAWJ, January 23, 1865, 18-20) The original note referred to in the article by Ord. is in the John Andrews papers and Andrews and Finch were close friends during the war. An obituary for Finch said that he had been a correspondent during the war. (*Atlanta Constitution*, June 18, 1918) This circumstantial evidence seems to lead to Finch. However, the meaning of "Ord." as a pseudonym for Finch is not apparent to me. I had initially thought that Ord. was Company C's Capt. Levi Force – an even closer friend of Andrews – on the theory that Ord. was short for Orderly Sergeant. Force had been Company C's Orderly Sergeant before being promoted. He had also previously served in the 23rd New York Volunteers, which Ord. mentioned in his letters. Both could also be said about Beekman King who succeeded Force as Orderly Sergeant, but King was a farmer and Force – as a medical student before the war – was more likely to be journalistically inclined. However, the fact that Ord. referred to Force as his friend in the February 2, 1865 letter and in a very complimentary way suggests that Ord. was someone other than Force (although that could have been a ploy to distract attention from Force).

(68) *Ibid.*

(69) Letter from George B. White to mother dated June 3, 1864, George White Pension File.

(70) Letter from Daniel Lee to wife dated May 1, 1864.

(71) Affidavit of Alexander Gardiner dated February 15, 1873, Francis Canfield Pension File.

(72) Affidavit of Ellen Williamson dated June 13, 1870, Edwin Williamson Pension File; The United States Express Co. envelope, Edwin Williamson Pension File.

(73) Letters from Daniel Lee to wife dated April 13, 1864, June 10, 1864 and June 26, 1864 and undated fragment (page 8 in my numbering, probably end of June 1864).

(74) Giesberg, 2. The role of private assistance should not be overlooked. The census enumerator for Angelica (Alleghany County) in the 1865 New York State Census noted that during the war there had been: "a greater degree of kindness and benevolence toward all who have stood in need of assistance and especially toward those whose husbands and fathers have been in the army." (Section X)

(75) *Buffalo Daily Courier*, December 20, 1864. These men are listed again in the February 1865 report. (*Buffalo Daily Courier*, February 21, 1865) Hugh McSarley (McSorley) is an enigma. His Carded Medical Record shows him being admitted to the Elmira Post Hospital with pneumonia on May 2, 1864 as a recruit before being assigned to a company and deserting on May 3, 1864. (CMR)

(76) Letter from Louise Bill to John Bill dated January 1, 1865, John Bill CMSR.

(77) Giesberg, 9.

(78) Letter from Daniel Lee to wife dated July 3, 1864 and undated fragment (page 8 in my numbering, probably end of June 1864).

(79) Letter from Sarah Larzelere to William Larzelere dated November 4, 1864.

(80). Letters from Daniel Lee to wife dated April 13, 1864 and May 13, 1864.

(81) Hardee, 128.

(82) The computation was based on the statements that officers made when they applied for furloughs as to the status of the regiment as a whole. These statements are in the officers' CMSRs.

(83) Letter from William Lamont to sister, dated February 27, 1865.

(84) Letter from Chauncey McKeever, AAG, to A. S. Diven dated October 24, 1863, RG110, Entry 2025, Box 31.

(85) Larzelere Diary, March 19, 1865.

(86) Letter dated January 28, 1865 with notation from Captain and Assistant Quartermaster to Commanding Officer, Company D, 179 Regiment, John Andrews Papers, Collection #3790, Cornell University, Box 3; Henry Mapes CMSR.

(87) Regimental History at 37. Perry later applied for a Presidential Pardon. (Lyman Perry CMSR)

(88) Gregg CMSR.

(89) Doty CMSR.

(90) Letter dated February 22, 1865 from Moses Van Benchoten; Letter dated January 27, 1865 from Levi Force; and Letter dated March 16, 1865 from James Farr, all in their CMSRs.

(91) Letter dated January 20, 1865 from Giles Holden in CMSR.

(92) Letter dated February 18, 1865 from Edwin Bowen in CMSR.

(93) Letter dated February 23, 1865 from Robert Hooper in CMSR.

(94) Letter dated December 14, 1864 from Davis Marshall in CMSR.

(95) Letter dated January 3, 1865 from Joseph Robinson in CMSR.

(96) Letter dated November 2, 1864 from William Hemstreet in CMSR.

Chapter Twenty-Three

—— *History of the 179th Regiment N.Y.S.V. – Rebellion of 1861-65*, E.D. Norton, Printer: Ithaca, New York (1900).

Beals, Thomas P., "In a Charge Near Fort Hell, Petersburg, April 2, 1865", *Maine MOLLUS*, Lefavor-Tower Company: Portland (1902).

Goodwin, Doris Kearns, *Team of Rivals: The Political Genius of Abraham Lincoln*, Simon & Schuster: New York (2005).

Greene, A. Wilson, "April 2, 1865: Day of Decision at Petersburg", *Blue & Gray*, Winter 2001.

Greene, A. Wilson, *Civil War Petersburg: Confederate City in the Crucible of War*, University of Virginia Press: Charlottesville (2006).

Greene, A. Wilson, *The Final Battles of the Petersburg campaign: Breaking the Backbone of Rebellion*, The University of Tennessee Press: Knoxville (Second Edition 2008).

Hess, Earl J., *In the Trenches at Petersburg: Field Fortifications & Confederate Defeat*, University of North Carolina Press: Chapel Hill (2009).

Hess, Earl J., *The Union Soldier in Battle: Enduring the Ordeal of Combat*, University Press of Kansas: Lawrence (1997).

Hopkins, William P., *The Seventh Regiment Rhode Island Volunteers in the Civil War, 1862-1865*.

Phisterer, Frederick, *New York in the War of the Rebellion 1861 to 1865*, D.B. Lyon Company, State Printers: Albany, New York (Third Ed. 1912).

Trudeau, Noel, *The Last Citadel: Petersburg, Virginia, June 1864-April 1865*, Little, Brown and Company: Boston (1991).

Wolcott, Walter, *The Military History of Yates County, N.Y., Comprising a Record of the Services Rendered by Citizens of This County in the Army and Navy, from the Foundation of the Government to the Present Time*, Express Book and Job Printing House: Penn Yan, New York (1895).

Photograph of Confederate position at Gracie's Salient

[Photo: Gracie's Salient]

(1) Regimental History, 6.
(2) JAWJ, Vol. III, March 25, 1865, 45.
(3) *Ibid.*, 43.
(4) *Ibid.*, 43-44.

[Map: March 24]

(5) JAWJ, March 25, 1865, 45; Larzelere Diary, March 25, 1865.
(6) JAWJ, March 25, 1865, 43-48.
(7) JAWJ, March 26, 27 and 28, 1865, 49-53; Larzelere Diary, March 27 and 28, 1865;
(8) JAWJ, March 28, 1865, 53.
(9) JAWJ, March 28 and 29, 1865, 53-54.
(10) JAWJ, March 29, 55-57.
(11) *Ibid.*

(12) *Ibid.* at 57.

(13) JAWJ, March 30, 1865, 58-59; Larzelere Diary, March 30, 1865.

(14) JAWJ, March 31, 1865, 59-60.

(15) *Ibid.*, 61; Larzelere Diary, March 31, 1865 .

(16) JAWJ, March 31, 1865, 61.

(17) *Ibid.*, 62.

(18) Hess, *In the Trenches*, xx.

(19) Greene, *The Final Battles*, 162.

(20) Greene, 182-88. See also Charles R. Bowery, Jr., *The Richmond-Petersburg campaign, 1864-65*, Praeger: Santa Barbara, California (2014), 130-142.

(21) OR, 46(1): 1054.

(22) Greene, "April 2, 1865", 49. See also Trudeau, 357 (Revised Edition, Savas Beatie: El Dorado, California (2014), 362; Beals. There was some confusion at the time as to which Confederate position was Fort Mahone and which was Fort Damnation and whether they were the same. It is agreed that Fort Mahone was Battery 29. (E.g. Wilson above and E. Hess, *Trenches*, 266) Captain Beals of the 31st Maine had thought that Fort Mahone was Fort Damnation, but concluded after the War that Battery No. 28 was Fort Damnation because they were attacking Fort Damnation and the battery they were attacking was along Jerusalem Plank Road. John Andrews also thought that the 179th was attacking Fort Damnation, which would make Battery No. 28 Fort Damnation. (JAWJ, April 1, 1865) Joseph Mathews, commanding the Second Brigade of Hartranft's Division, reported that they captured Fort Mahone, even though they were attacking to the right of Jerusalem Plank Road. (OR, Vol. 46, Part I at 1068.) Captain Raton of the 27th New York Battery referred to "Battery 27 formerly known to us as Fort Mahone." (*Ibid.*, 1087) Colonel Jacob Hardenbergh of the Eightieth New York Infantry (Twentieth Militia) in Hartranft's Division referred to a captured Confederate work "known as Battery 27, or Fort Damnation." (*Ibid.*, 1096.) William Hopkins of the 7th Rhode Island recalled that: "Fort Damnation was a title indefinitely applied to the rebel works opposite Fort Hell [Union Fort Sedgwick], and included Rives salient and the works extending west from that toward the Jerusalem Plank Road, it did not include Fort Mahone as many suppose." (Hopkins, 238)

(23) OR, 46(1): 1059. Trudeau concludes that the attack on the picket line was based on Meade's misinterpretation of Grant's order. (At 357. Revised edition, 361-362)

(24) Beals; OR, 46(1): 1072

(25) *The Hornellsville Tribune*, April 20, 1865; Letter from Samuel Coon to Commissioner of Pensions dated July 15, 1891, Samuel Coon Pension File. The moon was waxing crescent, just five days from a new moon, and was nearly set at 11:00 p.m. on April 1. There was almost no ambient light. When the full attack began at 4:30 a.m. on the morning of April 2, the sky was still completely dark, and with sunrise at 5:53 a.m., the Confederate defenses would not have been able easily to see the oncoming assault.

[Photo: April 2, 4:30 a.m.]

[Photo: April 2, 5:00 a.m.]

[Photo: April 2, 5:30 a.m.]

[Photo: April 2, 5:53 a.m. sunrise]

(26) OR, 46(1): 1054, 1058-1059; *The Hornellsville Tribune*, April 20, 1865.

(27) "Record of Events," Company B, Company E and Company H, April 1865, Janet Hewett (editor), *Supplement to the Official Records of the Union and Confederate Armies*, Broadfoot Publishing Company: Wilmington, North Carolina (1997) Vol. 47, 732, 735, 737. See also *The Hornellsville Tribune*, April 20, 1865.

(28) Letter from Samuel Coon to Commissioner of Pensions dated July 15, 1891, Samuel Coon Pension File; Letter from Samuel Musgrave to Commissioner of Pensions dated June 22, 1887, Peter Florean Pension File; Greene (Revised Edition), 377. The army made no effort to assess friendly fire incidents during the Civil War. Hess, *The Union Soldier*, 50.

(29) OR 46(3): 483 See also Parke's communications at 1:15 and 1:30 a.m. (At 482)

(30) Greene, *Backbone*, 446-47.

(31) OR, 46(1): 1059, 1056, 1058; Greene, *Backbone*, 446-47; Trudeau, 360.

(32) OR, 46(1): 1072.

(33) Beals; Hess at 267-68. Trudeau states that the Union forces reached the entanglements before the Confederate forces "became alive." (At 360. Revised edition 363) Similarly, *The Hornellsville Tribune* reported that: "the brigade advanced, took the picket line without firing a gun, ..., advanced to within five [gloss]rod[/gloss]s of the fort before being fired on. The first fire passed over them; some obstructions checked the advance, and the column fell back to the picket line, reformed and advanced." (April 20, 1865). Sixty years after the battle, Company H's Harry Ap Rees recalled that: "The Union Forces had climbed the steep ascent to the fort before the Southerners could load their guns." (The Niagara Falls Gazette, June 9, 1923)

(34) *Elmira Daily Advertiser*, January 23, 1880 (Letter from Albert Pierson dated January 21, 1880); *Dundee Record*, April 27, 1865; Beals.

(35) *Dundee Record*, April 27, 1865; Newspaper clipping in the John Andrews papers; *The Hornellsville Tribune*, April 20, 1865; *Elmira Daily Advertiser*, January 23, 1880; Wolcott, 111; *National Tribune*, September 17, 1881; Stephen Compton Diary, April 2, 1865. The *Elmira Daily Advertiser* erroneously reported that Gregg had been killed. (April 6 and April 7, 1865) Similarly, the *Yates County Chronicle* reported that: "Among the deaths reported in the late battle, we regret to observe the name of Col. William Gregg of the 179th, the regiment to which the brave Major Sloan belonged. He was a very valuable officer, formerly sheriff of Chemung County, and a man highly respected by those who knew him." (*Yates County Chronicle*, April 6, 1865.)

(36) Beals; JAWJ, April 3, and April 13, 1865; Letter from Harry Ap Rees to Editor dated July 23, 1865, Charles Flint Pension File.

(37) JAWJ, April 13, 1865. When Townsend rejoined the 179th ten days later, he had some interesting tales to relate. He insisted that General Lee was in the fort "earnestly endeavoring to rally his men who could not be prevailed upon to stand." Townsend said he heard a Confederate officer order ammunition sent to Fort Mahone saying that "if Fort Mahone fell Petersburg *must* fall with it." (emphasis in original) When Union forces entered Petersburg, Townsend was with about 1200 prisoners about a mile and a half away from Petersburg and could hear their shouts. From Sunday to Sunday all he had to eat was two small ears of corn and a very small piece of pork. During that time, he was marched constantly day and night. (*Ibid.*) Of all the men in the 179th New York who became prisoners of war, Townsend probably suffered the least.

(38) Beals. Griffen's official report collapsed these separate charges into a single successful attack. He also incorrectly stated that the storming party had been closely followed by the main body.

(See Hess, 267-68)

"The storming party dashed forward at a run, seizing and passing through an opening in the enemy's abatis, which had previously been observed and fixed upon as our point of attack, closely followed by the One hundred and seventy-ninth New York, Thirty-first Maine, Sixth New Hampshire, Second Maryland, and the whole column, which passed forward under a deadly fire of grape, canister and musketry in the most gallant and determined manner, carrying all before them, capturing guns and turning them upon the enemy, and sending hundreds of prisoners to the rear." (OR, 46(1): 1054).

(39) *Dundee Record*, April 27, 1865; Wolcott at 111; *Buffalo Daily Courier*, April 5, 1865; Affidavit of Alexander Chandler dated January 18, 1871 and Affidavit of Joseph Robinson dated January 24, 1872, both Alexander Chandler Pension File; Alexander Chandler CMR.

(40) OR, 46(1): 1054-55, 1057. Because General Potter was seriously wounded early in the day and Griffin succeeded him, Griffin filed two reports – one for the Second Division and one for the Second Brigade. His Second Brigade report stated that: "After seizing the line in our immediate front the head of the column turned to the left and swept the enemy's line for about one-quarter of a mile, while General Curtin's brigade, in support of mine, also attacked in that direction; the enemy however, were well posted, and checked our farther advance to the left; and, having collected a force at that point, attacked us furiously, but our troops held the ground with the utmost determination." (OR, 46(1): 1059)

(41) Beals.

(42) Company I Morning Report, April 1865; Terrill CMSR. In 1892 – sixteen years after he had died, Terrill was promoted to lieutenant colonel effective April 6, 1865, the day that Lieutenant Colonel Doty died. (Terrill CMSR)

(43) *Niagara Falls Gazette*, June 9, 1923 and November 18, 1927.

(44) OR, 46(1): 1054-55.

(45) OR, 46(1): 1057.

(46) OR, 46(3): 453. See also 483.

(47) OR, 46(3): 453, 484.

(48) OR, 46(3): 484.

(49) *Ibid.*

(50) OR, 46(3): 485.

(51) Letter from Samuel Coon to Commissioner of Pensions dated July 15, 1891, Samuel Coon Pension File.

(52) OR, 46(3): 485-86.

(53) Greene, "April 2, 1865," 50.

(54) OR, 46(3): 486.

(55) Affidavits of Jasper Jayne dated April 2, 1869 and George Lockwood dated August 5, 1869, both Jasper Jayne Pension File.

(56) Larzelere Diary, April 2, 1865.

(57) Affidavit of William Tuck dated December 2, 1893, William Tuck Pension File.

(58) *Buffalo Daily Courier*, April 5, 1865.

(59) Letter from William Lamont to Sister dated April 11, 1865.

(60) Greene, "April 2, 1865," 50.

(61) OR, 46(3): 1379, 1380.

(62) JAWJ, April 1, 1865.

(63) Transcription of letter from William Larzelere to Sarah Larzelere dated April 3, 1865.

(64) Greene, *Civil War Petersburg*, 252.

(65) *Dundee Record* , April 27, 1865; Company F Morning Report, April 1865, Regimental Books, Vol. 4.

(66) Company C Morning Report, April 1865, Regimental Books, Vol. 4; Transcription of letter from William Larzelere to Sarah Larzelere dated April 3, 1865.

(67) 11th NH, 451, 501; Co. F Morning Report, April 1865, "Remarks." President Lincoln spent an hour and a half in Petersburg on April 3, but the absence of any reference to Lincoln in William Larzelere's diary, John Andrews' War Journal or Stephen Compton's diary indicates that the 179th was either in the wrong part of town or had returned to Hancock Station before Lincoln arrived. (OR, 46(3): 509; See Goodwin, 715-716.

(68) *Dundee Record*, April 27, 1865. *The Hornellsville Tribune* similarly quoted the report in "a private letter received by one of our citizens," presumably from a local soldier:
"Cheers from our troops as they entered the city could be heard for miles. We were heartily welcomed by the poor people and the negroes. I think I never saw so much rejoicing among the latter as there was that morning. One colored woman remarked, 'I noes dey aint rebs, dey look too clean.' I don't think I ever saw so much universal poverty as I saw in Petersburg. Women and children could be seen begging of our commisarys for something to eat."
(*The Hornellsville Tribune*, April 13, 1865)

(69) *Dundee Record*, April 27, 1865. The letter quoted by *The Hornellsville Tribune* reported that:
"You would laugh to see the men buying and stealing tobacco. One brakeman stole 600 pounds yesterday." (*The Hornellsville Tribune*, April 13, 1865)

(70) See Greene, *Civil War Petersburg*, 254-256.

(71) *Ibid.*, 254.

(72) Phisterer, 4029; OR, 46(1): 1056.

(73) Compiled from CMRs; Regimental History, 8, 12, 18, 34.

(74) OR, 46(1): 1056.

(75) Phisterer, 4032-4038; Regimental History, 34.

(76) Regimental History, 11.

(77) *Elmira Daily Advertiser*, April 7, 1865.

(78) *Elmira Daily Advertiser*, October 12, 1883.

(79) *Elmira Daily Advertiser*, April 10, 1865.

(80) *Elmira Daily Advertiser*, April 18, 1865.

(81) CMSR; CMRs; Letter from Henry Rootkiskie to Capt. Messing dated May 23, 1865, Messing Mss., 1864-1917, Lilly Library Manuscript Collections, Indiana Universirty.

(82) Thomas Connor and William Gibson CMSRs and CMRs; Declaration of Thomas Connor dated April 14, 1879, Thomas Connor Pension File; Albert Havens CMSR and CMR.

(83) Smith McMaster CMR.

(84) Letter from Giles Holden to Miss Mary Ann Proper dated May 10, 1865, George Proper Pension File.

(85) See Consolidated Morning Report, March 31, 1865, Regimental Books. (25 officers and 439 enlisted men for a total of 469)

(86) OR 46(3): 510.

(87) JAWJ, April 3, 1865; Letter from Stephen Compton to Wife dated April 5, 1865.

(88) Company I Morning Report, "Remarks," April 1865, Regimental Books, Vol. 4.

(89) Stephen Compton Diary, April 3, 1865; JAWJ, April 3, 1865; OR 46(3), 514, 524. At this point, the Second Division was commanded by General Griffin. General Potter had been seriously wounded early in the April 2 assault. For convenience of reference, I continue to refer to the Second Division as Potter's division.

(90) Company C and Company F Morning Reports, "Remarks," April 1865, Regimental Books, Vol. IV.

(91) JAWJ, April 4, 1865; Compton Diary, April 4, 1865.

(92) *Ibid.*; Larzelere Diary, April 4, 1865; Letter from William Lamont to Sister dated April 11, 1865. Mapping troop movements to the current roads in the area:

[Map: April 1865]

(93) JAWJ, April 5 , 1865.

(94) Company F April 1865 Morning Report; Compton Diary, April 5, 1865 (14 miles); JAWJ, April 5, 1865.

(95) JAWJ, April 6, 1865.

(96) OR, 46(3): 608.

(97) JAWJ April 6, 1865; Compton Diary, April 6, 1865.

(98) Company F April 1865 Morning Report; JAWJ, April 6, 1865; Compton Diary, April 6, 1865.

(99) JAWJ, April 7, 1865; Compton Diary, April 7, 1865.

(100) JAWJ, April 8, 1865.

(101) OR, 46(3): 649-50, 674; *The Hornellsville Tribune*, April 27, 1865.

(102) JAWJ, April 8 and 12, 1865

(103) "Record of Events," Company D and Company I, April 1865, Janet Hewett (editor), *Supplement to the Official Records of the Union and Confederate Armies*, Broadfoot Publishing Company: Wilmington, North Carolina (1997) Vol. 47, 734, 738.

(104) JAWJ, April 9, 1865.

(105) Larzelere Diary, April 12 to 16, 1865.

(106) JAWJ, April 10, 1865; Compton Diary, April 10, 1865.

(107) JAWJ, April 10, 1865.

(108) Letter from William Lamont to Sister dated April 11, 1865.

(109) Larzelere Diary, April 4, 1865 to April 10, 1865.

(110) Larzelere Diary, April 4, 1865; Letter from William Lamont to Sister dated April 11, 1865.

(111) Lamont April 11, 1865 letter.

(112) *Ibid.*; JAWJ, April 5, 1865.

(113) JAWJ, April 11, 1865; Compton Diary, April 11, 1865.

(114) JAWJ, April 12, 1865; Compton Diary April 12, 1865.

(115) JAWJ, April 13, 1865.

(116) JAWJ, April 12, 1865.

(117) Compton Diary, April 14, 1865; JAWJ, April 9, 1865.

(118) Regimental History, 14; Affidavit of Chester Peckham dated January 20, 1876, Chester Peckham Pension File.

(119) JAWJ, April 16, 1865; Larzelere Diary, April 16, 1865.

(120) JAWJ, April 16, 1865.

(121) *Ibid.*

(122) Compton Diary, April 16, 1865.

(123) JAWJ, April 17, 1865; Larzelere Diary, April 17, 1865.

(124) JAWJ, April 17, 1865; Compton Diary, April 19, 1865.

(125) OR 46(3): 788.

(126) *The Hornellsville Tribune*, April 27, 1865; JAWJ, April 17, 1865.

(127) JAWJ, April 18, 1865.

(128) *The Hornellsville Tribune*, April 27, 1865.

(129) *The Hornellsville Tribune*, April 20 and 27, 1865.

(130) JAWJ, April 19, 1865.

(131) Compton Diary, April 20, 1865; Larzelere Diary, April 20, 1865.

(132) Larzelere Diary, April 20, 1865.

(133) JAWJ, April 21, 1865; Compton Diary, April 21, 1865; Larzelere Diary, April 21, 1865.

(134) JAWJ, April 21, 1865.

(135) JAWJ, April 22, 1865; Larzelere Diary, April 22 to 25, 1865; Compton Diary, April 22 to 25, 1865.

(136) Compton Diary, April 26, 1865; Larzelere Diary, April 26, 1865.

(137) JAWJ, October 3, 1864 at 30.

(138) Compton Diary, April 27, 1865; Larzelere Diary, April 27 and 28, 1865; Company I Morning Report, April 1865, Regimental Books, Vol. 4.

(139) Company H Morning Report, April 1865, Regimental Books, Vol. 4.

(140) Letter from Stephen Compton to Wife dated April 30, 1865.

(141) "Record of Events" of the Company Muster Rolls for Company B, Company E and for Company H, Compiled Records Showing Service of Military Units in Volunteer Union Organizations, Microfilm Reel 139, National Archives; Supplement to the Official Records, Vol. 47, 733, 735, 737.

(142) Compiled from the company rosters and the CMRs.

(143) Compiled from the Company Morning Reports for October 27, 1864. Companies A, B, C, D, E, H, I, and K reported 301 officers, non-commissioned officers and enlisted men present for duty. There are no morning reports for Companies F and G for October 1864, but assigning them the average for the other companies would bring the total to 367. The 179th's Consolidated Morning Report for November 1, 1864 showed 369 officers and men. (Regimental Books)

Chapter Twenty-Four

Clarke, N., "Ariel Standish Thurston: The Boy With the Awkward Mouth," *Chemung Historical Journal*, Vol. 57, No. 2 (December 2011).

Gallagher, Gary W., *The Union War*, Harvard University Press: Cambridge, Massachusetts (2011).

Goodwin, Doris Kearns, *Team of Rivals: The Political Genius of Abraham Lincoln*, Simon & Schuster: New York (2005).

Grant, Ulysses S., *Personal Memoirs of U.S. Grant*, Charles L. Webster & Company: New York (1886).

Holberton, William B., *The Demobilization of the Union and Confederate Armies 1865-1866*, Stackpole Books: Mechanicsburg, Pennsylvania (2001).

Ramold, Steven J., *Across the Divide: Union Soldiers View the Northern Home Front*, New York University Press: New York (2013).

Rudolph, J., "The Grand Review," *Civil War Times Illustrated*, Vol. XIX, No. 7 (November 1980).
Sears, Stephen W., *George B. McClellan: The Young Napoleon*, Ticknor & Fields: New York (1988).
Tarbell, Ida, "How the Union army Was Disbanded," *Civil War Times Illustrated*, Vol. VI, No. 8 (December 1967). (Originally published in *McClure's Magazine* in March 1901).
Waugh, John, *Lincoln and McClellan: The Troubled Relationship Between A President and His General*, Palgrave McMillan: New York (2010).

(1) Letter dated April 19, 1865 from Emma Andrews to John Andrews.

(2) Company Muster Rolls, for February 28, 1865 to April 30, 1865, Regimental Papers, Box 3406; Letter from John Andrews to Father dated May 6, 1865, Author's Collection.

(3) Larzelere Diary, May 13 to 16, 18, 1865; Letter from Stephen Compton to wife dated May 28, 1865.

(4) Letter dated May 6, 1865, from John Andrews to Father, Author's Personal Collection; Compton Letter, May 7, 1865; Larzelere Diary, May 4 to 8, 1865. See also Tarbell, 8; Holberton, 73.

(5) Davis Marshall CMSR.

(6) Letter dated May 26, 1865 from Albert Pierson to John Andrews, Andrews Papers, Collection #3790, Cornell University, Box 1.

(7) Letter dated May 7, 1865 from Stephen Compton to wife.

(8) Rudolph, 8; Goodwin, 745.

(9) Gallagher, 3. Gallagher provides a thought-provoking discussion of the historiography of the Grand Review in his first chapter. He notes that:
"Much recent commentary finds in the events of May 23-24 a template for what was wrong with the war's winning cause. Too militaristic, too avowedly nationalistic, and, most troubling, too white, the review laid bare the flawed nature of Union triumph. Strip away the waving flags and celebratory chest-thumping, and what remained was a soon-to-be reunited nation that looked much like the racist, exclusionary, oppressive United States of the prewar era." (At 8)
That scholarship is the starting point for Gallagher's "renewed exploration of the meaning of the Union, emancipation, black military service, and citizen-soldiers in the Civil War era and their legacy for America today." (At 32) Among other things, he discredits the thesis that the "United States Colored Troops" were deliberately excluded from the Grand Review by pointing out that none of these units were deployed close enough to Washington, D.C. to conveniently participate. (At 10-11, 170, n. 26) The idea for the Grand Review may have come from Lincoln's review of the Army of the Potomac in November 1861. Following their victory at the First Battle of Bull Run, Confederate forces had occupied Munson's Hill, a mere six miles from Washington. When the Confederates fell back to Centreville, Virginia in the Fall, President Lincoln decided to review the troops of the Army of the Potomac. Under General George McClellan's leadership, the Army of the Potomac was being trained and organized into an effective fighting force. Some 65,000 soldiers participated in the review by President Lincoln with 30,000 spectators in attendance. (Sears, 134-35; Waugh, 57)

(10) Tarbell, 8.

(11) Grant, Vol. II, 531.

(12) Gallagher, 8; Brian Jordan, *Marching Home: Union Veterans and Their Unending Civil War*, Liveright Publishing Corporation: Philadelphia (2014), 12-13.

(13) Rudolph, 36-37; Gallagher, 13; Jordan, 9. The *Elmira Daily Advertiser* reported on May 29,

1865 that: "Many of our citizens who went to Washington to witness the Grand Review, returned on Saturday, having been greatly delighted with their sight-seeing."

(14) Lamont Letter, May 24, 1865; Rudolph, 37. Company G's Private James Benton was one of the men who suffered sun stroke. (Benton CMR)

(15) Rudolph, 38.

(16) *Ibid.*; OR, 46(3): 1181.

(17) OR 46(3): 1189, 1208.

(18) *Harper's Weekly*, June 10, 1865 at 358.

(19) Goodwin, 746.

(20) *Harper's Weekly*, June 10, 1865, 358. See also Jordan, 10-11.

(21) Grant, Vol. II, 535-36.

(22) Rudolph, 39.

(23) Lamont Letter, May 24, 1865; Gallagher, 12.

(24) Larzelere Diary, May 24 and 29, 1865. See also *Albany Evening Journal*, May 30, 1865.

(25) Larzelere Diary, June 1, 1865.

(26) Tarbell, 4-6.

(27) *Ibid.*, 6.

(28) *Ibid.*, 5-6, 45.

(29) *Ibid.*, 45. See also Jordan, 30-31. One hundred sixteen thousand men were mobilized during the Mexican War. (Kreidberg and Henry, 78) Kreidberg and Henry do not indicate how many actually reached Mexico or moved significantly southward, but the number in Mexico probably did not exceed twenty thousand men. (See *Ibid.*, 74, 75, 77) The problems experienced by other countries demobilizing large numbers of soldiers raised concerns for many civilians in the United States at the end of the Civil War. The *New York Herald* attempted to assuage those concerns by pointing out that in the United States citizen-soldiers were involved.

These were fears justified to some extent by the experience of other countries that had suddenly disbanded large armies. But our experience has been very different from that of any other country in this respect. Men can be heroes without in the remotest degree losing a sense of their obligations as citizens. (*New York Herald*, June 14, 1865, quoted in Casey, *Marked by War*, 123) See also Jordan, 33-34.

(30) Tarbell, 8-9.

(31) Holberton, 6; Tarbell, 45.

(32) Holberton, 14; Tarbell, 7; Jordan, 24. The officers of the 179th New York deserve a good deal of credit for successfully negotiating the complexities of all that paperwork. See Casey, *Marked by War*, 129-30)

(33) Letter from Levi Force to Maj. Samuel Wright dated June 3, 1865, Regimental Papers, Box 3408.

(34) Letter from Giles Holden to Maj. Samuel Wright dated June 6, 1864, Regimental Papers, Box 3408.

(35) Rudolph, 37; Holberton, 81-82.

(36) Holberton, 83-84.

(37) Letter from Colonel Titus to Major White dated May 29, 1865, Regimental Papers, Box 3408.

(38) Notation by Captain Casey, May 31, 1865, Regimental Papers, Box 3408; Letter from General Vincent to General Augur dated May 31, 1865, Regimental Papers, Box 3408; Letter dated May 28, 1865 from Stephen Compton to wife. In the end, things went much more smoothly for the

179th New York than many other units being demobilized. (Jordan, 31-33)

(39) Court Martial File MM2203, Record Group 153, Records of the Office of the Judge Advocate General (Army), Court Martial Case Files, 1809-1894, MM2203-MM2211, Box 1117, National Archives.

(40) Larzelere Diary, June 3, 1865.

(41) Letter dated June 3, 1865 from Stephen Compton to wife.

(42) Notation by General Parke dated June 5, 1865, Regimental Papers, Box 3408; Letter from Thomas M. Vincent to James Casey dated June 6, 1865, Regimental Papers, Box 3408.

(43) Compton Diary, June 6, 1865.

(44) Letter from General Griffin to Lieutenant Bertolitte dated June 8, 1865, Regimental Papers, Box 3408; Larzelere Diary, June 8, 1865; Compton Diary, June 8, 1865.

(45) *Buffalo Daily Courier*, June 16, 1865.

(46) OR (46(3): 1248.

(47) *Elmira Daily Advertiser*, June 9, 1865.

(48) Larzelere Diary, June 8, 1865; *Elmira Daily Advertiser*, June 12, 1865.

(49) Lamont Letters, June 9 to sister Bell and June 19, 1865 to parents.

(50) Larzelere Diary, June 9, 1865; Compton Diary, June 9, 1865.

(51) Holberton, 144.

(52) Compton Diary, June 10, 1865; Holberton, 77-78; Tarbell, 44; Jordan, 36. However, not all communities provided "welcome-home ceremonies." (Jordan, 37-38)

(53) Larzelere Diary, June 11, 1865; Compton Diary, June 11, 1865.

(54) *Elmira Daily Advertiser*, June 12, 1865.

(55) *Ibid.*

(56) Compton Diary, June 12, 1865.

(57) Larzelere Diary, June 12, 1865; *Elmira Daily Advertiser*, June 12, 1865.

(58) *Elmira Daily Advertiser*, June 13, 1865.

(59) *Elmira Daily Advertiser*, June 12, 1865.

(60) Compton Diary, June 12, 1865.

(61) *Elmira Daily Advertiser*, June 13, 1865.

(62) For more information about Judge Thurston, see Clarke, 6373.

(63) Brigham's Elmira Directory, 1863-1864, Fairman & DeVoe's Steam Printing Establishment: Elmira, New York (1863), 119. When Dr. Lincoln spoke to the Watkins Temperance Society in 1864, the *Watkins Express* described him as "a very able and eloquent man and the friends of the cause should see that he has a full house." *Watkins Express*, April 28, 1864.

(64) *Elmira Daily Advertiser*, June 13, 1865. A Union artilleryman explained what a "Tiger" cheer meant: "...you wished to know what the term Tiger means... when a lot of soldiers are giving three cheers. After the third cheer is given one and all shout "Tiger" with a vengeance... When shouted by a large crowd [they] gives a very peculiar sound that can not be imitated by any other ..." (Letter from Thomas Corwin Potter to sister dated November 16, 1862, Raynor's Historical Collectible Auctions Catalogue (February 19, 2015), 67)

(65) *Ibid.*

(66) *Chemung Valley Reporter*, October 3, 1907.

(67) *Elmira Daily Advertiser*, June 22 and 26, 1865; Dennis Dempsey, Company G, 179th New York Volunteer Infantry, NARA Publication T289.

(68) *Elmira Daily Advertiser*, June 9, 1865.

(69) *Elmira Daily Advertiser*, June 12, 1865. See also Jordan, 46-50.

(70) *Elmira Daily Advertiser*, June 21, 1865.

(71) *Elmira Daily Advertiser*, June 13, 1865.

(72) *Elmira Daily Advertiser*, June 16, 1865.

(73) *Elmira Daily Advertiser*, June 18 (20), 1865.

(74) *Elmira Daily Advertiser*, June 19, 1865.

(75) *Elmira Daily Advertiser*, June 22, 1865; Ramold, 35. Zavin Carey apparently was not paid until June 23. (Form No. 5, To Zavin N. Carey from Franklin Ames, Paymaster, June 23, 1865, Author's Personal Collection). Private James Applegate was not paid ($200.29) until June 26. (Form No. 5, To James H. Applegate, from Franklin Ames, June 26, 1865, Author's Personal Collection). For reasons that are not apparent, Applegate was paid only the second installment of his federal bounty, while Carey was paid the full remaining amount. These amounts were typical of what a Union soldier received upon discharge. The average was about $250. (Marten, 33-34) However, it is not clear that the experience of Applegate and Carey was typical for the 179th New York. John Andrews recorded in his journal on March 2, 1865 that: "The Paymaster has been here all day paying the men." (JAWJ, March 2, 1865, 13. See also March 1, 1865, 12–"Regiment Paid"). The CMRs for Applegate suggest that he was at home on that date which would account for his not being paid. However, the CMRs for Carey suggest that he was in camp that day. (CMRs)

(76) Larzelere Diary, June 21, 1865. Larzelere did not break down the $305 amount. Larzelere had been on furlough on March 2, 1865 and had not been paid with the 179th New York on that date (see note 75 above), but had been paid in Washington on March 15, 1865 as he was returning–$112 comprising four months pay ($72) and $40 in bounty installments. (Larzelere Diary, March 15, 1865.

(77) *Elmira Daily Advertiser*, June 24, 1865, reprinting article from *Elmira Gazette*, June 22, 1865. Concern about returning soldiers being deceived by "sharpers" was not limited to Colonel Gregg. One of the reasons for the decision to delay payment until the soldiers were near home was to deprive "sharpers" of the means of taking advantage of soldiers en route. (Tarbell, 45. See also Marten, 33-34; Jordan, 27-28) Colonel Gregg's comments about "reputation" were followed in a similar vein by the commander of the 96th Illinois in his parting address: "I need not urge you to the fulfillment of every duty which pertains to the citizen. I know you will cherish your reputations as soldiers so highly that you will be especially careful to do nothing which will in the least tarnish or efface it." (Casey, *Marked by War*, 134)

(78) *Buffalo Daily Courier*, June 19, 1865.

(79) *The Hornellsville Tribune*, June 29, 1865, July 6, 1865 and July 13, 1865.

(80) *Elmira Daily Advertiser*, July 6, 1865; *Yates County Chronicle*, June 22, 1865 and July 6, 1865.

(81) *Yates County Chronicle*, June 22, 1865; *Broome Republican*, June 14, 1865. See also *Elmira Daily Advertiser*, June 12, 1864.

(82) Regimental History, 6. Ausburn Turner wrote in 1892 that: "For the brief period that the regiment was in the field there was crowded into the time a service of hardship and danger that many organizations did not experience during the whole war." (Towner, 247) The 179th New York was not included in "Fox's 300 Fighting Regiments" – regiments which had suffered at least 130 battle deaths. (Fox, 122-423) The number of men killed or mortally wounded in the 179th New York – sixty-eight according to Fox (at 481) and seventy-two according to Phisterer (at 302) – is only slightly more than half of Fox's threshold of 130. (At 122) However, most of the

regiment's in "Fox's 300 Fighting Regiments" served throughout the war. The newer regiments in the Army of the Potomac that qualified had gone through the Overland campaign as well as the Petersburg campaign. For the Petersburg campaign itself, the 179th New York suffered casualties in the same range as regiments from Potter's division that were included in "Fox's 300" – the 31st Maine, the 58th Massachusetts, the 6th and 9th New Hampshire and the 17th Vermont. (Compare Phisterer, 4029 with Fox, 136, 140, 142, 153, 176) Fox himself acknowledged that the "Fighting 300" regiments were not the only ones worthy of recognition:

"It is not claimed that these are *the* Three Hundred Fighting Regiments of the Army; but that they are three hundred regiments which evidently did considerable fighting. There were, undoubtedly, others which did equally good or, perhaps better fighting, and their gallant services will be fully recognized by the writers who are conversant with their history." (At 122) (emphasis in original) This book presents the 179th New York's record for consideration.

Chapter Twenty-Five

Bertuca, D., "The Fenian Invasion of Canada, 1866," *The Harp*, Buffalo & Erie County Historical Society, Ready Reference Files.

Boyko, J., *Blood and Daring: How Canada Fought the American Civil War and Forged A Nation*, Alfred A. Knopf, Canada: Toronto (2013).

Bradsby, H., *History of Bradford County, Pennsylvania with Biographical Sketches*, Public Member Trees, Ancestry.com.

Brandt, Nat, *Mr. Tubbs' Civil War*, Syracuse University Press: Syracuse, New York (1996).

Casey, John, "Marked by War: Demobilization, Disability and the Trope of the Citizen-Soldier in Miss Ravenel's Conversion", *Civil War History*, Volume 60, Number 2, June 2014. The Kent State University Press.

Glasson, William H., *Federal Military Pensions in the United States*, Oxford University Press: New York (1918).

Kelly, P., *Creating A National Home: Building the Veterans' Welfare State 1860-1900*, Harvard University Press: Cambridge, Massachusetts (1997).

Knight, Glenn B., "The Grand Army of the Republic: A Brief History," Internet suvcw.org/ny/gar/commanders/GARhistory.

MacDonald, John A., *Troublous Times in Canada: A History of the Fenian raids of 1866-1870*, W.S. Johnston and Company: Toronto (1910).

Marten, James, *Sing Not War: The Lives of Union & Confederate Veterans in Gilded Age America*, University of North Carolina Press: Chapel Hill (2011).

McPherson, James, *Battle Cry of Freedom: The Civil War Era*, Oxford University Press: Oxford (1988).

Owen, Thomas M., *History of Alabama and Dictionary of Alabama Biography*, The S.J. Clarke Publishing Company: Chicago (1921).

Ramold, Steven J., *Across the Divide: Union Soldiers View the Northern Home Front*, New York University Press: New York (2013).

Raymond, Andrew Van Vranken, *Union University: Its History, Influence, Characteristics, and Equipment*, Lewis Publishing Co.: New York (1907).

Schneirov, R., *The Pullman Strike and the Crisis of the 1890's*, Pullman Virtual Museum; 1892, 1893 and 1894 Wilmington Directories.

Smedberg, William R., "In Memorium: Levi Force," Military Order Loyal Legion of the United States, Headquarters Commandery of the State of California, series of 1891, no. 6, whole no. 256.

Sterling, Pound (Maxson, William P.), *Campfires of the Twenty-Third: Sketches of the Camp Life, Marches and Battles of the Twenty-Third Regiment, N.Y.V., During the Term of Two Years In The Service of the United States*, Davies & Kent, Printers: New York (1863).

Vinovskis, Maris A. (Ed.), *Toward a Social History of the American Civil War: Exploratory Essays*, Cambridge University Press: New York (1990).

Vronsky, Peter, *Ridgeway: The American Fenian Invasion and the 1866 Battle That Made Canada*, Allen Lane: Canada (2011).

Wilson, Sven Eric, "Prejudice & Policy: Racial Discrimination in the Union army Disability Pension System, 1865-1906", *American Journal of Public Health*, Vol. 0, No. 2010 (February 10, 2010)

(1) *The Hornellsville Tribune*, June 25, 1865. The tension between the soldiers about to return to civilian life and a society concerned about the harmful effects of military life on these men is described in Marten, *Sing Not War* and Casey, *Marked by War*.

(2) Marten, 4, 20.

(3) Marten, 284; Sterling, unnumbered first page of Preface.

(4) Letter dated January 19, 1866 from Levi Force to John Andrews, Cornell University Collection No. 3790, Box 2, Folder 2.

(5) Notecard, Cornell University Collection No. 3790, Box 2, Folder 2; Letter from John Andrews to Dr. John Taylor dated January 15, 1866, Box 2, Folder 2; Brandt, 200.

(6) Brandt, 199; Letter from H. D. Baldwin to John Andrews dated May 26, 1869, Cornell University Collection No. 3790, Box 2, Folder 4.

(7) Brandt, 199. In 1901, J.B. Sloan Post No. 93 in Penn Yan compiled a special volume of brief reminiscences by its members. Andrews wrote the following "Personal War Sketch: Entered service as Recruiting Officer at Owego, New York August 30, 1864 ... Was commissioned Second Lieutenant December 19, 1864 and First Lieutenant January 5, 1865. Took part in the engagement at Hatcher's Run October 1864; at Forts Haskell and Steadman before Petersburgh, Virginia and in the battles before that City in March and April 1865. In January 1865, I captured two confederates and was courtmartialed on charges of holding communications with the enemy growing out of this capture. I was honorably acquitted while under arrest and promoted to First Lieutenant. At the close of the war, I received a commission as Brevet Captain accompanied by a letter from the Colonel of the Regiment Bvt. Brig. General William Gregg stating that "no officer of the Regiment is better entitled to the honor nor has one more worthily earned it." (Yates County History Center)

[Photo: John Andrews' captain's bars]
The letter from Colonel Gregg was dated April 17, 1866. Gregg had obtained a brevet promotion to captain for Andrews from Gov. Fenton. (Cornell University Collection No. 3790, Box 2, Folder 2)

(8) Brandt, 199-200; Raymond, Vol. III, 185.

(9) Affidavit of William Norton dated February 22, 1890, William Norton Pension; *Watkins Express*, October 28, 1897; *Watkins Review*, October 27, 1897; [newspaper fragment], October 28, 1897, William Norton Pension File. Emma Robins Norton received an A.B. degree from Alfred

University. She was a strong advocate of Prohibition and published a book on temperance in 1882. (*Schuyler County Chronicle*, August 26, 1915.

(10) *Watkins Express*, October 9, 1879; *Watkins Express*, August 21, 1873.

(11) *Watkins Democrat*, September 20, 1882.

(12) *Watkins Express*, October 5, 1882, November 2, 1882 and November 9, 1882.

(13) *Watkins Review*, October 27, 1897.

(14) *Elmira Gazette*, January 24, 1896.

(15) *Watkins Review*, October 27, 1897; *Watkins Express*, October 28, 1897.

(16) *Watkins Express*, October 23, 1879; *Watkins Express*, November 2, 1882; *Havana Journal*, November 4, 1882.

(17) *Watkins Express*, September 14, 1882.

(18) *Penn Yan Democrat*, March 1, 1907; *(New York) Sun*, February 27, 1907; Reply by Newton Spencer dated May 1, 1898 to Bureau of Pensions questionnaire, Newton Spencer Pension File; *The Corning Journal*, May 9, 1879.

(19) *Penn Yan Democrat*, December 27, 1865.

(20) *Corning Journal*, [undated copy]; *Havana Journal*, January 24, 1880; *Geneva Daily Times*, February 28, 1907. See also *Rochester Democrat & Chronicle*, February 28, 1907: "He was a graceful writer and his [illegible] and other productions have been widely subscribed, especially his war poems."

(21) *Geneva Gazette*, November 16, 1877; *Corning Journal*, October 24, 1879; *Geneva Gazette*, August 16, 1878; *Watkins Express*, August 15, 1878; *Corning Journal*, August 16, 1877; *Corning Journal*, June 7, 1877; *Watkins Express*, August 7, 1879; *Watkins Democrat*, February 18, 1880.

(22) *Watkins Express*, January 14, 1885; *Rochester Democrat and Chronicle*, February 8, 1886; Surgeon's Certificate dated June 1, 1892, Newton Spencer Pension File; *Elmira Telegram*, March 3, 1907.

(23) *Elmira Telegram*, April 28, 1895.

(24) Declaration of Newton Spencer dated September 4, 1891, Newton Spencer Pension File.

(25) *The New York Times*, February 27, 1907; *New York Sun*, February 27, 1907; *Rochester Democrat & Chronicle*, February 28 , 1907; *Geneva Daily Times*, February 28, 1907; *Oswego Daily Palladium*, February 27, 1907; *The Rome Daily Sentinel*, February 27, 1907; *Penn Yan Democrat*, March 1, 1907; *Elmira Telegram*, March 3, 1907; *Elmira Gazette and Free Press*, February 27, 1907.

(26) Owen, Vol. III, 576; U.S. Census, 1850 (N. Talmage Finch), 1860 (Talmage Finch), 1870 and 1880, Ancestry.com; Affidavits of Nathaniel P. T. Finch dated June 10, 1909 and Mary Isabel Finch dated March 20, 1914, both Nathaniel P. T. Finch Pension File.

(27) Owen, 576; *Atlanta Constitution*, June 18, 1913. He continued his interest in libraries as director and president of the Young Men's Library Association of Atlanta.

(28) *Ibid*.

(29) Compiled from the Civil War Pension Index, fold3.com. The place of death is listed for 244 veterans of the 179th in the index. In that sample, 22% died in the states of California (6 men), Illinois (5), Indiana (1) Iowa (1), Kansas (3), Michigan (15), Minnesota (3), Missouri (1), Nebraska (1), Ohio (8), Oregon (3), South Dakota (2), Washington (3) and Wisconsin (2). Based on the Pension Index data, Michigan was the most popular state for emigration (6%). Ohio was next (3%), followed by California (2%). About 3% moved south to the states of the former Confederacy: Alabama (1 man), Arkansas (2), Florida (2), Texas (1) and Virginia (1). None of the men in the sample died in one of the New England states and only one each in New Jersey and Delaware. The claim by the *Chemung Valley Reporter* in 1907 that "there is not a state in the union that has not some of the old 179th regiment men as citizens." was a bit of an exaggeration.

(*Chemung Valley Reporter*, October 3, 1907)

(30) William Bird, 1860 Census, Ancestry.com; Various documents in William Bird, Jr. File, Martin County Historical Society.

(31) William Bird, Jr. CMSR; William Bird, Jr. Pension File; "Bird Family History," Martin County Historical Society.

(32) Letter from John P. Bird to Minnie dated November 8, 1930, Martin County Historical Society.

(33) William Bird, Jr., 1870 Federal Census, Ancestry.com; Bird reply dated July 4, 1898 to Bureau of Pensions questionnaire, William Bird Pension File.

(34) Letter from William Bird, Jr. to Wm. H. Dudley dated May 19, 1883, Bird Pension File. Bird had filed for an increased pension in 1877. (Application for the Increase of an Invalid Pension dated December 5, 1877, Bird Pension File)

(35) See William Bird, 1880 Census, Ancestry.com.

(36) Various materials in Martin County file; *The Sentinel*, June 29, 1908.

(37) *Portrait and Biographical Record of Saginaw and Bay Counties, Michigan*, Biographical Publishing Co.: Chicago (1892), 355-356; Chatford Howell CMSR and Pension File. Howell enlisted under the name of Hiram Puls, giving his birthplace as Canada, rather than Niagara County, New York where he in fact was born. The reason for giving an assumed name and birthplace is not contained in his CMSR or pension file.

(38) Letter from William Gregg to John L. Youngman dated February 3, 1865, Levi Force CMSR.

(39) JAWJ, October 6, 1864, 39; October 23, 1864, 88; and November 11, 1864, 26.

(40) Smedberg.

(41) William Lamont CMRs; Statement of Joseph Robinson dated September 20, 1879, William Lamont Pension File.

(42) Affidavit of William Lamont dated December 2, 1878, William Lamont Pension File.

(43) Affidavit of Jeanette Rich dated April 28, 1879 and Affidavit of Adams H. Bullis dated September 16, 1879, both William Lamont Pension File.

(44) 1875 Minnesota Census, Winnebago, Fairbault County; 1885 Minnesota Census, Jackson, Jackson County. He is not listed in either the 1870 or the 1880 Federal Censuses. (A William and Sarah A. Lamont are listed in the 1880 census for Springwater in Livingston County. While the names are correct, the ages are not quite right and there is a ten year-old daughter not referred to in either the 1875 or 1885 Minnesota censuses.)

(45) William Lamont file card, Civil War Pension Index, fold3.com.

(46) Jeanne L. Bloom notes.

(47) William Larzelere file card, Civil War Pension Index, fold3.com.

(48) Affidavit of James C. Rutan dated August 9, 1882, Affidavit of Joel M. Jansen dated September 8, 1883, and Response to Circular dated January 15, 1898, all James Rutan, Pension File.

(49) McPherson, *Battle Cry of Freedom*, 12-15. McPherson explains that as improved roads, then canals and then railroads significantly reduced transportation costs and opened up wider markets, the restructuring of the industrial system:

"took various forms, but had one dominant feature in common: the process of making a product (shoes or furniture, for example), which had previously been performed by one or a few skilled craftsmen, was broken down into numerous steps each requiring limited skills and performed by a separate worker. Sometimes the worker did his task with hand tools, but increasingly with the aid of power-driven machinery." (At 14)

(50) *Ibid.*, 18.

(51) Schneirov, 43; Wilmington City Directories, 1892 (Edward [Edwin] and Luther Rutan listed as carbuilders working for Pullman Palace Car Company; James Rutan as a carbuilder; and Frederick Rutan as a carpenter); 1893 (no Rutans listed), 1894 (Frederick and Luther Rutan listed as carpenters). In subsequent directories, Frederick was listed as working for Pullman (1895, and 1897), as was Edwin Rutan (1896 and 1897)and Luther Rutan (1896).

(52) Unsourced February 26, 1911 newspaper clipping, Author's collection.

(53) Of the 244 men from the 179th whose place of death is listed in the pension index, two-thirds died in New York. Another eight percent died in Pennsylvania. (Roughly six percent of the men in the 179th hailed from Pennsylvania.)

(54) Bradsby, 995-995; Huston McKinney CMSR.

(55) Deposition of Ambrose Worden dated April 20, 1896, 9, 12, Ambrose Worden Pension File.

(56) Stephen Compton CMSR; Stephen Compton file card, Civil War Pension Index, fold3.com.

(57) Boyd's Elmira Directory (1860)[not cite-checked]; 1860 United States Census, Horseheads, Chemung County, New York.

(58) Letter from James C. Rutan to Commissioner of Pensions dated February 15, 1888, Stephen Compton Pension File; Letter from Stephen Compton to Wife dated May 28, 1865.

(59) Affidavit of Stephen Compton dated August 6, 1888, Joseph Potter Pension File.

(60) McPherson, 16-17. To meet rapidly growing demand, a new style of construction – "balloon-frame" – first appeared in the 1830's in Chicago and nearby Rochester, both then rapidly growing boom towns. (*Ibid.*)

"These houses were constructed with the now familiar combination of machine- sawed boards fastened together with factory-produced nails to form the skeleton of a frame house. Machine-sawed siding and shingles and factory-made doors and window parts filled in the frame. Skeptics scoffed that these "balloon frames" would blow away in the first high wind. But in fact they were remarkably strong, for the boards were nailed together in such a way that every strain went against the grain of the wood. These houses could be put up in a fraction of the time and at a fraction of the cost of houses built by traditional methods." (At 17)

(61) Affidavit of George Kutz dated July 19, 1889 and Affidavit of George Dewey dated January 9, 1890, both James Wattleworth Pension File.

(62) Affidavits of Joseph Potter dated August 24, 1889 and May 2, 1890, Joseph Potter Pension File.

(63) Deposition of Jesse Cornell dated May 27, 1904, Jesse Cornell Pension File; "Paul Hildreth," Robert Graham, *Yates County's Boys in Blue, 1861-1865*, 137, ancestry.com; Giles Holden Pension File. In addition, William Jackson, Norton Sage, and Abraham Mills served in the 14th U.S. Infantry; Edward Jenkins served in the 2d U. S. Infantry; and Lewis Diar served in the 6th U.S. Infantry as well as the 179th New York, (Civil War and Later Veterans Pension Index, fold3. com), but I have not confirmed whether that service was after the war or during the war.

(64) Vronsky, 53, 81, 121. The name "Fenian" came from an "ancient warrior clans" that had defended the Irish coast from invaders. (*Ibid.*, 3)

(65) Vronsky, 3; Boyko, 257. The Fenian Brotherhood grew quickly and had fifty thousand members and four or five times as many sympathizers by 1861. The Fenian Brotherhood did not operate as an underground, secret society in Upstate New York. Its events were routinely covered by the local newspapers. (*Elmira Daily Advertiser*, September 19, 1864: "The Fenian Brotherhood

are to give a ball on the 29th of September. ... Such social gatherings, well conducted, have a good effect, and we trust this will be encouraged."; *Elmira Daily Advertiser*, May 29, 1865: "The Fenian Brotherhood will hold their Weekly Meeting this evening at half past seven o'clock. All members are requested to be present. By order of Centre.") During the Civil War, the Fenian Brotherhood encouraged its members to serve in the Union army to obtain military experience for use in future Fenian actions. Whether Hoy enlisted for that reason or not is unknown. After the Civil War, the Fenians became more aggressive, planning for the invasion of Canada from the United States. A Fenian song of the day proclaimed:

"We are a Fenian Brotherhood, skilled in the arts of war/ And we're going to fight for Ireland, the land that we adore/ Many battles we have won, along with the boys in blue/ And we'll go and capture Canada, for we've nothing else to do." (MacDonald, 16)

(66) Vronsky, 10, 30, 33; Boyko, 271; D. Bertuca, "The Fenian Movement," n.17. How to deal with the Fenians was a delicate matter for the United States government, which was trying to juggle enforcement of the Neutrality Act, lingering notions of Manifest Destiny that Canada be part of the United States, the growing political power of Irish-Americans, and international relations with Great Britain and the soon to confederate Canada. The crisis resulting from the Fenian invasion was serious enough to bring both Generals Grant and Meade to Buffalo. (Boyko, 273; Vronsky, 26-28) The Fenian invasion force was led by General John O'Neill, a former Union cavalry captain. The *U.S.S. Michigan* had been positioned in the area to prevent just such an attack, but the Fenian's had infiltrated the crew and were able to sidetrack the ship's pilot from boarding at the critical time. After landing in Canada, part of Hoy's regiment was deployed north of Fort Erie to secure the road from Chippewa. The main force moved westward toward the Welland Canal and dug in on a ridge just north of Ridgway. Hoy's regiment rejoined the main force in time to act as skirmishers at the Battle of Ridgway on June 2. Ever aware of the role of good press coverage, Hoy had signed the pass that gave reporters from the *Buffalo Express* access to the area. (Vronsky, 37-38, 43-44, 53, 121; Boyko, 272-274; *Buffalo Morning Express*, June 4, 1866)

(67) Vronsky, 197-98; Boyko, 273-74; *Buffalo Morning Express*, June 8 and June 15, 1866.

(68) Wilson, 2. By 1895, sixty-three percent of all Union veterans were receiving pension benefits. Vinovskis, 24. See also Kelly, 5-6.

(69) Compiled from Civil War Pension Index, fold3.com, which is searchable by regiment and by individual.

(70) Compiled from Civil War Pension Index, fold3.com; Robert Wilkens file card, Civil War Pension Index, fold3.com. Brian Jordan discusses the practical problems facing former prisoners of war in compiling the requisite evidence in *Marching Home: Union Veterans and Their Unending Civil War*, 148-49.

(71) Compiled from Civil War Pension Index, fold3.com.

(72) Glasson, 131; Vinovskis, 22, 23 & Fig. 1.3;

(73) Calculated from Civil War Pension Index, fold3.com and individual pension files.

(74) Affidavit of Felix Miller dated April 7, 1865; Affidavit of James Day, dated January 9, 1866; and Letter from Almon Webb to Commissioner of Pensions dated January 1, 1869, all Felix Miller Pension File; Felix Miller CMRs.

(75) Worksheets, James Fluent Pension File.

(76) Glasson, 126.

(77) Glasson, 150-151, 166, 186.

(78) Glasson, 149, 156-160, 164, 177. This was classic special interest legislation. The implications

and cost of the Arrears Act were not fully understood by Congress. When widespread public criticism developed and better estimates of the cost became available, Congress amended the law to close the window for arrears filings as of July 1, 1880. (*Ibid.*, 171-73)

(79) Glasson, 175-175.

(80) Compiled from Civil War Pension Index, fold3.com.

(81) Marten, 5.

(82) Affidavit of Edwin S. Rarrick dated April 26, 1882, Edwin Rarrick Pension File.

(83) Letter from Samuel Coon to Pension Commissioner dated July 15, 1891, Samuel Coon Pension File.

(84) Letter from Samuel Musgrave to E. McLean dated June 22, 1887, Peter Florean Pension File.

(85) Hadley and Gibson (alias Connor) Pension Index Cards, Civil War and Later Veterans Pension Index, fold3.com; Hadley and Connor CMRs; Hadley and Gibson (Connor) Pension Files; Hadley CMSR.

(86) Harvey Chapman Pension Index Card, Civil War Pension Index, fold3.com; Harvey Chapman CMR; Harvey Chapman Pension File.

(87) Compiled from Civil War Pension Index, Fold3. The outliers were Company H's Isaac Smith at one year and nine months and Company G's Russell Horton at eleven years and one month.

(88) Wilson, 6.

(89) Letter from J. H. Jennings to W. W. Dudley dated June 6, 1883, Samuel Parsons Pension File.

(90) *Ibid.* Jennings noted that "in this he succeeded." "[T]he claimant enlisted Sept 3d and was discharged Nov 19th 1864 whole term of service 77 days. Out of this period he was sick in Hospital from four to six weeks and was home on sick furlough twenty two days, leaving his term of duty in the service at about ten days."

(91) Cases where veterans of the 179th submitted affidavits in support of each others claims are common. See for example, Stephen Compton and George Carpenter; James Rutan and Stephen Compton; Willian Norton and John Price, Carpenter, Compton, Price, Rutan and Norton Pension Files.

(92) Special Examiner's Report dated April 30, 1886, Andrew Evarts Pension File.

(93) December 12, 1881 report, Charles Beckwith Pension File.

(94) Letter from James Spencer to Commissioner of Pensions dated October 22, 1888, Alvin Kilburn Pension File.

(95) Letter from Samuel Musgrave to E. McLean dated June 22, 1887, Peter Florean Pension File.

(96) Affidavit Of William Norton dated June 29, 1886, Ezra Northup Pension File.

(97) Special Examiner's Report dated December 18, 1881, Charles Beckwith Pension File.

(98) Affidavit of George Lake dated August 17, 1888 and Letter from Giles Holden to John Black dated December 8, 1888, both George D. Lake Pension File; George Lake CMSR. Even had Holden been silent, Lake's attempted fraud would not have succeeded. The Adjutant General's Office independently reported that Lake had deserted. (George Lake Pension File) Lake's application for removal of the charge of desertion was denied by the Adjutant General's Office on November 5, 1888. (George Lake CMSR)

(99) Affidavit of Alexander Gardner dated February 15, 1873, Francis Canfield Pension File.

(100) Deposition of David Meirthew dated March 6, 1899, David Meirthew Pension File.

(101) Letter from John Lawrence to Commissioner of Pensions dated March 4, 1903, John Lawrence Pension File.

(102) That may not be true for applications granted by the Harrison Administration. Harrison, a

general during the war, appointed James Tanner, a double amputee, as pension commissioner. He purportedly directed Tanner to "be liberal with the boys." (Glasson, 226)

(103) Compiled from Civil War Pension Index, fold3.com and individual pension files. Brian Jordan recently concluded that: "While the Pension Bureau no doubt had an obligation to foil scoundrels filing fraudulent claims, more often than not, these [evidentiary] provisions refused pensions to worthy ex-soldiers." (*Marching Home*, 156) With respect to the 179th New York, the impact of Pension Bureau scrutiny seems to be more one of delay rather than outright denial, although the old saw "justice delayed is justice denied" comes into play.

(104) Glasson, 180-181.

(105) Letter from Frank Tibbets to Hon. J.S. Black dated December 8, 1887, Charles Barnard Pension File.

(106) Letter from Thomas H. Pinch to John C. Black dated April 5, 1888, John Bills Pension File. See also Jordan, 157-58. Some men of the 179th took out their frustration by responding with sarcasm to the Pension Bureau's form questionnaire on vital statistics. In response to the question "Any children living?" Isaac Thompson, who never married, answered: "Not to my knowledge. There might be a stray one as I have been into a good many parts at different times." (May 4, 1898 response to January 15, 1898 questionnaire, Isaac Thompson Pension File) Thompson seems to have had a Puckish personality. Someone sent the Pension Bureau a newspaper article titled "Couldn't Foil Old Boy" about Thompson's success in obtaining liquor outside of the dry town where he lived in a soldiers' home. Martin Kellsy responded to the question "Were you previously married?" with "No, once was enough." (March 24, 1915 response to Questionnaire, Martin Kellsy Pension File) Newton Spencer answered the question "What record of marriage exists? " by referring to "A Marriage Certificate, and the 6 fine boys named below!" (emphasis in original) (May 11, 1898 response to questionnaire dated January 15, 1898, Newton Spencer Pension File)

(107) Wilson, 8; Glasson, 234-235. Glasson characterizes the 1890 Act as "really a service-pension law subject to a limitation – the existence in applicants of disabilities, regardless of origin." (234)

(108) Affidavit of Willard Stevens dated April 27, 1891 and Pension Bureau work papers, Willard Stevens Pension File.

(109) Affidavit of Charles Askay dated November 10, 1891 and Pension Bureau work papers, Charles Askay Pension File.

(110) Pension Bureau work papers, Charles Beckwith Pension File.

(111) Compiled from Civil War Pension Index, fold3.com.

(112) Glasson, 204-205, 238.

(113) Wilson, 6; Glasson, 204-205, 238.

(114) Wilson, 6. Membership was limited to honorably discharged veterans of the Union army, Navy, Marine Corps or Revenue Cutter Service who had served at any time from April 12, 1861 to April 9, 1865. Knight; S. (Wilson, 6)

(115) Glasson, 225.

(116) Glasson, 250. The Act of 1907 in effect codified an order issued by the Pension Bureau three years before. (*Ibid.*, 246, 248-49)

(117) Compiled from Civil War Pension Index, fold3.com; Marten, 17.

(118) Glasson, 250.

(119) Compiled from the Civil War Pension Index, fold3.com. A similar transfer occurred in 1912, when the rates were increased to $13, $18 and $21 and an intermediate step was added for

age sixty-six at $15. A increment was also created for length of service, which would have added a dollar per month for the men of the 179th. (See Glasson, 258-259)

(120) They are not listed in the Civil War Pension Index, fold3.com.

(121) Affidavit of William Norton dated February 22, 1890, William Norton Pension File. When the parents of Company F's George White, who was mortally wounded in the June 17, 1864 assault, filed for a military service pension in 1879, Norton filed an affidavit explaining that: "They are very respectable people, and *proud spirited*, the latter fact accounting for the delay in applying for a pension." (emphasis in original) (Affidavit of William Norton dated January 16, 1879, George White Pension File.

(122) Affidavit of Joseph Potter dated May 2, 1890, Joseph Potter Pension File.

(123) Marten, 13-14, 173, 191; Kelly, 133.

(124) Letter from Martin Kellsy to Comrade dated April 23, 1909 and July 15, 1898 Response to Circular Questionaire, both Martin Kellsy Pension File; Martin Kellsy CMSR.

(125) Martin Kellsy Pension File; Martin Kellsy Index Card, Civil War and Later Veterans Pension Index, fold3.com.

(126) Civil War Pension Index, fold3.com; Individual Pension Files. William Walker's wife was living in the Bradford County Poor House when he died. (William Walker Pension File).

(127) James Marten notes that:

"Specific issues – especially pensions and the behavior of the men who failed to flourish in postwar society – led to a clash between the nation's natural gratitude and deep-seated notions about independence, charity, and the role of government. Americans were uneasy about "volunteers" claiming pensions or other rewards." (Marten, 19)

Similarly, Brian Jordan recently concluded in *Marching Home: Civil War Soldiers and Their Unending Civil War*, that:

"Historians have long pointed out the "increasing liberality" of military pensions after the Civil War, marveling at the munificence of the federal government in an age of lemon-sucking fiscal conservatism. The persistent lobbying of Union veterans and their organizations no doubt secured upwardly adjusted rates, relaxed evidentiary requirements, and the full payment of arrears. But these legislative successes, only achieved after bruising political battles, failed to wrest from the public an enduring recognition of the human and emotional costs of the war: alternatively, they merely confirmed that there was indeed 'another' civil war–between Union veterans and northern civilians." (at 169)

For today's professional army, a service-based pension is no different from a private sector service-based pension, but the traditional private sector pension is rapidly disappearing today.

(128) Glasson, 262. The view was widespread that the Civil War veterans "had a preferred claim on any surplus that might accumulate in the Treasury." (*Ibid.*, 249, 263) A grateful nation granted special benefits to the "citizen-soldiers" of World War II, but these special benefits also arguably benefitted the nation as a whole. The "G.I. Bill" probably stimulated economic growth, for example, through the national investment in higher education. It would be interesting to study whether the Civil War pension payments and/or high bounties stimulated economic growth, for example, by enabling wider ownership of farmland or by just increasing consumption.

(129) Glasson, 177.

(130) Glasson, 130-131.

(131) Affidavit of William Hemstreet dated April 12, 1883, William Hemstreet Pension File.

(132) Glasson, 269, 238-239; Jordan,. 160. The per capita numbers for the other Confederate

states were: Alabama ($.29); Arkansas ($1.15); Florida ($.96); Georgia ($.21); Louisiana ($.57); Mississippi ($.42); North Carolina ($.30); and Texas ($.37). The Midwest (e.g. Indiana – $3.90 and Ohio – $3.36), the Northern New England states (e.g. Maine $4.08 and Vermont – $4.04) and surprisingly, California ($2.02) fared better than New York, Pennsylvania and Massachusetts ($1.93). (*Ibid.*)

(133) Glasson noted that "Southern members of Congress have usually been glad to support pension legislation for Union soldiers who were actually wounded or disabled in service. Their objections have been directed in the main at such service-pension legislation as has been developed out of the act of June 27, 1890." (At 267)

(134) Vinovskis, 27. But see Jordan, 158. William Mahone as a United States Senator from Virginia

[Photo: Sen. Mahone]

Chapter Twenty-Six

—— "The Army Civil War Campaign Medal", *Prologue*, Vol. 33, No. 2 (Summer 2001).

Dean Jr., Eric T., *Shook Over Hell: Post Traumatic Stress, Vietnam and the Civil War*, Harvard University Press: Cambridge (1997).

Fox, William F., *Regimental Losses in the American Civil War 1861-1865*, Albany Publishing Company: Albany, New York (1889).

Hess, Earl J., *The Union Soldier in Battle: Enduring the Ordeal of Combat*, University Press of Kansas: Lawrence (1997).

Knight, Glenn B., "The Grand Army of the Republic: A Brief History," Internet suvcw.org/ny/gar/commanders/GARhistory.

Marten, James, *Sing Not War: The Lives of Union & Confederate Veterans in Gilded Age America*, University of North Carolina Press: Chapel Hill (2011).

Wilkenson, Warren, *Mother, May You Never See the Sights I Have Seen: The Fifty-seventh Massachusetts Veteran Volunteers in the Last Year of the Civil War*, Harper & Row, Publishers: New York (1990).

Wilson, Sven Eric, "Prejudice & Policy: Racial Discrimination in the Union army Disability Pension System, 1865-1906", *American Journal of Public Health*, Vol. 0, No. 2010 (February 10, 2010)

(1) Marten, 284. Similarly, Eric Dean wrote:
"[M]any if not most soldiers in the Civil War era had an intense love-hate relationship with the service. On the one hand, they frequently deplored the hardships and the danger; on the other hand, perhaps because of their ability to withstand these tribulations, they considered the experience to be riveting, the most meaningful time of their lives, something that could never – for better or worse – be forgotten or trivialized." (Dean, 213)

(2) "Grand Army of the Republic," Wikipedia.

(3) Grand Army of the Republic (Series B1706), Box 31, New York State Archives.

(4) Wikipedia, "Memorial Day."

(5) Elmira *Daily Advertiser*, June 1, 1869.

(6) *Yates County Chronicle*, June 3, 1869.

(7) *Yates County Chronicle*, June 2, 1870.

(8) "Oration May 30, 1870," 10-11, 13-14, John Tuttle and Arvilla Raplee Andrews Papers, Box 3, Folder 10, Collection #3790, Cornell University Library. The text of Andrews' speech was not quoted in the *Yates County Chronicle*. I am assuming that he delivered the speech as he wrote it.

(9) Elmira *Daily Advertiser*, January 23, 1880.

(10) Elmira *Daily Advertiser*, January 23, 1880. Annual reunions of course were not the only times that veterans of the 179th got together. Many of the veterans remained in the hometowns that they had returned to and lived near fellow veterans of the 179th. In writing a supporting letter for John Price's pension application, Charles Beckwith noted that he and Price saw each other once a month. "We always talk of war times as is customary for the soldiers to do." (Letter dated April 23, 1888 from Charles Beckwith to John C. Black, John H. Price Pension File)

(11) Elmira *Daily Advertiser*, January 23, 1880.

(12) Elmira *Daily Advertiser*, February 18, 1881.

(13) Elmira *Daily Advertiser*, February 18, 1881.

(14) Regimental History, passim.

(15) Elmira *Daily Advertiser*, October 12, 1883. The reference to Spencer as "Lieutenant" was either a lighthearted comment by Norton or an error by the reporter.

(16) *Ontario Repository and Messenger*, September 11, 1884; Lesley Gordon, *A Broken Regiment: The 16th Connecticut's Civil War*, 5.

(17) Elmira *Daily Advertiser*, September 30, 1886; Elmira *Daily Advertiser*, September 28, 1894.

(18) Elmira *Daily Advertiser*, September 26, 1889.

(19) Marten, 251.

(20) *Ibid.*, 73.

(21) *Ibid.*, 265; Hess, 185-90.

(22) Wilkenson, 369.

(23) Notice, "23rd New York Volunteers," Folder 4, Chemung County Historical Museum. The 23rd New York and the 107th New York organized a joint railroad fare – $7.80 for a round trip to Antietam and $8.80 for a round trip to Gettysburg. (*Ibid.*)

(24) Marten, 135.

(25) Petersburg National Battlefield, crater site.

(26) Elmira *Daily Advertiser*, September 28, 1894.

(27) Elmira *Daily Advertiser*, September 30, 1897.

(28) Elmira *Daily Advertiser*, September 30, 1892.

(29) *Elmira Daily Gazette and Free Press*, September 28, 1893; *Elmira Daily Advertiser*, September 29, 1893.

(30) See photo; *Elmira Daily Gazette and Free Press*, September 27, 1894; *Elmira Daily News*, September 27, 1894; Undated [1894] and unsourced newspaper clipping, Author's collection.

(31) New York State Archives, B1706, Box 30, Folder 12. L.H. Bowers and Edward Lounsbery.

(32) Edwin Ellsworth Rutan's middle name came from Col. Ephraim Elmer Ellsworth, the Union's first war hero. His first name may have come from Secretary of War Edwin Stanton or Company A's Sgt. Edwin Lamberson.

(33) Regimental History, passim. Norton died in 1897 and Spencer had been committed to a mental hospital in 1891.

(34) *Elmira Daily Gazette and Free Press*, September 25, 1902.

(35) Fox, *Regimental Losses*, 122; Gordon, *A Broken Regiment*, 235-36, n.5; Michael P. Musick, "The Little Regiment: Civil War Units and Commands," *Prologue*, Vol. 27, No. 2 (Summer 1995), 1-2.

(36) *The Chemung Valley Reporter*, October 3, 1907; *Elmira Daily Advertiser*, September 27, 1907; *Elmira Star-Gazette*, September 26, 1907.

(37) "The Army Civil War Campaign Medal"; "Civil War Campaign Medal," Wikipedia.

(38) Chemung County Historical Museum.

(39) Elmira *Daily Advertiser*, September 29, 1911.

(40) *Elmira Star-Gazette*, September 26, 1912.

(41) *Ibid.*

(42) Elmira *Star Gazette*, July 30, 1914.

(43) *The [Elmira] Telegram*, September 3, 1916; *The Elmira Advertiser*, September 1, 1916. See also *The Elmira Advertiser*, August 27, 1915.

(44) *Penn Yan Democrat*, August 31, 1917.

(45) *Elmira Star-Gazette*, August 13, 1917; *Elmira Star-Gazette*, August 28, 1919; *Elmira Telegram*, August 29, 1920; *Elmira Star-Gazette*, August 25, 1921; *Elmira Star-Gazette*, August 20, 1923.

(46) Elmira *Daily Advertiser*, August 29, 1924; Elmira *Daily Advertiser*, August 28, 1925.

(47) CMSR, Edwin Morris.

(48) Elmira *Star Gazette*, May 25, 1943; Elmira *Daily Advertiser*, May 25, 1943.

(49) Elmira *Star Gazette*, May 25, 1943.

(50) Elmira *Star Gazette*, May 25, 1943.

Conclusion

Dean Jr., Eric T., "Reflections on the 'Trauma of War' and *Shook Over Hell*," *Civil War History*, Vol. 59, No. 4 (December 2013), 414.

Dunkelman, Mark H., *War's Relentless Hand: Twelve Tales of Civil War Soldiers*, Louisiana State University Press: Baton Rouge (2006).

Hess, Earl J., *In the Trenches at Petersburg: Field Fortifications & Confederate Defeat*, University of North Carolina Press: Chapel Hill (2009).

Howe, Thomas J., *The Petersburg campaign: Wasted Valor, June 15-18, 1864*, H.E. Howard, Inc.: Lynchburg, Virginia (Second Edition 1988).

Keegan, John, *The Face of Battle*, The Viking Press: New York (1976).

Liddell Hart, Basil Henry, *Sherman: Soldier, Realist, American*, Da Capo Press (1993 originally published 1929).

McPherson, James, *For Cause and Comrades: Why Men Fought in the Civil War*, Oxford University Press: New York (1997).

Phisterer, Frederick, *New York in the War of the Rebellion 1861 to 1865*, D.B. Lyon Company, State Printers: Albany, New York (Third Ed. 1912).

(1) Liddell Hart, 310. During correspondence between Sherman and the Mayor of Atlanta, Sherman wrote "You cannot qualify war in harsher terms than I will. War is cruelty and you cannot refine it; ..." From this Liddell Hart writes
... contains the nearest recorded words to the saying which all know who hardly know the name of Sherman – "War is hell." Earlier still at Jackson he had used the words "War is barbarism," and the theme was so constantly in his mind and on his lips that he may well have used the more "historic" phrase in informal addresses. He gave enough to gatherings of his old soldiers after the war to incline us to accept the testimony of his hearers that he did.
Thus, the phrase "War is hell" is literally hearsay.

(2) Goodwin, 628-29; *The Dunkirk Journal*, June 24, 1865.

(3) Phisterer, 4029; Regimental History, 5-6. See also Adams, *Living Hell*, 11-12. The number of amputees is based on the carded medical records. (Soldiers who died after amputation are not included.) The estimate for the number of widows is based on a sample of 117 hospital cards that indicated that 46% of the men of the 179th New York were married. This is much higher than the percentage for the Union army as a whole – 30%. McPherson, viii.

(4) Dunkelman, *Twelve Tales*, xii.

(5) See Hess, 264. On April 2, 1865, Grant sent the following message to Sheridan: "Wright and Parke attacked at daylight this morning and carried the enemy's works in their front. Wright's troops, some of them, pushed through to the Boydton road and cut the telegraph wire. Ord is now going in to re-enforce Wright, and Humphreys is feeling for a soft place in the line south of Hatcher's Run. I think nothing now is wanting but the approach of your force from the west to finish up the job on this side." OR 46(3): 488.

(6) Howe.

(7) *The Hornellsville Tribune*, August 25, 1864. In its report on the 179th's first reunion in 1880, the Elmira *Daily Advertiser* commented that the 179th "was badly used at the Poplar Grove Church fight," presumably a reference to sending the 179th into action when so many of its soldiers were raw recruits. (Elmira *Daily Advertiser*, January 23, 1880) The 16th Connecticut had been rushed into battle at Antietam only three weeks after being mustered in and Lt. Henry Beach used the same phrase that the 16th Connecticut had been "badly used." (Gordon, *A Broken Regiment*, 38)

(8) OR, 40(1): 128; OR, 42(3): 867, 896.

(9) Bartleby.com, Nonfiction, Ralph Waldo Emerson, The Complete Works, (1904), Vol. XI Miscellaneous, XVII. Dedication of the Soldiers' Monument in Concord.

(10) Grant, Vol. 1, 170. Grant's complete statement was that a "truthful history" "will do credit to the courage, endurance and soldierly ability of the American citizen, *no matter what section of the country he hailed from, or in what ranks he fought.*" (emphasis added) Thus Grant recognized that the South was also defended by citizen-soldiers who shared the same political tradition as the North. Grant concluded the point by stating:

The justice of the cause which in the end prevailed, will, I doubt not, come to be acknowledged by every citizen in the land, in time. For the present, and so long as there are living witnesses of the great war of sections, there will be people who will not be consoled for the loss of a cause which they believed to be holy. As time passes, people, even of the South, will begin to wonder how it was possible that their ancestors ever fought for or justified institutions which acknowledged the right of property in man. (*Ibid.*)

Appendix One

Petersburg Engagements

(1) Earl Hess, *In the Trenches at Petersburg: Field Fortifications & Confederate Defeat*, The University of North Carolina Press: Chapel Hill (2009), xvii.

(2) Hess, xvii, 25-28; Phisterer, 4029; *The History of the 179th Regiment N.Y.S.V., Rebellion of 1861-65*, E.D. Norton, Printer: Ithaca, N.Y. (1900) refers to "Before Petersburg, Va., June 16, 1864" and the "Assault of Petersburg, Va., June 16 and 19, 1864" as separate "engagements" of the 179th. (at 6) The 179th arrived "before Petersburg" the afternoon of June 16, but did not see action that day. After the attacks on June 17, Willcox's and Potter's divisions of the Ninth Corps did push the Confederate troops further west on June 18, but Ledlie's First Division, which included the 179th, essentially remained in the rear. (Hess, 29-33) On June 19, the 179th "rested". (Diary of William B. Larzelere, June 19, 1864)

(3) Hess, xvii-xviii; Regimental History, 6.

(4) Hess, xviii; Regimental History, 6.

(5) *Ibid.*

(6) Hess, xviii, 91; Regimental History, 6; Phisterer, 4029.

(7) Hess, xviii; Chris Calkins, "The Battle of Weldon Railroad" (or Globe Tavern")," *Blue & Gray*, Vol. XXIII, Issue 5, (Winter 2007), 7-23; Bruce Venter, "Hancock the (Not So) Superb: The Second Battle of Reams' Station, August 25, 1864," *Blue & Gray*, Vol. XXIII, Issue 5 (Winter 2007), 42-50; Regimental History, 6; Phisterer, 4029.

(8) Hess, xix; Richard Sommers, *Richmond Redeemed: The Siege at Petersburg*, Savas Beatie LLC: El Dorado, California (2014), 275-277; Regimental History, 6; Phisterer, 4029.

(9) Hess, xix; Regimental History, 6.

(10) Hess, xix; Hampton Newsome, *Richmond Must Fall: The Richmond-Petersburg campaign, October 1864*, The Kent State University Press: Kent, Ohio (2013), 133, 275-277, 293; Regimental History, 6; Phisterer, 4029.

(11) Hess, xix; Thomas Grace, "Wreck the Weldon Railroad," *America's Civil War*, Vol. 27, No. 6 (January 2015), 54; Memoranda, Regimental Books, Vol. 1; Regimental History, 6.

(12) Hess, xix; Regimental History, 6.

(13) Hess, xx; Regimental History 6.

(14) Hess, xx; Charles R. Bowery, Jr., *The Richmond-Petersburg campaign, 1864-65*, Praeger: Santa Barbara, California (2014), 130-142; Regimental History, 6.

(15) Hess, xx; A. Wilson Greene, "April 2, 1865: Day of Decision at Petersburg," *Blue & Gray*, Vol. XVIII, No. 3 (February 2001), 49-50; Regimental History, 6; Phisterer, 4029.

(16) Memoranda, Regimental Books, Vol. 1.

Appendix Seven

James C. Rutan's Pension Application

Vinovskis, Maris A. (Ed.), *Toward a Social History of the American Civil War: Exploratory Essays*, Cambridge University Press: New York (1990).

Wilson, Sven Eric, "Prejudice & Policy: Racial Discrimination in the Union army Disability Pension System, 1865-1906", *American Journal of Public Health*, Vol. 0, No. 2010 (February 10, 2010)

(1) Undated letter from James C. Rutan, to the U.S. Pension Commissioner, received by the Department of the Interior, Pension Division on July 26, 1879, James C. Rutan Pension File, 138 (Hereafter "JCRPF." Page references are to the author's numbered copy of the file). Rutan added a "P.S.": "Please send me blanks for Commutation of Rations while on furlough [in 1864]." It is not clear whether he ever filed that claim.

(2) Affidavit of James C. Rutan dated July 24, 1879, JCRPF, 135-37.

(3) Declaration for Original Invalid Pension, dated September 16, 1879, JCRPF, 35.

(4) *Ibid.*

(5) *Ibid.*

(6) *Elmira Weekly Gazette*, March 10, 1864.

(7) Form for Invalid Claim for Pension (printed instructions), JCRPF, 36.

(8) War Department, Adjutant General's Office, March 23, 1881, JCRPF, 97; War Department, Surgeon General's Office, Record and Pension Division, to the Commissioner of Pensions, April

9, 1881, JCRPF, 88.

(9) War Department, Surgeon General's Office, Record and Pension Division, to the Commissioner of Pensions, April 9, 1881, JCRPF, 88.

(10) Examining Surgeon Certificate, App. No. 310,919, June 15, 1881, JCRPF, 43; Enlistment Form, Rutan CMSR.

(11) Letter from Jno. Mitchell, U.S. Senate to the Commissioner of Pensions, dated January 14, 1882, JCRPF, 42.

(12) Affidavit of Dr. Mary Baldwin dated January 7, 1882, JCRPF, 41.

(13) January 19, 1882 file note, JCRPF, 24.

(14) Affidavit of James C. Rutan dated August 9, 1882, JCRPF, 105.

(15) Affidavit of James A. Christie dated July 25, 1882, JCRPF, 110-11.

(16) Affidavit of Stephen Compton dated July 25, 1882, JCRPF, 131; Affidavit of Harry Gardner dated July 25, 1882, JCRPF, 112-113.

(17) Affidavit of Dr. Orlando Groom dated July 25, 1882, JCRPF, 10; Statement of Dr. Orlando Groom dated August 8, 1882, JCRPF 12.

(18) Affidavit of William E. Wines dated July 29, 1882, JCRPF, 129-30.

(19) Affidavit of James C. Rutan dated August 9, 1882, JCRPF, 109.

(20) Lieutenat Colonel Doty was mortally wounded in the assault at Petersburg on April 2, 1865; Major Sloan was mortally wounded in the assault on June 17, 1864; and Major Barton was killed in the Battle of the Crater. (CMRs) Captain Terrill, who was ultimately promoted to Lt. Col. after Rutan was wounded and survived the war apparently had died in 1876. (Civil War and Later Veterans Pension Index, fold3.com) Rutan was confused in his reference to Cumberland Heights–the detachment from the 179th was at Cumberland Heights during the June 17, 1864 assault.

(21) Carpenter and Farr CMRs.

(22) Affidavit of Joseph W. Robinson dated February 20, 1884, JCRPF, 7-8; Affidavit of James Farr dated January 22, 1884, JCRPF, 115.

(23) Department of the Interior, Pension Office to Adjutant General, U.S.A. dated October 13, 1882, JCRPF, 103.

(24) War Department, Adjutant General's Office dated January 19, 1883, JCRPF, 102. This response was stamped received by the Pension Office the next day (JCRPF, 103), so it appears that interdepartmental mail in Washington moved quickly in that day.

(25) Department of the Interior, Pension Office to Postmaster, Horseheads, Chemung Co., N.Y. dated October 1882, JCRPF, 98.

(26) Letter from L.L. Curtis, Postmaster, to Commissioner of Pensions dated October 17, 1882, JCRPF, 99. The letter was stamped received by the Pension Office on October 19, 1882 (JCRPF, 98), indicating prompt mail service.

(27) Examining Surgeon's Certificate in the Case of an Original Applicant No. 310.919 dated October 18, 1882, JCRPF, 67.

(28) War Department, Adjutant General's Office, dated January 29, 1883, JCRPF, 126.

(29) February 11, 1883 file note, JCRPF, 24.

(30) James C. Rutan Additional Evidence: Inability Affidavit dated March 5, 1884, JCRPF, 33-34. However in his July 24, 1879 affidavit he had said that he had been treated by a Dr. Nichols in Minnesota. JCRPF, 137.

(31) Affidavit of Edwin Lambertson dated March 7, 1883, JCRPF, 117-19.

(32) Affidavit of William E. Wines dated August 29,1883, JCRPF, 5-6.

(33) Affidavit of Joel M. Jansen dated September 8, 1883, JCRPF, 77-78; Philena M. Brees, Public Member Trees, Ancestry.com. In the original set of copies the author ordered from the National Archives, this affidavit is missing some text. A complete copy is in the second set the author ordered at 49-50.

(34) Pension Bureau to Adjutant General, dated March 22, 1884, JCRPF, 76.

(35) Adjutant General to Pension Bureau, dated March 24, 1884, JCRPF, 75.

(36) Affidavit of Stephen Compton dated February 20, 1884, JCRPF, 100-101.

(37) Affidavit of James Farr dated January 20, 1884, JCRPF, 115.

(38) Affidavit of J.W. Robinson dated February 20, 1884, JCRPF, 7-8.

(39) Pension Bureau to Adjutant General, dated March 22, 1884, JCRPF, 76; Adjutant General to Pension Bureau, dated March 24, 1884, JCRPF, 75.

(40) JCRPF at 83. "Hon. Jno. J. Mitchell called up this case on Mar. 24, 1884 and should be informed of its adjudication." The Pension Office Form had the following instructions at the top: This slip should be attached to brief in admitted cases that have been called by members of present Congress."

(41) March 20, 1884 file note, JCRPF, 25.

(42) Affidavit of James M. Ormiston and David W. Budd dated April 21, 1884, JCRPF, 47-48; Undated [circa February 1911] and unsourced newspaper in author's personal collection; Fanny C. Brees, Public Member Trees, Ancestry.com; Peter Rutan of Sullivan County, posted by James Keegan, October 17, 2003, GenForum, Genealogy.com.

(43) Worksheet, JCRPF, 84; File Jacket Label, JCRPF, 141.

(44) Worksheet, JCRPF, 32.

(45) Department of the Interior, Pension Office, October 13, 1884, JCRPF, 52.

(46) Worksheet, JCRPF, 32.

(47) File Jacket Label, JCRPF, 141; Worksheet, JCRPF, 32.

(48) Declaration for the Increase of an Invalid Pension, Pension Certificate 266.854, dated June 27, 1887, JCRPF, 81.

(49) Surgeon's Certificate in the Case of James C. Rutan, October 12, 1887, United States of America, Department of the Interior, Bureau of Pensions, Certificate No. 266.854, dated November 5, 1887, JCRPF, 63; Certificate, JCRPF, 140.

(50) Declaration for the Increase of an Invalid Pension dated June 11, 1890, JCRPF, 38.

(51) Physician's Affidavit of E. Howe Davis dated July 2, 1890, JCRPF, 49; Worksheet, JCRPF, 40.

(52) 1891 Wilmington City Directory, 481; 1892 Wilmington City Directory, 549, Ancestry.com.

(53) Declaration for the Increase of an Invalid Pension, November 2, 1897, JCRPF, 79.

(54) Surgeon's Certificate, October 26, 1898, JCRPF, 54; Worksheet, JCRPF, 9.

(55) 1900 federal census, City of Philadelphia, County of Philadelphia, State of Pennsylvania, Ancestry.com.

(56) Declaration for the Increase of an Invalid Pension, May 4, 1905, JCRPF, 28; Cover sheet stamped "Nov 16 1905 REJECTED", JCRPF 27.

(57) Surgeon's Certificate, August 17, 1905, JCRPF, 15.

(58) Wilson, 3.

ILLUSTRATIONS & MAPS

Chapter One

Volunteer Enlistment Form (p.1)
Scanned by author from Stephen Compton CMSR, National Archives

Recruiting Advertisment (p.4)
Penn Yan Democrat, February 26, 1864, New York State Library

Chapter Two

Photograph of William Gregg (p.10)
Col. William M. Gregg previously served with the 23rd
New York Infantry Regiment of the Union army.
Descended from the John Gregg family (an early valley family), Gregg was a saddler
  and harness maker in Elmira.
He also served as the county's sheriff from 1858-61.

William M. Gregg, d. 1881
Date Created/Published: [no date recorded on caption card]
Reproduction Number: LC-USZ62-66074
Rights Advisory: No known restrictions on publication.
Repository: Library of Congress Prints and Photographs Division

[a]http://www.loc.gov/pictures/item/2003680449/[/a]

Photograph of John Andrews (p.12)
John Andrews Papers
Collection 3790
Cornell University

Photograph of William Bird, Jr. (p.16)
New York State Military Museum
PA.1999.0014.0384

United States. Army. New York Infantry Regiment, 37th, (1861-1863)

Residence was not listed; 30 years old.
Enlisted on 5/9/1861 at Ellicottville, NY as a 1st Sergeant.
On 6/7/1861 he mustered into "I" Co. NY 37th Infantry
He was Mustered Out on 6/22/1863 at New York, NY
He was listed as: Wounded 5/31/1862 Fair Oaks, VA
Promotions:
 2nd Lieut 5/5/1862

1st Lieut 9/13/1862 (As of Co. H)
Capt 12/2/1862
Intra Regimental Company Transfers: 9/13/1862 from company I to company H
Sources used by Historical Data Systems, Inc.:
New York: Report of the Adjutant-General
(c) Historical Data Systems, Inc.

[a]http://www.civilwardata.com[/a]

Chapter Three

Drawing of Barracks No. 1, Elmira Miliary Depot (circa 1861) (p.20)
National Archives, Records of the Quartermaster General, Records Group 92, 1.158-p

Photograph of Arnot Barracks 1864 (p.21)
Chemung County Historical Society

Camp No. 1 was named after John Arnot.
It was one of four camps in Elmira and the only one remaining as a training center by 1864.

Photograph of Giles Holden (p.22)
NYS Military Museum
PA.1999.0014.1288

United States. Army. New York Infantry Regiment, 179th, (1864-1865)

Giles H. Holden
Age, 35 years
Enrolled at Batavia, to serve three years, and mustered in
  as private, Co. F , February 26, 1864
  as second lieutenant, May 25, 1864
  as captain, Co. H, September 10, 1864
Mustered out with company, June 8, 1865, near Alexandria, Va

Commissioned second lieutenant, June 28, 1864, with rank from May 2, 1864, original
Captain, September 16, 1864, with rank from August 8, 1864, vice A . A. Terrill promoted
Major (not mustered) May 17, 1865, with rank from April 2, 1865, vice A. A. Terrill promoted

Photograph of William Hemstreet (p.30)
New York State Military Museum
PA.1999.0014.1291

William J. Hemstreet
Company G

Age, 31 years
Enrolled at Lockport, to serve three years
Mustered in as first lieutenant, Co. A, One Hundred and Eightieth Infantry, July 20, 1864
Transferred to Co. G, this regiment, July 23, 1864
Discharged to date, May 15, 1865
Prior service, second lieutenant, Co. F, One Hundred and Fourth Infantry.
Commissioned first lieutenant, September 27, 1861, with rank from July 18, 1864, original.

Chapter Four

Map of Southern Tier Counties (p.32)
from Map of the State of New York, 1865 showing the Population of Towns and Wards

New York State Library

Photo of Main Street, Penn Yan, New York (p.33)
Courtesy of Yates County History Center

Photograph of Scene in Horseheads 1860 (p.35)
Monisor Solomon's Rope Walking (June 23, 1860)

Horseheads Historical Society
scan of a photocopy of a photocopy

Photograph of Lake Street , Elmira
"Lake Street looking north from Water Street around 1858. ... Lake Street was once the main
business district in Elmira."

Michael Horigan, "Antebellum Elmira 1850-1860 Part One," [tb]The Chemung
Historical Journal[te], Vol. 48, No. 1 September 2002, 5272.

Chemung County Historical Society

Photograph of Buffalo circa 1860 (p.39)
The Buffalo History Museum

Photograph of Newfield, New York (p.41)
Courtesy of The History Center in Tompkins County

Photograph of Danby Federated Church (p.42)
General view from Southwest - Danby Federated Church 1859, Danby Road, Danby, Tompkins
County, NY.
Rights Advisory: No known restrictions.
Repository: Library of Congress Prints and Photographs Division
http://www.loc.gove/pictures/item/ny1327.photos1238506p/

Chapter Five

Lithograph of Soldiers Rest, Washington, D.C. (p.43)

Creator(s): Magnus, Charles, publisher
Date Created/Published: [New York and Washington, D.C.]
  Published by Chas. Mangus, 12 Frankfort St., New York,
  & 520 Seventh Street, Washington, D.C., c1864.
Summary: Print shows Union barracks between a railroad (bottom left) and the United
  States Capitol (top right). Soldiers in the camp are waving to soldiers riding on
  top of the railroad cars.
Reproduction Number: LC-DIG-ds-03472
Rights Advisory: No known restrictions on publication.
Repository: Library of Congress Prints and Photographs Division

[a]http://www.loc.gov/pictures/item/2011647024/[/a]

Photograph of Quartermaster's Wharf, Alexandria, Va.

Date Created/Published: photographed between 1861 and 1865, printed
  between 1880 and 1889
Summary: Photograph shows stacks of wood and cotton bales on the landing;
  steamer "John Brooks" in the distance.
Reproduction Number: LC-DIG-ppmsca-34823
Rights Advisory: No known restrictions on publication.
Repository: Library of Congress Prints and Photographs Division

[a]http://www.loc.gov/pictures/item/2014645755/[/a]

Chapter Six

Photograph of General Grant & his war horse Cincinatti (p.53)

Date Created/Published: Washington, D.C. :
  J. F. Jarvis' Stereoscopic Views, 135 Penn. Ave.,
  [1864 June 4, printed later]
Summary: Stereograph of General Grant in uniform, standing beside his horse, "Cincinnati."
Reproduction Number: LC-DIG-stereo-1s02872
Rights Advisory: No known restrictions on publication.
Repository: Library of Congress Prints and Photographs Division

[a]http://www.loc.gov/pictures/item/2011661093/[/a]

Photograph of Henry Menhenitt after the war (p.56)

Scanned by the author from Henry Menhenitt Pension File, National Archives.

Photograph of James River, Va. Pontoon bridge (p.57)

Creator(s): Gardner, James, b. 1832, photographer
Date Created/Published: 1864 June.
Reproduction Number: LC-DIG-cwpb-03994
Rights Advisory: No known restrictions on publication.
Repository: Library of Congress Prints and Photographs Division

[a]http://www.loc.gov/pictures/item/cwp2003000499/PP/[/a]

Chapter Seven

Map of the Petersburg Defenses--June 1864 (p.59)

adapted from Michler scanned at the National Archives
for the author July 2013

Showing the Dimmock Line, the intermediate Hagood Line, adopted for just a few days as reinforcements from the Army of Northern Virginia arrived, and the Harris Line, which formed the eastern front until April 3, 1865.

Chapter Eight

Photograph of John B. Sloan (p.69)
New York State Military Museum
PA.1999.0014.1287

United States. Army. New York Infantry Regiment, 179th, (1864-1865)
United States. Army. New York Infantry Regiment, 31st, (1861-1863)

John Barnet Sloan
Age, 26 years.
Enrolled at Wayland, to serve three years, and mustered in as major, May 26,1864
Killed in action, June 17, 1864, at Petersburg, Va
Prior service, as major, Thirty-first Infantry.
Commissioned major, July 9, 1864, with rank from May 17, 1864, original.

Photograph of Varnum Northup
Ancestry.com, "Varnum J. Northup," Barker-Northup member tree

Chapter Nine

Sketch of Mine, outline of crater (p.81)

Mine Sketch Scaled (p.82)

derived from Report 190, OR (40):556-563
Lt. Col. Henry Pleasants, 48th PA Infantry

The original drawing on page 559 shows a vertical scale of 20 feet to the inch where the horizontal is 100 feet to the inch. This allows a compact view which fits well on a sheet of paper. The version here compresses the vertical by a factor of 5, so the visual effect is more natural.

Chapter Ten

Sketch Ninth Corps Into The Crater (p.90)
From Frank Leslie's *Illustrations*, page 45.

The full caption for the engraving reads:

"THE NINTH ARMY CORPS charging into the crater at Petersburg, Va., July 30, 1864. -- Assault of General James H. Ledlie's brigade after the explosion of the mine. The assaulting party was chosen by lot from the colored troops of the Ninth corps and fell upon Ledlie. His men dashed over the lip of the crater immediately upon the lifting of the smoke from theexplosion and plunged wildly into its depths, then found to be a yawning chasm 185 feet long, 97 feet wide, and 30 feet deep. The explosion had buried the Confederate batteries and separated the troops oneither side of the crater, where they reorganized, asbrigade after brigade followed into the crater, crowded in disorganized mass. A hand-to-hand fight ensued, when a cross fire from the Confederate batteries effectually emptied the crater; only 30 menand three stands of color were captured. General Meadereported 4,400 killed, wounded, and missing. General Beauregard gives the Confederate loss as 1,172.
From a sketch by A. McCallum."

Observations:
It was Ledlie's First Division, not a brigade, and was all white.

The USCT brigades formed Ferrero's Fourth Division, last into the assault.

Andrew McCallum's sketch can be found in the Becker Collection in Boston, MA. McCallum was a private in the 50th NY Volunteers, assigned to Willcox's Third Division. There are roughly 120 soldiers shown in the this sketch.

Photograph of Edward Gyles (p.98)
Scanned by author from Edward Gyles Pension File, National Archives.

Chapter Eleven

Court-martial Transcript (p. 106)
Scanned by author from Newton Spencer file copy, U. S. Army Military History Institute, CWTIColl, Pvts court-martial papers 1864.

Photograph of Robert Potter (p.112)

Gen. Robert B Potter

Date Created/Published: [between 1860 and 1870]
Reproduction Number: LC-DIG-cwpb-05593
Rights Advisory: No known restrictions on publication.
Repository: Library of Congress Prints and Photographs Division

[a]http://www.loc.gov/pictures/item/cwp2003002514/PP/[/a]

Chapter Twelve

Sketch of Blick's Station (p.117)

Siege of Petersburg - Scenes of the Construction of Grant's Railroad. Terminus and Junction with Weldon RR at Blick Station

Ref No.: (Becker Collection)CW-AM-VA-10/1/64b
Artist: McCallum, Andrew.
Date: October 1, 1864.
Medium: graphite on wove paper ;
Original Size: 12.25 x 2.75 and 6.75 in.
Transcribed Text:

Recto: [Four vignettes, each with a caption]
 "Crossing Jerusalem Plank Road
 // [Pass]ing the Gurley House
 // Looking down the Weldon RR from the junction with Grant's RR at Blick House
 // Terminus and junction with Weldon RR at Blick Station.
Verso: no text.

Condition: Large section torn from upper left (prob. by artist); loss of paper at left
 lower corner; dog ear at lower right; folds.
Location: Petersburg, Dinwiddie, Virginia, United States

Chapter Thirteen

Photograph of Joseph W. Robinson (p.120)
with handwritten note of James C. Rutan.
W. L. Sutton, Photographer, Hornellsville, N.Y.

Author's Collection

Photograph of Martin V. Doty (p.121)
New York State Military Museum
PA.1999.0014.1292

Martin V. Doty
Company B

United States. Army. New York Infantry Regiment, 179th, (1864-1865)

Martin V. Doty
Age, 31 years. Enrolled, March 31, 1861, at Hornellsville, to serve three years,
and mustered in as private, Co. C, April 23, 1864;
promoted hospital steward, same date;
mustered in; as first lieutenant, Co. C, January 16, 1865, as captain Co. B, April 22, 1865
mustered out with company, June 8, 1865, near Alexandria, Va.;

prior service, as first sergeant, Co. G, Twenty third Infantry.
Commissioned first lieutenant, January 13, 1865, with rank from December 23, 1864,
vice L. Force, promoted; captain, March 30, 1865, with rank from February 21, 1865,
vice G. H . Holden promoted.

Photograph of Edgar Lattin (p.126)
New York State Military Museum
PA.1999.0014.1293

Edgar Lattin

Age, 22 years. Enlisted, February 29, 1864, at Dunkirk, to serve three years.
Mustered in as private, Co. D, May 11, 1864.
Promoted corporal, May 13, 1864.
Wounded in action, July 30, 1864, at Petersburg, Va.
Discharged, December 3, 1864
Prior service, in Co. B, One Hundred and Fifty Fourth Infantry (1862-1863)

Photograph of Martin Wilkins (p.128)
also Wilkens
New York State Military Museum

PA.1999.0014.1289

Martin Wilkin
Company F

Martin Wilkin
Age, 21 years.
Enlisted, March 28, 1864, at Benton, to serve three years
Mustered in as private, Co. F, May 25, 1864
Mustered out with company, June 8, 1865, near Alexandria, Va.

Jacob Hausner Furlough document (p.131)
Scanned by author from Jacob Hausner CMSR, National Archives.

Chapter Fourteen

Photograph of William Gregg (p.132)
No data on photographer.
Donated by author to New York State Military Museum

Photograph of Regimental Guidon (p.133)
New York State Military Museum

Photograph of William Howell (p. 137)
William Howell

Company I
Tolles & Seely, Photographists, 388-40 Owego Street,
Ithaca, New York

Donated by author to New York State Military Museum.

Photograph of "Fitz" Culver (p. 138)
New York State Military Museum

[a]http://dmna.ny.gov/historic/reghist/civil/infantry/179thInf/179thInfPersonCulver.htm[/a]

Photograph of George Pratt (p.140)
New York State Military Museum
PA.1999.0014.1294

George Lancing Pratt

Company A

Age, 23 years. Enlisted at Ulysses, to serve one year
Mustered in as private, Co. A, August 30, 1864
Mustered out with company, June 8, 1865, near Alexandria, Va

Chapter Fifteen

Sketch of Poplar Spring Church (p.142)

Frank Leslie's Scenes and Portraits of the Civil War,
Mrs. Frank Leslie, Publisher: New York (1894), page 474.

Author's collection

Photograph of Elihu Linkletter (p.147)

Ancestry.com, provided to the author
by Corinne DeGraaf

Chapter Sixteen

Lithograph of Salisbury Prison (p.149)

Bird's eye view of Confederate prison pen at Salisbury, N.C., taken in 1864.
Contributor Names: Kraus, C. A.
Created / Published: Boston ; New York : J.H. Bufford's Sons Lith., c1886.
Repository: Library of Congress Geography and Map Division

[a]http://hdl.loc.gov/loc.gmd/g3904s.cw0317350[/a]

[a]http://lccn.loc.gov/84692279[/a]

Photograph of Charles Johnson (p.151)

Scanned by author from E-J Workers' Review,
Vol. One, Number 6 (August 20, 1919)

Photograph of Daniel Hazelton (p.160)
New York State Military Museum
PA.1999.0014.2396

Daniel S. Hazelton
Company C

Age, 31 years.
Enlisted, March 18, 1864, at Dix, to serve three years

Mustered in as private, Co, C, April 23, 1864
Captured in action, July 30, 1864, at Petersburg, Va
Paroled, no date
Mustered out, May 25, 1865, at Elmira, N.Y.

Also borne as Daniel C. Hazelton

Photograph of Howland Washburn (p.161)
Enlisted Feb. 26, 1864 for three years
Age: 34 Occupation: farmer

Donated by author to New York State Military Museum.

Chapter Seventeen

Photograph of Ninth Corps Chaplains (p. 162)
Petersburg, Va. Chaplains of the 9th Corps
Date Created/Published: 1864 October.
Summary: Photograph from the main eastern theater of war, the siege of Petersburg,
 June 1864-April 1865.
Reproduction Number: LC-DIG-cwpb-03666
Rights Advisory: No known restrictions on publication.
Repository: Library of Congress Prints and Photographs Division
[a]http://www.loc.gov/pictures/item/cwp2003000584/PP/[/a]

Photograph of Ezra Tinker (p.163)
Enlisted September 8, 1864 for one year
Age: 22 Occupation: teacher

Photograph taken 1907, Mansfield, Pennsylvania.
Donated by author to New York State Military Museum.

Chapter Eighteen

Sketch of Working Parties (p.169)
Ref No.: (Becker Collection)CW-EM-VA-9/10/64
Artist: Mullen, E. F.
Date: September 9, 1864.
Medium: Graphite on heavy gauge wove paper ;
Original Size: 6.5 x 13.25 in.
Transcribed Text:

Recto: No text.
Verso: "In Front of Petersburg. Working Party Going through the Covered Way to the Trenches
at Night."

Condition: Vertical folds; dog ear at lower right corner; ripping along right margin.
Location: Petersburg, Dinwiddie, Virginia, United States

Photograph of Benjamin Hadley (p.170)
New York State Military Museum
PA.1999.0014.1286

Benjamin F. Hadley
Company F

Age, 19 years.
Enlisted at Dryden, to serve one year
Mustered in as private, Co. F, September 2, 1864
Wounded while on picket, February 1, 1865, at Petersburg, Va
Discharged for wounds, June 10, 1865.

Photograph of Elias Beach (p. 175)
Enlisted August 9, 1864 for one year
Age: 20 Occupation: farmer

Provided to the author by Donald Tubbs.

Chapter Nineteen

Sketch of Firing Squad (p.177)

Siege of Petersburg - Military Execution of a Deserter near Peebles House, Virginia

Ref No.: (Becker)CW-AM-VA-10/14/64
Artist: McCallum, Andrew.
Date: October 14, 1864.
Medium: graphite on wove paper ;
Original Size: 9.5 x 6.5 in.
Transcribed Text:

Recto: no text.
Verso: "Military execution of a Deserter taken in the enemies ranks belonging to the
2nd Div. 9th A.C. he was shot near the Peebles House, Va. October 14 1864
- this is a correct sketch, a great many soldiers witnessing the sight."

Condition: Two vertical folds; yellowing.
Location: Petersburg, Dinwiddie, Virginia, United States

Chapter Twenty

Political Cartoon--1864 Election (p.190)
Harpers Weekly, October 8, 1864, p. 656
Author's collection

Chapter Twenty-One

Map of Hancock Station/Jones House Vicinity (p.199)

adapted from Michler for the time frame, with later fortifications and entrenched lines removed.

Sketch of Hancock Station (p. 199)
Harper's Weekly, December 24, 1864, p. 821

Author's collection

Chapter Twenty-Two

Photograph of James C. and Amelia Breese Rutan (April 1864)

Author's collection

Chapter Twenty-Three

Sketch of April 2, 1865 Assault (p.218)
Sketched by A.R. Waud

Harper's Weekly, May 27, 1865
Author's collection

Photograph of Albert Havens (p.225)

Enlisted September 5, 1864 for one year
Age: 32 Occupation: farmer

Scanned by author from Albert Havens CMSR, National Archives.

Photograph of Smith McMasters and wife (p.225)
Provided to author by Pam Anderson

Chapter Twenty-Four

Photograph of Grand Review (p.237)
Washington, D.C. Maj. Gen. Horatio G. Wright, staff and units of 9th Army Corps
passing on Pennsylvania Avenue near the Treasury

Creator(s): Brady, Mathew B., ca. 1823-1896, photographer
Date Created/Published: 1865 May 23.
Summary: Washington, 1862-1865, the grand review of the Army, May, 1865.
Reproduction Number: LC-DIG-cwpb-02938
Rights Advisory: No known restrictions on publication.
Repository: Library of Congress Prints and Photographs Division

[a]http://www.loc.gov/pictures/item/cwp2003001021/PP/[/a]

Photograph of Judge Ariel Thurston (p.241)
Chemung County Historical Society
Judge Ariel Thurston, d. 1894

Chapter Twenty-Five

Gardner & Compton Advertisement (p.246)
Advertisement for Garder & Compton Furniture

Waite Brothers & Co., Compilers
Elmira Directory with A Business Directory of Chemung Co.
Preswick & Dudley: Elmira, New York (1866/67), 110.

Scanned by author

Photograph of Frederick Bates (p.247)
Scanned by the author from the *Elmira Telegram*, October 28, 1917.

Image reproduced from microfilm of the newspaper
by permission of ProQuest LLC.

Photograph of Chatford Howell (p.250)
Enlisted as Hiram Puls on April 23, 1864 to serve three years
Age: 22 Occupation: farmer

Provided to author by Bruce Haynes and Maureen Walters
(whose great-grandfather was Chatford Howell, Company G)

Photograph of William Lamont (p.251)
Wisconsin Historical Society Image Caption

Image Number: WHi-110542
Format #:WHi PH 4195.435 - cased images
Format #:WHi 9999015607 - digital temp
Title: William Lamont
Created by: Unknown
Collection:
Date of Subject:
Description: A dagguerreotype print of William Lamont. This image is issued by the
Wisconsin Historical Society. Use of the image requires written permission from the
staff of the Division of Library-Archives. It may not be sold or redistributed, copied or
distributed as a photograph, electronic file, or any other media.
The image should not be significantly altered through conventional or electronic means.
Images altered beyond standard cropping and resizing require further negotiation
with a staff member. The user is responsible for all issues of copyright.

Credit: Wisconsin Historical Society.

Image ID: 110542

Photographs of Rutans Young/Old (p.253)
James and Amelia Rutan (April 1864)
James and Amelia Rutan (circa 1900)

Author's collection.

Photographs of Francis Thorne Young/Old (p.253)
"Young" -- Hall's Ground Floor Gallery, Meadville, Penna.
Donated by author to New York State Military Museum.

Photographs of Elihu Linkletter Young/Old (p.253)
Provided to the author by Corinne DeGraaf

Photographs of Johnsons Young/Old (p.253)
Copied by Author from *E-J Workers' Review.*

Photographs of Elias Beach Young/Old (p.253)
Provided to the author by Donald Tubbs.

Chapter Twenty-Six

Reunion Invite (p.261)
John Andrews Papers, Collection 3790, Cornell University.

Photographed by author.

Photograph of Leander Bowers (p.269)
New York State Military Museum
P.A.1999.0014.1290
Leander H. Bowers
Company I

Leander H. Bowers
Age, 25 years. Enlisted, August 27, 1864, at Newfield, to serve one year;
mustered in as private, Co. I, September 13,1864; promoted, corporal, same date; mustered out,
May 20,1865, at Elmira, N . Y .

BIBLIOGRAPHY

◆━◆━◆

Archival Sources

A. B., "Story of A Civil War Veteran," *E. J. Workers Review*, Vol. One, Number 6 (August 20, 1919), George F. Johnson Papers, E - J Workers Review, Aug – Dec, 1919, Syracuse University Library, Special Collections Research Center.

Ancestry.com, Internet United States Census, 1860, 1870, 1880

Andrews, John Tuttle and Arvilla Rapleee Andrews Papers, Collection No. 3790, Cornell University, Carl A. Kroch Library, Division of Rare and Manuscript Collections.

Buffalo History Museum, Buffalo, New York. Civil War Collection, Mss COO-3 (179th New York Volunteers) Buffalo photo

Chemung County Historical Society, Elmira, New York; Elmira Military Depot; 23rd New York Volunteers; 179th New York Volunteers; Photos of Elmira Armory, New England Kitchen and Ariel Thurston

Chemung Valley Library, (Steele Memorial Library), Elmira, New York. *Boyd's Elmira Directory* (1860) *Brigham's Elmira Directory 1863-1864*, Fairman & DeVoe's Steam Printing Establishment: Elmira, New York (1863).

Daughters of Charity Archives, Albany, New York. St. Mary's Hospital Register.

Family History Library, Salt Lake City, Utah. New York State Census: 1865 (microfilm). *A Record of the Commissioned Officers, Non-Commissioned Officers, and Privates of the regiments Which Were Organized in the State of New York and Called into the Service of the United States to Assist in Suppressing the Rebellion Caused by the Secession of Some of the Southern States from the Union, A.D. 1861, As Taken from the Muster-In Rolls on File in the Adjutant General's Office*, S.N.Y., Weed, Parsons and Company, Printers: Albany (1866). *Complete Record as Required by Chapter 690, of the Laws of 1865, Relating to the Officers, Soldiers and Seamen Comprising the Quotas of the Troops Furnished to the United States By the Town of [X], County of [Y], State of New York in the War of the Rebellion Covering the Period from the 15th day of April 1861, to the date of the Certificate of the Town Clerk*, Microfilm Nos. 1,993,431 and 1,993,407.

Fold3.com, Internet. Civil War and Later Veterans Pension Index.

Hamilton College, Archives, Hamilton College Library, Clinton, New York. E.A. Taft Letter.

Indiana University, The Lilly Library, Bloomington, Indiana. Papers of Henry J. Messing, Messing, mss., 1864-1917.

Martin County Historical Society, Fairmont, Minnesota. William Bird, Jr. file.

Minnesota Historical Society, St. Paul, Minnesota. William Bird, Jr. Papers, A/m.B618.

National Archives, Washington, D.C.; College Park, Maryland; and New York City. Record Group 15, Pension Files Record Group 94, Records of the Adjutant General Record Group 110, Quartermaster Records Record Group 153, Records of the Judge Advocate Gen'l Cartographic Section

New York State Archives, New York State Library, Manuscripts & Special Collections, Albany, New York. Grand Army of the Republic Papers, Department of New York, 1866-1948 (B1706) Photos of Horatio Seymour and Reuben Fenton Maps of New York State

New York State Military Museum and Veterans Research Center, Saratoga Springs, New York. Unit History Project website (179th New York Volunteers and 23rd New York Volunteers.

The Library of Virginia, Richmond, Virginia. John T. Andrews Letters, 1864-1865, Accession 50258, Location: 4/C/41/6/7.

U. S. Military History Institute, Carlisle, Pennsylvania. Letters of Daniel B. Lee, CWMiscColl (Enlisted Man's letters, Jan. 10, 1863-Jan. 14, 1883); Newton Spencer court-martial transcript.

Virginia Historical Society, Richmond, Virginia. Martin, John Marshall Papers, Collection Number 643, MssM3643b. Younger Letters, 1864, Collection Number 610, MssZL8585b.

Wisconsin Historical Society, Madison, Wisconsin. William Lamont Papers.

Yates County History Center, Penn Yan, New York. Personal War Sketches, J. Barnett Sloan G.A.R. Post No. 93 (1892). Town of Jerusalem Military Record.

NEWSPAPERS

[Batavia] *Spirit of the Times*	FultonHistory.com
Binghamton Daily Democrat	Broome County Historical Society Binghamton, New York
Binghamton Daily Republican	Broome County Historical Society Binghamton, New York
Binghamton Daily Standard	Broome County Historical Society Binghamton, New York
Binghamton Standard	Broome County Historical Society Binghamton, New York
Bradford Argus	Bradford County Historical Society Towanda, Pennsylvania
The Bradford Reporter	Bradford County Historical Society Towanda, Pennsylvania
Broome Republican	Broome County Historical Society Binghamton, New York
Broome Weekly Republican	Broome County Historical Society Binghamton, New York
[Buffalo] *Commercial Advertiser*	The Buffalo History Museum Buffalo, New York
[Buffalo] *Courier and Republican*	The Buffalo History Museum Buffalo, New York
Buffalo Daily Courier	The Buffalo History Museum Buffalo, New York
Buffalo Morning Express	The Buffalo History Museum Buffalo, New York
Chemung County Republican	The Chemung County Library (Steele Memorial Library) Elmira, New York

Chemung Valley Reporter	The Chemung County Library (Steele Memorial Library) Elmira, New York
Corning Journal	New York State Library Albany, New York
Dryden Weekly News	New York State Library Albany, New York Cornell University Ithaca, New York
Dundee Record	Clipping in John Andrews papers Cornell University Ithaca, New York
Dunkirk Journal	New York State Library Albany, New York
Elmira Advertiser and Republican	The Chemung County Library (Steele Memorial Library) Elmira, New York
Elmira Daily Advertiser	The Chemung County Library (Steele Memorial Library) Elmira, New York
Elmira Daily Gazette	The Chemung County Library (Steele Memorial Library) Elmira, New York
Elmira Star Gazette	The Chemung County Library (Steele Memorial Library) Elmira, New York
Elmira Telegram	The Chemung County Library (Steele Memorial Library) Elmira, New York
The [Elmira] *Telegram*	The Chemung County Library (Steele Memorial Library) Elmira, New York
Elmira Weekly Gazette	The Chemung County Library (Steele Memorial Library) Elmira, New York
Harper's Weekly	Compact Disk
Havana Journal	Montour Falls Public Library Montour Falls, New York

The Hornellsville Tribune	New York State Library Albany, New York Cornell University Ithaca, New York Hornell Public Library Hornell, New York
Ithaca Journal	Cornell University Ithaca, New York
National Tribune	Online
Niagara Falls Gazette	New York State Library Albany, New York
The New York Times	Online
Ontario County Times	Ontario County Historical Society Canandaigua, New York
Ontario Repository and Messenger	Ontario County Historical Society Museum and Research Center, Canandaigua, New York
Owego Gazette	Tioga County Historical Society Owego, New York
Penn Yan Democrat	New York State Library Albany, New York
Sunday Spectator	Wellsville, New York
The [Warsaw] *Western New Yorker*	FultonHistory.com
Watkins Express	Cornell University, Ithaca, New York
Yates County Chronicle	Yates County History Center, Penn Yan, New York (original)

BOOK, ARTICLES AND OTHER PRINTED MATERIALS

—— "The Army Civil War Campaign Medal", *Prologue*, Vol. 33, No. 2 (Summer 2001).

—— "The Court-Martial of Private Spencer," *Civil War Times Illustrated*, Vol. XXVII, No. 10 (February 1989)

—— *The First Half Century of Madison University*, 1819-1869.

—— *History of the 179th Regiment N.Y.S.V. – Rebellion of 1861-65*, E.D. Norton, Printer: Ithaca, New York (1900).

—— "Member Conrad Bush – New York", *The Prison Exchange*, Vol. XII, No. 3 (Winter 2011).

—— *Official Records of the Union and Confederate Navies in the War of the Rebellion*, Government Printing Office: Washington, D.C.

—— *Portrait and Biographical Record of Saginaw and Bay Counties, Michigan*, Biographical Publishing Co.: Chicago (1892).

—— *Report of the Joint Committee on the Conduct of the War at the Second Session, Thirty Eighth Congress*, Government Printing Office: Washington, D. C. (1865) (Vol 1).
—— *The War of the Rebellion: A Compilation of the Official Records of the Union and Confederate Armies*, Government Printing Office: Washington, D.C.

Adams, William (Ed.), *Historical Gazeteer and Biographical Memoir of Cattaraugus County*, Lyman, Horton & Co. (1893).

Adams, George W., *Doctors in Blue: The Medical History of the Union army in the Civil War*, Louisiana State University Press: Baton Rouge (1952).

Adams, Michael C. C., *Living Hell: The Dark Side of the Civil War*, Johns Hopkins University Press: Baltimore (2014)

Alotta, Robert I., *Civil War Justice: Union army Executions Under Lincoln*, White Mane Publishing Co., Inc.:Shippensburg, Pennsylvania (1989).

Ambrose, Stephen, *Band of Brothers: E Company, 506th Regiment, 101st Airborne, From Normandy to Hitler's Eagle's Nest*, Simon & Schuster: New York (2001).

Ambrose, Stephen, *Citizen-Soldiers: The U.S. Army from the Normandy Beaches to the Bulge to the Surrender of Germany, June 7, 1944-May 7, 1945*, Simon & Schuster: New York (1997).

Anderson, John, *The Fifty-Seventh Regiment of Massachusetts Volunteers in the War of the Rebellion*, E.B. Stillings & Co, Printers: Boston (1896).

Armstrong, Warren B., *For Courageous Fighting and Confident Dying: Union Chaplains in the Civil War*, University Press of Kansas: Lawrence (1998).

Axelrod, Alan *The Horrid Pit: The Battle of the Crater. the Civil War's Cruelest Mission*, Carroll & Graf Publishers: New York (2007).

Baker, Charles B., ðPersonal War Sketch of Charles B. Baker,ð August 25, 1901, J. B. Sloan G.A.R. Post, Yates County Genealogical & Historical Society.

Barber, W. Charles, "The Civil War Years", *The Chemung Historical Journal*, Vol. 6, No. 1 (September 1960).

Barber, W. Charles, "Elmira as Civil War Depot and Prison Camp," *The Chemung Historical Journal*, Vol. 6, No. 1 (September 1960).

Basler, Roy P. (ed.), *The Collected Works of Abraham Lincoln*, Rutgers University Press: New Brunswick, New Jersey (1953).

Beals, Thomas P., "In a Charge Near Fort Hell, Petersburg, April 2, 1865", *Maine MOLLUS*, Lefavor-Tower Company: Portland (1902).

Bearss, Edwin C. with Suderow, Bryce A., *The Petersburg campaign, Volume I, The Eastern Front Battles, June-August 1864*, Savas Beatie LLC: El Dorado Hills, California (2012).

Benton, Josiah H., *Voting in the Field: A Forgotten Chapter of the Civil War*, reprinted General Books: Memphis (2010). (originally privately published in 1915).

Bernstein, Peter L., *Wedding of the Waters: The Erie Canal and the Making of A Great Nation*, W. W. Norton & Company: New York (2005).

Bertuca, D., "The Fenian Invasion of Canada, 1866," *The Harp*, Buffalo & Erie County Historical Society, Ready Reference Files.

Boatner III, Mark M., *The Civil War Dictionary*, Vintage Press: New York (Rev. Ed. 1991).

Bollet, Alfred J., *Civil War Medicine: Challenges and Triumphs*, Galen Press, Ltd.: Tucson, Arizona (2002)

Booth, Benjamin F. and Meyer, Steve, *Dark Days of the Rebellion: Life in Southern Military Prisons*, Meyer Publishing: Garrison, Iowa (1995).

Bowery, Charles R. Jr., *The Richmond-Petersburg campaign, 1864-65*, Praeger: Santa Barbara, California (2014).

Boyko, J., *Blood and Daring: How Canada Fought the American Civil War and Forged A Nation*, Alfred A. Knopf, Canada: Toronto (2013).

Bradsby, H., *History of Bradford County, Pennsylvania with Biographical Sketches*, Public Member Trees, Ancestry.com.

Brandt, Nat, *Mr. Tubbs' Civil War*, Syracuse University Press: Syracuse, New York (1996).

Brown, Louis A., *The Salisbury Prison: A Case Study of Confederate Military Prisons, 1861-1865*, Broadfoot Publishing Company: Wilmington, North Carolina (Revised and Enlarged 1992).

Byrne, Thomas E., "Elmira 1861-1865; Civil War Rendezvous," *The Chemung Historical Journal*, Vol. 9, No. 4 (June 1964).

Calkins, Chris, "The Battle of Weldon Railroad (or 'Globe Tavern')", *Blue & Gray*, Vol. XXIII, Issue 5 (Winter 2007).

Casey, John, "Marked by War: Demobilization, Disability and the Trope of the Citizen-Soldier in Miss Ravenel's Conversion", *Civil War History*, Volume 60, Number 2, June 2014. The Kent State University Press.

Catton, Bruce, *The Army of the Potomac: Glory Road*, Doubleday & Company: Garden City, New York (1952).

Catton, Bruce, *The Army of the Potomac: Mr. Lincoln's Army*, Doubleday & Company, Inc.: Garden City, New York (1951).

Catton, Bruce, *Grant Moves South*, Little Brown & Company: Boston (1960).

Catton, Bruce, *The Army of the Potomac: A Stillness at Appomattox*, Doubleday & Company: Garden City, New York (1953).

Catton, Bruce, *Grant Takes Command*, Little, Brown and Company: Boston (1969).

Cavanaugh, Michael A. and Marvel, William, *The Petersburg campaign: The Battle of the Crater 'The Horrid Pit' June 25-August 6, 1864*, H. E. Howard, Inc.: Lynchburg, Virginia (Second Edition 1989).

Childs, H., *Gazetteer and Business Directory of Chemung and Schuyler Counties, N.Y., for 1868-69*, Journal Office: Syracuse, New York (1868).

Clarke, N., "Ariel Standish Thurston: The Boy With the Awkward Mouth," *Chemung Historical Journal*, Vol. 57, No. 2 (December 2011).

Clayton, Henry, *History of Steuben County, New York*, Lewis Peck & Co.: Philadelphia (1879).

Cleaves, Freeman, *Meade of Gettysburg*, University of Oklahoma Press: Norman (1960).

Cogswell, Leander W., *A History of the Eleventh New Hampshire Regiment Volunteer Infantry in the Rebellion War 1861-1865*, Republican Press Association: Concord, New Hampshire (1891).

Connor Jr., Albert Z. and Mackowski, Chris, "Burnside's Bleak Midwinter", *America's Civil War* (January 2014).

Cross, Whitney R., *The Burned-Over District: The Social and Intellectual History of Enthusiastic Religion in Western New York, 1800-1850*, Cornell University Press: Ithaca New York (1950).

Cullen, Joseph P., "The Siege of Petersburg," *Civil War Times Illustrated*, Vol. IX, No. 5 (August 1970).

Dabney, Emmanuel, "A Federal Opportunity Lost: The Battle of the Crater," *Blue & Gray*, Vol. XXX, #5 (2014).

Dean Jr., Eric T., "Reflections on the 'Trauma of War' and *Shook Over Hell*," *Civil War History*, Vol. 59, No. 4 (December 2013), 414.

Dean Jr., Eric T., *Shook Over Hell: Post Traumatic Stress, Vietnam and the Civil War*, Harvard University Press: Cambridge (1997).

Dieckmann, Jane M., *A Short History of Tompkins County*, DeWitt Historical Society of Tompkins County: Ithaca, New York (1986)

Duff, J., "David Wilmot, the Statesman and Political Leader," Bradford County Historical Society (1946).

Dunkelman, Mark H., *Brothers One and All: Esprit de Corps in a Civil War Regiment*, Louisiana State University Press: Baton Rouge (2004).

Dunkelman, Mark H., *The Hardtack Regiment: An Illustrated History of the 154th Regiment, New York State Infantry Volunteers*, Associated University Presses, Inc.: East Brunswick, New Jersey (1981).

Dunkelman, Mark H., *War's Relentless Hand: Twelve Tales of Civil War Soldiers*, Louisiana State University Press: Baton Rouge (2006).

Emerson, Gary, *A Link in the Great Chain: A History of the Chemung Canal*, Purple Mountain Press: Fleischmanns, New York (2005)

Fantina, Robert, *Desertion and the American Soldier, 1776-2006*, Algora Publishing: New York (2006).

Faust, Drew Gilpin, *This Republic of Suffering: Death and the American Civil War*, Alfred A. Knopf: New York (2008).

Field, Ron, *Petersburg: The Longest Siege*, Osprey Publishing: Oxford (2009).

Foner, Eric, *The Fiery Trial: Abraham Lincoln and American Slavery*, W.W. Norton & Company: New York (2010).

Fox, William F., *Regimental Losses in the American Civil War 1861-1865*, Albany Publishing Company: Albany, New York (1889).

Freeman, Douglas Southall, *R. E. Lee: A Biography*, Charles Scribnerðs Sons: New York (1935).

French, John Homer, *Gazetteer of the State of New York: Embracing A Comprehensive View of the Geography, Geology, and General History of the State, and A Complete History and Description of Every County, City, Town, Village, and Locality, With Full Tables of Statistics*, R. Pearsall Smith: Syracuse (1860).

Gallagher, Gary W., "To love or loathe McClellan?", *Civil War Times*, Vol. 51, No. 2 (April 2012)

Gallagher, Gary W., *The Union War*, Harvard University Press: Cambridge, Massachusetts (2011).

Gavin, William G., *Campaigning with the Roundheads: The History of the Hundreth Pennsylvania Veteran Volunteer Regiment in the American Civil War 1861-1865*, Morningside House, Inc.: Dayton, Ohio (1989).

Giesberg, Judith, *Army at Home: Women and the Civil War on the Northern Home Front*, The University of North Carolina Press: Chapel Hill (2009).

Glasson, William H., *Federal Military Pensions in the United States*, Oxford University Press: New York (1918).

Goodwin, Doris Kearns, *Team of Rivals: The Political Genius of Abraham Lincoln*, Simon & Schuster: New York (2005).

Gordon, Lesley J., *A Broken Regiment: The 16th Connecticut's Civil War*, Louisiana State University Press: Baton Rouge (2014).

Grace, Thomas, "Wreck the Weldon Railroad," *America's Civil War*, Vol. 27, No. 6 (January 2015).

Graham, Robert H., *Yates County's Boys in Blue, 1861-1865: Who They Were – What They Did*, [self-published]: Penn Yan, New York (1926).

Grant, Ulysses S., *Personal Memoirs of U.S. Grant*, Charles L. Webster & Company: New York (1886).

Gray, Michael P., *The Business of Captivity: Elmira and Its Civil War Prison*, The Kent State University Press: Kent, Ohio (2001).

Greene, A. Wilson, "April 2, 1865: Day of Decision at Petersburg", *Blue & Gray*, Winter 2001.

Greene, A. Wilson, *Breaking the Backbone of the Rebellion: The Final Battles of the Petersburg campaign*, Savas Publishing Company: Mason City, Iowa (2000).

Greene, A. Wilson, *Civil War Petersburg: Confederate City in the Crucible of War*, University of Virginia Press: Charlottesville (2006).

Greene, A. Wilson, *The Final Battles of the Petersburg campaign: Breaking the Backbone of Rebellion*, The University of Tennessee Press: Knoxville (Second Edition 2008).

Hallock, Judith Lee, "The Role of the Community in Civil War Desertion," *Civil War History*, Vol. 29, No. 2 (June 1983).

Hardee, William J., *Hardee's Rifle and Light Infantry Tactics for the Instructions, Exercises and Manoeuvres of Riflemen and Light Infantry, Including School of the Soldier and School of the Company, To Which Is added, Duties of Non-Commissioned Officers, Military Honors to Be Paid By Troops, the Articles of War*, J. O. Kane, Publisher: New York (1862) (reprinted by H-Bar Enterprises: Silver Spring, Maryland).

Hess, Earl J.,*The Civil War in the West: Victory and Defeat from the Appalachians to the Mississippi*, The University of North Carolina Press: Chapel Hill (2012).

Hess, Earl J., *Field Armies and Fortifications in the Civil War: The Eastern Campaigns, 1861-1864*, The University of North Carolina Press: Chapel Hill: (2005).

Hess, Earl J., *Into the Crater: The Mine Attack at Petersburg*, The University of South Carolina Press: Columbia (2010).

Hess, Earl J., *In the Trenches at Petersburg: Field Fortifications & Confederate Defeat*, University of North Carolina Press: Chapel Hill (2009).

Hess, Earl J., *The Union Soldier in Battle: Enduring the Ordeal of Combat*, University Press of Kansas: Lawrence (1997).

Heverly, Clement Ferdinand, *Our Boys in Blue. Heroic Deeds, Sketches and Reminiscences of Bradford County Soldiers in the Civil War*, The Bradford Star Print., Towanda, Pennsylvania (1898, reprinted 1998, Murrelle Printing Co., Inc., Sayre, Pennsylvania)

Hewett, Janet B., *Supplement to the Official Records of the Union and Confederate Armies*, Broadfoot Publishing Company: Wilmington, North Carolina (1997).

Hoffsommer, R., "The Wreck of the Prisoners' Train," *Civil War Times Illustrated*, Vol. 3, No. 2 (May 1964).

Holberton, William B., *The Demobilization of the Union and Confederate Armies 1865-1866*, Stackpole Books: Mechanicsburg, Pennsylvania (2001).

Hopkins, William P., *The Seventh Regiment Rhode Island Volunteers in the Civil War, 1862-1865*.

Horigan, Michael, "Antebellum Elmira: 1850-1860 (Part One)," *The Chemung Historical Journal*, Vol. 48, No. 1 (September 2002).

Horigan, Michael, "Antebellum Elmira: 1850-1860 (Part Two)," *The Chemung Historical Journal*, Vol. 48, No. 2 (December 2002).

Horigan, Michael, *Elmira: Death Camp of the North*, Stackpole Books: Mechanicsburg, Pennsylvania (2002).

Howe, Thomas J., *The Petersburg campaign: Wasted Valor, June 15-18, 1864*, H.E. Howard, Inc.: Lynchburg, Virginia (Second Edition 1988).

Humphreys, Margaret, *Marrow of Tragedy: The Health Crisis of the American Civil War*, The Johns Hopkins University Press: Baltimore (2013).

Johnston, Jenny, "Living History: Witness to the 154th," *The Civil War Monitor*, Vol. 4, No. 4 (Winter 2014),16.

Brian Jordan, *Marching Home: Union Veterans and Their Unending Civil War* Liveright Publishing Corporation: New York (2014).

Katz, Michael B., Doucet, Michael J. and Stern, Mark J., "Migration and the Social Order in Erie County, New York: 1855," *Journal of Interdisciplinary History*, Volume 8, Issue 4, Spring 1978.

Kautz, August V., *The Company Clerk*, J. B. Lippincott & Co.: Philadelphia (1864).

Keegan, John, *The Face of Battle*, The Viking Press: New York (1976).

Keen, William W., "Military Surgery in 1861 and 1918", *Annals of the American Academy of Political and Social Science*, Vol. LXXX, No. 169 (November 1918).

Kelly, P., *Creating A National Home: Building the Veterans' Welfare State 1860-1900*, Harvard University Press: Cambridge, Massachusetts (1997).

King, Curtis S., Robertson, William Glenn and Clay, Steven E., *Staff Ride Handbook for the Overland campaign, Virginia, 4 May to 15 June, 1865: A Study in Operational-Level Command*, Combat Studies Institute Press: Fort Leavenworth, Kansas (Second Edition 2009).

King, W. Robertson and Clay, S., *Staff Ride Handbook for the Overland campaign, Virginia, 4 May to 15 June 1864: A Study in Operational-Level Command*, Combat Studies Institute Press: Fort Leavenworth, Kansas (2d Ed. 2009).

Klein, Fredic S., " ... Lost Opportunity at Petersburg," *Civil War Times Illustrated*, Vol. V, No. 5 (August 1966).

Kling, Warren, *Americaôs First Boomtown – Rochester, NY: The Early Years and the Notables Who Shaped It*, Rochester History Alive Publications: Rochester (1908).

Knight, Glenn B., "The Grand Army of the Republic: A Brief History," Internet suvcw.org/ny/gar/commanders/GARhistory.

Kostyal, Karen M., *Field of Battle: The Civil War Letters of Major Thomas J. Halsey*, National Geographic Society (1996).

Krick, Robert K., *Civil War Weather in Virginia*, University of Alabama Press: Tuscaloosa (2007).

Kriedberg, Marvin A. and Henry, Merton G., *History of Military Mobilization in the United States Army 1775-1945*, Department of the Army: Washington (DOD Pamphlet No. 20-212) (1955).

Leech, M., *Reveille in Washington: 1860-1865*, Grosset & Dunlap: New York (1941).

Levin, Kevin, *Remembering the Battle of the Crater: War as Murder*, The University Press of Kentucky: Lexington (2012).

Liddell Hart, Basil Henry, *Sherman: Soldier, Realist, American*, Da Capo Press (1993 originally published 1929).

Lind, Michael,_Land of Promise: An Economic History of the United States_, Harper: New York (2013).

Lonn, Ella, _Desertion During the Civil War_, University of North Carolina Press: Lincoln (1998 originally published 1928).

Lord, Edward O. (Ed.), _History of the Ninth Regiment New Hampshire Volunteers in the War of the Rebellion_, Republican Press Associaiton: Concord, New Hampshire (1895).

Lowry, Thomas P., _Irish & German: Whiskey & Beer Drinking Patterns in the Civil War_, T. Lowrey: Lexington, Kentucky (2011).

MacDonald, John A., _Troublous Times in Canada: A History of the Fenian raids of 1866-1870_, W.S. Johnston and Company: Toronto (1910).

Manchester, William, _The Last Lion: Winston Spencer Churchill: Visions of Glory, 1874-1932_, Little, Brown and Company: Boston (1983).

Marten, James, _Sing Not War: The Lives of Union & Confederate Veterans in Gilded Age America_, University of North Carolina Press: Chapel Hill (2011).

Marvel, William, _Burnside_, The University of North Carolina Press: Chapel Hill (1991).

McClintock, Megan J., "The Impact of the Civil War on Nineteenth Century Marriages," in Paul A. Cimbala and Randall M. Miller (eds.), _Union Soldiers and the Northern Home Front: Wartime Experiences, postwar adjustments_, Fordham University Press: New York (2002).

McKelvey, Blake, _A Panoramic History of Rochester and Monroe County New York_, Windsor Publications: Woodland Hills California (1979).

McNamara, Robert F., _Saint Mary's Hospital and the Civil War_, Rochester: St. Mary's Hospital (1961), Rochester Historical Society.

McPherson, James, _Battle Cry of Freedom: The Civil War Era_, Oxford University Press: Oxford (1988).

McPherson, James, _For Cause and Comrades: Why Men Fought in the Civil War_, Oxford University Press: New York (1997).

McPherson, James, _Tried By War: Abraham Lincoln as Commander in Chief_, The Penguin Press: New York (2008).

McWhiney, Grady and Jenkins, Jack Jay, "The Union̓s Worst General", _Civil War Times Illustrated_, Vol. XIV, No. 3 (June 1975).

Meier, Michael, T., "Civil War Draft Records: Exemptions and Enrollments", _Prologue_, Winter 1994, Vol. 26 No. 4.

Miller, Robert J., _Both Prayed to the Same God: Religion and Faith in the Civil War_, Lexington Books: New York (2007).

Miller, Richard F., _Harvard̓s Civil War: A History of the Twentieth Massachusetts Volunteer Infantry_, University Press of New England: Lebanon, New Hampshire (2005).

Mills, J., _Chronicles of the Twenty-First Regiment New York State Volunteers_, The 21st Reg't Veteran Association: Buffalo (1887).

Moe, Richard, _The Last Full Measure: The Life and Death of the First Minnesota Volunteers_, Minnesota Historical Society Press: St. Paul (1993).

Morris, R., _A Low, Dirty Place: The Parole Camps of Annapolis, MD 1862-1865_, Ann Arrundell County Historical Society: Linthicum, MD (2012).

Murdock, Eugene C., "New York̓s Civil War Bounty Brokers", _The Journal of American History_, Vol. 53, No. 2 (Sept. 1966).

Murdock, Eugene C., _Patriotism Limited – 1862-1865 – The Civil War Draft and Bounty System_, The

Kent State University Press: Kent, Ohio (1967).

Musick, Michael P., "The Little Regiment: Civil War Units and Commands," *Prologue*, Vol. 27, No. 2 (Summer 1995), 2.

Newsome, Hampton, *Richmond Must Fall: The Richmond-Petersburg campaign, October 1864*, The Kent State University Press: Kent, Ohio (2013).

Oakes, Robert F., "Historically Speaking", *Sunday Spectator*, July 8, 1973.

Oakes, Robert F., "Historically Speaking", *The [Hornell] Evening Tribune*, January 23, 1984.

Owen, Thomas M., *History of Alabama and Dictionary of Alabama Biography*, The S.J. Clarke Publishing Company: Chicago (1921).

Parker, Sandra V., *Richmond's Civil War Prisons*, H.E. Howard, Inc.: Lynchburg, Virginia (1990).

Person, Gustav J., "Crossing the James River, June 1864 '...the real crisis of the war' " in *Engineer: The Professional Bulletin for Army Engineers*, Sep-Dec 2009.

Phisterer, Frederick, *New York in the War of the Rebellion 1861 to 1865*, D.B. Lyon Company, State Printers: Albany, New York (Third Ed. 1912).

Poche, D., "Ain't No Company J in This Man's Army," wwwpochefamily.org/Books/NoCompanyJ.html.

Rafuse, Ethan, "Lincoln, Grant and the Trouble with Robert E. Lee," *America's Civil War*, (September 2014).

Ramold, Steven J., *Across the Divide: Union Soldiers View the Northern Home Front*, New York University Press: New York (2013).

Raney, David A., "In the Lord's Army: The United States Christian Commission, Soldiers, and the Union War Effort" in Paul A. Cimbala and Randall M. Miller (eds.), *Union Soldiers and the Northern Home Front: Wartime experiences, postwar adjustments*, Fordham University Press: New York (2002).

Rappaport, Armin, "The Replacement System During the Civil War," *Military Affairs*, Vol. 15, No. 2 (Summer 1951).

Raymond, Andrew Van Vranken, *Union University: Its History, Influence, Characteristics, and Equipment*, Lewis Publishing Co.: New York (1907).

Reed, Robert, *Old Washington, D.C. in Early Photographs: 1846-1932*, Dover Publications, Inc.: New York (1980).

Reid, Brian Holden and White, John, " 'A Mob of Stragglers and Cowards': Desertion from the Union and Confederate Armies, 1861-65", *The Journal of Strategic Studies*, Vol. 8, Issue 1 (1985).

Robertson, James I., "Introduction" in Robert Lester, *Civil War Unit Histories: Regimental Histories and Personal Narratives, Part 5, The Union–Higher and Independent Commands and Naval Forces*, University Publications of America: Bethesda, Maryland.

Rolph, Gerald Vern and Clark, Noel, *The Civil War Soldier*, Historical Impressions Co.: Washington (1961).

Rosenheim, Jeff, *Photography and the American Civil War*, The Metropolitan Museum of Art: New York (2013).

Rudolph, J., "The Grand Review," *Civil War Times Illustrated*, Vol. XIX, No. 7 (November 1980).

Rutan II, Edwin P., "The 179th New York Volunteers," *The Chemung Historical Journal*, Vol. 58, No. 3 (March 2013).

Sartin, Jeffrey S., "Infectious Diseases During the Civil War: The Triumph of the 'Third Army'", *Clinical Infectious Diseases*, Vol. 16, No. 4 (April 1993).

Schmutz, John F., *The Battle of the Crater: A Complete History*, McFarland & Company, Inc., Publishers: Jefferson, North Carolina (2009).

Schneirov, R., *The Pullman Strike and the Crisis of the 1890's*, Pullman Virtual Museum; 1892, 1893 and 1894 Wilmington Directories.

Schroeder-Lein, Glenna R., *The Encyclopedia of Civil War Medicine*, M.E. Sharpe: Armonk, New York (2008).

Scott, Robert Garth (ed.), *Forgotten Valor: The Memoirs, Journals, & Civil War Letters of Orlando B. Willcox*, The Kent State University Press, 1999.

Sears, Stephen W., *George B. McClellan: The Young Napoleon*, Ticknor & Fields: New York (1988).

Sears, Stephen W., "Major General Philip Kearny: 'A One-Armed Jersey Son-of-A-Gun'", *The Civil War Monitor*, Vol. 4, No. 1 (Spring 2014).

Selkreg, John H.(Ed.), *Landmarks of Tompkins County*, New York, D. Mason & Company, Publishers: Syracuse (1894)

Shannon, Fred A., *The Organization and Administration of the Union army 1861-1865*, The Arthur H. Clark Company: Cleveland (1928).

Simons, Ezra de Freest, *A Regimental History: The One Hundred and Twenty Fifth New York State Volunteers*, Ezra D. Simons: New York (1888).

Simpson, Brooks D., *Campaign Promise*, The Civil War Monitor, Vol. 4, No. 4 (Winter 2014), 30.

Simpson, Brooks D., *Ulysses S. Grant: Triumph Over Adversity, 1822-1865*, Houghton Mifflin Company: Boston (2000).

Slotkin, Richard, *No Quarter: The Battle of the Crater*, 1864, Random House: New York (2009).

Smedberg, William R., "In Memorium: Levi Force," Military Order Loyal Legion of the United States, Headquarters Commandery of the State of California, series of 1891, no. 6, whole no. 256.

Smith, H. Perry (ed.), *History of the City of Buffalo and Erie County with Illustrations and Biographical Sketches of Some of Its Prominent Men and Pioneers*, D.Mason & Co., Publishers: Syracuse, New York (1884).

Sommers, Richard J., *Richmond Redeemed: The Siege at Petersburg*, Savas Beatie LLC: El Dorado Hills, California (150th Anniversary Edition 2014).

Sommers, Richard, *Richmond Redeemed: The Siege at Petersburg*, Doubleday & Company, Inc.: Garden City, New York (1981).

Starr, F., *The Loyal Soldier. A Discourse Delivered in the First Presbyterian Church in Penn Yan, New York, at the Funeral of Major John Barnet Sloan, of the 179th Regiment, N.Y.V. Infantry*, C.D.A. Bridgman, Book and Job Printer: Penn-Yan, New York (1864).

Steiner, Paul E., *Disease in the Civil War: Natural Biological Warfare in 1861-1865*, Charles C. Thomas, Publisher: Springfield, Illinois (1968),

Sterling, Pound (Maxson, William P.), *Campfires of the Twenty-Third: Sketches of the Camp Life, Marches and Battles of the Twenty-Third Regiment, N.Y.V., During the Term of Two Years In The Service of the United States*, Davies & Kent, Printers: New York (1863).

Street, Jr., J., "Under the Influence: Did Vivil War Soldiers Depend on Drugs and Alcohol?", *Civil War Times Illustrated*, Vol. XXVII, No. 3, (May 1988).

Tarbell, Ida, "How the Union army Was Disbanded," *Civil War Times Illustrated*, Vol. VI, No. 8 (December 1967). (Originally published in *McClureõs Magazine* in March 1901).

Taylor, George Rogers, *The Transportation Revolution, 1815 - 1860*, Holt, Rinehart and Winston: New York (1951, reprinted Harper & Rowe 1968).

Thomas, Emory, *Robert E. Lee: A Biography*, W. W. Norton & Company: New York (1995).

Trudeau, Noah Andre, *The Last Citadel: Petersburg June 1864-April 1865*, Savas Beatie LLC: El Dorado Hills, California (150th Anniversary Edition 2014).

Trudeau, Noel, *The Last Citadel: Petersburg, Virginia, June 1864-April 1865*, Little, Brown and Company: Boston (1991).

Venter, Bruce M., "Hancock the (Not So) Superb: The Second Battle of Reams' Station", *Blue & Gray*, Vol. XXIII, Issue 5 (Winter 2007).

Vinovskis, M., "Have Social Historians Lost the Civil War?: Some Preliminary Demographic Speculations", *Toward a Social History of the American Civil War: Exploratory Essays*, Cambridge University Press: New York (1990).

Vinovskis, Maris A. (Ed.), *Toward a Social History of the American Civil War: Exploratory Essays*, Cambridge University Press: New York (1990).

Vronsky, Peter, *Ridgeway: The American Fenian Invasion and the 1866 Battle That Made Canada*, Allen Lane: Canada (2011).

Wagner, Margaret E., Gallagher, Gary W. and Finkelman, Paul (Eds.), *The Library of Congress Civil War Desk Reference*, Simon & Schuster: New York, Reprint edition (2009).

Walcott, *History of the Twenty-First Regiment Massachusetts Volunteers in the War for Preservation of the Union 1861-1865*, Houghton, Mifflin and Company: Boston (1882).

Walling, Henry Francis, *Walling's 1867 Guide to The Erie Railway and Its Branches with Descriptive Sketches of the Cities, Villages and Stations and of Scenery and Object of Interest Along the Route*, Taintor Brothers & Co.: New York (1867).

Ward, Geoffrey C., *The Civil War: An Illustrated History*, Alfred A. Knopf: New York (1990).

Waugh, John, *Lincoln and McClellan: The Troubled Relationship Between A President and His General*, Palgrave McMillan: New York (2010).

Weber, Thomas, *The Northern Railroads in the Civil War, 1861-1865*, Indiana University Press: Bloomington (1999).

White, Daniel, "Charging The Crater", *National Tribune*, June 21, 1883.

Wiley, Bell Irvin, *The Life of Billy Yank: The Common Soldier of the Union*, Louisiana State University Press: Baton Rouge (1952, 1971).

Wilkenson, Warren, *Mother, May You Never See the Sights I Have Seen: The Fifty-seventh Massachusetts Veteran Volunteers in the Last Year of the Civil War*, Harper & Row, Publishers: New York (1990).

Wilson, Sven Eric, "Prejudice & Policy: Racial Discrimination in the Union army Disability Pension System, 1865-1906", *American Journal of Public Health*, Vol. 0, No. 2010 (February 10, 2010)

Winther, Oscar O., "The Soldier Vote in the Election of 1864," *New York History*, 25 (1944).

Wolcott, Walter, *The Military History of Yates County, N.Y., Comprising a Record of the Services Rendered by Citizens of This County in the Army and Navy, from the Foundation of the Government to the Present Time*, Express Book and Job Printing House: Penn Yan, New York (1895).

Woodworth, Steven E., *While God Is Marching On: The Religious World of Civil War Soldiers*, University Press of Kansas: Lawrence (2001).

Writers' Group of the Chemung County Historical Society, *Chemung County... its History*, Commercial Press of Elmira, Inc.: Elmira, New York (2d printing 1963).

INDEX

248

Crawford, Sgt. Robert O. (CoD), 159, 160, 294, 295, 297, 299, 302, 304

Crawford, Cpl. William (CoD), 159

Crocker, Sgt. Eben (CoK), 300, 303, 306

Cross, Cpl. George (CoA), 113, 114, 187, 382n55

Culver, Lt. Fitz E. (CoH), 138, 291, 300, 305, 468

Cumberland Heights/ Landing, VA, 48, 51, 52, 62, 232, 350n77, 353n91. See also One hundred seventy-ninth New York Volunteer Infantry, Cumberland Heights Detachment

Curry, Pvt. Volney (CoD), 290

Curtin, Col. John I. (1st Brigade, Potter's Div.), 219, 222

Dains, Pvt. Bryant (CoD), 158, 159

Danby (Tompkins Co., NY), 34, 41, 42, 135, 136, 137, 138, 139, 343n50, 343n51, 462

Danville Military Prison (VA), 159-61

Davis, Roswell (recruit), 18, 19, 30, 329n40

Day, Capt. James (CoG), 31, 101, 117, 119, 203, 259, 291, 296, 298, 300, 302, 337n106

Dean, Sgt. Theodore (CoK), 300, 303, 306

Decoration Day, xiv, 263, 264, 311

DeFord, Pvt. Dennis (CoG), 102, 159

DeKay, Cpl. Stephen (CoA), 52

demobilization, 238-40, 246, 441n29

demographics of soldiers. See One hundred seventy-ninth New York Volunteer Infantry, demographics of soldiers

Dempsey, Pvt. Dennis (CoG), 243

Dence, Pvt. Tuthill (CoF), 67

desertion: Confederate, 177, 181, 206, 413n1; Union, xiii, 25-27, 42, 43, 50, 51, 86, 117, 138-39, 177-189, 216, 271, 326n1, 333n45, 334n46, 334n51, 335n61, 350n78, 351n79, 351n82, 352n85, 352n86, 352n87, 352n89, 363n47, 416n70 . See also bounty jumpers

Dexter, Pvt. Denton (CoH), 201

Diar, Pvt. Lewis (CoH), 291, 448n63

diarrhea. See disease

Dicker, Pvt. James (CoF), 109, 110

Dickey, Pvt. William H. (CoH), 187-88, 386n31, 418n76

Disability Pension Act of 1890, 258, 259

disease : 77, 117, 120, 122-23, 254, 270, diarrhea, 120, 122, 123, 124, 127, 154, 158, 159, 160, 165, 312, 314, 386n33, 419n83; dysentery, 122; typhoid fever, 70-71, 122, 123, 124, 168

Diven, Maj. /Gen. A.S. (Provost Marshal General and Superintendent of Volunteer Recruiting Service, Western New York), 4, 12, 29, 133, 134, 204, 324n49, 390n14

Dodzell, Pvt. Nicholas (CoD), 290

Doty, Lt. Col. Franklin B. (F&S), 13, 14, 15, 16, 47, 66, 75, 76, 79, 86, 91, 112, 118, 119, 121, 145, 147-48, 181, 186, 205, 215, 216, 221-22, 224, 225, 226, 228, 230-31, 232, 233, 242, 246, 262, 288, 293, 295, 296, 298, 301, 303, 313, 326n7, 327n19, 350n77, 355n24, 428n63, 436n42

Doty, Capt. Martin (CoC, F&S), 13, 29, 75, 121, 174, 194, 228, 289, 427n47

draft, 2-3, 5-7, 8, 9, 10, 17, 23, 136-37, 139, 192, 257, 271, 322n13, 324n49,393n50, 394n71

Drake, Pvt. John (CoI), 154

drug usage, 386n31, 418n76

Dryden (Tompkins Co. , NY): 34, 136, 137; Dryden Weekly News, civilian morale, 382n1, Moses Brown death, 77

Dudley, George. See Lake, George D.

Dundee Record: April 1-2, 221; Newton Spencer, 221, 224, 249

Dunkirk , Chautauqua Co., NY: 33, 34; Dunkirk Journal, Crater and colored troops, 379n13; draft, 3; soldiers' vote, 191

Dunn, Sgt. Edward S. (CoF), 109, 294, 296, 298, 300, 302, 305, 378n4

Dunn, Pvt. William (CoG), 27

Dunton, Pvt. Eugene (CoB), 92, 95, 102, 122, 211, 383n3

Durham, Sgt. John W. (CoF), 28, 63, 130, 290, 294, 296, 298, 300, 302, 305 dysentery. See disease

Made in United States
North Haven, CT
13 June 2022

20155255R00314